Mike Meyers'

CompTIA A+®
Guide to 801: Managing
and Troubleshooting PCs

Fourth Edition
(Exam 220-801)

Mike Meyers'

CompTIA A+®
Guide to 801: Managing and Troubleshooting PCs

Fourth Edition
(Exam 220-801)

Mike Meyers

New York Chicago San Francisco
Lisbon London Madrid Mexico City Milan
New Delhi San Juan Seoul Singapore Sydney Toronto

Library of Congress Cataloging-in-Publication Data

Meyers, Michael, 1961-
 Mike Meyers' CompTIA A+ guide to 801 : managing and troubleshooting PCs
(exam 220-801) / Mike Meyers. — Fourth edition.
 pages cm
 Includes index.
 ISBN 978-0-07-179600-2 — ISBN 0-07-179600-2 — ISBN 978-0-07-179602-6
(set) — ISBN 0-07-179602-9 (set) — ISBN 978-0-07-179601-9 (CD) — ISBN
0-07-179601-0 (CD)
 1. Microcomputers—Maintenance and repair—Examinations—Study guides. 2. Computer technicians—Certification. 3. Computing Technology Industry
Association—Examinations—Study guides. I. Title. II. Title : CompTIA
A+ guide to 801.
TK7887.M458 2013
004.165—dc23

2012040812

McGraw-Hill books are available at special quantity discounts to use as premiums and sales promotions, or for use in corporate training programs. To contact a representative, please e-mail us at bulksales@mcgraw-hill.com.

Mike Meyers' CompTIA A+® Guide to 801: Managing and Troubleshooting PCs, Fourth Edition (Exam 220-801)

2 3 4 5 6 7 8 9 0 QVS QVS 1 0 9 8 7 6 5 4

ISBN: Book p/n 978-0-07-179600-2 and CD p/n 978-0-07-179601-9
of set 978-0-07-179602-6

MHID: Book p/n 0-07-179600-2 and CD p/n 0-07-179601-0
of set 0-07-179602-9

Sponsoring Editor
TIMOTHY GREEN

Editorial Supervisor
PATTY MON

Project Manager
YASHMITA HOTA,
CENVEO PUBLISHER SERVICES

Acquisitions Coordinator
STEPHANIE EVANS

Technical Editor
CHRISTOPHER A. CRAYTON

Copy Editor
BILL MCMANUS

Proofreader
CLAIRE SPLAN

Indexer
TED LAUX

Production Supervisor
JAMES KUSSOW

Composition
CENVEO PUBLISHER SERVICES

Illustration
FORD PIERSON & CENVEO PUBLISHER SERVICES

Art Director, Cover
JEFF WEEKS

■ About the Author

Mike Meyers, lovingly called the "AlphaGeek" by those who know him, is the industry's leading authority on CompTIA A+ certification. He is the president and co-founder of Total Seminars, LLC, a provider of PC and network repair seminars, books, videos, and courseware for thousands of organizations throughout the world. Mike has been involved in the computer and network repair industry since 1977 as a technician, instructor, author, consultant, and speaker.

Author of numerous popular PC books and videos, including the best-selling *CompTIA A+ Certification All-in-One Exam Guide*, Mike is also the series editor for the highly successful *Mike Meyers' Certification Passport* series, the *Mike Meyers' Computer Skills* series, and the *Mike Meyers' Guide to* series, all published by McGraw-Hill.

As well as writing, Mike has personally taught (and continues to teach) thousands of students, including U.S. senators, U.S. Supreme Court justices, the United Nations, every branch of the U.S. Armed Forces, most branches of the Department of Justice, hundreds of corporate clients, academic students at every level, prisoners, and pensioners.

 E-mail: michaelm@totalsem.com
 Facebook: Mike Meyers (Houston, TX)
 Twitter/Skype/most instant messaging clients: desweds
 Web forums: www.totalsem.com/forums

About the Editor in Chief

Scott Jernigan wields a mighty red pen as Editor in Chief for Total Seminars. With a Master of Arts degree in Medieval History, Scott feels as much at home in the musty archives of London as he does in the warm CRT glow of Total Seminars' Houston headquarters. After fleeing a purely academic life, he dove headfirst into IT, working as an instructor, editor, and writer.

Scott has written, edited, and contributed to dozens of books on computer literacy, hardware, operating systems, networking, and certification, including *Computer Literacy—Your Ticket to IC³ Certification*, and co-authoring with Mike Meyers the *All-in-One CompTIA Strata® IT Fundamentals Exam Guide*.

Scott has taught computer classes all over the United States, including stints at the United Nations in New York and the FBI Academy in Quantico. Practicing what he preaches, Scott is a CompTIA A+ and CompTIA Network+ certified technician, a Microsoft Certified Professional, a Microsoft Office User Specialist, and Certiport Internet and Computing Core Certified.

About the Technical Editor

Chris Crayton (CompTIA A+, CompTIA Network+, MCSE) is an author, editor, technical consultant, and trainer. Mr. Crayton has worked as a computer and networking instructor at Keiser University, as network administrator for Protocol, an eCRM company, and as a computer and network

specialist at Eastman Kodak. Mr. Crayton has authored several print and online books on PC Repair, CompTIA A+, CompTIA Security+, and Microsoft Windows. Mr. Crayton has served as technical editor on numerous professional technical titles for leading publishing companies, including the *CompTIA A+ All-in-One Exam Guide*, the *CompTIA A+ Certification Study Guide,* and the *Mike Meyers' CompTIA A+ Certification Passport.*

Peer Reviewers

Thank you to the reviewers, past and present, who contributed insightful reviews, criticisms, and helpful suggestions that continue to shape this textbook.

Donat Forrest
Broward County Community College
Pembroke Pines, FL

Brian Ives
Finger Lakes Community College
Canadaigua, NY

Farbod Karimi
Heald College
San Francisco, CA

Tamie Knaebel
Jefferson Community College
Louisville, KY

Keith Lyons
Cuyahoga Community College
Parma, OH

Winston Maddox
Mercer County Community College
West Windsor, NJ

Rajiv Malkan
Montgomery College
Conroe, Texas

Scott Sweitzer
Indiana Business College
Indianapolis, IN

Randall Stratton
DeVry University
Irving, TX

Thomas Trevethan
CPI College of Technology
Virginia Beach, VA

■ Acknowledgments

Scott Jernigan, my Editor in Chief at Total Seminars and boon companion on many an evening, worked his *usual* magic *again* pulling together this latest edition. My thanks, amigo!

My acquisitions editor, Tim Green, and his trusty assistant, Stephanie Evans, had this book schedule dialed in from day one and never let up. I mean, *never* let up. Better still, they browbeat me into working with their incessantly chirpy voices. I long for the mean Tim of old who just yelled at me.

Chris Crayton, my technical editor, did a great job once again. Thank you for helping make this book happen.

Aaron Verber stepped up in a big way for this edition, with stellar editing, writing, and research. You did a great job with every chapter thrown at you (and managed to pull together the lab manual at the same time). Let's do this again!

Michael Smyer devoted his superb skills in photography and tech to making this book the best edition ever. He kept me on my toes on the tech and helped greatly with the research. Excellent work, Michael.

Ford Pierson, my in-house editor and illustrator, worked very hard to upgrade the line art in this book, including turning man in the box into Mini Me, a touch that displays his wit, cleverness, and complete lack of fear. Great job, Ford.

Scott Strubberg, Doug Jones, and Dave Rush, instructors at Total Seminars, were my sounding boards and research partners for this book, helping me turn the complicated into the understandable on many subjects. Thank you all very much!

On the McGraw-Hill side, the crew once again demonstrated why McGraw-Hill is the best in show as a publisher. With excellent work and even better attitude, this book came together smoothly.

■ *To my daughter Emily: Beautiful, happy, healthy, and successful—with a clear path ahead. I am content.*

—Dad

ABOUT THIS BOOK

■ Important Technology Skills

Information technology (IT) offers many career paths, leading to occupations in such fields as PC repair, network administration, telecommunications, Web development, graphic design, and desktop support. To become competent in any IT field, however, you need certain basic computer skills. Mike Meyers' CompTIA A+ Guide to 801: Managing and Troubleshooting PCs builds a foundation for success in the IT field by introducing you to fundamental technology concepts and giving you essential computer skills.

Try This! exercises apply core skills in a new setting.

Key Terms, identified in red, point out important vocabulary and definitions that you need to know.

Tech Tip sidebars provide inside information from experienced IT professionals.

Cross Check questions develop reasoning skills: ask, compare, contrast, and explain.

Engaging and Motivational—
Using a conversational style and proven instructional approach, the author explains technical concepts in a clear, interesting way using real-world examples.

Makes Learning Fun!—
Rich, colorful text and enhanced illustrations bring technical subjects to life.

Proven Learning Method Keeps You on Track

Mike Meyers' CompTIA A+ Guide to 801: Managing and Troubleshooting PCs is structured to give you comprehensive knowledge of computer skills and technologies. The textbook's active learning methodology guides you beyond mere recall and, through thought-provoking activities, labs, and sidebars, helps you develop critical-thinking, diagnostic, and communication skills.

Effective Learning Tools

This pedagogically rich book is designed to make learning easy and enjoyable and to help you develop the skills and critical-thinking abilities that will enable you to adapt to different job situations and troubleshoot problems.

Mike Meyers' proven ability to explain concepts in a clear, direct, even humorous way makes these books interesting, motivational, and fun.

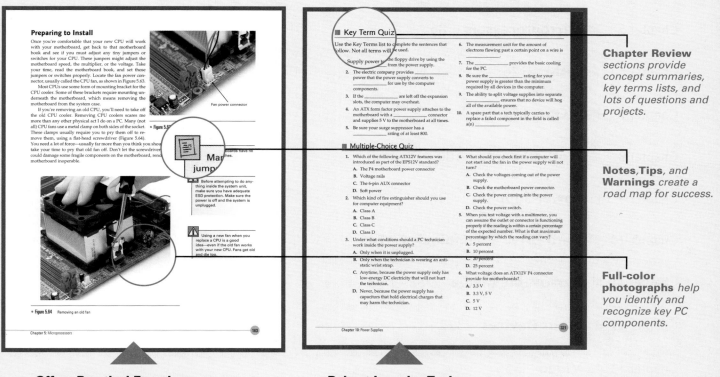

Chapter Review sections provide concept summaries, key terms lists, and lots of questions and projects.

Notes, Tips, and **Warnings** create a road map for success.

Full-color photographs help you identify and recognize key PC components.

Offers Practical Experience—
Tutorials and lab assignments develop essential hands-on skills and put concepts in real-world contexts.

Robust Learning Tools—
Summaries, key terms lists, quizzes, essay questions, and lab projects help you practice skills and measure progress.

Each chapter includes

- **Learning objectives** that set measurable goals for chapter-by-chapter progress
- **Try This!, Cross Check,** and **Tech Tip** sidebars that encourage you to practice and apply concepts in real-world settings
- **Notes, Tips,** and **Warnings** that guide you through difficult areas
- **Exam-driven organization** that divides chapters into Historical/Conceptual, 801, and Beyond A+ sections, making it easy to focus study time on the core and specialization areas of the exams

- Plenty of full-color **photographs** and **illustrations** that provide clear, up-close pictures of the technology, making difficult concepts easy to visualize and understand
- **Highlighted Key Terms, Key Terms lists,** and **Chapter Summaries** that provide you with an easy way to review important concepts and vocabulary
- **Challenging End-of-Chapter Quizzes** that include vocabulary-building exercises, multiple-choice questions, essay questions, and on-the-job lab projects

CONTENTS AT A GLANCE

CONTENTS

Chapter 15
■ Wireless Networking 456

Chapter 16
■ The Internet 474

Chapter 17
■ Multimedia 522

Chapter 18
■ Portable Computing 556

I started writing computer books for the simple reason that no one wrote the kind of books I wanted to read. The books were either too simple (Chapter 1, "Using Your Mouse") or too complex (Chapter 1, "TTL Logic and Transistors"), and none of them provided a motivation for me to learn the information. I believed that there were geeky readers just like me who wanted to know *why* they needed to know the information in a computer book.

Good books motivate readers to learn what they are reading. If a book discusses binary arithmetic but doesn't explain why I need to learn it, for example, that's not a good book. Tell me that understanding binary makes it easier to understand how a CPU works or why a megabyte is different from a million bytes—then I get excited, no matter how geeky the topic. If I don't have a good motivation to do something, then I'm simply not going to do it (which explains why I haven't jumped out of an airplane!).

In this book, I teach you why you need to understand the technology that runs almost every modern business. You'll learn to build and fix computers, exploring every nook and cranny, and master the art of the PC tech. In the process, you'll gain the knowledge you need to pass the CompTIA A+ certification exams.

Enjoy, my fellow geek.

Michael D. Meyers

■ It Pays to Get Certified

In a digital world, digital literacy is an essential survival skill. Certification proves you have the knowledge and skill to solve business problems in virtually any business environment. Certifications are highly valued credentials that qualify you for jobs, increased compensation, and promotion.

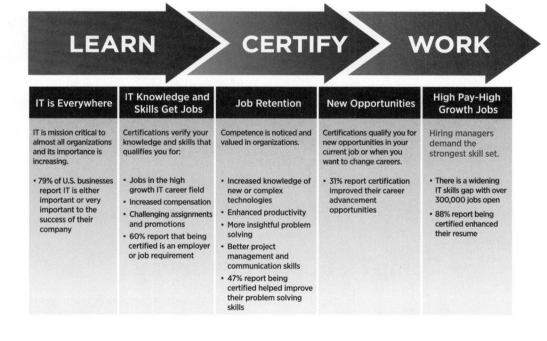

IT is Everywhere	IT Knowledge and Skills Get Jobs	Job Retention	New Opportunities	High Pay-High Growth Jobs
IT is mission critical to almost all organizations and its importance is increasing.	Certifications verify your knowledge and skills that qualifies you for:	Competence is noticed and valued in organizations.	Certifications qualify you for new opportunities in your current job or when you want to change careers.	Hiring managers demand the strongest skill set.
• 79% of U.S. businesses report IT is either important or very important to the success of their company	• Jobs in the high growth IT career field • Increased compensation • Challenging assignments and promotions • 60% report that being certified is an employer or job requirement	• Increased knowledge of new or complex technologies • Enhanced productivity • More insightful problem solving • Better project management and communication skills • 47% report being certified helped improve their problem solving skills	• 31% report certification improved their career advancement opportunities	• There is a widening IT skills gap with over 300,000 jobs open • 88% report being certified enhanced their resume

■ CompTIA A+ Certification Advances Your Career

- **The CompTIA A+ credential**—provides foundation-level knowledge and skills necessary for a career in PC repair and support.

- **Starting Salary**—CompTIA A+ Certified individuals can earn as much as $65,000 per year.

- **Career Pathway**—CompTIA A+ is a building block for other CompTIA certifications such as Network+, Security+ and vendor specific technologies.

- **More than 850,000**—individuals worldwide are CompTIA A+ certified.

- **Mandated/Recommended by organizations worldwide**—such as Cisco and HP and Ricoh, the U.S. State Department, and U.S. government contractors such as EDS, General Dynamics, and Northrop Grumman.

- **Some of the primary benefits individuals report from becoming CompTIA A+ certified are:**
 - More efficient troubleshooting
 - Improved career advancement
 - More insightful problem solving

■ CompTIA Career Pathway

CompTIA offers a number of credentials that form a foundation for your career in technology and that allow you to pursue specific areas of concentration. Depending on the path you choose to take, CompTIA certifications help you build upon your skills and knowledge, supporting learning throughout your entire career.

■ Steps to Getting Certified and Staying Certified

1. **Review exam objectives.** Review the certification objectives to make sure you know what is covered in the exam: www.comptia.org/certifications/testprep/examobjectives.aspx

2. **Practice for the exam.** After you have studied for the certification, take a free assessment and sample test to get an idea what type of questions might be on the exam: www.comptia.org/certifications/testprep/practicetests.aspx

3. **Purchase an exam voucher.** Purchase your exam voucher on the CompTIA Marketplace, which is located at: www.comptiastore.com

4. **Take the test!** Select a certification exam provider and schedule a time to take your exam. You can find exam providers at the following link: www.comptia.org/certifications/testprep/testingcenters.aspx

5. **Stay Certified!** Continuing education is required. Effective January 1, 2011, CompTIA A+ certifications are valid for three years from the date of certification. There are a number of ways the certification can be renewed. For more information go to: http://certification.comptia.org/getCertified/steps_to_certification/stayCertified.aspx

■ Join the Professional Community

The free online IT Pro Community provides valuable content to students and professionals. Join the IT Pro Community:

> http://itpro.comptia.org

Career IT job resources include:

- Where to start in IT
- Career assessments
- Salary trends
- U.S. job board

Join the IT Pro Community and get access to:

- Forums on networking, security, computing, and cutting-edge technologies
- Access to blogs written by industry experts
- Current information on cutting edge technologies
- Access to various industry resource links and articles related to IT and IT careers

■ Content Seal of Quality

This courseware bears the seal of CompTIA Approved Quality Content. This seal signifies this content covers 100 percent of the exam objectives and implements important instructional design principles. CompTIA recommends multiple learning tools to help increase coverage of the learning objectives.

Why CompTIA?

- **Global recognition**—CompTIA is recognized globally as the leading IT nonprofit trade association and has enormous credibility. Plus, CompTIA's certifications are vendor-neutral and offer proof of foundational knowledge that translates across technologies.

- **Valued by hiring managers**—Hiring managers value CompTIA certification because it is vendor- and technology-independent validation of your technical skills.

- **Recommended or required by government and businesses**—Many government organizations and corporations (for example, Dell, Sharp, Ricoh, the U.S. Department of Defense, and many more) either recommend or require technical staff to be CompTIA certified.

- **Three CompTIA certifications ranked in the top 10**—In a study by DICE of 17,000 technology professionals, certifications helped command higher salaries at all experience levels.

How to Obtain More Information

- *Visit CompTIA online*
 Go to www.comptia.org to learn more about getting CompTIA certified.

- *Contact CompTIA*
 Please call 866-835-8020, ext. 5 or e-mail questions@comptia.org.

- *Join the IT Pro Community*
 Go to http://itpro.comptia.org to join the IT community to get relevant career information.

- *Connect with CompTIA*
 Find us on Facebook, LinkedIn, Twitter, and YouTube.

CAQC Disclaimer

The logo of the CompTIA Approved Quality Curriculum (CAQC) program and the status of this or other training material as "Approved" under the CompTIA Approved Quality Curriculum program signifies that, in CompTIA's opinion, such training material covers the content of CompTIA's related certification exam.

The contents of this training material were created for the CompTIA A+ exams covering CompTIA certification objectives that were current as of the date of publication.

CompTIA has not reviewed or approved the accuracy of the contents of this training material and specifically disclaims any warranties of merchantability or fitness for a particular purpose. CompTIA makes no guarantee concerning the success of persons using any such "Approved" or other training material in order to prepare for any CompTIA certification exam.

For instructor and student resources, please visit:

www.mhprofessional.com/certification801

Students will find the chapter quizzes from the end of each chapter, and teachers can access instructor support materials.

■ Additional Resources for Teachers

The Online Learning Center provides resources for teachers in a format that follows the organization of the textbook.

This site includes the following:

- Answer keys to the end-of-chapter activities in the textbook
- Answer keys to the Mike Meyers' Lab Manual activities (Lab Manual available separately)
- Access to test bank files and software that allows you to generate a wide array of paper- or network-based tests, and that features automatic grading. The test bank includes:
 - Hundreds of practice questions and a wide variety of question types categorized by exam objective, enabling you to customize each test to maximize student progress
 - Blackboard cartridges and other formats may also be available upon request; contact your sales representative
- Engaging PowerPoint slides on the lecture topics that include full-color artwork from the book
- Instructor's Manual that contains learning objectives, classroom preparation notes, instructor tips, and a lecture outline for each chapter

Please contact your McGraw-Hill sales representative for details.

The Path of the PC Tech

"Never trust a computer you can't throw out a window."

—STEVE WOZNIAK

In this chapter, you will learn how to

- **Explain the importance of skill in managing and troubleshooting PCs**
- **Explain the importance of CompTIA A+ certification**
- **Describe how to become CompTIA A+ certified**

Computers have taken over the world, or at least many professions. Everywhere you turn, a quick dig beneath the surface sawdust of construction, the grease of auto mechanics, and the hum of medical technology reveals one or more personal computers (PCs) working away, doing essential jobs. Because the PC evolved from novelty item to essential science tool to everyday object in a short period of time, there's a huge demand for a workforce that can build, maintain, troubleshoot, and repair PCs.

■ The Importance of Skill in Managing and Troubleshooting PCs

The people who work with computers, often lumped into a single group known as the **Information Technology (IT)** workforce, do an amazingly varied number of jobs. These include diverse pursuits such as designing hardware, writing computer programs, and creating **networks** (groups of computers connected together to share data or programs). IT people built the Internet and maintain the millions of computers that keep it running.

But for all this IT diversity, it's the computer technicians (or **PC techs**, as those of us in the field call each other) who make up the core of the IT workforce. Without us techs, none of the other stuff would work, so none of the other jobs could exist. Getting workers with skill in building, maintaining, troubleshooting, and fixing PCs is essential for the success of every modern business. We need more PC techs. We need you!

In the early days of the personal computer, anyone who used a PC had to have skills as a PC tech. The PC was new, buggy, and prone to problems. If you owned a PC back then, you didn't want to rely on others to fix your PC when the inevitable problems arose. Today's PCs are much more robust and have fewer problems, so *using* one no longer requires having PC tech skills, but they're also much more complex machines. Today's IT industry, therefore, needs specialized workers who know how to make the machines run well and fix them when they break for the millions of users who lack PC tech skills.

Every profession requires specialized skills. For the most part, if you want to *get* or *keep* a job that requires those specialized skills, you need some type of **certification** or license. If you want a job fixing automobiles in the United States, for example, you get the Automotive Service Excellence (ASE) certification. If you want to perform companies' financial audits in the United Kingdom, you get your Chartered Accountant certification.

Nearly every profession has some criteria that you must meet to show your competence and ability to perform at a certain level. Although the way this works varies widely from one profession to another, all of them will at some point make you take an exam or series of exams. Passing these exams proves that you have the necessary skills to work at a certain level in your profession, whether you're an aspiring plumber, teacher, barber, or lawyer.

If you successfully pass these exams, the organization that administers them grants you a certification. You receive some piece of paper or pin or membership card that you can show to potential clients or employers. This certification gives those potential clients or employers a level of confidence that you can do what you say you can do. Without this certification, either you will not find suitable work in that profession or no one will trust you to do the work. Until relatively recently, PC technicians have been the exception to this rule.

■ The Importance of CompTIA A+ Certification

Microcomputers were introduced in the late 1970s, and for many years PC technicians did not have a universally recognized way to show clients or employers that they knew what to do under the hood of a personal computer. Sure, vendor-specific certifications existed, but the only way to get them was to get a job at an authorized warranty or repair facility first and then get the certification. There's nothing wrong with vendor-specific training, but no single manufacturer has taken enough market share to make IBM training, for example, something that works for any job. (Then there is always that little detail of getting the job first before you can be certified...)

The software and networking sides of our business have not suffered from the same lack of certifications. Due to the dominance of certain companies at one time or another (for example, Microsoft and Cisco), the vendor-specific certifications have provided a great way to get and keep a job. For example, Microsoft's Microsoft Certified IT Professional (MCITP) and Cisco's Cisco Certified Internetwork Expert (CCIE) certifications have opened the employment doors for many.

But what about the person who runs around all day repairing printers, repartitioning hard drives, upgrading device drivers, and assembling systems? What about the PC hobbyists who want to be paid for their skills? What about the folks who, because they had the audacity to show that they knew the difference between a homegroup and a workgroup, find themselves with a new title such as PC Support Technician or Electronic Services Specialist? On the other hand, how about the worst title of them all: "The Person Who Doesn't Get a Nickel Extra but Who Fixes the Computers?" CompTIA A+ certification gives these people a universally recognized way to prove their PC technical proficiency to employers or clients (and to seek due compensation for their skills).

What Is CompTIA A+ Certification?

CompTIA A+ certification is an industry-wide, vendor-neutral certification program developed and sponsored by the **Computing Technology Industry Association (CompTIA)**. The CompTIA A+ certification shows that you have a basic competence in supporting microcomputers. You achieve this certification by taking two computer-based, multiple-choice exams. The tests cover what technicians should know after 12 months of hands-on work on PCs, either from a job or as a student in the lab. CompTIA A+ certification enjoys wide recognition throughout the computer industry. To date, more than 800,000 technicians have become CompTIA A+ certified, making it the most popular of all IT certifications.

Who Is CompTIA?

CompTIA is a nonprofit industry trade association based in Oakbrook Terrace, Illinois. It consists of over 20,000 members in 102 countries. You'll

find CompTIA offices in such diverse locales as Amsterdam, Dubai, Johannesburg, Tokyo, and São Paulo.

CompTIA provides a forum for people in these industries to network (as in meeting people), represents the interests of its members to the government, and provides certifications for many aspects of the computer industry. CompTIA sponsors CompTIA A+, CompTIA Network+, CompTIA Security+, and other certifications. CompTIA works hard to watch the IT industry and constantly looks to provide new certifications to meet the ongoing demand from its membership. Check out the CompTIA Web site at **www.comptia.org** for details on the other certifications you can obtain from CompTIA.

Virtually every company of consequence in the IT industry is a member of CompTIA. Here are a few of the biggies:

Adobe Systems	AMD	Best Buy	Brother International
Canon	Cisco Systems	CompUSA	Fujitsu
Gateway	Hewlett-Packard	IBM	Intel
Kyocera	McAfee	Microsoft	NCR
Novell	Panasonic	Sharp Electronics	Siemens
Symantec	Toshiba	Total Seminars, LLC (that's my company)	Plus many thousands more

CompTIA began offering CompTIA A+ certification back in 1993. When it debuted, the IT industry largely ignored CompTIA A+ certification. Since that initial stutter, however, the CompTIA A+ certification has grown to become the de facto requirement for entrance into the PC industry. Many companies require CompTIA A+ certification for all of their PC support technicians, and the CompTIA A+ certification is widely recognized both in the United States and internationally. Additionally, many other certifications recognize CompTIA A+ certification and use it as credit toward their certifications.

The Path to Other Certifications

Most IT companies—big and small—see CompTIA A+ certification as the entry point to IT. From CompTIA A+, you have a number of certification options, depending on whether you want to focus more on hardware and operating systems or move into network administration (although these aren't mutually exclusive goals). The following three certifications are worth serious consideration:

- CompTIA Network+ certification
- Microsoft technical certifications
- Cisco certifications

CompTIA Network+ Certification

If you haven't already achieved CompTIA Network+ certification, make it your next certification goal after CompTIA A+ certification. Just as CompTIA A+ certification shows that you have solid competency as a PC

CompTIA A+ is the entry point to IT, though definitely not the only route for learning about computers and having certifications to prove that knowledge. Several certifications cover computer literacy or digital literacy, the phrase that means "what every person needs to know about computers to survive in the 21st century." The most popular computer literacy certification is Certiport's IC³ certification that tests on general computer knowledge; office productivity applications, such as Word and PowerPoint; and Internet applications such as Web browsers and e-mail clients.

CompTIA has a pre–CompTIA A+ exam (*not* a certification), called the *CompTIA Strata IT Fundamentals exam*, that's geared a bit more to a user preparing to become a tech. It's designed to check basic knowledge levels for people getting into IT.

technician, **CompTIA Network+ certification** demonstrates your skills as a network technician, including your understanding of network hardware, installation, and troubleshooting. CompTIA's Network+ certification is a natural step for continuing toward your Microsoft or Cisco certifications. Take the CompTIA Network+: it's your obvious next certification.

Microsoft Technical Certifications

Microsoft operating systems control a huge portion of all installed networks, and those networks need qualified support people to make them run. Pursuing Microsoft's series of certifications for networking professionals is a natural next step after completing the CompTIA certifications. They offer a whole slew of tracks and exams, ranging from simple specializations in Windows 7 to numerous **Microsoft Certified IT Professional (MCITP)** certifications and beyond. You can find more details on the Microsoft Learning Web site at www.microsoft.com/learning/en/us/certification/cert-overview.aspx.

Cisco Certification

Let's face it: Cisco routers pretty much run the Internet and most intranets in the world. A *router* is a networking device that controls and directs the flow of information over networks, such as e-mail messages, Web browsing, and so on. Cisco provides five levels of IT certification for folks who want to show their skills at handling Cisco products, such as the **Cisco Certified Network Associate (CCNA)**, plus numerous specialty certifications. See the Cisco IT Certification Web site here for more details: www.cisco.com/web/learning/le3/learning_career_certifications_and_learning_paths_home.html.

■ How Do I Become CompTIA A+ Certified?

You become CompTIA A+ certified, in the simplest sense, by taking and passing two computer-based, multiple-choice exams. No prerequisites are required for taking the CompTIA A+ certification exams (although there's an assumption of computer literacy, whether or not you have one of the computer literacy certifications). There is no required training course and no training materials to buy. You *do* have to pay a testing fee for each of the two exams. You pay your testing fees, go to a local testing center, and take the tests. You immediately know whether you have passed or failed. By passing both exams, you become CompTIA A+ certified.

What's the Deal with "No More Lifetime Certification"?

In early 2010, CompTIA announced that, effective January 1, 2011, CompTIA A+, CompTIA Network+, and CompTIA Security+ certifications would no longer be considered "certified for life." If you passed any of these exams before the deadline, you're still certified for life for those exams. For any

exams that you pass on or after January 1, 2011, to stay certified, every three years you'll need to either retake the exam or perform sufficient continuing education as specified by CompTIA.

Retaking the exams isn't that hard to understand, but the continuing education requirement is a bit more complex. Instead of trying to explain it all here, please review CompTIA's documentation at http://certification .comptia.org/Libraries/Certification_Documents/ceu_faq.sflb.ashx.

Most importantly, if you pursue the continuing education path, you'll need to earn 20 continuing education units (CEUs) each three-year period to renew your CompTIA A+ certification. How do you earn these CEUs? You can participate in industry events and seminars, complete a presentation, participate in IT training, teach a course, or earn another higher-level certification. The number of CEUs that you earn by completing each of these requirements varies, and each requires that you submit documentation to CompTIA for their review.

Personally, I think this is a long-overdue feature. Someone who took the CompTIA A+ exam in 2010 had no way to distinguish himself from a person who took the exam in 1997, and that wasn't fair. By no longer awarding "certified for life" status, CompTIA's certifications are now in line with Microsoft, Cisco, and other industry certifications.

The Basic Exam Structure

The two exams introduced by CompTIA in 2012 are **CompTIA A+ 220-801** (Hardware) and **CompTIA A+ 220-802** (Operating Systems). The terms "Hardware" and "Operating Systems" are not officially part of the exam names, but I've included them here because they're commonly used to reference the exams. It's also common to refer to these two exams as the "2012" exams to differentiate them from older CompTIA exams. Although you may take either of the two exams first, I recommend taking 220-801 followed by 220-802. The 220-801 exam (covered by this book) concentrates on understanding terminology and technology, how to do fundamental tasks such as upgrading RAM, and basic network and laptop support. The 220-802 exam builds on the first exam, concentrating on Windows support, advanced configuration, and troubleshooting scenarios.

Both of the exams are extremely practical, with little or no interest in history. All questions are multiple-choice, simulation, or "click on the right part of the picture" questions. The following is an example of the type of questions you will see on the exams:

Your laser printer is printing blank pages. Which item should you check first?

A. Printer drivers

B. Toner cartridge

C. Printer settings

D. Paper feed

The correct answer is B, the toner cartridge. You can make an argument for any of the others, but common sense (and skill as a PC technician) tells you to check the simplest possibility first.

The 2012 exams use a regular test format in which you answer a set number of questions and are scored based on how many correct answers you give. These exams have no more than 100 questions each. (Both exams have 100 questions each at the time of this writing.)

Be aware that CompTIA may add new questions to the exams at any time to keep the content fresh. The subject matter covered by the exams won't change, but new questions may be added periodically at random intervals. This policy puts strong emphasis on understanding concepts and having solid PC-tech knowledge rather than on trying to memorize specific questions and answers that may have been on the tests in the past. No book or Web resource will have all the "right answers" because those answers change constantly. Luckily for you, however, this book not only teaches you what steps to follow in a particular case, but also explains how to be a knowledgeable tech who understands *why* you're doing those steps. That way when you encounter a new problem (or test question), you can work out the answer. This will help you not only to pass the exams, but also to be a better PC tech!

To keep up to date, we monitor the CompTIA A+ exams for new content and update the special Tech Files section of the Total Seminars Web site (www.totalsem.com) with new articles covering subjects we believe may appear on future versions of the exams.

Windows-Centric

The CompTIA A+ exams focus on the Microsoft Windows operating systems you would expect to find on a PC at a workstation or in a home. There are no Linux questions. There are no Mac OS X questions. The 802 exam will ask you about the common mobile device operating systems, iOS and Android, but the vast majority of operating system questions on both exams address Windows. Objectives in the exams cover the following operating systems:

- Windows XP Home, Windows XP Professional, Windows XP Media Center, Windows XP 64-bit Professional
- Windows Vista Home Basic, Windows Vista Home Premium, Windows Vista Business, Windows Vista Ultimate, Windows Vista Enterprise
- Windows 7 Starter, Windows 7 Home Premium, Windows 7 Professional, Windows 7 Ultimate, Windows 7 Enterprise

Windows 8

CompTIA has the darnedest luck when it comes to the timing of new CompTIA A+ exams compared to releases of new Windows versions. In 2006, CompTIA released an update to the CompTIA A+ exams about four months before Microsoft released Windows Vista. In 2009, CompTIA missed Windows 7 by about one month (though CompTIA released a Windows 7 update to the exams in late 2009).

It seems that CompTIA will once again run into what I'm going to call the "CompTIA Windows Curse." As the new 220-801 and 220-802 exams come out in late 2012, it looks like Windows 8 will come out just a few

months later. Assuming CompTIA stays true to form, there's a very good chance that you'll see a Windows 8 update on the exams within a year or two of the Windows 8 rollout. Be sure to check the CompTIA Web site or contact me directly at michaelm@totalsem.com to see if any Windows 8 updates have taken place.

Exam 220–801

The book you're reading covers the CompTIA A+ 220-801 Exam. The questions on this exam fit into one of five domains. The number of questions for each domain is based on the percentages shown in Table 1.1.

The 220-801 exam tests your knowledge of computer components, expecting you to be able to identify just about every common device on PCs, including variations within device types. Here's a list:

- Floppy drives
- Hard drives
- Optical drives
- Solid state drives
- Motherboards
- Power supplies
- CPUs
- RAM
- Monitors
- Input devices, such as keyboards, mice, and touchscreens
- Video and multimedia cards
- Network and modem cards
- Cables and connectors
- Heat sinks, fans, and liquid cooling systems
- Laptops and portable devices
- Printers
- Scanners
- Network switches, cabling, and wireless adapters
- Biometric devices

The 220-801 exam tests your ability to install, configure, and maintain all the hardware technology involved in a personal computer. You need to be able to install and set up a hard drive, for example, and configure devices in Windows XP, Windows Vista, and Windows 7. You have to understand device drivers. Additionally, this exam puts a lot of emphasis on operational procedures, such as safety and environmental issues, communication, and professionalism. You need to understand how to avoid hazardous situations. The exam tests your ability to communicate effectively with customers and coworkers. You need to understand professional behavior and demonstrate that you have tact, discretion, and respect for others and their property.

Table 1.1	Exam 220-801 Domains and Percentages
Domain	**Percentage**
1.0 PC Hardware	40%
2.0 Networking	27%
3.0 Laptops	11%
4.0 Printers	11%
5.0 Operational Procedures	11%

Exam 220-802

The CompTIA A+ 220-802 exam covers four domains. Table 1.2 lists the domains and the percentage of questions dedicated to each domain.

The 220-802 exam covers the configuration, repair, and troubleshooting of the Windows operating system. You have to know your way around Windows and understand the tasks involved in updating, upgrading, and installing Windows XP, Windows Vista, and Windows 7. You need to know the standard diagnostic tools available in Windows so that you can fix problems and work with higher-level techs. Make sure you know Windows; 33% of the 220-802 questions are going to challenge you on this.

The biggest part of the 220-802 exam is dedicated to troubleshooting. Think in terms of a hands-on approach to determining the appropriate technology for a situation—running diagnostics and troubleshooting—rather than identification of hardware or operating system utilities. You need to understand how all the technology should work, know the proper steps to figure out why something doesn't work, and then know how to fix it.

The 220-802 exam adds mobile devices to the objectives, a new topic for 2012. While the smartphone and tablet market covers an impossibly wide array of hardware and software, the 220-802 exam focuses on Apple iOS and Google Android devices. You'll need to know how to interact with the hardware and software, as well as configure personal settings, such as those for e-mail clients and security.

Security is a big topic on the 220-802 exam. You need to know quite a bit about computer security, from physical security (door locks to retinal scanners), to knowledge of security threats (malware and viruses), to the ways in which to secure an individual computer. This also includes coverage of how to recycle and dispose of computer gear properly.

You'll also be tested on methods of securing networks. You'll need to know how to access a small office/home office (SOHO) router or wireless access point and configure that device to protect your network.

How Do I Take the Exams?

Pearson VUE administers the CompTIA A+ testing at over 5000 testing centers in 165 countries. You may take the exams at any testing center. You can select the closest training center and schedule your exams right from the comfort of your favorite Web browser by going to the Pearson VUE Web site:

www.vue.com

Alternatively, in the United States and Canada, call Pearson VUE at 877-551-PLUS (7587) to schedule the exams and to locate the nearest testing

Table 1.2	Exam 220-802 Domains and Percentages
Domain	**Percentage**
1.0 Operating Systems	33%
2.0 Security	22%
3.0 Mobile Devices	9%
4.0 Troubleshooting	36%

center. International customers can find a list of Pearson VUE international contact numbers for various regions of the world on CompTIA's Web site at www.comptia.org.

You must pay for the exam when you call to schedule. Be prepared to sit on hold for a while. Have your Social Security number (or international equivalent) and a credit card ready when you call. Pearson VUE will be glad to invoice you, but you won't be able to take the exam until they receive full payment.

Pearson VUE will accommodate any special needs, although this may limit your selection of testing locations.

How Much Does the Exam Cost?

The cost of the exam depends on whether you work for a CompTIA member or not. At this writing, the cost for non-CompTIA members is $178 (U.S.) for each exam. International prices vary, but you can check the CompTIA Web site for international pricing. Of course, the prices are subject to change without notice, so always check the CompTIA Web site for current pricing.

Very few people pay full price for the exam. Virtually every organization that provides CompTIA A+ training and testing also offers discount **vouchers**. You buy a discount voucher and then use the voucher number instead of a credit card when you schedule the exam. Vouchers are sold per exam, so you'll need two vouchers to take the two CompTIA A+ exams. Total Seminars is one place to get discount vouchers. You can call Total Seminars at 800-446-6004 or 281-922-4166, or get vouchers via the Web site: www.totalsem.com. No one should ever pay full price for CompTIA A+ exams.

How to Pass the CompTIA A+ Exams

The single most important thing to remember about the CompTIA A+ certification exams is that CompTIA designed the exams to test the knowledge of a technician with only 12 months of experience, so keep it simple! The exams aren't interested in your ability to overclock DDR3 CAS timings in CMOS or whether you can explain the exact difference between the Intel ICH10 and the AMD 790 southbridges. Think in terms of practical knowledge and standards. Read this book, do whatever works for you to memorize the key concepts and procedures, take the practice exams on the media accompanying this book, review any topics you miss, and you should pass with no problem.

Those of you who just want more knowledge in managing and troubleshooting PCs can follow the same strategy as certification-seekers. Think in practical terms and work with the PC as you go through each chapter.

Some of you may be in or just out of school, so studying for exams is nothing novel. But if you haven't had to study for and take an exam in a while, or if you think maybe you could use some tips, you may find the next section valuable. It lays out a proven strategy for preparing to take and pass the CompTIA A+ exams. Try it. It works.

Obligate Yourself

The very first step you should take is to schedule yourself for the exams. Have you ever heard the old adage, "Heat and pressure make diamonds"? Well, if you don't give yourself a little "heat," you'll end up procrastinating

and delay taking the exams, possibly forever. Do yourself a favor. Using the following information, determine how much time you'll need to study for the exams, and then call Pearson VUE and schedule the exams accordingly. Knowing the exams are coming up makes it much easier to turn off the television and crack open the book. You can schedule an exam as little as a few weeks in advance, but if you schedule an exam and can't take it at the scheduled time, you must reschedule at least a day in advance or you'll lose your money.

Set Aside the Right Amount of Study Time

After helping thousands of techs get their CompTIA A+ certification, we at Total Seminars have developed a pretty good feel for the amount of study time needed to pass the CompTIA A+ certification exams. The following table provides an estimate to help you plan how much study time you must commit to the CompTIA A+ certification exams. Keep in mind that these are averages. If you're not a great student or if you're a little on the nervous side, add 10 percent; if you're a fast learner or have a good bit of computer experience, you may want to reduce the figures.

To use Table 1.3, just circle the values that are most accurate for you and add them up to get your estimated total hours of study time.

To that value, add hours based on the number of months of direct, professional experience you have had supporting PCs, as shown in Table 1.4.

A total neophyte often needs roughly 240 hours of study time. An experienced tech shouldn't need more than 60 hours.

Total hours for you to study: _____.

A Strategy for Study

Now that you have a feel for how long it's going to take to prepare for the exams, you're ready to develop a study strategy. I'd like to suggest a strategy that has worked for others who've come before you, whether they were experienced techs or total newbies.

This book is designed to accommodate the different study agendas of these two groups of students. The first group is experienced techs who already have strong PC experience but need to be sure they're ready to be tested on the specific subjects covered by the CompTIA A+ exams. The second group is those with little or no background in the computer field. These techs can benefit from a more detailed understanding of the history and concepts that underlie modern PC technology, to help them remember the specific subject matter information they must know for the exams. I'll use the shorthand terms Old Techs and New Techs for these two groups. If you're not sure which group you fall into, pick a few chapters and go through some end-of-chapter questions. If you score less than 70%, go the New Tech route.

I have broken most of the chapters into three distinct parts:

Not all chapters have all three parts.

- **Historical/Conceptual** Topics that are not on the CompTIA A+ exams but will help you understand more clearly what is on the CompTIA A+ exams

- **801** Topics that clearly fit under the CompTIA A+ 220-801 exam domains

- **Beyond A+** More advanced issues that probably will not be on the CompTIA A+ exams—yet

Table 1.3	Analyzing Skill Levels			
		Amount of Experience		
Tech Task	**None**	**Once or Twice**	**Every Now and Then**	**Quite a Bit**
Installing an adapter card	6	4	2	1
Installing and configuring hard drives	12	10	8	2
Installing modems and NICs	8	6	6	3
Connecting a computer to the Internet	16	10	8	4
Installing printers and scanners	16	8	4	2
Installing RAM	8	6	4	2
Installing CPUs	8	7	5	3
Repairing printers	6	5	4	3
Repairing boot problems	8	7	7	5
Repairing portable computers	8	6	4	2
Configuring mobile devices	4	3	2	1
Building complete systems	12	10	8	6
Using the command line	8	8	6	4
Installing and optimizing Windows	10	8	6	4
Using Windows XP	6	6	4	2
Using Windows Vista	8	6	4	2
Using Windows 7	8	6	4	2
Configuring NTFS, Users, and Groups	6	4	3	2
Configuring a wireless network	6	5	3	2
Configuring a software firewall	6	4	2	1
Configuring sound	2	2	1	0
Removing malware	4	3	2	0
Using OS diagnostic tools	8	8	6	4
Using a multimeter	4	3	2	1

Table 1.4	Adding Up Your Study Time
Months of Direct, Professional Experience...	**Hours to Add to Your Study Time...**
0	50
Up to 6	30
6 to 12	10
Over 12	0

The beginning of each of these parts is clearly marked with a large banner that looks like this:

Historical/Conceptual

Those of you who fall into the Old Tech group may want to skip everything except the 801 parts in each chapter. After reading the sections in those parts, jump immediately to the questions at the end of the chapter. The end-of-chapter questions concentrate on information in the 801 sections. If you run into problems, review the Historical/Conceptual sections in that chapter. Note that you may need to skip back to previous chapters to get the Historical/Conceptual information you need for later chapters.

After going through every chapter as described, Old Techs can move directly to testing their knowledge by using the free practice exams on the media that accompanies the book. Once you start scoring above 90%, you're ready to take the exams. If you're a New Tech—or if you're an Old Tech who wants the full learning experience this book can offer—start by reading the book, *the whole book*, as though you were reading a novel, from page one to the end without skipping around. Because so many computer terms and concepts build on each other, skipping around greatly increases the odds that you will become confused and end up closing the book and firing up your favorite PC game. Not that I have anything against PC games, but unfortunately that skill is *not* useful for the CompTIA A+ exams!

Your goal on this first read is to understand concepts, the *whys* behind the *hows*. Having a PC nearby as you read is helpful so you can stop and inspect the PC to see a piece of hardware or how a particular concept manifests in the real world. As you read about hard drives, for example, inspect the cables. Do they look like the ones in the book? Is there a variation? Why? It is imperative that you understand why you are doing something, not just how to do it on one particular system under one specific set of conditions. Neither the exams nor real life as a PC tech works that way.

If you're reading this book as part of a managing and troubleshooting PCs class rather than a certification-prep course, I highly recommend going the New Tech route, even if you have a decent amount of experience. The book contains a lot of details that can trip you up if you focus only on the test-specific sections of the chapters. Plus, your program might stress historical and conceptual knowledge as well as practical, hands-on skills.

The CompTIA A+ certification exams assume that you have basic user skills. The exams really try to trick you with questions on processes that you may do every day and not think much about. Here's a classic: "To move a file from the C:\DATA folder to the D:\ drive using Windows Explorer, what key must you hold down while dragging the file?" If you can answer that without going to your keyboard and trying a few likely keys, you're better than most techs! In the real world, you can try a few wrong answers before you hit on the right one, but for the exams, you have to *know* it. Whether Old Tech or New Tech, make sure you are proficient at user-level Windows skills, including the following:

- Recognizing all the components of the standard Windows desktop (Start menu, notification area, etc.)
- Manipulating windows—resizing, moving, and so on
- Creating, deleting, renaming, moving, and copying files and folders within Windows
- Understanding file extensions and their relationship with program associations
- Using common keyboard shortcuts/hotkeys
- Installing, running, and closing a Windows application

Any PC technician who has been around a while will tell you that one of the great secrets in the computer business is that there's almost never anything completely new in the world of computer technology. Faster, cleverer, smaller, wider—absolutely—but the underlying technology, the core of what makes your PC and its various peripheral devices operate, has changed remarkably little since PCs came into widespread use a few decades ago. When you do your initial read-through, you may be tempted to skip the Historical/Conceptual sections—don't! Understanding the history and technological developments behind today's PCs helps you understand why they work—or don't work—the way they do. Basically, I'm passing on to you the kind of knowledge you might get by apprenticing yourself to an older, experienced PC tech.

After you've completed the first read-through, go through the book again, this time in textbook mode. If you're an Old Tech, start your studying here. Try to cover one chapter at a sitting. Concentrate on the 801 section. Get a highlighter and mark the phrases and sentences that bring out major points. Be sure you understand how the pictures and illustrations relate to the concepts being discussed.

Once you feel you have a good grasp of the material in the book, you can check your knowledge by using the practice exams included on the media accompanying this book. You can take these in Practice mode or Final mode. In Practice mode, you can use the Assistance window to get a helpful hint for the current questions, use the Reference feature to find the chapter that covers the question, check your answer for the question, and see an explanation of the correct answer. In Final mode, you answer all the questions and receive an exam score at the end, just like the real thing. You can also adjust the number of questions on a Practice or Final mode exam with the Customize option.

Both modes show you an overall grade, expressed as a percentage, as well as a breakdown of how well you did on each exam domain. The Review Questions feature lets you see which questions you missed and what the correct answers are. Use these results to guide further studying. Continue reviewing the topics you miss and taking additional exams until you are consistently scoring in the 90% range. When you get there, you are ready to pass the CompTIA A+ certification exams.

Study Tactics

Perhaps it's been a while since you had to study for a test. Or perhaps it hasn't, but you've done your best since then to block the whole experience from your mind. Either way, savvy test-takers know that certain techniques make studying for tests more efficient and effective.

Here's a trick used by students in law and medical schools who have to memorize reams of information: write it down. The act of writing something down (not typing, *writing*) in and of itself helps you to remember it, even if you never look at what you wrote again. Try taking separate notes on the material and re-creating diagrams by hand to help solidify the information in your mind.

Another oldie but goodie: Make yourself flash cards with questions and answers on topics you find difficult. A third trick: Take your notes to bed and read them just before you go to sleep. Many people find they really do learn while they sleep!

Contact

If you have any problems, any questions, or if you just want to argue about something, feel free to send an e-mail to the author—michaelm@totalsem.com— or to the editor—scottj@totalsem.com.

For any other information you might need, contact CompTIA directly at their Web site: www.comptia.org.

■ Chapter Summary

After reading this chapter and completing the exercises, you should understand the following about the path of the PC tech.

Explain the importance of skill in managing and troubleshooting PCs

- The IT workforce designs, builds, and maintains computers, computer programs, and networks. PC techs take care of personal computers, thus representing an essential component in that workforce. As PCs become more complex, the IT workforce needs specialized PC techs.

- Certifications prove to employers that you have the necessary skills to perform the job. If you want a job fixing automobiles in the United States, for example, you get the Automotive Service Excellence (ASE) certification. To become certified, you take and successfully pass exams. Then the organization that developed those exams grants you certification. Gaining certification is particularly important for IT workers.

Explain the importance of CompTIA A+ certification

- In the early days of the personal computer, you could get vendor-specific certifications, such as IBM Technician, but nothing general for PC techs. Worse, you often had to have a job at an authorized warranty or repair facility to get the vendor-specific certification. The software and networking side of IT has not suffered from the same lack of certifications. To prove skill in working with Windows, for example, you could become a Microsoft Certified IT Professional (MCITP).

- CompTIA A+ certification is an industry-wide, vendor-neutral certification program that shows that you have a basic competence in supporting microcomputers. You achieve this certification by taking two computer-based, multiple-choice exams. The tests cover what technicians should know after 12 months of hands-on work on PCs, either from a job or as a student in the lab. CompTIA A+ certification enjoys wide recognition throughout the computer industry.

- CompTIA is a nonprofit, industry trade association based in Oakbrook Terrace, Illinois. It consists of over 20,000 members in 102 countries. CompTIA provides a forum for people in these industries to network, represents the interests of its members to the government, and provides certifications for many aspects of the computer industry. CompTIA sponsors CompTIA A+, CompTIA Network+, CompTIA Security+, and other certifications.

- The CompTIA A+ certification is the de facto entry point to IT. From CompTIA A+, you have a number of certification options, depending on whether you want to focus more on hardware and operating systems or move into network administration. You can get CompTIA Network+ certification, for example, or go on to get Microsoft or Cisco certified. CompTIA Network+ certification is the most obvious certification to get after becoming CompTIA A+ certified.

Describe how to become CompTIA A+ certified

- You become CompTIA A+ certified, in the simplest sense, by taking and passing two computer-based, multiple-choice exams. No prerequisites are required for taking the CompTIA A+ certification exams. There is no required training course and no training materials to buy. You *do* have to pay a testing fee for each of the two exams. To stay current, you need to retest every three years or gain continuing education credits.

- The CompTIA exams introduced in 2012 are *220-801* and *220-802*. It's common to refer to these two exams as the 2012 exams to differentiate them from older CompTIA exams. Although you may take either of the two exams first, I recommend taking the 220-801 followed by the 220-802.

- Both of the exams are extremely practical, with little or no interest in theory. All questions are multiple-choice, simulation, or "click on the right part of the picture" questions. CompTIA may add new questions to the exams at any time to keep the content fresh, although the subject matter covered by the exams won't change.

- The Pearson VUE company administers the CompTIA A+ exams. You can schedule the exam times and location via the Pearson VUE Web site at www.vue.com. Check CompTIA's Web site for international links.

- To achieve success with the CompTIA A+ certification exams, think in terms of practical knowledge. Read the book. Work through the problems. Work with computers. Take the practice exams. You should obligate yourself by scheduling your exams. This keeps you focused on study.

- Read the book all the way through once. Experienced techs ("Old Techs") should then concentrate on the test-specific sections to prepare for the exams. Less experienced techs ("New Techs") should read the book all the way through again until everything makes sense.

- If you're reading this book as part of a managing and troubleshooting PCs class rather than a certification-prep course, I highly recommend going the New Tech route, even if you have a decent amount of experience. The book contains a lot of details that can trip you up if you focus only on the test-specific sections of the chapters.

■ Key Terms

certification *(1)*
Cisco Certified Network Associate (CCNA) *(4)*
CompTIA A+ 220-801 *(5)*
CompTIA A+ 220-802 *(5)*
CompTIA A+ certification *(2)*
CompTIA Network+ certification *(4)*
Computing Technology Industry Association (CompTIA) *(2)*

Information Technology (IT) *(1)*
Microsoft Certified IT Professional (MCITP) *(4)*
network *(1)*
PC tech *(1)*
Pearson VUE *(8)*
voucher *(9)*
www.comptia.org *(3)*

■ Key Term Quiz

Use the Key Terms list to complete the sentences that follow. Not all terms will be used.

1. You can lump together all the folks who design, build, program, and fix computers into the _____ workforce.

2. You become CompTIA A+ certified by passing the _____ and CompTIA A+ 220-802 exams.

3. A(n) _____ gives clients and employers a level of confidence that you can do what you say you can do.

4. A casual term for a person who builds and maintains computers is _____.

5. The _____ company administers the CompTIA A+ certification exams.

6. You can use a(n) _____ when you schedule your exam to save some money.

7. Persons desiring to work in Windows-based networking should pursue _____ certification after completing their CompTIA certifications.

8. You can find the latest information about the CompTIA A+ certification exams here: _____.

9. Typically, techs who attain CompTIA A+ certification then pursue _____ to add to their computer credentials.

10. A grouping of computers that enables people to share resources is called a(n) _____.

■ Multiple-Choice Quiz

1. Which of the following is a vendor-specific certification? (Select all that apply.)

 A. Cisco Certified Network Associate

 B. CompTIA A+

 C. CompTIA Network+

 D. Microsoft Certified IT Professional

2. Which of the following certifications is the de facto requirement for entrance into the PC industry?

 A. Certified Cisco Network Associate

 B. CompTIA A+

 C. CompTIA Network+

 D. Microsoft Certified IT Professional

3. John loves the Internet and wants a career working on the machines that make the Internet work. He has completed both CompTIA A+ and CompTIA Network+ certifications. Which of the following certifications would make a good next step?

 A. Cisco Certified Network Associate

 B. Certified Cisco Network Professional

 C. CompTIA Security+

 D. Microsoft Certified IT Professional

4. Which of the following exams focuses on installing, configuring, and maintaining all the standard technology involved in a personal computer?

 A. Certified Cisco Network Associate

 B. CompTIA A+ 220-801

 C. CompTIA A+ 220-802

 D. Microsoft Certified IT Professional

5. At which of the following Web sites can you register to take the CompTIA A+ certification exams?

 A. www.comptia.org

 B. www.microsoft.com

 C. www.totalsem.com

 D. www.vue.com

6. How many exams must you pass to become CompTIA A+ certified?

 A. One

 B. Two

 C. Three

 D. Four

7. How much practical IT experience do you need to become CompTIA A+ certified?

 A. Six months

 B. One year

 C. Two years

 D. None

8. How many questions should you expect on the 220-801 exam?

 A. 25

 B. 50

 C. 100

 D. The number of questions varies because the exams are adaptive.

9. The CompTIA A+ certification covers which of the following operating systems? (Select two.)

 A. Linux

 B. Mac OS X

 C. Windows XP Media Center

 D. Windows 7

10. What percentage of questions should you expect on operating systems in the 220-802 exam?

 A. 15%

 B. 22%

 C. 30%

 D. 33%

11. What percentage of questions should you expect on networking in the 220-801 exam?

 A. 10%

 B. 17%

 C. 25%

 D. 27%

12. How much does it cost to take each exam (at the time of this book's publication)?

 A. $100 each

 B. $138 each

 C. $178 each

 D. $150 each

13. What percentage of questions should you expect on Windows 8 in the 220-802 exam?

 A. 10%

 B. 13%

 C. 20%

 D. 0%

14. The 220-801 exam will *not* test you on which of the following computer components?

 A. Biometric devices

 B. Keyboards

 C. Printers

 D. Zip drives

15. If you skip the continuing education path to recertify, how often do you need to take the CompTIA A+ exams to retain your status as a CompTIA A+ certified technician?

 A. Every year

 B. Every three years

 C. Every ten years

 D. Never

■ Essay Quiz

1. Write a short essay on the benefits of certification in the field of computers. Include discussion on how the CompTIA certifications function within the broader category of computer certification. Why do you suppose people get certifications rather than (or in addition to) two- and four-year college degrees in IT?

Lab Project

• Lab Project 1.1

If you have access to the Internet, do some searching on computer certifications. Make a personal certification tree or pathway that maps out a series of certifications to pursue that might interest you.

Which certifications would be useful if you want to be a graphics designer, for example? What if you want to create computer games?

Operational Procedures

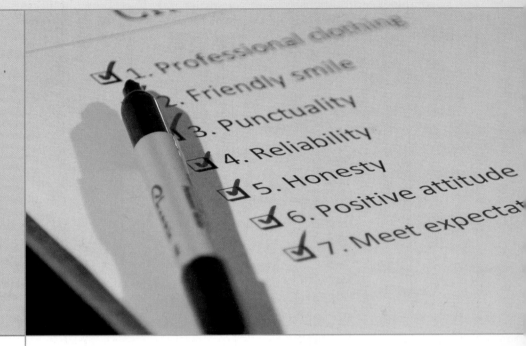

"The real problem is not whether machines think but whether men do."

—B. F. SKINNER

In this chapter, you will learn how to

- **Present yourself with a proper appearance and professional manner**
- **Talk to customers in a professional, productive manner**
- **Work with PCs safely using the proper tools**

Teaching new techs helps me keep up with the skills that get a tech a job and the issues that cause them to lose the jobs they get. To me, the number one reason techs fail to get or hold onto a job isn't lack of technical skill; it's a lack of what CompTIA calls "operational procedures." Personally, I think a better name might be "life skills and basic safety," but it boils down to the same thing: nontechnical skills that technicians are famous for lacking.

I like to describe myself as a "nerd" and I consider it a compliment if you call me one. Nerds are smart and like to work with technology—these are the good aspects of nerd-dom. On the other hand, most people would think of the term nerd as an insult. Nerds are rarely portrayed in a positive manner in the media, and I think I know why. Nerds generally suffer from some pretty serious social weaknesses. These weaknesses are classics: bad clothing, shyness, and poor communication skills. If you've ever seen an episode of the TV show *The Big Bang Theory*, you know what I'm talking about.

This chapter covers some basic life skills to enable you to enjoy your nerdiness and yet function out in the real world. You'll learn how to dress, how to act, and how to communicate. After you're well on your way to the beginnings of social graces, we'll discuss some of the hazards (such as static electricity) you may run into in your job and the tools you can use to prevent problems. After all, nerds who cannot stay organized—or who break equipment or themselves—need to learn some tricks to keep everything organized and safe.

■ The Professional Tech

A professional tech displays professionalism, which might seem a little trite if it weren't absolutely true. The tech presents a professional appearance and follows a proper ethical code. I call the latter the Traits of a Tech. Let's take a look at these two areas in more detail.

Appearance

Americans live in a casual society, and I think that's great, because I prefer dressing casually. The problem with casual is that perhaps our society is becoming *too* casual. New techs sometimes fail to appreciate that customers equate casual clothing with a casual attitude. You might think you're just fixing somebody's computer, but you're doing much more than that. You are saving precious family photos. You are keeping a small business in operation. This is serious stuff, and nobody wants an unclean, slovenly person doing these important jobs. Take a look at Figure 2.1. This is our resident illustrator (among other job descriptions), Ford Pierson, casually dressed to hang with his buddies.

I have a question for you. If you ran a small business and your primary file server died, leaving 15 employees with nothing to do, how would you feel about Ford as a tech coming into your office looking like this? I hope your answer would be "not too confident." Every company has some form of dress code for techs. Figure 2.2 shows Ford dressed in a fairly typical example, with a company polo shirt, khaki pants, and dark shoes (trust me on that score). Please also note that both his shirt and his pants are wrinkle free. All techs should either know how to iron or know the location of the nearest cleaners.

While we are looking at this model of a man, do you appreciate that his hair is combed and his face is cleanly shaven? It's too bad I can't use scratch-and-sniffs, but if I could, you'd also notice that Professional Ford took a shower, used some deodorant, and brushed his teeth.

I hope that most of the people who read this smile quietly to themselves and say, "Well, of course." The sad truth tells me otherwise. Next time you look at a tech, ask yourself how many of these simple appearance and hygiene issues were missed. Then make a point not to be one of the unkempt techs.

• **Figure 2.1** Casual Ford

• **Figure 2.2** Professional Ford

The Traits of a Tech

When I was a Boy Scout in the United States, we learned something called the Boy Scout Law, a list of traits that define the ethics of a Boy Scout. Even though I haven't been active in Boy Scouts for a long time, I still have the Scout Law memorized: "A Scout is trustworthy, loyal, helpful, friendly, courteous, kind, obedient, cheerful, thrifty, brave, clean, and reverent."

My goal here isn't a sales pitch for scouting in any form, but rather to give you an idea of what we are trying to achieve: a list of ethics that will help you be a better technician. The list you are about to see is my own creation, but it does a great job of covering the CompTIA A+ objectives. Let's dive into the traits of a tech: honesty/integrity, dependability/responsibility, adaptability/versatility, and sensitivity.

Honesty/Integrity

Honesty and integrity are not the same thing, but for a tech, they are so closely related that it is best to think of them as one big ethic. **Honesty** means telling the truth, and **integrity** means doing the right thing.

It's simple to say you have to be honest, but be warned that our industry often makes it difficult. IT technicians get a lot of leeway compared to most starting jobs, making dishonesty tempting. One of the biggest temptations is lying to your boss. A new tech driving around in a van all day may find it convenient to stretch the truth on how long he took for lunch or how far along he is on the next job. Being up front and honest with your boss is pretty obvious and easy to understand.

Being honest with your customers is a lot harder. Don't sell people goods and services they don't need, even if you get a cut of what you sell. Don't lie to your customers about a problem. If you can't explain the problem to them in plain English, don't create techno-babble (see note) and don't be afraid to say, "I don't know." Too many techs seem to think that not knowing exactly what a problem might be is a reflection of their skill. In your humble author's opinion, there is no greater proof of a quality technician than the ability to say "I don't know, but I know how to figure it out, and I will get you the right answer."

A computer tech must bring *integrity* to the job, just like any other service professional. You should treat anything said to you and anything you see as a personal confidence, not to be repeated to customers, co-workers, or bosses. Here's Mike's Rule of Confidentiality: "Unless it's a felony or an imminent physical danger, you didn't see nothin'." You'll learn more about dealing with prohibited content in Chapter 20.

There is an exception to this rule. Sometimes you need to separate paying customers from in-house users. A paying customer is someone who doesn't work for your company and is paying for your services. An in-house user is someone who works for the same company you work for and is not directly paying for your services. It's often your job (but not always) to police in-house IT policies. Here's a great example. If you are at a customer's site and you see a Post-it note with a password on a user's monitor, you say nothing. If you are in-house and you see the same thing, you probably need to speak to the user about the dangers of exposing passwords.

You have a lot of power when you sit in front of someone's computer. You can readily read private e-mail, discover Web sites surfed, and more.

> *Techno-babble* is the use of (often nonsensical) jargon and technical terms to intimidate and silence a challenge to a technical issue.

With a click of the Start button, you can know the last five programs the user ran, including Word and Solitaire, and the last few documents the user worked on. Don't do this; you really don't want to know. Plus, if you are caught violating a customer's privacy, you not only will lose credibility and respect, but you could also lose your job.

Passwords are a big issue for techs. We have to reboot computers and access shares and other jobs that require passwords. The rule here is to *avoid learning other folks' passwords at all costs* (see Figure 2.3). If you know a password to access a mission-critical machine and that machine ends up compromised or with data missing, who might be blamed? You, that's who, so avoid learning passwords! If you only need a password once, let the user type it in for you. If you anticipate accessing something multiple times (the more usual situation), ask the user to change the password temporarily.

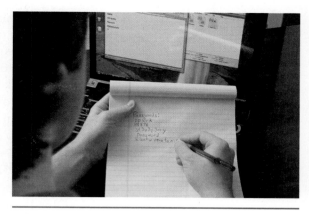

• **Figure 2.3** Don't do this!

It's funny, but people assume ownership of things they use at work. John in accounting doesn't call the computer he uses anything but "my PC." The phone on Susie's desk isn't the company phone, it's "Susie's phone." Regardless of the logic or illogic involved with this sense of ownership, a tech needs to respect that feeling. You'll never go wrong if you follow the **Ethic of Reciprocity**, also known as the *Golden Rule:* "Do unto others as you would have them do unto you." In a tech's life, this can translate as "treat people's things as you would have other people treat yours." Don't use or touch anything—keyboard, printer, laptop, monitor, mouse, phone, pen, paper, or cube toy—without first asking permission. Follow this rule at all times, even when the customer isn't looking.

Dependability/Responsibility

Dependability and responsibility are another pair of traits that, while they don't mean the same thing, often go together. A responsible person is answerable for her actions. A dependable person can be counted on to perform those acts. Again, the freedom of the typical IT person's job makes dependability and responsibility utterly critical.

The single biggest dependability issue for an IT technician is to show up for job appointments and to show up on time. It seems to me we now live in a society where not showing up and not letting anyone know is normal. I call it the "Age of the Blow-Off." We've all had an experience where we counted on someone to show up to get work done, and we can all share experiences when they simply did not show up. Failure to show up for an appointment not only is inconvenient, but also can cost your customer a lot of money in lost time and productivity.

If you or your company makes an appointment for you, show up. Be there. Don't let simple problems (such as bad traffic) prevent you from showing up on time. Take some time to prepare. Figure out traffic times. Figure out if preceding appointments will cause a problem, and check for traffic. There is a popular old saying in the United States, "Five minutes early is on time, and on time is late." Sometimes events take place that prevent you from being on time. When that happens, call the customer immediately and give them your best estimate of when you can be there. A simple apology wouldn't hurt, either.

Responsibility is a tricky subject for IT folks. Certainly you should be responsible for your actions, but the stakes are high when critical data and expensive equipment are at risk. Before you work on a computer, always ask the customer if there are up-to-date backups of the data. If there aren't, offer to make backups for the customer, even if this incurs an extra charge for the customer. If the customer chooses not to make a backup, make sure he or she understands, very clearly, the risk to the data on the system you are about to repair.

Adaptability/Versatility

Adaptability defines how someone adjusts to changes. Versatility, at least within the scope of an IT technician, is bringing a broad set of skills to the PC repair process. Every PC repair is to some degree a guessing game. No one knows all the possible problems that can go wrong with a computer. There is no universal PC repair manual to which you can refer to tell you how to fix computers. Good techs must be able to adapt to any situation, both technically and in the environment. For example, good techs should be able to fix most peripherals, even if they are not experts on that particular device. As you progress through the book, you'll discover that most devices fit into one family or another and that there are certain diagnostic/repair steps that you can at least try to enact a repair.

Adaptability isn't required just for technical issues. PCs find themselves broken in the strangest places and ways. An adaptable tech doesn't have a problem if a computer sits at the top of a suspension bridge or behind a desk. An adaptable tech can work around mean dogs, broken water lines, and noisy little kids. (But there are some very important rules to dealing with kids. See later in this chapter.)

A technician has to be versatile. The best example of this is what I call the User Advocate. User Advocates are technicians who not only take the time to learn the processes of whatever organization they work for, but also look to create technology solutions for problems and inefficiencies. This also means a tech should be at least competent if not expert at working with all the computer applications used by the organization. When you combine your IT skills with an understanding of how the business works, you become amazingly versatile, quickly finding yourself with more responsibility and (hopefully) more money.

A big part of versatility is offering different repair options in certain situations. When there is more than one way to fix things, make sure the customer knows all the options, but also give them your recommendation. Tell him why you feel your recommendation is the best course of action, but give them knowledge necessary to make their own decision.

A tech's versatility isn't limited to IT skills. Woe to the tech who doesn't understand basic electrical wiring and building codes. I've had hundreds of repair scenarios where the fix was as simple as knowing how to turn on an electrical breaker or moving a PC away from an electrical motor. No, these aren't IT skills, but a versatile tech knows these problems exist.

Sensitivity

Sensitivity is the ability to appreciate another's feeling and emotions. Sensitivity requires observing others closely, taking time to appreciate their feelings, and acting in such a way that makes them feel comfortable. I've rarely

Tech Tip

Paperwork

Most PC repair companies require a signed Authorization of Work or Work Authorization form to document the company name, billing information, date, scope of work, and that sort of thing. Even if you do your own repairs, these forms can save you from angst and from litigation. You can create your own or do an Internet search for examples.

felt that technicians I've met were good at sensitivity. The vast majority of nerds I know, including myself, tend to be self-centered and unaware of what's going on around them. Let me give you a few tips I've learned along the way.

Understand that the customer is paying for your time and skills. Also understand that your presence invariably means something is wrong or broken, and few things make users more upset than broken computers. When you are "on the clock," you need to show possibly very upset customers that you are giving their problem your full attention. To do this, you need to avoid distractions. If you get a personal call, let it roll over to voicemail. If you get a work-related call, politely excuse yourself, walk away for privacy, and keep the call brief. Never talk to co-workers in a place where your customer can hear. Never speak badly of a customer; you never know where you'll run into them next.

Last, be culturally sensitive. We live in a diverse world of races, religions, etiquettes, and traditions. If a customer's religious holiday conflicts with your work schedule, the customer wins. If the customer wants you to take off your shoes, take them off. If the customer wants you to wear a hat, wear one. When in doubt, always ask the customer for guidance.

■ Communication

When you deal with users, managers, and owners who are frustrated and upset because a computer or network is down and they can't work, your job requires you to take on the roles of detective and psychologist. Talking with frazzled and confused people and getting answers to questions about how the PC got into the state it's in takes skill. Communicating clearly and effectively is important. Plus, you need to follow the rules of tech-person decorum, acting with personal integrity and respect for the customer. Finally, use assertive communication to empathize with and educate the user. Great techs spend the time needed to develop these essential skills.

Assertive Communication

In many cases, a PC problem results from user error or neglect. As a technician, you must show users the error of their ways without creating anger or conflict. You do this by using assertive communication. **Assertive communication** isn't pushy or bossy, but it's also not the language of a pushover. Assertive communication first requires you to show the other person that you understand and appreciate the importance of his feelings. Use statements such as "I know how frustrating it feels to lose data," or "I understand how infuriating it is when the network goes out and you can't get your job done." Statements like these cool off the situation and let customers know you are on their side. Avoid using the word "you," as it can sound accusatory.

The second part of assertive communication is making sure you state the problem clearly without accusing the user directly: "Not keeping up with defragmenting your hard drive slows it down," or "Help me understand how the network cable keeps getting unplugged during your lunch

hour." Last, tell the user what you need to prevent this error in the future. "Please call me whenever you hear that buzzing sound," or, "Please check the company's approved software list before installing anything." Always use "I" and "me," and never make judgments. "I can't promise the keyboard will work well if it's always getting dirty," is much better than, "Stop eating cookies over the keyboard, you slob!"

Respectful Communication

The final key in communicating with users revolves around **respect**. You don't do the user's job, but you should respect that job and person as an essential cog in the organization. Communicate with users the way you would like them to communicate with you, were the roles reversed. Again, this follows the Ethic of Reciprocity.

Generally, IT folks are there to support the people doing a company's main business. You are there to serve their needs and, all things being equal, to do so at their convenience, not yours.

Don't assume the world stops the moment you walk in the door and that you may immediately interrupt their work to do yours. Although most customers are thrilled and motivated to help you the moment you arrive, this may not always be the case. Ask the magic question, "May I start working on the problem now?" Give customers a chance to wrap up, shut down, or do anything else necessary to finish their business and make it safe for you to do yours.

Engage the user with the standard rules of civil conversation. Take the time to listen. Don't interrupt customers as they describe a problem; just listen and take notes. You might hear something that leads to resolving the problem. Rephrase and repeat the problems back to the customer to verify you understand the issue ("So the computer is locking up three times a day?"). Use an even, nonaccusatory tone, and although it's okay to try to explain a problem if the user asks, never condescend and never argue.

Remain positive in the face of adversity. Don't get defensive if you can't figure something out quickly and the user starts hassling you. Remember that an angry customer isn't really angry with you—he's just frustrated—so don't take his anger personally. Take it in stride; smile, and assure him that computer troubleshooting sometimes takes a while.

Avoid letting outside interruptions take your focus away from the user and her computer problem. Things that break your concentration slow down the troubleshooting process immensely. Plus, customers will feel insulted if you start chatting on your cell phone with your significant other about a movie date later that night when you're supposed to be fixing their computers! You're not being paid to socialize, so turn those cell phones and pagers to vibrate. That's why the technogods created voicemail. Never take any call except one that is potentially urgent. If a call

Try This!

Apply the Ethic of Reciprocity

The Ethic of Reciprocity appears in almost every religion on the planet, with versions attributed to Confucius, Jesus, Moses, and Mohammed, among others. Just for practice, try the Ethic of Reciprocity out in nontechnical situations, such as when buying something from the corner store or grocery. Consciously analyze how the clerk behind the counter would want a customer to interact with him. Now put yourself in the clerk's shoes. How would you want a customer to communicate with you? Act accordingly!

Mike Meyers' CompTIA A+ Guide to 801: Managing and Troubleshooting PCs

is potentially urgent, explain the urgency to the customer, step away, and deal with the call as quickly as possible.

If you discover that the user caused the problem, either through ignorance or by accident, don't minimize the importance of the problem, but don't be judgmental or insulting about the cause. We all screw up sometimes, and these kinds of mistakes are your job security. *You get paid because people make mistakes and machines break.* Chances are you'll be back at that workstation six months or a year later, fixing something else. By becoming the user's advocate and go-to person, you create a better work environment. If a mistaken action caused the problem, explain in a positive and supportive way how to do the task correctly, and then have the user go through the process while you are there to reinforce what you said.

Eliciting Answers

Your job as a tech is to get the computer fixed, and the best way to start that process is to determine what the computer is doing or not doing. You must start by talking to the customer. Allow the customer to explain the problem fully while you record the information. Once the person has described the situation, you must then ask questions. This process is called **eliciting answers**.

Although each person is different, most users with a malfunctioning computer or peripheral will be distraught and perhaps defensive about the problem. To overcome this initial attitude, you need to ask the right questions *and* listen to the customer's answers. Then ask the proper follow-up questions.

Always avoid accusatory questions, because they won't help you in the least (see Figure 2.4). "What did you do?" generally gets a confused or defensive "Nothing" in reply, which doesn't get you closer to solving the problem. First, ask questions that help clarify the situation. Repeat what you think is the problem after you've listened all the way through the user's story.

• **Figure 2.4** Never accuse!

Follow up with fact-seeking questions. "When did it last work?" "Has it ever worked in this way?" "Has any software changed recently?" "Has any new hardware been added?" Ask open-ended questions to narrow the scope ("Which applications are running when the computer locks up?").

By keeping your questions friendly and factual, you show users that you won't accuse them or judge their actions (see Figure 2.5). You also show them that you're there to help them. After the initial tension drops away, you'll often get more information: for instance, a recitation of something the user might have tried or changed. These clues can help lead to a quick resolution of the problem.

Remember that you may know all about computer technology, but the user probably does not. This means a user will often use vague and/or incorrect terms to describe a particular computer component or function. That's just the way it works, so don't bother to correct them. Wherever possible, avoid using jargon, acronyms, or abbreviations specific

• **Figure 2.5** Keeping it friendly

to computers. They simply confuse the already upset user and can make you sound like you're talking down to them. Just ask direct, factual questions in a friendly tone, using simple, non-jargon language to zero in on what the user was trying to accomplish and what happened when things went wrong. Use visual aids when possible. Point at the machine or go to a working PC to have the user show what went wrong or what she did or tried to do.

People do usually want to get a handle on what you are doing—in a simplified way. You don't want to overwhelm them, but don't be afraid to use simple analogies or concepts to give them an idea of what is happening. If you have the time (and the skills), use drawings, equipment, and other visual aids to make technical concepts more clear. If a customer is a closet tech and is really digging for answers—to the point that it's affecting your ability to do your job—compliment her initiative and then direct her to outside training opportunities. Better yet, tell her where she can get a copy of this book!

Beyond basic manners, never assume that just because you are comfortable with friendly or casual behavior, the customer will be too. Even an apparently casual user will expect you to behave with professional decorum. On the flip side, don't allow a user to put you in an awkward or even potentially dangerous or illegal situation. Never do work outside the scope of your assigned duties without the prior approval of your supervisor (when possible in such cases, try to direct users to someone who *can* help them). You are not a babysitter; never volunteer to "watch the kids" while the customer leaves the job site or tolerate a potentially unsafe situation if a customer isn't properly supervising a child. Concentrate on doing your job safely and efficiently, and maintain professional integrity.

Expectations and Follow-up

Users are terrified when their PCs and networks go down so hard that they need to call in a professional. Odds are good that they've left critical, or at least important, data on the computer. Odds are equally good they need this computer to work to do their job. When they're ready to lay down money for a professional, they're expecting you to make their system exactly the way it was before it broke.

Hopefully, you can do exactly that for them, but you also must deal with their expectations and let them know what to expect. Equally, you should give your customers some follow-up after the job is finished. We've already covered data backups and Authorization of Work forms (and those are very important), but you need to keep the customer's needs in mind. You also want to keep them thinking about you, should they need more help in the future. Here are a few items you should consider.

Time Frame

If you can give the customer a best guess as to how long the repair will take, you'll be a hero. Don't be afraid to hold off on your time-frame prediction until you've diagnosed the machine. If you truly don't have a feel for the time involved, tell the customer that and then tell them what you'll need to know before you can make the prediction.

Stick to the timeline. If you finish more quickly, great! People love a job that goes faster than predicted. If you're moving past the predicted time frame, contact the customer and tell him as soon as possible. Let him know what's happened, explain why you need more time, and give him a new time frame. The biggest secret here is to keep in communication with the customer on any change in status. People understand delays—they take place in our lives daily. People resent not knowing why a delay is occurring, especially when a precious computer is at stake.

Documentation

At the completion of work, document the problem, including the time and day you started work, the solution (again including the time and day the work ended), the number of hours you worked, and a list of all parts you replaced. If the customer owns the replaced parts, offer them to the customer (this is especially true if you replace any storage media). This documentation may or may not include your charges.

Follow-Up

I call follow-up the Lost Art: a simple follow-up, usually just a phone call, to confirm that the customer is happy with your work. This gives the customer a chance to detail any special issues that may have arisen, and it also adds that final extra touch that ensures they will call you again when they encounter a technical problem.

■ Safety and Tools

Effective communication with your customer enables you to *start* the troubleshooting process, getting details about the problem and clues about things that happened around the same time. To continue troubleshooting, though, you need to be adept at handling the computer. That starts with knowing how to handle computer components safely and how to use the tools of a tech. Let's begin by identifying and discussing some of the problems you may run into and how to deal with them.

Electrostatic Discharge (ESD)

If you decide to open a PC while reading this chapter, as I encourage you to do, you must take proper steps to avoid the greatest killer of PCs: **electrostatic discharge (ESD)**. ESD simply means the passage of a static electrical charge from one item to another. Have you ever rubbed a balloon against your shirt, making the balloon stick to you? That's a classic example of static electricity. When that static charge discharges, you may not notice it happening—although on a cool, dry day, I've been shocked so hard by touching a doorknob that I could see a big, blue spark! I've never heard of a human being getting anything worse than a rather nasty shock from ESD, but I can't say the same thing about computers. ESD will destroy the sensitive parts of your PC, so it is essential that you take steps to avoid ESD when working on your PC.

> All PCs are well protected against ESD on the outside. Unless you take a screwdriver and actually open up your PC, you don't need to concern yourself with ESD.

Anti-static Tools

ESD only takes place when two objects that store different amounts (the hip electrical term to use is **potential**) of static electricity come in contact. The secret to avoiding ESD is to keep you and the parts of the PC you touch at the same electrical potential, otherwise known as grounding yourself to the PC. You can accomplish this by connecting yourself to the PC via a handy little device called an **anti-static wrist strap**. This simple device consists of a wire that connects on one end to an alligator clip and on the other end to a small metal plate that secures to your wrist with an elastic strap. You snap the alligator clip onto any handy metal part of the PC and place the wrist strap on either wrist. Figure 2.6 shows a typical anti-static wrist strap in use.

Anti-static wrist straps are standard equipment for anyone working on a PC, but other tools might also come in handy. One of the big issues when working with a PC occurs if you find yourself pulling out parts from the PC and setting them aside. The moment you take a piece out of the PC, it no longer has contact with the systems and may pick up static from other sources. Techs use anti-static mats to eliminate this risk. An **anti-static mat** acts as a point of common potential; it's typical to purchase a combination anti-static wrist strap and mat that all connect to keep you, the PC, and any loose components at the same electrical potential (see Figure 2.7).

Anti-static wrist straps and mats use tiny **resistors**— devices that stop or *resist* the flow of electricity—to prevent a static charge from racing through the device. These resistors can fail over time, so it's always a good idea to read the documentation that comes with your anti-static tools to see how to test those small resistors properly.

• **Figure 2.6** Anti-static wrist strap in use

Any electrical component not in a PC needs to be stored in an **anti-static bag**, a specially designed bag that sheds whatever static electricity you have when you touch it, thus preventing any damage to components stored within (see Figure 2.8). Almost all PC components come in an anti-static bag when purchased. Experienced techs never throw these bags away, as you never know when you'll want to pull a part out and place it on a shelf for a while.

Although having an anti-static wrist strap with you at all times would be ideal, the reality is that from time to time you'll find yourself in a situation where you lack the proper anti-static tools. This shouldn't keep you from working on the PC—if you're careful! Before working on a PC in such

• **Figure 2.7** Anti-static wrist strap and mat combination

Try This!

Anti-static Protection Devices

In some circumstances, an anti-static wrist strap could get in the way. Manufacturers have developed some alternatives to the wrist strap, so try this:

1. Take a field trip to a local computer or electronics store.

2. Check out their selection of anti-static devices. Can you find anything other than wrist straps or mats?

3. Do a Web search for "static control products." Can you find anything other than wrist straps or mats?

4. Report what options you can find for protecting your equipment from ESD. Weigh the pros and cons and decide what you would use in various situations.

• **Figure 2.8** Anti-static bag

a situation, take a moment to touch the power supply every once in a while as you work—I'll show you where it is in Chapter 3—to keep yourself at the same electrical potential as the PC. Although this isn't as good as a wrist strap, it's better than nothing at all.

The last issue when it comes to preventing ESD is that never-ending question—should you work with the PC plugged in or unplugged? The answer is simple: Do you really want to be physically connected to a PC that is plugged into an electrical outlet? Granted, the chances of electrocution are slim, but why take the risk?

Always unplug a PC when working inside it.

Electromagnetic Interference (EMI)

A magnetic field interfering with electronics is **electromagnetic interference (EMI)**. EMI isn't nearly as dangerous as ESD, but it can cause permanent damage to some components and erase data on some storage devices. You can prevent EMI by keeping magnets away from computer equipment. Certain components are particularly susceptible to EMI. Never get a magnet close to

- Floppy disks
- Hard drives
- Flash drives
- CRT (tube) monitors

The biggest problem with EMI is that we often use magnets without even knowing we are doing so. Any device with an electrical motor has a magnet. Many telephones have magnets. Power bricks for laptops and speakers also have magnets. Keep them away!

Radio Frequency Interference (RFI)

Do you ever hear strange noises on your speakers even though you aren't playing any sounds? Do you ever get strange noises on your cell phone?

Tech Tip

Protective Bag Types

Computer gear manufacturers package their product in a variety of ways to shield against accidental damage, whether that's physical damage, ESD, EMI, or RFI. The typical pink translucent computer bag is coated with a film that prevents the bag from producing static electricity and mildly protects the contents against physical contact (and thus damage). The two types of metal bags offer shielding against EMI and RFI as well as ESD. These are the silvery bags (such as in Figure 2.8) you'll see hard drives packed in, for example, and the black and silver woven bags you'll sometimes see.

A word of caution is in order here. The metal bags provide proper protection only when sealed, so fold the open end over and slap a piece of tape on it when storing a component.

When thinking about safety, keep in mind any local government regulations. You may be required to wear certain protective gear or take extra precautions while in the workplace. Make sure you also follow any environmental rules for the disposal of old parts, especially with things like CRT monitors, which may contain hazardous materials. Check with your employer or your local government's Web site for more information.

If so, you've probably run into **radio frequency interference (RFI)**. Many devices emit radio waves:

- Cell phones
- Wireless network cards
- Cordless phones
- Baby monitors
- Microwave ovens

In general, the radio waves that these devices emit are very weak, and almost all electronic devices are shielded to prevent RFI. A few devices, speakers in particular, are susceptible to RFI. RFI will never cause any damage, but it can be incredibly irritating. The best way to prevent RFI is to keep radio-emitting devices as far away as possible from other electronics.

RFI becomes a big problem when two devices share the same frequencies. Cordless phones, baby monitors, and wireless networks share the same range of frequencies. They sometimes interfere with each other, causing poor signals or even blocking signals completely. These devices need to be tuned to avoid stomping on each other's frequencies. In Chapter 15, you'll see how to tune a wireless network to prevent RFI.

Physical Safety

IT techs live in a dangerous world. We're in constant danger of tripping, hurting our backs, and getting burned by hot components. You also need to keep in mind what you wear (in a safety sense). Let's take a moment to discuss these physical safety issues and what to do about them.

If you don't keep organized, hardware technology will take over your life. Figure 2.9 shows a corner of my office, a painful example of a cable "kludge."

Cable messes such as these are dangerous tripping hazards. While I may allow a mess like this in my home office, all cables in a business environment are carefully tucked away behind computer cases, run into walls, or placed under cable runners. If you see a cable that is an obvious tripping hazard, contact the person in charge of the building (CompTIA calls these folks

• **Figure 2.9**　Mike's cable kludge

● **Figure 2.10** What a strange, bad trip it's been.

"building services") to take care of it immediately. The results of ignoring such hazards can be catastrophic (see Figure 2.10).

Another physical safety issue is heavy boxes. Computers, printers, monitors—everything we use—all seem to come to us in heavy boxes. Remember never to lift with your back; lift with your legs, and always use a hand truck if available. You are never paid enough to risk your own health.

You also need to watch out for hot components. It's hard to burn yourself unless you actually open up a computer, printer, or monitor. First, watch for anything with a cooling fin like the one shown in Figure 2.11. If you see a cooling fin, odds are good that something is hot enough to burn you. Also look for labels or stickers warning about hot components. Last, when in doubt, move your hand over components as if you were checking the heat on a stove.

Finally, remove any jewelry or loose-hanging clothing before working on a computer. If you have long hair, you might consider tying it back in a ponytail. You don't want anything getting caught in a fan or stuck on a component. This can save you and your components a lot of pain.

● **Figure 2.11** Checking for hot cooling fins

Tools of the Trade

The basic **tech toolkit** consists of a **Phillips-head screwdriver** and not much else—seriously—but a half-dozen tools round out a fully functional toolkit. Most kits have a star-headed Torx wrench, a nut driver or two, a pair of plastic tweezers, a little grabber tool (the technical term is *parts retriever*), a hemostat, an IC extractor for removing various chips, and both Phillips-head and flat-head screwdrivers (see Figure 2.12).

A lot of techs throw in an extension magnet to grab hard-to-reach bits that drop into cases (an exception to the "no magnets" rule). Many also add a magnifying glass and a flashlight for those hard-to-read numbers and text on the printed circuit boards (PCBs) that make up a large percentage of devices inside the system unit. Contrary to what you might think, techs rarely need a hammer.

• **Figure 2.12** Typical technician toolkit

Chapter 2 Review

■ Chapter Summary

After reading this chapter and completing the exercises, you should understand the following about operational procedures.

Present yourself with a proper appearance and professional manner

■ Professional techs dress appropriately. This means decent, clean clothes that are wrinkle-free, such as khaki trousers and a polo or button-down shirt. Professional techs bathe. Regularly.

■ Professional techs cultivate proper traits, such as honesty/integrity, dependability/responsibility, adaptability/versatility, and sensitivity.

Talk to customers in a professional, productive manner

■ Techs should use effective communication techniques such as assertive communication to interact with customers. Assertive communication means showing empathy for the customer's plight and clearly stating the perceived problem without directly accusing the customer. Assertive communication also means telling the user what needs to happen to avoid the problem in the future.

■ A good tech respects the customer, following the Ethic of Reciprocity. Do not interrupt the customer. Engage in conversation, using proper manners and actively listening. Remain positive, even when the customer gets upset. Avoid letting outside interruptions take your focus away from the user and the user's computer problem.

■ When eliciting answers, ask questions to help clarify the situation. Follow up with fact-seeking questions. Always explain what you're doing, but avoid excessive jargon.

■ Never do work outside the scope of your assigned duties without the prior approval of your supervisor. Don't babysit the kids while the customer wanders off.

■ Manage your customer's expectations by explaining how much time you expect to take and the price. Document everything you do to solve the problem, including the time you spend. Follow up with the customer after solving the problem—a quick phone call will do—to make certain nothing has gone wrong and that he is satisfied with your work.

Work with PCs safely using the proper tools

■ Take precautionary measures when working on computers. Use best practices for avoiding electrostatic discharge. Put unused components in anti-static bags. Protect sensitive equipment from electromagnetic interference.

■ Use the right tools to get the job done, especially your Phillips-head screwdriver!

■ Key Terms

anti-static bag (30)
anti-static mat (30)
anti-static wrist strap (30)
assertive communication (25)
electromagnetic interference (EMI) (31)
electrostatic discharge (ESD) (29)
eliciting answers (27)
Ethic of Reciprocity (23)
honesty (22)

integrity (22)
passwords (23)
Phillips-head screwdriver (34)
potential (30)
radio frequency interference (RFI) (32)
resistor (30)
respect (26)
tech toolkit (34)

■ Key Term Quiz

Use the Key Terms list to complete the sentences that follow. Not all terms will be used.

1. Always place an expansion card or other computer part into a(n) _____ when it's not in use to protect against electrostatic discharge.

2. A few screwdrivers and an anti-static wrist strap should be in your _____.

3. An effective use of _____ means clearly stating a problem without accusing the user of creating that problem.

4. Accomplished computer techs should treat anything said to them as a personal confidence, not to be repeated to co-workers or bosses. A tech brings _____ to the job.

5. You should avoid learning _____ to other folks' computers so you don't get blamed if something happens to those computers.

6. Treating other people the way you want to be treated is an example of the _____.

7. A magnetic field interfering with electronics is _____.

8. A(n) _____ is a device that stops the flow of electricity.

9. To begin troubleshooting a computer problem, start by talking to the customer and allowing the customer to explain the problem fully, and then ask follow-up questions. This process is called _____.

10. A customer complains that he can hear music coming from his computer speakers, even though the computer is not playing any music. This is most likely caused by _____.

■ Multiple-Choice Quiz

1. While troubleshooting a fairly routine printing problem, the customer explains in great detail precisely what he was trying to do, what happened when he tried to print, and what he had attempted as a fix for the problem. At what point should you interrupt him?

 A. After he describes the first problem

 B. As soon as you understand the problem

 C. As soon as you have a solution

 D. Never

2. While manning the help desk, you get a call from a distraught user who says she has a blank screen. What would be a useful follow-up question? (Select two.)

 A. Is the computer turned on?

 B. Is the monitor turned on?

 C. Did you reboot?

 D. What did you do?

3. While manning the help desk, you get a call from Sharon in accounting. She's lost a file that she knows she saved to her hard drive. Which of the following statements would direct Sharon in the most efficient and professional manner to open her My Documents folder?

 A. Sharon, check My Documents.

 B. Sharon, a lot of programs save files to a default folder, often to a folder called My Documents. Let's look there first. Click on the Start button and move the mouse until the cursor hovers over My Documents. Then press the left mouse button and tell me what you see when My Documents opens.

 C. It probably just defaulted to My Docs. Why don't you open Excel or whatever program you used to make the file, and then open a document and point it to My Documents?

 D. Look, Sharon, I know you're a clueless noob when it comes to computers, but how could somebody lose a file? Just open up My Documents and look there for the file.

4. Al in marketing calls in for tech support, complaining that he has a dead PC. What is a good first question or set of questions to begin troubleshooting the problem?

 A. Did the computer ever work?

 B. When did the computer last work?

 C. When you say "dead," what do you mean? What happens when you press the power button?

 D. What did you do?

5. While manning the help desk, you get a call from Bryce in sales complaining that he can't print and every time he clicks on the network shared drive, his computer stops and freezes. He says he thinks it's his hard driver. What would be a good follow-up question or statement?

 A. Bryce, you're an idiot. Don't touch anything. I'll be there in five minutes.

 B. Okay, let's take this one step at a time. You seem to have two problems, one with printing and the second with the network shared drive, right?

 C. First, it's not a hard *driver*; it's a hard *drive*. It doesn't have anything to do with the network share or printing, so that's just not right.

 D. When could you last print?

6. When troubleshooting a software problem on Phoebe's computer and listening to her describe the problem, your beeper goes off. It's your boss. What would be an acceptable action for you to take?

 A. Excuse yourself, walk out of the cube, and use a cell phone to call your boss.

 B. Pick up Phoebe's phone and dial your boss's number.

 C. Wait until Phoebe finishes her description and then ask to use her phone to call your boss.

 D. Wait until Phoebe finishes her description, run through any simple fixes, and then explain that you need to call your boss on your cell phone.

7. While fixing a printing problem on Paul's computer, you check his e-mail out of curiosity to see if there are any interesting messages there. You find several personal e-mails he has sent. Using the company computer for personal e-mail is against regulations, so what should you do?

 A. Leave the e-mail on the computer and notify your boss.

 B. Delete the e-mails from the computer and notify your boss.

 C. Delete the e-mails from the computer and remind Paul of the workplace regulations.

 D. You shouldn't be looking in his e-mail folders at all as it compromises your integrity.

8. Upon responding to a co-worker's request for help, you find that she is away from her desk and Microsoft Excel is on the computer screen with a spreadsheet open. How do you proceed?

 A. Go find the co-worker and ask her to exit her applications before you touch her computer.

 B. Exit Excel and save changes to the document and begin troubleshooting the computer.

 C. Exit Excel without saving changes to the document and begin troubleshooting the computer.

 D. Use the Save As command to save the file with a new name, exit Excel, and begin troubleshooting the computer.

9. You are solving a problem on Kate's computer that requires you to reboot several times. Upon each reboot, the logon screen appears and prompts you for a username and password before you can continue working. Kate has gone to another office to continue her work on another computer. How do you proceed?

 A. Call Kate, ask her for her password, type it in, and continue working on the problem.

 B. Insist that Kate stay with you and have her type the password each time it is needed.

 C. Call Kate and have her come in to type the password each time it is needed.

 D. Have Kate temporarily change her password for you to use as you work; then have her change it back when you are through.

10. You are working in a customer's home and his five-year-old child continues to scream and kick the back of your chair. What do you do?

 A. Ignore the child and finish your work as quickly as you can.

 B. Discipline the child as you see fit.

 C. Politely ask your client to remove the child from your work area.

 D. Tell your client you refuse to work under such conditions and leave the premises with the job half done.

11. After replacing a keyboard a user has spilled coffee on for the fifth time, what should you say to the user?

 A. I can't guarantee the new keyboard will work if it gets dirty.

 B. I can't guarantee the new keyboard will work if you continue to spill coffee on it.

 C. These keyboards are expensive. Next time we replace one because you spilled coffee, it's coming out of your paycheck.

 D. You need to be more careful with your coffee.

12. When is it appropriate to yell at a user?

 A. When he screws up the second time.

 B. When he interrupts your troubleshooting.

 C. When he screws up the fifth time.

 D. Never.

13. What's the best practice when working inside a system unit and installing and removing components?

 A. Wear an anti-static wrist strap.

 B. Touch a doorknob to ground yourself before going into the case.

 C. Place components on the motherboard to keep them grounded.

 D. Use plastic tools.

14. Which of the following tools would you find in a typical PC tech's toolkit? (Select two.)

 A. Phillips-head screwdriver

 B. Torx wrench

 C. Hammer

 D. File

15. What term describes the flow of a static electrical charge from a person to the inside of the PC?

 A. EMI

 B. ESD

 C. HDMI

 D. TTFN

■ Essay Quiz

1. Your worksite currently has no ESD protection. In fact, your supervisor doesn't feel that such protection is necessary. Write a proposal to purchase ESD protection equipment for the computer assembly/repair facility that will convince your supervisor that ESD protection is necessary and cost-effective in the long run. What kinds of protection will you recommend?

2. A friend is considering turning his computer hobby into a career and has asked your advice on outfitting himself as a freelance computer technician. What tools can you recommend to your friend?

3. A user phones you at your desk and reports that after pressing the power button on his computer and hearing the hard drive spin up, his screen remains blank. What questions can you ask to determine the problem?

Lab Projects

• Lab Project 2.1

Visit your local computer store or hardware store and purchase the items for a hardware tech toolkit. You may want to include a variety of screwdrivers, an anti-static wrist strap, tweezers, or other items.

• Lab Project 2.2

Visit your local computer store to observe how techs interact with people and how professionally they dress and appear. I suggest this not to judge the store's techs, but simply to watch and learn. How do the techs talk to customers? How do the customers react? How would you handle the same situation if you followed the guidelines in this chapter?

chapter 3

The Visible PC

In this chapter, you will learn how to

- **Describe how the PC works**
- **Identify all the connectors and devices on a typical PC system unit**
- **Discuss the major internal components of a PC**

Mastering the craft of a PC technician requires you to learn a lot of details about the many pieces of hardware in the typical PC. Even the most basic PC contains hundreds of discrete hardware components, each with its own set of characteristics, shapes, sizes, colors, connections, and so on. By the end of this book, you will be able to discuss all of these components in detail. This chapter takes you on a tour of a typical PC, starting with an overview of how computers work, and then examining both external connectors and internal components.

Remember the children's song that goes, "Oh, the leg bone connects to the thigh bone..."? Well, think of the rest of the chapter in that manner, showing you what the parts look like and giving you a rough idea about how they work and connect. In later chapters, you'll dissect all of these PC "leg bones" and "thigh bones" and reach the level of detail you need to install, configure, maintain, and fix computers. Even if you are an expert, do not skip this chapter! It introduces a large number of terms used throughout the rest of the book. You might know some of these terms already, but reading about them again won't hurt.

It is handy, although certainly not required, to have a PC that you can take the lid off of and inspect as you progress. Almost any old PC will help—it doesn't even need to work. So get thee a screwdriver, grab your PC, and see if you can recognize the various components as you read about them.

Historical/Conceptual

■ How the PC Works

You've undoubtedly seen a PC in action: a nice, glossy monitor displaying a picture that changes according to the actions of the person sitting in front of it, typing away on a keyboard and clicking on a mouse. Sound pours out of tiny speakers that flank the screen, and a box whirs happily beneath the table. The PC is a computer: a machine that enables you to do work, produce documents, play games, balance your checkbook, and look up the latest sports scores on the Internet.

Although the computer is certainly a machine, it's also **programming**: the commands that tell the computer what to do to get work done. These commands are just ones and zeros that the computer's hardware understands, enabling it to do amazing actions, such as perform powerful mathematical functions, move data (also ones and zeros), realize the mouse has moved, and put pretty icons on the screen. So a computer is a complex interaction between hardware and computer programming, created by your fellow humans.

Ever heard of Morse code? Morse code is nothing more than dots and dashes to those who do not understand it, but if you send dots and dashes (in the right order) to someone who understands Morse code, you can tell the recipient a joke. Think of programming as Morse code for the computer (see Figure 3.1). You may not understand those ones and zeros, but your computer certainly does!

There's more to the ones and zeros than just programming. All of the data on the computer—the Web pages, your documents, your e-mail—is also stored as ones and zeros. Programs know how to translate these ones and zeros into a form humans understand.

Programming comes in two forms. First are the applications: the programs that get work done. Word processing programs, Web browsers, and e-mail programs are all considered applications. But applications need a main program to support them. They need a program that enables you to start and stop applications, copy, move, and delete data, talk to the hardware, and perform lots of other jobs. This program is called the operating system (OS). Microsoft Windows is the most popular OS today, but there are other computer operating systems, such as Apple Mac OS X and the popular (and free) Linux (see Figure 3.2). Computer people lump operating systems and applications into the term **software** to differentiate them from the hardware of the computer.

I know this. This is binary! It all makes sense now.

• **Figure 3.1** Computer musing that a string of ones and zeros makes perfect sense

• **Figure 3.2** Typical Mac OS X (left), Linux (middle), and Windows (right) interfaces

The CompTIA A+ 801 exam only covers the Windows operating system in regard to PCs, so you won't see much discussion of Mac OS X or Linux in this book. Nevertheless, a good tech should possess a basic understanding of these two excellent operating systems.

Understanding the computer at this broad conceptual level—in terms of hardware, OS, and programs—can help you explain things to customers, but good techs have a much more fundamental appreciation and understanding of the complex interplay of all of the software and the individual pieces of hardware. In short, techs need to know the processes going on behind the scenes.

From the CompTIA A+ tech's perspective, the computer functions through four stages: input, processing, output, and storage. Knowing which parts participate in a particular stage of the computing process enables you to troubleshoot on a fundamental and decisive level.

To illustrate this four-step process, let's walk through the steps involved in a fairly common computer task: preparing your taxes. [Insert collective groan here.] February has rolled around and, at least in the United States, millions of people install their favorite tax software, TurboTax from Intuit, onto their computers to help them prepare their taxes.

Input

After starting TurboTax, your first job is to provide the computer with data: essential information, such as your name, where you live, how much you earned, and how many dollars you gave to federal and state governments.

Various pieces of hardware enable you to input data, the most common of which are the keyboard and mouse. Most PCs won't react when you say, "Hey you!"—at least not anywhere outside of a *Star Trek* episode. Although that day will come, you must still use something decidedly more mechanical: a keyboard to type in your data. The OS provides a fundamental service in this process as well. You can bang on a keyboard all day and accomplish nothing unless the OS translates your keystrokes into code that the rest of your computer's hardware understands.

Processing

Next, the computer processes your data. After you place information in various appropriate "boxes" in TurboTax, the computer does the math for you. Processing takes place inside the system unit—the box under your desk (see Figure 3.3)—and happens almost completely at a hardware level, although that hardware functions according to rules laid out in the OS. Thus you have another complex interaction between hardware and software.

The processing portion is the magical part—you can't see it happen. The first half of this book demystifies this stage, because good techs understand all of the pieces of the process. I won't go through the specific hardware involved in the processing stage here, because the pieces change according to the type of process.

• **Figure 3.3** Processing takes place somewhere in here!

Output

Simply adding up your total tax for the year is useless unless the computer shows you the result. That's where the third step—output—comes into play (see Figure 3.4). Once the computer finishes processing data, it must put the information somewhere for you to inspect it. Often it places data on the monitor so you can see what you've just typed. It might send the data over to the printer if you tell it to, so you can print out copies of your tax return to mail to the Internal Revenue Service (or whatever the Tax Man is called where you live). A hardware device does the actual printing, but the OS controls the printing process. Again, it's a fundamental interaction of hardware and software.

Printer

Monitor

Speaker

• **Figure 3.4** Output devices

Storage

Once you've sent in your tax return, you most likely do not want all that work simply to disappear. What happens if the IRS comes back a couple of months later with a question about your return? Yikes! You need to keep permanent records and a copy of the tax program. The fourth stage in the computing process is storage. A lot of devices are used in the storage process, the most visible of which are the external storage parts, such as a thumb drive or recordable CD discs (see Figure 3.5).

■ The Art of the PC Technician

Using the four stages of the computing process—input, processing, output, and storage—to master how the PC works and, in turn, become a great technician requires that you understand all of the pieces of hardware and software involved *and* the interactions between them that make up the various stages. You have to know what the parts do, in other words, and how they work together. The best place to start is with a real computer. Let's go through the process of inspecting a typical, complete PC, including opening

• **Figure 3.5** Typical storage (CD-R discs)

up a few important pieces to see the components inside. Hopefully, you have a real computer in front of you right now that you may dismantle a bit. No two computers are exactly the same, so you'll see differences between your PC and the one in this chapter—and that's okay. You'll come to appreciate that all computers have the same main parts that do the same jobs even though they differ in size, shape, and color.

By the time you reach the end of this book, you'll have a deeper, more nuanced understanding of the interaction of hardware and software in the four-stage computing process. Just as great artists have mastered fundamental skills of their trade before creating a masterpiece, you'll have the fundamentals of the art of the computer technician and be on your road to mastery.

801

■ The Complete PC

Sometimes I hate the term "personal computer." That term implies a single device, like a toaster. A typical PC is more than one device, and you need all of the parts (or at least most) to make the PC work. The most important part of the PC is the box that usually sits under your desk: the one that all of the other parts connect to, called the **system unit**. All of the processing and storage takes place in the system unit. All of the other parts of the PC— the printer, the keyboard, the monitor—connect to the system unit and are known collectively as **peripherals**. Figure 3.6 shows a typical desktop PC, with the system unit and peripherals as separate pieces.

Most computers have a standard set of peripherals to provide input and output. You'll see some variation in color, bells, and whistles, but here's the standard set:

- **Monitor** The big television thing that provides a visual output for the computer.

- **Keyboard** Keypad for providing keyed input. Based on a typewriter.

- **Mouse** Pointing device used to control a graphical pointer on the monitor for input.

- **Speakers** Provide sound output.

- **Printer** Provides printed paper output.

A typical PC has all of these peripherals, but no law requires a PC to have them. Plenty of PCs don't have a printer. Some PCs don't have speakers, just headphones. Some computers don't even have a keyboard, mouse, or monitor—but they tend to hide in unlikely places, such as the inside of a jet fighter or next to the engine in an automobile.

Other PCs may have many more peripherals. Installing four or five printers on a single PC is easy,

System unit Peripherals

• **Figure 3.6** Typical desktop computer with peripherals

if you so desire. You'll also find hundreds of other types of peripherals, such as Web cameras and microphones, on many PCs. You add or remove peripherals depending on what you need from the system. The only limit is the number of available connections.

External Connections

Every peripheral connects to the system unit through one of the many types of ports. The back of a typical system unit (see Figure 3.7) has many cables running from the system unit to the various peripherals. You may even have a few connectors in the front. All of these connectors and ports have their own naming conventions, and a good tech knows all of them. It's not acceptable to go around saying such things as "That's a printer port," or "That's a little-type keyboard connector." You need to be comfortable with the more commonly used naming conventions so you can say "That's a female DB-25," or "That's a USB connector."

Plugs, Ports, Jacks, and Connectors

Although PCs use close to 50 different types of connections, almost all fit into one of six major types: DIN, USB, FireWire, DB, RJ, and audio. Read the next paragraphs to get your terminology straight so that you can then jump into the details of the various connectors with gusto.

No one seems to use the terms *plug*, *port*, *jack*, or *connector* correctly, so let's get these terms straight right from the start. To connect one device to another, you need a cable containing the wires that make the connection. On each device, as well as on each end of the connecting cable, you need standardized parts to make that connection. Because these are usually electrical connections, one part needs to fit inside another to make a snug, safe connection.

A **plug** is a part with some type of projection that goes into a *port*. A **port** is a part that has some type of matching hole or slot that accepts the plug. You never put a port into a plug; it's always the other way around. The term **jack** is used as an alternative to *port*, so you may also put a plug into a jack. The term **connector** describes either a port (jack) or a plug. As you progress though this chapter and see the various plugs and ports, this will become clearer (see Figure 3.8).

• **Figure 3.7** Connections in the back of a PC

• **Figure 3.8** Plug, port, and jack

• **Figure 3.9** DIN (top) and mini-DIN (bottom) connectors

Mini-DIN Connectors

Most PCs sport the European-designed **mini-DIN connectors**. The original Deutsche Industrie Norm (DIN) connector was replaced by mini-DIN a long time ago, so you'll only see mini-DIN connectors on your PC (see Figure 3.9 bottom). Older-style keyboards and mice plugged into DIN ports (Figure 3.9 top). You'll hear many older techs refer to a mini-DIN keyboard connector as a *PS/2* connector. That's what IBM called the port when it released the Personal System 2 (PS/2) computer way back in 1987 and the name stuck.

The standard mini-DIN connector has six pins and has been used for many devices aside from mice and keyboards. Some ancient video cards used the mini-DIN connector for output to a television, for example, and a lot of speaker sets use it to connect satellites to a subwoofer or to a control box. In uses other than keyboard or mouse, the mini-DIN gets yet another name, *DIN-6*.

USB Connectors

Universal serial bus (USB) provides the most common general-purpose connection for PCs. You'll find USB versions of many devices, such as mice, keyboards, scanners, cameras, and printers. USB connections come in three sizes: A, B, and mini-B. The USB A connector's distinctive rectangular shape makes it easily recognizable (see Figure 3.10).

You never see a USB B connector on your computer. USB B connecters are for the other end of the USB cable, where it attaches to the USB device (see Figure 3.11).

The USB B connector's relatively large size makes it less than optimal for small devices such as cameras, so the USB folks also make the smaller mini-B–style connector shown in Figure 3.12.

USB has a number of features that make it particularly popular on PCs. First, USB devices are **hot-swappable**, which means you can insert or remove them without restarting your PC. Almost every other type of connector requires you to turn the system off, insert or remove the connector, and then turn the system back on. Hot-swapping completely eliminates this process.

Second, many USB devices get their electrical power through the USB connection, so they don't need batteries or a plug for an electrical outlet.

• **Figure 3.10** USB A connector and port

• **Figure 3.11** USB B connector

• **Figure 3.12** USB mini-B connector

You can even recharge some devices, such as cellular phones, by plugging them into a USB port (see Figure 3.13).

FireWire Connectors

FireWire, also known as **IEEE 1394**, moves data at incredibly high speeds, making it the perfect connection for highly specialized applications such as streaming video from a digital video camera onto a hard drive. FireWire consists of a 6-wire connector, as shown in Figure 3.14, or a 9-wire connector for devices that need more speed and power. A smaller 4-pin version is usually seen on peripherals. Like USB, FireWire devices are hot-swappable.

DB Connectors

Over the years, **DB connectors** have been used for almost any type of peripheral you can think of, with the exception of keyboards. They have a slight *D* shape, which allows only one proper way to insert a plug into the socket and makes it easier to remember what they're called. Technically, they're known as D-sub or **D-subminiature** connectors, but most techs call them DBs. CompTIA calls them *D-shell* connectors, so don't be surprised by that term either.

Each male DB plug has a group of small pins that connect to DB ports. Female DB plugs connect to male DB ports on the system unit. DB connectors in the PC world can have from 9 to 37 pins or sockets, although you rarely see a DB connector with more than 25 pins or sockets. Figure 3.15 shows an example. DB-type connectors are some of the oldest and most common connectors used in the back of PCs.

• **Figure 3.13** Cell phone charging via a USB connection

In addition to mini-B USB connectors, you'll also see mini-A, micro-A, and micro-B connectors, though they're much less common.

Tech Tip

D-Subminiature Naming Scheme
Each D-sub connector size—called the shell size*—has a specific name in the D-sub manufacturing world. A two-row, 9-pin connector, for example, is officially a DE-9 connector rather than a DB-9. The E refers to the 9-pin shell size. Why all of the DA, DB, DC, DD, and DE connectors became DB-x in the world of personal computers is a mystery, but most techs simply call them DB connectors.*

• **Figure 3.14** FireWire connector and port

• **Figure 3.15** DB-25 connector and port

Keep in mind that the variety of connectors is virtually endless. The preceding types of connectors cover the vast majority, but you'll find many others on PCs as a tech. No law or standard requires device makers to use a particular connector, especially if they have no interest in making that device interchangeable with similar devices from other manufacturers.

Almost all connectors are now color-coordinated to help users plug the right device into the right port. These color codes are not required, and not all PCs and devices use them.

It wasn't that long ago that a typical PC used at least three or more different DB connectors. Over the past few years, the PC world has moved away from DB connectors. A typical modern system has only one or two, usually for video.

RJ Connectors

You have more than likely seen an **RJ connector**, whether or not you knew it by that name. The little plastic plug used to connect your telephone cord to the jack (techs don't use the word "port" to describe RJ connectors) is a classic example of an RJ plug. Modern PCs use only two types of RJ jacks: the RJ-11 and the RJ-45. The phone jack is an RJ-11. It is used almost exclusively for modems. The slightly wider RJ-45 jack is used for your network connection. Figure 3.16 shows an RJ-11 plug (top) and an RJ-45 plug (bottom).

Audio Connectors

Speakers and microphones connect to audio jacks on the system unit. The most common type of sound connector in popular use is the *3.5-mm* connector, also called a **mini-audio connector**. These small connectors have been around for years; they're just like the plug you use to insert headphones into a radio, music player, or similar device (see Figure 3.17). Traditionally, you'd find the audio jacks on the back of the PC, but many newer models sport front audio connections as well.

Devices and Their Connectors

Now that you have a sense of the connectors, let's turn to the devices common to almost every PC to learn which connectors go with which device.

Cards Versus Onboard

All of the connectors on the back of the PC are just that: connectors. Behind those connectors are the actual devices that support whatever peripherals plug into those connectors. These devices might be built into the computer, such as a keyboard port. Others might be add-on expansion cards that a tech installed into the PC.

 Try This!

Feeling Your Way Around Connectors

Given that most PCs tend to sit on the floor under desks, a good PC tech learns to recognize most every PC connector by touch. This is a great exercise to do with a partner.

1. Look at all of the connectors on the back of any PC's system unit.
2. Turn the system unit around so you can no longer see the connections.
3. Try to identify the connectors by feel.

Most PCs have special **expansion slots** inside the system unit that enable you to add more devices on expansion cards. Figure 3.18 shows a typical card. If you want some new device that your system unit doesn't have built into the PC, you just go to the store, buy a card version of that device, and snap it in. Later chapters of the book go into great detail on how to do this, but for now just appreciate that a device might be built in or might come on a card.

Be careful handling cards. Touch the metal plate with the 90-degree bend and try to avoid touching any of the electronics. As mentioned in Chapter 2, you can protect your cards by keeping them in an anti-static bag when moving them.

• **Figure 3.18** Typical expansion card

Keyboard

Today's keyboards come in many shapes and sizes, but they always connect to your computer by either a mini-DIN port or a USB port. Many keyboards ship with an adapter so you can use either port. Most keyboard plugs and mini-DIN keyboard ports are colored purple (see Figure 3.19).

Monitor

A monitor connects to the video connector on the system unit. You'll usually see one of two types of video connectors: the older, 15-pin female DB **Video Graphics Array (VGA)** connector or the unique **digital visual interface (DVI)** connector. VGA connectors are colored blue, whereas DVI connectors are white. Many video cards have both types of connectors (see Figure 3.20) or two VGA or two DVI connectors. Other video cards also add S-Video, component, or composite ports. Video cards with two connectors support two monitors, a very cool setup to have!

The newest video connector is called **High-Definition Multimedia Interface (HDMI)**, shown in Figure 3.21. HDMI brings a number of enhancements, such as the ability to carry both video and sound on the same cable. Primarily designed for home theaters, computers with HDMI connectors grow more common every year.

• **Figure 3.19** Keyboard plug and port

> The DVI connector comes in three flavors, DVD-D (all digital), DVD-A (analog), and DVI-I (both digital and analog).

> There are two smaller versions of HDMI called Mini-HDMI and Micro-HDMI. You'll find these primarily on high-end cell phones.

Sound

The sound device in a computer performs two functions. First, it takes digital information and turns it into sound, outputting the sound through speakers. Second, it takes sound that is input through a microphone or some other audio source and turns it into digital data.

To play and record sounds, your sound device needs to connect to a set of speakers and a microphone or more. All PCs have at least two miniature audio jacks: one for a microphone and another for stereo speakers. Better cards provide extra miniature

• **Figure 3.20** Video card with (from left to right) S-Video, DVI, and VGA ports

• **Figure 3.21** HDMI connector

• Figure 3.22 Typical bank of 3.5-mm audio jacks

• Figure 3.23 Legacy joystick/MIDI port

Modern PCs have built-in network connections, but this is a fairly recent development. For many years, network devices only came on an expansion card, called a **network interface card (NIC)**. The term is so common that even built-in network connections—which most certainly are not cards—are still called NICs.

audio jacks for surround sound. Figure 3.22 shows a typical onboard sound card with six different 3.5-mm jacks. Four of these are for speakers and two are for input (such as microphones). The color scheme for sound connections is complex, but for now remember one color—green. That's the one you need to connect a standard pair of stereo speakers.

An older sound card may have a female 15-pin DB port that enables you to attach a musical instrument digital interface (MIDI) device or add a joystick to your PC (see Figure 3.23). These multi-function joystick/MIDI ports are rare today.

Adding more and more audio jacks to sound cards made the back of a typical sound card a busy place. In an effort to consolidate the various sound signals, the industry invented the **Sony/Philips Digital Interface Format (S/PDIF)** connection. S/PDIF comes in coaxial and optical versions. Figure 3.24 shows a motherboard with both (the coaxial connection is on the left). One S/PDIF connection replaces all of the mini-audio connections, assuming your surround speaker system also comes with an S/PDIF connection.

Network

Networks are groups of connected PCs that share information. The PCs most commonly connect via some type of cabling that usually looks like an extra-thick phone cable. A modern PC uses an RJ-45 connection to connect to the network. Figure 3.25 shows a typical RJ-45 network connector. Network connectors do not have a standard color.

Mouse

Most folks are pretty comfortable with the function of a mouse—it enables you to select graphical items on a graphical screen. A PC mouse has at least two buttons (as opposed to the famous one-button mouse that came with Apple computers until recently), while a better mouse provides a scroll

S/PDIF

• Figure 3.24 S/PDIF connection

Figure 3.25 Typical network connection

Figure 3.26 Mouse with mini-DIN connection

wheel and extra buttons. A mouse uses either a USB port or a dedicated, light-green mini-DIN connector (see Figure 3.26).

A variation of the mouse is a **trackball**. A trackball does the same job as a mouse, but instead of pushing it around like a mouse, the trackball stays in one place as you roll a ball with your fingers or thumb (see Figure 3.27).

Modem

A **modem** enables you to connect a PC to a network via a standard telephone line. Modems are another easily identifiable device in PCs as they have one or two RJ-11 jacks. One jack is to connect the modem to the telephone jack on the wall. If the modem has a second RJ-11 jack, it is for an optional telephone so you can use the phone line when the modem is not in use (see Figure 3.28).

Figure 3.27 Trackball

Figure 3.28 Internal modem

Tech Tip

Serial Ports

External modems traditionally connected to a male 9-pin or 25-pin D-sub port on the system unit called a **serial port***. Although just about every external modem today connects to USB, a few computers still come with a serial port for legacy devices.*

• **Figure 3.29** Parallel port

• **Figure 3.30** Joystick

Printer

For many years, printers only used a special connector called a **parallel port**. Parallel ports use a 25-pin female DB (DB-25) connector that's usually colored fuchsia (see Figure 3.29).

After almost 30 years of domination by parallel ports, most printers now come with USB, Ethernet, and Wi-Fi 802.11 b/g/n connectivity options. Parallel ports are quickly fading away from the backs of most computers.

Joystick

Joysticks weren't supposed to be used just for games (see Figure 3.30). When the folks at IBM added the two-row, 15-pin female DB joystick connector to PCs, they envisioned joysticks as hard-working input devices, just as the mouse is today. Except in the most rare circumstances, however, the only thing a **joystick** does today is enable you to turn your PC into a rather expensive game machine. But is there a more gratifying feeling than easing that joystick over, pressing the Fire button, and watching an enemy fighter jet get blasted by a well-placed Sidewinder missile? I think not. Traditional joystick connecters are colored orange, but most joysticks today connect to USB ports.

eSATA

More and more PCs are showing up with eSATA ports like the one shown in Figure 3.31. Some external hard drives and optical drives can connect via eSATA.

Plenty More!

Keep in mind that there are lots more devices and connectors out there. This section includes only the most common and the ones you're most likely to see. As you progress through this book, you'll see some less common connecters and where they are used.

• **Figure 3.31** eSATA port

■ Inside the System Unit

Now that you've seen the devices that connect to the PC, it's time to open up the system unit to inspect the major internal components of a typical PC. A single PC is composed of thousands of discrete components. Although no one can name every tiny bit of electronics in a PC, a good technician should be able to name the major internal components that make up the typical PC. Let's open and inspect a system unit to see these components and see what they do. In later chapters, you'll see all of these components in much more detail.

Case

The system unit's case is both the internal framework of the PC and the external skin that protects the internal components from the environment. Cases come in an amazing variety of styles, sizes, and colors. Figure 3.32 shows the front and back of a typical PC case. The front of the case holds the buttons for turning the system on and off, lights to tell you the status of the system, and doors for accessing removable media drives such as digital versatile disc (DVD) drives. This system also provides USB, FireWire, and audio connections in the front for easy access if you want to use a device that needs these connections.

The back of the case holds the vast majority of the system unit connections. You will also notice the power supply—almost always at the top of the case—distinguished by its cooling fan and power plug. Note that one area of the back, the input/output (I/O) area, holds all of the onboard connections (see Figure 3.33), while another area in the back contains slots for cards. Similarly, the case uses slots to enable access to the external connectors on cards installed in the system unit.

Opening a case is always…interesting. There's no standard way to open a case, and I'm convinced that the folks making system units enjoy some sick humor inventing new and complex ways to open them. In general, you detach the sides of a case by removing a few screws in the back of the system unit, as shown in Figure 3.34. Use common sense and you won't have too many problems. Just don't lose track of your screws or where each one was inserted!

• **Figure 3.32** Case—front and back

You'll hear the PC case called the *enclosure*, especially at the more expensive end of the spectrum. Case, enclosure, and system unit are interchangeable terms.

• **Figure 3.33** Onboard connections

• **Figure 3.34** Opening a system unit

Cross Check

Tools for Opening Cases

You read about the standard tools for opening cases and working on the inside of a system unit in Chapter 2, so check your memory now. What types of screwdrivers might you use? (Name three.) What tool would you use if you dropped a screw inside a case?

Once you've opened the case, take a look inside. You'll see metal framework, all kinds of cables, and a number of devices. As you inspect the devices, you may gently push cables to the side to get a better view. Don't forget to wear an anti-static wrist strap (attaching it to any handy metal part of the case) or touch the metal case occasionally to prevent ESD.

CPU

The **central processing unit (CPU)**, also called the **microprocessor**, performs all of the calculations that take place inside a PC. CPUs come in a variety of shapes and sizes, as shown in Figure 3.35.

Modern CPUs generate a lot of heat and thus require a cooling fan and heat sink assembly to avoid overheating (see Figure 3.36). A *heat sink* is a big slab of copper or aluminum that helps draw heat away from the processor. The fan then blows the heat out into the case. You can usually remove this cooling device if you need to replace it, although some CPU manufacturers have sold CPUs with a fan permanently attached.

CPUs have a make and model, just like automobiles do. When talking about a particular car, for example, most people speak in terms of a Ford

• **Figure 3.35** Typical CPUs still in protective packaging

• **Figure 3.36** CPU with fan

Taurus or a Toyota Camry. When they talk about CPUs, people say Intel Core i7 or AMD Phenom. Over the years, there have been only a few major CPU manufacturers, just as there are only a few major auto manufacturers. The two most common makes of CPUs used in PCs are AMD and Intel.

Although only a few manufacturers of CPUs have existed, those manufacturers have made hundreds of models of CPUs. Some of the more common models made over the past few years have names such as Core 2 Duo, Core i5, Core i7, Phenom II, and AMD-FX.

Finally, CPUs come in a variety of packages. The package defines how the CPU looks physically and how it connects to the computer. Intel CPUs currently use a package type called *land grid array* (*LGA*), and AMD likes *pin grid array* (*PGA*). Every CPU package type has a number of versions, and each package type is designed to fit into a particular connection called a *socket*. Sockets have such names as Socket AM3 or Socket B. Figure 3.37 shows a CPU with its matching socket.

Chapter 5 goes into great detail on CPUs, but for now remember that every CPU has a make, a model, and a package type.

• **Figure 3.37** CPU and matching socket

RAM

Random access memory (RAM) stores programs and data currently being used by the CPU. The maximum amount of programs and data that a piece of RAM can store is measured in units called *bytes*. Modern PCs have many millions, even billions, of bytes of RAM, so RAM is measured in units called *megabytes* (*MB*) or *gigabytes* (*GB*). An average PC will have from 1 to 4 GB of RAM, although PCs may have more or less. Each piece of RAM is called a *stick*. One common type of stick found in today's PC is called a *dual inline memory module* (*DIMM*). Figure 3.38 shows two examples of DIMMs used in PCs.

Your PC takes only one type of DIMM, and you must know the type so you can add or replace RAM when needed. Chapter 6 covers everything you need to know to work comfortably with RAM.

> ⚠️ Some parts of your PC are much more sensitive to ESD than others. Your CPU and RAM are very sensitive to ESD. If you touch the metal parts of your CPU or RAM and you have even the tiniest amount of charge, you can destroy them.

• **Figure 3.38** Two DIMMs

● **Figure 3.39** Typical motherboard

● **Figure 3.40** Placing a card into an expansion slot

Motherboard

You can compare a motherboard to the chassis of an automobile. In a car, everything connects to the chassis either directly or indirectly. In a PC, everything connects to the motherboard either directly or indirectly. A **motherboard** is a thin, flat piece of circuit board, usually green or gold, and often slightly larger than a typical piece of notebook paper (see Figure 3.39).

A motherboard contains a number of special sockets that accept various PC components. The CPU and RAM, for example, plug directly into the motherboard. Other devices, such as floppy drives, hard drives, and CD and DVD drives, connect to the motherboard sockets through short cables. Motherboards also provide onboard connectors for external devices such as mice, printers, joysticks, and keyboards.

All motherboards use multipurpose expansion slots in which you can add adapter cards. Different types of expansion slots exist for different types of cards (see Figure 3.40).

Power Supply

The **power supply**, as its name implies, provides the necessary electrical power to make the PC operate. The power supply takes standard electrical power and converts it into power your PC can use. Most power supplies are about the size of a shoebox cut in half and are usually a gray or metallic color (see Figure 3.41).

A number of connectors lead out of the power supply. Every power supply provides special connectors to power the motherboard and a number of other general-use connectors that provide power to any device that needs electricity. Check out Chapter 9 for more information.

● **Figure 3.41** Power supply

Floppy Drive

The **floppy drive** enables you to access removable floppy disks. The floppy drives used in today's PCs (and I use the term loosely—you'll have trouble finding a floppy drive on most modern computers) are 3.5-inch floppy drives. Floppy drives only store a tiny amount of data and have all but disappeared from PCs.

Floppy drives connect to the computer via a ribbon cable, which in turn connects to the motherboard. The connection to the motherboard is known as the *floppy drive controller* (see Figure 3.42).

• **Figure 3.42** Floppy drive connected to motherboard

Hard Drive

A **hard drive** stores programs and data that are not currently being used by the CPU. Although RAM storage is measured in megabytes and gigabytes, a PC's hard drive stores much more data than a typical PC's RAM—hundreds of gigabytes to *terabytes*. A terabyte is 1000 gigabytes.

An average PC has one hard drive, although most PCs accept more. Special PCs that need to store large amounts of data, such as a large corporation's main file-storage computer, can contain many hard drives—8 to 16 drives in some cases.

The two most common types of hard drives seen in today's PCs are the older *Parallel Advanced Technology Attachment* (*PATA*) and the more modern *Serial Advanced Technology Attachment* (*SATA*). PATA drives use a ribbon cable very similar to the one used by floppy drives, whereas SATA drives use a very narrow cable. Figure 3.43 shows a SATA drive (left) next to a PATA drive (right). Most motherboards only come with SATA connections, but if you look around, you can find one that supports PATA as well.

Optical drives, introduced next, use the same PATA or SATA connections used with hard drives. Figure 3.44 shows a DVD drive sharing a single ribbon cable with a PATA hard drive—a common sight inside a PC.

Tech Tip

SCSI

Very few PCs use small computer system interface (SCSI) *drives. SCSI drives are generally faster and more expensive, so they usually show up only in high-end PCs such as network servers or graphics workstations.*

• **Figure 3.43** SATA and PATA drives showing data connectors

• **Figure 3.44** Hard drive and DVD drive

Optical Drives

Optical drives enable a computer to read one or more types of optical discs, such as CD, DVD, or Blu-ray Disc (see Figure 3.45). CDs store around 700 MB and come in three varieties: CD-ROM (*read only memory*: you can't change the data on them), CD-R (*recordable*: you can change the data once), and CD-RW (*rewritable*: you can change the data on them over and over). DVDs store much more data—the smallest capacity DVDs store around 4 GB, enough for a Hollywood movie—and come in even more varieties: DVD-ROM, DVD+R, DVD-R, DVD+RW, and DVD-RW, just to name the more famous ones. Blu-ray Discs are popular for high-definition movies, but there are also Blu-ray Discs for storing data with capacities starting at 25 GB.

• **Figure 3.45** Assorted optical discs

Chapter 11 goes into great detail on the assorted discs and drive types.

All of these optical discs require an optical drive that knows how to read them. If you want to do anything with a CD-RW disc, for example, you need a CD-RW drive. If you want to use a DVD+R disc, you need a DVD+R drive. Luckily, most optical drives support many different types of discs, and some support every common type of optical disc available. Figure 3.46 shows typical optical drives. Note that some of them advertise what disc types they use. Others give no clue whatsoever.

Know Your Parts

The goal of this chapter was to get you to appreciate the names and functions of the various parts of the PC: peripherals, connectors, and components. By starting with the Big Picture view, you may now begin breaking down the individual components on a chapter-by-chapter basis and truly understand at great depth how each component works and how it interconnects with the PC system as a whole.

• **Figure 3.46** Optical drives

Chapter 3 Review

■ Chapter Summary

After reading this chapter and completing the exercises, you should understand the following about the visible PC.

Describe how the PC works

■ The two parts of the PC—hardware and software—work intimately together to enable you to do work.

■ The computer tech knows the four stages of computing: input, processing, output, and storage. Understanding how the various pieces of hardware and software interact in each stage enables you to master the art of the PC tech.

Identify all the connectors and devices on a typical PC system unit

■ Most computers have a standard set of peripherals to provide input and output. Typical devices include the monitor, keyboard, mouse, speakers, and printer.

■ PCs use many kinds of external connectors, but most fit into one of six major types: mini-DIN, USB, FireWire, DB, RJ, and mini-audio. A plug goes into a port or jack. Connectors are often identified by their shape (such as DB connectors that look like a capital D), by their gender (male or female), and by the number of pins. Most PCs have two round mini-DIN connectors, one for the keyboard and the other for the mouse.

■ Universal serial bus (USB) connectors come in six forms, A, B, mini-A, mini-B, micro-A, and micro-B. Many devices plug into USB ports, including keyboards and cameras. USB is hot-swappable, so you may insert or remove devices without restarting the computer.

■ Also known as IEEE 1394, the FireWire interface is perfect for high-speed devices such as digital video cameras. FireWire consists of a 6-wire or 9-wire connector. A smaller 4-pin version is usually seen on peripherals.

■ DB connectors come in a variety of sizes but only one shape. You'll find only a few DB connectors on modern PCs, primarily for printers and video.

■ The telephone jack is an RJ connector, called an RJ-11. Most network interface cards have a wider RJ-45 jack.

■ Speakers and microphones connect to mini-audio jacks. You'll always find these on the back of the system unit; newer models have connectors on the front as well.

■ Keyboards connect into either a dedicated mini-DIN keyboard port or a USB port. Monitors connect to VGA or DVI ports. Mice and trackballs use the mini-DIN or USB ports as well. The majority of modern printers connect either to a USB, Ethernet, or Wi-Fi connection. A joystick plugs into either a 15-pin female DB port or a USB port.

Discuss the major internal components of a PC

■ Everything fits inside or connects to the case, more technically called a system unit. The system unit provides the framework for buttons, lights, drives, access doors, and so forth. Opening the case is usually a matter of unscrewing screws and pulling one side open.

■ The central processing unit (CPU), also called the microprocessor or brain of the computer, has a make, a model, and a package type. AMD and Intel are the two most common makers of CPUs. The pin grid array (PGA) is the most common CPU package. A CPU cooling fan or heat sink is essential to dissipate the heat.

■ Random access memory (RAM) contains the current programs and data that the CPU is using. Most PC memory is installed on sticks called dual inline memory modules (DIMMs). RAM capacity is measured in megabytes (MB) or gigabytes (GB).

■ The motherboard contains components, expansion slots, and sockets for the CPU, RAM, and other components. Expansion slots are connectors for expansion cards that enable optional devices to communicate with the PC.

- A floppy drive uses a ribbon cable to connect to the floppy drive controller on the motherboard. The most common type is the 3.5-inch floppy drive.

- Hard drives store programs and data that the CPU is not currently using. An average PC has one hard drive, although most PCs accept more. Most PCs use either PATA or SATA drives, both of which commonly connect to controllers built into the motherboard.

- Optical drives enable the computer to access optical discs. Some optical drives can record CDs, such as the compact disc-recordable (CD-R) drive or the compact disc-rewritable (CD-RW) drive. Most PCs now have digital versatile disc (DVD) drives that support capacities large enough for a full-length movie.

■ Key Terms

central processing unit (CPU) *(54)*
connector *(45)*
DB connector *(47)*
digital visual interface (DVI) *(49)*
D-subminiature *(47)*
expansion slot *(49)*
FireWire *(47)*
floppy drive *(57)*
hard drive *(57)*
High-Definition Multimedia Interface (HDMI) *(49)*
hot-swappable *(46)*
IEEE 1394 *(47)*
jack *(45)*
joystick *(52)*
keyboard *(44)*
microprocessor *(54)*
mini-audio connector *(48)*
mini-DIN connector *(46)*
modem *(51)*
monitor *(44)*
motherboard *(56)*

mouse *(44)*
network interface card (NIC) *(50)*
optical drives *(58)*
parallel port *(52)*
peripheral *(44)*
plug *(45)*
port *(45)*
power supply *(56)*
printer *(44)*
programming *(41)*
random access memory (RAM) *(55)*
RJ connector *(48)*
serial port *(51)*
software *(41)*
Sony/Philips Digital Interface Format (S/PDIF) *(50)*
speakers *(44)*
system unit *(44)*
trackball *(51)*
universal serial bus (USB) *(46)*
Video Graphics Array (VGA) *(49)*

■ Key Term Quiz

Use the Key Terms list to complete the sentences that follow. Not all terms will be used.

1. A monitor can attach to a video card with a 15-pin female DB connector called a(n) _____ connector.

2. If you install a DIMM stick, your computer will have more _____.

3. The _____ has a make, a model, and a package type.

4. Two RJ-11 connectors identify the _____.

5. When attaching a peripheral, put the plug into the _____ or jack.

6. The _____ takes standard electrical power from a wall outlet and converts it to power your PC can use.

7. If an expansion card contains an RJ-45 jack, it is a(n) _____.

8. A 25-pin female DB connector with a printer attached to it is a(n) _____.

9. An internal storage device that typically holds 200 GB or more is a(n) _____.

10. The box that all the other components plug into is called the _____.

■ Multiple-Choice Quiz

1. Which of the following connections can replace all of the mini-audio jacks on a system unit?
 - A. FireWire
 - B. HDMI
 - C. S/PDIF
 - D. VGA

2. A modern keyboard generally connects to which of the following ports? (Select two.)
 - A. FireWire
 - B. Mini-DIN
 - C. USB
 - D. VGA

3. USB connectors come in which of the following sizes? (Select three.)
 - A. A
 - B. B
 - C. Nano-B
 - D. Mini-B

4. Which of the following devices attaches with a ribbon cable?
 - A. CPU
 - B. CD-ROM drive
 - C. RAM
 - D. Sound card

5. Which of the following devices measure(s) storage capacity in megabytes or gigabytes?
 - A. Floppy disk and hard drive
 - B. NIC
 - C. CPU
 - D. Modem

6. Which of the following devices has enough storage capacity to hold a movie?
 - A. CD-ROM
 - B. CD-R
 - C. CD-RW
 - D. DVD

7. Which of the following connector types enable you to plug a device into them and have the device function without your restarting the computer? (Select two.)
 - A. FireWire
 - B. Mini-DIN
 - C. Serial
 - D. USB

8. Which of the following ports would you most likely find built into a motherboard?
 - A. Keyboard port
 - B. DVI port
 - C. HDMI port
 - D. RDA port

9. Which of the following connectors is used mostly for external hard drives?
 - A. PATA
 - B. eSATA
 - C. HDMI
 - D. PS/2

10. Which of the following ports can handle a connection from a monitor?
 - A. DVI
 - B. FireWire
 - C. Mini-DIN
 - D. USB

11. Which of the following ports enables a modern PC to connect to a network?

 A. Mini-audio

 B. Mini-DIN

 C. RJ-13

 D. RJ-45

12. Which of the following connectors is used for hard drives?

 A. Parallel

 B. SATA

 C. HDMI

 D. TTFN

13. Of the following, what do USB and FireWire connections have in common?

 A. Both are used for connecting keyboards

 B. Both support dual monitors

 C. Both support hot-swapping devices

 D. Both use D-subminiature connectors

14. Which devices enable you to select graphical items on a graphical screen? (Select two.)

 A. Modem

 B. Mouse

 C. Touchball

 D. Trackball

15. Which device traditionally used a two-row, 15-pin DB connector (though current models connect through USB)?

 A. Joystick

 B. Keyboard

 C. Mouse

 D. Printer

■ Essay Quiz

1. Although serial and parallel ports have been around forever, newer and faster ports such as USB and FireWire are available. At the same time, new computers have faster CPUs, more RAM, and larger-capacity hard drives. What factors do you think are driving the PC market for these improvements? Do you feel that you need to have the newest and the greatest PC? Why or why not?

2. Jason, one of your coworkers who knows nothing about computer hardware, needs to move his computer and will be responsible for reassembling it himself in his new office across town. What advice can you give him about disassembly steps that will help him reassemble the computer successfully? List at least five things Jason should do as he disassembles the computer, transports it, and reassembles it. Do shapes and colors help him?

3. A floppy drive was a standard component for personal computers from their beginning. Today, most manufacturers build PCs without a floppy drive. Would you want to purchase a PC without a floppy drive? Why or why not? If you don't want a floppy drive, what kinds of alternative devices would you want your computer to have?

4. Hearing that you are taking a computer hardware course, Aunt Sally approaches you about helping her select a new computer. She wants to use the computer primarily for office applications, to track her budget, to receive and send e-mail, and to surf the Internet. What are you going to tell her about the kind of PC to buy? What peripherals should she purchase? Why?

Lab Projects

• Lab Project 3.1

Many personal computers do not normally include the relatively new eSATA port. Check the following three Web sites: www.dell.com, www.hp.com, and www.lenovo.com. Is an eSATA port standard built-in equipment on their new computers? If so, how many eSATA ports are included? If not, do the sites offer eSATA as an optional add-on?

• Lab Project 3.2

Find an advertisement for a new personal computer in a current newspaper or magazine and examine it to determine the following:

- What is the make, model, and package type of the CPU?

- How much RAM does it have?

- What is the storage capacity of the hard drive?

- Does it include a Blu-ray Disc, CD-RW, or DVD drive?

- Does it come with a network interface card?

- Is a monitor included? If so, what kind and size?

chapter

4

Visible Networks

"Information at your fingertips."

—BILL GATES

In this chapter, you will learn how to

- **Describe the basic functions of a network, including identifying common devices and connectors**
- **Discuss the differences between a LAN and a WAN and the importance of TCP/IP**

It's hard to find a computer that's not connected to a network. Whether your system is part of a large enterprise network or a single PC with an Internet connection, every computer has some form of network connection. CompTIA has wisely added quite a bit of networking coverage to the CompTIA A+ 801 exam, and a number of chapters toward the back of this book cover networking in great detail. By covering the basic or "user level" networking topics early in the book, however, you'll see how networking impacts every facet of modern computing.

I didn't name this chapter "Visible Networks" simply as a clever follow-up to the titles of the previous chapters. The primary goal of this chapter is to cover the more visible parts of the network: the connections and settings that enable you and me to set up simple networks. Let's begin by answering a big question: Why do we network?

Historical/Conceptual

Take a moment to think about what you do on a network. Most of us, when asked, would say, "surf the Internet," or "watch YouTube videos," or maybe "print to the printer downstairs." These are all good reasons to use a network, but what ties them together? In each of these situations, you are using your computer (the local computer) to access "stuff" stored on a remote computer (not your local computer). So what do remote computers have that you might want (see Figure 4.1)?

A remote computer called a **Web server** stores the files that make up a Web site. The Web server uses server programs to store and share the data. The two most famous Web server programs are Apache HTTP Server and Internet Information Server (IIS). When you access a Web site, your **Web browser** (likely Internet Explorer, Mozilla Firefox, or Google Chrome) asks the Web server to share the Web page files and then displays them (see Figure 4.2). Because your computer asks for the Web page, we call it the **client**. The remote computer that serves the Web site is a **server**.

 Any computer that's running a sharing program is by definition a server.

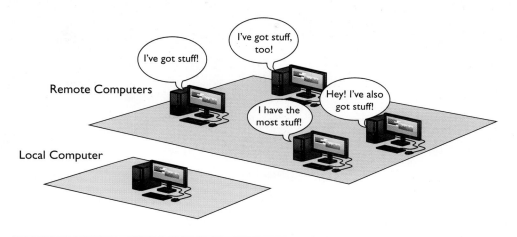

• **Figure 4.1** Accessing remote computers

• **Figure 4.2** Accessing a Web page

But what about YouTube? YouTube also uses Web servers, but these Web servers connect to massive video databases. Like a normal Web server, these remote computers share the videos with your client PC, but they use special software capable of sending video fast enough that you can watch it without waiting (see Figure 4.3).

But we don't need the Internet to share stuff. Figure 4.4 shows a small home network with each computer running Windows 7. One of the computers on the network has a printer connected via a USB port. This computer has enabled a printer-sharing program built into Windows so that the other computers on the network can use the printer.

No matter how big the network, we use networks to share stuff. This stuff might be Web pages, videos, printers, folders, e-mail messages, music—what you can share is limited only by your ability to find a server program capable of sharing it and a client program that can access it.

● **Figure 4.3** Accessing a YouTube page

● **Figure 4.4** Sharing a printer in Windows 7

Network people call anything that one computer might share with another a **resource**. Therefore, the goal of networking is to connect computers so that they can share resources or access other shared resources.

To share and access resources, a network must have the following:

1. Something that defines and standardizes the design and operation of cabling, network cards, and the interconnection of multiple computers

2. An addressing method that enables clients to find servers and enables servers to send data to clients, no matter the size of the network

3. Some method of sharing resources and accessing those shared resources

■ Networking Technologies

When the first network designers sat down at a café to figure out how to get two or more PCs to share data and peripherals, they had to write a lot of notes on little white napkins to answer even the most basic questions. The first question was: *How?* It's easy to say, "Well, just run a wire between them!" But that doesn't tell us how the wire works or how the computers connect to the wire. Here are some more big-picture questions:

- How will each computer be identified?

- If two or more computers want to talk at the same time, how do you ensure that all conversations are understood?

- What kind of wire? What gauge? How many wires in the cable? Which wires do what? How long can the cable be? What type of connectors?

Clearly, making a modern PC network entails a lot more than just stringing up some cable! As you saw a bit earlier, most networks have one or more *client machines,* PCs that request information or services, and a *server,* the machine that hosts and shares the data. Both clients and servers need **network interface controllers (NICs)** that define or label the machine on the network. A NIC also breaks files into smaller data units, called **frames**, to send across the network and reassembles the frames it receives into whole files. You also need some medium for delivering the frames between two or more PCs—most often this is a wire that can carry electrical pulses; sometimes it's radio waves or other wireless methods. Finally, your PC's operating system has to be able to communicate with its own networking hardware and with other machines on the network. Figure 4.5 shows a typical network layout.

This section of the chapter looks at the inventive solutions network engineers found to handle frames and cabling. After a brief look at the core technology, the chapter dives into four specific types of networks. You'll dig into the software side of things later in the chapter.

 Not too many years ago, every NIC came on an expansion card that you added to a motherboard. Most techs called that card a *network interface card* or *NIC*. Now that just about every motherboard has the networking feature built in, the acronym has shifted to network interface *controller*. You're likely only to see the term *NIC* on the exam, though I call them *network cards*, too.

Windows 7 Workstations

Windows Server
2008

• **Figure 4.5** A typical network

Topology

If a bunch of computers connect together to make a network, some logic or order must influence the way they connect. Perhaps each computer connects to a single main line that snakes around the office. Each computer might have its own cable, with all of the cables coming together at a central point. Or maybe all of the cables from all of the computers connect to a main loop that moves data along a track, picking up and dropping off data like a circular subway line.

A network's **topology** describes the way that computers connect to each other in that network. The most common network topologies are called *bus*, *ring*, *star*, and *mesh*. Figure 4.6 shows the four types: a **bus** topology, where all computers connect to the network via a main line called a *bus cable*; a **ring** topology, where all computers on the network attach to a central ring of cable; a **star** topology, where the computers on the network connect to a central wiring point (usually called a *switch*); and a **mesh** topology, where each computer has a dedicated line to every other computer. There are also **hybrid** topologies, such as star bus or star ring, which combine aspects of the other topologies to capitalize on their strengths and minimize their weaknesses. You'll look at the most important hybrid topology, star bus, in a moment, but for now, make sure you know the four main topologies!

Look at Figure 4.6. A mesh topology looks amazingly resilient and robust, doesn't it? And it is, at least on paper. Every computer physically connects to every other computer on the network, so even if half of the PCs crash, the network functions as well as ever (for the survivors). In a practical sense, however, implementing a mesh topology network would be an expensive mess. For example, a tiny network with only 10 PCs would need 45 distinct pieces of cable to connect every PC to every other PC. What a mesh mess! Because of this, mesh topologies have never been practical in a cabled network.

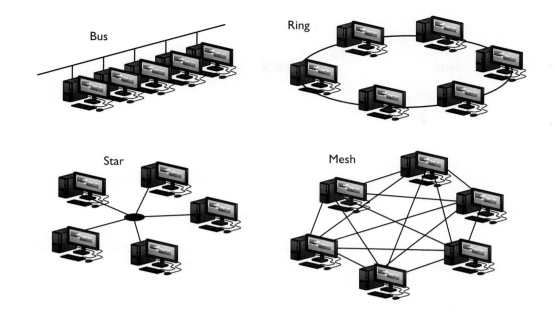

● **Figure 4.6** Clockwise from top left: bus, ring, mesh, and star topologies

Although a topology describes the method by which systems in a network connect, the topology alone doesn't describe all of the features necessary to make a cabling system work. The term *bus topology*, for example, describes a network that consists of some number of machines connected to the network via the same piece of cable. Notice that this definition leaves a lot of questions unanswered. What is the cable made of? How long can the cable be? How do the machines decide which machine should send data at a specific moment? A network based on a bus topology can answer these questions in a number of different ways.

Most techs make a clear distinction between the *logical topology* of a network—how the network is laid out on paper, with nice straight lines and boxes, similar to an electronic schematic—and the physical topology. The *physical topology* describes the typically messy computer network, with cables running diagonally through the ceiling space or snaking their way through walls. If someone describes the topology of a particular network, make sure you understand whether they're talking about the logical topology or the physical topology.

Over the years, manufacturers and standards bodies created several specific network technologies based on different topologies. A **network technology** is a practical application of a topology and other critical standards to provide a method to get data from one computer to another on a network. It defines many aspects of a network, from the topology, to the frame type, to the cabling and connectors used. A network technology defines everything necessary to get data from one computer to another.

Frames and NICs

Data is moved from one PC to another in discrete chunks called *frames*. You'll sometimes hear the word *packet* used instead of frames—this is incorrect. Packets are a part of the frame. You'll find more information about packets in Chapter 14.

Every NIC in the world has a built-in identifier, an address unique to that single network card, called a **media access control (MAC) address**. You read that right—every network card in the world has its own unique MAC address!

A MAC address is a *binary number*, meaning it's a string of 1s and 0s. Each 1 or 0 is called a *bit*. (You'll learn more about binary in Chapter 5.)

The MAC address is 48 bits long, providing more than 281 *trillion* MAC addresses, so there are plenty of MAC addresses to go around. Because people have trouble keeping track of that many 1s and 0s, we need another way to display the addresses. *Hexadecimal* is shorthand for representing strings of 1s and 0s. One hex character is used to represent four binary characters. Here's the key:

0000 = 0	0100 = 4	1000 = 8	1100 = C
0001 = 1	0101 = 5	1001 = 9	1101 = D
0010 = 2	0110 = 6	1010 = A	1110 = E
0011 = 3	0111 = 7	1011 = B	1111 = F

Even though MAC addresses are embedded into the NIC, some NICs allow you to change the MAC address on the NIC. This is rarely done.

So, MAC addresses may be binary, but we represent them by using 12 hexadecimal characters. These MAC addresses are burned into every NIC, and some NIC makers print the MAC address on the card. Figure 4.7 shows the System Information utility description of a NIC, with the MAC address highlighted.

Hey! I thought we were talking about frames! Well, we are, but you need to understand MAC addresses to understand frames. The many varieties of frames share common features (see Figure 4.8). First, frames contain the MAC address of the network card to which the data is being sent. Second, they have the MAC address of the network card that sent the data. Third is the data itself (at this point, we have no idea what the data is—certain software handles that question), which can vary in size depending on the type of frame. Finally, the frame must contain some type of data check to verify that the data was received in good order. Most frames use a

• **Figure 4.7** MAC address

clever mathematical algorithm called a **cyclic redundancy check (CRC)**.

This discussion of frames raises the question, how big is a frame? Or more specifically, how much data do you put into each frame? How do you ensure that the receiving PC understands the *way* the data was broken down by the sending machine and can thus put the pieces back together? The problem in answering these questions is that they encompass so many items. When the first networks were created, *everything* from the frames to the connectors to the type of cable had to be invented from scratch.

To make a successful network, you need the sending and receiving PCs to use the same network technology.

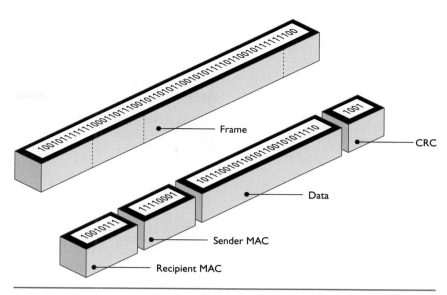

• **Figure 4.8** Generic frame

Over the years, many hardware protocols have been implemented, with such names as Token Ring, FDDI, and ARCnet, but today only one hardware protocol dominates the modern PC computing landscape: *Ethernet*.

Introducing Ethernet

A consortium of companies centered on Digital Equipment Corporation, Intel, and Xerox invented the first network in the mid-1970s. More than just create a network, they wrote a series of standards that defined everything necessary to get data from one computer to another. This series of standards was called **Ethernet**. Over the years, Ethernet has gotten faster and has used different types of cabling. As a result, the Ethernet folks have a number of Ethernet versions, often called *Ethernet flavors*. Even though there are various speeds and cable types, all flavors of Ethernet use the same frame. This is very important: you can have any combination of hardware devices and cabling using different Ethernet flavors on a single Ethernet network and, in most cases, the PCs will be able to communicate just fine.

Most modern Ethernet networks employ one of three speeds (and sometimes all three), **10BaseT**, **100BaseT**, or **1000BaseT**. As the numbers in the names suggest, 10BaseT networks run at 10 Mbps, 100BaseT networks run at 100 Mbps, and 1000BaseT networks—called Gigabit Ethernet—run at 1000 Mbps, or 1 Gbps. All three technologies—sometimes referred to collectively as *10/100/1000BaseT* or just plain Ethernet—use a *star bus* topology and connect via a type of cable called *unshielded twisted pair (UTP)*.

 Ethernet developers continue to refine the technology. 1000BaseT might be the most common standard now, but 10-Gigabit Ethernet is starting to make inroads today.

Star Bus

Imagine taking a bus network (where every computer connects to a common wire) and shrinking the bus down so it fits inside a box. Then, instead of attaching each PC directly to the wire, you attach them via cables to special ports on the box (see Figure 4.9). The box with the bus takes care of all of the tedious details required by a bus network. The bus topology would look a lot like a star topology, wouldn't it? Modern Ethernet networks all use **star bus** topology.

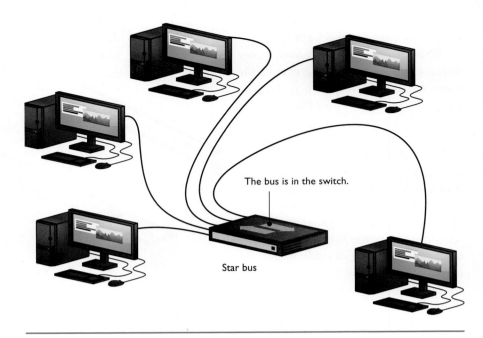

The bus is in the switch.

Star bus

• **Figure 4.9** Star bus

The central box with the bus—a **switch**—provides a common point of connection for network devices. Switches can have a wide variety of ports. Most consumer-level switches have 4 or 8 ports, but business-level switches can have 32 or more ports.

Early Ethernet networks used a **hub**. A switch is a far superior and far more common version of a hub. Figure 4.10 shows a typical consumer-level switch.

A simple example demonstrates the difference between hubs and switches. Let's say you have a network of 32 PCs, all using 100-Mbps NICs attached to a 100-Mbps hub or switch. We would say the network's **bandwidth** is 100 Mbps. If you put the 32 PCs on a 32-port 100-Mbps hub, you have 32 PCs sharing the 100 Mbps of bandwidth. A switch addresses this problem by making each port its own separate network. Each PC gets to use the full bandwidth. The bottom line? Once switches became affordable, hubs went away.

The connection between a computer and a switch is called a **segment**. With most cable types, Ethernet segments are limited to 100 meters or less.

Cheap and centralized, a star bus network does not go down if a single cable breaks. True, the network would go down if the switch failed, but that is rare. Even if a switch fails, replacing a switch in a closet is much easier than tracing a bus running through walls and ceilings and trying to find a break!

Unshielded Twisted Pair

Unshielded twisted pair (UTP) cabling is the specified cabling for 10/100/1000BaseT and is the predominant

• **Figure 4.10** A switch

cabling system used today. Many types of twisted pair cabling are available, and the type used depends on the needs of the network. Twisted pair cabling consists of AWG 22–26 gauge wire twisted together into color-coded pairs. Each wire is individually insulated and encased as a group in a common jacket.

CAT Levels UTP cables come in categories that define the maximum speed at which data can be transferred (also called *bandwidth*). The major categories (CATs) are outlined in Table 4.1.

Table 4.1	CAT levels
CAT 1	Standard telephone line
CAT 3	Designed for 10-Mbps networks; a variant that used all four pairs of wires supported 100-Mbps speeds
CAT 5	Designed for 100-Mbps networks
CAT 5e	Enhanced to handle 1000-Mbps networks
CAT 6	Supports 1000-Mbps networks at 100-meter segments; 10-Gbps networks up to 55-meter segments
CAT 6a	Supports 10-Gbps networks at 100-meter segments

> Although these days you'll only find CAT 3 installed for telephones and in very old network installations, CompTIA traditionally enjoys tripping up techs who don't know it could handle 100-Mbps networks.

The CAT level should be clearly marked on the cable, as Figure 4.11 shows.

The *Telecommunication Industry Association/Electronics Industries Alliance (TIA/EIA)* establishes the UTP categories, which fall under the TIA/EIA 568 specification. Currently, most installers use CAT 5e or CAT 6 cable.

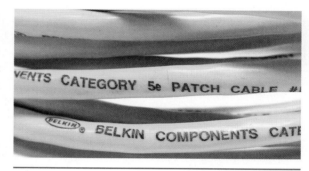

• **Figure 4.11** Cable markings for CAT level

Shielded Twisted Pair

Shielded twisted pair (STP), as its name implies, consists of twisted pairs of wires surrounded by shielding to protect them from EMI, or electromagnetic interference. STP is pretty rare, primarily because there's so little need for STP's shielding; it only really matters in locations with excessive electronic noise, such as a shop floor area with lots of lights, electric motors, or other machinery that could cause problems for other cables.

Implementing 10/100/1000BaseT

The 10BaseT and 100BaseT standards require two pairs of wires: a pair for sending and a pair for receiving. 10BaseT ran on an ancient CAT version called CAT 3, but typically used at least CAT 5 cable. 100BaseT requires at least CAT 5 to run. 1000BaseT needs all four pairs of wires in a CAT 5e or CAT 6 cable. These cables use a connector called an **RJ-45** connector. The *RJ (registered jack)* designation was invented by Ma Bell (the phone company, for you youngsters) years ago and is still used today.

> There are CAT levels for connectors as well as cables. Don't even try to use a CAT 5e RJ-45 connector with a CAT 6 cable.

Currently only two types of RJ connectors are used for networking: RJ-11 and RJ-45 (see Figure 4.12). **RJ-11** connects your telephone to the telephone jack in the wall of your house. It supports up to two pairs of wires, though most phone lines use only one pair. The other pair is used to support a second phone line. RJ-11 connectors are primarily used for telephone-based

• **Figure 4.12** RJ-11 and RJ-45

• **Figure 4.13** RJ-45 pin numbers

Internet connections (see Chapter 16) and are not used in any common LAN installation, although a few weird (and out of business) "network in a box" companies used them. RJ-45 is the standard for UTP connectors. RJ-45 has connections for up to four pairs and is visibly much wider than RJ-11. Figure 4.13 shows the position of the #1 and #8 pins on an RJ-45 jack.

The TIA/EIA has two standards for connecting the RJ-45 connector to the UTP cable: the TIA/EIA 568A (**T568A**) and the TIA/EIA 568B (**T568B**). Both are acceptable. You do not have to follow any standard as long as you use the same pairings on each end of the cable; however, you will make your life simpler if you choose a standard. Make sure that all of your cabling uses the same standard and you will save a great deal of work in the end. Most importantly, *keep records*!

Like all wires, the wires in UTP are numbered. A number does not appear on each wire, but rather each wire has a standardized color. Table 4.2 shows the official TIA/EIA Standard Color Chart for UTP.

Understanding Ethernet is critical in your understanding of how networks function. But when we talk about networking, there are two interconnected but very different worlds: the small local area networks where nearby users connect their computers via switches, and the Internet. Let's make sure we understand the differences by exploring the world of LANs and WANs in the next section.

Tech Tip

Plenum Versus PVC Cabling

Most workplace installations of network cable go up above the ceiling and then drop down through the walls to present a nice port in the wall. The space in the ceiling, under the floors, and in the walls through which cable runs is called the plenum *space. The potential problem with this cabling running through the plenum space is that the protective sheathing for networking cables, called the jacket, is made from plastic, and if you get any plastic hot enough, it creates smoke and noxious fumes.*

Standard network cables usually use PVC *(polyvinyl chloride) for the jacket, but PVC produces noxious fumes when burned. Fumes from cables burning in the plenum space can quickly spread throughout the building, so you want to use a more fire-retardant cable in the plenum space.*

Plenum-grade cable is simply network cabling with a fire-retardant jacket and is required for cables that go in the plenum space. Plenum-grade cable costs about three to five times more than PVC, but you should use it whenever you install cable in a plenum space.

■ Network Protocols, LANs, and WANs

The whole idea of networking is often confusing to new techs simply because there are two seemingly different ways to look at networking: small networks that share resources like documents, music, and printers, and big networks like the Internet where you share Web pages, e-mail, and just about anything you want. Let's take a moment to clarify how these two very different networks are very similar because today both use the same language or protocol.

Table 4.2	**UTP Cabling Color Chart**				
Pin	**T568A**	**T568B**	**Pin**	**T568A**	**T568B**
1	White/Green	White/Orange	5	White/Blue	White/Blue
2	Green	Orange	6	Orange	Green
3	White/Orange	White/Green	7	White/Brown	White/Brown
4	Blue	Blue	8	Brown	Brown

A Short History of the War of the Network Protocols and Why TCP/IP Won

Ethernet does a fine job of moving data from one machine to another, but Ethernet alone isn't enough to make a complete network; many other functions need to be handled. For example, an Ethernet frame holds a maximum of 1500 bytes. What if the data being moved is larger than 1500 bytes? Something has to chop up the data into chunks on one end and something else needs to reassemble those chunks on the other end so the file can be properly reassembled.

Another issue arises if one of the machines on the network has its network card replaced. Up to this point, the only way to distinguish one machine from another was by the MAC address on the network card. To solve this, each machine must have a name, an identifier for the network, which is "above" the MAC address. Something needs to keep track of the MAC addresses on the network and the names of the machines so that frames and names can be correlated. If you replace a PC's network card, the network will, after some special queries, update the list to associate the name of the PC with the new network card's MAC address.

Network protocol software takes the incoming data received by the network card, keeps it organized, sends it to the application that needs it, and then takes outgoing data from the application and hands it to the NIC to be sent out over the network. All networks use some protocol. Over the years there have been many network protocols, most combining multiple simple protocols into groups, called *protocol stacks*. This lead to some crazily named network protocols, such as NetBIOS/NetBEUI and TCP/IP.

> A *node* is any device that has a network connection—usually this means a PC, but other devices can be nodes. For example, many printers connect directly to a network and can therefore be deemed nodes.

NetBIOS/NetBEUI

During the 1980s, IBM developed the **NetBIOS Extended User Interface (NetBEUI)**, the default protocol for early versions of Windows. NetBEUI offered small size, easy configuration, and a relatively high speed. The underlying protocol stack was called *NetBIOS/NetBEUI*. The NetBIOS protocol handled naming conventions, while NetBEUI chopped up data for delivery via frames.

NetBIOS names were very simple. You could call your computer TIMMY or MIKESPC. NetBIOS didn't allow names to include anything but letters (uppercase only), numbers, and a very few special characters. NetBIOS/NetBEUI was great for little networks, but it relied on individual computers to send out frames addressed to the MAC address FF-FF-FF-FF-FF-FF—which meant *everybody*. The official term for this is a **broadcast**. Broadcasts eat up bandwidth, but they're great for a node that's trying to get a MAC address for another node, as shown in Figure 4.14.

Broadcasts are useful, but the larger the network is, the more bandwidth broadcasts eat up. In general, NetBIOS could handle about 300 computers on a single network before the broadcast became too much. By the mid-

> Could the computer called MIKESPC please send me a frame back to tell me your MAC address?

• **Figure 4.14** A broadcast in action

> NetBIOS stands for *networked basic input/output system*, which is why everyone always just called it NetBIOS.

1980s, it was clear NetBIOS wasn't going to work for really large networks, so a new network protocol was in the works. Plus, scaling required new hardware as well.

LANs, Routing, and WANs

For the CompTIA A+ 220-801 exam, remember that a LAN is a group of networked computers that are close to each other. Also, remember that a LAN is almost always a broadcast domain.

A **local area network (LAN)** is a group of computers that are located physically close to each other—no more than a few hundred meters apart at most. A LAN might be in a single room, on a single floor, or in a single building. But I'm going to add that a LAN is almost always a group of computers that are able to "hear" each other when one of them sends a broadcast. A group of computers connected by one or more switches is a broadcast domain (see Figure 4.15).

A **wide area network (WAN)** is a widespread group of computers connected using long-distance technologies. You connect LANs into a WAN with a magical box called a **router** (see Figure 4.16). The best example of a WAN is the Internet.

You can connect multiple smaller networks into a bigger network, turning a group of LANs into one big WAN, but this raises a couple of issues with network traffic. A computer needs some form of powerful, flexible addressing to address a frame so that it goes to a computer within its own LAN or to a computer on another LAN on the same WAN. Broadcasting is also unacceptable, at least between LANs. If every computer saw every frame, the network traffic would quickly spin out of control! Plus, the addressing scheme needs to work so that routers can sort the frames and send them along to the proper LAN. This process, called *routing*, requires routers and a routing-capable protocol to function correctly.

Routers destroy any incoming broadcast frames by design. No broadcast frame can ever go through a router. This makes broadcasting still quite common within a single broadcast domain, but never anywhere else.

NetBIOS/NetBEUI was great for a single LAN, but it lacked the extra addressing capabilities needed for a WAN. A new protocol was needed, one that could handle routing.

• **Figure 4.15** Two broadcast domains—two separate LANs

Mike Meyers' CompTIA A+ Guide to 801: Managing and Troubleshooting PCs

• **Figure 4.16** Two broadcast domains connected by a router—a WAN

TCP/IP

Transmission Control Protocol/Internet Protocol (TCP/IP) was originally developed for the Internet's progenitor, the *Advanced Research Projects Agency Network* (*ARPANET*) of the U.S. Department of Defense. In 1983, TCP/IP became the built-in protocol for the popular BSD (Berkeley Software Distribution) UNIX, and other flavors of UNIX quickly adopted it as well. The biggest network of all, the Internet, uses TCP/IP as its protocol. All versions of Windows (in fact, all operating systems today) use TCP/IP as the default protocol.

The reason TCP/IP has a slash in the middle is to reflect that TCP/IP isn't a single network protocol. It's a number of protocols that all work together. TCP handles getting the data between computers, while IP handles the addressing scheme that gives us something more powerful and flexible than MAC addresses. Let's cover IP addresses in this chapter and save some of the other protocols for Chapter 14.

Chapter 14 covers TCP/IP in much greater detail.

IP Addresses and Subnet Masks In a TCP/IP network, the systems don't have names but rather have IP addresses. The **IP address** is the unique identification number for your system on the network. Part of the address identifies the network, and part identifies the local computer (host) address on the network. IP addresses consist of four sets of eight binary numbers (octets), with each set separated by a period. The numbers range from 0 to 255. This is called *dotted-decimal notation*. Every computer on a network running TCP/IP gets an IP address like so:

202.34.16.11

Every computer in the same broadcast domain as this computer will have some numbers in common. If the network is small, then all the computers will share the first three octets. In this case, a computer with the IP address of 202.34.16.123 is in the same broadcast domain as 202.34.16.11.

The part of the IP address that is common for all the computers in the same broadcast domain is called the **network ID**. The network ID for this example is 202.34.16.

Are these example computers part of the same broadcast domain as a device with an IP address of 202.34.15.33? No. In this example, only computers that are part of 202.34.16 are part of the same broadcast domain as 202.34.16.11. But how does every computer know which part of its IP address identifies the network ID? The **subnet mask** tells the computer which part of its IP address is the network ID. A typical subnet mask looks like this:

255.255.255.0

The network ID is determined by the number of 255 octets in the subnet mask. If there is a 255, that part of your address is the network ID. If your IP address were 190.24.16.11 and your subnet mask were 255.255.0.0, your network ID would be 190.24. If the subnet mask were 255.255.255.0, the same IP address would have a network ID of 190.24.16.

Default Gateway Sometimes you'll want to talk to computers that are outside your network. In that case, you'll need to connect to a router. I can now give another description of a router. A router has at least two IP addresses: one that connects to your LAN's switch and one that connects to the "next network." That next network could be your Internet service provider (ISP) or another router at your company—who knows (and more importantly, who cares, as long as it gets there)? The port on your router that connects to your LAN is given an IP address that's part of your network ID. In most cases, this is the first address shown in Figure 4.17.

The IP address of the "LAN" side of your router (the port connected to your LAN) is the address your computer uses to send data to anything outside your network ID. This is called the **default gateway**.

So far, I've only discussed Internet Protocol version 4 (IPv4) addresses. A newer version, known as Internet Protocol version 6 (IPv6), doesn't follow the same conventions. You'll learn a lot more about IPv6 in Chapter 14.

• **Figure 4.17** Default gateway

Domain Name Service (DNS) Knowing that users could not remember lots of IP addresses, early Internet pioneers came up with a way to correlate those numbers with more human-friendly designations. Special computers, called **domain name service (DNS)** servers, keep databases of IP addresses and their corresponding names. For example, let's say a machine with the IP address 209.34.45.163 hosts a Web site and we want it to be known as www.totalsem.com. When we set up the Web site, we pay money for a DNS server to register the DNS name www.totalsem.com to the IP address 209.34.45.163. So instead of typing "http://209.34.45.163" to access the Web page, you can type "www.totalsem.com." Your system will then query the DNS server to get www.totalsem.com's IP address and use that to find the right machine. Unless you want to type in IP addresses all the time, you'll need to use DNS servers (see Figure 4.18).

The Internet has regulated domain names. If you want a domain name that others can access on the Internet, you must register your domain name and pay a small yearly fee. Originally, DNS names all ended with one of the following seven domain name qualifiers, called *top-level domains* (*TLDs*):

.com	General business	**.mil**	Military organizations
.edu	Educational organizations	**.net**	Internet organizations
.gov	Government organizations	**.org**	Nonprofit organizations
.int	International		

As more and more countries joined the Internet, a new level of domains was added to the original seven to indicate a DNS name from a particular country, such as .uk for the United Kingdom. It's common to see DNS names such as www.bbc.co.uk or www.louvre.fr. The *Internet Corporation for Assigned Names and Numbers* (*ICANN*) has added several

• **Figure 4.18** Domain name service

new domains over the years, including .name, .biz, .info, .tv, and others. Given the explosive growth of the Internet, these are unlikely to be the last ones! For the latest developments, check ICANN's Web site at www .icann.org.

Entering the IP Information When you configure a computer to connect to a network, you must enter the IP address, the subnet mask, the default gateway, and at least one DNS server. Let's review:

- **IP address** A computer's unique address on the network
- **Subnet mask** Identifies your network ID
- **Default gateway** IP address or the LAN side of your router
- **DNS server** Tracks easy-to-remember DNS names for IP addresses

Configuring the IP address differs between each version of Windows. Figure 4.19 shows the IP settings on a Windows 7 system.

As you look at Figure 4.19, note the radio button for *Obtain an IP address automatically*. This is a common setting for which you don't need to enter any information. You can use this setting if your network uses Dynamic

> CompTIA uses the term *client-side* DNS to describe DNS configuration done on a local machine.

• **Figure 4.19** IP settings on a Windows 7 system

• **Figure 4.20** A DHCP server handing out an IP address

Host Configuration Protocol (DHCP). If you have DHCP (most networks do) and your computer is configured to obtain an IP address automatically, your computer boots up and will broadcast a DHCP request. The DHCP server provides your computer with all the IP information it needs to get on the network (see Figure 4.20).

Refer to Chapter 14 for more details on IP addresses, subnet masks, default gateways, and DNS servers.

Chapter 4 Review

■ Chapter Summary

After reading this chapter and completing the exercises, you should understand the following facts about networks.

Describe the basic functions of a network, including identifying common devices and connectors

■ Topologies define how data is moved between computers in a network. The most important types of topology are bus, ring, mesh, and star. Almost all networks today use the hybrid star bus topology.

■ Networks have one or more client machines with NICs for both defining the nodes and creating frames for sending data to other nodes. Some kind of network cabling or wireless signal connects the nodes together.

■ Each NIC has a unique MAC address that identifies a node. Frames include the MAC address for both the sender and recipient, some kind of data payload, and a data check.

■ Most networks today employ some form of Ethernet to define things like frame type and cabling. The vast majority of 10/100/1000BaseT networks run on unshielded twisted-pair cabling. Switches provide the central connection point in the Ethernet star bus topology. Most network cables connect with RJ-45 connectors.

■ Varieties of UTP include CAT 1, CAT 3, CAT 5, CAT 5e, and CAT 6. Each can be plenum-grade or use a PVC jacket.

Discuss the differences between a LAN and a WAN and the importance of TCP/IP

■ Network protocols enable you to name and address computers within a network, removing the need to rely solely on the MAC address to get data from one node to another.

■ NetBIOS/NetBEUI protocols were used on early Windows networks for naming purposes. Because they relied on broadcasts, the move to scale up in size required a new protocol for the larger network.

■ You can connect LANs together to form a WAN using routers to make the connections. Routers don't pass broadcast frames.

■ All modern operating systems use TCP/IP as the default protocol. TCP is the part that handles getting the data between computers, while IP handles the addressing scheme that gives us something more powerful and flexible than MAC addresses. Other protocols in the protocol stack handle other duties.

■ The IP address is the unique identification number for your system on the network. Part of the address identifies the network, and part identifies the local computer (host) address on the network. The subnet mask tells the computer which part of its IP address is the network ID.

■ DNS servers enable users to type in names for remote nodes rather than having to remember and type the numerical IP addresses. Many systems are set up with DHCP enabled, where a DHCP server will provide all the TCP/IP settings needed by the systems at boot.

■ Key Terms

10BaseT *(71)*

100BaseT *(71)*

1000BaseT *(71)*

bandwidth *(72)*

broadcast *(75)*

bus *(68)*

client *(65)*

cyclic redundancy check (CRC) *(71)*

default gateway *(78)*

domain name service (DNS) *(79)*

Ethernet *(71)*

frame *(67)*

hub *(72)*

hybrid *(68)*

IP address *(77)*

local area network (LAN) *(76)*

media access control (MAC) address *(70)*

mesh *(68)*

NetBIOS Extended User Interface (NetBEUI) *(75)*

network ID *(78)*

network interface controller (NIC) *(67)*

network protocol *(75)*

network technology *(69)*

resource *(67)*

RJ-11 *(73)*

RJ-45 *(73)*

ring *(68)*

router *(76)*

segment *(72)*

server *(65)*

shielded twisted pair (STP) *(73)*

star *(68)*

star bus *(71)*

subnet mask *(78)*

switch *(72)*

T568A *(74)*

T568B *(74)*

topology *(68)*

Transmission Control Protocol/Internet Protocol (TCP/IP) *(77)*

unshielded twisted pair (UTP) *(72)*

Web browser *(65)*

Web server *(65)*

wide area network (WAN) *(76)*

■ Key Term Quiz

Use the Key Terms list to complete the sentences that follow. Not all terms will be used.

1. The _____ version of Ethernet runs at 100 Mbps.

2. Ethernet cables typically use a(n) _____ connector.

3. The most common Ethernet topology is _____.

4. The _____ tells the computer which part of its IP address is the network ID.

5. Most Ethernet networks have a central box called a(n) _____.

6. All NICs have a unique identifier called a(n) _____.

7. Routers enable multiple LANs to connect into a(n) _____.

8. A _____ topology connects every computer on the network to every other computer on the network.

9. A computer that hosts HTML files is called a _____.

10. The numbers 192.168.5.36 are an example of a(n) _____.

■ Multiple-Choice Quiz

1. How many bits are in a MAC address?

 A. 24

 B. 36

 C. 48

 D. 64

2. Which protocol enables the use of names such as www.totalsem.com rather than IP addresses?

 A. DNS

 B. MAC

 C. IP

 D. TCP

3. What is the minimum CAT level cable required for a 100BaseT network?

 A. CAT 1

 B. CAT 5

 C. CAT 5e

 D. CAT 6

4. What do you call the IP address of your router?

 A. Router address

 B. Subnet mask

 C. Workgroup name

 D. Default Gateway

5. Which of the following is an example of a hybrid topology?

 A. Bus

 B. Ring

 C. Star

 D. Star bus

6. What top-level domain is used by non-profit organizations?

 A. .com

 B. .org

 C. .net

 D. .non

7. A typical CAT 6 cable uses which connector?

 A. RJ-11

 B. RJ-45

 C. Plenum

 D. PVC

8. Why would you use STP over UTP cabling?

 A. Cheaper

 B. Easier to install

 C. Better to avoid interference

 D. They're interchangeable terms

9. What kind of frame gets received by all NICs in a LAN?

 A. Ethernet

 B. Broadcast

 C. WAN

 D. DNS

10. Internet Explorer, Mozilla Firefox, and Google Chrome are all examples of what?

 A. Web servers

 B. DNS

 C. Web browsers

 D. IP addresses

11. Which of the following does 255.255.255.0 most probably represent?

 A. An IP address

 B. A subnet mask

 C. A default gateway

 D. A DNS address

12. What do you call the way IP addresses are written?

 A. Dotted-decimal notation

 B. Hexadecimal notation

 C. Base-ten notation

 D. Dots and bits notation

13. What is a remote computer providing resources called?

 A. Web browser

 B. DNS

 C. Server

 D. Router

14. What is the total amount of data that a network can handle called?

 A. Protocol

 B. Broadcast

 C. Bandwidth

 D. Client

15. What do you call the discrete "chunks" of data that networks transmit?

 A. Frames

 B. Stacks

 C. LANs

 D. Workgroups

■ Essay Quiz

1. Most computers come with onboard NICs. Check out your NIC and determine its fastest speed. Can your NIC support lower speeds as well? Show how you came to this determination.

2. Mike's office is composed of roughly ten PCs all running 100BaseT NICs and a 100BaseT switch on CAT 5 cable. He wants to "speed up the network" by going up to 1000BaseT. Explain to him the process of doing this upgrade and give him your opinion of whether this is a good idea.

3. Even though NetBIOS/NetBEUI is long gone, Windows systems still use computer names. Do some research on the term SMB and explain how modern Windows systems still support network names.

Lab Projects

• Lab Project 4.1

To access the Internet, you must have a DNS server address. Typically this is automatically configured when your system starts, but you can add custom DNS servers to increase your Internet speed.

1 Go to www.grc.com and download the Domain Name Speed Benchmark utility. This utility compares your DNS server to alternatives that may be faster.

2 Run the utility. Did the utility find a faster DNS server? (Google has some very popular, very fast DNS servers.)

3 Figure out how to replace your DNS server for your system with one of these alternatives. Be sure to remember how to return to the original DNS settings in case this doesn't work!

4 Try browsing with your new settings. Do you notice a difference?

Microprocessors

chapter 5

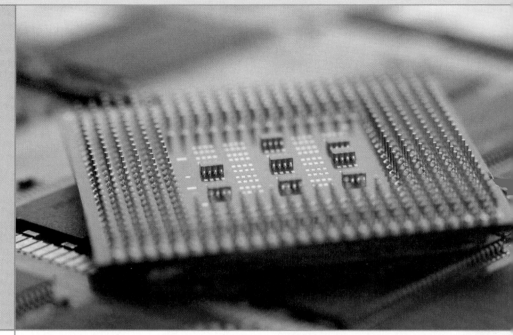

"I'm going to give you a little advice. There's a force in the universe that makes things happen. And all you have to do is get in touch with it, stop thinking, let things happen, and be the ball."

—Ty Webb, *Caddyshack*

In this chapter, you will learn how to

- **Identify the core components of a CPU**
- **Describe the relationship of CPUs and memory**
- **Explain the varieties of modern CPUs**
- **Select and install a CPU**
- **Troubleshoot CPUs**

For all practical purposes, the terms **microprocessor** and **central processing unit (CPU)** mean the same thing: it's that big chip inside your computer that many people often describe as the brain of the system. You know from Chapter 3 that CPU makers name their microprocessors in a fashion similar to the automobile industry: CPUs get a make and a model, such as Intel Core i7 or AMD Phenom II X4. But what's happening inside the CPU to make it able to do the amazing things asked of it every time you step up to the keyboard?

This chapter delves into microprocessors in detail. We'll first discuss how processors work and the components that enable them to interact with the rest of the computer. The second section describes how CPUs work with memory. The third section takes you on a tour of modern CPUs. The final section gets into practical work: selecting and installing CPUs.

Historical/Conceptual

■ CPU Core Components

Although the computer might seem to act quite intelligently, comparing the CPU to a human brain hugely overstates its capabilities. A CPU functions more like a very powerful calculator than like a brain—but, oh, what a calculator! Today's CPUs add, subtract, multiply, divide, and move billions of numbers per second. Processing that much information so quickly makes any CPU look intelligent. It's simply the speed of the CPU, rather than actual intelligence, that enables computers to perform feats such as accessing the Internet, playing visually stunning games, or editing photos.

A good PC technician needs to understand some basic CPU functions to support PCs, so let's start with an analysis of how the CPU works. If you wanted to teach someone how an automobile engine works, you would use a relatively simple example engine, right? The same principle applies here. Let's begin our study of the CPU with the granddaddy of all PC CPUs: the famous Intel 8088, invented in the late 1970s. Although this CPU first appeared over 30 years ago, it defined the idea of the modern microprocessor and contains the same basic parts used in even the most advanced CPUs today. Prepare to enter that little bit of magic called the CPU.

• **Figure 5.1** Imagine the CPU as a man in a box.

The Man in the Box

Let's begin by visualizing the CPU as a man in a box (see Figure 5.1). This is one clever guy. He can perform virtually any mathematical function, manipulate data, and give answers *very quickly*.

This guy is potentially very useful to us, but there's a catch—he lives closed up in a tiny box. Before he can work with us, we must come up with a way to exchange information with him (see Figure 5.2).

Imagine that we install a set of 16 light bulbs, 8 inside his box and 8 outside his box. Each of the 8 light bulbs inside the box connects to one of the 8 bulbs outside the box to form a pair. Each pair of light bulbs is always either on or off. You can control the 8 pairs of bulbs by using a set of 8 switches outside the box, and the Man in the Box can also

• **Figure 5.2** How do we talk to the Man in the Box?

• **Figure 5.3** Cutaway of the external data bus—note that one light bulb pair is on

control them by using an identical set of 8 switches inside the box. This light-bulb communication device is called the **external data bus (EDB)**.

Figure 5.3 shows a cutaway view of the external data bus. When either you or the Man in the Box flips a switch on, *both* light bulbs go on, and the switch on the other side is also flipped to the on position. If you or the Man in the Box turns a switch off, the light bulbs on both sides are turned off, along with the other switch for that pair.

Can you see how this works? By creating on/off patterns with the light bulbs that represent different pieces of data or commands, you can send that information to the Man in the Box, and he can send information back in the same way—*assuming that you agree ahead of time on what the different patterns of lights mean.* To accomplish this, you need some sort of codebook that assigns meanings to the many patterns of lights that the EDB might display. Keep this thought in mind while we push the analogy a bit more.

Before going any further, make sure you're clear on the fact that this is an analogy, not reality. There really is an EDB, but you won't see any light bulbs or switches on the CPU. You can, however, see little wires sticking out of the CPU (see Figure 5.4). If you apply voltage to one of these wires, you in essence flip the switch. Get the idea? So if that wire had voltage, and if a tiny light bulb were attached to the wire, that light bulb would glow, would it not? By the same token, if the wire had no power, the light bulb would not glow. That is why the switch-and-light-bulb analogy may help you picture these little wires constantly flashing on and off.

Now that the EDB enables you to communicate with the Man in the Box, you need to see how it works by placing voltages on the wires. This brings up a naming problem. It's a hassle to say something like "on-off-on-off-on-on-off-off" when talking about which wires have voltage. Rather than saying that one of the EDB wires is on or off, use the number 1 to represent on and the number 0 to represent off (see Figure 5.5). That way, instead of describing the state of the lights as "on-off-on-off-on-on-off-off," I can instead describe them by writing "10101100."

In the world of computers, we constantly turn wires on and off. As a result, we can use this "1 and 0" or **binary** system to describe the state of these wires at any given moment. (See, and you just thought computer geeks spoke in binary to confuse normal people. Ha!) There's much more to binary numbering in the world of computing, but this is a great place to start.

Registers

The Man in the Box provides good insight into the workspace inside a CPU. The EDB gives you a way to

• **Figure 5.4** Close-up of the underside of a CPU

● **Figure 5.5** Here "1" means on, "0" means off.

communicate with the Man in the Box so you can give him work to do. But to do this work, he needs a worktable; in fact, he needs at least four worktables. Each of these four worktables has 16 light bulbs. These light bulbs are not in pairs; they're just 16 light bulbs lined up straight across the table. Each light bulb is controlled by a single switch, operated only by the Man in the Box. By creating on/off patterns like the ones on the EDB, the Man in the Box can use these four sets of light bulbs to work math problems. In a real computer, these worktables are called **registers** (see Figure 5.6).

Registers provide the Man in the Box with a workplace for the problems you give him. All CPUs contain a large number of registers, but for the moment let's concentrate on the four most common ones: the *general-purpose registers*. Intel named them AX, BX, CX, and DX.

Great! We're just about ready to put the Man in the Box to work, but before you close the lid on the box, you must give the Man one more tool. Remember the codebook I mentioned earlier? Let's make one to enable us to communicate with him. Figure 5.7 shows the codebook we'll use. We'll give one copy to him and make a second for us.

● **Figure 5.6** The four general-purpose registers

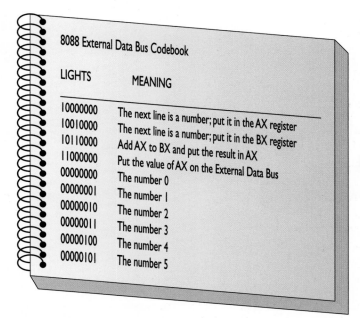

8088 External Data Bus Codebook

LIGHTS	MEANING
10000000	The next line is a number; put it in the AX register
10010000	The next line is a number; put it in the BX register
10110000	Add AX to BX and put the result in AX
11000000	Put the value of AX on the External Data Bus
00000000	The number 0
00000001	The number 1
00000010	The number 2
00000011	The number 3
00000100	The number 4
00000101	The number 5

• **Figure 5.7** CPU codebook

In this codebook, for example, 10000111 means *Move the number 7 into the AX register*. These commands are called the microprocessor's **machine language**. The commands listed in the figure are not actual commands; as you've probably guessed, I've simplified dramatically. The Intel 8088 CPU actually used commands very similar to these, plus a few hundred others.

Here are some examples of real machine language for the Intel 8088:

10111010	The next line of code is a number. Put that number into the DX register.
01000001	Add 1 to the number already in the CX register.
00111100	Compare the value in the AX register with the next line of code.

By placing machine language commands—called *lines of code*—onto the EDB one at a time, you can instruct the Man in the Box to do specific tasks. All of the machine language commands that the CPU understands make up the CPU's **instruction set**.

So here is the CPU so far: the Man in the Box can communicate with the outside world via the EDB; he has four registers he can use to work on the problems you give him; and he has a codebook—the instruction set—so he can understand the different patterns (machine language commands) on the EDB (see Figure 5.8).

• **Figure 5.8** The CPU so far

Clock

Okay, so you're ready to put the Man in the Box to work. You can send the first command by lighting up wires on the EDB. How does he know when you've finished setting up the wires and it's time to act?

Have you ever seen one of those old-time manual calculators with the big crank on one side? To add two numbers, you pressed a number key, the + key, and another number key, but then to make the calculator do the calculation and give you the answer, you had to pull down the crank. That was the signal that you had finished entering data and instructions and were ready for the calculator to give you an answer.

A CPU also has a type of crank. To return to the Man in the Box, imagine there's a bell inside the box activated by a button on the outside of the box. Each time you press the button to sound the bell, the Man in the Box reads the next set of lights on the EDB. Of course, a real computer doesn't use a bell. The bell on a real CPU is a special wire called the **clock wire** (most diagrams label the clock wire CLK). A charge on the CLK wire tells the CPU that another piece of information is waiting to be processed (see Figure 5.9).

For the CPU to process a command placed on the EDB, a certain minimum voltage must be applied to the CLK wire. A single charge to the CLK wire is called a **clock cycle**. Actually, the CPU requires at least two clock cycles to act on a command, and usually more. Using the manual calculator analogy, you need to pull the crank at least twice before anything happens. In fact, a CPU may require hundreds of clock cycles to process some commands (see Figure 5.10).

The maximum number of clock cycles that a CPU can handle in a given period of time is referred to as its **clock speed**. The clock speed is the fastest speed at which a CPU can operate, determined by the CPU manufacturer. The Intel 8088 processor had a clock speed of 4.77 MHz (4.77 million cycles

• **Figure 5.9** The CPU does nothing until activated by the clock.

• **Figure 5.10** The CPU often needs more than one clock cycle to get a result.

Aggressive users sometimes intentionally overclock CPUs by telling the clock chip to multiply the pulse faster than the CPU's designed speed. They do this to make slower (cheaper) CPUs run faster and to get more performance in demanding programs. See the "Overclocking" section later in this chapter.

per second), extremely slow by modern standards, but still a pretty big number compared to using a pencil and paper. CPUs today run at speeds in excess of 3 GHz (3 billion cycles per second). You'll see these "hertz" terms a lot in this chapter, so here's what they mean:

- 1 hertz (1 Hz) = 1 cycle per second
- 1 megahertz (1 MHz) = 1 million cycles per second
- 1 gigahertz (1 GHz) = 1 billion cycles per second

A CPU's clock speed is its *maximum* speed, not the speed at which it *must* run. A CPU can run at any speed, as long as that speed does not exceed its clock speed. Manufacturers used to print the CPU's clock speed directly onto the CPU, but for the past few years they've used cryptic codes (see Figure 5.11). As the chapter progresses you'll see why they do this.

The **system crystal** determines the speed at which a CPU and the rest of the PC operate. The system crystal is usually a quartz oscillator, very similar to the one in a wristwatch, soldered to the motherboard (see Figure 5.12).

The quartz oscillator sends out an electric pulse at a certain speed, many millions of times per second. This signal goes first to a clock chip that adjusts the pulse, usually increasing the pulse sent by the crystal by some large multiple. (The folks who make motherboards could connect the crystal directly to the CPU's clock wire, but then if you wanted to replace your CPU with a CPU with a different clock speed, you'd need to replace the crystal too.) As long as the PC is turned on, the quartz oscillator, through the clock chip, fires a charge on the CLK wire, in essence pushing the system along.

AMD Phenom™ II
HDX810WFK4FGI
CACZC AC 0904GPMW
9069529A90617

• **Figure 5.11** Where is the clock speed?

Visualize the system crystal as a metronome for the CPU. The quartz oscillator repeatedly fires a charge on the CLK wire, setting the beat, if you will, for the CPU's activities. If the system crystal sets a beat slower than the CPU's clock speed, the CPU will work just fine, though at the slower speed of the system crystal. If the system crystal forces the CPU to run faster than its clock speed, it can overheat and stop working. Before you install a CPU into a system, you must make sure that the crystal and clock chip send out the correct clock pulse for that particular CPU. In the old days, this required very careful adjustments. With today's systems, the motherboard talks to the CPU. The CPU tells the motherboard the clock speed it needs, and the clock chip automatically adjusts for the CPU, making this process now invisible.

• **Figure 5.12** One of many types of system crystals

Back to the External Data Bus

One more reality check. We've been talking about tables with racks of light bulbs, but of course real CPU registers don't use light bulbs to represent on/1 and off/0. Registers are tiny storage areas on the CPU made up of microscopic semiconductor circuits that hold charges. It's just easier to imagine a light bulb lit up to represent a circuit holding a charge; when the light bulb is off, there is no charge.

Figure 5.13 is a diagram of a real 8088 CPU, showing the wires that comprise the external data bus and the single clock wire. Because the registers are inside the CPU, you can't see them in this figure.

Now that you have learned what components are involved in the process, try the following simple exercise to see how the process works. In this example, you tell the CPU to add 2 + 3. To do this, you must send a series of commands to the CPU; the CPU will act on each command, eventually giving you an answer. Refer to the codebook in Figure 5.7 to translate the instructions you're giving the Man in the Box into binary commands.

Did you try it? Here's how it works:

1. Place 10000000 on the external data bus (EDB).
2. Place 00000010 on the EDB.
3. Place 10010000 on the EDB.
4. Place 00000011 on the EDB.
5. Place 10110000 on the EDB.
6. Place 11000000 on the EDB.

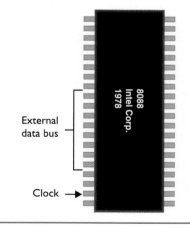

• **Figure 5.13** Diagram of an Intel 8088 showing the external data bus and clock wires

When you finish step 6, the value on the EDB will be 00000101, the decimal number 5 written in binary.

Congrats! You just added 2+3 by using individual commands from the codebook. This set of commands is known as a **program**, which is a series of commands sent to a CPU in a specific order for the CPU to perform work. Each discrete setting of the EDB is a line of code. This program, therefore, has six lines of code.

■ Memory

Now that you've seen how the CPU executes program code, let's work backward in the process for a moment and think about how the program code gets to the external data bus. The program itself is stored on the hard drive. In theory, you could build a computer that sends data from the hard drive directly to the CPU, but there's a problem—the hard drive is too slow. Even the ancient 8088, with its clock speed of 4.77 MHz, could conceivably process several million lines of code every second. Modern CPUs crank out billions of lines every second. Hard drives simply can't give the data to the CPU at a fast enough speed.

Computers need some other device that takes copies of programs from the hard drive and then sends them, one line at a time, to the CPU quickly enough to keep up with its demands. Because each line of code is nothing more than a pattern of eight ones and zeros, any device that can store ones and zeros eight-across will do. Devices that in any way hold ones and zeros that the CPU accesses are known generically as **memory**.

Many types of devices store ones and zeros perfectly well—technically even a piece of paper counts as memory—but computers need memory that does more than just store groups of eight ones and zeros. Consider this pretend program:

1. Put 2 in the AX register.
2. Put 5 in the BX register.
3. If AX is greater than BX, run line 4; otherwise, go to line 6.
4. Add 1 to the value in AX.
5. Go back to line 1.
6. Put the value of AX on the EDB.

This program has an IF statement, also called a *branch* by CPU makers. The CPU needs a way to address each line of this memory—a way for the CPU to say to the memory, "Give me the next line of code" or "Give me line 6." Addressing memory takes care of another problem: the memory must not only store programs but also store the result of the programs. If the CPU adds 2 + 3 and gets 5, the memory needs to store that 5 in such a way that other programs may later read that 5, or possibly even store that 5 on a hard drive. By addressing each line of memory, other programs will know where to find the data.

Memory and RAM

Memory must store not only programs, but also data. The CPU needs to be able to read and write to this storage medium. Additionally, this system must enable the CPU to jump to *any* line of stored code as easily as to any other line of code. All of this must be done at or at least near the clock speed of the CPU. Fortunately, this magical device has existed for many years: **random access memory (RAM)**.

Chapter 6 develops the concept of RAM in detail, so for now let's look at RAM as an electronic spreadsheet, like one you can generate in Microsoft Excel (see Figure 5.14). Each cell in this spreadsheet can store only a one or a zero. Each cell is called a **bit**. Each row in the spreadsheet is eight bits across to match the EDB of the 8088. Each row of eight bits is called a **byte**. In the PC world, RAM transfers and stores data to and from the CPU in byte-sized chunks. RAM is therefore arranged in byte-sized rows. Here are the terms used to talk about quantities of bits:

- Any individual 1 or 0 = a bit
- 4 bits = a nibble
- 8 bits = a byte
- 16 bits = a word
- 32 bits = a double word
- 64 bits = a paragraph or quad word

The number of bytes of RAM varies from PC to PC. In earlier PCs, from around 1980 to 1990, the typical system would have only a few hundred thousand bytes of RAM. Today's systems often have billions of bytes of RAM.

Let's stop here for a quick reality check. Electronically, RAM looks like a spreadsheet, but real RAM is made of groups of semiconductor chips soldered onto small cards that snap into your computer (see Figure 5.15). In Chapter 6, you'll see how these groups of chips actually make themselves look like a spreadsheet. For now, don't worry about real RAM and just stick with the spreadsheet idea.

The CPU accesses any one row of RAM as easily and as fast as any other row, which explains the "random access" part of RAM. Not only is RAM randomly accessible, it's also fast. By storing programs on RAM, the CPU can access and run them very quickly. RAM also stores any data that the CPU actively uses.

Computers use **dynamic RAM (DRAM)** for the main system memory. DRAM needs both a constant electrical charge and a periodic refresh of the circuits; otherwise, it loses data—that's what makes it dynamic rather than static in content.

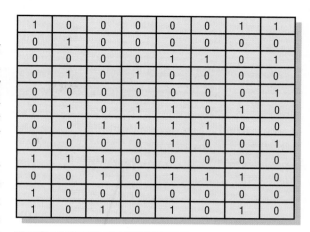

1	0	0	0	0	0	1	1
0	1	0	0	0	0	0	0
0	0	0	0	1	1	0	1
0	1	0	1	0	0	0	0
0	0	0	0	0	0	0	1
0	1	0	1	1	0	1	0
0	0	1	1	1	1	0	0
0	0	0	0	1	0	0	1
1	1	1	0	0	0	0	0
0	0	1	0	1	1	1	0
1	0	0	0	0	0	0	0
1	0	1	0	1	0	1	0

• **Figure 5.14** RAM as a spreadsheet

• **Figure 5.15** Typical RAM

The refresh can cause some delays, because the CPU has to wait for the refresh to happen, but modern CPU manufacturers have clever ways to get by this issue, as you'll see when you read about modern processor technology later in this chapter.

Don't confuse RAM with mass storage devices such as hard drives and flash drives. You use hard drives and flash drives to store programs and data permanently. Chapters 10 and 11 discuss permanent storage in intimate detail.

✓ **Cross Check**

RAM

You learned a few essentials about RAM in Chapter 3, so check back in that chapter and see if you can answer these questions. How is RAM packaged? Where do you install the PC's primary RAM, called the *system RAM*, in the system unit?

Address Bus

So far, the entire PC consists of only a CPU and RAM. But the CPU and the RAM need some connection so they can talk to each other. To do so, extend the external data bus from the CPU so it can talk to the RAM (see Figure 5.16).

Wait a minute. This is not a matter of just plugging the RAM into the EDB wires! RAM is a spreadsheet with thousands and thousands of discrete rows, and you need to look at the contents of only one row of the spreadsheet at a time, right? So how do you connect the RAM to the EDB in such a way that the CPU can see any one given row but still give the CPU the capability to look at *any* row in RAM? We need some type of chip between the RAM and the CPU to make the connection. The CPU needs to be able to say which row of RAM it wants, and the chip should handle the mechanics of retrieving that row of data from the RAM and putting it on the EDB. Wouldn't you know I just happen to have such a chip? This chip comes with many names, but for right now just call it the **memory controller chip (MCC)**.

The MCC contains special circuitry so it can grab the contents of any single line of RAM and place that data or command on the EDB. This in turn enables the CPU to act on that code (see Figure 5.17).

Once the MCC is in place to grab any discrete byte of RAM, the CPU needs to be able to tell the MCC which line of code it needs. The CPU therefore gains a second set of wires, called the **address bus**, with which it can communicate with the MCC. Different CPUs have different numbers of

• **Figure 5.16** Extending the EDB

wires (which, you will soon see, is very significant). The 8088 had 20 wires in its address bus (see Figure 5.18).

By turning the address bus wires on and off in different patterns, the CPU tells the MCC which line of RAM it wants at any given moment. Every different pattern of ones and zeros on these 20 wires points to one byte of RAM. There are two big questions here. First, how many different patterns of on-and-off wires can exist with 20 wires? And second, which pattern goes to which row of RAM?

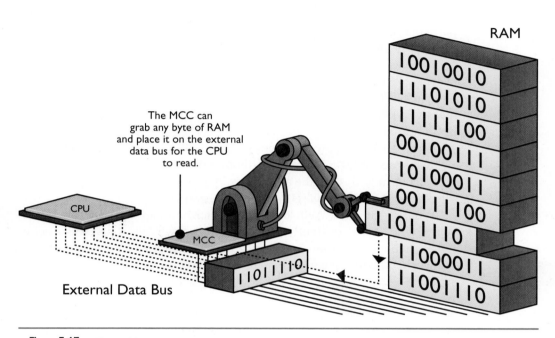

• **Figure 5.17** The MCC grabs a byte of RAM.

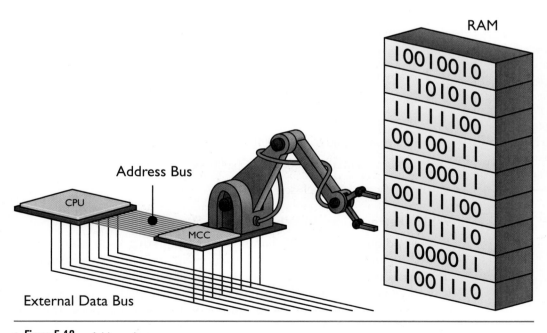

• **Figure 5.18** Address bus

How Many Patterns?

Mathematics can answer the first question. Each wire in the address bus exists in only one of two states: on or off. If the address bus consisted of only one wire, that wire would at any given moment be either on or off. Mathematically, that gives you (pull out your old pre-algebra books) $2^1 = 2$ different combinations. If you have two address bus wires, the address bus wires create $2^2 = 4$ different combinations. If you have 20 wires, you would have 2^{20} (or 1,048,576) combinations. Because each pattern points to one line of code and each line of RAM is one byte, if you know the number of wires in the CPU's address bus, you know the maximum amount of RAM that a particular CPU can handle.

Because the 8088 had a 20-wire address bus, the most RAM it could handle was 2^{20} or 1,048,576 bytes. The 8088, therefore, had an *address space* of 1,048,576 bytes. This is not to say that every computer with an 8088 CPU had 1,048,576 bytes of RAM. Far from it! The original IBM PC only had a measly 64 kilobytes—but that was considered plenty back in the Dark Ages of Computing in the early 1980s.

Okay, so you know that the 8088 had 20 address wires and a total address space of 1,048,576 bytes. Although this is accurate, no one uses such an exact term to discuss the address space of the 8088. Instead you say that the 8088 had one *megabyte* (1 MB) of address space.

What's a "mega"? Well, let's get some terminology down. Dealing with computers means constantly dealing with the number of patterns a set of wires can handle. Certain powers of 2 have names used a lot in the computing world. The following list explains.

1 kilo = 2^{10} = 1024 (abbreviated as "K")

1 kilobyte = 1024 bytes (abbreviated as "KB")

1 mega = 2^{20} = 1,048,576 (abbreviated as "M")

1 megabyte = 1,048,576 bytes (abbreviated as "MB")

1 giga = 2^{30} = 1,073,741,824 (abbreviated as "G")

1 gigabyte = 1,073,741,824 bytes (abbreviated as "GB")

1 tera = 2^{40} = 1,099,511,627,776 (abbreviated as "T")

1 terabyte = 1,099,511,627,776 bytes (abbreviated as "TB")

1 kilo is *not* equal to 1000 (one thousand)

1 mega is *not* equal to 1,000,000 (one million)

1 giga is *not* equal to 1,000,000,000 (one billion)

1 tera is *not* equal to 1,000,000,000,000 (one trillion)

(But they are pretty close!)

Which Pattern Goes to Which Row?

The second question is a little harder: "Which pattern goes to which row of RAM?" To understand this, let's take a moment to discuss binary counting. In binary, only two numbers exist, 0 and 1, which makes binary a handy way to work with wires that turn on and off. Let's try to count in binary: 0, 1...what's next? It's not 2—you can only use zeros and ones. The next

number after 1 is 10! Now let's count in binary to 1000: 0, 1, 10, 11, 100, 101, 110, 111, 1000. Try counting to 10000. Don't worry; it hardly takes any time at all.

Super; you now count in binary as well as any math professor. Let's add to the concept. Stop thinking about binary for just a moment and think about good old base 10 (regular numbers). If you have the number 365, can you put zeros in front of the 365, like this: 000365? Sure you can—it doesn't change the value at all. The same thing is true in binary. Putting zeros in front of a value doesn't change a thing! Let's count again to 1000 in binary. In this case, add enough zeros to make 20 places:

00000000000000000000

00000000000000000001

00000000000000000010

00000000000000000011

00000000000000000100

00000000000000000101

00000000000000000110

00000000000000000111

00000000000000001000

Hey, wouldn't this be a great way to represent each line of RAM on the address bus? The CPU identifies the first byte of RAM on the address bus with 00000000000000000000. The CPU identifies the last RAM row with 11111111111111111111. When the CPU turns off all of the address bus wires, it wants the first line of RAM; when it turns on all of the wires, it wants the 1,048,576th line of RAM. Obviously, the address bus also addresses all of the rows of RAM in between. So, by lighting up different patterns of ones and zeros on the address bus, the CPU can access any row of RAM it needs.

 Bits and bytes are abbreviated differently. Bits get a lowercase b, whereas bytes get a capital B. So for example, 4 Kb is four kilobits, but 4 KB is four kilobytes.

801

■ Modern CPUs

CPU manufacturers have achieved stunning progress with microprocessors since the days of the Intel 8088, and the rate of change doesn't show any signs of slowing. At the core, though, today's CPUs function similarly to the processors of your forefathers. The arithmetic logic unit (ALU)—that's the Man in the Box—still crunches numbers many millions of times per second. CPUs rely on memory to feed them lines of programming as quickly as possible.

This section brings the CPU into the present. We'll first look at models you can buy today, and then we'll turn to essential improvements in technology you should understand.

Manufacturers

When IBM awarded Intel the contract to provide the CPUs for its new IBM PC back in 1980, it established for Intel a virtual monopoly on all PC CPUs. The other home-computer CPU makers of the time faded away: MOS Technology, Zilog, Motorola—no one could compete directly with Intel. Over time, other competitors have risen to challenge Intel's market-segment share dominance. In particular, a company called Advanced Micro Devices (AMD) began to make clones of Intel CPUs, creating an interesting and rather cutthroat competition with Intel that lasts to this day.

Intel

Intel Corporation thoroughly dominated the personal computer market with its CPUs and motherboard support chips. At nearly every step in the evolution of the PC, Intel has led the way with technological advances and surprising flexibility for such a huge corporation. Intel CPUs—and more specifically, their instruction sets—define the personal computer. Intel currently produces a dozen or so models of CPU for both desktop and portable computers. Most of Intel's desktop and laptop processors are sold under the Celeron, Pentium, and Core brands. Their very low-power portable/smartphone chips are branded Atom; their high-end workstation/server chips are called Xeon and Itanium.

AMD

You can't really talk about CPUs without mentioning Advanced Micro Devices. AMD makes superb CPUs for the PC market and provides competition that keeps Intel on its toes. Like Intel, AMD doesn't just make CPUs, but their CPU business is certainly the part that the public notices. AMD has made CPUs that clone the function of Intel CPUs. If Intel invented the CPU used in the original IBM PC, how could AMD make clone CPUs without getting sued? Well, chipmakers have a habit of exchanging technologies through cross-license agreements. Way back in 1976, AMD and Intel signed just such an agreement, giving AMD the right to copy certain types of CPUs.

The trouble started with the Intel 8088. Intel needed AMD's help to supply enough CPUs to statisfy IBM's demands. But after a few years, Intel had grown tremendously and no longer wanted AMD to make CPUs. AMD said, "Too bad. See this agreement you signed?" Throughout the 1980s and into the 1990s, AMD made pin-for-pin identical CPUs that matched the Intel lines of CPUs (see Figure 5.19). You could yank an Intel CPU out of a system and snap in an AMD CPU—no problem!

In January 1995, after many years of legal wrangling, Intel and AMD settled and decided to end the licensing agreements. As a result of this settlement, AMD chips are no longer compatible with sockets or motherboards made for Intel CPUs—even though in

• **Figure 5.19** Identical Intel and AMD 486 CPUs from the early 1990s

Mike Meyers' CompTIA A+ Guide to 801: Managing and Troubleshooting PCs

some cases the chips look similar. Today, if you want to use an AMD CPU, you must purchase a motherboard designed for AMD CPUs. If you want to use an Intel CPU, you must purchase a motherboard designed for Intel CPUs. So you now have a choice: Intel or AMD.

Model Names

Intel and AMD differentiate product lines by using different product names, and these names have changed over the years. For a long time, Intel used *Pentium* for its flagship model, just adding model numbers to show successive generations—Pentium, Pentium II, Pentium III, and so on. AMD used the *Athlon* brand in a similar fashion.

Most discussions on PC CPUs focus on four end-product lines: desktop PC, budget PC, portable PC, and server computers. Table 5.1 displays many of the current product lines and names.

Table 5.1	Current Intel and AMD Product Lines and Names	
Market	**Intel**	**AMD**
Mainstream and enthusiast desktop	Core i7/i5/i3, Core 2 Duo	Phenom II, A-Series, Phenom, Athlon X2
Budget desktop	Pentium, Celeron	Sempron, Athlon II
Mobile	Core i7/i5/i3 (mobile), Core 2 Duo (mobile), Atom	Turion
Server	Xeon/Itanium	Opteron

You'll notice that both Intel and AMD reuse model names for products aimed at different markets. Yesterday's Pentium brand used to be for the highest end, for example, but now Intel uses the brand for its budget market. The same thing happened to the Athlon brand. To add a little more confusion, the budget CPUs are not the older CPUs still being sold, but low-end versions of current model lines.

Code Names

Both Intel and AMD continue to refine the CPU manufacturing process after releasing a new model, but they try to minimize the number of model names in use. This means that they release CPUs labeled as the same model, but the CPUs inside can be very different from earlier versions of that model. Both companies use **code names** to keep track of different variations within models (see Figure 5.20). As a tech, you need to know both the models and code names to be able to make proper recommendations for your clients. One example illustrates the need: the Intel Core i7.

Intel released the first Core i7 in the summer of 2008. By spring of 2012, the original microarchitecture—code

• **Figure 5.20** Same branding, but different capabilities

named Nehalem—had gone through five variations, none of which worked on motherboards designed for one of the other variations. Plus, in 2011, Intel introduced the Sandy Bridge version of the Core i7 that eventually had two desktop versions and a mobile version, all of which used still other sockets. (And I'm simplifying the variations here.)

At this point, a lot of new techs throw their hands in the air. How do you keep up? How do you know which CPU will give your customer the best value for his or her money and provide the right computing firepower for his or her needs? Simply put, you need to *research efficiently*.

Your first stop should be the manufacturers' Web sites. Both companies put out a lot of information on their products.

- www.intel.com
- www.amd.com

You can also find many high-quality tech Web sites devoted to reporting on the latest CPUs. When a client needs an upgrade, surf the Web for recent articles and make comparisons. Because you'll understand the underlying technology from your CompTIA A+ studies, you'll be able to follow the conversations with confidence. Here's a list of some of the sites I use:

- www.arstechnica.com
- www.hardocp.com
- www.tomshardware.com
- www.bit-tech.net

Finally, you can find great, exhaustive articles on all things tech at Wikipedia:

- www.wikipedia.org

Desktop Versus Mobile

Mobile devices, such as portable computers, have needs that differ from those of desktop computers, notably the need to consume as little electricity as possible. This helps in two ways: extending battery charge and creating less heat.

Both Intel and AMD have engineers devoted to making excellent mobile versions of their CPUs that sport advanced energy-saving features (see Figure 5.21). Intel's SpeedStep technology, for example, enables the

 Wikipedia is a user-generated, self-regulated resource. I've found it to be accurate on technical issues the vast majority of the time, but you should always check other references as well. Nicely, most article authors on the site will tell you their sources through footnotes. You can often use the Wikipedia articles as jump-off points for deeper searches.

• **Figure 5.21** Desktop vs. mobile, fight!

CPU to run in very low power mode and scale up automatically if the user demands more power from the CPU. If you're surfing the Web at an airport terminal, the CPU doesn't draw too much power. When you switch to playing an action game, the CPU kicks into gear. Saving energy by making the CPU run more slowly when demand is light is generically called **throttling**.

Many of the technologies developed for mobile processors have migrated into their more power-hungry desktop siblings, too. That's an added bonus for the planet.

Technology

Although microprocessors today still serve the same function as the venerable 8088—crunching numbers—they do so far more efficiently. Engineers have altered, enhanced, and improved CPUs in a number of ways. This section looks at seven features:

- Clock multipliers
- 64-bit processing
- Virtualization support
- Parallel execution
- Multicore processing
- Integrated memory controller (IMC)
- Integrated graphics processing unit (GPU)

Clock Multipliers

All modern CPUs run at some multiple of the system clock speed. The system bus on my Core i7 machine, for example, runs at 100 MHz. The clock multiplier goes up to ×35 at full load to support the 3.4 GHz maximum speed. Originally, CPUs ran at the speed of the bus, but engineers early on realized the CPU was the only thing doing any work much of the time. If the engineers could speed up just the internal operations of the CPU and not anything else, they could speed up the whole computing process. Figure 5.22 shows a nifty program called CPU-Z displaying my CPU details. Note that all I'm doing is typing at the moment, so SpeedStep has dropped the clock multiplier down to ×16 and the CPU core speed is only 1600 MHz.

• **Figure 5.22** CPU-Z showing the clock speed, multiplier, and bus speed of a Core i7 processor hardly breaking a sweat

● **Figure 5.23** DIP switches on a motherboard

The clock speed and the multiplier on early clock-multiplying systems had to be manually configured via jumpers or dual in-line package (DIP) switches on the motherboard (see Figure 5.23). Today's CPUs report to the motherboard through a function called CPUID (CPU identifier), and the speed and multiplier are set automatically. (You can manually override this automatic setup on many motherboards. See "Overclocking," later in this chapter, for details.)

64-Bit Processing

Over successive generations of microprocessors, engineers have upgraded many physical features of CPUs. The EDB gradually increased in size, from 8- to 16- to 32- to 64-bits wide. The address bus similarly jumped, going from 20- to 24- to 32-bits wide (where it stayed for a decade).

The technological features changed as well. Engineers added new and improved registers, for example, that used fancy names like multimedia extensions (MMX) and Streaming SIMD Extensions (SSE). A mighty shift started a couple of years ago and continues to evolve: the move to 64-bit computing.

Most new CPUs support **64-bit processing**, meaning they can run a compatible 64-bit operating system, such as Windows 7, and 64-bit applications. They also support 32-bit processing for 32-bit operating systems, such as Windows XP, and 32-bit applications. The general-purpose registers also make the move up to 64-bit. The primary benefit to moving to 64-bit computing is that modern systems can support much more than the 4 GB of memory supported with 32-bit processing.

With a 64-bit address bus, CPUs can address 2^{64} bytes of memory, or more precisely, 18,446,744,073,709,551,616 bytes of memory—that's a lot of RAM! This number is so big that gigabytes and terabytes are no longer convenient, so we now go to an exabyte (2^{60}), abbreviated *EB*. A 64-bit address bus can address 16 EB of RAM.

In practical terms, 64-bit computing greatly enhances the performance of programs that work with large files, such as video editing applications. You'll see a profound improvement moving from 4 GB to 8 GB or 12 GB of RAM with such programs.

Virtualization Support

Intel and AMD have built in support for running more than one operating system at a time, a process called *virtualization*. The key issue from a CPU standpoint is that virtualization used to work entirely through software. Programmers had to write a ton of code to enable a CPU—that was designed to run one OS at a time—to run more than one OS at the same time. Think about the issues involved. How does the memory get allocated, for example, or how does the CPU know which OS to update when you type something or click an icon? With hardware-based virtualization support, CPUs took a lot of the burden off the programmers and made virtualization a whole lot easier.

Parallel Execution

Modern CPUs can process multiple commands and parts of commands in parallel, known as **parallel execution**. Early processors had to do everything in a strict, linear fashion. The CPUs accomplish this parallelism through multiple pipelines, dedicated cache, and the capability to work with multiple threads or programs at one time. To understand the mighty leap in efficiency gained from parallel execution, you need insight into the processing stages.

Pipelining To get a command from the data bus, do the calculation, and then get the answer back out on the data bus, a CPU takes at least four steps (each of these steps is called a *stage*):

1. **Fetch** Get the data from the EDB.
2. **Decode** Figure out what type of command needs to be executed.
3. **Execute** Perform the calculation.
4. **Write** Send the data back onto the EDB.

Smart, discrete circuits inside the CPU handle each of these stages. In early CPUs, when a command was placed on the data bus, each stage did its job and the CPU handed back the answer before starting the next command, requiring at least four clock cycles to process a command. In every clock cycle, three of the four circuits sat idle. Today, the circuits are organized in a conveyer-belt fashion called a **pipeline**. With pipelining, each stage does its job with each clock-cycle pulse, creating a much more efficient process. The CPU has multiple circuits doing multiple jobs, so let's add pipelining to the Man in the Box analogy. Now, it's *Men* in the Box (see Figure 5.24)!

Pipelines keep every stage of the processor busy on every click of the clock, making a CPU run more efficiently without increasing the clock speed. Note that at this point, the CPU has four stages: fetch, decode, execute,

Fetch
Decode
Execute
Write

• **Figure 5.24** Simple pipeline

and write—a four-stage pipeline. No CPU ever made has fewer than four stages, but advancements in caching (see "Cache," next) have increased the number of stages over the years. Current CPU pipelines contain many more stages, up to 20 in some cases.

Pipelining isn't perfect. Sometimes a stage hits a complex command that requires more than one clock cycle, forcing the pipeline to stop. Your CPU tries to avoid these stops, or *pipeline stalls*. The decode stage tends to cause the most pipeline stalls; certain commands are complex and therefore harder to decode than other commands. Current processors use multiple decode stages to reduce the chance of pipeline stalls due to complex decoding.

The inside of the CPU is composed of multiple chunks of circuitry to handle the many types of calculations your PC needs to do. For example, one part, the **arithmetic logic unit (ALU)** (or *integer unit*), handles integer math: basic math for numbers with no decimal point. A perfect example of integer math is $2 + 3 = 5$. The typical CPU spends most of its work doing integer math. CPUs also have special circuitry to handle complex numbers, called the **floating point unit (FPU)**. With a single pipeline, only the ALU or the FPU worked at any execution stage. Worse yet, floating point calculation often took many, many clock cycles to execute, forcing the CPU to stall the pipeline until the FPU finished executing the complex command (see Figure 5.25). Current CPUs offer multiple pipelines to keep the processing going (see Figure 5.26).

• **Figure 5.25** Bored integer unit

Cache When you send a program to the CPU, you actually run lots of little programs all at the same time. Okay, let's be fair here: *you* didn't run all of these little programs—you just started your Web browser or some other program. The moment you double-clicked that icon, Windows started sending many programs to the CPU. Each of these programs breaks down into some number of little pieces, called *threads*, and data. Each thread is a series of instructions designed to do a particular job with the data.

Modern CPUs don't execute instructions sequentially—first doing step 1, then step 2, and so on—but rather process all kinds of instructions. Most applications have certain instructions and data that get reused, sometimes many times.

Pipelining CPUs work fantastically well as long as the pipelines stay filled with instructions. Because the CPU runs faster than the RAM can supply it with code, you'll always get pipeline stalls—called **wait states**—because the RAM can't keep up with the CPU. To reduce wait states, CPUs come with built-in, very high-speed RAM called **static RAM (SRAM)**. This SRAM preloads as many instructions as possible and keeps copies of already run instructions and data in case the CPU needs to work on them again (see Figure 5.27). SRAM used in this fashion is called a **cache**.

● **Figure 5.26** Multiple pipelines

● **Figure 5.27** RAM cache

The SRAM cache inside the early CPUs was tiny, only about 16 KB, but it improved performance tremendously. In fact, it helped so much that many motherboard makers began adding a cache directly to the motherboards. These caches were much larger, usually around 128 to 512 KB. When the CPU looked for a line of code, it first went to the built-in cache; if the code wasn't there, the CPU went to the cache on the motherboard. The cache on the CPU was called the *L1 cache* because it was the one the CPU first tried to use. The cache on the motherboard was called the *L2 cache*, not because it was on the motherboard, but because it was the second cache the CPU checked.

Eventually, engineers took this cache concept even further and added the L2 cache onto the CPU package (see Figure 5.28). Some CPUs even include three caches: an L1, an L2, and an L3 cache.

The L2 cache on the early CPUs that had L2 cache included on the CPU package ran at a slower clock speed than the L1 cache. The L1 cache was in the CPU and thus ran at the speed of the CPU. The L2 cache connected to the CPU via a tiny set of wires on the CPU package. The first L2 caches ran at half the speed of the CPU.

The inclusion of the L2 cache on the chip gave rise to some new terms to describe the connections between the CPU, MCC, RAM, and L2 cache. The address bus and external data bus (connecting the CPU, MCC, and RAM) were lumped into a single term called the **frontside bus**, and the connection between the CPU and the L2 cache became known as the **backside bus** (see Figure 5.29).

The end of the road for the terms frontside bus and backside bus seems to be at the Intel Core 2 Duo and Core 2 Quad processors, as far as the CompTIA A+ certification exams are concerned. The terms are also used

To keep up with faster processors, motherboard manufacturers began to double and even quadruple the size of the frontside bus. Techs sometimes refer to these as *double-pumped* and *quad-pumped* frontside buses.

Typically, the CompTIA A+ exams expect you to know that L1 cache will be the smallest and fastest cache; L2 will be bigger and slower than L1; and L3 will be the biggest and slowest cache.

• **Figure 5.28** CPU-Z displaying the cache information for a Core i7 processor

Mike Meyers' CompTIA A+ Guide to 801: Managing and Troubleshooting PCs

• Figure 5.29 Frontside and backside buses

by a lot of techs to refer to simply "the connection between the CPU and system RAM."

Multithreading At the peak of the single-CPU 32-bit computing days, Intel released a CPU called the Pentium 4 that took parallelism to the next step with Hyper-Threading. *Hyper-Threading* enabled the Pentium 4 to run multiple threads at the same time, what's generically called *simultaneous multithreading*, effectively turning the CPU into two CPUs on one chip—with a catch.

Figure 5.30 shows the Task Manager in Windows XP on a system running a Hyper-Threaded Pentium 4. Note how the CPU box is broken into two groups—Windows thinks this one CPU is two CPUs.

• Figure 5.30 Windows Task Manager with the Performance tab displayed for a system running a Hyper-Threaded Pentium 4

Multithreading enhances a CPU's efficiency, but with a couple of limitations. First, the operating system and the application have to be designed to take advantage of the feature. Second, although the CPU simulates the actions of a second processor, it doesn't double the processing power because the main execution resources are not duplicated.

Multicore Processing

CPU clock speeds hit a practical limit of roughly 4 GHz around 2002–2003, motivating the CPU makers to find new ways to get more processing power for CPUs. Although Intel and AMD had different opinions about 64-bit CPUs, both decided at virtually the same time to combine two CPUs (or *cores*) into a single chip, creating a **dual-core** architecture. A dual-core CPU has two execution units—two sets of pipelines—but the two sets of pipelines share caches and RAM.

Today, dual-core CPUs like the Intel Core 2 Duo are common, and multicore CPUs—with four, six, or eight cores—grace the desktop PCs of many enthusiasts. With each generation of multicore CPU, both Intel and AMD have tinkered with the mixture of how to allocate the cache among the cores. Figure 5.31 shows another screenshot of CPU-Z, this time displaying the cache breakdown of a Core i7.

Figure 5.31 reveals specific details about how this Intel CPU works with cache. The Core i7 has L1, L2, and L3 caches of 64 KB, 256 KB, and 8 MB, respectively. (The L1 cache divides into 32 KB to handle data—the

• **Figure 5.31** CPU-Z showing the cache details of a Sandy Bridge Core i7

D-Cache—and another 32 KB for instructions—the *I-Cache*.) Each core has dedicated L1 and L2 caches. (You can tell this by the ×4 to the right of the capacity listing.) All four cores share the giant L3 cache. That pool of memory enables the cores to communicate and work together without having to access the radically slower main system RAM as much. CPU manufacturers engineered the cores in multicore CPUs to divide up work independently of the OS, known as **multicore processing**. This differs from Hyper-Threading, where the OS and applications have to be written specifically to handle the multiple threads. Note that even with multicore processors, applications have to be modified or optimized for this parallelism to have a huge impact on performance.

Integrated Memory Controller

Almost all current microprocessors have an **integrated memory controller (IMC)**, moved from the motherboard chip into the CPU to optimize the flow of information into and out from the CPU. An IMC enables faster control over things like the large L3 cache shared among multiple cores.

Just like in so many other areas of computing, manufacturers implement a variety of IMCs in their CPUs. In practice, this means that different CPUs handle different types and capacities of RAM. I'll save the details on those RAM variations for Chapter 6. For now, add "different RAM support" to your list of things to look at when making a CPU recommendation for a client.

Integrated Graphics Processing Unit

As you'll read about in much more detail in Chapter 13, the video processing portion of the computer—made up of the parts that put a changing image on the monitor—traditionally has a discrete microprocessor that differs in both function and architecture from the CPUs designed for general-purpose computing. The generic term for the video processor is a **graphics processing unit (GPU)**. I'll spare you the details until we get to video in Chapter 13, but it turns out that graphics processors can handle certain tasks much more efficiently than the standard CPU. Integrating a GPU into the CPU enhances the overall performance of the computer while at the same time reducing energy use, size, and cost. With the proliferation of mobile devices and portable computers today, all of these benefits have obvious merit.

Both major CPU manufacturers have released CPUs with integrated GPUs. The architecture differs in some ways, such as how they use the cache on the chip. The *Intel HD Graphics* integrated into many Core i3/i5/i7 processors, for example, has the CPU cores and the GPU core sharing the "last level cache," which is either L2 or L3, depending on the processor (see Figure 5.32). With the AMD *accelerated processing unit*

Tech Tip

NVIDIA Tegra and "Project Denver"
One of the two major players in the performance GPU market, NVIDIA, also manufactures microprocessors that have combined CPUs and GPUs. The current offering, called the Tegra, is almost a complete computer on a single chip. You'll find it in many mobile devices. NVIDIA hasn't made a push for the PC desktop market yet, although that might change with the release of their integrated microprocessor code named "Project Denver" in 2013.

Last Level Cache

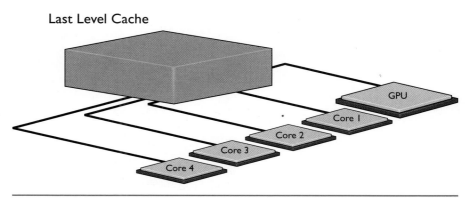

• **Figure 5.32** Dedicated cache (in each core) and shared cache

(*APU*), such as the AMD Fusion, the GPU has access to all levels of cache on the CPU.

■ Selecting and Installing CPUs

Now that you know how CPUs work, it's time to get practical. This last section discusses selecting the proper CPU and installing several types of processors.

Selecting a CPU

When selecting a CPU, you need to make certain you get one that the motherboard can accommodate. Or, if you're buying a motherboard along with the CPU, then get the right CPU for the intended purpose. Chapter 21 discusses computer roles and helps you select the proper components for each role. You need to have a lot more knowledge of all the pieces around the CPU to get the full picture, so we'll wait until then to discuss the "why" of a particular processor. Instead, this section assumes you're placing a new CPU in an already-acquired motherboard. You need to address two key points in selecting a CPU that will work. First, does the motherboard support Intel or AMD CPUs? Second, what socket does the motherboard have?

To find answers to both those questions, you have two sources: the motherboard book or manual and the manufacturer's Web site. Figure 5.33 shows a manual for an Asus motherboard open to reveal the supported processors and the socket type.

Just as Intel and AMD make many types of CPUs, motherboards are manufactured with various different types of sockets. The CompTIA A+ exams expect you to know which sockets go with which family of CPU. Table 5.2 charts the important Intel ones; Table 5.3 lists the AMD-based sockets. I would show you all the pictures, but, frankly, CPU sockets aren't the sexiest part of the computer.

I've included the number of socket pins for the AMD-based sockets because related questions have been on the CompTIA A+ certifications in exam objectives prior to 801. You don't need to memorize the Intel numbers, because Intel names the sockets by the number of pins.

1.3 Special features

1.3.1 Product highlights

LGA1155 socket for Intel® Second Generation Core™ i7 / Core™ i5 / Core™ i3 Processors

This motherboard supports the Intel® second generation Core™ i7 / Core™ i5 / Core™ i3 processors in LGA1155 package with memory and PCI Express controllers integrated to support 2-channel (4 DIMMs) DDR3 memory and 16 PCI Express 2.0 lanes. This provides great graphics performance. Intel® second generation Core™ i7 / Core™ i5 / Core™ i3 processors are among the most powerful and energy efficient CPUs in the world. Refer to page 2-4 for details.

Intel® P67 Express Chipset

The Intel® P67 Express Chipset is the latest single-chipset design to support the new 1155 Intel® Core™ i7 / Core™ i5 / Core™ i3 second generation processors. It uses serial allows increased bandwidth and stability, and provides an improved and four SATA 3.0 Gb/s ports for faster data

• **Figure 5.33** Supported processors and socket type

Table 5.2	Intel-based Sockets
Socket	**CPU**
LGA 775[1]	Pentium 4, Celeron, Pentium 4 Extreme Edition, Core 2 Duo, Core 2 Quad, Xeon, and many others
LGA 1155[2]	Core i3/i5/i7, Pentium, Celeron, Xeon
LGA 1156[3]	Core i3/i5/i7, Pentium, Celeron, Xeon
LGA 1366[4]	Core i7, Xeon, Celeron

1 The LGA 775 socket was the only desktop or server socket used for many years by Intel and thus just about every branded Intel CPU used it at one time or another.

2 Socket LGA 1155 CPUs are based on Sandy Bridge or Ivy Bridge architecture.

3 Socket LGA 1156 CPUs are based on the pre–Sandy Bridge architecture.

4 The very first Core i7 processors used LGA 1366.

This list of Intel CPUs covers only those listed on the CompTIA A+ 801 exam objectives. The CompTIA A+ 701/702 exams mentioned a couple of other processors, such as the *Pentium Pro* (very old, 32-bit) and the *Itanium* (also old; used for servers exclusively). You might see them as incorrect answers on the 801 exam.

Table 5.3	AMD-based Sockets	
Socket	**Pins**	**CPU**
940[1]	940	Opteron, Athlon 64 FX
AM2[2]	940	Athlon 64, Athlon 64 X2, Athlon 64 FX, Opteron, Sempron, Phenom
AM2+[2]	940	Athlon 64, Athlon 64 X2, Athlon II, Opteron, Phenom, Phenom II
AM3[3]	941	Phenom II, Athlon II, Sempron, Opteron
AM3+[4]	942	FX
FM1	905	A[5]
F	1207	Opteron, Athlon FX

1 You would usually find only an Opteron server-based CPU in a socket 940. The Athlon 64 FX was a super high-end CPU for the day and is very unlikely to be on the exams.

2 AMD says that CPUs designed for AM2 sockets will work in a Socket AM2+ and vice versa, though at the slower memory movement speeds of the AM2 component (socket or CPU). Many manufacturers have not released motherboard updates that would enable support for a Socket AM2+ CPU on a Socket AM2 motherboard, thus making it impossible to upgrade just the CPU.

3 Though the names of some of the processors designed for Socket AM3 match the names of CPUs designed for earlier sockets, they're *not* the same CPUs. They are specific to AM3 because they support different types of RAM (see Chapter 6). Just to make things even crazier, though, AM3 CPUs work just fine in Socket AM2/2+ motherboards.

4 AMD had only released the FX-branded CPUs that use the Bulldozer core at the time of this writing. Motherboards with AM3+ sockets already available tout support for Phenom II, Athlon II, and Sempron CPUs, in addition to the FX series.

5 The A series features integrated GPUs and other chips.

This list of AMD CPUs covers only those listed on the CompTIA A+ 801 exam objectives. As with the Intel processors, the CompTIA A+ 700-series exams mentioned a couple of other processors, such as the *Athlon XP* (old, 32-bit) and the *Duron* (also old; label used for low-end CPUs). You might see them as incorrect answers on the 801 exam.

Installation Issues

When installing a CPU, you need to use caution with the tiny pins. Plus, you must make certain that the power supply can supply enough electricity for the processor to function along with all the other components on the computer. You have to provide adequate cooling. Finally, you can decide whether to leave the CPU at stock settings or overclock it.

Socket Types

When installing a CPU, you need to exercise caution not to bend any of the tiny pins. The location of the pins differs between Intel and AMD.

● **Figure 5.34** Intel-based socket with pins

● **Figure 5.35** AMD-based socket without pins

With Intel-based motherboards, the sockets have hundreds of tiny pins that line up with contacts on the bottom of the CPU (see Figure 5.34). Intel CPUs use a *land grid array* (*LGA*) package, where the underside of the CPU has hundreds of contact points that line up with the socket pins.

AMD CPUs have the pins (see Figure 5.35); the sockets have holes. The pins on the AMD *pin grid array* (*PGA*) CPUs align with the holes in the sockets.

All CPUs and sockets are keyed so you can't (easily) insert them incorrectly. Look at the underside of the CPU in Figure 5.36 (left). Note that

● **Figure 5.36** Underside and top of a CPU

the pins do not make a perfect square, because a few are missing. Now look at the top of the CPU (right). See the little mark at the corner? The socket also has tiny markings so you can line the CPU up properly with the socket.

In both socket styles, you release the retaining mechanism by pushing the little lever down slightly and then away from the socket (see Figure 5.37). You next raise the arm fully, and then move the retaining bracket (see Figure 5.38).

Align the processor with the socket and gently drop the processor into place. If it doesn't go in easily, check the orientation and try again. These sockets are generically called **zero insertion force (ZIF) sockets**, which means you never have to use any force at all.

Cooling

CPUs work very hard and thus require power to function. In electrical terms, CPUs consume *wattage* or *watts*, a unit of electrical power, just like a 100-watt light bulb consumes power whenever it's on. (See Chapter 9 for more details about electricity.) Have you ever touched a light bulb after it's been on for a while? Ouch! CPUs heat up, too.

To increase the capability of the CPUs to handle complex code, CPU manufacturers have added a lot of microscopic transistors over the years. The more transistors the CPU has, the more power they need and thus the hotter they get. CPUs don't tolerate heat well, and modern processors need active cooling solutions just to function at all. Almost every CPU uses a combination of a heat-sink and fan assembly to wick heat away from the CPU. Figure 5.39 shows the standard Intel heat sink and fan.

There was a time, long ago, when CPUs didn't need any type of cooling device. You just snapped in the CPU and it worked. Well, those days are gone. Long gone. If you're installing a modern CPU, you will have to cool it. Fortunately, you have choices.

● **Figure 5.37** Moving the release arm

● **Figure 5.38** Fully opened socket

Figure 5.39 Intel OEM heat-sink and fan assembly

- **OEM CPU coolers** OEM heat-sink and fan assemblies are included with a retail-boxed CPU. OEM CPUs, on the other hand, don't normally come bundled with CPU coolers. Crazy, isn't it? OEM CPU coolers have one big advantage: you know absolutely they will work with your CPU.

- **Specialized CPU coolers** Many companies sell third-party heat-sink and fan assemblies for a variety of CPUs. These usually exceed the OEM heat sinks in the amount of heat they dissipate. These CPU coolers invariably come with eye-catching designs to look really cool inside your system—some are even lighted (see Figure 5.40).

The last choice is the most impressive of all: liquid cooling! **Liquid cooling** works by running some liquid—usually water—through a metal block that sits on top of your CPU, absorbing heat. The liquid gets heated by the block, runs out of the block and into something that cools the liquid, and is then pumped through the block again. Any liquid-cooling system consists of three main parts:

- A hollow metal block that sits on the CPU
- A pump to move the liquid around
- Some device to cool the liquid

Figure 5.40 Cool retail heat sink

And of course, you need plenty of hosing to hook them all together. Figure 5.41 shows a typical liquid-cooled CPU.

A number of companies sell these liquid-based cooling systems. Although they look impressive and certainly cool your CPU, unless you're overclocking or want a quiet system, a good fan will more than suffice.

Once you've got a heat-sink and fan assembly sorted out, you need to connect them to the motherboard. To determine the orientation of the heat-sink and fan assembly, check the power cable from the fan. Make sure it can easily reach the three- or four-wire standout on the motherboard (see Figure 5.42). If it can't, rotate the heat sink until it can. (Check the motherboard manual if you have trouble locating the CPU fan power standout.)

• **Figure 5.41** Liquid-cooled CPU

Next, before inserting the heat sink, you need to add a small amount of **thermal compound** (also called *heat dope* or *nasty silver goo*). Many heat sinks come with some thermal compound already on them; the thermal compound on these pre-doped heat sinks is covered by a small square of tape—take the tape off before you snap it to the CPU. If you need to put heat dope on from a tube, know that you need to use only a tiny amount of this compound (see Figure 5.43). Spread it on as thinly, completely, and evenly as you can. Unlike so many other things in life, you *can* have too much heat dope!

• **Figure 5.42** CPU fan power standout on motherboard

• **Figure 5.43** Applying thermal compound

You secure heat sinks in various ways, depending on the manufacturer. Stock Intel heat sinks have four plungers that you simply push until they click into place in corresponding holes in the motherboard. AMD stock heat sinks generally have a bracket that you secure to two points on the outside of the CPU socket and a latch that you swivel to lock it down (see Figure 5.44).

Finally, you can secure many aftermarket heat-sink and fan assemblies by screwing them down from the underside of the motherboard (see Figure 5.45). You have to remove the motherboard from the case or install the heat sink before you put the motherboard in the case.

For the final step, plug the fan power connector into the motherboard standout. It won't work if you don't!

Overclocking

For the CPU to work, the motherboard speed, multiplier, and voltage must be set properly. In most modern systems, the motherboard uses the CPUID functions to set these options automatically. Some motherboards enable you to adjust these settings manually by moving a jumper, changing a CMOS setting, or using software; many enthusiasts deliberately change these settings to enhance performance.

Tech Tip

CMOS

Chapter 7 goes into gory detail about the system setup utility and the area in which it stores important data (called CMOS), but invariably students want to experiment at this point, so I'll give you some information now. You can access the system setup utility by pressing some key as the computer starts up. This is during the text phase, well before it ever says anything about starting Windows. Most systems require you to press the DELETE key, but read the screen for details. Just be careful once you get into the system setup utility not to change anything you don't understand. And read Chapter 7!

• **Figure 5.44** AMD OEM heat-sink and fan assembly

Starting way back in the days of the Intel 80486 CPU, people intentionally ran their systems at clock speeds higher than the CPU was rated, a process called **overclocking**, and it worked. Well, *sometimes* the systems worked, and sometimes they didn't. Intel and AMD have a reason for marking a CPU at a particular clock speed—that's the highest speed they guarantee will work.

Before I say anything else, I must warn you that intentional overclocking of a CPU immediately voids most warranties. Overclocking has been known to destroy CPUs. Overclocking might make your system unstable and prone to lockups and reboots. I neither applaud nor decry the practice of overclocking. My goal here is simply to inform you of the practice. You make your own decisions.

CPU makers dislike overclocking. Why would you pay more for a faster processor when you can take a cheaper, slower CPU and just make it run faster? To that end, CPU makers, especially Intel, have gone to great lengths to discourage the practice. For example, both AMD and Intel now make almost all of their CPUs with locked multipliers and special overspeed electronics to deter the practice.

Most people make a couple of adjustments to overclock successfully. First, through jumpers, CMOS settings, or software configuration, you would increase the bus speed for the system. Second, you often have to increase the voltage going into the CPU by just a little to provide stability. You do that by changing a jumper or CMOS setting (see Figure 5.46).

• Figure 5.45 Heat-sink and fan assembly mounted to motherboard with screws

If you want to know exactly what type of CPU you're running, download a copy of the very popular and free CPU-Z utility from www.cpuid.com. CPU-Z gives you every piece of information you'll ever want to know about your CPU.

• Figure 5.46 Manually overriding CPU settings in the system setup utility

CMOS-clear jumper

● **Figure 5.47** CMOS-clear jumper

Overriding the defaults can completely lock up your system, to the point where even removing and reinstalling the CPU doesn't bring the motherboard back to life. (There's also a slight risk of toasting the processor, although all modern processors have circuitry that shuts them down quickly before they overheat.) Most motherboards have a jumper setting called *CMOS clear* (see Figure 5.47) that makes the CMOS go back to default settings. Before you try overclocking on a modern system, find the CMOS-clear jumper and make sure you know how to use it! Hint: Look in the motherboard manual.

To clear the CMOS, turn off the PC. Then locate one of those tiny little plastic pieces (officially called a *shunt*) and place it over the two jumper wires for a moment. Next, restart the PC and immediately go into CMOS and restore the settings you need.

Chapter 5 Review

■ Chapter Summary

After reading this chapter and completing the exercises, you should understand the following facts about microprocessors.

Identify the core components of a CPU

- The central processing unit performs calculations on binary numbers to make the magic of computers work. The CPU interfaces with the motherboard and other components through the external data bus.

- CPUs contain several areas of internal memory, known as registers, in which data and addresses are stored while processing. The commands a CPU knows how to perform are dictated by its instruction set.

- A quartz crystal soldered to the motherboard and known as the system crystal provides a constant pulse known as the clock. The frequency of this pulse, or clock speed, dictates the maximum speed at which a processor can run, measured in megahertz or gigahertz. The processor typically runs at some multiple of this clock pulse, known as the internal clock speed. You can set the internal clock speed by adjusting the multiplier (which multiplies the clock speed by some number) or by configuring motherboard jumpers or making a change to a CMOS setting, or it is set automatically via CPU circuitry. Setting the clock speed higher to force the CPU to run faster than its rating is known as overclocking.

Describe the relationship of CPUs and memory

- A computer uses random access memory to take copies of programs from the hard drive and send them, one line at a time, to the CPU quickly enough to keep up with its demands. The CPU accesses any one row of RAM as easily and as quickly as any other row, which explains the "random access" part of RAM. RAM is not only randomly accessible, but also fast. By storing programs on RAM, the CPU can access and run them very quickly. RAM also stores any data that the CPU actively uses.

- The CPU communicates with RAM on the motherboard via the address bus. The number of wires comprising the address bus dictates the amount of memory the CPU can access.

Explain the varieties of modern CPUs

- Most CPUs in modern PCs are manufactured by Intel or AMD. Both companies use code names to differentiate among different models within a CPU family name. That way techs can tell the difference between, for example, a Nehalem-based Core i7 and a Sandy Bridge Core i7. Both companies offer low-power mobile versions of their desktop CPU architectures.

- Although they share the same function as early CPUs, modern CPUs offer a lot more efficiency. Seven architectural changes define modern CPUs. All are clock multipliers, running at some multiple of the system bus speed. Most current CPUs support 64-bit processing and can handle much more RAM than the 4 GB that 32-bit processors supported.

- With parallel execution and multicore processing, modern CPUs can handle many simultaneous applications efficiently. One Intel-only parallel execution technology, Hyper-Threading, makes a single CPU function like two CPUs if the OS and applications support the technology. A multicore CPU, in contrast, functions as multiple CPUs regardless of the OS, though the applications still need optimization.

Select and install a CPU

- Consult your motherboard documentation to see which CPUs are compatible with your system. Not all CPUs are compatible with all motherboards.

- Cooling is critical. Make sure you have a fan rated to work with your CPU.

- A CPU fits only one way in the ZIF socket. Don't force it. If you find the CPU will not seat properly, take a second look at the orientation markers and verify the CPU is in the correct direction. Check the pins on the underside to make sure none are bent.

- There should be a small amount of heat-sink compound between the CPU and heat-sink and fan assembly. If your fan came with the compound already applied, be sure to remove the protective tape covering the compound before attaching the fan to the CPU. If you are using your own heat dope from a tube, spread it thinly and evenly.

■ Key Terms

<div style="display:flex">

64-bit processing *(104)*
address bus *(96)*
arithmetic logic unit (ALU) *(106)*
backside bus *(108)*
binary *(88)*
bit *(95)*
byte *(95)*
cache *(106)*
central processing unit (CPU) *(86)*
clock cycle *(91)*
clock speed *(91)*
clock wire *(91)*
code name *(101)*
dual-core *(110)*
dynamic RAM (DRAM) *(95)*
external data bus (EDB) *(88)*
floating point unit (FPU) *(106)*
frontside bus *(108)*
graphics processing unit (GPU) *(111)*
instruction set *(90)*

integrated memory controller (IMC) *(111)*
liquid cooling *(116)*
machine language *(90)*
memory *(94)*
memory controller chip (MCC) *(96)*
microprocessor *(86)*
multicore processing *(111)*
overclocking *(119)*
parallel execution *(105)*
pipeline *(105)*
program *(94)*
random access memory (RAM) *(95)*
registers *(89)*
static RAM (SRAM) *(106)*
system crystal *(92)*
thermal compound *(117)*
throttling *(103)*
wait state *(106)*
zero insertion force (ZIF) socket *(115)*

</div>

■ Key Term Quiz

Use the Key Terms list to complete the sentences that follow. Not all terms will be used.

1. All of the machine language commands that the CPU understands make up the CPU's _____.

2. By lifting the arm on the _____, you can easily install a PGA CPU.

3. Computers use _____ for main system memory.

4. Computers use the _____ numbering system.

5. Areas inside the CPU where it temporarily stores internal commands and data while it is processing them are called _____.

6. Divided into L1 and L2, the _____ consists of a small amount of _____ that serves as a holding area. This provides data to the CPU faster than getting it from regular memory or when RAM is unavailable because of refreshes.

7. A CPU with a(n) _____ can handle RAM directly.

8. If a stock heat-sink and fan assembly can't handle an overclocked CPU, a solution based on _____ might do the trick.

9. In a process known as _____, a CPU can slow itself down in low-demand times or if it gets too hot.

10. An Intel Core 2 Duo is an example of a(n) _____ processor.

■ Multiple-Choice Quiz

1. What device enables a PC to retrieve a specific row of data from system memory and place it on the external data bus?

 A. Advanced micro device

 B. Arithmetic logic unit

 C. Floating point processor

 D. Memory controller chip

2. Which of the following statements is true?

 A. The address bus enables the CPU to communicate with the MCC.

 B. The external data bus enables the CPU to communicate with the MCC.

 C. The address bus enables the CPU to communicate with the hard drive.

 D. The system bus enables the CPU to communicate with the memory.

3. What do 64-bit processors expand beyond what 32-bit processors have?

 A. System bus

 B. Frontside bus

 C. Address bus

 D. Registers

4. What is the first stage in a typical four-stage CPU pipeline?

 A. Decode

 B. Execute

 C. Fetch

 D. Write

5. Which of the following terms are measures of CPU speed?

 A. Megahertz and gigahertz

 B. Megabytes and gigabytes

 C. Megahertz and gigabytes

 D. Frontside bus, backside bus

6. Which of the following statements is true?

 A. If you have an AMD-compatible motherboard, you can install a Celeron processor.

 B. You should always overclock your CPU.

 C. As the size of the address bus increases, the amount of RAM the CPU can use decreases.

 D. You can upgrade your CPU if you make sure that a new CPU will fit into the socket on your motherboard.

7. Which CPU feature enables the microprocessor to support running multiple operating systems at the same time?

 A. Clock multiplying

 B. Caching

 C. Pipelining

 D. Virtualization support

8. Into which socket could you place an AMD Phenom II?

 A. Socket LGA 775

 B. Socket LGA 1154

 C. Socket AM2+

 D. Socket A

9. Joey has a motherboard that advertises support for x64 processors. Which CPU will definitely work in that motherboard?

 A. Athlon 64 X2

 B. Core 2 Duo

 C. Core i7

 D. There's not enough information to answer the question.

10. Which feature enables a single-core CPU to function like two CPUs?

 A. Hyper-Threading

 B. SpeedStep

 C. Virtualization

 D. x64

11. What connects on the backside bus?

 A. CPU, MCC, RAM

 B. CPU, MCC, L1 cache

 C. CPU, L1 cache

 D. CPU, L2 cache

12. What improvement have CPU manufacturers put into processors to deal with pipeline stalls?

 A. Added multiple pipelines

 B. Increased the speed of the SRAM

 C. Created new die sizes with more pins

 D. Bundled better fans with their retail CPUs

13. What steps do you need to take to install an Athlon 64 X2 CPU into an LGA 775 motherboard?

 A. Lift the ZIF socket arm; place the CPU according to the orientation markings; snap on the heat-sink and fan assembly.

 B. Lift the ZIF socket arm; place the CPU according to the orientation markings; add a dash of heat dope; snap on the heat-sink and fan assembly.

 C. Lift the ZIF socket arm; place the CPU according to the orientation markings; snap on the heat-sink and fan assembly; plug in the fan.

 D. Take all of the steps you want to take because it's not going to work.

14. How many bits are in a byte?

 A. 1024

 B. 64

 C. 32

 D. 8

15. What do you need to install on top of your CPU to keep it from overheating?

 A. RAM

 B. Heatsink assembly

 C. Thermal dissipator

 D. CPU disperser

■ Essay Quiz

1. It is important for the CPU to stay cool. A number of technical advances have been made in the design of CPUs, along with various devices made to keep the CPU from overheating. Discuss at least two cooling features or cooling options.

2. Where do code names for CPUs come from? Write up a comparison of the code names used by Intel and AMD for their processors. What other aspects of computing use code names?

3. Compare parallel execution with multicore processing. How are they similar? How do they differ?

4. Write a brief essay on the benefits and risks of overclocking a CPU.

5. Do we need 64-bit computing? What can you do with 64-bit that you can't do with 32-bit? What applications do you use on a regular basis that could take advantage of 64-bit versions? If the answer is "none," explain.

Lab Projects

• Lab Project 5.1

Perhaps newer and faster CPUs have come out recently. Go to www.intel.com and www.amd.com and investigate the newest CPUs for desktop computers from each manufacturer. Write a paragraph comparing the newest Intel CPU with the newest AMD CPU. Try to include the following information:

- What is the size of the system bus?
- What is the size of the address bus?

- What is the speed of the CPU?
- What are the sizes of the L1 and L2 caches?
- Does either CPU offer an L3 cache?
- What kind of chip package houses each CPU?
- What kind of socket does each use?
- What other new features does each site advertise for its newest CPU?

• Lab Project 5.2

Imagine that you are going to buy components to build your own computer. What processor will you use? Typically, the latest and greatest CPU is a lot more expensive than less recent models. Intel processors usually cost more than comparable AMD processors. Check CPU features and prices in newspapers or magazines or on the Internet at a site such as www.newegg.com. Decide what CPU you want to use for your computer. Write a paragraph explaining why you selected it and how much you will spend for the CPU.

• Lab Project 5.3

If your school hardware lab has motherboards and processors for hands-on labs, practice removing and installing LGA and PGA processors on the motherboards. Take note of how the mechanical arm on a ZIF socket works. Answer the following about your experience:

- How do you know in which direction to place the CPU?

- How does the mechanical arm lift up? Does it lift straight up or must it clear a lip?
- What effect does lifting the arm have on the socket?
- How does the ZIF socket hold the CPU in place?

chapter
6

RΛM

"The memory be green."

—William Shakespeare, *Hamlet*,
Act I, Scene 2

In this chapter, you will learn how to

- Identify the different types of DRAM packaging
- Explain the varieties of RAM
- Select and install RAM

Whenever people come up to me and start professing their computer savvy, I ask them a few questions to see how much they really know. In case you and I ever meet and you decide you want to "talk tech" with me, I'll tell you my first two questions now so you'll be ready. Both involve *random access memory (RAM)*, the working memory for the CPU.

1. "How much RAM is in your computer?"
2. "What is RAM and why is it so important that every PC has some?"

Can you answer either of these questions? Don't fret if you can't—you'll know how to answer both of them before you finish this chapter. Let's start by reviewing what you know about RAM thus far.

Cross Check

Dynamic and Random Access

You encountered DRAM back in Chapter 5, so see if you can answer these questions: What makes DRAM dynamic? What does random access mean?

The CompTIA A+ certification domains use the term *memory* to describe the short-term storage used by the PC to load the operating system and running applications. The more common term in the industry is *RAM*, for random access memory. More specifically, the primary system RAM is **dynamic random access memory (DRAM)**. For the most part, this book uses the terms RAM and DRAM.

When not in use, programs and data are held in a mass storage device such as a hard drive, USB thumb drive, optical drive, or some other device that can hold data while the computer is off. When you load a program in Windows, your PC copies the program from the mass storage device to RAM and then runs it (see Figure 6.1).

You saw in Chapter 5 that the CPU uses dynamic random access memory (DRAM) as RAM for all PCs. Just like CPUs, DRAM has gone through a number of evolutionary changes over the years, resulting in improved DRAM technologies such as SDRAM, RDRAM, and DDR RAM. This chapter starts by explaining how DRAM works, and then discusses the types of DRAM used over the past several years and how they improve on the original DRAM. The third section, "Working with RAM," goes into the details of finding and installing RAM.

Historical/Conceptual

• **Figure 6.1** Mass storage holds programs, but programs need to run in RAM.

■ Understanding DRAM

As discussed in Chapter 5, DRAM functions like an electronic spreadsheet, with numbered rows containing cells and each cell holding a one or a zero. Now let's look at what's physically happening. Each spreadsheet cell is a special type of semiconductor that can hold a single bit—one or zero—by using microscopic capacitors and transistors. DRAM makers put these semiconductors into chips that can hold a certain number of bits. The bits inside the chips are organized in a rectangular fashion, using rows and columns.

Each chip has a limit on the number of lines of code it can contain. Think of each line of code as one of the rows on the electronic spreadsheet; one chip might be able to store a million rows of code while another chip might be able to store over a billion lines. Each chip also has a limit on the width of the lines of code it can handle. One chip might handle 8-bit-wide data while another might handle 16-bit-wide data. Techs describe chips by bits rather than bytes, so they refer to *×8* and *×16*, respectively. Just as you could describe a spreadsheet by the number of rows and columns—John's accounting spreadsheet is huge, 48 rows × 12 columns—memory makers describe RAM chips the same way. An individual DRAM chip that holds 1,048,576 rows and 8 columns, for example, would be a *1M×8* chip, with "M" as shorthand for "mega," just like in megabytes (2^{20} bytes). It is difficult if not impossible to tell the size of a DRAM chip just by looking at it—only

• **Figure 6.2** What do these numbers mean?

the DRAM makers know the meaning of the tiny numbers on the chips (see Figure 6.2), although sometimes you can make a good guess.

Organizing DRAM

Because of its low cost, high speed, and capability to contain a lot of data in a relatively small package, DRAM has been the standard RAM used in all computers—not just PCs—since the mid-1970s. DRAM can be found in just about everything, from automobiles to automatic bread makers.

The PC has very specific requirements for DRAM. The original 8088 processor had an 8-bit frontside bus. Commands given to an 8088 processor were in discrete 8-bit chunks. You needed RAM that could store data in 8-bit (1-byte) chunks, so that each time the CPU asked for a line of code, the memory controller chip (MCC) could put an 8-bit chunk on the data bus.

> **✓ Cross Check**
>
> ### Riding the 8088 Bus
>
> You first saw the Intel 8088 CPU in Chapter 5, and now it pops up again. Which components inside the 8088 handle the data once the CPU gets it from RAM? How does the CPU know when the data is complete and ready to take?

This optimized the flow of data into (and out from) the CPU. Although today's DRAM chips may have widths greater than 1 bit, all DRAM chips back then were 1 bit wide, meaning only sizes such as 64 K × 1 or 256 K × 1 existed—always 1 bit wide. So how was 1-bit-wide DRAM turned into 8-bit-wide memory? The solution was quite simple: just take eight 1-bit-wide chips and use the MCC to organize them electronically to be eight wide (see Figure 6.3).

Practical DRAM

Okay, before you learn more about DRAM, I need to clarify a critical point. When you first saw the 8088's machine language in Chapter 5, all the examples in the "codebook" were exactly 1-byte commands. Figure 6.4 shows the codebook again—see how all the commands are 1 byte?

The MCC can produce byte-sized pieces out of eight bit-sized RAM chips.

The CPU requires data in byte-sized pieces.

Address Bus

CPU

MCC

External Data Bus

• **Figure 6.3** The MCC accessing data on RAM soldered onto the motherboard

Well, the reality is slightly different. Most of the 8088 machine language commands are 1 byte, but more-complex commands need 2 bytes. For example, the following command tells the CPU to move 163 bytes "up the RAM spreadsheet" and run whatever command is there. Cool, eh?

1110100110100011

The problem here is that the command is 2 bytes wide, not 1 byte. So how did the 8088 handle this? Simple—it just took the command 1 byte at a time. It took twice as long to handle the command because the MCC had to go to RAM twice, but it worked.

So if some of the commands are more than 1 byte wide, why didn't Intel make the 8088 with a 16-bit frontside bus? Wouldn't that have been better? Well, Intel did. Intel invented a CPU called the 8086. The 8086 actually predates the 8088 and was absolutely identical to the 8088 except for one small detail: it had a 16-bit frontside bus. IBM could have used the 8086 instead of the 8088 and used 2-byte-wide RAM instead of 1-byte-wide RAM. Of course, they would have needed to invent an MCC that handled that kind of RAM (see Figure 6.5).

Why did Intel sell to IBM the 8088 and not the 8086? Nobody had invented an affordable MCC or RAM that handled 2 bytes at a time. Sure, chips had been invented, but they were *expensive* and IBM didn't think anyone would want to pay $12,000 for a personal computer. So IBM bought the Intel 8088, not the Intel 8086, and all our RAM came in bytes. But as you might imagine, it didn't stay that way for long.

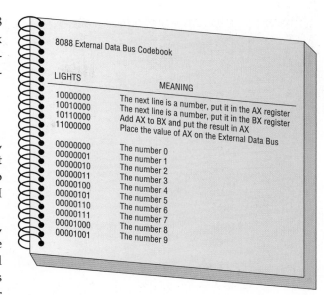

• **Figure 6.4** Codebook again

DRAM Sticks

As CPU data bus sizes increased, so too did the need for RAM wide enough to fill the bus. The Intel 80386 CPU, for example, had a 32-bit data bus and thus the need for 32-bit-wide DRAM. Imagine having to line up 32 one-bit-wide DRAM chips on a motherboard. Talk about a waste of space! Figure 6.6 shows motherboard RAM run amuck.

DRAM manufacturers responded by creating wider DRAM chips, such as ×4, ×8, and ×16, and putting multiples of them on a small circuit board called a **stick** or **module**. Figure 6.7 shows an early stick, called a **single inline memory module (SIMM)**, with eight DRAM chips. To add RAM to a modern machine, you need to get the right stick or sticks for the particular motherboard. Your motherboard manual tells you precisely what sort of module you need and how much RAM you can install.

• **Figure 6.5** Pumped-up 8086 MCC at work

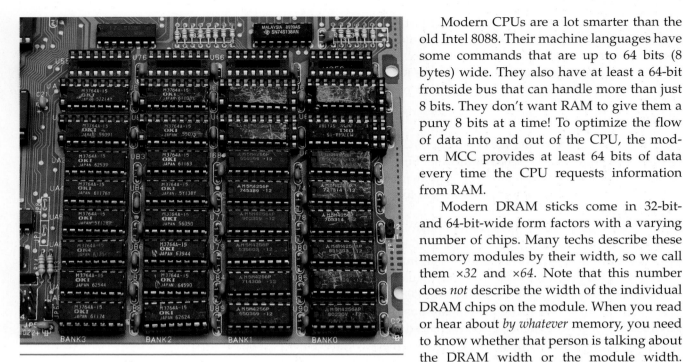

• Figure 6.6 That's a lot of real estate used by RAM chips!

• Figure 6.7 A 72-pin SIMM

 Some MCCs are 128 bits wide.

Modern CPUs are a lot smarter than the old Intel 8088. Their machine languages have some commands that are up to 64 bits (8 bytes) wide. They also have at least a 64-bit frontside bus that can handle more than just 8 bits. They don't want RAM to give them a puny 8 bits at a time! To optimize the flow of data into and out of the CPU, the modern MCC provides at least 64 bits of data every time the CPU requests information from RAM.

Modern DRAM sticks come in 32-bit- and 64-bit-wide form factors with a varying number of chips. Many techs describe these memory modules by their width, so we call them ×32 and ×64. Note that this number does *not* describe the width of the individual DRAM chips on the module. When you read or hear about *by whatever* memory, you need to know whether that person is talking about the DRAM width or the module width. When the CPU needs certain bytes of data, it requests those bytes via the address bus. The CPU does not know the physical location of the RAM that stores that data, nor the physical makeup of the RAM—such as how many DRAM chips work together to provide the 64-bit-wide memory rows. The MCC keeps track of this and just gives the CPU whichever bytes it requests (see Figure 6.8).

 Try This!

Dealing with Old RAM

Often in the PC world, old technology and ways of doing things are reimplemented with some newer technology. A tech who knows these ancient ways will have extra opportunities. Many thousands of companies—including hospitals, auto repair places, and more—use very old proprietary applications that keep track of medical records, inventory, and so on. If you're called to work on one of these ancient systems, you need to know how to work with old parts, so try this.

Obtain an old computer. Ask your uncle, cousin, or Great Aunt Edna if they have a PC collecting dust in a closet that you can use. Failing that, go to a secondhand store or market and buy one for a few dollars.

Open up the system and check out the RAM. Remove the RAM from the motherboard and then replace it to familiarize yourself with the internals. You never know when some critical system will go down and need repair immediately—and you're the one to do it!

• Figure 6.8 The MCC knows the real location of the DRAM.

Consumer RAM

If modern DRAM modules come in sizes much wider than a byte, why do people still use the word "byte" to describe how much DRAM they have? Convention. Habit. Rather than using a label that describes the electronic structure of RAM, common usage describes the *total capacity of RAM on a stick in bytes*. John has a single 2-GB stick of RAM on his motherboard, for example, and Sally has two 1-GB sticks. Both systems have a total of 2 GB of system RAM. That's what your clients care about. Having enough RAM makes their systems snappy and stable; not enough RAM means their systems run poorly. As a tech, you need to know more, of course, to pick the right RAM for many different types of computers.

801

■ Types of RAM

Development of newer, wider, and faster CPUs and MCCs motivate DRAM manufacturers to invent new DRAM technologies that deliver enough data at a single pop to optimize the flow of data into and out of the CPU.

SDRAM

Most modern systems use some form of **synchronous DRAM (SDRAM)**. SDRAM is still DRAM, but it is *synchronous*—tied to the system clock, just like the CPU and MCC, so the MCC knows when data is ready to be grabbed from SDRAM. This results in little wasted time.

SDRAM made its debut in 1996 on a stick called a **dual inline memory module (DIMM)**. The early SDRAM DIMMs came in a wide variety of pin sizes. The most common pin sizes found on desktops were the 168-pin variety. Laptop DIMMs came in 68-pin, 144-pin (see Figure 6.9), or 172-pin

• Figure 6.9 144-pin micro-DIMM (photo courtesy of Micron Technology, Inc.)

• Figure 6.10 A 168-pin DIMM above a 144-pin SO-DIMM

The 400-MHz frontside bus speed wasn't achieved by making the system clock faster—it was done by making CPUs and MCCs capable of sending 64 bits of data two or four times for every clock cycle, effectively doubling or quadrupling the system bus speed.

• Figure 6.11 RDRAM

micro-DIMM packages; and the 72-pin, 144-pin, or 200-pin **small-outline DIMM (SO-DIMM)** form factors (see Figure 6.10). With the exception of the 32-bit 72-pin SO-DIMM, all these DIMM varieties delivered 64-bit-wide data to match the 64-bit data bus of every CPU since the Pentium.

To take advantage of SDRAM, you needed a PC designed to use SDRAM. If you had a system with slots for 168-pin DIMMs, for example, your system used SDRAM. A DIMM in any one of the DIMM slots could fill the 64-bit bus, so each slot was called a **bank**. You could install one, two, or more sticks and the system would work. Note that on laptops that used the 72-pin SO-DIMM, you needed to install two sticks of RAM to make a full bank, because each stick only provided half the bus width.

SDRAM was tied to the system clock, so its clock speed matched the frontside bus. Five clock speeds were commonly used on the early SDRAM systems: 66, 75, 83, 100, and 133 MHz. The RAM speed had to match or exceed the system speed or the computer would be unstable or wouldn't work at all. These speeds were prefixed with a "PC" in the front, based on a standard forwarded by Intel, so SDRAM speeds were PC66 through PC133. For a Pentium III computer with a 100-MHz frontside bus, you needed to buy SDRAM DIMMs rated to handle it, such as PC100 or PC133.

RDRAM

When Intel was developing the Pentium 4, they knew that regular SDRAM just wasn't going to be fast enough to handle the quad-pumped 400-MHz frontside bus. Intel announced plans to replace SDRAM with a very fast, new type of RAM developed by Rambus, Inc., called **Rambus DRAM**, or simply **RDRAM** (see Figure 6.11). Hailed by Intel as the next great leap in DRAM technology, RDRAM could handle speeds up to 800 MHz, which gave Intel plenty of room to improve the Pentium 4.

RDRAM was greatly anticipated by the industry for years, but industry support for RDRAM proved less than enthusiastic due to significant delays in development and a price many times that of SDRAM. Despite this grudging support, almost all major PC makers sold systems that used RDRAM—for a while. From a tech's standpoint, RDRAM shares almost all of the characteristics of SDRAM. A stick of RDRAM is called a **RIMM**. In this case, however, the letters don't actually stand for anything; they just rhyme: SIMMs, DIMMs, and now RIMMs, get it?

RIMMs came in two sizes: a 184-pin for desktops and a 160-pin SO-RIMM for laptops. RIMMs were keyed differently from DIMMs to ensure that even though they are the same basic size, you couldn't accidentally install a RIMM in a DIMM slot or vice versa. RDRAM also had a speed rating: 600 MHz, 700 MHz, 800 MHz, or 1066 MHz. RDRAM employed an interesting **dual-channel architecture**. Each RIMM was 64 bits wide, but the Rambus MCC alternated between two sticks to increase the speed of data retrieval. You were required to install RIMMs in pairs to use this dual-channel architecture.

RDRAM motherboards also required that all RIMM slots be populated. Unused pairs of slots needed a passive device called a **continuity RIMM (CRIMM)** installed in each slot to enable the RDRAM system to terminate properly. Figure 6.12 shows a CRIMM.

• **Figure 6.12** CRIMM

RDRAM offered dramatic possibilities for high-speed PCs but ran into three roadblocks that Betamaxed it. First, the technology was owned wholly by Rambus; if you wanted to make it, you had to pay the licensing fees they charged. That led directly to the second problem, expense. RDRAM cost substantially more than SDRAM. Third, Rambus and Intel made a completely closed deal for the technology. RDRAM worked only on Pentium 4 systems using Intel-made MCCs. AMD was out of luck. Clearly, the rest of the industry had to look for another high-speed RAM solution.

 On the CompTIA A+ 220-801 exam, you'll see RDRAM referred to as RAMBUS RAM. Don't get thrown by the odd usage.

DDR SDRAM

AMD and many major system and memory makers threw their support behind **double data rate SDRAM (DDR SDRAM)**. DDR SDRAM basically copied Rambus, doubling the throughput of SDRAM by making two processes for every clock cycle. This synchronized (pardon the pun) nicely with the Athlon and later AMD processors' double-pumped frontside bus. DDR SDRAM could not run as fast as RDRAM—although relatively low frontside bus speeds made that a moot point—but cost only slightly more than regular SDRAM.

"Betamaxed" is slang for "made it obsolete because no one bought it, even though it was a superior technology to the winner in the marketplace." It refers to the VHS versus Betamax wars in the old days of video cassette recorders.

DDR SDRAM for desktops comes in 184-pin DIMMs. These DIMMs match 168-pin DIMMs in physical size but not in pin compatibility (see Figure 6.13). The slots for the two types of RAM appear similar as well but have different guide notches, so you can't insert either type of RAM into the other's slot. DDR SDRAM for laptops comes in either 200-pin SO-DIMMs or 172-pin micro-DIMMs (see Figure 6.14).

• **Figure 6.13** DDR SDRAM

DDR sticks use a rather interesting naming convention—actually started by the Rambus folks—based on the number of bytes per second of data throughput the RAM can handle. To determine the bytes per second, take the MHz speed and multiply by 8 bytes (the width of all DDR SDRAM sticks). So 400 MHz multiplied by 8 is 3200 megabytes per second (MBps). Put the abbreviation "PC" in the front to make the new term: PC3200. Many techs also use the naming convention used for the individual DDR chips; for example, *DDR400* refers to a 400-MHz DDR SDRAM chip running on a 200-MHz clock.

Even though the term DDR*xxx* is really just for individual DDR chips and the term

• **Figure 6.14** 172-pin DDR SDRAM micro-DIMM (photo courtesy of Kingston/ Joint Harvest)

RAM makers use the term *single data rate SDRAM* (*SDR SDRAM*) for the original SDRAM to differentiate it from DDR SDRAM.

PC*xxxx* is for DDR sticks, this tradition of two names for every speed of RAM is a bit of a challenge because you'll often hear both terms used interchangeably. Table 6.1 shows all the speeds for DDR—not all of these are commonly used.

Table 6.1	DDR Speeds	
Clock Speed	**DDR Speed Rating**	**PC Speed Rating**
100 MHz	DDR200	PC1600
133 MHz	DDR266	PC2100
166 MHz	DDR333	PC2700
200 MHz	DDR400	PC3200
217 MHz	DDR433	PC3500
233 MHz	DDR466	PC3700
250 MHz	DDR500	PC4000
275 MHz	DDR550	PC4400
300 MHz	DDR600	PC4800

Following the lead of AMD, VIA, and other manufacturers, the PC industry adopted DDR SDRAM as the standard system RAM. In the summer of 2003, Intel relented and stopped producing motherboards and memory controllers that required RDRAM.

One thing is sure about PC technologies: any good idea that can be copied will be copied. One of Rambus' best concepts was the dual-channel architecture—using two sticks of RDRAM together to increase throughput. Manufacturers have released motherboards with MCCs that support dual-channel architecture using DDR SDRAM. Dual-channel DDR motherboards use regular DDR sticks, although manufacturers often sell RAM in matched pairs, branding them as dual-channel RAM.

Dual-channel DDR works like RDRAM in that you must have two identical sticks of DDR and they must snap into two paired slots. Unlike RDRAM, dual-channel DDR doesn't have anything like CRIMMs—you

Try This!

DRAM Availability

The DRAM market changes fairly rapidly at the higher end, but products tend to linger at the low end, seemingly well past their usefulness. What do your class systems need? What's available in your area today? Try this.

Check out the RAM requirements for the PCs available in your class (or home or office). You can open them up for physical examination or read the motherboard books. Then go to your friendly neighborhood computer store and see what's available. Does the store offer memory that your system cannot use, such as EDO DRAM on 72-pin SIMMs or registered DDR SDRAM? What does this tell you about the PCs available to you?

don't need to put anything into unused slot pairs. Dual-channel DDR technology is very flexible, but it also has a few quirks that vary with each system. Some motherboards have three DDR SDRAM slots, but the dual-channel DDR works only if you install DDR SDRAM in two of the slots. Other boards have four slots and require that you install matching pairs in the same-colored slots to run in dual-channel mode (see Figure 6.15). If you populate a third slot, the system uses the full capacity of RAM installed, but turns off the dual-channel feature.

DDR2

The fastest versions of DDR RAM run at a blistering PC4800. That's 4.8 gigabytes per second (GBps) of data throughput! You'd think that kind of speed would satisfy most users, and to be honest, DRAM running at approximately 5 GBps really is plenty fast—for yesterday. However, the ongoing speed increases ensure that even these speeds won't be good enough in the future. Knowing this, the RAM industry came out with DDR2, the successor to DDR. *DDR2* is DDR RAM with some improvements in its electrical characteristics, enabling it to run even faster than DDR while using less power. The big speed increase from DDR2 comes by clock doubling the input/output circuits on the chips. This does not speed up the core RAM—the part that holds the data—but speeding up the input/output and adding special buffers (sort of like a cache) makes DDR2 run much faster than regular DDR. DDR2 uses a 240-pin DIMM that's not compatible with DDR (see Figure 6.16). Likewise, the DDR2 200-pin SO-DIMM is incompatible with the DDR SO-DIMM. You'll find motherboards running both single-channel and dual-channel DDR2.

Table 6.2 shows some of the common DDR2 speeds.

• **Figure 6.15** A motherboard showing four RAM slots. By populating the same-colored slots with identical RAM, you can run in dual-channel mode.

• **Figure 6.16** 240-pin DDR2 DIMM

DDR2 RAM sticks will not fit into DDR sockets, nor are they electronically compatible.

Table 6.2	DDR2 Speeds		
Core RAM Clock Speed	DDR I/O Speed	DDR2 Speed Rating	PC Speed Rating
100 MHz	200 MHz	DDR2-400	PC2-3200
133 MHz	266 MHz	DDR2-533	PC2-4200
166 MHz	333 MHz	DDR2-667	PC2-5300
200 MHz	400 MHz	DDR2-800	PC2-6400
250 MHz	500 MHz	DDR2-1000	PC2-8000

DDR3

DDR3 boasts higher speeds, more efficient architecture, and around 30 percent lower power consumption than DDR2 RAM, making it a compelling choice for system builders. Just like its predecessor, DDR3 uses a 240-pin DIMM, albeit one that is slotted differently to make it difficult for users to install the wrong RAM in their system without using a hammer (see Figure 6.17). DDR3 SO-DIMMs for portable computers have 204 pins. Neither fits into a DDR2 socket.

DDR3 doubles the buffer of DDR2 from 4 bits to 8 bits, giving it a huge boost in bandwidth over older RAM. Not only that, but some DDR3 modules also include a feature called *XMP*, or *extended memory profile*, that enables power users to overclock their RAM easily, boosting their already fast memory to speeds that would make Chuck Yeager nervous. DDR3 modules also use higher-density memory chips, which means we may eventually see 16-GB DDR3 modules.

• **Figure 6.17** DDR2 DIMM on top of a DDR3 DIMM

Some chipsets that support DDR3 also support a feature called *triple-channel memory*, which works a lot like dual-channel before it, but with three sticks of RAM instead of two. Intel's LGA 1366 platform supports triple-channel memory; no AMD processors support a triple-channel feature. You'll need three of the same type of memory modules and a motherboard that supports it, but triple-channel memory can greatly increase performance for those who can afford it.

In keeping with established tradition, Table 6.3 is a chart of common DDR3 speeds. Note how DDR3 I/O speeds are quadruple the clock speeds, whereas DDR2 I/O speeds are only double the clock. This speed increase is due to the increased buffer size, which enables DDR3 to grab twice as much data every clock cycle as DDR2 can.

> Do not confuse DDR3 with GDDR3; the latter is a type of memory used solely in video cards. See Chapter 13 for the scoop on video-specific types of memory.

> Quad-channel memory also exists, but as of 2012, you'll only find it in servers.

Table 6.3	DDR3 Speeds		
Core RAM Clock Speed	**DDR I/O Speed**	**DDR3 Speed Rating**	**PC Speed Rating**
100 MHz	400 MHz	DDR3-800	PC3-6400
133 MHz	533 MHz	DDR3-1066	PC3-8500
166 MHz	667 MHz	DDR3-1333	PC3-10667
200 MHz	800 MHz	DDR3-1600	PC3-12800
233 MHz	933 MHz	DDR3-1866	PC3-14900
266 MHz	1066 MHz	DDR3-2133	PC3-17000

RAM Variations

Within each class of RAM, you'll find variations in packaging, speed, quality, and the capability to handle data with more or fewer errors. Higher-end systems often need higher-end RAM, so knowing these variations is of crucial importance to techs.

Double-Sided DIMMs

Every type of RAM stick, starting with the old FPM SIMMs and continuing through to 240-pin DDR3 SDRAM, comes in one of two types: **single-sided RAM** and **double-sided RAM**. As their name implies, single-sided sticks have chips on only one side of the stick. Double-sided sticks have chips on both sides (see Figure 6.18). The vast majority of RAM sticks are single-sided, but plenty of double-sided sticks are out there. Double-sided sticks are basically two sticks of RAM soldered onto one board. There's nothing wrong with double-sided RAM sticks other than the fact that some motherboards either can't use them or can only use them in certain ways—for example, only if you use a single stick and it goes into a certain slot.

• **Figure 6.18** Double-sided DDR SDRAM

Latency

If you've shopped for RAM lately, you may have noticed terms such as "CL2" or "low latency" as you tried to determine which RAM to purchase. You might find two otherwise identical RAM sticks with a 20 percent price difference and a salesperson pressuring you to buy the more expensive one because it's "faster" even though both sticks say DDR3200 (see Figure 6.19).

RAM responds to electrical signals at varying rates. When the memory controller starts to grab a line of memory, for example, a slight delay occurs; think of it as the RAM getting off the couch. After the RAM sends out the requested line of memory, there's another slight delay before the memory controller can ask for another line—the RAM sat back down. The delay in RAM's response time is called its **latency**. RAM with a lower latency—such

> ### Tech Tip
>
> **Latency Is Relative**
> *Latency numbers reflect how many clicks of the system clock it takes before the RAM responds. If you speed up the system clock, say from 166 MHz to 200 MHz, the same stick of RAM might take an extra click before it can respond. When you take RAM out of an older system and put it into a newer one, you might get a seemingly dead PC, even though the RAM fits in the DIMM slot. Many motherboards enable you to adjust the RAM timings manually. If yours does so, try raising the latency to give the slower RAM time to respond. See Chapter 7 to learn how to make these adjustments (and how to recover if you make a mistake).*

• **Figure 6.19** Why is one more expensive than the other?

as CL2—is faster than RAM with a higher latency—such as CL3—because it responds more quickly. The CL refers to clock cycle delays. The 2 means that the memory delays two clock cycles before delivering the requested data; the 3 means a three-cycle delay.

From a tech's standpoint, you need to get the proper RAM for the system you're working on. If you put a high-latency stick in a motherboard set up for a low-latency stick, you'll get an unstable or completely dead PC. Check the motherboard manual and get the quickest RAM the motherboard can handle, and you should be fine.

Parity and ECC

Given the high speeds and phenomenal amount of data moved by the typical DRAM chip, a RAM chip might occasionally give bad data to the memory controller. This doesn't necessarily mean that the RAM has gone bad. It could be a hiccup caused by some unknown event that makes a good DRAM chip say a bit is a zero when it's really a one. In most cases you won't even notice when such a rare event happens. In some environments, however, even these rare events are intolerable. A bank server handling thousands of online transactions per second, for example, can't risk even the smallest error. These important computers need a more robust, fault-resistant RAM.

The first type of error-detecting RAM was known as parity RAM (see Figure 6.20). **Parity RAM** stored an extra bit of data (called the parity bit) that the MCC used to verify whether the data was correct. Parity wasn't perfect. It wouldn't always detect an error, and if the MCC did find an error, it couldn't correct the error. For years, parity was the only available way to tell if the RAM made a mistake.

Today's PCs that need to watch for RAM errors use a special type of RAM called **error correction code RAM (ECC RAM)**. ECC is a major advance in error checking on DRAM. First, ECC detects any time a single bit is incorrect. Second, ECC fixes these errors on-the-fly. The checking and fixing come at a price, however, as ECC RAM is always slower than non-ECC RAM.

ECC DRAM comes in every DIMM package type and can lead to some odd-sounding numbers. You can find DDR2 or DDR3 RAM sticks, for example, that come in 240-pin, 72-bit versions. Similarly, you'll see 200-pin, 72-bit SO-DIMM format. The extra 8 bits beyond the 64-bit data stream are for the ECC.

You might be tempted to say "Gee, maybe I want to try this ECC RAM." Well, don't! To take advantage of ECC RAM, you need a motherboard with an MCC designed to use ECC. Only expensive motherboards for high-end systems use ECC. The special-use-only nature of ECC makes it fairly rare. Plenty of techs with years of experience have never even seen ECC RAM.

• **Figure 6.20** Ancient parity RAM stick

■ Working with RAM

Whenever someone comes up to me and asks what single hardware upgrade they can do to improve their system performance, I always tell them the same thing—add more RAM. Adding more RAM can improve overall system performance, processing speed, and stability—if you get it right. Botching the job can cause dramatic system instability, such as frequent, random crashes and reboots. Every tech needs to know how to install and upgrade system RAM of all types.

To get the desired results from a RAM upgrade, you must first determine if insufficient RAM is the cause of system problems. Second, you need to pick the proper RAM for the system. Finally, you must use good installation practices. Always store RAM sticks in anti-static packaging whenever they're not in use, and use strict ESD handling procedures. Like many other pieces of the PC, RAM is *very* sensitive to ESD and other technician abuse (see Figure 6.21).

● **Figure 6.21** Don't do this! Grabbing the contacts is a bad idea!

Do You Need More RAM?

Two symptoms point to the need for more RAM in a PC: general system sluggishness and excessive hard drive accessing. If programs take forever to load and running programs seem to stall and move more slowly than you would like, the problem could stem from insufficient RAM. A friend with a Windows Vista system complained that her PC seemed snappy when she first got it but now takes a long time to do the things she wants to do with it, such as photograph retouching in Adobe Photoshop and document layout for an online magazine she produces. Her system had only 1 GB of RAM, sufficient to run Windows Vista, but woefully insufficient for her tasks—she kept maxing out the RAM and thus the system slowed to a crawl. I replaced her stick with a pair of 2-GB sticks and suddenly she had the powerhouse workstation she desired.

Excessive hard drive activity when you move between programs points to a need for more RAM. Every Windows PC has the capability to make a portion of your hard drive look like RAM in case you run out of real RAM.

The default and recommended page-file size is 1.5 times the amount of installed RAM on your computer.

Page File

Windows uses a portion of the hard drive as an extension of system RAM, through what's called a *RAM cache*. A RAM cache is a block of cylinders on a hard drive set aside as what's called a **page file**, **swap file**, or *virtual memory*. When the PC starts running out of real RAM because you've loaded too many programs, the system swaps programs from RAM to the page file, opening more space for programs currently active. All versions of Windows use a page file, so here's how one works.

Let's assume you have a PC with 4 GB of RAM. Figure 6.22 shows the system RAM as a thermometer

● **Figure 6.22** A RAM thermometer showing that more programs take more RAM

• **Figure 6.23** Not enough RAM to load program D

Virtual memory is a fully automated process and does not require any user intervention. Tech intervention is another story!

• **Figure 6.24** Program B being unloaded from memory

• **Figure 6.25** Program B stored in the page file, making room for Program D

with gradients from 0 to 4 GB. As programs load, they take up RAM, and as more and more programs are loaded (labeled A, B, and C in the figure), more RAM is used.

At a certain point, you won't have enough RAM to run any more programs (see Figure 6.23). Sure, you could close one or more programs to make room for yet another one, but you can't keep all of the programs running simultaneously. This is where virtual memory comes into play.

Windows' virtual memory starts by creating a page file that resides somewhere on your hard drive. The page file works like a temporary storage box. Windows removes running programs temporarily from RAM into the page file so other programs can load and run. If you have enough RAM to run all your programs, Windows does not need to use the page file—Windows brings the page file into play only when insufficient RAM is available to run all open programs.

To load, Program D needs a certain amount of free RAM. Clearly, this requires unloading some other program (or programs) from RAM without actually closing any programs. Windows looks at all running programs—in this case A, B, and C—and decides which program is the least used. That program is then cut out of or swapped from RAM and copied into the page file. In this case, Windows has chosen Program B (see Figure 6.24). Unloading Program B from RAM provides enough RAM to load Program D (see Figure 6.25).

It is important to understand that none of this activity is visible on the screen. Program B's window is still visible, along with those of all the other running programs. Nothing tells the user that Program B is no longer in RAM (see Figure 6.26).

So what happens if you click on Program B's window to bring it to the front? The program can't actually

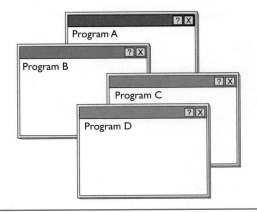

• **Figure 6.26** You can't tell whether a program is swapped or not.

run from the page file; it must be loaded back into RAM. First, Windows decides which program must be removed from RAM, and this time Windows chooses Program C (see Figure 6.27). Then it loads Program B into RAM (see Figure 6.28).

Swapping programs to and from the page file and RAM takes time. Although no visual clues suggest that a swap is taking place, the machine slows down quite noticeably as Windows performs the swaps. Page files are a crucial aspect of Windows operation.

Windows handles page files automatically, but occasionally you'll run into problems and need to change the size of the page file or delete it and let Windows re-create it automatically. The page file is pagefile.sys. You can often find it in the root directory of the C: drive, but again, that can be changed. Wherever it is, the page file is a hidden system file, which means in practice that you'll have to play with your folder-viewing options to see it.

If Windows needs to access the page file too frequently, you will notice the hard drive access LED going crazy as Windows rushes to move programs between RAM and the page file in a process called **disk thrashing**. Windows uses the page file all the time, but excessive disk thrashing suggests that you need more RAM.

You can diagnose excessive disk thrashing through simply observing the hard drive access LED flashing or through various third-party tools. I like FreeMeter (www.tiler.com/freemeter/). It's been around for quite a while, runs on all versions of Windows, and is easy to use (see Figure 6.29). Notice on the FreeMeter screenshot that some amount of the page file is being used. That's perfectly normal.

System RAM Recommendations

Microsoft sets very low the minimum RAM requirements listed for the various Windows operating systems to get the maximum number of users to upgrade or convert, and that's fine. A Windows XP Professional machine runs well enough on 128 MB of RAM. Just don't ask it to do any serious computing, such as running Crysis 2! Windows Vista and Windows 7 raised the bar considerably, especially with the 64-bit versions of the operating system. Table 6.4 lists my recommendations for system RAM.

If you have a second hard drive installed in your PC, you can often get a nice performance boost by moving your page file from the C: drive (the default) to the second drive. To move your page file in all versions of Windows, open the System Control Panel applet and select the Advanced tab in Windows XP or Advanced system settings menu in Windows Vista/7. This opens the System Properties dialog box. In the Performance section of the Advanced tab, click the Settings button to open the Performance Options dialog box. Select the Advanced tab, and then click the Change button in the Virtual memory section. In the Virtual Memory dialog box, select a drive from the list and give it a size or range, and you're ready to go.

Just don't turn virtual memory off completely. Although Windows can run without virtual memory, you will definitely take a performance hit.

• **Figure 6.27** Program C is swapped to the page file.

• **Figure 6.28** Program B is swapped back into RAM.

Table 6.4	Windows RAM Recommendations			
Operating System	Minimum System Requirements	Reasonable Minimum	Solid Performance	Power User
Windows XP	64 MB	256 MB	1 GB	2 GB
Windows Vista	1 GB (32-bit), 2 GB (64-bit)	2 GB	4 GB	8 GB
Windows 7	1 GB (32-bit), 2 GB (64-bit)	2 GB	4 GB	8 GB

• **Figure 6.29** FreeMeter

Determining Current RAM Capacity

Before you go get RAM, you obviously need to know how much RAM you currently have in your PC. Windows displays this amount in the System Control Panel applet (see Figure 6.30). You can also access the screen with the WINDOWS-PAUSE/BREAK keystroke combination.

Windows also includes the handy Performance tab in the Task Manager (as shown in Figure 6.31). The Performance tab includes a lot of information about the amount of RAM being used by your PC. Access the Task Manager by pressing CTRL-SHIFT-ESC and selecting the Performance tab.

ReadyBoost

Windows Vista and Windows 7 offer a feature called **ReadyBoost** that enables you to use flash media devices—removable USB thumb drives or memory cards—as super fast, dedicated virtual memory. The performance gain over using only a typical hard drive for virtual memory can

 Try This!

Checking the Page File

How much of your hard drive does Windows use for a page file? Does the level change dramatically when you open typical applications, such as Microsoft Word, Solitaire, and Paint Shop Pro? The answers to these questions can give a tech a quick estimation about RAM usage and possible RAM needs for a particular system, so try this.

In Windows XP, you can easily glance at your page file usage through the Task Manager. To access the Task Manager, press CTRL-ALT-DEL simultaneously once. Click the Performance tab. The second box on the left, titled PF Usage, displays the amount of hard drive the page file is currently using. In Windows Vista and Windows 7, the process of viewing the page file is exactly the same, but they use a less descriptive way of displaying its usage. In the bottom-right corner of the Performance tab, you'll see the title "Page File," which gives you a numeric representation.

1. How big is the page file when you have no applications open?

2. How much does it change when you open applications?

• **Figure 6.30** Mike has a lot of RAM!

be significant with ReadyBoost because read/write speeds on flash memory blow hard drive read/write speeds away. Plus, the added ReadyBoost device or devices means Windows has multiple sources of virtual memory that it can use at the same time.

Windows 7 can handle up to eight flash devices, whereas Windows Vista can benefit from only one device. Devices can be between 1–32 GB in capacity. The flash device's file system matters in terms of how much memory Windows can use. Typically, the most you'll get out of a flash drive is 4 GB without manually changing the file system. Finally, Microsoft recommends using 1–3× the amount of system RAM for the ReadyBoost drives or devices to get optimal performance.

Plug a ReadyBoost-approved device into a USB port or built-in flash memory card reader slot. Right-click the device in Computer and select Properties. Click the ReadyBoost tab and select the radio button next to either *Dedicate this device to ReadyBoost* or *Use this device* (see Figure 6.32). Click Apply to enhance your system's performance.

• **Figure 6.31** Performance tab in Windows 7 Task Manager

Getting the Right RAM

To do the perfect RAM upgrade, determine the optimum capacity of RAM to install and then get the right RAM for the motherboard. Your first two

• **Figure 6.32** Dedicating a flash drive to ReadyBoost to enhance system performance

stops toward these goals are the inside of the case and your motherboard manual. Open the case to see how many sticks of RAM you have installed currently and how many free slots you have open.

Check the motherboard book to determine the total capacity of RAM the system can handle and what specific technology works with your system.

You can't put DDR2 into a system that can only handle DDR SDRAM, after all, and it won't do you much good to install a pair of 2-GB DIMMs when your system tops out at 1.5 GB. Figure 6.33 shows the RAM limits for my ASUS Crosshair motherboard.

Mix and Match at Your Peril

All motherboards can handle different capacities of RAM. If you have three slots, you may put a 512-MB stick in one and a 1-GB stick in the other with a high chance of success. To ensure maximum stability in a system, however, shoot for as close as you can get to uniformity of RAM. Choose RAM sticks that match in technology, capacity, and speed.

Mixing Speeds

With so many different DRAM speeds available, you may often find yourself tempted to mix speeds of DRAM in the same system. Although

Tech Tip

CPU-Z

The freeware CPU-Z program tells you the total number of slots on your motherboard, the number of slots used, and the exact type of RAM in each slot—very handy. CPU-Z not only determines the latency of your RAM but also lists the latency at a variety of motherboard speeds. The media accompanying this book has a copy of CPU-Z, so check it out.

you may get away with mixing speeds on a system, the safest, easiest rule to follow is to use the speed of DRAM specified in the motherboard book, and make sure that every piece of DRAM runs at that speed. In a worst-case scenario, mixing DRAM speeds can cause the system to lock up every few seconds or every few minutes. You might also get some data corruption. Mixing speeds sometimes works fine, but don't do your tax return on a machine with mixed DRAM speeds until the system has proven to be stable for a few days. The important thing to note here is that you won't break anything, other than possibly data, by experimenting.

Okay, I have mentioned enough disclaimers. Modern motherboards provide some flexibility regarding RAM speeds and mixing. First, you can use RAM that is faster than the motherboard specifies. For example, if the system needs PC3200 DDR2 SDRAM, you may put in PC4200 DDR2 SDRAM and it should work fine. Faster DRAM is not going to make the system run any faster, however, so don't look for any system improvement.

Second, you can sometimes get away with putting one speed of DRAM in one bank and another speed in another bank, as long as all the speeds are as fast as or faster than the speed specified by the motherboard. Don't bother trying to put different-speed DRAM sticks in the same bank with a motherboard that uses dual-channel DDR.

Crosshair specifications summary

CPU	Support AMD® Socket AM2 Athlon 64 X2 / Athlon 64 FX / Athlon 64/ Sempron AMD Cool 'n' Quiet™ Technology AMD64 architecture enables simultaneous 32-bit and 64-bit computing AMD Live!™ Ready
Chipset	NVIDIA nForce® 590 SLI™ MCP NVIDIA LinkBoost™ Technology
System bus	2000 / 1600 MT/s
Memory	Dual channel memory architecture 4 x DIMM, max. 8GB, DDR2-800/667/533, ECC and non-ECC, un-buffered memory
Expansion slots	2 x PCI Express x16 slot with NVIDIA® SLI™ technology support, at full x16, x16 speed 1 x PCI Express x4 3 x PCI 2.2
Scalable Link Interface (SLI™)	Support two identical NVIDIA SLI-Ready graphics cards (both at x16 mode) ASUS two-slot thermal design ASUS PEG Link
High Definition Audio	SupremeFX Audio Card featuring ADI 1988B 8-channel High Definition Audio CODEC Support Jack-Sensing, Enumeration, Multi-streaming and Jack-Retasking 8 channel audio ports Coaxial, Optical S/PDIF out on back I/O port * ASUS Array Mic * Noise Filter
Storage	NVIDIA nForce® 590 SLI™ MCP supports: * 1 x Ultra DMA 133 / 100 / 66 / 33 * 6 x Serial ATA 3.0Gb/s with NCQ * NVIDIA MediaShield™ RAID supports RAID 0, 1, 0+1, 5 and JBOD span cross Serial ATA drives Silicon Image® 3132 SATA controller supports: * 2 x External Serial ATA 3.0Gb/s port on back I/O (SATA On-the-Go) * Support RAID 0, 1, JBOD, RAID 0+1(10) and 5 through multiplier

(continued on the next page)

xi

• **Figure 6.33** The motherboard book shows how much RAM the motherboard will handle.

Installing DIMMs and RIMMs

Installing DRAM is so easy that it's one of the very few jobs I recommend to non-techie folks. First, attach an anti-static wrist strap or touch some bare metal on the power supply to ground yourself and avoid ESD. Then swing the side tabs on the RAM slots down from the upright position. Pick up a stick of RAM—don't touch those contacts—and line up the notch or notches with the raised portion(s) of the DIMM socket (see Figure 6.34). A good hard push down is usually all you need to ensure a solid connection. Make sure that the DIMM snaps into position to show it is completely seated. Also, notice that the two side tabs move in to reflect a tight connection.

Serial Presence Detect (SPD)

Your motherboard should detect and automatically set up any DIMM or RIMM you install, assuming you have the right RAM for the system, using a technology called **serial presence detect (SPD)**. RAM makers add a handy

● **Figure 6.34** Inserting a DIMM

chip to modern sticks called the SPD chip (see Figure 6.35). The SPD chip stores all the information about your DRAM, including size, speed, ECC or non-ECC, registered or unregistered, and a number of other more technical bits of information.

When a PC boots, it queries the SPD chip so that the MCC knows how much RAM is on the stick, how fast it runs, and other information. Any program can query the SPD chip. Take a look at Figure 6.36 with the results of the popular CPU-Z program showing RAM information from the SPD chip.

All new systems count on SPD to set the RAM timings properly for your system when it boots. If you add a RAM stick with a bad SPD chip, you'll get a POST error message and the system will not boot. You can't fix a broken SPD chip; you just buy a new stick of RAM.

The RAM Count

After installing the new RAM, turn on the PC and watch the boot process closely. If you installed the RAM correctly, the RAM count on the PC

● **Figure 6.35** SPD chip on a stick

reflects the new value (compare Figures 6.37 and 6.38). If the RAM value stays the same, you probably have installed the RAM in a slot the motherboard doesn't want you to use (for example, you may need to use a particular slot first) or have not installed the RAM properly. If the computer does not boot and you've got a blank screen, you probably have not installed all the RAM sticks correctly. Usually, a good second look is all you need to determine the problem. Reseat or reinstall the RAM stick and try again. RAM counts are confusing because RAM uses megabytes and gigabytes as opposed to millions and billions. Here are some examples of how different systems would show 256 MB of RAM:

268435456 (exactly 256 × 1 MB)

256M (some PCs try to make it easy for you)

262,144 (number of KB)

You should know how much RAM you're trying to install and use some common sense. If you have 512 MB and you add another 512-MB stick, you should end up with a gigabyte of RAM. If you still see a RAM count of 524582912 after you add the second stick, something went wrong!

• **Figure 6.36** CPU-Z showing RAM information

Installing SO-DIMMs in Laptops

It wasn't that long ago that adding RAM to a laptop was either impossible or required you to send the system back to the manufacturer. For years, every laptop maker had custom-made, proprietary RAM packages that were difficult to handle and staggeringly expensive. The wide acceptance of SO-DIMMs over the past few years has virtually erased these problems. All laptops now provide relatively convenient access to their SO-DIMMs, enabling easy replacement or addition of RAM.

Access to RAM usually requires removing a panel or lifting up the keyboard—the procedure varies among laptop manufacturers. Figure 6.39 shows a typical laptop RAM access panel. You can slide the panel off to reveal the SO-DIMMs. SO-DIMMs usually insert exactly like the old SIMMs;

```
Award Modular BIOS v6.00PG, An Energy Star Ally
Copyright (C) 1984-2005, Award Software, Inc.

GA-K8NP F13

Processor : AMD Athlon(tm) 64 Processor 3200+
<CPUID:0000F4A Patch ID:003A>
Memory Testing : 1048576K OK
CPU clock frequency : 200 Mhz

Detecting IDE drives ...
```

• **Figure 6.37** Hey, where's the rest of my RAM?!

```
Award Modular BIOS v6.00PG, An Energy Star Ally
Copyright (C) 1984-2005, Award Software, Inc.

GA-K8NP F13

Processor : AMD Athlon(tm) 64 Processor 3200+
<CPUID:0000F4A Patch ID:003A>
Memory Testing : 3145728K OK
CPU clock frequency : 200 Mhz

Detecting IDE drives ...
```

• **Figure 6.38** RAM count after proper insertion of DIMMs

slide the pins into position and snap the SO-DIMM down into the retaining clips (see Figure 6.40).

Before doing any work on a laptop, turn the system off, disconnect it from the AC wall socket, and remove all batteries. Use an anti-static wrist strap because laptops are far more susceptible to ESD than desktop PCs.

• **Figure 6.39** A RAM access panel on a laptop

• **Figure 6.40** Snapping in a SO-DIMM

Chapter 6 Review

■ Chapter Summary

After reading this chapter and completing the exercises, you should understand the following about RAM.

Identify the different types of DRAM packaging

- The sticks of RAM snapped into your motherboard are DRAM. Think of DRAM as a spreadsheet in which each cell holds a one or a zero. Each cell represents a single bit. The number of columns and rows is finite.

- If a chip contains 1,048,576 rows and 8 columns, it can be described as a 1M×8 chip. A chip containing 2,097,152 rows and 16 columns can be described as a 2M×16 chip.

- DRAM needs to be able to fill the data bus. A 1M×8 DRAM chip is only 8 bits wide and would provide the CPU with only 8 bits of data. You would need eight of the 1M×8 chips to fill a 64-bit data bus.

- DRAM chips are soldered to a circuit board called a stick or module, and when these chips are combined, a single stick can fill the data bus. Modern DRAM sticks come in 32-bit- and 64-bit-wide varieties.

Explain the varieties of RAM

- Synchronous dynamic random access memory, or SDRAM, is tied to the system clock. The CPU, memory controller, and RAM all work in tandem with the clock pulse. This results in little wasted time when the CPU requests data from RAM.

- SDRAM comes in sticks called dual inline memory modules (DIMMs). SDRAM DIMMs come in a variety of pin sizes, with 168 pins being the most common for desktop systems. DIMMs are 64 bits wide so that they match the 64-bit data bus of modern CPUs. DIMMs snap into slots on the motherboard. Each DIMM is 64 bits, so snapping in a single DIMM fills the data bus; therefore, each slot is called a *bank*.

- SDRAM is advertised by capacity and speed. The capacity is measured in megabytes or gigabytes. The speed is measured in MHz (the DDR speed rating) or MBps (the PC-speed rating).

- RAM speed must match or exceed that of the system. For example, DDR-400 runs at 200 MHz (the double data rate speeds it up to DDR-400 instead of DDR-200), so the motherboard must run at 200 MHz, too.

- Rambus DRAM (RDRAM) was created by Rambus, Inc., and came in sticks called RIMMs. Due to cost, licensing issues, and compatibility, RDRAM is now obsolete.

- RIMMs were 64 bits wide and came in speeds of 600 MHz, 700 MHz, 800 MHz, and 1066 MHz. Differences in the notches prevented you from snapping a RIMM into a motherboard DIMM slot or vice versa.

- The RIMM memory controller uses a dual-channel architecture: it alternates between two banks to increase the speed of data retrieval. You need to install RIMMs in pairs to accommodate this feature.

- All RIMM slots on the motherboard must be filled with either a RIMM or a CRIMM. A CRIMM, or continuity RIMM, is simply a stick with no memory chips on it.

- Double data rate SDRAM (DDR RAM) is faster than regular SDRAM because it doubles the throughput. Desktop PCs use 184-pin DDR DIMMs, whereas laptops use either 200-pin small-outline DIMMs (SO-DIMM) or 172-pin micro-DIMMs. DDR RAM modules have notches that differ from both regular SDRAM and RDRAM, so DDR RAM only snaps into DDR slots on a motherboard.

- DDR RAM is advertised in one of two ways. One way is with "DDR" followed by the speed; for example, DDR400 for a stick of RAM runs at 400 MHz. Because DDR RAM runs at twice the clock speed, DDR400 is meant for a 200-MHz frontside bus. DDR RAM is also advertised by "PC" followed by the throughput; for example, PC3200. The number is determined by multiplying the speed by eight (as all DDR sticks are 64 bits, or 8 bytes, wide). Thus, DDR400 has a throughput of 3200 bytes per second (400 MHz × 8 bytes). DDR400 and PC3200 are equivalent.

- Dual-channel DDR improves upon DDR by using the DIMMs in pairs, much like RDRAM. For systems to use dual-channel DDR, the motherboard and memory controller must support dual-channel DDR RAM, and the DDR DIMMs must be identical. Dual-channel DDR does not require dummy modules such as CRIMMs.

- DDR2 is an improvement of DDR. DDR2 runs faster than DDR and uses a 240-pin form factor that is not compatible with DDR. You need a motherboard with DDR2 slots to use DDR2 RAM. DDR2 is rated by speed or throughput. Thus DDR2-400 is the same as PC2-3200 and is meant for a 200-MHz frontside bus.

- DDR3 boasts higher speeds, more efficient architecture, and around 30 percent lower power consumption than DDR2 RAM. DDR3 doubles the buffer of DDR2 from 4 bits to 8 bits, giving it a huge boost in bandwidth over older RAM. Some chipsets that support DDR3 also support triple-channel memory, which works a lot like dual-channel but with three sticks of RAM instead of two.

- RAM modules are either single-sided or double-sided. Single-sided sticks have chips on only one side, whereas double-sided sticks have chips on both sides. Most RAM is single-sided.

- Latency refers to the time lag between when the memory controller starts to fetch data from RAM and when RAM actually sends out the requested data. Another lag occurs when the memory controller asks for the next line from RAM. The shorter this lag time, the faster the system. CL2 indicates a shorter lag time, or lower latency, than CL3, so CL2 is faster. Check your motherboard documentation and get the lowest-latency RAM your system will support.

- Error correction code (ECC) RAM improved upon parity RAM by being able to fix single-bit errors on-the-fly. ECC RAM is always slower than non-ECC RAM due to the overhead of the correcting code. Only high-end motherboards and memory controllers can use ECC RAM.

Select and install RAM

- Windows uses a portion of the hard drive as an extension of system RAM, through what's called a *RAM cache*. A RAM cache is a block of cylinders on a hard drive set aside for what's called a page file, swap file, or virtual memory.

- Disk thrashing is excessive hard drive activity symptomatic of insufficient RAM. It occurs when Windows repeatedly uses up all available RAM space and has to move data not immediately needed out of the RAM into the page file, and then swap the data back into RAM when it is needed by the program.

- You must know what type of RAM (such as regular SDRAM, DDR, DDR2, or DDR3) your motherboard accepts before you purchase a RAM upgrade. You also need to know the maximum amount of RAM your motherboard supports and the maximum supported per slot.

- Though not required, it is good practice to make sure all sticks of RAM in any system are as close to identical as possible. Matching your RAM modules in technology, capacity, speed, and manufacturer lessens the chance of problems and incompatibility.

- The serial presence detect (SPD) chip on modern DIMMs automatically supplies all the information about the RAM to the system, such as the size, speed, ECC or non-ECC, registered or unregistered, and other details.

- To install SO-DIMMs in a laptop, you must remove a panel on the underside of the laptop or remove the keyboard to find the RAM slots. The SO-DIMM slides into the slot and snaps down into position. Unplug the laptop and remove the battery before attempting a RAM upgrade, and protect the RAM from ESD by wearing an anti-static wristband.

■ Key Terms

bank *(132)*

continuity RIMM (CRIMM) *(133)*

disk thrashing *(141)*

double data rate SDRAM (DDR SDRAM) *(133)*

double-sided RAM *(137)*

dual-channel architecture *(132)*

dual inline memory module (DIMM) *(131)*

dynamic random access memory (DRAM) *(127)*

error correction code RAM (ECC RAM) *(138)*

latency *(137)*

module *(129)*
page file *(139)*
parity RAM *(138)*
Rambus DRAM (RDRAM) *(132)*
ReadyBoost *(142)*
RIMM *(132)*
serial presence detect (SPD) *(145)*

single inline memory module (SIMM) *(129)*
single-sided RAM *(137)*
small-outline DIMM (SO-DIMM) *(132)*
stick *(129)*
swap file *(139)*
synchronous DRAM (SDRAM) *(131)*

■ Key Term Quiz

Use the Key Terms list to complete the sentences that follow. Not all terms will be used.

1. If your motherboard uses RDRAM, you must fill each slot with either a(n) _____ or a(n) _____.

2. If the LED for your hard drive stays on most of the time, your computer is suffering from _____, a sure sign you need to add more memory.

3. A special kind of memory stick for laptops is called a(n) _____.

4. Memory that makes two data accesses during each clock tick is called _____.

5. Unlike regular DRAM, _____ is tied to the system clock.

6. Unlike regular DRAM, _____ enables error checking and correcting.

7. The time lag between when the memory controller starts to fetch a line of data from RAM and when the RAM actually starts to deliver the data is known as _____.

8. Systems automatically detect new RAM by polling the module's _____ chip.

9. The _____ uses a portion of the hard drive as an extension of your physical RAM.

10. Memory chips are soldered to a small circuit board called a(n) _____ or a(n) _____.

■ Multiple-Choice Quiz

1. What is the correct throughput of DDR-SDRAM, and what is the speed of PC1600 RAM?

 A. 4 bytes per second, 133 MHz

 B. 8 bytes per second, 200 MHz

 C. 4 bits per second, 400 MHz

 D. 8 bits per second, 200 MHz

2. How many sticks of RAM do you need to fill a bank in a computer that can use 168-pin DIMMs?

 A. One

 B. Two

 C. Four

 D. Eight

3. If you upgrade your memory but notice that the RAM count does not reflect the additional memory, what should you do?

 A. Remove the RAM and try to reinstall it.

 B. Restart the computer.

 C. Return the memory because it's probably bad.

 D. Go to Setup and configure the memory to reflect the new amount.

4. How should you handle RAM?

 A. Touch only the gold contacts at the bottom of the stick.

 B. Touch only the edges, never the gold contacts.

 C. You should only use special tongs when handling RAM.

 D. It is unsafe to ever handle RAM.

5. What does the CPU use to access the system's RAM?

 A. The system bus

 B. The MCC

 C. The address bus

 D. The expansion bus

6. Which of the following statements is true about RDRAM?

 A. It uses dual-channel architecture.

 B. It offers speeds ranging from 200 MHz to 600 MHz.

 C. It is less expensive than SDRAM.

 D. It is used by AMD but not Intel processors.

7. Which of the following PC speed ratings matches up with DDR3-1600 RAM?

 A. PC3-6400

 B. PC3-8500

 C. PC3-10600

 D. PC3-12800

8. Which of the following is a valid package size for DDR2 DIMMs?

 A. 168-pin

 B. 172-pin

 C. 184-pin

 D. 240-pin

9. If you are running Windows 7, which of the following methods does not enable you to find out how much RAM is installed in your computer?

 A. From the Control Panel, select System and Security and then the Action Center.

 B. Use the Performance tab under the Task Manager.

 C. Select Properties from Computer.

 D. With a newer keyboard, press the WINDOWS-PAUSE/BREAK keystroke combination.

10. What package does DDR3 SDRAM use for desktop PCs?

 A. 30-pin

 B. 168-pin

 C. 172-pin

 D. 240-pin

11. What happens if you mix RAM sticks of different speeds?

 A. Your computer will work fine as long as it uses dual-channel architecture.

 B. Your computer may slow down.

 C. Your computer will work fine if all the memory sticks are slower than the speed of the motherboard.

 D. Your computer may lock up every few seconds or provide corrupted data.

12. Why is SDRAM faster than regular DRAM?

 A. It makes two processes per clock cycle.

 B. It runs synchronously with the system clock.

 C. It uses dual-channel architecture.

 D. It has fewer pins, resulting in fewer corrupt bits.

13. What is true about a double-sided DIMM?

 A. It has memory chips on the front and back.

 B. It can be installed forward or backward.

 C. It is twice as fast as a single-sided DIMM.

 D. It has half the capacity of a quad-sided DIMM.

14. What is the minimum requirement for RAM for Windows 7?

 A. 128 MB

 B. 256 MB

 C. 512 MB

 D. 1 GB

15. What happens if you add two RAM sticks to your PC, and one has a bad SPD?

 A. When your system boots, it will recognize both RAM sticks but will not register any special features (such as ECC) of the stick with the bad SPD.

 B. When your system boots, it will only register the presence of the RAM stick with the good SPD.

 C. When your system boots, it won't register the presence of the RAM stick with the bad SPD until you configure the RAM settings by using the Setup utility.

 D. When you try to boot the system, you will get a POST error message and the system will not boot.

■ Essay Quiz

1. Celia tells you she just received a new motherboard for the system she is building. She knows the motherboard is capable of using triple-channel memory, but she only has two sticks of RAM. She wonders if her PC will still work. What can you tell her to clear up the confusion?

2. Your cousin James recently bought a computer with 512 MB of RAM and a Windows Vista operating system. He's complaining about how slow his new computer is, especially when he's working with his graphics applications. How can you convince him that he needs more memory?

3. Now that you've convinced your cousin James that he needs more memory for his new PC, how will you explain what kind he should buy and how he should install it? You may assume that he has the motherboard book and that his computer has a 166-MHz system bus and can support DDR2 RAM.

Lab Projects

● Lab Project 6.1

To learn more about memory, read TechRadar's RAM upgrade guide at www.techradar.com/news/computing-components/ram-upgrade-the-complete-guide-951495. The article discusses all aspects of computer memory. After reading the article, answer the following questions:

① Why are dual-channel memory controllers so much more popular than triple-channel memory controllers, even though the triple-channel technology is newer and faster? Provide at least two reasons.

② Why have PC users and manufacturers not rushed to adopt DDR4 RAM?

BIOS

7

"I am the virus,
I am a siren in the rain.
I am a courier bring the
Spiral into your brain.
Alter connections, encoding now,
Initial sequence is loading down
Into the BIOS
Into the BIOS
Into the BIOS"

—DURAN DURAN, "VIRUS," *ASTRONAUT*

In this chapter, you will learn how to

- **Explain the function of BIOS**
- **Distinguish among various CMOS setup utility options**
- **Describe option ROM and device drivers**

In Chapter 5, you saw how the address bus and external data bus connect RAM to the CPU via the memory controller chip (MCC) to run programs and transfer data. Assuming you apply power in the right places, you don't need anything else to make a simple computer. The only problem with such a simple computer is that it would bore you to death—there's no way to do anything with it! A PC needs devices such as keyboards and mice to provide input, and output devices such as monitors and sound cards to communicate the current state of the running programs to you. A computer also needs permanent storage devices, such as hard drives, USB drives, and optical drives, to store programs and data when you turn off the computer.

Historical/Conceptual

■ We Need to Talk

Simply placing a number of components into a computer is useless if the CPU can't communicate with them. Getting the CPU to communicate with a device starts with some kind of interconnection—a communication bus that enables the CPU to send commands to and from devices. To make this connection, let's promote the MCC, giving it extra firepower to act as not only the interconnection between the CPU and RAM, but also the interconnection between the CPU and the other devices on the PC. The MCC isn't just the memory controller anymore, so let's now call it the **Northbridge** because it acts as the primary bridge between the CPU and the rest of the computer (see Figure 7.1).

Your PC uses so many devices, the PC industry decided to delegate some of the interconnectivity work to a second chip called the **Southbridge**. The Northbridge deals with high-speed interfaces such as the connection to your video card and RAM. The Southbridge works mainly with lower-speed devices such as the USB controller and hard drive controllers. Chip makers design matched sets of particular models of Northbridge and Southbridge to work together. You don't buy a Northbridge from one company and a Southbridge from another—they're sold as a set. We call this set of Northbridge and Southbridge the **chipset**.

The chipset extends the data bus to every device on the PC. The CPU uses the data bus to move data to and from all of the devices of the PC. Data constantly flows on the external data bus among the CPU, chipset, RAM, and other devices on the PC (see Figure 7.2).

The first use for the address bus, as you know, is for the CPU to tell the chipset to send or store data in memory and to tell the chipset which section of memory to access or use. Just as with the external data bus, the chipset extends the address bus to all of the devices (see Figure 7.3). That way, the CPU can use the address bus to send commands to devices, just as it sends commands to the chipset.

It's not too hard to swallow the concept that the CPU uses the address bus to talk to devices, but how does it know what to *say* to them? How does it know all of the patterns of ones and zeros to place on the address bus to tell the hard drive it needs to send a file? Let's look at the interaction between the keyboard and CPU for insight into this process.

Talking to the Keyboard

The keyboard provides a great example of how the buses and support programming help the CPU get the job done. In early computers, the keyboard

RAM

10010010
01010011
11011110
10010010
01010011
11011110
10101101
10010010
01010011
11011110
10101101
00110011
01010000
11110010
10010101

Address bus

CPU

Northbridge

• **Figure 7.1** Meet the Northbridge

Modern processors include the functions of the Northbridge directly on the CPU. The Southbridge is now called the *Input/Output Controller Hub* (*ICH*) in new Intel systems and the *Fusion Controller Hub* (*FCH*) in new AMD systems. To help you understand their function, however, I'll still refer to the Northbridge and Southbridge as distinct elements.

Techs commonly talk about various functions of the chipset as if those functions were still handled by discrete chips. So you'll hear about memory controllers, keyboard controllers, mouse controllers, USB controllers, and so on, even though they're all just circuits on the Northbridge or Southbridge.

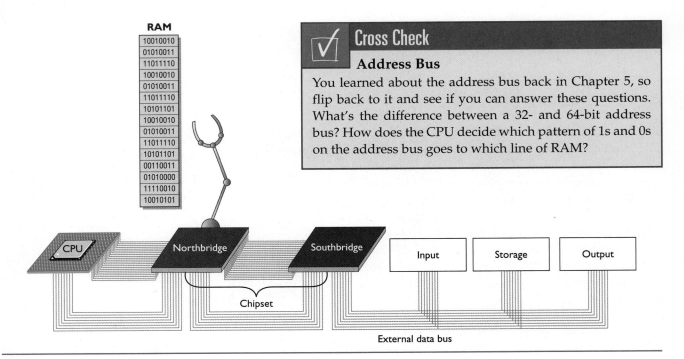

Cross Check

Address Bus

You learned about the address bus back in Chapter 5, so flip back to it and see if you can answer these questions. What's the difference between a 32- and 64-bit address bus? How does the CPU decide which pattern of 1s and 0s on the address bus goes to which line of RAM?

• **Figure 7.2** The chipset extending the data bus

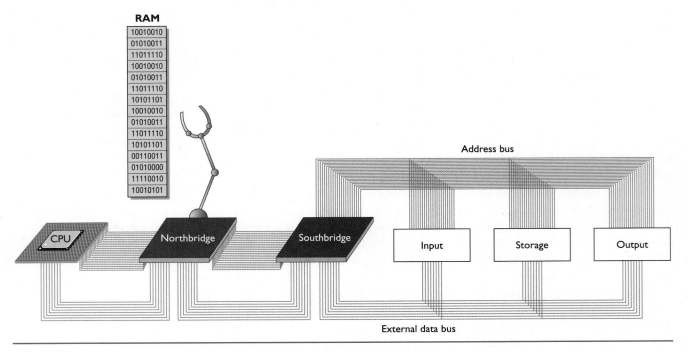

• **Figure 7.3** Every device in your computer connects to the address bus.

connected to the external data bus via a special chip known as the *keyboard controller*. Don't bother looking for this chip on your motherboard—the Southbridge now handles keyboard controller functions. The way the keyboard controller—or technically, the keyboard controller *circuitry*—works with the CPU, however, has changed only a small amount in the past 25+ years, making it a perfect tool to illustrate how the CPU talks to a device.

● **Figure 7.4** A keyboard chip on a Pentium motherboard

The keyboard controller was one of the last single-function chips to be absorbed into the chipset. For many years—in fact, well into the Pentium III/Early Athlon era—most motherboards had separate keyboard controller chips. Figure 7.4 shows a typical keyboard controller from those days. Electronically, it looked like Figure 7.5.

Every time you press a key on your keyboard, a scanning chip in the keyboard notices which key you pressed. Then the scanner sends a coded pattern of ones and zeros—called the **scan code**—to the keyboard controller. Every key on your keyboard has a unique scan code. The keyboard controller stores the scan code in its own register. Does it surprise you that the lowly keyboard controller has a register similar to a CPU? Lots of chips have registers—not just CPUs (see Figure 7.6).

How does the CPU get the scan code out of the keyboard controller (see Figure 7.7)? While we're at it, how does the CPU tell the keyboard to change

Tech Tip

The 8042

Even though the model numbers changed over the years, you'll still hear techs refer to the keyboard controller as the 8042, after the original keyboard controller chip.

● **Figure 7.5**

• Figure 7.6 Scan code stored in keyboard controller's register

the typematic buffer rate (when you hold down a key and the letter repeats) or to turn the number lock LED on and off, to mention just a few other jobs the keyboard needs to do for the system? The point is that the keyboard controller must be able to respond to multiple commands, not just one.

The keyboard controller accepts commands exactly as you saw the CPU accept commands in Chapter 5. Remember when you added 2 to 3 with

• Figure 7.7 The CPU ponders the age-old dilemma of how to get the 8042 to cough up its data.

the 8088? You had to use specific commands from the 8088's codebook to tell the CPU to do the addition and then place the answer on the external data bus. The keyboard controller has its own codebook—much simpler than any CPU's codebook, but conceptually the same. If the CPU wants to know what key was last pressed on the keyboard, the CPU needs to know the command (or series of commands) that orders the keyboard controller to put the scan code of the letter on the external data bus so the CPU can read it.

801

■ BIOS

The CPU doesn't magically or otherwise automatically know how to talk with any device; it needs some sort of support programming loaded into memory that teaches it about a particular device. This programming is called **basic input/output services (BIOS)**. The programs dedicated to enabling the CPU to communicate with devices are called services (or device drivers, as you'll see later in the chapter). This goes well beyond the keyboard, by the way. In fact, *every* device on the computer needs BIOS! But let's continue with the keyboard for now.

Bringing BIOS to the PC

A talented programmer could write BIOS for a keyboard if the programmer knew the keyboard's codebook; keyboards are pretty simple devices. This begs the question: where would this support programming be stored? Well, programming could be incorporated into the operating system. Storing programming to talk to the hardware of your PC in the operating system is great—all operating systems have built-in code that knows how to talk to your keyboard, your mouse, and just about every piece of hardware you may put into your PC.

That's fine once the operating system's up and running, but what about a brand new stack of parts you're about to assemble into a new PC? When a new system's being built, it has no operating system. The CPU must have access to BIOS for the most important hardware on your PC: not only the keyboard, but also the monitor, hard drives, optical drives, USB ports, and RAM. This code can't be stored on a hard drive or optical disc—these important devices need to be ready at any time the CPU calls them, even before installing a mass storage device or an operating system.

The perfect place to store the support programming is on the motherboard. That settles one issue, but another looms: What storage medium should the motherboard use? DRAM won't work, because all of the data would be erased every time you turned off the computer. You need some type of permanent program storage device that does not depend on other peripherals to work. And you need that storage device to sit on the motherboard.

• Figure 7.8 Typical flash ROM

ROM

Motherboards store the keyboard controller support programming, among other programs, on a special type of device called a **read-only memory (ROM)** chip. A ROM chip stores programs, called **services**, exactly like RAM: that is, like an 8-bit-wide spreadsheet. But ROM differs from RAM in two important ways. First, ROM chips are **nonvolatile**, meaning that the information stored on ROM isn't erased when the computer is turned off. Second, traditional ROM chips are read-only, meaning that once you store a program on one, you can't change it. Modern motherboards use a type of ROM called **flash ROM** that differs from traditional ROM in that you can update and change the contents through a very specific process called "flashing the ROM." Figure 7.8 shows a typical flash ROM chip on a motherboard. When the CPU wants to talk to the keyboard controller, it goes to the flash ROM chip to access the proper programming.

Every motherboard has a flash ROM chip, called the **system ROM** chip because it contains code that enables your CPU to talk to the basic hardware of your PC (see Figure 7.9). As alluded to earlier, the system ROM holds BIOS for more than just the keyboard controller. It also stores programs for communicating with the floppy drive, hard drives, optical drives, display devices, USB ports, and other basic devices on your motherboard.

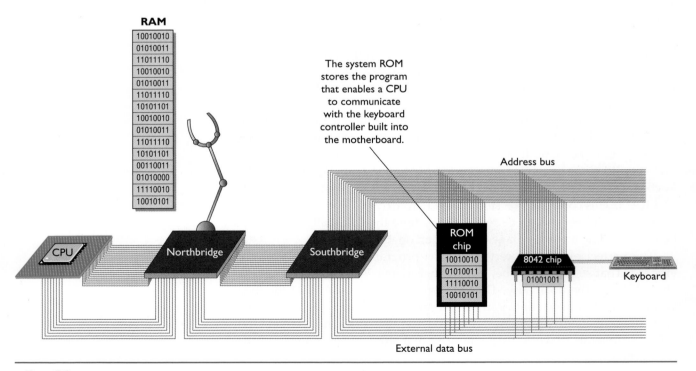

• Figure 7.9 Function of the flash ROM chip

To talk to all of that hardware requires hundreds of little services (2 to 30 lines of code each). These hundreds of little programs stored on the system ROM chip on the motherboard are called, collectively, the **system BIOS** (see Figure 7.10). Techs call programs stored on ROM chips of any sort **firmware**.

The system ROM chips used on modern PCs store as much as 2 MB of programs, although only 65,536 bytes are used to store the system BIOS. This allows for backward compatibility with earlier systems. The rest of the ROM space is put to good use doing other jobs.

Programs stored on ROM chips—flash or any other kind of ROM chip—are known collectively as *firmware*, as opposed to programs stored on erasable media, which are collectively called *software*.

System BIOS Support

Every system BIOS has two types of hardware to support. First, the system BIOS supports all of the hardware that never changes, such as the keyboard. (You can change your keyboard, but you can't change the keyboard controller built into the Southbridge.) Another example of hardware that never changes is the PC speaker (the tiny one that beeps at you, not the ones that play music). The system ROM chip stores the BIOS for these and other devices that never change.

Second, the system BIOS supports all of the hardware that might change from time to time. This includes RAM (you can add RAM), hard drives (you can replace your hard drive with a larger drive or add a second hard drive), and floppy drives (you can add another floppy drive, although that's not common today). The system ROM chip stores the *BIOS* for these devices, but the system needs another place to store information about the specific *details* of a piece of hardware. This enables the system to differentiate between a Western Digital Caviar Black 1.5-TB hard drive and a Seagate Barracuda 1-TB drive, and yet still support both drives right out of the box.

• **Figure 7.10** CPU running BIOS service

■ CMOS

A separate memory chip, called the **complementary metal-oxide semiconductor (CMOS)** chip, stores the information that describes specific device parameters. CMOS does *not* store programs; it only stores data that is read by BIOS to complete the programs needed to talk to changeable hardware. CMOS also acts as a clock to keep the current date and time.

Years ago, CMOS was a separate chip on the motherboard, as shown in Figure 7.11. Today, the CMOS is almost always built into the Southbridge.

Most CMOS chips store around 64 KB of data, but the PC usually needs only a very small amount—about 128 bytes—to store all of the necessary information on the changeable hardware. Don't let the tiny size fool you. The information stored in CMOS is absolutely necessary for the PC to function!

If the data stored on CMOS about a particular piece of hardware (or about its fancier features) is different from the specs of the actual hardware, the computer cannot access that piece of hardware (or use its fancier features). It is crucial that this information be correct. If you change any of the previously mentioned hardware, you must update CMOS to reflect those changes. You need to know, therefore, how to change the data on CMOS.

• **Figure 7.11** Old-style CMOS

The terms *CMOS setup program*, *CMOS*, and *system setup utility* are functionally interchangeable today. You'll even hear the program referred to as the *BIOS setup utility*. Most techs just call it the CMOS.

Modify CMOS: The Setup Program

Every PC ships with a program built into the system ROM called the **CMOS setup program** or the **system setup utility** that enables you to access and modify CMOS data. When you fire up your computer in the morning, the first thing you likely see is the BIOS information. It might look like the example shown in Figure 7.12 or perhaps like the example shown in Figure 7.13.

Who or what is AMIBIOS, and who or what is Phoenix Technologies? These are brand names of BIOS companies. They write BIOS programs and sell them to computer manufacturers. In today's world, motherboard makers rarely write their own BIOS. Instead, they buy their BIOS from specialized third-party BIOS makers such as Award Software and Phoenix Technologies. Although several companies write BIOS, two big companies control 99 percent of the BIOS business: American Megatrends (AMI) and Phoenix Technologies. Phoenix

Tech Tip

Term Limits

Okay, I've thrown a whole bunch of terms at you describing various pieces of hardware and software and what does what to whom. Here's the scorecard so you can sort out the various pieces of data.

1. *The system ROM chip stores the system BIOS, programs needed by the CPU to communicate with devices.*

2. *The system ROM chip also holds the program that accesses the information stored on the CMOS chip to support changeable pieces of hardware. This program is called the CMOS setup program or the system setup utility.*

3. *The CMOS holds a small amount of data that describes the changeable pieces of hardware supported by the system BIOS. The CMOS today is a part of the Southbridge.*

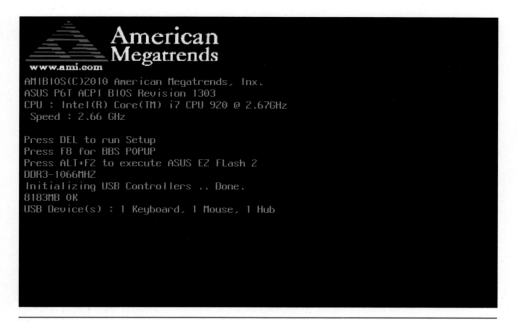

• **Figure 7.12** AMI BIOS information

bought Award Software and still sells the Award brand name as a separate product line. These three are the most common brand names in the field.

You always access a system's CMOS setup program at boot. The real question is how to access the CMOS setup at boot for your particular PC. AMI, Award, and Phoenix use different keys to access the CMOS setup program. Usually, BIOS manufacturers tell you how to access the CMOS setup right on the screen as your computer boots. For example, at the bottom of the screen in Figure 7.13, you are instructed to instructed to press the DEL key to enter BIOS Setup. Keep in mind that this is only one possible example. Motherboard manufacturers can change the key combinations for entering CMOS setup. You can even set up the computer so the message does not show—a smart idea if you need to keep nosy people out of your CMOS setup! If you don't see an "enter setup" message, wait until the RAM count starts and then try one of the following keys or key combinations: DEL, ESC, F1, F2, CTRL-ALT-ESC, CTRL-ALT-INS, CTRL-ALT-ENTER, or CTRL-S. It may take a few tries, but you will eventually find the right key or key combination. If not, check the motherboard book or the manufacturer's Web site for the information.

If your system clock keeps resetting itself, check the CMOS battery on the motherboard. It's the large coin battery on your motherboard that gives the CMOS the charge it needs when the computer is turned off.

• **Figure 7.13** Award/Phoenix BIOS information

 Try This!

Accessing CMOS Setup

The key or key combination required to access CMOS setup varies depending on your particular BIOS. It's important to know how to access CMOS setup, and how to find the BIOS information once you're in, so try this:

1. Boot your system and turn on your monitor. Watch the information that scrolls by on the screen as your computer boots. Most BIOS makers include a line indicating what key(s) to press to access the CMOS setup program. Make a note of this useful information! You can also check your motherboard book to determine the process for accessing the CMOS setup program.

2. Reboot the system, and this time watch for information on the BIOS manufacturer. If you don't see it, and if it's okay to do so, open the system case and check the name printed on the system ROM chip. Make a note of this useful information.

3. Reboot one more time, and this time use the key or key combination you found to run the CMOS setup program. Locate and make a note of the manufacturer, date, and version number of your PC's current BIOS.

4. If you can, make a note of the exact model information for your system and visit the Web site of the company that manufactured your PC. Search their support files for the specs on your specific system and see if you can locate your BIOS information. Now take the detailed BIOS information and search the BIOS manufacturer's Web site for the same information.

A Quick Tour Through a Typical CMOS Setup Program

Every BIOS maker's CMOS setup program looks a little different, but don't let that confuse you. They all contain basically the same settings; you just have to be comfortable poking around. To avoid doing something foolish, *do not save anything* unless you are sure you have it set correctly.

As an example, let's say your machine has Award BIOS. You boot the system and press DEL to enter CMOS setup. The screen shown in Figure 7.14 appears. You are now in the main menu of the Award CMOS setup program. The setup program itself is stored on the ROM chip, but it edits only the data on the CMOS chip.

If you select the Standard CMOS Features option, the Standard CMOS Features screen appears (see Figure 7.15). On this screen you can change floppy drive, hard drive, and optical drive settings, as well as the system's date and time. You will learn how to set up the CMOS for these devices in later chapters. At this point, your only goal is to understand CMOS and know how to access the CMOS setup on your PC, so don't try to change

⚠ Accessing the CMOS setup utility for a system is perfectly fine, but do not make changes unless you fully understand that system!

• Figure 7.14 Typical CMOS main screen by Award

anything yet. If you have a system that you are allowed to reboot, try accessing the CMOS setup now.

Does it look anything like these examples? If not, can you find the screen that enables you to change the floppy drives, hard drives, and optical drives? Trust me, every CMOS setup has that screen somewhere! Figure 7.16 shows the same standard CMOS setup screen on a system with Phoenix BIOS. Note that this CMOS setup utility calls this screen "Main."

The first BIOS was nothing more than this standard CMOS setup. Today, all computers have many extra CMOS settings. They control items such as memory management, password and booting options, diagnostic and error handling, and power management. The following section takes a quick tour of an Award CMOS setup program. Remember that your CMOS setup

• Figure 7.15 Standard CMOS Features screen

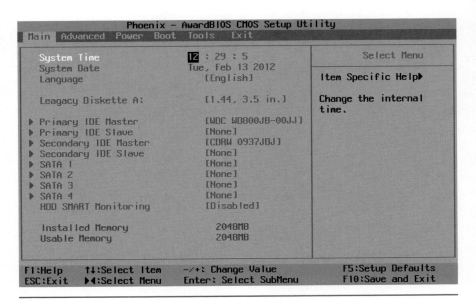

```
                  Phoenix - AwardBIOS CMOS Setup Utility
    Main  Advanced  Power  Boot  Tools  Exit

      System Time              12 : 29 : 5          Select Menu
      System Date              Tue, Feb 13 2012
      Language                 [English]          Item Specific Help▶

      Leagacy Diskette A:      [1.44, 3.5 in.]    Change the internal
                                                  time.
    ▶ Primary IDE Master       [WDC WD800JB-00JJ]
    ▶ Primary IDE Slave        [None]
    ▶ Secondary IDE Master     [CDRW 0937JDJ]
    ▶ Secondary IDE Slave      [None]
    ▶ SATA 1                   [None]
    ▶ SATA 2                   [None]
    ▶ SATA 3                   [None]
    ▶ SATA 4                   [None]
      HDD SMART Monitoring     [Disabled]

      Installed Memory             2048MB
      Usable Memory                2048MB

    F1:Help        ↑↓:Select Item    -/+: Change Value    F5:Setup Defaults
    ESC:Exit       ▶◀:Select Menu    Enter: Select SubMenu  F10:Save and Exit
```

• **Figure 7.16** Phoenix BIOS CMOS setup utility Main screen

All of these screens tend to overwhelm new techs. When they first encounter the many options, some techs feel they need to understand every option on every screen to configure CMOS properly. Relax—if I don't talk about a particular CMOS setting somewhere in this book, it's probably not important, either for the CompTIA A+ 801 exam or to a real tech.

almost certainly looks at least a little different from mine, unless you happen to have the *same* BIOS. The chances of that happening are quite slim.

Phoenix has virtually cornered the desktop PC BIOS market with its Award Modular BIOS. Motherboard makers buy a boilerplate BIOS, designed for a particular chipset, and add or remove options (Phoenix calls them *modules*) based on the needs of each motherboard. This means that seemingly identical CMOS setup utilities can be extremely different. Options that show up on one computer might be missing from another. Compare the older Award screen in Figure 7.17 with the more modern Award CMOS screen in Figure 7.14. Figure 7.17 looks different—and it should—as this much older system simply doesn't need the extra options available on the newer system.

The next section starts the walk-through of a CMOS setup utility with the MB Intelligent Tweaker, followed by some of the Advanced screens. Then you'll go through other common screens, such as Integrated Peripherals, Power, and more.

MB Intelligent Tweaker

You can use MB Intelligent Tweaker (M.I.T.) to change the voltage and multiplier settings on the motherboard for the CPU from the defaults. Motherboards that cater to overclockers tend to have this option. Usually you just set this to Auto or Default and stay away from this screen (see Figure 7.18).

```
                ROM PCI/ISA BIOS (2A69HQ1A)
                    CMOS SETUP UTILITY
                   AWARD SOFTWARE, INC.

    ┌─────────────────────────────┬────────────────────────────┐
    │  STANDARD CMOS SETUP         │  INTEGRATED PERIPHERALS     │
    │                              │                             │
    │  BIOS FEATURES SETUP         │  SUPERVISOR PASSWORD        │
    │                              │                             │
    │  CHIPSET FEATURES SETUP      │  USER PASSWORD              │
    │                              │                             │
    │  POWER MANAGEMENT SETUP      │  IDE HDD AUTO DETECTION     │
    │                              │                             │
    │  PNP/PCI CONFIGURATION       │  HDD LOW LEVEL FORMAT       │
    │                              │                             │
    │  LOAD BIOS DEFAULTS          │  SAVE & EXIT SETUP          │
    │                              │                             │
    │  LOAD SETUP DEFAULTS         │  EXIT WITHOUT SAVING        │
    ├─────────────────────────────┴────────────────────────────┤
    │  Esc : Quit              ↑ ↓ → ←   : Select Item           │
    │  F10 : Save & Exit Setup (Shift)F2 : Change Color          │
    │                                                            │
    └────────────────────────────────────────────────────────────┘
```

• **Figure 7.17** Older Award setup screen

```
CMOS Setup Utility - Copyright (C) 1984-2009 Award Software
                 MB Intelligent Tweaker(M.I.T.)
  ▶ Advanced Clock Calibration[Press Enter]        ▲        Item Help
    CPU Clock Ratio          [Auto]       2600Mhz
    CPU NorthBridge Freq.    [Auto]       2000Mhz    Menu Level   ▶
    CPU Host Clock Control   [Auto]
  x CPU Frequency(MHz)        200
    PCIE Clock(MHz)          [Auto]
    HT Link Width            [Auto]
    HT Link Frequency        [Auto]       2000Mhz
    Set Memory Clock         [Auto]
  x Memory Clock             x5.33        1066Mhz
  ▶ DRAM Configuration       [Press Enter]
    ******** System Voltage Optimized ********
    System Voltage Control   [Auto]
  x DDR3 Voltage Control      Auto
  x SB/HT Voltage Control     Auto
  x NB/PCIe/PLL Voltage Contro Auto
  x CPU PLL Voltage Control    Auto
  x DDR VTT Voltage Control    Auto
  x NB Voltage Control         Auto        ▼

  ↑↓→←:Move  Enter:Select  +/-/PU/PD:Value  F10:Save  ESC:Exit  F1:General Help
        F5:Previous Values  F6:Fail-Safe Defaults  F7:Optimized Defaults
```

• **Figure 7.18** MB Intelligent Tweaker (M.I.T.)

Advanced BIOS Features

Advanced BIOS Features is the dumping ground for all of the settings that aren't covered in the Standard menu and don't fit nicely under any other screen. This screen varies wildly from one system to the next. You most often use this screen to select the boot options (see Figure 7.19).

Virtualization Support You've already learned a lot about how an operating system interacts with hardware and software, but did you know you can also recreate an entire PC (including the hardware, software, and operating system) *virtually* as a program on your PC? A *virtual machine* is a powerful type of program that enables you to run a second (or third or fourth), software-based machine inside your physical PC. It recreates the motherboard, hard drives, RAM, network adapters, and more, and is just as powerful as a real PC. To run these virtual machines, however, you'll need a very powerful PC—you are trying to run multiple PCs at the same time, after all.

> In Advanced BIOS Features, you might also find several diagnostic tools. I'll discuss a common hard drive diagnostic tool, the Self-Monitoring, Analysis and Reporting Technology (S.M.A.R.T.), in Chapter 10.

```
CMOS Setup Utility - Copyright (C) 1984-2009 Award Software
                  Advanced BIOS Features
    Virtualization           [Disabled]           Item Help
    AMD K8 Cool&Quite control [Auto]
  ▶ Hard Disk Book Priority   [Press Enter]     Menu Level   ▶
    First Boot Device         [CDROM]
    Second Boot Device        [Hard Disk]       Hardware assisted
    Third Boot Device         [CDROM]           Virtualization
    Password Check            [Setup]           Technology which help
    HDD S.M.A.R.T. Capability [Enabled]         improve performance of
    Away Mode                 [Disabled]        system running
    Full Screen LOGO Show     [Enabled]         Virtual Machine
    Init Display First        [PEG]             Softwares.

                                                Virtual Machine
                                                allows multiple OS
                                                on one computer
                                                simultaneously.

  ↑↓→←:Move  Enter:Select  +/-/PU/PD:Value  F10:Save  ESC:Exit  F1:General Help
        F5:Previous Values  F6:Fail-Safe Defaults  F7:Optimized Defaults
```

• **Figure 7.19** Advanced BIOS Features

To support this, CPU manufacturers have added *hardware-assisted virtualization*. Intel calls their version Intel Virtualization Technology, and AMD calls theirs AMD Virtualization Technology—perhaps the only time these two companies have agreed on a name. This technology helps the virtual machines use your hardware more efficiently and is controlled by the BIOS. This feature is off by default in BIOS, so if your

```
SB750 Spread Spectrum        [Disabled]              Item Help

                                                   Menu Level    ▶

                                                   [Disabled]
                                                   Disabled southbridge
                                                   spread spectrum

                                                   [Enabled]
                                                   Enable southbridge
                                                   spread spectrum

↑↓→←:Move  Enter:Select  +/-/PU/PD:Value  F10:Save  ESC:Exit  F1:General Help
           F5:Previous Values  F6:Fail-Safe Defaults  F7:Optimized Defaults
```

• **Figure 7.20** Advanced Chipset Features

```
  SB750 Spread Spectrum       [Enabled]               Item Help
  OnChip SATA Type            [Native IDE]
x OnChip SATA Port4/5 Type    IDE                    Menu Level    ▶
  Onboard SATA/IDE Device     [Enabled]
  Onboard SATA/IDE Ctrl Mode[IDE]                    [Disabled]
▶ Smart Backup                [Press Enter]          Disable the onboard
  Onboard Audio Function      [Enabled]              parallel IDE Channel0.
▶ Onboard LAN device          [Press Enter]
  Onboard 1394 Function       [Enabled]              [Enabled]
  OnChip USB Controller       [Enabled]              Enabled the onboard
  USB EHCI Controller         [Enabled]              parallel IDE Channel0.
  USB Keyboard Support        [Enabled]
  USB Mouse Support           [Enabled]
  Legacy USB storage detect   [Enabled]
  Onboard Serial Port 1       [3F8/IRQ4]
  Onboard Parallel Port       [378/IRQ7]
  Parallel Port Mode          [SPP]
x ECP Mode Use DMA            3

↑↓→←:Move  Enter:Select  +/-/PU/PD:Value  F10:Save  ESC:Exit  F1:General Help
           F5:Previous Values  F6:Fail-Safe Defaults  F7:Optimized Defaults
```

• **Figure 7.21** Integrated Peripherals

> When overclocking your PC, look for settings that adjust the CPU's clock and bus speeds. The higher you push these, the faster your PC will go.

virtual machine requires hardware-assisted virtualization, you'll need to activate it here.

Chassis Intrusion Detection Many motherboards support the **chassis intrusion detection** feature provided by the computer case, or chassis. Compatible cases contain a switch that trips when someone opens the case. With motherboard support and a proper connection between the motherboard and the case, the CMOS logs whether the case has been opened and, if it has, posts a notification to the screen on the subsequent boot. How cool is that?

Advanced Chipset Features

The Advanced Chipset Features screen (see Figure 7.20) strikes fear into most everyone, because it deals with extremely low-level chipset functions. Avoid this screen unless a high-level tech (such as a motherboard maker's support tech) explicitly tells you to do something in here.

Integrated Peripherals

You will use the Integrated Peri-pherals screen quite often. Here you configure, enable, or disable the onboard devices, such as the integrated sound card (see Figure 7.21).

Power Management Setup

As the name implies, you can use the Power Management Setup screen (see Figure 7.22) to set up the power management settings for the system. These settings work in concert (sometimes in conflict) with Windows' power management settings to control how and when devices turn off and back on to conserve power.

Overclocking

Many PCs have CMOS setup menus that display information about the CPU, RAM, and GPU and include controls for overclocking them. You learned about overclocking in Chapter 5, so you already know what it does and how dangerous it can be. Overclocking works by changing the bus speeds, clock multipliers, and voltage for the desired component. Be very careful when overclocking or you could end up with a dead CPU!

PnP/PCI Configurations

All CMOS setup utilities come with menu items that are for the most part no longer needed, but no one wants to remove them. The PnP/PCI Configurations screen is a perfect example (see Figure 7.23). Plug and play (PnP) is how devices automatically work when you snap them into your PC. PCI is a type of slot used for cards. Odds are very good you'll never deal with this screen.

And the Rest of the CMOS Settings...

The other options on the main menu of an Award CMOS do not have their own screens. Rather,

these simply have small dialog boxes that pop up, usually with "Are you sure?" messages. The Load Fail-Safe/Optimized default options keep you from having to memorize all of those weird settings you'll never touch. Fail-Safe sets everything to very simple settings—you might occasionally use this setting when very low-level problems such as freeze-ups occur and you've checked more obvious areas first. Optimized sets the CMOS to the best possible speed/stability for the system. You would use this option after you've tampered with the CMOS too much and need to put it back like it was!

Many CMOS setup programs enable you to set a password in CMOS to force the user to enter a password every time the system boots. Don't confuse this with the Windows logon password. This CMOS password shows up at boot, long before Windows even starts to load. Figure 7.24 shows a typical CMOS password prompt.

Some CMOS setup utilities enable you to create two passwords: one for boot and another for accessing the CMOS setup program. This extra password just for entering CMOS setup is a godsend in schools, for example, where nontechs tend to wreak havoc in areas (such as CMOS) that they should not access!

Many CMOS setup utilities also enable you to monitor CPU temperature, system temperature, and the voltages of the CPU and RAM. This menu, usually called PC Health

• **Figure 7.22** Power Management Setup

• **Figure 7.23** PnP/PCI Configurations

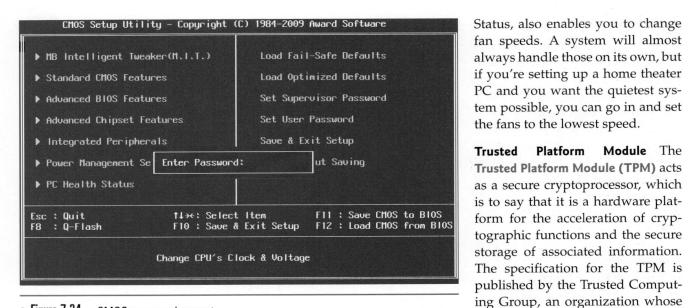

• **Figure 7.24** CMOS password prompt

On some motherboards, the CMOS setup program enables you to control the ATA Security Mode Feature Set, also commonly referred to as drive lock or **DriveLock**. ATA Security Mode is the first line of defense for protecting hard disks from unwanted access when a system is lost or stolen.

Some PC manufacturers also include *LoJack* security features in their BIOS—this way, if your PC is stolen, you can track its location, install a key logger, or even remotely shut down your computer.

Status, also enables you to change fan speeds. A system will almost always handle those on its own, but if you're setting up a home theater PC and you want the quietest system possible, you can go in and set the fans to the lowest speed.

Trusted Platform Module The **Trusted Platform Module (TPM)** acts as a secure cryptoprocessor, which is to say that it is a hardware platform for the acceleration of cryptographic functions and the secure storage of associated information. The specification for the TPM is published by the Trusted Computing Group, an organization whose corporate members include Intel, Microsoft, AMD, IBM, Lenovo, Dell, Hewlett-Packard, and many others.

The TPM can be a small circuit board plugged into the motherboard, or it can be built directly into the chipset. The CMOS setup program usually contains settings that can turn the TPM on or off and enable or disable it.

TPMs can be used in a wide array of cryptographic operations, but one of the most common uses of TPMs is hard disk encryption. For example, the BitLocker Drive Encryption feature of Microsoft's Windows Vista and Windows 7 can be accelerated by a TPM, which is more secure because the encryption key is stored in the tamper-resistant TPM hardware rather than on an external flash drive. Other possible uses of TPMs include digital rights management (DRM), network access control, application execution control, and password protection.

Exiting and Saving Settings

Of course, all CMOS setups provide some method to Save and Exit or to Exit *Without* Saving. Use these as needed for your situation. Exit Without Saving is particularly nice for those folks who want to poke around the CMOS setup utility but don't want to mess anything up. Use it!

The CMOS setup utility would meet all of the needs of a modern system for BIOS if manufacturers would just stop creating new devices. That's not going to happen, of course, so let's turn now to devices that need to have BIOS loaded from elsewhere.

■ Option ROM and Device Drivers

Every piece of hardware in your computer needs some kind of programming that tells the CPU how to talk to that device. When IBM invented the PC more than 30 years ago, they couldn't possibly have included all of the necessary BIOS routines for every conceivable piece of hardware on

the system ROM chip. How could they? Most of the devices in use today didn't exist on the first PCs. When programmers wrote the first BIOS, for example, network cards, mice, and sound cards did not exist. Early PC designers at IBM understood that they could not anticipate every new type of hardware, so they gave us a few ways to add programming other than on the BIOS. I call this *BYOB*—Bring Your Own BIOS. You can BYOB in two ways: option ROM and device drivers. Let's look at both.

Option ROM

The first way to BYOB is to put the BIOS on the hardware device itself. Look at the card displayed in Figure 7.25. This is a serial ATA RAID hard drive controller—basically just a card that lets you add more hard drives to a PC. The chip in the center with the wires coming out the sides is a flash ROM that stores BIOS for the card. The system BIOS does not have a clue about how to talk to this card, but that's okay, because this card brings its own BIOS on what's called an **option ROM** chip.

Most BIOS that come on option ROMs tell you that they exist by displaying information when you boot the system. Figure 7.26 shows a typical example of an option ROM advertising itself.

In the early days of the PC, you could find all sorts of devices with BIOS on option ROMs. Today, option ROMs have mostly been replaced by more flexible software methods (more on device driver software in the next section), with one major exception: video cards. Every video card made today contains its own BIOS. Option ROMs work well but are hard to upgrade. For this reason, most hardware relies on software for BYOB.

• **Figure 7.25** Option ROM

```
System Memory Size: 4.0 GB, System Memory Speed: 800 MHz, Voltage: 1.5V

Broadcom NetXtreme II Ethernet Boot Agent v5.2.7
Copyright (C) 2000-2009 Broadcom Corporation
All rights reserved.
Press Ctrl-S to Configure Device (MAC Address - 0024E867D111)

Adaptec 1225SA SATA HostRAID BIOS V6.0-0 B2328
(c) 1998-2007 Adaptec, Inc. All Rights Reserved.

◄◄◄ Press <Ctrl><A> for Adaptec RAID Configuration Utility! ►►►

Controller #00: Adaptec 1225SA at PCI Bus:03, Dev:00, Func:00
SerialNumber = 0KX0B0040013
Loading Configuration...
00:00 WDC WD20EADS-00R6B0 01.00A01        1.81 TB Healthy       3.0 Gb/s

SATA JBOD- PORT-0    WDC WD20EADS-00R     1.81 TB        Legacy

1 JBOD Device(s) Found.

_
```

• **Figure 7.26** Option ROM at boot

Device Drivers

A **device driver** is a file stored on the PC's hard drive that contains all of the commands necessary to talk to whatever device it was written to support. All operating systems employ a method of loading these device drivers into RAM every time the system boots. They know which device drivers to install by reading a file (or files) that lists which device drivers the system needs to load at boot time. All operating systems are designed to look at this list early on in the boot process and copy the listed files into RAM, thereby giving the CPU the capability to communicate with the hardware supported by

Hardware Update Wizard

This wizard helps you install software for:

Silicon Image Sil 3512 SATALink Controller

If your hardware came with an installation CD or floppy disk, insert it now.

What do you want the wizard to do?

◉ Install the software automatically (Recommended)
○ Install from a list or specific location (Advanced)

Click Next to continue.

< Back Next > Cancel

• **Figure 7.27** Windows asking for the installation disc

the device driver. Device drivers come with the device when you buy it. When you buy a sound card, for example, it comes with a disc that holds all of the necessary device drivers (and usually a bunch of extra goodies). The generic name for this type of CD-ROM is **installation disc**. In most cases, you install a new device, start the computer, and wait for Windows to prompt you for the installation disc (see Figure 7.27).

You might want to add or remove device drivers manually at times. Windows uses a special database called the **Registry** that stores everything you want to know about your system, including the device drivers. You shouldn't access the Registry directly to access these drivers, but instead use the venerable Device Manager utility (accessed by right-clicking on Computer, selecting Manage, and navigating to the Device Manager tool on the left).

BIOS, BIOS, Everywhere!

As you should now understand, every piece of hardware on a system must have an accompanying program that provides the CPU with the code necessary to communicate with that particular device. This code may reside on the system ROM on the motherboard, on ROM on a card, or in a device driver file on the hard drive loaded into RAM at boot. BIOS is everywhere on your system, and you need to deal with it occasionally.

Beyond A+

■ UEFI

Your computer's system BIOS is one very old piece of programming. BIOS hasn't changed much since it was conceived with the 286-based IBM AT computer back in the 1980s. As a result, BIOS works only in 16-bit mode and depends on *x*86-compliant hardware. In addition, if you have more than one operating system loaded on a single drive, you need one of those installed OSes to "take charge" and act as a boot loader.

If computing was going to move forward, a new type of BIOS needed to come along. Intel's **Extensible Firmware Interface (EFI)** fills that role. In 2005, Intel released EFI for public standards, creating the Unified EFI forum

Even though it's really called UEFI, most techs use the term EFI.

to manage the specification. EFI was then renamed **Unified Extensible Firmware Interface (UEFI)**.

UEFI acts as a super-BIOS, doing the same job as BIOS, but in a 32- or 64-bit environment. UEFI, though, does much more than just fill in for BIOS. Think of UEFI as a not yet extremely well-defined, industry-standard, mini–operating system that runs on top of the firmware of your computer, enabling you to do some pretty cool things at boot. Here are some of the things UEFI does:

- UEFI supports 32-bit or 64-bit booting.

- UEFI handles all boot-loading duties.

- UEFI is not dependent on *x86* firmware.

UEFI became a standard years ago, so why did no one see a UEFI motherboard until 2011? The answer is simple: 3-TB hard drives. Regular BIOS will only boot to master boot record (MBR) drives, and MBR drives don't support partitions greater than 2.2 TB. As 3-TB and larger drives began to appear in 2011, people using traditional BIOS discovered that strange issues popped up when they wanted to boot off of a 3-TB hard drive (see Figure 7.28). Instead of a 3-TB volume, you'd find a 2.2-TB volume and unpartitioned space.

UEFI motherboards support booting a newer type of hard drive partitioning called *GUID Partition Table* (*GPT*) that supports partitions larger than 2.2 TB. If you want to boot off of a hard drive using a single partition greater than 2.2 TB, you must use a UEFI motherboard and the hard drive must be blank. If your system meets these two criteria, the Windows 7 installation routine will automatically make a GPT drive for you (see Figure 7.29).

While UEFI works both for 32-bit and 64-bit operating systems, Microsoft decided to enable UEFI support only for 64-bit editions of Windows 7.

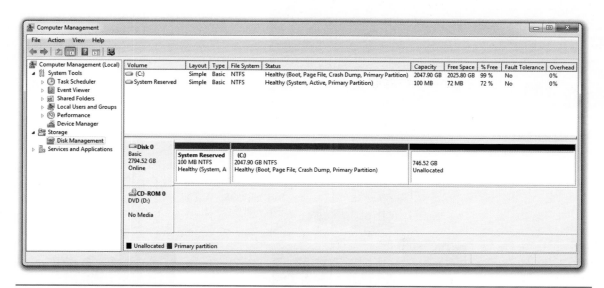

• **Figure 7.28** Here's what happens when you install Windows 7 on a greater-than-2.2-TB drive using regular BIOS.

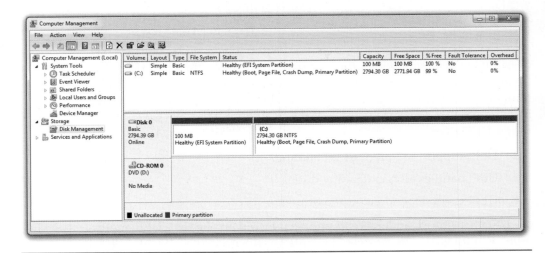

• Figure 7.29 Here's what happens when you install Windows 7 on a greater-than-2.2-TB drive using UEFI.

Although the EFI folks clearly defined issues such as booting and accessing firmware, they didn't define issues such as the graphical user interface or audio. If you think UEFI possesses a standard interface similar to the Windows desktop, forget it. Figure 7.30 shows an ASUS motherboard's UEFI interface. UEFI serves as a non-hardware-specific, non-OS-specific, 32- or 64-bit bootloader. This doesn't make things we know and love such as POST or system setup go away. They still exist, but now UEFI runs the show instead of BIOS (see Figure 7.31).

• Figure 7.30 ASUS EFI BIOS Utility

• Figure 7.31 POST and system setup are still here.

Chapter 7 Review

■ Chapter Summary

After reading this chapter and completing the exercises, you should understand the following about BIOS and CMOS.

Explain the function of BIOS

■ The CPU must be able to communicate with all devices in a computer system. The Northbridge chip is the primary communication bridge between the CPU and the rest of the computer. The Northbridge deals with high-speed devices such as the video card, RAM, and PCIe bus. A second chip, the Southbridge, works with the other devices. The Northbridge and Southbridge chips are manufactured as a set called the chipset. The chipset extends the data and address buses to every device in the PC.

■ A ROM (read-only memory) chip is nonvolatile, meaning it retains the information stored on it even when the power is turned off. Usually attached to the Southbridge, the ROM chip stores hundreds of little programs that enable the CPU to communicate with basic devices such as the floppy drive, optical drives, hard drives, video card, and others. These programs, called services, are collectively referred to as the basic input/output services (BIOS). These programs are stored on a read-only medium and can't be changed by the user, so they are known as firmware, in contrast to software, which is programs stored on erasable media. The term "system ROM" refers to the ROM chip on the motherboard.

■ Although the system ROM chip has room for as much as 2 MB of programs, only 65,536 bytes store the BIOS.

■ The ROM BIOS includes programs that enable the CPU to talk to many basic hardware devices such as the keyboard, but other devices not supported by the ROM BIOS may have their own ROM chips.

■ Each piece of hardware in the computer needs programs for everything that piece of hardware does. The CPU must access these programs to get the hardware to do its job. IBM also devised other methods to get BIOS to the hardware of the computer. If the hardware is common, necessary, and does not change, such as the keyboard, the system ROM chip stores the BIOS. If the hardware is common and necessary but may change from time to time, such as when you install a larger hard drive or add more RAM, the BIOS for the general type of device (e.g., a hard drive) can be on the system ROM chip. The information describing specific features unique to that particular device (e.g., a Seagate Barracuda 1-TB drive), however, must be stored on a changeable storage medium such as a complementary metal-oxide semiconductor (CMOS) chip.

Distinguish among various CMOS setup utility options

■ Your motherboard includes a changeable chip, capable of storing about 64 KB of data, called the complementary metal-oxide semiconductor (CMOS) chip. CMOS does not store programs. It stores the data that is read by BIOS, and that data is used by the programs residing in BIOS. Although CMOS used to be a separate chip on the motherboard, it is almost always built into the Southbridge on modern motherboards. The CMOS chip also keeps track of the date and time. To maintain its date, CMOS requires a constant trickle of electricity supplied by a small battery on the motherboard. If the data you have stored in CMOS continues to disappear or if the date/time resets itself, it may be time to change the motherboard battery.

■ Within the system ROM is a CMOS setup program that lets you access and update the data on the CMOS chip. The terms CMOS setup program, CMOS, and system setup utility are functionally interchangeable today. Most techs just call it the CMOS. Two major manufacturers control 99 percent of the BIOS business: American Megatrends (AMI) and Phoenix Technology (which includes Award Software). The CMOS setup program can be started in many different ways, depending on the brand of BIOS you have on your computer. Pressing DEL when the computer boots is the most common way to access the CMOS setup program. The screen itself usually tells you how to access setup. If it doesn't, you can check the motherboard book or the Web site of your PC or BIOS manufacturer.

- All CMOS setup programs have basically the same main options. On the Standard CMOS Features screen, you can change floppy drive, hard drive, and date/time settings. Today's setup programs have extra CMOS settings that control such items as memory management, password and booting options, diagnostic and error handling, and power management. The Award Modular BIOS enables motherboard manufacturers to add or remove options from the setup program.

- Among the other things you can configure in CMOS setup are the voltage and multiplier settings for the CPU (the MB Intelligent Tweaker), boot options (check the Advanced BIOS Features menu), power management, password protection, and ports (the Integrated Peripherals menu). All setup programs include options to *Save and Exit* or *Exit Without Saving*. You should not change CMOS settings unless you know exactly what you're doing.

- On older systems, if the information on the CMOS chip was lost or erased, the computer would not boot. The most common cause was a dead onboard battery, but other factors such as electrical surges or a dirty motherboard could also erase CMOS data. Lost CMOS information produces errors such as *No boot device available* or *CMOS date/time not set*. Making a backup copy of the CMOS data enabled you to restore the information and recover from this catastrophe.

- Unlike earlier ROM chips that you had to replace when you wanted to upgrade the BIOS programs, today's computers use flash ROM chips that you can reprogram without removing. If you install a CPU or other new hardware that the flash ROM chip does not support, you can run a small command-line program combined with an update file to change your BIOS. The exact process varies from one motherboard maker to another. If the flash ROM utility allows you to make a backup of your BIOS, you should always do so. Don't update your BIOS unless you have a good reason. As the old saying goes, "If it ain't broke, don't fix it!"

- Many CMOS setup programs enable you to set a boot password, a password to enter the CMOS setup program itself, or both. These passwords are stored in CMOS. If you forget your password, you simply need to clear the CMOS data. Alternatively, many motherboards provide a clear CMOS jumper you can use to clear the CMOS data without removing the battery.

Describe option ROM and device drivers

- Newer hardware devices that are not supported by the system BIOS have other ways to BYOB—bring your own BIOS. A hardware device may contain its own BIOS chip or ROM chip known as option ROM. Every video card contains its own BIOS for internal functions. A more flexible way to BYOB is to use files called device drivers that contain instructions to support the hardware device. Device drivers load when the system boots.

- Many devices come with device driver files on installation discs. These drivers must be loaded for the PC to recognize and use the devices. In a database called the Registry, Windows keeps a list of what drivers should be loaded. Editing the Registry directly is dangerous (a mistake can prevent Windows from booting), but you can safely install or remove drivers by using Device Manager.

■ Key Terms

basic input/output services (BIOS) *(159)*
chassis intrusion detection *(168)*
chipset *(155)*
CMOS setup program *(162)*
complementary metal-oxide semiconductor (CMOS) *(162)*
device driver *(171)*
DriveLock *(170)*
Extensible Firmware Interface (EFI) *(172)*

firmware *(161)*
flash ROM *(160)*
installation disc *(172)*
nonvolatile *(160)*
Northbridge *(155)*
option ROM *(171)*
read-only memory (ROM) *(160)*
Registry *(172)*
scan code *(157)*

services *(160)*
Southbridge *(155)*
system BIOS *(161)*
system ROM *(160)*

system setup utility *(162)*
Trusted Platform Module (TPM) *(170)*
Unified Extensible Firmware Interface (UEFI) *(173)*

■ Key Term Quiz

Use the Key Terms list to complete the sentences that follow. Not all terms will be used.

1. Loaded when the system boots, a(n) _____ is a file that contains instructions to support a hardware device.

2. If you set up _____ on your computer, you'll be alerted whenever the case is opened.

3. The combination of a specific Northbridge and a specific _____ is collectively referred to as the _____.

4. To change settings in CMOS, you would use the _____, also known as the _____.

5. You can reprogram a(n) _____ chip without removing the chip.

6. Unlike RAM, which loses all data when the computer is shut down, a ROM chip is _____, retaining the information even when the power is off.

7. The hundreds of programs in the system ROM chip are collectively called the _____.

8. The generic term for a program stored on a ROM chip is _____.

9. The low-energy chip that holds configuration information and keeps track of date and time is called the _____ chip.

10. BIOS stored on a device (as opposed to on a motherboard) is called _____.

■ Multiple-Choice Quiz

1. A user calls first thing Monday morning saying she has an error message at boot-up that says her case was opened. She's looked at the computer, but it seems normal. What does this tell you about her computer?

 A. Her computer has TPM enabled in the CMOS.

 B. Her computer has fan monitoring enabled in CMOS and the fan stopped over the weekend.

 C. Her computer case has chassis intrusion detection and the feature is enabled in CMOS.

 D. It doesn't tell you anything about the computer, only that the user has a problem.

2. Which of the following can a PC boot to?

 A. Hard drive

 B. DVD-ROM

 C. USB drive

 D. All of the above

3. Imogen just bought a fancy new sound card, so she changed CMOS to disable her onboard sound card. However, when she booted into Windows, the onboard card was still showing up! What did Imogen probably do wrong?

 A. She didn't set "Allow disabling of onboard devices" to "True."

 B. She pressed the wrong key to get into CMOS setup.

 C. She forgot to save her changes when exiting CMOS setup.

 D. She made the changes in the General section of CMOS setup, and not the Advanced section.

4. Jack decided to go retro and added a second floppy disk drive to his computer. He thinks he has it physically installed correctly, but it doesn't show up in Windows. Which of the following options will most likely lead Jack where he needs to go to resolve the issue?

 A. Reboot the computer and press the F key on the keyboard twice. This signals that the computer has two floppy disk drives.

 B. Reboot the computer and watch for instructions to enter the CMOS setup utility (for example, a message may say to press the DELETE key). Do what it says to go into CMOS setup.

 C. In Windows, press the DELETE key twice to enter the CMOS setup utility.

 D. In Windows, go to Start | Run and type **floppy**. Click OK to open the Floppy Disk Drive Setup Wizard.

5. What does BIOS provide for the computer? (Choose the best answer.)

 A. BIOS provides the physical interface for various devices such as USB and FireWire ports.

 B. BIOS provides the programming that enables the CPU to communicate with other hardware.

 C. BIOS provides memory space for applications to load into from the hard drive.

 D. BIOS provides memory space for applications to load into from the main system RAM.

6. Which two manufacturers control about 99% of the PC BIOS business? (Select two.)

 A. American Megatrends

 B. ASUS

 C. Phoenix Technology

 D. Firebird Software

7. Which of the following statements is true about CMOS?

 A. CMOS is a configuration program that runs from the hard drive during booting.

 B. CMOS is a low-energy chip that draws power from a battery while the computer is turned off.

 C. CMOS includes the power-on self test (POST) routines.

 D. CMOS is the Southbridge chip that controls input and output devices.

8. How do you enter CMOS setup?

 A. Open the Start Menu, then go to All Programs | CMOS setup.

 B. Hold down CTRL-ALT-DEL while rebooting the computer.

 C. You have to set the CMOS setup jumper on the motherboard.

 D. Press a shortcut key, usually DEL or F2.

9. Henry bought a new card for capturing television on his computer. When he finished going through the packaging, though, he found no driver disc, only an application disc for setting up the TV capture software. After installing the card and software, it all works flawlessly. What's the most likely explanation?

 A. The device doesn't need BIOS, so there's no need for a driver disc.

 B. The device has an option ROM that loads BIOS, so there's no need for a driver disc.

 C. Windows supports TV capture cards out of the box, so there's no need for a driver disc.

 D. The manufacturer made a mistake and didn't include everything needed to set up the device.

10. Which chip does the CPU use to communicate with high-speed devices such as video cards or RAM?

 A. Complementary metal-oxide semiconductor

 B. Northbridge

 C. Southbridge

 D. Scan code

11. When your computer boots and you press the appropriate key to enter the CMOS setup utility, a small program loads, allowing you to specify settings for various hardware devices. Where is this small program permanently stored?

 A. In the ROM

 B. In CMOS

 C. On the hard drive

 D. In RAM

12. When you enter the CMOS setup utility (as in the previous question) and make changes, where are your settings stored?

 A. In the BIOS

 B. In CMOS

 C. On the hard drive

 D. In RAM

■ Essay Quiz

1. From this chapter you learned that every piece of hardware in the computer needs BIOS to make it work. Explain three ways in which these essential programs may be provided to the CPU.

2. You've been hired as a tutor for Tom, a fellow student in your hardware class. He's having a difficult time understanding the role that the system BIOS plays in booting the computer. How will you explain this process to him? Be sure to explain in order the step-by-step process that the BIOS goes through from the time you turn on the computer until it relinquishes control to the operating system.

3. Your instructor has asked you to give a report on the Northbridge and Southbridge chips, their functions, and how they use the address bus. Write a short essay on the subject that you can use in class.

Lab Projects

• Lab Project 7.1

Use the motherboard book (if you have one or can download one) or check the Web site of your BIOS manufacturer to identify what each of the following POST error messages means:

- A numeric message of 301
- One long beep followed by three short beeps
- A numeric message of 601
- HDD controller failure

• Lab Project 7.2

Watch closely as your computer boots to see if it displays a message about how to reach the setup program. If it does not, consult your motherboard book to try to locate this information. Then, using the method appropriate for your system BIOS chip, access the setup program and examine the various screens. Do not change anything! Usually, your motherboard book includes default settings for the various setup screens and perhaps includes explanations of the various choices. Compare what you see on the screen with what the book says. Do you see any differences? If so, how do you account for these differences? As you examine the setup program, answer the following questions:

1. How do you navigate from one screen to the next? Are there menus across the top or do you simply jump from one page of options to the next? Are there instructions on the screen for navigating the setup program?

2. What is the boot sequence for your computer? In other words, in what order does the BIOS look for a bootable device?

3. What is the core voltage of the CPU?

4. How many SATA drives does the BIOS list?

When you have finished, choose Exit Without Saving.

Motherboards

chapter 8

"Did anybody hear that?"

—Michael "Motherboard" Pampin,
Rainbow Six: Vegas

In this chapter, you will learn how to

- **Explain how motherboards work**
- **Recognize modern expansion buses**
- **Upgrade and install motherboards**

The motherboard provides the foundation for the personal computer. Every piece of hardware, from the CPU to the lowliest expansion card, directly or indirectly plugs into the motherboard. The motherboard contains the wires—called traces—that make up the buses of the system. It holds the vast majority of the ports used by the peripherals, and it distributes the power from the power supply (see Figure 8.1). Without the motherboard, you literally have no PC.

This chapter starts with an explanation of how motherboards work, identifying various types or form factors of motherboards, including distinguishing features. The second section examines expansion capabilities on motherboards, specifically the types of expansion slots you'll run into in the wild and how to install expansion cards. The final section goes through the pragmatic steps of upgrading and installing motherboards.

• **Figure 8.1** Traces visible beneath the CPU socket on a motherboard

Historical/Conceptual

■ How Motherboards Work

Three variable and interrelated characteristics define modern motherboards: form factor, chipset, and components. The **form factor** determines the physical size of the motherboard as well as the general location of components and ports. The **chipset** defines the type of processor and RAM the motherboard requires and determines to a degree the built-in devices the motherboard supports, including the expansion slots. Finally, the built-in components determine the core functionality of the system.

Any good tech should be able to make a recommendation to a client about a particular motherboard simply by perusing the specs. Because the motherboard determines function, expansion, and stability for the whole PC, it's essential to know motherboards!

Form Factors

Form factors are industry-standardized shapes and layouts that enable motherboards to work with cases and power supplies. A single form factor applies to all three components. Motherboards come in a basic rectangular or square shape but vary in overall size and in the layout of built-in components (see Figure 8.2). You need to install a motherboard in a case designed

Tech Tip

Layers of the PCB
Modern motherboards are layered **printed circuit boards (PCBs)**, *copper etched onto a nonconductive material and then coated with some sort of epoxy for strength. The layers mask some of their complexity. You can see some of the traces on the board, but every motherboard is four or more layers thick. The layers contain a veritable highway of wires, carrying data and commands back and forth between the CPU, RAM, and peripherals.*

The layered structure enables multiple wires to send data without their signals interfering with each other. The layered approach allows the manufacturer to add complexity and additional components to the board without extending the overall length and width of the board. Shorter traces also allow signals to travel faster than they would if the wires were longer, as would be necessary if motherboards did not use layers. The multiple layers also add strength to the board itself, so it doesn't bend easily.

● **Figure 8.2** Typical motherboard

All AT motherboards had a split power socket called *P8/P9.* You can see the white P8/P9 socket near the keyboard port in Figures 8.3 and 8.4.

to fit it, so the ports and slot openings on the back fit correctly.

The power supply and the motherboard need matching connectors, and different form factors define different connections. Given that the term "form factor" applies to the case, motherboard, and power supply—the three parts of the PC most responsible for moving air around inside the PC—the form factor also defines how the air moves around in the case.

To perform motherboard upgrades and provide knowledgeable recommendations to clients, techs need to know their form factors. The PC industry has adopted—and dropped—a number of form factors over the years with such names as AT, ATX, and BTX. Let's start with the granddaddy of all PC form factors, AT.

AT Form Factor

The **AT** form factor (see Figure 8.3), invented by IBM in the early 1980s, was the predominant form factor for motherboards through the mid-1990s. AT is now obsolete.

The AT motherboard had a few size variations (see Figure 8.4), ranging from large to very large. The original AT motherboard was huge, around 12 inches wide by 13 inches deep. PC technology was new and needed lots of space for the various chips necessary to run the components of the PC.

The single greatest problem with AT motherboards was the lack of external ports. When PCs were first invented, the only devices plugged into the average PC were a monitor and a keyboard. That's what the AT was designed to handle—the only dedicated connector on an AT motherboard was the keyboard port (see Figure 8.5).

P8/P9 socket

● **Figure 8.3** AT-style motherboard

• **Figure 8.4** AT motherboard (bottom) and Baby AT motherboard (top)

Over the years, the number of devices plugged into the back of the PC has grown tremendously. Your average PC today has a keyboard, a mouse, a printer, some speakers, a monitor, and—if your system's like mine—four to six USB devices connected to it at any given time. These added components created a demand for a new type of form factor, one with more dedicated connectors for more devices. Many attempts were made to create a new standard form factor. Invariably, these new form factors integrated dedicated connectors for at least the mouse and printer, and many even added connectors for video, sound, and phone lines.

• **Figure 8.5** Keyboard connector on the back of an AT motherboard

One variation from the AT form factor that enjoyed a degree of success was the **slimline** form factor. The first slimline form factor was known as **LPX** (defined in some sources as *low profile extended*, although there's some disagreement). It was replaced by the **NLX** form factor. (NLX apparently stands for nothing, by the way. It's just a cool grouping of letters.) The LPX and NLX form factors met the demands of the slimline market by providing a central riser slot to enable the insertion of a special **riser card** (see Figure 8.6) or, as it's sometimes called, a *daughterboard*. Expansion cards then fit into the riser card horizontally. Combining built-in connections with a riser card enabled manufacturers to produce PCs shorter than 4 inches.

The main problem with form factors such as LPX and NLX was their inflexibility. Certainly, no problem occurred with dedicated connections for such devices as mice or printers, but the new form factors also added connectors for such devices as video and sound—devices that were prone to obsolescence, making the motherboard out of date the moment a new type of video or sound card came into popularity.

• **Figure 8.6** Riser card on an older motherboard

ATX Form Factor

The demand for a form factor that had more standard connectors and was also flexible enough for possible changes in technology led to the creation of the ATX form factor in 1995 (see Figure 8.7). ATX got off to a slow start, but by around 1998, ATX overtook AT to become the most common form factor, a distinction it holds today.

ATX is distinct from AT in the lack of an AT keyboard port, replaced with a rear panel that has all necessary ports built in. Note the mini-DIN (PS/2) keyboard and mouse ports at the left of Figure 8.8, until recently, standard features on almost all ATX boards. You recall those from Chapter 3, right?

The ATX form factor includes many improvements over AT. The position of the power supply creates better air movement. The CPU and RAM are placed to provide easier access, and the rearrangement of components prevents long expansion cards from colliding with the CPU or Northbridge. Other improvements, such as placing the RAM closer to the Northbridge and CPU than on AT boards, offer users enhanced performance as well. The shorter the wires, the easier to shield them and make them capable of

• **Figure 8.7** Early ATX motherboard

• Figure 8.8 ATX ports

handling double or quadruple the clock speed of the motherboard. Figure 8.9 shows AT and ATX motherboards—note the radical differences in placement of internal connections.

ATX motherboards come in three variations to accommodate different types of cases. So far, you've seen the full-sized ATX form factor, which is 12 by 9.6 inches.

• Figure 8.9 AT (left) and ATX (right) motherboards for quick visual comparison

 Cross Check

High-Speed CPUs and RAM

Modern CPUs incorporate the memory controller on the processor rather than locating it on the Northbridge. This move has facilitated even further increases in the speed at which the processor can fetch data from RAM. Refer to Chapters 5 and 6 and see if you can answer these questions.

1. What different clock frequencies are supported by DDR2 and DDR3 types of memory?

2. What processors support DDR3 memory?

The **microATX (μATX)** motherboard (see Figure 8.10) floats in at a svelte 9.6 by 9.6 inches (usually), or about 30 percent smaller than standard ATX, yet uses the standard ATX connections. A microATX motherboard fits into a standard ATX case or in the much smaller microATX cases. Note that not all microATX motherboards have the same physical size. You'll sometimes see micro-ATX motherboards referred to with the Greek symbol for micro, as in μATX.

In 1999, Intel created a variant of the microATX called the FlexATX. **FlexATX** motherboards have maximum dimensions of just 9 by 7.5 inches, which makes them the smallest motherboards in the ATX standard. Although FlexATX motherboards can use a standard ATX power supply, most FlexATX

• Figure 8.10 A microATX motherboard

Many techs and Web sites use the term *mini-ATX* to refer to motherboards smaller than a full ATX board. This is technically incorrect. The specifications for these small boards use only the terms *microATX* and *FlexATX*.

systems use a special FlexATX-only power supply. This diminutive power supply fits into tight FlexATX cases.

Keep in mind that each main type of form factor requires its own case. AT motherboards go into AT cases, NLX motherboards go into NLX cases, and ATX motherboards go into ATX cases. You cannot replace one form factor with another without purchasing a new case (see Figure 8.11). The exception to this rule is that larger form factor ATX cases can handle any smaller-sized ATX form factor motherboards.

ITX

Not everyone wants or needs a huge desktop system. From the beginning of PCs, there's always been a demand for smaller computers. While a number of companies have made proprietary motherboards to support smaller computers, it wasn't until around 2001 that the chipset maker VIA Technologies started the process to create a small form factor (SFF) motherboard, the ITX. The ITX itself wasn't a success, but VIA in turn created a number of even smaller form factors that today populate the SFF market: Mini-ITX, Nano-ITX, and Pico-ITX.

Mini-ITX is the largest and the most popular of the three ITX form factors. At a miniscule 6.7 by 6.7 inches, Mini-ITX competes head to head with the virtually identical microATX (see Figure 8.12).

If you think that's small, **Nano-ITX** at 4.7 by 4.7 inches and **Pico-ITX** at 3.8 by 2.8 inches are even smaller (see Figure 8.13). These tiny

• **Figure 8.11** That's not going to fit!

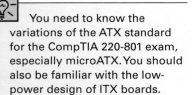

You need to know the variations of the ATX standard for the CompTIA 220-801 exam, especially microATX. You should also be familiar with the low-power design of ITX boards.

• **Figure 8.12** Mini-ITX (photo courtesy of VIA Technologies, Inc.)

• **Figure 8.13** Pico-ITX (photo courtesy of VIA Technologies, Inc.)

motherboard form factors are commonly used for embedded systems and highly specialized devices such as routers.

One of the great benefits of these SFF motherboards is the tiny amount of power needed to support them. ITX power supplies are quite small compared to a typical power supply. Lower power usage produces less heat, thus enabling passive cooling on many SFF systems. The lack of fan noise makes them ideal for media center PCs.

Proprietary Form Factors

Several major PC makers, including Dell and Sony, make motherboards that work only with their cases. These *proprietary* motherboards enable these companies to create systems that stand out from the generic ones and, not coincidently, push you to get service and upgrades from their authorized dealers. Some of the features you'll see in proprietary systems are riser boards like you saw with the NLX form factor—part of a motherboard separate from the main one but connected by a cable of some sort—and unique power connections. Proprietary motherboards drive techs crazy because replacement parts tend to cost more and are not readily available.

> **Try This!**
>
> ### Motherboard Varieties
>
> Motherboards come in a wide variety of form factors. Go to your local computer store and check out what is on display. Note the different features offered by ATX, microATX, and FlexATX (if any) motherboards.
>
> 1. Does the store stock Mini-ITX or proprietary motherboards?
>
> 2. Did the clerk use tech slang and call the motherboards "mobos"? (It's what most of us call them outside of formal textbooks, after all!)

Chipset

Every motherboard has a chipset, one or more discrete integrated circuit chips that support the CPU's interfacing to all the other devices on the

Northbridge

Southbridge

• **Figure 8.14** Northbridge and Southbridge

motherboard. The chipset determines the type of processor the motherboard accepts, the type and capacity of RAM, and the sort of internal and external devices that the motherboard supports. As you learned in earlier chapters, the chips in a PC's chipset serve as electronic interfaces through which the CPU, RAM, and input/output devices interact. Chipsets vary in features, performance, and stability, so they factor hugely in the purchase or recommendation of a particular motherboard. Good techs know their chipsets!

Because the chipset facilitates communication between the CPU and other devices in the system, its component chips are relatively centrally located on the motherboard (see Figure 8.14). For over a decade, chipsets were composed of two primary chips: the Northbridge and the Southbridge.

The **Northbridge** chip on traditional Intel-based motherboards helped the CPU work with RAM, as mentioned in earlier chapters. On newer motherboards, however, the CPU has taken on the role of the memory controller so the Northbridge either no longer exists or mainly just provides the communication with the video card. Northbridge chips did a lot and thus got pretty hot, requiring their own heat-sink and fan assembly.

The **Southbridge** handles some expansion devices and mass storage drives, such as hard drives. Most Southbridge chips don't need extra cooling, leaving the chip exposed or passively cooled with only a heat sink. This makes the Southbridge a great place for you to see the manufacturer of the chipset, as the name of the manufacturer is always right on the chip.

Some motherboards support very old technologies such as floppy drives, infrared connections, parallel ports, and modems. Although supporting these old devices was once part of the Southbridge's job, hardly any modern chipsets still support these devices. Motherboard manufacturers add a third chip called the **super I/O chip** to handle these chores. Figure 8.15 shows a typical super I/O chip.

The system ROM chip provides part of the BIOS for the chipset, but only at a barebones, generic level. The chipset still needs support for the rest of the things it can do. So how do expansion devices get BIOS? From software drivers, of course, and the same holds true for modern chipsets. You have to load the proper drivers for the specific OS to support all of the features of today's chipsets. Without software drivers, you'll never create a stable,

• **Figure 8.15** Super I/O chip on ASUS motherboard

fully functional PC. Most motherboards ship with an optical disc with drivers, support programs, and extra-special goodies such as antivirus software (see Figure 8.16).

There are a limited number of chipset makers. The dominant chipset vendors today are Intel and AMD, although several other companies continue to produce chipsets, such as NVIDIA. Motherboard manufacturers incorporate the chipsets into motherboards that match the feature set of the chipset. Chipset companies rise and fall every few years, with one company seeming to hold the hot position for a while until another company comes along to unseat them.

Chipset makers don't always use the terms Northbridge and Southbridge. Chipsets for AMD-based motherboards tend to use these terms, but Intel-based motherboards tend to say **Memory Controller Hub (MCH)** for the Northbridge and **I/O Controller Hub (ICH)** for the Southbridge. With the launch of the X58 Express Chipset, Intel further refined their terminology, calling the Northbridge simply the *I/O Hub (IOH)* since the memory controller is located on the CPU. Sometimes Intel refers to the Southbridge as the *Legacy I/O Controller Hub*. Regardless of the official name, Northbridge and Southbridge are the commonly used terms. Figure 8.17 shows a schematic with typical chipset chores for an Intel X79 chipset.

• **Figure 8.16** Driver disc for ASUS motherboard

Super I/O chips work with chipsets, but are not part of the chipset. Motherboard makers purchase them separately from chipsets.

PCI Express * 2.0 Graphics

Support for multi-card configurations
2×16 & 1×8
or
1×16 & 3×8
or
1×16 & 2×8 & 2×4

40 lanes total

1 GB/s each ×1 bi-directional

2nd Gen Intel® Core™ i7 Processors LGA 2011

DDR3 memory 12.8 GB/s
DDR3 memory 12.8 GB/s
DDR3 memory 12.8 GB/s
DDR3 memory 12.8 GB/s

DMI 20 GB/s

14 Hi-Speed USB 2.0 Ports; Dual EHCI; USB Port Disable

480 MB/s each

Intel® X79 Express Chipset

Intel® High Definition Audio

1 GB/s each ×1

8 PCI Express* 2.0

Intel® Integrated 10/100/1000 MAC

up to 6 GB/s²

6 Serial ATA Ports; eSATA; Port Disable

PCIe* ×1 SM Bus

SPI

Intel® Gigabit LAN Connect

Intel® ME Firmware and BIOS Support

Intel® Rapid Storage Technology enterprise 3.0

Intel® Extreme Tuning Suppport

....Optional

¹Theoretical maximum bandwidth
²All SATA ports capable of 3 Gb/s. 2 ports capable of 6 Gb/s.

Intel® X79 Express Chipset Block Diagram

• **Figure 8.17** Schematic of a modern chipset (courtesy of Intel Corporation)

So why do good techs need to know the hot chipsets in detail? The chipset defines almost every motherboard feature short of the CPU itself. Techs love to discuss chipsets and expect a fellow tech to know the differences between one chipset and another. You also need to be able to recommend a motherboard that suits a client's needs. Chapter 21 covers choosing components and building PCs for specific purposes, such as video editing and gaming. One of the most important choices you'll make in building a custom rig is selecting a chipset.

Motherboard Components

The connections and capabilities of a motherboard sometimes differ from those of the chipset the motherboard uses. This disparity happens for a couple of reasons. First, a particular chipset may support eight USB ports, but to keep costs down, the manufacturer might include only four ports. Second, a motherboard maker may choose to install extra features—ones not supported by the chipset—by adding additional chips. A common example is a motherboard that supports FireWire. Other technologies you might find are built-in sound, hard drive RAID controllers, and AMR or CNR slots for modems, network cards, and more. Some motherboards have added convenience features, such as case fan power connectors and running lights so you can see what you're working on.

• **Figure 8.18** USB/FireWire dongle for rear connectors

• **Figure 8.19** Front USB and FireWire drive bay device

USB/FireWire

Most chipsets support USB, and many motherboards come with FireWire as well, but it seems no two motherboards offer the same port arrangement. My motherboard supports eight USB ports and two FireWire ports, for example, but if you look on the back of the motherboard, you'll only see four USB ports and one FireWire port. So, where are the other ports? Well, this motherboard has special connectors for the other ports, and the motherboard comes with the dongles you need to connect them (see Figure 8.18). These dongles typically use an extra slot on the back of the case.

These dongle connectors are standardized, so many cases have built-in front USB/FireWire ports that have dongles attached. This is very handy for USB or FireWire devices you might want to plug and unplug frequently, such as thumb drives or digital cameras. You can also buy add-on front USB and FireWire devices that go into a 3.5-inch drive bay (see Figure 8.19).

Sound

Quite a few motherboards come with onboard sound chips. These sound chips are usually pretty low quality compared to even a lower-end sound card, but onboard sound is cheap and doesn't take up a slot. As with USB, a lot of motherboards have a port for connecting to audio jacks on the front of the case. These enable you to plug headphones or microphones into the front rather than the rear of the case, a very convenient feature. These

connectors are identical to the ones used on sound cards, so we'll save more discussion for Chapter 17.

RAID

RAID stands for *redundant array of independent (or inexpensive) disks* and is very common on motherboards. There are many types of RAID, but the RAID found on motherboards usually only supports *mirroring* (the process of using two drives to hold the same data, which is good for safety, because if one drive dies, the other still has all of the data) or *striping* (making two drives act as one drive by spreading data across them, which is good for speed). RAID is a very cool but complex topic that's discussed in detail in Chapter 10.

AMR/CNR

The U.S. Federal Communications Commission (FCC) must certify any electronic device to ensure that it does not transmit unwanted electronic signals. This process is a bit expensive, so in the very late 1990s, Intel came up with a special slot called the **audio modem riser (AMR)**, shown in Figure 8.20. An AMR slot was designed to take specialized AMR devices (modems, sound cards, and network cards). An AMR device would get one FCC certification and then be used on as many motherboards as the manufacturer wanted without going through the FCC certification process again. AMR was quickly replaced with the more advanced **communications and networking riser (CNR)**. Many motherboard manufacturers used these slots in the early 2000s, but they've lost popularity because most motherboard makers simply use onboard networking and sound.

• **Figure 8.20** AMR slot

Case Fan Support

Every motherboard has a CPU fan power connector, as you'll recall from Chapter 5 in the CPU installation process, usually a four-wire connector that supports three-wire fans too. Some motherboards offer one or more fan power connectors for case fans. These are almost always only three-wire connectors. The case fans plugged into the motherboard can be monitored and controlled in Windows, unlike case fans connected only to the power supply, so they add a nice feature.

■ Expansion Bus

Expansion slots have been part of the PC from the very beginning. Way back then, IBM created the PC with an eye to the future; the original IBM PC had slots built into the motherboard—called **expansion slots**—for adding

expansion cards and thus new functions to the PC. The slots and accompanying wires and support chips on the first PC and on the latest and greatest PC are called the **expansion bus**.

Structure and Function of the Expansion Bus

As you've learned, every device in the computer—whether soldered to the motherboard or snapped into a socket—connects to the external data bus and the address bus. The expansion slots are no exception. They connect to the rest of the PC through the chipset. Exactly *where* on the chipset varies depending on the system. On some systems, the expansion slots connect to the Southbridge (see Figure 8.21). On other systems, the expansion slots connect to the Northbridge (see Figure 8.22). Finally, many systems have more than one type of expansion bus, with slots of one type connecting to the Northbridge and slots of another type connecting to the Southbridge (see Figure 8.23).

The chipset provides an extension of the address bus and data bus to the expansion slots, and thus to any expansion cards in those slots. If you plug a hard drive controller card into an expansion slot, it functions just as if it were built into the motherboard, albeit with one big difference: speed. As you'll recall from Chapter 5, the system crystal—the clock—pushes the CPU. The system crystal provides a critical function for the

• **Figure 8.21** Expansion slots connecting to Southbridge

• **Figure 8.22** Expansion slots connecting to Northbridge

entire PC, acting like a drill sergeant calling a cadence, setting the pace of activity in the computer. Every device soldered to the motherboard is designed to run at the speed of the system crystal. A 133-MHz motherboard, for example, has its chipset chips all timed by a 133-MHz crystal (see Figure 8.24).

Clock crystals aren't just for CPUs and chipsets. Pretty much every chip in your computer has a CLK wire and needs to be pushed by a clock chip, including the chips on your expansion cards. Suppose you buy a device that did not come with your computer—say, a sound card. The chips on the sound card need to be pushed by a CLK signal from a crystal. If PCs were designed to use the system crystal to push that sound card, sound card manufacturers would need to make sound cards for every possible motherboard speed. You would have to buy a 100-MHz sound card for a 100-MHz system or a 133-MHz sound card for a 133-MHz system.

• **Figure 8.23** Expansion slots connecting to both Northbridge and Southbridge

That would be ridiculous, and IBM knew it when they designed the PC. They had to make an extension to the external data bus that *ran at its own standardized speed*. You would use this part of the external data bus to snap new devices into the PC. IBM achieved this goal by adding a different crystal, called the **expansion bus crystal**, which controlled the part of the external data bus connected to the expansion slots (see Figure 8.25).

The expansion slots run at a much slower speed than the frontside bus. The chipset acts as the divider between the two buses, compensating for the speed difference with wait states and special buffering (storage) areas. No matter how fast the motherboard runs, the expansion slots run at a standard speed. In the original IBM PC, that speed was about 14.318 MHz ÷ 2, or about 7.16 MHz. Luckily, modern expansion buses run much faster! Let's start with the oldest of the modern expansion slots, PCI.

The system crystal sits on its own bus.

• **Figure 8.24** The system crystal sets the speed.

System crystal

Sound card

Modem card

CPU

Expansion crystal

● **Figure 8.25** Function of system and expansion bus crystals

PCI

Intel introduced the **Peripheral Component Interconnect (PCI)** bus architecture (see Figure 8.26) in the early 1990s, and the PC expansion bus was never again the same. Intel made many smart moves with PCI, not the least of which was releasing PCI to the public domain to make PCI very attractive to manufacturers. PCI provided a wider, faster, more flexible alternative than any previous expansion bus. The exceptional technology of the new bus, combined with the lack of a price tag, made manufacturers quickly drop older buses and adopt PCI.

PCI really shook up the PC world with its capabilities. The original PCI bus was 32 bits wide and ran at 33 MHz, which was superb, but these features were expected and not earth-shattering. The coolness of PCI came from its capability to coexist with other expansion buses. When PCI first came out, you could buy a motherboard with both PCI and older slots. This was important because users could keep their old expansion cards and slowly migrate to PCI. Equally impressive was that PCI devices were (and still are) self-configuring, a feature that led to the industry standard that became known as plug and play (PnP). Finally, PCI had a powerful burst-mode feature that enabled very efficient data transfers.

The original PCI expansion bus has soldiered on in PCs for almost twenty years at the time of this writing. Recently, more advanced forms have begun to appear. Although these new PCI expansion buses are faster than the original PCI, they're only improvements to

● **Figure 8.26** PCI expansion bus slots

PCI, not entirely new expansion buses. The original PCI might be fading away, but PCI in its many new forms is still "King of the Motherboard."

AGP

When video started going graphical with the introduction of Windows, the current buses were too slow and graphics looked terrible. PCI certainly improved graphics when it came out, but Intel was thinking ahead. Shortly after Intel invented PCI, they presented a specialized, video-only version of PCI called the **Accelerated Graphics Port (AGP)**. An AGP slot is a PCI slot, but one with a direct connection to the Northbridge. AGP slots are only for video cards—don't try to snap a sound card or modem into one. You'll learn much more about this fascinating technology in Chapter 13. Figure 8.27 shows a typical AGP slot.

There was a 64-bit version of the original PCI standard, but it was quite rare.

The AGP slot is almost universally brown in color, making it easy to spot.

• **Figure 8.27** AGP slot

PCI-X

PCI Extended (PCI-X) is a huge enhancement to PCI that is also fully backward compatible in terms of both hardware and software. PCI-X is a 64-bit-wide bus (see Figure 8.28). Its slots will accept regular PCI cards. The real bonus of PCI-X is its much enhanced speed. The PCI-X 2.0 standard features four speed grades (measured in MHz): PCI-X 66, PCI-X 133, PCI-X 266, and PCI-X 533.

• **Figure 8.28** PCI-X slot

The obvious candidates for PCI-X are businesses using workstations and servers, because they have the "need for speed" and also the need for backward compatibility. Large vendors, especially in the high-end market, are already on board. HP, Dell, and Intel server products, for example, support PCI-X. A quick online shopping trip reveals tons of PCI-X stuff for sale: gigabit NICs, Fibre Channel cards, video adapters, and more.

Mini-PCI

PCI has even made it into laptops in the specialty **Mini-PCI** format (see Figure 8.29). You'll find Mini-PCI in just about every laptop these days. Mini-PCI is designed to use low power and to lie flat—both good features for a laptop expansion slot. Mini-PCI returns in Chapter 18.

PCI Express

PCI Express (PCIe) is the latest, fastest, and most popular expansion bus in use today. As its name implies, PCI Express is still PCI, but it uses a point-to-point serial connection instead of PCI's shared parallel communication. Consider a single 32-bit chunk of data moving from a device to the CPU. In PCI parallel communication, 32 wires each carry one bit of that chunk

• **Figure 8.29** Tiny card in Mini-PCI slot. See the contacts at the bottom of the picture?

When you talk about the lanes, such as ×1 or ×8, use "by" rather than "ex" for the multiplication mark. So "by 1" and "by 8" is the correct pronunciation. You'll of course hear it spoken as both "by 8" and "8 ex" for the next few years until the technology has become a household term.

of data. In serial communication, only one wire carries those 32 bits. You'd think that 32 wires are better than one, correct? Well, first of all, PCIe doesn't share the bus. A PCIe device has its own direct connection (a point-to-point connection) to the Northbridge, so it does not wait for other devices. Plus, when you start going really fast (think gigabits per second), getting all 32 bits of data to go from one device to another at the same time is difficult, because some bits get there slightly faster than others. That means you need some serious, high-speed checking of the data when it arrives to verify that it's all there and in good shape. Serial data doesn't have this problem, as all of the bits arrive one after the other in a single stream. When data is really going fast, a single point-to-point serial connection is faster than a shared 32-wire parallel connection.

And boy howdy, is PCIe ever fast! A PCIe connection uses one wire for sending and one for receiving. Each of these pairs of wires between a PCIe controller and a device is called a *lane*. Each direction of a lane runs at 2.5 Gbps, or 5 Gbps with PCIe 2.0. Better yet, each point-to-point connection can use 1, 2, 4, 8, 12, 16, or 32 lanes to achieve a maximum theoretical bandwidth of 320 Gbps. The effective data rate drops a little bit because of the *encoding scheme*—the way the data is broken down and reassembled—but full-duplex data throughput can go up to a whopping 16 GBps on a ×16 connection.

The most common PCIe slot is the 16-lane (×16) version most commonly used for video cards, as shown in Figure 8.30. The first versions of PCIe motherboards used a combination of a single PCIe ×16 slot and a number of standard PCI slots. (Remember, PCI is designed to work with other expansion slots, even other types of PCI.) There is also a small form factor version of PCI Express for mobile computers called PCI Express Mini Card.

The bandwidth generated by a ×16 slot is far more than anything other than a video card would need, so most PCIe motherboards also contain slots with fewer lanes. Currently ×1 is the most common general-purpose PCIe slot (see Figure 8.31).

• **Figure 8.30** PCIe ×16 slot (black) with PCI slots (blue)

• **Figure 8.31** PCIe ×1 slot (top)

Try This!

Shopping Trip

So, what's the latest PCIe motherboard out there? Get online or go to your local computer store and research higher-end motherboards. What combinations of PCIe slots can you find on a single motherboard? Jot them down and compare your findings with your classmates' findings.

Installing Expansion Cards

Installing an expansion card successfully—another one of those bread-and-butter tasks for the PC tech—requires at least four steps. First, you need to know that the card works with the PC and the operating system. Second, you have to insert the card in an expansion slot properly and without damaging the card or the motherboard. Third, you need to provide drivers for the operating system—*proper* drivers for the *specific* OS. Fourth, you should always verify that the card functions properly before you walk away from the PC.

Step 1: Knowledge

Learn about the device you plan to install—preferably before you purchase it! Does the device work with the PC and the OS? Does it have drivers for the operating system? If you use Windows, the answer to these questions is almost always "yes." If you use an old operating system such as Windows XP or a less common operating system such as Linux, these questions become important. A lot of older hardware simply won't work with Windows Vista or Windows 7 at all, especially if you go for the 64-bit versions. Check the device's documentation and check the device manufacturer's Web site to verify that you have the correct drivers. While you're checking, make sure you have the latest version of the driver; most devices get driver updates more often than the weather changes in Texas.

For Windows systems, your best resource for this knowledge is the Microsoft Web site. The specific list of supported hardware has changed names many times. Currently for Windows 7 it's called the *Windows 7 Compatibility Center*. Earlier operating systems called it the *Hardware*

The four steps involved in installing expansion cards apply to all types of expansion cards. The CompTIA A+ 220-801 exam will ask you about cards ranging from the common—sound, video, and networking—to the legacy—serial, parallel, and modem. It will ask about wireless networking cards, TV tuner cards, video capture cards, and more, all of which we'll cover in their proper chapters in this book. You install any of them using the same four steps: knowledge, physical installation, device drivers, and verification.

• **Figure 8.32** Works with Windows 7!

• **Figure 8.33** Where to handle a card

Compatibility List (HCL) or *Windows Logo'd Product List*, and you'll still hear lots of people refer to it by one of those names, especially the former. You can check out the Web site here:

www.microsoft.com/windows/compatibility/windows-7/ en-us/default.aspx

This might list your product, but most people just look on the box of the device in question (see Figure 8.32)—all Windows-certified devices proudly display that they work with Windows.

Step 2: Physical Installation

To install an expansion card successfully, you need to take steps to avoid damaging the card, the motherboard, or both. This means knowing how to handle a card and avoiding electrostatic discharge (ESD) or any other electrical issue. You also need to place the card firmly and completely into an available expansion slot.

Optimally, a card should always be in one of two places: in a computer or in an anti-static bag. When inserting or removing a card, be careful to hold the card only by its edges. Do not hold the card by the slot connectors or touch any components on the board (see Figure 8.33).

Use an anti-static wrist strap if possible, properly attached to the PC, as noted in Chapter 2. If you don't have a wrist strap, you can use the tech way of avoiding ESD by touching the power supply after you remove the expansion card from its anti-static bag. This puts you, the card, and the PC at the same electrical potential and thus minimizes the risk of ESD.

Modern systems have a trickle of voltage on the motherboard at all times when the computer is plugged into a power outlet. Chapter 9 covers power for the PC and how to deal with it in detail, but here's the short version: *Always unplug the PC before inserting an expansion card!* Failure to do so can destroy the card, the motherboard, or both. It's not worth the risk.

Never insert or remove a card at an extreme angle. This may damage the card. A slight angle is acceptable and even necessary when removing a card. Always secure the card to the case with a connection screw or other retaining mechanism. This keeps the card from slipping out and potentially shorting against other cards. Also, many cards use the screw connection to ground the card to the case (see Figure 8.34).

Many technicians have been told to clean the slot connectors if a particular card is not working. This is almost never necessary after a card is installed and, if done improperly, can cause damage. You should clean slot connectors only if you have a card that's been on the shelf for a while and the contacts are obviously dull.

Never use a pencil eraser for this purpose. Pencil erasers can leave behind bits of residue that wedge between the card and slot, preventing contact and causing the card to fail. Grab a can of contact cleaning solution and use it instead. Contact cleaning solution is designed exactly for this purpose,

• **Figure 8.34** Always secure all cards properly.

cleans contacts nicely, and doesn't leave any residue. You can find contact cleaning solution at any electronics store.

A fully inserted expansion card sits flush against the back of the PC case—assuming the motherboard is mounted properly, of course—with no gap between the mounting bracket on the card and the screw hole on the case. If the card is properly seated, no contacts are exposed above the slot. Figure 8.35 shows a properly seated (meaning fitted snugly in the slot) expansion card.

 Cross Check

BIOS

Although most devices bring their own BIOS in the form of device drivers, that's not always the case, as you know from Chapter 7. So turn there now and see if you can answer these questions. Aside from device drivers, how can a device bring BIOS to a system so the device will work properly? What about devices that are common and necessary, such as the keyboard? How do they bring their own BIOS to a system? Or do they?

Step 3: Device Drivers

You know from Chapter 7 that all devices, whether built into the motherboard or added along the way, require BIOS. For almost all expansion

• **Figure 8.35** Properly seated expansion card; note the tight fit between case and mounting bracket and the evenness of the card in the slot.

cards, that BIOS comes in the form of **device drivers**—software support programs—loaded from an optical disc provided by the card manufacturer.

Installing device drivers is fairly straightforward. You should use the correct drivers—kind of obvious, but you'd be surprised how many techs mess this up—and, if you're upgrading, you might have to unload current drivers before loading new drivers. Finally, if you have a problem, you may need to uninstall the drivers you just loaded or roll back to earlier, more stable drivers.

Getting the Correct Drivers To be sure you have the best possible driver you can get for your device, you should always check the manufacturer's Web site. The drivers that come with a device may work well, but odds are good that you'll find a newer and better driver on the Web site. How do you know that the drivers on the Web site are newer? First, take the easy route: look on the disc. Often the version is printed right on the CD or DVD. If it's not printed there, you're going to have to load the disc in your optical drive and poke around. Many driver discs have an AutoRun screen that advertises the version. If nothing is on the pop-up screen, look for a Readme file (see Figure 8.36).

Driver or Device? In almost all cases, you should install the device driver after you install the device. Without the device installed, the driver installation will not see the device and will give an error screen. The only exceptions to this rule are USB and FireWire devices—with these you should always install the driver first.

Removing the Old Drivers Some cards—and this is especially true with video cards—require you to remove old drivers of the same type before you install the new device. To do this, you must first locate the driver in Device Manager. Right-click the device driver you want to uninstall and select Uninstall (see Figure 8.37). Many devices, especially ones that come with a lot of applications, will have an uninstall option in the Add or

• **Figure 8.36** Part of a Readme file showing the driver version

Remove Programs (Windows XP) or Programs and Features (Windows Vista/7) applet in the Control Panel (see Figure 8.38).

Unsigned Drivers Microsoft truly wants your computer to work, so they provide an excellent and rigorous testing program for hardware manufacturers called the **Windows Certification Program**. Developers initially use software to test their devices and, when they're ready, submit the device for further testing. Hardware and drivers that survive the testing get to wear the *Designed for Windows* logo. The drivers get a digital signature that says Microsoft tested them and found all was well.

Not all driver makers go through the rather involved process of the Windows Certification Program, so their software does not get a digital signature from Microsoft. When Windows runs into such a driver, it brings up a scary-looking screen (see Figure 8.39) that says you're about to install an **unsigned driver**.

The fact that a company refuses to use the Windows Certification Program doesn't mean their drivers are bad—it simply means they haven't gone through Microsoft's exhaustive quality-assurance certification procedure. If I run into this, I usually check the driver's version to make sure I'm not installing something outdated, and then I just take my chances and

• **Figure 8.37** Uninstalling a device

• **Figure 8.38** The Uninstall/Change option in Programs and Features

• Figure 8.39 Unsigned driver warning

install it. (I've yet to encounter a problem with an unsigned driver that I haven't also seen with *Designed for Windows* drivers.)

With the 64-bit versions of Windows Vista and Windows 7, Microsoft tightened the rules to try to provide the most stable platform possible. You simply cannot install unsigned drivers without clunky workarounds. Microsoft must approve each 64-bit driver.

Installing the New Driver You have two ways to install a new driver: by using the installation disc directly or by using the Add Hardware Wizard in the Control Panel. Most experienced techs prefer to run from the installation disc. Most devices come with extra programs. My motherboard comes with a number of handy applications for monitoring temperature and overclocking. The Add Hardware Wizard does not install anything but the drivers. Granted, some techs find this a blessing because they don't want all of the extra junk that sometimes comes with a device, but most installation discs give clear options so you can pick and choose what you want to install (see Figure 8.40).

The other reason to use installation discs instead of the Add Hardware Wizard stems from the fact that many expansion cards are actually many devices in one, and each device needs its own drivers. Some video cards have built-in TV tuners, for example. The Add Hardware Wizard will install all of the devices, but the installation disc brings them to your attention. Go for the optical disc installation program first and save the Add Hardware Wizard for problems, as you'll see in the next section.

Driver Rollback All versions of Windows offer the nifty feature of rolling back to previous drivers after an installation or driver upgrade. If you

Tech Tip

Permissions

To install drivers in a Windows computer, you need to have the proper permission. I'm not talking about asking somebody if you're allowed to install the device. Permissions are granted in Windows to enable people to do certain things, such as add a printer to a local computer or install software, or to stop people from being able to do such tasks. Specifically, you need administrative permissions to install drivers.

• Figure 8.40 Installation menu

decide to live on the edge and install beta drivers for your video card, for example, and your system becomes frightfully unstable, you can roll back to the drivers that worked before. (Not that I've ever had to use that feature....) To access the rollback feature, simply open Device Manager and access the properties for the device you want to adjust. On the Driver tab (see Figure 8.41), you'll find the Roll Back Driver button.

Step 4: Verify

As a last step in the installation process, inspect the results of the installation and verify that the device works properly. Immediately after installing, you should open Device Manager and verify that Windows sees the device (see Figure 8.42). Assuming that Device Manager shows the device working properly, your next check is to put the device to work by making it do whatever it is supposed to do. If you installed a printer, print something; if you installed a scanner, scan something. If it works, you're finished!

Troubleshooting Expansion Cards

A properly installed expansion card rarely makes trouble; it's the botched installations that produce headaches. Chances are high that you'll have to troubleshoot an expansion card installation at some point, usually from an installation you botched personally.

The first sign of an improperly installed card usually shows up the moment you try to get that card to do whatever it's supposed to do and it doesn't do it. When this happens, your primary troubleshooting process is a reinstallation—after checking in with Device Manager.

Other chapters in this book cover specific hardware troubleshooting: sound cards in Chapter 17, for example, and video cards in Chapter 13. Use

Tech Tip

Beta Drivers
Many PC enthusiasts try to squeeze every bit of performance out of their PC components, much as auto enthusiasts tinker with engine tunings to get a little extra horsepower out of their engines. Expansion card manufacturers love enthusiasts, who often act as free testers for their unpolished drivers, known as beta drivers. Beta drivers are fine for the most part, but they can sometimes cause amazing system instability—never a good thing! If you use beta drivers, make sure you know how to uninstall or roll back to previous drivers.

• **Figure 8.41** Driver rollback feature

• **Figure 8.42** Device Manager shows the device working properly.

this section to help you decide what to look for and how to deal with the problem.

Device Manager provides the first diagnostic and troubleshooting tool in Windows. After you install a new device, Device Manager gives you many clues if something has gone wrong.

Occasionally, Device Manager may not even show the new device. If that happens, verify that you inserted the device properly and, if needed, that the device has power. Run the Add Hardware Wizard and see if Windows recognizes the device. You'll find the wizard as a Control Panel applet in Windows XP and Windows Vista. In Windows 7, you run the program by clicking Start and typing the name of the executable in the Search bar: **hdwwiz.exe**.

If Device Manager doesn't recognize the device at this point, you have one of two problems: either the device is physically damaged and you must replace it, or the device is an onboard device, not a card, and is turned off in CMOS.

Device Manager rarely completely fails to see a device. More commonly, device problems manifest themselves in Device Manager via error icons:

- A black "!" on a yellow circle (Windows XP) or triangle (Windows Vista/7) indicates that a device is missing (see Figure 8.43), that Windows does not recognize a device, or that there's a device driver problem. A device may still work even while producing this error.

- A black downward-pointing arrow on a white field in Windows Vista and Windows 7 indicates a disabled device. This usually points to a device that's been manually turned off, or a damaged device. A device producing this error will not work. Windows XP uses a red "X" for the same status indicator.

The "!" symbol is the most common error symbol and usually the easiest to fix. First, double-check the device's connections. Second, try reinstalling the driver with the Update Driver button. To get to the Update Driver button, right-click the desired device in Device Manager and select Properties. In the Properties dialog box, select the Driver tab. On the Driver tab, click the Update Driver button to open the updating wizard (see Figure 8.44).

If you get a downward-pointing arrow or a red "X" error, first check that the device isn't disabled. Right-click on the device and select Enable. If that doesn't work (it often does not), try rolling back the driver (if you updated the driver) or uninstalling (if it's a new install). Shut the system down and make triple-sure you have the card physically installed. Then redo the entire driver installation procedure, making sure you have the most current driver for that device. If none of these procedures works, return the card—it's almost certainly bad.

As you look at the errors in Device Manager, you'll notice error codes for the device that does not work properly. Windows has about 20 error codes, but the fixes still boil down to the same methods just shown. If you really want to frustrate yourself, try the Troubleshooter. It starts most fixes the same way: by reinstalling the device driver.

• **Figure 8.43** An "!" in Device Manager, indicating a problem with the selected device

• **Figure 8.44** Updating the driver

■ Upgrading and Installing Motherboards

To most techs, the concept of adding or replacing a motherboard can be extremely intimidating. It really shouldn't be; motherboard installation is a common and necessary part of PC repair. It is inexpensive and easy, although it can sometimes be a little tedious and messy because of the large number of parts involved. This section covers the process of installation and replacement and shows you some of the tricks that make this necessary process easy to handle.

Choosing the Motherboard and Case

Choosing a motherboard and case can prove quite a challenge for any tech, whether newly minted or a seasoned veteran. You first have to figure out the type of motherboard you want, such as AMD- or Intel-based. Then you need to think about the form factor, which of course influences the type of case you'll need. Third, how rich in features is the motherboard and how tough is it to configure? You have to read the motherboard manual to find out. Finally, you need to select the case that matches your space needs, budget, and form factor. Now look at each step in a little more detail.

 Being able to select and install a motherboard appropriate for a client or customer is something every CompTIA A+ technician should know.

Try This!

Building a Recommendation

Family, friends, and potential clients often solicit the advice of a tech when they're thinking about upgrading their PC. This solicitation puts you on the spot to make not just any old recommendation, but one that works with the needs and budget of the potential upgrader. To do this successfully, you need to manage expectations and ask the right questions, so Try This!

What does the upgrader want to do that compels him or her to upgrade? Write it down! Some of the common motivations for upgrading are to play that hot new game or to take advantage of new technology. What's the minimum system needed to run tomorrow's action games? What do you need to make multimedia sing? Does the motherboard need to have SuperSpeed USB 3.0 built in to accommodate digital video or some other special purpose?

How much of the current system does the upgrader want to save? Upgrading a motherboard can very quickly turn into a complete system rebuild. What form factor is the old case? If it's a microATX case, that constrains the motherboards you can use with it to microATX or the smaller FlexATX. If the desired motherboard is a full-sized ATX board, you'll need to get a new case. Does the new motherboard possess the same type of CPU socket as the old motherboard? If not, that's a sure sign you'll need to upgrade the CPU as well. What about RAM? If the old motherboard was using DDR SDRAM, and the new motherboard requires DDR2 or DDR3 SDRAM, you'll need to replace the RAM. If you need to upgrade the memory, it is best to know how many channels the new RAM interface supports, because performance is best when all channels are populated. What if the old motherboard was using an AGP graphics accelerator that the new motherboard does not support, but you don't want to splurge on a PCI Express graphics accelerator right now? In this situation you might want to consider moving to a motherboard with integrated graphics. What's great about integrated graphics is that if the motherboard also possesses a ×16 PCI Express slot, you can upgrade to a more powerful discrete graphics accelerator later.

Once you've gathered information on motivation and assessed the current PC of the upgrader, it's time to get down to business: field trip time! This is a great excuse to get to the computer store and check out the latest motherboards and gadgets. Don't forget to jot down notes and prices while you're there. By the end of the field trip, you should have the information to give the upgrader an honest assessment of what an upgrade will entail, at least in monetary terms. Be honest—in other words, don't just tell upgraders what you think they want to hear—and you won't get in trouble.

First, determine what motherboard you need. What CPU are you using? Will the motherboard work with that CPU? Because most of us buy the CPU and the motherboard at the same time, make the seller guarantee that the CPU will work with the motherboard. If you can, choose a motherboard that works with much higher speeds than the CPU you can afford; that way

you can upgrade later. How much RAM do you intend to install? Are extra RAM sockets available for future upgrades?

A number of excellent motherboard manufacturers currently exist. Some of the more popular brands are ASUS, BIOSTAR, DFI, GIGABYTE, Intel, MSI, and Shuttle. Your supplier may also have some lesser-known but perfectly acceptable brands of motherboards. As long as the supplier has an easy return policy, it's perfectly fine to try one of these.

Second, make sure you're getting a form factor that works with your case. Don't try to put a regular ATX motherboard into a microATX case!

Third, all motherboards come with a technical manual, better known as the **motherboard book** (see Figure 8.45). You must have this book! This book is your primary source for all of the critical information about the motherboard. If you set up CPU or RAM timings incorrectly in CMOS, for example, and you have a dead PC, where would you find the CMOS-clear jumper? Where do you plug in the speaker? Even if you let someone else install the motherboard, insist on the motherboard book; you will need it.

Fourth, pick your case carefully. Cases come in many sizes: slimline, desktop, mini-tower, mid-tower, tower, and cube. Plus you can get specialized cases, such as tiny cases for entertainment systems or ones that fit the same format as a stereo receiver or DVD player. Slimline and desktop models generally sit on the desk, beneath the monitor. The various tower cases usually occupy a bit of floor space next to the desk. The mini-tower and mid-tower cases are the most popular choices. Make sure you get a case that fits your motherboard—most microATX and all FlexATX cases are too small for a regular ATX motherboard. Cube cases generally require a specific motherboard, so be prepared to buy both pieces at once. A quick test-fit before you buy saves a lot of return trips to the supplier.

Cases come with many options, but three more common options point to a better case. One option is a removable face (see Figure 8.46) to make disassembly much easier.

Chapter 21 covers items needed for specialized PCs.

Tech Tip

Replacement Motherboard Books
If you have a motherboard with no manual, you can usually find a copy of the manual in Adobe Acrobat (.PDF) format online at the manufacturer's Web site. It's a good idea to grab and print a copy to keep with the motherboard. I often tape a copy (either hard copy or burned onto a disc) of the manual in the case where I installed the motherboard. Just don't cover any vents!

• **Figure 8.45** Motherboard box and book

• **Figure 8.46** Removable face

• **Figure 8.47** Case with both front-mounted ports and an add-on flash memory card reader

 The CompTIA A+ 801 exam will test you on the basics of installing a motherboard.

 Watch out for ESD here! Remember that it's very easy to damage or destroy a CPU and RAM with a little electrostatic discharge. It's also fairly easy to damage the motherboard with ESD. Always wear an anti-static wrist strap.

 Pay attention to the location of the standouts if you're swapping a motherboard. If you leave a screw-type standout beneath a spot on the motherboard where you can't add a screw and then apply power to the motherboard, you run the risk of shorting the motherboard.

Another common feature, front-mounted ports for USB, FireWire, and headphones, can make using a PC much easier. Better cases offer these ports, although you can also get add-on components that fit into the now-useless floppy drive bay to bring added front connectivity to the PC. Figure 8.47 shows a case with both types of front connectors.

Better cases offer tool-free component installation, so you don't have to screw down cards or drives. They just snap into place. (You'll still need a trusty screwdriver to secure the motherboard, though. No installation is completely tool-free yet.)

Power supplies often come with the case. Watch out for "really good deal" cases because that invariably points to a cheap or missing power supply. You also need to verify that the power supply has sufficient wattage. This issue is handled in Chapter 9.

Installing the Motherboard

If you're replacing a motherboard, first remove the old motherboard. Begin by removing all of the cards. Also remove anything else that might impede removal or installation of the motherboard, such as a hard drive. Keep track of the screws—a good idea is to return the screws to their mounting holes temporarily, at least until you can reinstall the parts. Sometimes you even have to remove the power supply temporarily to enable access to the motherboard.

Unscrew the motherboard. *It will not simply lift out.* The motherboard mounts to the case via small connectors called **standouts** that slide into keyed slots or screw into the bottom of the case (see Figure 8.48). Screws then go into the standouts to hold the motherboard in place. Be sure to place the standouts properly before installing the new motherboard.

When you insert the new motherboard, do not assume that you will put the screws and standouts in the same place as they were in your old motherboard. When it comes to the placement of screws and standouts, only one rule applies: anywhere it fits. Do not be afraid to be a little tough here! Installing motherboards can be a wiggling, twisting, knuckle-scraping process.

The next part of motherboard installation is connecting the LEDs, buttons, and front-mounted ports on the front of the box. This is sometimes easier to do before you install the motherboard fully in the case. You can trace the wire leads from the front of the case to the appropriate standouts on the motherboard. These usually include the following:

- Soft power button
- Reset button
- Speaker
- Hard drive activity light
- Power light
- USB
- FireWire
- Sound

Before the Case

A lot of techs install the CPU, CPU fan, and RAM into the motherboard before installing the motherboard into the case. This helps in several ways, especially with a new system. First, you want to make certain that the CPU and RAM work well with the motherboard and with each other—without that, you have no hope of setting up a stable system. Second, installing these components first prevents the phenomenon of flexing the motherboard. Some cases don't provide quite enough support for the motherboard, and pushing in RAM can make the board bend. Third, attaching a CPU fan can be a bear of a task, one that's considerably easier to do on a table top than within the confines of a case.

• **Figure 8.48** Standout in a case, ready for the motherboard

These wires have specific pin connections to the motherboard. Although you can refer to the motherboard book for their location, usually a quick inspection of the motherboard will suffice for an experienced tech (see Figure 8.49).

You need to follow a few rules when installing these wires. First, the lights are LEDs, not light bulbs; they have a positive side and a negative side. If they don't work one way, turn the connector around and try the other. Second, when in doubt, guess. Incorrect installation only results in the device not working; it won't damage the computer. Refer to the motherboard book for the correct installation. The third and last rule is that, with the exception of the soft power switch on an ATX system, you do not need any of these wires for the computer to run. Many techs often simply ignore these wires, although this would not be something I'd do to any system but my own.

No hard-and-fast rule exists for determining the function of each wire. Often the function of each wire is printed on the connector (see Figure 8.50). If not, track each wire to the LED or switch to determine its function.

Finally, install the motherboard into the case fully and secure it with the appropriate screws. Once you get the motherboard mounted in the case, with the CPU and RAM

• **Figure 8.49** Motherboard wire connections labeled on the motherboard

Very old motherboards used to require techs to set jumpers to determine the bus speed for the motherboard. This enabled these motherboards to accommodate CPUs that needed a 100-MHz bus, for example, and other CPUs that needed a 66-MHz bus. The CompTIA A+ exams might refer to these kinds of manual adjustments needed for installation.

Setting these jumpers incorrectly resulted in bizarre behavior. First, if you set the bus speed too high, many CPUs wouldn't even try to power up. If you set the speed too low, you wouldn't get optimal use out of the CPU. The motherboard manuals had extensive charts for settings for the CPUs supported.

Modern motherboards autodetect CPU and RAM settings and adjust accordingly, so these errors only happen when you intentionally overclock or underclock a CPU through the CMOS setup utility.

properly installed, it's time to insert the power connections and test it. A POST card can be helpful with the system test because you won't have to add the speaker, a video card, monitor, and keyboard to verify that the system is booting. If you have a POST card, start the system, and watch to see if the POST takes place—you should see a number of POST codes before the POST stops. If you don't have a POST card, install a keyboard, speaker, video card, and monitor. Boot the system and see if the BIOS information shows up on the screen. If it does, you're probably okay. If it doesn't, it's time to refer to the motherboard book to see where you made a mistake.

If you get no power at all, check to make sure you plugged in all the necessary power connectors. If you get power to fans but get nothing on the screen, you could have several problems. The CPU, RAM, or video card might not be connected to the motherboard properly. The only way to determine the problems is to test. Check the easy connections first (RAM and video) before removing and reseating the CPU. (Also, see Chapter 9 for power issues.)

• **Figure 8.50** Sample of case wires

Chapter 8 Review

■ Chapter Summary

After reading this chapter and completing the exercises, you should understand the following about motherboards.

Explain how motherboards work

- Every piece of hardware connects either directly or indirectly to the motherboard. Wires called traces make up the buses on the system, enabling hardware to communicate. Motherboards are several layers thick, with traces running across each layer, creating a veritable highway of wires.

- Motherboards are defined by their form factor, chipset, and components. The form factor defines the physical size and airflow; the chipset defines the type of CPU, the type and amount of RAM, and the components a motherboard will support.

- The Advanced Technology (AT) form factor, though now obsolete, was the predominant form factor for motherboards through the mid-1990s. Its identifying features included a large keyboard plug and a split power socket called P8/P9.

- LPX and NLX were slimline form factors, meaning they were ideal for low-profile cases. They offered a central riser slot to accept a special riser card into which expansion cards fit horizontally.

- The Advanced Technology Extended (ATX) form factor replaced AT as the form factor of choice by the late 1990s. It offered several improvements over AT, including repositioning the power supply for better airflow, easier access to CPU and RAM slots, and better performance by moving RAM closer to the Northbridge and CPU. MicroATX (µATX) and FlexATX are subtypes of ATX and are considerably smaller.

- The ITX form factor is newer than ATX and is designed to support small form factor (SFF) systems. While the regular ITX form factor never gained acceptance, the Mini-ITX, Nano-ITX, and Pico-ITX form factors are quite popular.

- Several PC manufacturers make proprietary motherboards, meaning they do not adhere to a standard form factor such as ATX or ITX. Servicing a system like this can be frustrating, as parts may be difficult to find and are often available only from authorized dealers.

- Motherboards come with differing features or components such as USB/FireWire ports, audio, video, RAID, and AMR or CNR slots for modems and network cards. Sometimes a motherboard supports several USB/FireWire ports but does not have rear ports for all of them. In this case, the motherboard likely has connections for the additional ports to be used in conjunction with a dongle to create front-mounted ports.

- Popular motherboard manufacturers include ASUS, BIOSTAR, DFI, GIGABYTE, Intel, MSI, VIA, and Shuttle.

Recognize modern expansion buses

- Every device in the computer connects to the external data bus and the address bus. Expansion slots enable expansion cards to connect to these same buses. Depending on the system, the expansion slots may connect to the Southbridge or the Northbridge. Many systems have more than one type of expansion bus, with slots connecting to both the Southbridge and the Northbridge. It is the chipset that extends the address bus and data bus to the expansion slots.

- Expansion buses run at a standardized speed, depending on the type of expansion bus. This speed, which is much slower than the frontside bus, is dictated by the expansion bus crystal. The chipset uses wait states and buffers to compensate for the difference in speed between the expansion and frontside buses.

- PCI is 32 bits, runs at 33 MHz, and is self-configuring (no more manual configuration of expansion card jumpers). Additionally, it coexists with other expansion buses.

- AGP is a special PCI slot for video cards, with a direct connection to the Northbridge. You can easily find the AGP slot on a motherboard: a lone slot that's brown in color.

- Enhancements to the PCI bus paved the way for a few modern variations. PCI-X is 64 bits wide, backward compatible with PCI, and available in a variety of speeds up to 533 MHz. Mini-PCI is designed for laptops with an emphasis on low power consumption and a small, flat physical design. Finally, PCIe, with its point-to-point serial connection, touts speeds as high as 16 GBps.

Upgrade and install motherboards

- Not all motherboards fit in all cases. If you upgrade a motherboard, make sure the new motherboard fits in the existing case. If you purchase a new motherboard and a new case, make sure you purchase a case that supports the form factor of your motherboard.

- Determine the CPU you or your client wants before purchasing a motherboard. Not all CPUs are supported by, or even fit in, all motherboards. Make sure your motherboard supports your CPU and, if possible, purchase a motherboard that supports higher speeds than your CPU in case you want to upgrade the processor at a later time.

- To replace a motherboard, first remove all of the expansion cards from the old motherboard. Unscrew the motherboard and remove it from the case.

- Before installing a new motherboard in the case, attach the CPU, heat sink/fan, and RAM. Check the standouts in the case—you might have to add or remove a few to accommodate the new motherboard. Once installed, boot the system and make sure there are no POST errors and the BIOS information appears on the screen. Then install any expansion cards.

- Cases come with a series of little wires that connect to LEDs on the front of the case. You need to plug these wires in to the motherboard for the LEDs to function. LEDs have a positive side and a negative side, so the wires must be connected the right way or the LEDs will not work. If you find that the LEDs are not working, turn the connector around to reverse the positive/negative connection. Getting it wrong will not damage your system; it will only cause the LEDs not to light up.

■ Key Terms

Accelerated Graphics Port (AGP) *(195)*
AT *(182)*
ATX *(184)*
audio modem riser (AMR) *(191)*
chipset *(181)*
communications and networking riser (CNR) *(191)*
device driver *(200)*
expansion bus *(192)*
expansion bus crystal *(193)*
expansion slot *(191)*
FlexATX *(185)*
form factor *(181)*
I/O Controller Hub (ICH) *(189)*
LPX *(183)*
Memory Controller Hub (MCH) *(189)*
microATX (μATX) *(185)*
Mini-ITX *(186)*
Mini-PCI *(195)*
motherboard *(180)*

motherboard book *(207)*
Nano-ITX *(186)*
NLX *(183)*
Northbridge *(188)*
P8/P9 *(182)*
PCI Express (PCIe) *(195)*
PCI Extended (PCI-X) *(195)*
Peripheral Component Interconnect (PCI) *(194)*
Pico-ITX *(186)*
printed circuit board (PCB) *(181)*
riser card *(183)*
slimline *(183)*
Southbridge *(188)*
standouts *(208)*
super I/O chip *(188)*
traces *(180)*
unsigned driver *(201)*
Windows Certification Program *(201)*

Key Term Quiz

Use the Key Terms list to complete the sentences that follow. Not all terms will be used.

1. The _____ defines the type of processor and RAM required for the motherboard and determines to a degree the built-in devices supported by a motherboard, including the expansion slots.

2. The most common bus on today's computers is the flexible _____ and its derivatives.

3. The _____ form factor replaced the LPX slimline form factor.

4. The _____ bus was designed for laptop computers.

5. The _____ determines the physical size of the motherboard as well as the general location of components and ports.

6. The smallest ATX motherboard form factor is the _____.

7. The newest and fastest expansion bus in use today, with speeds up to 16 Gbps, is _____.

8. A device driver for a device manufactured by a company that is not participating in the Windows Certification Program is reported as a(n) _____.

9. The _____ is your primary source for all of the critical information about the motherboard.

10. The motherboard mounts to the case via small connectors called _____ that slide into keyed slots or screw into the bottom of the case.

Multiple-Choice Quiz

1. Which of the following are part of the ATX form factor? (Select two.)
 A. FlexATX
 B. macroATX
 C. microATX
 D. picoATX

2. Which of the following form factors dominates the PC market?
 A. AT
 B. ATX
 C. Mini-ITX
 D. NLX

3. Which of the following slots features serial data transfers?
 A. AGP
 B. PCI
 C. PCIe
 D. PCI-X

4. A client brought in an old computer that won't boot. He wants to see if any data can be recovered from the hard drive. When the tech opened the case, he noted that two expansion cards were plugged into some kind of circuit board that plugged into the motherboard. The expansion cards were parallel with the motherboard, in other words, rather than perpendicular. Into what kind of circuit board did the expansion cards most likely connect? (Select two.)
 A. Daughterboard
 B. Expansion board
 C. Riser card
 D. Southbridge

5. In a routine check of a system newly built by her latest intern, Sarah discovers that everything works except the hard drive and power LEDs on the front of the case. What could be the problem? (Select two.)
 A. The intern forgot to connect the LED leads to the motherboard.
 B. The intern reversed the LED leads to the motherboard.
 C. There is no power to the motherboard.
 D. There is no activity on the hard drive.

6. Robert installed a new motherboard, CPU, and RAM into his old case. After he attached the power correctly and pressed the power button, not only did the system not boot up, but he smelled ozone and realized the motherboard had shorted out. What could have been the cause?

 A. Robert installed an ATX motherboard into an ITX case.

 B. Robert installed an ITX motherboard into an ATX case.

 C. Robert used an ITX power supply on an ATX motherboard.

 D. Robert left a standout in the wrong place under the motherboard.

7. Which of the following enables you to access the Add Hardware Wizard in Windows 7 Professional?

 A. addhdware.exe

 B. hdware.exe

 C. hdwwiz.exe

 D. addhwiz.exe

8. Brian bought a new motherboard that advertised support for eight USB ports. When he pulled the motherboard out of the box, though, he found that it only had four USB ports. What's likely the issue here?

 A. The extra four USB ports will connect to the front of the case or via a dongle to an expansion slot.

 B. The extra four USB ports require an add-on expansion card.

 C. The FireWire port will have a splitter that makes it four USB ports.

 D. The motherboard chipset might support eight USB ports, but the manufacturer only included four ports.

9. Martin bought a new motherboard to replace his older ATX motherboard. As he left the shop, the tech on duty called after him, "Check your standouts!" What could the tech have meant?

 A. Standouts are the connectors on the motherboard for the front panel buttons, such as the on/off switch and reset button.

B. Standouts are the metal edges on some cases that aren't rolled.

C. Standouts are the metal connectors that attach the motherboard to the case.

D. Standouts are the dongles that enable a motherboard to support more than four USB ports.

10. What should you always do before installing an expansion card?

 A. Reboot the PC

 B. Install device drivers

 C. Unplug the PC

 D. Update Windows

11. Solon has a very buggy computer that keeps locking up at odd moments and rebooting spontaneously. He suspects the motherboard. How should he test it?

 A. Check settings and verify good components.

 B. Verify good components and document all testing.

 C. Replace the motherboard first to see if the problems disappear.

 D. Check settings, verify good components, replace components, and document all testing.

12. As tech support for a computer shop, you receive a call from an irate customer insisting that you sent him the wrong motherboard, because it won't fit in his old case. Which of the following questions might enable you to determine the problem? Select the best answer.

 A. Will you describe the location of the connectors on the back of the motherboard?

 B. Will you describe the location of the standouts on the case?

 C. What kind of CPU are you using?

 D. What type of RAM are you using?

13. Which of the following companies makes chipsets?

 A. AMI

 B. GIGABYTE

 C. MSI

 D. AMD

14. What purpose does the Super I/O chip serve?

 A. The Super I/O chip handles the communication with RAM.

 B. The Super I/O chip handles the communication with video.

 C. The Super I/O chip handles the communication with legacy devices.

 D. The Super I/O chip handles the communication between the Northbridge and Southbridge chips.

15. What should you do *before* installing an expansion card? (Select two.)

 A. Attach an anti-static wrist strap

 B. Install the drivers

 C. Plug the PC into a grounded outlet

 D. Unplug the PC

■ Essay Quiz

1. This chapter talks about motherboards made in layers that contain the wires or traces. Find an Internet site that talks about the motherboard manufacturing process. Why do you think motherboards are made in layers? What advantages do the layers provide?

2. Some people believe that selecting a motherboard based on the motherboard chipset is even more important than basing the decision on the kind of processor. Do you agree or disagree, and why?

3. Prepare a PowerPoint presentation or write a paper that would help your classmates select and replace a bad motherboard. Be sure to walk through all of the necessary steps.

4. Your neighbors Dora and Jim just learned that you're studying computer hardware. They feel that their computer is slightly out of date. They want to upgrade the processor, but not the motherboard. Prepare a list of at least five questions you should ask them before you know what CPU they can choose or whether it is feasible to upgrade their system.

Lab Projects

• Lab Project 8.1

Examine all of the ports and connectors on the back of your computer. With the computer turned off, you may disconnect the cables from the ports. (If necessary, document where and how the cables are connected so you can replace them correctly.) Determine the kinds of ports that are built in and those that are provided by expansion cards. From this information alone, can you ascertain whether your motherboard is an ATX or ITX form factor? What else would you need to know, if anything? Draw a diagram of the back of your system and label every port and all connectors. State if their sources are from the motherboard or from an expansion card. Last, state the form factor of the motherboard.

• Lab Project 8.2

One of the most important skills a PC technician can possess is the ability to read and interpret documentation. No single piece of documentation is as important as the motherboard book. Let's see how well you can understand this documentation. Consult your motherboard book or use one that your instructor provides. (If you do not have the motherboard book, try to download it from the manufacturer's Web site.) Then write a paragraph about your motherboard that includes answers to the following questions:

- What make and model is the motherboard?
- What chipset does it use?
- What kinds of RAM slots does it contain?
- What kinds of expansion slots does your motherboard have and how many of each kind does it have?

- What kinds of onboard ports does it have?
- What kinds of CPUs does it support and what kind of processor slot does it have?
- Does your motherboard use jumpers or dip switches for configuration? If so, what do the jumpers or dip switches control?
- The motherboard book probably contains an illustration of the way the motherboard components are laid out. By examining this illustration, determine what form factor your motherboard uses.
- Does your motherboard have any unusual or proprietary features?

• Lab Project 8.3

You know now how important the motherboard chipset is in determining the kind of CPU and RAM that you can install in the computer. You also know that motherboards may look similar but have very different features and prices. Imagine that you are going to build a new computer by ordering the components. Price is not a problem, so you will want to select the best and most powerful components. On the Internet, search sites such as www.intel.com or www.amd.com along with sites such as www.newegg.com to select a motherboard and a particular chipset. Then select a compatible CPU and RAM. Explain where you found the information about the components, what brands/models you selected, and how much each will cost.

Now imagine that your budget will not allow you to buy these components at this time. In fact, you've decided that you can afford only 75 percent of the cost of these components. What will you do to save money? Will you change the motherboard and the chipset or will you use a less powerful CPU with a smaller amount of RAM? Consider what you can upgrade at a later time when you have more available cash. Again search the Internet and select components that would be satisfactory but are not the latest and the greatest. Be sure that the CPU and RAM you select are indeed compatible with your motherboard and chipset. What did you select and how much will it cost you?

Lab Projects

• Lab Project 8.4

Open your computer case and determine the kind of expansion slots available on your motherboard. How many of each kind are available? What cards are installed in the slots? Now examine the back and front of the computer case to see what ports are available. What devices do you have plugged into the ports?

Power Supplies

In this chapter, you will learn how to

- **Explain the basics of electricity**
- **Describe the details about powering the PC**
- **Install and maintain power supplies**

Powering the PC requires a single box—the power supply—that takes electricity from the wall socket and transforms it into electricity to run the motherboard and other internal components. Figure 9.1 shows a typical power supply inside a case. All of the wires dangling out of it connect to the motherboard and peripherals.

As simple as this appears on the surface, power supply issues are of critical importance for techs. Problems with power can create system instability, crashes, and data loss—all things most computer users would rather avoid! Good techs therefore know an awful lot about powering the PC, from understanding the basic principles of electricity to knowing the many variations of PC power supplies. Plus, you need to know how to recognize power problems and implement the proper solutions. Too many techs fall into the "just plug it in" camp and never learn how to deal with power, much to their clients' unhappiness.

• **Figure 9.1** Typical power supply mounted inside the PC system unit

Historical/Conceptual

■ Understanding Electricity

Electricity is a flow of negatively charged particles, called electrons, through matter. All matter enables the flow of electrons to some extent. This flow of electrons is very similar to the flow of water through pipes; so similar that the best way to learn about electricity is by comparing it to how water flows though pipes. So let's talk about water for a moment.

Water comes from the ground, through wells, aquifers, rivers, and so forth. In a typical city, water comes to you through pipes from the water supply company that took it from the ground. What do you pay for when you pay your water bill each month? You pay for the water you use, certainly, but built into the price of the water you use is the surety that when you turn the spigot, water will flow at a more or less constant rate. The water sits in the pipes under pressure from the water company, waiting for you to turn the spigot.

Electricity works essentially the same way as water. Electric companies gather or generate electricity and then push it to your house under pressure through wires. Just like water, the electricity sits in the wires, waiting for you to plug something into the wall socket, at which time it'll flow at a more or less constant rate. You plug a lamp into an electrical outlet and flip the switch, electricity flows, and you have light. You pay for reliability, electrical pressure, and electricity used.

The pressure of the electrons in the wire is called *voltage* and is measured in units called **volts (V)**. The amount of electrons moving past a certain point on a wire is called the *current* or *amperage*, which is measured in units called **amperes (amps or A)**. The amount of amps and volts needed

so that a particular device will function is expressed as how much **wattage (watts or W)** that device needs. The correlation between the three is very simple math: V × A = W (or VA = W). You'll learn more about wattage a little later in this chapter.

Wires of all sorts—whether copper, tin, gold, or platinum—have a slight **resistance** to the flow of electrons, just as water pipes have a slight amount of friction that resists the flow of water. Resistance to the flow of electrons is measured in **ohms (Ω)**.

- Pressure = voltage (V)
- Volume flowing = amperes (A)
- Work = wattage (W)
- Resistance = ohms (Ω)

A particular thickness of wire only handles so much electricity at a time. If you push too much through, the wire will overheat and break, much as an overloaded water pipe will burst. To make sure you use the right wire for the right job, all electrical wires have an amperage rating, such as 20 amps. If you try to push 30 amps through a 20-amp wire, the wire will break and electrons will seek a way to return into the ground. Not a good thing, especially if the path back to the ground is through you!

Circuit breakers and ground wires provide the basic protection from accidental overflow. A circuit breaker is a heat-sensitive electrical switch rated at a certain amperage. If you push too much amperage through the circuit breaker, the wiring inside detects the increase in heat and automatically opens, stopping the flow of electricity before the wiring overheats and breaks. You reset the circuit breaker to reestablish the circuit, and electricity flows once more through the wires. A ground wire provides a path of least resistance for electrons to flow back to ground in case of an accidental overflow.

An electrical outlet must have a ground wire to be suitable for PC use.

Many years ago, your electrical supply used fuses instead of circuit breakers. Fuses are small devices with a tiny filament designed to break if subjected to too much current. Unfortunately, fuses had to be replaced every time they blew, making circuit breakers much more preferable. Even though you no longer see fuses in a building's electrical circuits, many electrical devices—such as a PC's power supply—often still use fuses for their own internal protection.

Electricity comes in two flavors: **direct current (DC)**, in which the electrons flow in one direction around a continuous circuit, and **alternating current (AC)**, in which the flow of electrons alternates direction back and forth in a circuit (see Figure 9.2). Most electronic devices use DC power, but all power companies supply AC power because AC travels long distances much more efficiently than DC.

Constant voltage in one direction

Voltage in both directions, constantly switching back and forth

• **Figure 9.2** Diagrams showing DC and AC flow of electrons

■ Powering the PC

Your PC uses DC voltage, so some conversion process must take place before the PC can use AC power from the power company. The power supply in a computer converts high-voltage AC power from the wall socket to low-voltage DC. The first step in powering the PC, therefore, is to get and maintain a good supply of AC power. Second, you need a power supply to convert AC to the proper voltage and amperage of DC power for the motherboard and peripherals. Finally, you need to control the byproduct of electricity use, namely heat. Let's look at the specifics of powering the PC.

Supplying AC

Every PC power supply must have standard AC power from the power company, supplied steadily rather than in fits and spurts, and protection against accidental blurps in the supply. The power supply connects to the power cord (and thus to an electrical outlet) via a standard **IEC-320** connector. In the United States, standard AC comes in somewhere between 110 and 120 V, often written as ~115 VAC (volts of alternating current). The rest of the world uses 220–240 VAC, so most power supplies are dual-voltage and compatible with both. Power supplies with voltage-selection switches are referred to as fixed-input. Power supplies that you do not have to manually switch for different voltages are known as auto-switching. Figure 9.3 shows the back of a power supply. Note the three components, from top to bottom: the hard on/off switch, the 115/230 switch, and the IEC-320 connector.

Flipping the AC switch on the back of a power supply can wreak all kinds of havoc on a PC. Moving the switch to ~230 V in the United States makes for a great practical joke (as long as the PC is off when you do it)—the PC might try to boot up but probably won't get far. You don't risk damaging anything by running at half the AC the power supply is expecting. In countries that run ~230 standard, on the other hand, firing up the PC with the AC switch set to ~115 can cause the power supply to die a horrid, smoking death. Watch that switch!

• **Figure 9.3** Back of fixed-input power supply, showing typical switches and power connection

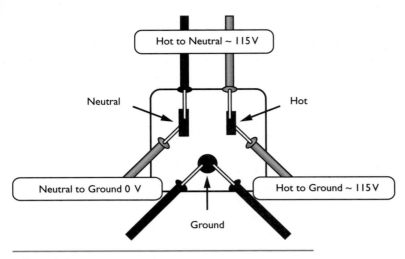

Hot to Neutral ~ 115V

Neutral

Hot

Neutral to Ground 0 V

Hot to Ground ~ 115V

Ground

• **Figure 9.4** Outlet voltages

Before plugging any critical components into an AC outlet, take a moment to test the outlet first by using a multimeter or a device designed exclusively to test outlets. Failure to test AC outlets properly can result in inoperable or destroyed equipment, as well as possible electrocution. The IEC-320 plug has three holes, called hot, neutral, and ground. These names describe the function of the wires that connect to them behind the wall plate. The hot wire carries electrical voltage, much like a pipe that delivers water. The neutral wire carries no voltage, but instead acts like a water drain, completing the circuit by returning electricity to the local source, normally a breaker panel.

The ground wire makes it possible for excess electricity to return safely to the ground. When testing AC power, you want to check for three things: that the hot outputs approximately 115 V (or whatever the proper voltage is for your part of the world), that the neutral connects to ground (0 V output), and that the ground connects to ground (again, 0 V). Figure 9.4 shows the voltages at an outlet. You can use a **multimeter**—often also referred to as a *volt-ohm meter* (*VOM*) or *digital multimeter* (*DMM*)—to measure a number of aspects of electrical current. A multimeter consists of two probes, an analog or digital meter, and a dial to set the type of test you want to perform. Refer to Figure 9.5 to become familiar with the components of the multimeter.

Note that some multimeters use symbols rather than letters to describe AC and DC settings. The *V* with the solid line above a dashed line, for example, in Figure 9.6, refers to direct current. The *V~* stands for alternating current.

Every multimeter offers at least four types of electrical tests: continuity, resistance, AC voltage (VAC), and DC voltage (VDC). Continuity tests whether electrons can flow from one end of a wire to the other end. If so,

• **Figure 9.5** Digital multimeter

• **Figure 9.6** Multimeter featuring DC and AC symbols

Try This!

Using a Multimeter to Test AC Outlets

Every competent technician knows how to use a multimeter, so if you haven't used one in the past, get hold of one and Try This!

First you need to set up the meter for measuring AC. Follow these steps:

1. Move the selector switch to the AC V (usually red). If multiple settings are available, put it into the first scale higher than 120 V (usually 200 V). *Auto-range* meters set their own range; they don't need any selection except AC V.

2. Place the black lead in the common (–) hole. If the black lead is permanently attached, ignore this step.

3. Place the red lead in the V-Ohm-A (+) hole. If the red lead is permanently attached, ignore this step.

Once you have the meter set up for AC, go through the process of testing the various wires on an AC socket. Just don't put your fingers on the metal parts of the leads when you stick them into the socket! Follow these steps:

1. Put either lead in hot, the other in neutral. You should read 110 to 120 V AC.

2. Put either lead in hot, the other in ground. You should read 110 to 120 V AC.

3. Put either lead in neutral, the other in ground. You should read 0 V AC.

If any of these readings is different from what is described here, it's time to call an electrician.

Tech Tip

AC Adapters

Many devices in the computing world use an AC adapter rather than an internal power supply. Even though it sits outside a device, an AC adapter converts AC current to DC, just like a power supply. Unlike power supplies, AC adapters are rarely interchangeable. Although manufacturers of different devices often use the same kind of plug on the end of the AC adapter cable, these adapters are not necessarily interchangeable. In other words, just because you can plug an AC adapter from your friend's laptop into your laptop does not mean it's going to work.

You need to make sure that three things match before you plug an AC adapter into a device: voltage, amperage, and polarity. If either the voltage or amperage output is too low, the device won't run. If the polarity is reversed, it won't work, just like putting a battery in a flashlight backwards. If either the voltage or amperage—especially the latter—is too high, on the other hand, you can very quickly toast your device. Don't do it! Always check the voltage, amperage, and polarity of a replacement AC adapter before you plug it into a device.

you have continuity; if not, you don't. You can use this setting to determine if a fuse is good or to check for breaks in wires. If your multimeter doesn't have a continuity tester (many cheaper multimeters do not), you can use the resistance tester. A broken wire or fuse will show infinite resistance, while a good wire or fuse will show no resistance. Testing AC and DC voltages is a matter of making sure the measured voltage is what it should be.

Using Special Equipment to Test AC Voltage

A number of good AC-only testing devices are available. With these devices, you can test all voltages for an AC outlet by simply inserting them into the outlet. Be sure to test all of the outlets the computer system uses: power supply, external devices, and monitor. Although convenient, these devices aren't as accurate as a multimeter. My favorite tester is made by Radio Shack, a simple-seeming tool (see Figure 9.7). This handy device provides three light-emitting diodes (LEDs) that describe everything that can go wrong with a plug.

Protecting the PC from Spikes and Sags in AC Power

If all power companies could supply electricity in smooth, continuous flows with no dips or spikes in pressure, the next two sections of this chapter would be irrelevant. Unfortunately, no matter how clean the AC supply appears to a multimeter, the truth is that voltage from the power company tends to drop well below (sag) and shoot far above (surge or spike) the standard 115 V (in the United States). These sags and spikes usually don't affect lamps and refrigerators, but they can keep your PC from running or can even destroy a PC or peripheral device. Two essential devices handle spikes and sags in the supply of AC: surge suppressors and uninterruptible power supplies.

Surge Suppressors Surges or spikes are far more dangerous than sags. Even a strong sag only shuts off or reboots your PC; any surge can harm your computer, and a strong surge destroys components. Given the seriousness of surges, every PC should use a **surge suppressor** device that absorbs the extra voltage from a surge to protect the PC. The power supply does a good job of surge suppression and can handle many of the smaller surges that take place fairly often. But the power supply takes a lot of damage from this and will eventually fail. To protect your power supply, a dedicated surge suppressor works between the power supply and the outlet to protect the system from power surges (see Figure 9.8).

Most people tend to spend a lot of money on their PC and for some reason suddenly get cheap on the surge suppressor. Don't do that! Make sure your surge suppressor has the Underwriters Laboratories UL 1449 for 330-V rating to ensure substantial protection for your system. Underwriters Laboratories (www.ul.com) is a U.S.-based, not-for-profit, widely recognized industry testing laboratory whose testing standards are very important to the consumer electronics industry. Additionally, check the joules rating before buying a new surge suppressor. A **joule** is a unit of electrical energy. How much energy a surge suppressor can handle before it fails is described in joules. Most authorities agree that your surge suppressor should rate at a minimum of 800 joules—and the more joules, the better the protection. My surge suppressor rates out at 1,750 joules.

While you're protecting your system, don't forget that surges also come from telephone and cable connections. If you use a modem, DSL, or cable modem, make sure to get a surge suppressor that includes support for these types of connections. Many manufacturers make surge suppressors with telephone line protection (see Figure 9.9).

No surge suppressor works forever. Make sure your surge suppressor has a test/reset button so you'll know when the device has—as we say in the business—turned into an extension cord. If your system takes a hit

• **Figure 9.7** Circuit tester

• **Figure 9.8** Surge suppressor

• **Figure 9.9** Surge suppressor with telephone line protection

and you have a surge suppressor, call the company! Many companies provide cash guarantees against system failure due to surges, but only if you follow their guidelines.

If you want really great surge suppression, you need to move up to **power conditioning**. Your power lines take in all kinds of strange signals that have no business being in there, such as electromagnetic interference (EMI) and radio frequency interference (RFI). Most of the time, this line noise is so minimal it's not worth addressing, but occasionally events (such as lightning) generate enough line noise to cause weird things to happen to your PC (keyboard lockups, messed-up data). All better surge suppressors add power conditioning to filter out EMI and RFI.

UPS An **uninterruptible power supply (UPS)** protects your computer (and, more importantly, your data) in the event of a power sag or power outage. Figure 9.10 shows a typical UPS. A UPS essentially contains a big battery that provides AC power to your computer regardless of the power coming from the AC outlet.

All uninterruptible power supplies are measured in both watts (the true amount of power they supply in the event of a power outage) and in *volt-amps* (*VA*). Volt-amps is the amount of power the UPS could supply if the devices took power from the UPS in a perfect way. Your UPS provides perfect AC power, moving current smoothly back and forth 60 times a second. Power supplies, monitors, and other devices, however, may not take all of the power the UPS has to offer at every point as the AC power moves back and forth, resulting in inefficiencies. If your devices took all of the power the UPS offered at every point as the power moved back and forth, VA would equal watts.

If the UPS makers knew ahead of time exactly what devices you planned to plug into their UPS, they could tell you the exact watts, but different devices have different efficiencies, forcing the UPS makers to go by what they can offer (VAs), not what your devices will take (watts). The watts value they give is a guess, and it's never as high as the VAs. The VA rating is always higher than the watt rating.

Because you have no way to calculate the exact efficiency of every device you'll plug into the UPS, go with the wattage rating. You add up the total wattage of every component in your PC and buy a UPS with a higher wattage. You'll spend a lot of time and mental energy figuring precisely how much wattage your computer, monitor, drives, and so on require to get the proper UPS for your system. But you're still not finished! Remember that the UPS is a battery with a limited amount of power, so you then need to figure out how long you want the UPS to run when you lose power.

The quicker and far better method to use for determining the UPS you need is to go to any of the major surge suppressor/UPS makers' Web sites and use their handy power calculators. My personal favorite is on the American Power Conversion Web site: www.apc.com. APC makes great surge suppressors and UPSs, and the company's online calculator will show you the true wattage you need—and teach you about whatever new thing is happening in power at the same time.

• **Figure 9.10** Uninterruptible power supply

Tech Tip

UPS Technologies
There are two main types of UPS: online, *where devices are constantly powered through the UPS's battery, and* standby, *where devices connected to the UPS receive battery power only when the AC sags below ~80–90 V. Another type of UPS is called* line-interactive, *which is similar to a standby UPS but has special circuitry to handle moderate AC sags and surges without the need to switch to battery power.*

No surge suppressor in the world can handle the ultimate surge, the ESD of a lightning strike. If your electrical system takes such a hit, you can kiss your PC goodbye if it was plugged in at the time. Always unplug electronics during electrical storms!

Shopping for a UPS

When it comes to getting a UPS for yourself or a client, nothing quite cuts through the hype and marketing terms like a trip to the local computer store to see for yourself. You need excuses to go to the computer store, so Try This!

1. Go to your local computer store—or visit an online computer site if no stores are nearby—and find out what's available.

2. Answer this question: How can you tell the difference between an online and a standby UPS?

Every UPS also has surge suppression and power conditioning, so look for the joule and UL 1449 ratings. Also look for replacement battery costs—some UPS replacement batteries are very expensive. Last, look for a UPS with a USB or serial port connection. These handy UPSs come with monitoring and maintenance software (see Figure 9.11) that tells you the status of your system and the amount of battery power available, logs power events, and provides other handy options.

Table 9.1 gives you a quick look at the low end and the very high end of UPS products (as of early 2012).

• **Figure 9.11** APC PowerChute software

Supplying DC

After you've assured the supply of good AC electricity for the PC, the power supply unit (PSU) takes over, converting high-voltage AC into several DC voltages (notably, 5.0, 12.0, and 3.3 V) usable by the delicate interior components. Power supplies come in a large number of shapes and sizes, but the most com-

Table 9.1	**Typical UPS Devices**				
Brand	**Model**	**Outlets Protected**	**Backup Time**	**Price**	**Type**
APC	BE350G	3 @ 120 V	3 min @ 200 W, 10 min @ 100 W	$33.99	Standby
APC	Pro 1000	4 @ 120 V	4 min @ 600 W, 64 min @ 100 W	$129.99	Standby
CyberPower	CPS1500AVR	6 @ 120 V	18 min @ 950 W, 6 min @ 475 W	$279.99	Line-interactive

mon size by far is the standard 150 mm × 140 mm × 86 mm desktop PSU shown in Figure 9.12.

The PC uses the 12.0-V current to power motors on devices such as hard drives and optical drives, and it uses the 5.0-V and 3.3-V current for support of onboard electronics. Manufacturers may use these voltages any way they wish, however, and may deviate from these assumptions. Power supplies also come with standard connectors for the motherboard and interior devices.

Power to the Motherboard

Modern motherboards use a 20- or 24-pin **P1 power connector**. Some motherboards may require special 4-, 6-, or 8-pin connectors to supply extra power (see Figure 9.13). We'll talk about each of these connectors in the form factor standards discussion later in this chapter.

• **Figure 9.12** Desktop PSU

Power to Peripherals: Molex, Mini, and SATA

Many devices inside the PC require power. These include hard drives, floppy drives, optical drives, and fans. The typical PC power supply has up to three types of connectors that plug into peripherals: Molex, mini, and SATA.

Molex Connectors The most common type of power connection for devices that need 5 or 12 V of power is the **Molex connector** (see Figure 9.14). The Molex connector has notches, called *chamfers*, that guide its installation. The tricky part is that Molex connectors require a firm push to plug in properly, and a strong person can defeat the chamfers, plugging a Molex in upside down. Not a good thing. *Always* check for proper orientation before you push it in!

Mini Connectors All power supplies have a second type of connector, called a **mini connector** (see Figure 9.15), that supplies 5 and 12 V to peripherals, although only floppy disk drives in modern systems use this connector. Drive manufacturers adopted the mini as the standard connector on 3.5-inch floppy disk drives. Often these mini connectors are referred to as *floppy power connectors*.

Modern power supplies include a lot of connectors. You'll find cheaper ones with as few as 10 connectors. More powerful models could have 25 or more.

• **Figure 9.13** Motherboard power connectors

• **Figure 9.14** Molex connector

• **Figure 9.15** Mini connector

Try This!

Testing DC

A common practice for techs troubleshooting a system is to test the DC voltages coming out of the power supply. Even with good AC, a bad power supply can fail to transform AC to DC at voltages needed by the motherboard and peripherals. So grab your trusty multimeter and Try This! on a powered-up PC with the side cover removed. Note that you must have P1 connected to the motherboard and the system must be running (you don't have to be in Windows, of course).

1. Switch your multimeter to DC, somewhere around 20 V DC if you need to make that choice. Make sure your leads are plugged into the multimeter properly: red to hot, black to ground. The key to testing DC is that which lead you touch to which wire matters. Red goes to hot wires of all colors; black *always* goes to ground.

2. Plug the red lead into the red wire socket of a free Molex connector and plug the black lead into one of the two black wire sockets. You should get a reading of ~5 V. What do you have?

3. Now move the red lead to the yellow socket. What voltage do you get?

4. Testing the P1 connector is a little more complicated. You push the red and black leads into the top of P1, sliding in alongside the wires until you bottom out. Leave the black lead in one of the black wire ground sockets. Move the red lead through all of the colored wire sockets. What voltages do you find?

As with any power connector, plugging a mini connector into a device the wrong way will almost certainly destroy the device. Check twice before you plug one in!

Be extra careful when plugging in a mini connector! Whereas Molex connectors are difficult to plug in backward, you can insert a mini connector incorrectly with very little effort. As with a Molex connector, doing so will almost certainly destroy the floppy drive. Figure 9.16 depicts a correctly oriented mini connection, with the small ridge on the connector away from the body of the data socket.

• **Figure 9.16** Correct orientation of a mini connector

SATA Power Connectors Serial ATA (SATA) drives need a special 15-pin **SATA power connector** (see Figure 9.17). The larger pin count supports the SATA hot-swappable feature and 3.3-, 5.0-, and 12.0-V devices. SATA power connectors are *L* shaped, making it almost impossible to insert one incorrectly into a SATA drive. No other device on your computer uses the SATA power connector. For more information about SATA drives, see Chapter 10.

Splitters and Adapters You may occasionally find yourself without enough connectors to power all of the devices inside your PC. In this case, you can purchase splitters to create more connections (see Figure 9.18). You might also run into the phenomenon of needing a SATA connector but having only a spare Molex. Because the voltages on the wires are the same, a simple adapter will take care of the problem nicely.

ATX

The original ATX power supplies had two distinguishing physical features: the motherboard power connector and soft power. Motherboard power came from a single cable with a 20-pin P1 motherboard power connector. ATX power supplies also had at least two other cables, each populated with two or more Molex or mini connectors for peripheral power.

When plugged in, ATX systems have 5 V running to the motherboard. They're always "on" even when powered down. The power switch you press to power up the PC isn't a true power switch like the light switch on the wall in your bedroom. The power switch on an ATX system simply tells the computer whether it has been pressed. The BIOS or operating system takes over from there and handles the chore of turning the PC on or off. This is called **soft power**.

Using soft power instead of a physical switch has a number of important benefits. Soft power prevents a user from turning off a system before the operating system has been shut down. It enables the PC to use power-saving modes that put the system to sleep and then wake it up when you press a key, move a mouse, or receive an e-mail (or other network traffic). (See Chapter 18 for more details on sleep mode.)

All of the most important settings for ATX soft power reside in CMOS setup. Boot into CMOS and look for a Power Management section. Take a look at the Power Button Function option in Figure 9.19. This determines the function of the on/off switch. You may set this switch to turn off the computer, or you may set it to the more common *4-second delay*.

ATX did a great job supplying power for more than a decade, but over time more powerful CPUs, multiple CPUs, video cards, and other components began to need more current than the original ATX

• **Figure 9.17** SATA power connector

• **Figure 9.18** Molex splitter

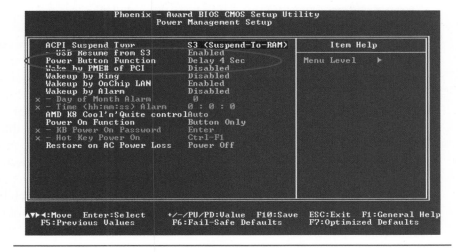

• **Figure 9.19** Soft power setting in CMOS

provided. This motivated the industry to introduce a number of updates to the ATX power standards: ATX12V 1.3, EPS12V, multiple rails, ATX12V 2.0, other form factors, and active PFC.

ATX12V 1.3 The first widespread update to the ATX standard, ATX12V 1.3, came out in 2003. This introduced a 4-pin motherboard power connector, unofficially but commonly called the P4, that provided more 12-V power to assist the 20-pin P1 motherboard power connector. Any power supply that provides a P4 connector is called an ATX12V power supply. The term "ATX" was dropped from the ATX power standard, so if you want to get really nerdy you can say—accurately—that there's no such thing as an ATX power supply. All power supplies—assuming they have a P4 connector—are ATX12V or one of the later standards.

The ATX12V 1.3 standard also introduced a 6-pin auxiliary connector—commonly called an *AUX* connector—to supply increased 3.3- and 5.0-V current to the motherboard (see Figure 9.20). This connector was based on the motherboard power connector from the precursor of ATX, called *AT*.

 SATA also supports a slimline connector that has a 6-pin power segment and a micro connector that has a 9-pin power segment.

 It's normal and common to have unused power connectors inside your PC case.

The introduction of these two extra power connectors caused the industry some teething problems. In particular, motherboards using AMD CPUs tended to need the AUX connector, while motherboards using Intel CPUs needed only the P4. As a result, many power supplies came with only a P4 or only an AUX connector to save money. A few motherboard makers skipped adding either connector and used a standard Molex connector so people with older power supplies wouldn't have to upgrade just because they bought a new motherboard (see Figure 9.21).

The biggest problem with ATX12V was its lack of teeth—it made a lot of recommendations but few requirements, giving PSU makers too much choice (such as choosing or not choosing to add AUX and P4 connectors) that weren't fixed until later versions.

EPS12V Server motherboards are thirsty for power, and sometimes ATX12V 1.3 just didn't cut it. An industry group called the Server System Infrastructure (SSI) developed a non-ATX standard motherboard and power supply called EPS12V. An EPS12V power supply came with a 24-pin main motherboard power connector that resembled a 20-pin ATX connector, but it offered more current and thus more stability for motherboards. It also came with an AUX connector, an ATX12V P4 connector, and a unique 8-pin connector. That's a lot of connectors! EPS12V power supplies were not interchangeable with ATX12V power supplies.

EPS12V may not have seen much life beyond servers, but it introduced a number of power features, some of which eventually became part of the ATX12V standard. The most important issue was something called **rails**.

Rails Generally, all of the PC's power comes from a single transformer that takes the AC current from a wall socket and converts it into DC current

Cross Check

ATX Form Factor

The power supply form factor alone does not define a system as ATX or one of the later varieties; you have to discuss the motherboard as well. Flip back to Chapter 8 and see if you can put the full picture of the ATX standard together. What defines a system as ATX? What improvements did ATX incorporate over AT? What ATX form factors can you purchase?

• **Figure 9.20** Auxiliary power connector

that is split into three primary DC voltage rails: 12.0 V, 5.0 V, and 3.3 V. Groups of wires run from each of these voltage rails to the various connectors. In ideal circumstances, these rails are wholly independent: an overtaxed 12-V rail shouldn't draw power from the 3.3-V rail. Many power supply manufacturers, however, do not follow this rule, especially when making cheap power supplies.

Each rail has a maximum amount of power it can supply. Normal computer use rarely approaches this ceiling, but powerful computers with advanced processors and graphics cards require more power than some rails can provide. In the past, 12-V rails only supplied about 18 amps, which wasn't enough to power all that high-end equipment.

• **Figure 9.21** Molex power on motherboard

The most popular solution was to include multiple 12-V rails in the power supply. This worked fine, but you needed to make sure that you weren't drawing all of your power from the same 12-V rail. Most power supplies failed to mark which power cables connected to which rail, so it became a confusing mess of trial and error to work out how to power your components.

Today's power supply manufacturers seem more interested in single, high-amperage, 12-V rails, ignoring the 16–18 amp rule. You can find power supplies now with 12-V rails pushing 50 amps or more!

ATX12V 2.0 The ATX12V 2.0 standard incorporated many of the good ideas of EPS12V into the ATX world, starting with the 24-pin connector. This 24-pin motherboard power connector is backward compatible with the older 20-pin connector, so users don't have to buy a new motherboard if they use an ATX12V 2.0 power supply. ATX12V 2.0 requires two 12-V rails for any power supply rated higher than 230 W. ATX12V 2.0 dropped the AUX connector and requires SATA hard drive connectors.

In theory, a 20-pin motherboard power supply connector will work on a motherboard with a 24-pin socket, but doing this is risky because the 20-pin connector may not provide enough power to your system. Try to use the right power supply for your motherboard to avoid problems. Many ATX12V 2.0 power supplies have a convertible 24-to-20-pin converter. These are handy if you want to make a nice "clean" connection, because many 20-pin connectors have capacitors that prevent plugging in a 24-pin connector. You'll also see the occasional 24-pin connector constructed in such a way that you can slide off the extra four pins. Figure 9.22 shows 20-pin and 24-pin connectors; Figure 9.23 shows a convertible connector. Although they look similar, those extra four pins won't replace the P4 connector. They are incompatible!

Many modern ATX motherboards feature an 8-pin CPU power connector like the one found in the EPS12V standard to help support high-end CPUs that demand a lot of power. This connector is referred to by several names, including EPS12V, EATX12V, and ATX12V 2x4. One half of this connector will be pin compatible with the P4 power connector and the other half may be under a protective cap. Be sure to check the motherboard installation manuals for recommendations on if and when you need to use the

• **Figure 9.22** 20- and 24-pin connectors

• **Figure 9.23** Convertible motherboard power connector

• **Figure 9.24** PCI Express 6-pin power connector

full 8 pins. For backward compatibility, some power supplies provide an 8-pin power connector that can split into two 4-pin sets, one of which is the P4 connector.

Another notable connector is the auxiliary PCI Express (PCIe) power connector. Figure 9.24 shows the 6-pin PCIe power connector. Some motherboards add a Molex socket for PCIe, and some cards come with a Molex socket as well. Higher-end cards have a dedicated 6-pin or 8-pin PCIe power connector. The 8-pin PCIe connector should not be confused with the EPS12V connector, as they are not compatible. Some PCIe devices with the 8-pin connector will accept a 6-pin PCIe power connection instead, but this may put limits on their performance. Often you'll find that 8-pin PCIe power cables have two pins at the end that you can detach for easy compatibility with 6-pin devices.

Niche-Market Power Supply Form Factors The demand for smaller and quieter PCs has led to the development of a number of niche-market power supply form factors. All use standard ATX connectors but differ in size and shape from standard ATX power supplies.

Here are some of the more common specialty power supply types:

- **Mini-ATX** and **micro-ATX** Smaller power supply form factors designed specifically for mini-ATX and micro-ATX cases, respectively
- **TFX12V** A small power supply form factor optimized for low-profile ATX systems
- **SFX12V** A small power supply form factor optimized for systems using FlexATX motherboards (see Figure 9.25)

You'll commonly find niche-market power supplies bundled with computer cases (and often motherboards as well). These form factors are rarely sold alone.

• **Figure 9.25** SFX power supply

Active PFC Visualize the AC current coming from the power company as water in a pipe, smoothly moving back and forth, 60 times a second. A PC's power supply, simply due to the process of changing this AC current into DC current, is like a person sucking on a straw on the end of this pipe. It takes gulps only when the current is fully pushing or pulling at the top and bottom of each cycle and creating an electrical phenomena—sort of a back pressure—that's called *harmonics* in the power industry. These harmonics create the humming sound you hear from electrical components. Over time, harmonics damage electrical equipment, causing serious problems with the power supply and other electrical devices on the circuit. Once you put a few thousand PCs with power supplies in the same local area, harmonics can even damage the electrical power supplier's equipment!

Good PC power supplies come with **active power factor correction (active PFC)**, extra circuitry that smooths out the way the power supply takes power from the power company and eliminates harmonics (see Figure 9.26). Never buy a power supply that does not have active PFC—all power supplies with active PFC will announce it on the box.

Wattage Requirements

Every device in a PC requires a certain amount of wattage to function. A typical hard drive draws 15 W of power when accessed, for example, whereas a quad-core AMD Phenom II X4 draws a whopping 125 W at peak usage. The total wattage of all devices combined is the minimum you need the power supply to provide.

If the power supply cannot produce the wattage a system needs, that PC won't work properly. Because most devices in the PC require maximum wattage when first starting, the most common result of insufficient wattage is a paperweight that looks like a PC. This can lead to some embarrassing moments. You might plug in a new hard drive for a client, push the power button on the case, and nothing happens—a dead PC! Eek! You can quickly determine if insufficient wattage is the problem. Unplug the drive and power up the system. If the system boots up, the power supply is a likely suspect. The only fix for this problem is to replace the power supply with one that provides more wattage (or leave the new drive out—a less-than-ideal solution).

No power supply can turn 100 percent of the AC power coming from the power company into DC current, so all power supplies provide less power to the system than the wattage advertised on the box. ATX12V 2.0 standards require a power supply to be at least 70 percent efficient, but you can find power supplies with better than 80 percent efficiency. More efficiency can tell you how many watts the system puts out to the PC in actual use. Plus, the added efficiency means the power supply uses less power, saving you money.

[ENGLISH] Model: Neo HE 550

- ATX12V v2.2 and EPS12V compliant.
- Dual CPU and dual core ready.
- **Advanced cable management system** improves internal airflow and reduces system clutter by allowing you to use only the cables that you need.
- **Universal Input** automatically accepts line voltages from 100V to 240V AC.
- **Active PFC** (Power Factor Correction) delivers environmentally-friendlier power.
- **Up to 85% efficiency** reduces heat generation and saves power and money.
- **Dedicated voltage outputs** to deliver more stable power.
- **Voltage feedback** and tight ±3% regulation for improved system stability.
- **Three +12V output circuits** provide maximum stable power for the CPU independently and for other peripherals.
- **Dual PCI Express** graphics card power connectors.
- **Low-speed 80mm fan** delivers whisper-quiet cooling and ensures quiet operation by varying fan speed in response to load and conditions.
- **SATA connectors** for your Serial ATA drives.
- **Industrial grade protection circuitry** prevents damage resulting from short circuits (SCP), power overloads (OPP), excessive current (OCP), excessive voltages (OVP), and under voltage (UVP).
- **Approvals:** UL, CUL, CE, CB, FCC Class B, TÜV, CCC, C-tick.
- **MTBF:** 80,000 hrs.
- **Size:** 5.9" (D) x 5.9" (W) x 3.4" (H) 15cm (D) x 15cm (W) x 8.6cm (H)
- **AQ3*** – Antec's unbeatable three-year parts and labor warranty.

• **Figure 9.26** Power supply advertising active PFC

 The CompTIA A+ 220-801 exam does not require you to figure precise wattage needs for a particular system. When building a PC for a client, however, you do need to know this stuff!

One common argument these days is that people buy power supplies that provide far more wattage than a system needs and therefore waste power. This is untrue. A power supply provides only the amount of power your system needs. If you put a 1000-W power supply (yes, they really exist) into a system that needs only 250 W, that big power supply will put out only 250 W to the system. So buying an efficient, higher-wattage power supply gives you two benefits. First, running a power supply at less than 100 percent load helps it live longer. Second, you'll have plenty of extra power when adding new components.

As a general recommendation for a new system, use at least a 500-W power supply. This is a common wattage and gives you plenty of extra power for booting as well as for whatever other components you might add to the system in the future.

■ Installing and Maintaining Power Supplies

Although installing and maintaining power supplies takes a little less math than selecting the proper power supply for a system, they remain essential skills for any tech. Installing takes but a moment, and maintaining is almost as simple. Let's take a look.

Installing

The typical power supply connects to the PC with four standard computer screws, mounted in the back of the case (see Figure 9.27). Unscrew the four screws and the power supply lifts out easily (see Figure 9.28). Insert a new power supply that fits the case and attach it by using the same four screws.

Handling ATX power supplies requires special consideration. Understand that an ATX power supply *never turns off*. As long as that power

• **Figure 9.27** Mounting screws for power supply

• **Figure 9.28** Removing power supply from system unit

supply stays connected to a power outlet, the power supply will continue to supply 5 V to the motherboard. Always unplug an ATX system before you do any work! For years, techs bickered about the merits of leaving a PC plugged in or unplugged when servicing it. ATX settled this issue forever. Many ATX power supplies provide a real on/off switch on the back of the PSU (see Figure 9.29). If you really need the system shut down with no power to the motherboard, use this switch.

When working on an ATX system, you may find using the power button inconvenient because you're not using a case or you haven't bothered to plug the power button's leads into the motherboard. That means there is no power button. One trick when in that situation is to use a set of car keys or a screwdriver to contact the two wires to start and stop the system (see Figure 9.30).

Your first task after acquiring a new power supply is simply making sure it works. Insert the motherboard power connectors before starting the system. If you have video cards with power connectors, plug them in too. Other connectors such as hard drives can wait until you have one successful boot—or if you're cocky, just plug everything in!

Cooling

Heat and computers are not the best of friends. Cooling is therefore a vital consideration when building a computer. Electricity equals heat. Computers, being electrical devices, generate heat as they operate, and too much heat can seriously damage a computer's internal components.

The **power supply fan** provides the basic cooling for the PC (see Figure 9.31). It not only cools the voltage regulator circuits *within* the power supply but also provides a constant flow of outside air throughout the interior of the computer case. A dead power supply fan can rapidly cause tremendous problems, even equipment failure. If you ever turn on a computer and it boots just fine but you notice that it seems unusually quiet, check to see if the power supply fan has died. If it has, quickly turn off the PC and replace the power supply.

Some power supplies come with a built-in sensor to help regulate the airflow. If the system gets too hot, the power supply fan spins faster. The 3-pin, 3-wire fan sensor connector plugs into the motherboard directly (see Figure 9.32).

Case fans are large, square fans that snap into special brackets on the case or screw directly to the case, providing extra cooling for key components (see Figure 9.33). Most cases come with a case fan, and no modern computer should really be without one or two.

• **Figure 9.29** On/off switch for an ATX system

• **Figure 9.30** Shorting the soft on/off jumpers

• **Figure 9.31** Power supply fan

The single biggest issue related to case fans is where to plug them in. Most case fans come with standard Molex connectors, which are easy to plug in, but other case fans come with special three-pronged power connectors that need to connect to the motherboard. You can get adapters to plug three-pronged connectors into Molex connectors or vice versa.

Maintaining Airflow

A computer is a closed system, and computer cases help the fans keep things cool: everything is inside a box. Although many tech types like to run their systems with the side panel of the case open for easy access to the components, in the end they are cheating themselves. Why? A closed case enables the fans to create airflow. This airflow substantially cools off interior components. When the side of the case is open, you ruin the airflow of the system, and you lose a lot of cooling efficiency.

An important point to remember when implementing good airflow inside your computer case is that hot air rises. Warm air always rises above cold air, and you can use this principle to your advantage in keeping your computer cool.

In the typical layout of case fans for a computer case, an intake fan is located near the bottom of the front bezel of the case. This fan draws cool air in from outside the case and blows it over the components inside the case. Near the top and rear of the case (usually near the power supply), you'll usually find an exhaust fan. This fan works the opposite of the intake fan: it takes the warm air from inside the case and sends it to the outside.

Another important part of maintaining proper airflow inside the case is ensuring that **slot covers** are covering all empty expansion bays (see Figure 9.34). To maintain good airflow inside your case, you shouldn't provide too many opportunities for air to escape. Slot covers not only assist in maintaining a steady airflow; they also help keep dust and smoke out of your case.

Always be sure to have a class C fire extinguisher ready in case of an electrical fire.

Missing slot covers can cause the PC to overheat!

Reducing Fan Noise

Fans generate noise. In an effort to ensure proper cooling, many techs put several high-speed fans into a case, making the PC sound like a jet engine. You can reduce fan noise by using manually adjustable fans, larger fans, or specialty "quiet" fans. Many motherboards enable you to control fans through software.

Manually adjustable fans have a little knob you can turn to speed up or slow down the fan (see Figure 9.35). This kind of fan can reduce some of the noise, but you run the risk of slowing down the fan too much and thus letting the interior of the case heat up. A better solution is to get quieter fans.

Larger fans that spin more slowly are another way to reduce noise while maintaining good airflow. Fans sizes are measured in millimeters (mm) or centimeters (cm). Traditionally, the industry used 80-mm power supply and cooling fans, but today you'll find 100-mm, 120-mm, and even larger fans in power supplies and cases.

Many companies manufacture and sell higher-end low-noise fans. The fans have better bearings than run-of-the-mill fans, so they cost a little more, but they're definitely worth it. They market these fans as "quiet" or "silencer" or other similar adjectives. If you run into a PC that sounds like a jet, try swapping out the case fans for a low-decibel fan from Papst, Panasonic, or Cooler Master. Just check the decibel rating to decide which one to get. Lower, of course, is better.

Because the temperature inside a PC changes depending on the load put on the PC, the best solution for noise reduction combines a good set of fans with temperature sensors to speed up or slow down the fans automatically. A PC at rest uses less than half of the power of a PC running a video-intensive computer game and therefore makes a lot less heat. Virtually all modern systems support three fans through three 3-pin fan connectors on the motherboard. The CPU fan uses one of these connectors, and the other two are for system fans or the power supply fan.

Most CMOS setup utilities provide a little control over fans plugged into the motherboard. Figure 9.36 shows a typical CMOS setting for the fans. Note that you can't tell the fans when to come on or off—only when to set off an alarm when they reach a certain temperature.

Software is the best way to control your fans. Some motherboards come with system-monitoring software that enables you to set the temperature at which you want the fans to come on and off. If no

• **Figure 9.34** Slot covers

Knob for adjusting fan speed

• **Figure 9.35** Manual fan adjustment device

> When shopping for fans, remember your metric system: 80 mm = 8 cm; 120 mm = 12 cm. You'll find fans marketed both ways.

• **Figure 9.36** CMOS fan options

SpeedFan is a powerful tool that does far more than work with fans. Don't tweak any settings you don't understand!

program came with your motherboard, and the manufacturer's Web site doesn't offer one for download, try the popular freeware SpeedFan utility (see Figure 9.37). Written by Alfredo Milani Comparetti, SpeedFan monitors voltages, fan speeds, and temperatures in computers with hardware monitor chips. SpeedFan can even access S.M.A.R.T. information (see Chapter 10) for hard disks that support this feature and show hard disk temperatures, too. You can find SpeedFan at www.almico.com/speedfan.php.

Even if you don't want to mess with your fans, always make a point to turn on your temperature alarms in CMOS. If the system gets too hot, an alarm will warn you. There's no way to know if a fan dies other than to have an alarm.

• **Figure 9.37** SpeedFan

Beyond A+

Power supplies provide essential services for the PC, creating DC out of AC and cooling the system, but that utilitarian role does not stop the power supply from being an enthusiast's plaything. Plus, servers and high-end workstations have somewhat different needs than more typical systems, so naturally they need a boost in power. Let's take a look Beyond A+ at these issues.

It Glows!

The enthusiast community has been modifying, or *modding*, their PCs for years: cutting holes in the cases, adding fans to make overclocking feasible, and slapping in glowing strips of neon and cold cathode tubes. The power supply escaped the scene for a while, but it's back. A quick visit to a good computer store off- or online, such as http://directron.com, reveals power supplies that light up, sport a fancy color, or have more fans than some rock stars. Figure 9.38 shows a see-through PSU.

You can also find super-quiet stealth power supplies, with single or double high-end fans that react to the temperature inside your PC—speeding up when necessary but running slowly and silently when not. One of these would make a perfect power supply for a home entertainment PC because it would provide function without adding excessive noise.

Modular Power Supplies

It's getting more and more popular to make PCs look good on both the inside and the outside. Unused power cables dangling around inside PCs creates a not-so-pretty picture. To help stylish people, manufacturers created power supplies with modular cables (see Figure 9.39).

Modular cables are pretty cool, because you add only the lines you need for your system. On the other hand, some techs claim that modular cables hurt efficiency because the modular connectors add resistance to the lines. You make the choice; is a slight reduction in efficiency worth a clean look?

• Figure 9.38 See-through power supply that glows blue

Temperature and Efficiency

Watch out for power supplies that list their operating temperature at 25° C—about room temperature. A power supply that provides 500 W at 25° C will supply substantially less in warmer temperatures, and the inside of your PC is usually 15° C warmer than the outside air. Sadly, many power supply makers—even those who make good power supplies—fudge this fact.

• Figure 9.39 Modular-cable power supply

Chapter 9 Review

■ Chapter Summary

After reading this chapter and completing the exercises, you should understand the following about power supplies.

Explain the basics of electricity

■ The power supply takes electricity from the wall outlet and transforms it into the kind of electricity that the motherboard and other internal components use. To remove the power supply, unscrew the four screws in the back of the case and lift it out. Installing it is just as simple. Be careful never to open the power supply itself, as the capacitors inside can store a dangerous electrical charge.

■ Techs need to know basic principles of electricity and how to recognize power problems. Electricity is a flow of negatively charged particles or electrons through matter. Metallic wire is a good conductor, allowing electrons to move freely. The pressure of the electrons in the wire is called voltage and is measured in volts (V). Measured in units called amperes (amps or A), current or amperage is the amount of electrons flowing past a certain point on a wire. Wattage (watts or W) refers to the amount of amps and volts a particular device needs. The formula VA = W expresses the correlation among the three. Resistance to the flow of electrons is measured in ohms (Ω). Fuses and ground wires set limits for the flow of electrons. A ground wire provides a path of least resistance to allow the electrons to flow to the ground.

■ Electricity may be either direct current (DC), with electrons flowing in one direction around a continuous circuit, or alternating current (AC), with electrons flowing back and forth in a circuit.

Describe the details about powering the PC

■ Because power companies supply high-voltage AC, the computer's power supply converts AC to low-voltage DC that is then portioned out to the internal devices. Heat is a byproduct of electricity and must be controlled in the computer.

■ The power supply connects to the electrical outlet via a standard IEC-320 connector. Although power in the U.S. ranges from 110 to 120 V, the rest of the world uses 200 to 240 VAC. Most power supplies can switch between 115 and 230 V. The IEC-320 plug has three holes, called hot, neutral, and ground. The hot carries electrical voltage and should output approximately 115 V in the U.S. The neutral returns electricity to the breaker panel and should have 0 V output. The ground wire returns excess electricity to the ground and should also have a 0 V output. You can use a multimeter to test voltages at the outlet.

■ A multimeter, also called a volt-ohm meter (VOM), uses two probes to provide at least four measurements: AC voltage (V~), DC voltage (V with a solid line above a dashed line), continuity (whether electrons flow from one end of a wire to the other end), and resistance (whether a fuse is good or blown or whether a wire has breaks). Some AC-only testing devices are available that simply plug into the AC outlet and may display results via three light-emitting diodes (LEDs).

■ A surge suppressor is an inexpensive device that protects your computer from voltage spikes. Inserted between the wall outlet and the power supply, a surge suppressor has a joule rating that measures how much electrical energy it can suppress. Be sure your surge suppressor has at least an 800 joules rating. Because telephone lines and cable connections also produce spikes, your surge suppressor should include connections for a modem, DSL, or cable modem. Make sure you purchase a surge suppressor that has the UL 1449 for 330-V rating, as this will ensure substantial protection for your system. Because surge suppressors work for only a limited time, you should check the manufacturer's recommended replacement schedules. If your surge suppressor comes with a cash guarantee against system failure due to surges, be aware that manufacturers honor it only if you follow their guidelines.

■ Because the AC supply lacks consistency and actually provides power with sags and spikes, it is important that you use two devices with a computer: an uninterruptible power supply and a surge suppressor. An uninterruptible power supply (UPS) continues to supply AC power

to your computer during both brownouts and blackouts via a battery that is charged from the AC current. All UPSs measure the amount of power or watts they supply, as well as listing the number of minutes the UPS will last with a certain voltage. It's difficult to estimate exactly how much wattage your computer and devices will require, so the better method to determine the UPS you need is to go to the UPS makers' Web sites and use their power calculators.

- The power supply converts AC into several DC voltages (5.0, 12.0, and 3.3 V). Devices such as hard drives and optical drives require 12.0 V, and onboard electronics use 3.3- and 5.0-V currents.

- The power supply has several standard connectors for the motherboard and interior devices. Today's motherboards have a P1 socket that uses the P1 connector from the power supply. A standard ATX power supply has a 20-pin P1 connector, while the newer ATX12V 2.0 power supplies come with a 24-pin P1 connector. Some motherboards also need a 4-, 6-, or 8-pin connector to provide an additional 12 V of power.

- Peripherals use two or possibly three different kinds of connectors: the larger Molex connector, the smaller mini connector, and the SATA connector. Used with hard drives and optical drives, the Molex has chamfers to ensure that it is connected properly. Used today only for floppy drives, the mini connector can easily be inserted incorrectly, thus destroying the floppy drive. The SATA connector is used for SATA drives. If you do not have enough connectors for all of the devices inside your PC, you can create more connections with a splitter. Similarly, if your power supply does not have the connector a device needs, you can purchase adapters to convert one type to another.

- The ATX power supply includes full support for power-saving functions and waking from sleep due to incoming network traffic. Using the soft power feature, the ATX power supply puts a 5-V charge on the motherboard as long as there is AC from the wall socket. You can configure the ATX soft power through the Power Management section of the CMOS setup. Always unplug an ATX system before you work on it. ATX power supplies use a single P1 connector for motherboard power.

- The ATX standard has undergone several updates. ATX12V 1.3 introduced additional 4-pin (P4) and 6-pin auxiliary (AUX) connectors. ATX12V 2.0 introduced the 24-pin connector (inspired by EPS12V), dropped the AUX connector, and required SATA connectors. Additionally, ATX12V 2.0 requires two 12-V rails for any power supply rated higher than 230 W.

- The non-ATX standard EPS12V introduced a 24-pin motherboard connector and a unique 8-pin connector. It was not swappable with ATX power supplies, and while its popularity was short-lived, it introduced several features that became part of the ATX12V standard, including rails.

- The demand for smaller and quieter PCs led to the development of niche-market power supply form factors. MiniATX, microATX, TFX12V, and SFX12V have the same connectors as standard ATX power supplies but differ in size or shape.

- Active power factor correction (active PFC) helps to eliminate harmonics, which can damage electrical components. Never buy a power supply that does not have active PFC.

- Power supplies are rated in watts. If you know the amount of wattage that every device in the PC needs, you can arrive at the total wattage required for all devices, and that is the minimum wattage your power supply should provide. If the power supply does not provide sufficient wattage, the computer will not work. For a new computer system, you should select at least a 500-W power supply to have extra power for adding components in the future.

- Because converting from AC to DC may result in a significant loss of wattage, purchase a power supply that offers a high percentage of efficiency. The ATX12V 2.0 standard requires a power supply to be at least 70 percent efficient, but you can find power supplies with better than 80 percent efficiency. Be aware that power supplies produce less wattage over time, so don't cut the wattage specification too tightly. While power supplies range from 200 to 600 W, you should know that the more AC the power supply draws, the more heat it produces.

Install and maintain power supplies

- Power supplies connect to the PC case via four screws mounted in the rear of the case. Unscrew the four screws and the power supply will lift out. Because an ATX power supply is always on, be sure to unplug it from the wall outlet before working on it.

- Adequate cooling is important to prevent damage to the computer's internal components. The fan inside the power supply itself cools the voltage regulator circuits within the power supply and provides a constant flow of outside air throughout the interior of the computer case. If the fan is not working, turn the computer off before you experience equipment failure. Some power supplies regulate airflow by using a sensor with a three-wire connector that plugs into the motherboard.

- To improve cooling, most cases come with a case fan. If the case does not have one, you should add one. Most case fans use standard Molex connectors, but some use a special three-pronged power connector that plugs directly into the motherboard. To enable the fans to create airflow, the case needs to be closed. If slot covers are left off of empty expansion bays, the computer can overheat. Slot covers also help keep dust and smoke out of the case. Beware of "great deals" on cases that come with power supplies, because the included power supply is often substandard.

- Electrical problems range from irregular AC to dying or faulty power supplies. Power supplies may fail suddenly or slowly over time. After you make sure that the wall outlet is providing electricity, checking voltages from the power supply with a voltmeter is the best way to verify that the power supply is working or has failed. A power supply is functioning properly if the output voltages are within 10 percent over or under the expected voltage. Be sure to check all of the connections on the power supply. If you determine that the power supply is bad, the most economical solution is to throw it away and replace it with a new one.

- Power supplies will not start unless they are connected to a motherboard. If you need to test a power supply but don't have a motherboard, use an ATX tester.

■ Key Terms

active power factor correction (active PFC) *(233)*	**power conditioning** *(225)*
alternating current (AC) *(220)*	**power supply fan** *(235)*
amperes (amps or A) *(219)*	**power supply unit (PSU)** *(219)*
direct current (DC) *(220)*	**rails** *(230)*
field replaceable unit (FRU) *(219)*	**resistance** *(220)*
IEC-320 *(221)*	**SATA power connector** *(229)*
joule *(224)*	**slot covers** *(236)*
mini connector *(227)*	**soft power** *(229)*
Molex connector *(227)*	**surge suppressor** *(224)*
multimeter *(222)*	**uninterruptible power supply (UPS)** *(225)*
ohms (Ω) *(220)*	**volts (V)** *(219)*
P1 power connector *(227)*	**wattage (watts or W)** *(220)*

■ Key Term Quiz

Use the Key Terms list to complete the sentences that follow. Not all terms will be used.

1. Supply power to the floppy drive by using the _____ from the power supply.

2. The electric company provides _____ power that the power supply converts to _____ for use by the computer components.

3. If the _____ are left off the expansion slots, the computer may overheat.

4. An ATX form factor power supply attaches to the motherboard with a(n) _____ and supplies 5 V to the motherboard at all times.

5. Be sure your surge suppressor has a(n) _____ rating of at least 800.

6. The measurement unit for the amount of electrons flowing past a certain point on a wire is _____ .

7. The _____ provides the basic cooling for the PC.

8. Be sure the _____ rating for your power supply is greater than the minimum required by all devices in the computer.

9. The ability to split voltage supplies into separate _____ ensures that no device will hog all of the available power.

10. A spare part that a tech typically carries to replace a failed component in the field is called a(n) _____.

■ Multiple-Choice Quiz

1. Which of the following ATX12V features was introduced as part of the EPS12V standard?

 A. The P4 motherboard power connector

 B. Voltage rails

 C. The 6-pin AUX connector

 D. Soft power

2. Where can you control the speed of the fans plugged into the motherboard?

 A. CMOS setup

 B. The little knob in the middle of every fan

 C. The fan speed jumper on your motherboard

 D. In Device Manager

3. Under what conditions should a PC technician work inside the power supply?

 A. Only when it is unplugged.

 B. Only when the technician is wearing an anti-static wrist strap.

 C. Anytime, because the power supply only has low-energy DC electricity that will not hurt the technician.

 D. Never, because the power supply has capacitors that hold electrical charges that may harm the technician.

4. What should you check first if a computer will not start and the fan in the power supply will not turn?

 A. The voltages coming out of the power supply

 B. The motherboard power connector

 C. The power coming into the power supply

 D. The power switch

5. When you test voltage with a multimeter, you can assume the outlet or connector is functioning properly if the reading is within a certain percentage of the expected number. What is that maximum percentage by which the reading can vary?

 A. 5 percent

 B. 10 percent

 C. 20 percent

 D. 25 percent

6. What voltage does an ATX12V P4 connector provide for motherboards?

 A. 3.3 V

 B. 3.3 V, 5 V

 C. 5 V

 D. 12 V

7. When testing an AC outlet, what voltage should the multimeter show between the neutral and ground wires?

 A. 120 V

 B. 60 V

 C. 0 V

 D. −120 V

8. What sort of power connector does a traditional hard drive typically use?

 A. Molex

 B. Mini

 C. Sub-mini

 D. Micro

9. Arthur installed a new motherboard in his case and connected the ATX power, but his system would not turn on. He sees an extra 4-wire port on the motherboard. What's he missing?

 A. He needs to plug in the P2 connector for powering auxiliary components.

 B. He needs to plug in the P3 connector to power the case fans.

 C. He needs to plug in the P4 connector to power the processor.

 D. He needs to plug in the Aux connector to connect to a secondary power supply.

10. What is the effect of exceeding the wattage capabilities of a power supply by inserting too many devices?

 A. The system will boot normally, but some of the devices will not function properly.

 B. The system will boot normally and all of the devices will work, but only for a limited time. After an hour or so, the system will spontaneously shut down.

 C. The system will not boot or turn on at all.

 D. The system will try to boot, but the overloaded power supply will fail, burning up delicate internal capacitors.

11. Where do you put the multimeter leads when you test a Molex connector?

 A. The red lead should always touch the red wire; the black lead should touch a black ground wire.

 B. The red lead should always touch the black ground wire; the black lead should always touch the red hot wire.

 C. The red lead should always touch the yellow hot wire; the black lead should touch the red hot wire.

 D. The red lead should touch either the red or yellow hot wire; the black lead should touch a black ground wire.

12. What is the minimum PSU required for an ATX system that requires Molex, mini, and SATA connectors?

 A. ATX

 B. ATX12V 1.3

 C. ATX12V 2.0

 D. EPS12V

13. Which of the following is not a PSU form factor?

 A. TFX12V

 B. SFX12V

 C. CFX12V

 D. LPX12V

14. Which statement is true?

 A. Removing the expansion slot covers on the back of your case will improve cooling by allowing hot air to escape.

 B. Shop around when purchasing a case; you will often find good deals that include a powerful PSU.

 C. Always keep the power supply plugged in to the wall outlet when working on the inside of a computer, as this helps to ground it.

 D. If your power supply fails, don't try to repair it; buy a new one.

■ Essay Quiz

1. Jack and Denise have joined your study group. Because neither has any previous experience with basic electricity and its jargon, they want you to explain voltage, amperage, and wattage. In plain language, define these terms and explain what VA = W means.

2. In the computer field, advances in one area often lead to advances in another area. Do you think improvements in the CPU and other computer devices and functions made the ATX form factor power supply necessary?

3. Because microprocessors have become more powerful and more devices have been invented for the computer, the wattage demands for the PC have gone up. So has the need for cooling. Discuss the cooling devices that come with today's PCs and what the user needs to know about keeping the PC cool.

4. Helene's computer worked fine last week. Although she has not changed anything since then, today her computer won't even boot. You suspect that the power supply died. You know she does not have a multimeter. What will you tell her to check to confirm this opinion? If she does need to replace the power supply, how can she be sure the new one will work with her PC?

Lab Projects

• Lab Project 9.1

This chapter recommends a 500-W power supply for a new computer. Is that the wattage that manufacturers usually offer with their computers? Check the following Web sites to see what wattage comes with a new PC:

- www.dell.com

- www.gateway.com
- www.hp.com

Do any of these companies mention a power supply upgrade with a higher wattage rating? If so, what are the wattages and what are the additional costs?

• Lab Project 9.2

Every technician needs a multimeter. Visit a local electronics store and look at its line of multimeters. (If a store is not nearby, you may use the Internet instead.) What features do the various multimeters offer? What kinds of measurements do they provide? Is the output from some in digital format and others in analog? Which output do you find easier to read? Is one kind more accurate than another? What price ranges are available for multimeters? Then, select the multimeter you would like to add to your toolkit. Why did you choose that model? Now start saving your pennies so you can buy it!

Hard Drive Technologies

"Any sufficiently advanced technology is indistinguishable from magic."

—Arthur C. Clarke

In this chapter, you will learn how to

■ **Explain how hard drives work**

■ **Identify and explain the PATA and SATA hard drive interfaces**

■ **Identify and explain the SCSI hard drive interfaces**

■ **Describe how to protect data with RAID**

■ **Install hard drives**

■ **Configure CMOS and install drivers**

Of all the hardware on a PC, none gets more attention—or gives more anguish—than the hard drive. There's a good reason for this: if the hard drive breaks, you lose data. As you probably know, when the data goes, you have to redo work or restore from a backup—or worse. It's good to worry about the data, because the data runs the office, maintains the payrolls, and stores the e-mail. This level of concern is so strong that even the most neophyte PC users are exposed to terms such as *IDE*, *PATA*, *SATA*, and *controller*—even if they don't put the terms into practice.

This chapter focuses on how hard drives work, beginning with the internal layout and organization of hard drives. You'll look at the different types of hard drives used today (PATA, SATA, SSD, and SCSI), how they interface with the PC, and how to install them properly into a system. The chapter covers how more than one drive may work with other drives to provide data safety and improve speed through a feature called RAID. Let's get started.

■ How Hard Drives Work

Hard drives come in two major types. The most common type has moving parts; the newer and more expensive technology has no moving parts. Let's look at both.

Platter-Based Hard Drives

A traditional **hard disk drive (HDD)** is composed of individual disks, or *platters*, with read/write heads on actuator arms controlled by a servo motor—all contained in a sealed case that prevents contamination by outside air (see Figure 10.1).

The aluminum platters are coated with a magnetic medium. Two tiny read/write heads service each platter, one to read the top and the other to read the bottom of the platter (see Figure 10.2).

The coating on the platters is phenomenally smooth. It has to be, as the read/write heads actually float on a cushion of air above the platters, which spin at speeds between 3500 and 15,000 RPM. The distance (flying height) between the heads and the disk surface is less than the thickness of a fingerprint. The closer the read/write heads are to the platter, the more densely the data packs onto the drive. These infinitesimal tolerances demand that the platters never be exposed to outside air. Even a tiny dust particle on a platter would act like a mountain in the way of the read/write heads and would cause catastrophic damage to the drive. To keep the air clean inside the drive, all hard drives use a tiny, heavily filtered aperture to keep the air pressure equalized between the interior and the exterior of the drive.

• **Figure 10.1** Inside the hard drive

• **Figure 10.2** Read/write heads on actuator arms

Data Encoding

Although the hard drive stores data in binary form, visualizing a magnetized spot representing a one and a non-magnetized spot representing a zero grossly oversimplifies the process. Hard drives store data in tiny magnetic fields—think of them as tiny magnets that can be placed in either direction on the platter. Each tiny magnetic field, called a *flux*, can switch north/south polarity back and forth through a process called *flux reversal*. When a read/write head goes over an area where a flux reversal has occurred, the head reads a small electrical current.

Today's hard drives use a complex and efficient method to interpret flux reversals. Instead of reading individual flux reversals, a modern hard drive reads groups of them called *runs*. Starting around 1991, hard drives began using a data encoding system known as *run length limited* (*RLL*). With RLL, any combination of ones and zeros can be stored in a preset combination of about 15 different runs. The hard drive looks for these runs and reads them as a group, resulting in much faster and much more densely packed data.

Current drives use an extremely advanced method of RLL called **Partial Response Maximum Likelihood (PRML)** encoding. As hard drives pack more and more fluxes on the drive, the individual fluxes start to interact with each other, making it more and more difficult for the drive to verify where one flux stops and another starts. PRML uses powerful, intelligent circuitry to analyze each flux reversal and make a "best guess" as to what type of flux reversal it just read. As a result, the maximum run length for PRML drives reaches up to 16 to 20 fluxes, far more than the 7 or so on RLL drives. Longer run lengths enable the hard drive to use more complicated run combinations so the hard drive can store a phenomenal amount of data. For example, a run of only 12 fluxes on a hard drive might equal a string of 30 or 40 ones and zeros when handed to the system from the hard drive.

The size required by each magnetic flux on a hard drive has reduced considerably over the years, resulting in higher capacities. As fluxes become smaller, they begin to interfere with each other in weird ways. I have to say *weird* because to make sense of what's going on at this subatomic level (I told you these fluxes are small!) would require you to take a semester of quantum mechanics. Let's just say that laying fluxes flat against the platter has reached its limit. To get around this problem, hard drive makers began to make hard drives that store their fluxes vertically (up and down) rather than longitudinally (forward and backward), enabling them to make hard drives in the 1 terabyte (1024 gigabyte) range. Manufacturers call this vertical storage method *perpendicular recording*.

For all this discussion and detail on data encoding, the day-to-day PC technician never deals with encoding. Sometimes, however, knowing what you don't need to know helps as much as knowing what you do need to know. Fortunately, data encoding is inherent to the hard drive and completely invisible to the system. You're never going to have to deal with data encoding, but you'll sure sound smart when talking to other PC techs if you know your RLL from your PRML!

Moving the Arms

The read/write heads move across the platter on the ends of *actuator arms* or **head actuators**. In the entire history of hard drives, manufacturers have

used only two technologies to move the arms: **stepper motor** and **voice coil**. Hard drives first used stepper motor technology, but today they've all moved to voice coil.

Stepper motor technology moved the arm in fixed increments or steps, but the technology had several limitations that doomed it. Because the interface between motor and actuator arm required minimal slippage to ensure precise and reproducible movements, the positioning of the arms became less precise over time. This physical deterioration caused data transfer errors. Additionally, heat deformation wreaked havoc with stepper motor drives. Just as valve clearances in automobile engines change with operating temperature, the positioning accuracy changed as the PC operated and various hard drive components got warmer. Although very small, these changes caused problems. Accessing the data written on a cold hard drive, for example, became difficult after the disk warmed. In addition, the read/write heads could damage the disk surface if not parked (set in a non-data area) when not in use, requiring techs to use special parking programs before transporting a stepper motor drive.

All magnetic hard drives made today employ a linear motor to move the actuator arms. The linear motor, more popularly called a voice coil motor, uses a permanent magnet surrounding a coil on the actuator arm. When an electrical current passes, the coil generates a magnetic field that moves the actuator arm. The direction of the actuator arm's movement depends on the polarity of the electrical current through the coil. Because the voice coil and the actuator arm never touch, no degradation in positional accuracy takes place over time. Voice coil drives automatically park the heads when the drive loses power, making the old stepper motor park programs obsolete.

Lacking the discrete steps of the stepper motor drive, a voice coil drive cannot accurately predict the movement of the heads across the disk. To make sure voice coil drives land exactly in the correct area, the drive reserves one side of one platter for navigational purposes. This area essentially maps the exact location of the data on the drive. The voice coil moves the read/write head to its best guess about the correct position on the hard drive. The read/write head then uses this map to fine-tune its true position and make any necessary adjustments.

Now that you have a basic understanding of how a drive physically stores data, let's turn to how the hard drive organizes that data so we can use that drive.

Geometry

Have you ever seen a cassette tape? If you look at the actual brown Mylar (a type of plastic) tape, nothing will tell you whether sound is recorded on that tape. Assuming the tape is not blank, however, you know *something* is on the tape. Cassettes store music in distinct magnetized lines. You could say that the physical placement of those lines of magnetism is the tape's "geometry."

Geometry also determines where a hard drive stores data. As with a cassette tape, if you opened up a hard drive, you would not see the geometry. But rest assured that the drive has geometry; in fact, every model of hard drive uses a different geometry. We describe the geometry for a particular hard drive with a set of numbers representing three values: heads, cylinders, and sectors per track.

Tech Tip

Fluid Bearings

Currently, almost all hard drives (except solid state) use a motor located in the center spindle supporting the drive platters. Traditionally, tiny ball bearings support the spindle motor, and as disk technology has advanced, these ball bearings have become the limiting factor in the three critical design criteria for hard drives: rotational speed, storage capacity, and noise levels. The higher the rotational speed of a drive, the more the metal-on-metal contact creates heat and lubricant problems that impact the lifespan of the bearings. However precisely machined, ball bearings are not perfectly round. Runout, the measurement of how much the ball bearings wobble (and thus how much the drive platters wobble), is now the limiting factor on how densely you can pack information together on a disk drive.

The technological fix for this comes in the form of fluid bearings. A fluid bearing is basically a small amount of lubricant trapped in a carefully machined housing. The use of fluid in place of metal balls means that no contact occurs between metal surfaces to generate heat and wear. The fluid also creates no mechanical vibration, so fluid bearings can support higher rotational speeds. The runout of a fluid bearing is about one-tenth that of the best ball bearing, significantly increasing potential information density. The absence of a mechanical connection between moving parts also dramatically reduces noise levels, and the fluid itself acts to dampen the sound further. Finally, liquid bearings provide better shock resistance than ball bearings.

• **Figure 10.3** Two heads per platter

Heads The number of **heads** for a specific hard drive describes, rather logically, the number of read/write heads used by the drive to store data. Every platter requires two heads. If a hard drive has four platters, for example, it needs eight heads (see Figure 10.3).

Based on this description of heads, you would think that hard drives would always have an even number of heads, right? Wrong! Most hard drives reserve a head or two for their own use. Therefore, a hard drive can have either an even or an odd number of heads.

Cylinders To visualize cylinders, imagine taking an empty soup can and opening both ends. Look at the shape of the can; it is a geometric shape called a cylinder. Now imagine taking that cylinder and sharpening one end so that it easily cuts through the hardest metal. Visualize placing the ex–soup can over the hard drive and pushing it down through the drive. The can cuts into one side and out the other of each platter. Each circle transcribed by the can is where you store data on the drive, and is called a **track**.

All tracks of the same diameter are called a cylinder.

Track

Each side of each platter contains tens of thousands of tracks. Interestingly enough, the individual tracks themselves are not directly part of the drive geometry. Our interest lies only in the groups of tracks of the same diameter, going all of the way through the drive. Each group of tracks of the same diameter is called a **cylinder** (see Figure 10.4). There's more than one cylinder. Go get yourself about a thousand more cans, each one a different diameter, and push them through the hard drive.

• **Figure 10.4** Cylinder

Sectors per Track Now imagine cutting the hard drive like a birthday cake, slicing all of the tracks into tens of thousands of small slivers. Each sliver then has many thousands of small pieces of track. The term **sector** refers to a specific piece of track on a sliver, and each sector stores 512 bytes of data.

The sector is the universal atom of all hard drives. You can't divide data into anything smaller than a sector. Although sectors are important, the number of sectors is not a geometry value that describes a hard drive. The geometry value is called **sectors per track (sectors/track)**. The sectors/track value describes the number of sectors in each track (see Figure 10.5).

The Big Three Cylinders, heads, and sectors/track combine to define the hard drive's geometry. In most cases, these three critical values are referred to as *CHS*. The three values are important because the PC's BIOS needs to know the drive's geometry to know how to talk to the drive. Back in the old days, a technician needed to enter these values into the CMOS setup program manually. Today, every hard drive stores the CHS information in the drive itself, in an electronic format that enables the BIOS to query the drive automatically to determine these values. You'll see more on this later in the chapter, in the "Autodetection" section.

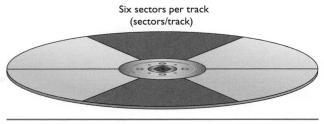

Six sectors per track
(sectors/track)

Two other values—write precompensation cylinder and landing zone—are no longer relevant in today's PCs. People still toss around these terms, however, and a few

• **Figure 10.5** Sectors per track

CMOS setup utilities still support them—another classic example of a technology appendix. Let's look at these two holdouts from another era so when you access CMOS, you won't say, "What the heck are these?"

Write Precompensation Cylinder Older hard drives had a real problem with the fact that sectors toward the inside of the drives were much smaller than sectors toward the outside. To handle this, an older drive would spread data a little farther apart once it got to a particular cylinder. This cylinder was called the write precompensation (write precomp) cylinder, and the PC had to know which cylinder began this wider data spacing. Hard drives no longer have this problem, making the write precomp setting obsolete.

Landing Zone On older hard drives with stepper motors, the landing zone value designated an unused cylinder as a "parking place" for the read/write heads. As mentioned earlier, before moving old stepper motor hard drives, the read/write heads needed to be parked to avoid accidental damage. Today's voice coil drives park themselves whenever they're not accessing data, automatically placing the read/write heads on the landing zone. As a result, the BIOS no longer needs the landing zone geometry.

801

Spindle (or Rotational) Speed

Hard drives run at a set spindle speed, measured in *revolutions per minute (RPM)*. Older drives ran at a speed of 3600 RPM, but new drives are hitting 15,000 RPM. The faster the spindle speed, the faster the controller can store and retrieve data. Here are the common speeds: 5400, 7200, 10,000 and 15,000 RPM.

Faster drives mean better system performance, but they can also cause the computer to overheat. This is especially true in tight cases, such as minitowers, and in cases containing many drives. Two 5400-RPM drives might run forever, snugly tucked together in your old case. But slap a hot new 15,000 RPM drive in that same case and watch your system start crashing right and left!

You can deal with these very fast drives by adding drive bay fans between the drives or migrating to a more spacious case. Most enthusiasts end up doing both. Drive bay fans sit at the front of a bay and blow air across the drive. They range in price from $10 to $100 (U.S.) and can lower the temperature of your drives dramatically. Some cases come with a bay fan built in (see Figure 10.6).

Airflow in a case can make or break your system stability, especially when you add new drives that increase the ambient temperature. Hot systems get flaky and lock up at odd moments. Many things can impede the airflow— jumbled-up ribbon cables, drives squished together in a tiny case, fans clogged by dust or animal hair, and so on.

• **Figure 10.6** Bay fan

Technicians need to be aware of the dangers when adding a new hard drive to an older system. Get into the habit of tying off ribbon cables, adding front fans to cases when systems lock up intermittently, and making sure any fans run well. Finally, if a client wants a new drive for a system in a tiny minitower with only the power supply fan to cool it off, be gentle, but definitely steer the client to one of the slower drives!

Solid-State Drives

Booting up a computer takes time in part because a traditional hard drive needs to first spin up before the read/write heads can retrieve data off the drive and load it into RAM. All of the moving metal parts of a platter-based drive use a lot of power, create a lot of heat, take up space, wear down over time, and take a lot of nanoseconds to get things done. A **solid-state drive (SSD)** addresses all of these issues nicely.

In technical terms, solid-state technology and devices are based on the combination of semiconductors, transistors, and bubble memory used to create electrical components with no moving parts. That's a mouthful! Here's the translation.

In simple terms, SSDs (see Figure 10.7) use memory chips to store data instead of all those pesky metal spinning parts used in platter-based hard drives. Solid-state technology has been around for many moons. It was originally developed to transition vacuum tube–based technologies to semiconductor technologies, such as the move from cathode ray tubes (CRTs) to liquid crystal displays (LCDs) in monitors. (You'll get the scoop on monitor technologies in Chapter 13.)

Solid-state devices use current flow and negative/positive electron charges to achieve their magic. Although Mr. Spock may find the physics of how this technology actually works "fascinating," it's more important for you to know the following points regarding solid-state drives, devices, and technology.

- Solid-state technology is commonly used in desktop and laptop hard drives, memory cards, cameras, USB thumb drives, and other handheld devices.

- SSD form factors are typically 1.8-inch, 2.5-inch, or 3.5-inch.

- SSDs can be PATA, SATA, eSATA, SCSI, or USB for desktop systems. Some portable computers have mini-PCI Express versions. You can also purchase SSD cards built onto PCIe cards (which you would connect to your PC like any other expansion card).

- SSDs that use SDRAM cache are volatile and lose data when powered off. Others that use nonvolatile flash memory such as NAND retain data when power is turned off or disconnected. (See Chapter 11 for the scoop on flash memory technology.)

- SSDs are more expensive than traditional HDDs. Less expensive SSDs typically implement less reliable multi-level cell (MLC) memory technology in place of the more efficient single-level cell (SLC) technology to cut costs.

• **Figure 10.7** A solid-state drive (photo courtesy of Corsair)

With solid-state drives coming into more regular use, you see the initials HDD used more frequently than in previous years to refer to the traditional, platter-based hard drives. Thus we have two drive technologies: SSDs and HDDs.

Tech Tip

IDE

The term IDE *(integrated drive electronics) refers to any hard drive with a built-in controller. All hard drives are technically IDE drives, although we only use the term IDE when discussing ATA drives.*

■ Parallel and Serial ATA

Over the years, many interfaces existed for hard drives, with such names as ST-506 and ESDI. Don't worry about what these abbreviations stood for; neither the CompTIA A+ 220-801 exam nor the computer world at large have an interest in these prehistoric interfaces. Starting around 1990, an interface called **advanced technology attachment (ATA)** appeared that now virtually monopolizes the hard drive market. ATA hard drives are often referred to as **integrated drive electronics (IDE)** drives. Only one other type of interface, the moderately popular small computer system interface (SCSI), has any relevance for hard drives.

ATA drives come in two basic flavors. The older **parallel ATA (PATA)** drives send data in parallel, on a 40- or 80-wire data cable. PATA drives dominated the industry for more than a decade but have been mostly replaced by **serial ATA (SATA)** drives that send data in serial, using only one wire for data transfers. The leap from PATA to SATA is only one of a large number of changes that have taken place with ATA. To appreciate these changes, we'll run through the many ATA standards that have appeared over the years.

ATA-1

When IBM unveiled the 80286-powered IBM PC AT in the early 1980s, it introduced the first PC to include BIOS support for hard drives. This BIOS supported up to two physical drives, and each drive could be up to 504 MB—far larger than the 5-MB and 10-MB drives of the time. Although having built-in support for hard drives certainly improved the power of the PC, installing, configuring, and troubleshooting hard drives could at best be called difficult at that time.

To address these problems, Western Digital and Compaq developed a new hard drive interface and placed this specification before the *American National Standards Institute (ANSI)* committees, which in turn put out the AT Attachment (ATA) interface in March of 1989. The ATA interface specified a cable and a built-in controller on the drive itself. Most importantly, the ATA standard used the existing AT BIOS on a PC, which meant that you didn't have to replace the old system BIOS to make the drive work—a very important consideration for compatibility but one that would later haunt ATA drives. The official name for the standard, ATA, never made it into the common vernacular until recently, and then only as PATA to distinguish it from SATA drives.

Early ATA Physical Connections

The first ATA drives connected to the computer with a **40-pin ribbon cable** that plugged into the drive and into a hard drive controller. The cable has a colored stripe down one side that denotes pin 1 and should connect to the drive's pin 1 and to the controller's pin 1. Figure 10.8 shows the business end of an early ATA drive, with the connectors for the ribbon cable and the power cable.

Tech Tip

External Hard Drives
A quick trip to any major computer store will reveal a thriving trade in external hard drives. You used to be able to find external drives that connected to the slow parallel port, but external drives today connect to a FireWire, USB, or eSATA port. All three interfaces offer high data transfer rates and hot-swap capability, making them ideal for transporting huge files such as digital video clips. Regardless of the external interface, however, you'll find an ordinary PATA or SATA drive inside the **external enclosure** *(the name used to describe the casing of external hard drives).*

• **Figure 10.8** Back of IDE drive showing 40-pin connector (left), jumpers (center), and power connector (right)

• **Figure 10.9** Relation of drive, controller, and bus

• **Figure 10.10** A typical hard drive with directions (top) for setting a jumper (bottom)

The controller is the support circuitry that acts as the intermediary between the hard drive and the external data bus. Electronically, the setup looks like Figure 10.9.

Wait a minute! If ATA drives are IDE (see the earlier Tech Tip), they already have a built-in controller. Why do they then have to plug into a *controller* on the motherboard? Well, this is a great example of a term that's not used properly, but everyone (including the motherboard and hard drive makers) uses it this way. What we call the ATA controller is really no more than an interface providing a connection to the rest of the PC system. When your BIOS talks to the hard drive, it actually talks to the onboard circuitry on the drive, not the connection on the motherboard. But, even though the *real* controller resides on the hard drive, the 40-pin connection on the motherboard is called the controller. We have a lot of misnomers to live with in the ATA world.

The ATA-1 standard defined that no more than two drives attach to a single IDE connector on a single ribbon cable. Because up to two drives can attach to one connector via a single cable, you need to be able to identify each drive on the cable. The ATA standard identifies the two drives as "master" and "slave." You set one drive as master and one as slave by using tiny jumpers on the drives (see Figure 10.10).

The controllers are on the motherboard and manifest themselves as two 40-pin male ports, as shown in Figure 10.11.

PIO and DMA Modes

If you're making a hard drive standard, you must define both the method and the speed at which the data's going to move.

ATA-1 defined two methods, the first using programmed I/O (PIO) addressing and the second using direct memory access (DMA) mode.

The ANSI subcommittee directly responsible for the ATA standard is called Technical Committee T13. If you want to know what's happening with ATA, check out the T13 Web site: www.t13.org.

• **Figure 10.11** IDE interfaces on a motherboard

PIO is nothing more than the traditional I/O addressing scheme, where the CPU talks directly to the hard drive via the BIOS to send and receive data. Three different PIO speeds called **PIO modes** were initially adopted:

- PIO mode 0: 3.3 MBps (megabytes per second)
- PIO mode 1: 5.2 MBps
- PIO mode 2: 8.3 MBps

DMA modes defined a method to enable the hard drives to talk to RAM directly, using old-style DMA commands. (The ATA folks called this *single-word DMA*.) This old-style DMA was slow, and the resulting three ATA single-word DMA modes were also slow:

- Single-word DMA mode 0: 2.1 MBps
- Single-word DMA mode 1: 4.2 MBps
- Single-word DMA mode 2: 8.3 MBps

When a computer booted up, the BIOS queried the hard drive to see what modes it could use and then automatically adjusted to the fastest possible mode.

ATA-2

In 1990, the industry adopted a series of improvements to the ATA standard called ATA-2. Many people called these new features **Enhanced IDE (EIDE)**. EIDE was really no more than a marketing term invented by Western Digital, but it caught on in common vernacular and is still used today, although its use is fading. Regular IDE drives quickly disappeared, and by 1995, EIDE drives dominated the PC world. Figure 10.12 shows a typical EIDE drive.

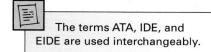
The terms ATA, IDE, and EIDE are used interchangeably.

ATA-2 was the most important ATA standard, as it included powerful new features such as higher capacities, support for non–hard drive storage devices, support for two more ATA devices for a maximum of four, and substantially improved throughput.

Higher Capacity with LBA

IBM created the AT BIOS to support hard drives many years before IDE drives were invented, and every system had that BIOS. The developers of IDE made certain that the new drives would run from the same AT BIOS command set. With this capability, you could use the same CMOS and BIOS routines to talk to a much more advanced drive. Your motherboard or hard drive controller wouldn't become instantly obsolete when you installed a new hard drive.

Unfortunately, the BIOS routines for the original AT command set allowed a hard drive size of only up to 528 million bytes (or 504 MB—remember

• **Figure 10.12** EIDE drive

that a mega = 1,048,576, not 1,000,000). A drive could have no more than 1024 cylinders, 16 heads, and 63 sectors/track:

1024 cylinders × 16 heads × 63 sectors/track × 512 bytes/sector = 504 MB

For years, this was not a problem. But when hard drives began to approach the 504-MB barrier, it became clear that there needed to be a way of getting past 504 MB. The ATA-2 standard defined a way to get past this limit with **logical block addressing (LBA)**. With LBA, the hard drive lies to the computer about its geometry through an advanced type of sector translation. Let's take a moment to understand sector translation, and then come back to LBA.

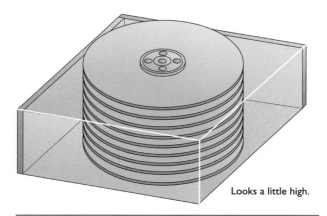

Looks a little high.

● **Figure 10.13** Too many heads

16 sectors/track

8 sectors/track

● **Figure 10.14** Multiple sectors/track

Sector Translation Long before hard drives approached the 504-MB limit, the limits of 1024 cylinders, 16 heads, and 63 sectors/track gave hard drive makers fits. The big problem was the heads. Remember that every two heads means another platter, another physical disk that you have to squeeze into a hard drive. If you wanted a hard drive with the maximum number of 16 heads, you would need a hard drive with eight physical platters inside the drive. Nobody wanted that many platters: it made the drives too tall, it took more power to spin up the drive, and that many parts cost too much money (see Figure 10.13).

Manufacturers could readily produce a hard drive that had fewer heads and more cylinders, but the stupid 1024/16/63 limit got in the way. Plus, the traditional sector arrangement wasted a lot of useful space. Sectors toward the inside of the drive, for example, are much shorter than the sectors on the outside. The sectors on the outside don't need to be that long, but with the traditional geometry setup, hard drive makers had no choice. They could make a hard drive store a lot more information, however, if they could make hard drives with more sectors/track on the outside tracks (see Figure 10.14).

The ATA specification was designed to have two geometries. The *physical geometry* defined the real layout of the CHS inside the drive. The *logical geometry* described what the drive told the CMOS. In other words, the IDE drive "lied" to the CMOS, thus side-stepping the artificial limits of the BIOS. When data was being transferred to and from the drive, the onboard circuitry of the drive translated the logical geometry into the physical geometry. This function was, and still is, called **sector translation**.

Let's look at a couple of hypothetical examples in action. First, pretend that Seagate came out with a new, cheap, fast hard drive called the ST108. To get the ST108 drive fast and cheap, however, Seagate had to use a rather strange geometry, shown in Table 10.1.

Table 10.1	Seagate's ST108 Drive Geometry		
ST108 Physical		**BIOS Limits**	
Cylinders	2048	Cylinders	1024
Heads	2	Heads	16
Sectors/track	52	Sectors/track	63
Total capacity	108 MB	Total capacity	504 MB

Notice that the cylinder number is greater than 1024. To overcome this problem, the IDE drive performs a sector translation that reports a geometry to the BIOS that is totally different from the true geometry of the drive. Table 10.2 shows the physical geometry and the "logical" geometry of our mythical ST108 drive. Notice that the logical geometry is now within the acceptable parameters of the BIOS limitations. Sector translation never changes the capacity of the drive; it changes only the geometry to stay within the BIOS limits.

Hard drive makers talk about hard drive capacities in millions and billions of bytes, not megabytes and gigabytes.

Back to LBA Now let's watch how the advanced sector translation of LBA provides support for hard drives greater than 504 MB. Let's use an old drive, the Western Digital WD2160, a 2.1-GB hard drive, as an example. This drive is no longer in production, but its smaller CHS values make understanding LBA easier. Table 10.3 lists its physical and logical geometries.

Table 10.2	Physical and Logical Geometries of the ST108 Drive		
Physical		**Logical**	
Cylinders	2048	Cylinders	512
Heads	2	Heads	8
Sectors/track	52	Sectors/track	52
Total capacity	108 MB	Total capacity	108 MB

Note that, even with sector translation, the number of heads is greater than the allowed 16. So here's where the magic of LBA comes in. When the computer boots up, the BIOS asks the drives if they can perform LBA. If they say yes, the BIOS and the drive work together to change the way they talk to each other. They can do this

Table 10.3	Western Digital WD2160's Physical and Logical Geometries		
Physical		**Logical**	
Cylinders	16,384	Cylinders	1024
Heads	4	Heads	64
Sectors/track	63	Sectors/track	63
Total capacity	2.1 GB	Total capacity	2.1 GB

without conflicting with the original AT BIOS commands by taking advantage of unused commands to use up to 256 heads. LBA enables support for a maximum of $1024 \times 256 \times 63 \times 512$ bytes = 8.4-GB hard drives. Back in 1990, 8.4 GB was hundreds of times larger than the drives used at the time. Don't worry, later ATA standards will get the BIOS up to today's huge drives.

Not Just Hard Drives Anymore: ATAPI

ATA-2 added an extension to the ATA specification, called **advanced technology attachment packet interface (ATAPI)**, that enabled non–hard drive devices such as CD-ROM drives and tape backups to connect to the PC via the ATA controllers. ATAPI drives have the same 40-pin interface and master/slave jumpers as ATA hard drives. Figure 10.15 shows an ATAPI CD-RW drive attached to a motherboard. The key difference between hard drives and every other type of drive that attaches to the ATA controller is in how the drives get BIOS support. Hard drives get it through the system BIOS, whereas non–hard drives require the operating system to load a software driver.

With the introduction of ATAPI, the ATA standards are often referred to as ATA/ATAPI instead of just ATA.

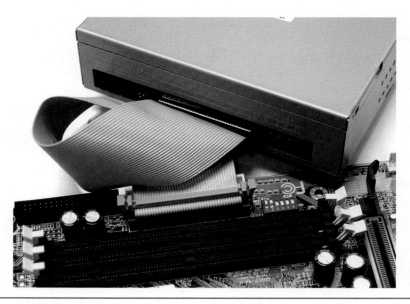

• **Figure 10.15** ATAPI CD-RW drive attached to a motherboard via a standard 40-pin ribbon cable

Tape drives are still available for purchase, but they're barely used. The only kind you'll need to know about for the CompTIA A+ 801 exam is the Digital Linear Tape (DLT) format.

More Drives with ATA-2

ATA-2 added support for a second controller, raising the total number of supported drives from two to four. Each of the two controllers is equal in power and capability. Figure 10.16 is a close-up of a typical motherboard, showing the primary controller marked as *PRI_IDE* and the secondary marked as *SEC_IDE*.

Increased Speed

ATA-2 defined two new PIO modes and a new type of DMA called *multi-word DMA* that was a substantial improvement over the old DMA. Technically, multi-word DMA was still the old-style DMA, but it worked in a much more efficient manner, so it was much faster.

- PIO mode 3: 11.1 MBps
- PIO mode 4: 16.6 MBps
- Multi-word DMA mode 0: 4.2 MBps
- Multi-word DMA mode 1: 13.3 MBps
- Multi-word DMA mode 2: 16.6 MBps

• **Figure 10.16** Primary and secondary controllers labeled on a motherboard

ATA-3

ATA-3 came on quickly after ATA-2 and added one new feature called **Self-Monitoring, Analysis, and Reporting Technology (S.M.A.R.T.)**, one of the few PC acronyms that requires the use of periods after each letter. S.M.A.R.T. helps predict when a hard drive is going to fail by monitoring the hard drive's mechanical components.

S.M.A.R.T. is a great idea and is popular in specialized server systems, but it's complex, imperfect, and hard to understand. As a result, only a few utilities can read the S.M.A.R.T. data on your hard drive. Your best sources are the hard drive manufacturers. Every hard drive maker has a free diagnostic tool (which usually works only for their drives) that will do a S.M.A.R.T. check along with other tests. Figure 10.17 shows Western Digital's Data Lifeguard Tools in action. Note that it says only whether the drive has passed or not. Figure 10.18 shows some S.M.A.R.T. information.

Although you can see the actual S.M.A.R.T. data, it's generally useless or indecipherable. Your best choice is to trust the manufacturer's opinion and run the software provided.

ATA-4

Anyone who has opened a big database file on a hard drive appreciates that a faster hard drive is better. ATA-4 introduced a new DMA mode called Ultra DMA that is now the primary way a hard drive communicates with a PC. **Ultra DMA** uses DMA bus mastering to achieve far faster speeds than were possible with PIO or old-style DMA. ATA-4 defined three Ultra DMA modes:

- Ultra DMA mode 0: 16.7 MBps
- Ultra DMA mode 1: 25.0 MBps
- Ultra DMA mode 2: 33.3 MBps

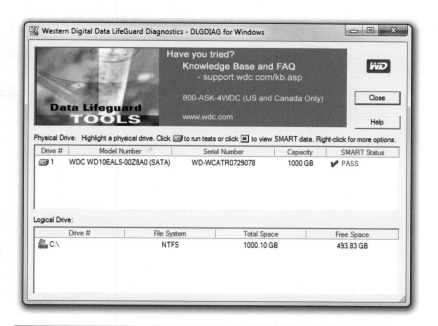

• **Figure 10.17** Data Lifeguard Tools

• **Figure 10.18** S.M.A.R.T. information

Ultra DMA mode 2, the most popular of the ATA-4 DMA modes, is also called ATA/33.

INT13 Extensions

Here's an interesting factoid for you: The original ATA-1 standard allowed for hard drives up to 137 GB. It wasn't the ATA standard that caused the 504-MB size limit; the standard used the old AT BIOS, and the BIOS, not the

ATA standard, could support only 504 MB. LBA was a work-around that told the hard drive to lie to the BIOS to get it up to 8.4 GB. But eventually hard drives started edging close to the LBA limit and something had to be done. The T13 folks said, "This isn't *our* problem. It's the ancient BIOS problem. You BIOS makers need to fix the BIOS." And they did.

In 1994, Phoenix Technologies (the BIOS manufacturer) came up with a new set of BIOS commands called **Interrupt 13 (INT13) extensions**. INT13 extensions broke the 8.4-GB barrier by completely ignoring the CHS values and instead feeding the LBA a stream of addressable sectors. A system with INT13 extensions can handle drives up to 137 GB. The entire PC industry quickly adopted INT13 extensions, and every system made since 2000–2001 supports INT13 extensions.

ATA-5

Ultra DMA was such a huge hit that the ATA folks adopted two faster Ultra DMA modes with ATA-5:

- Ultra DMA mode 3: 44.4 MBps
- Ultra DMA mode 4: 66.6 MBps

Ultra DMA mode 4 ran so quickly that the ATA-5 standard defined a new type of ribbon cable that could handle the higher speeds. This **80-wire cable** still has 40 pins on the connectors, but it also includes another 40 wires in the cable that act as grounds to improve the cable's capability to handle high-speed signals. The 80-wire cable, just like the 40-pin ribbon cable, has a colored stripe down one side to give you proper orientation for pin 1 on the controller and the hard drive. Previous versions of ATA didn't define where the various drives were plugged into the ribbon cable, but ATA-5 defined exactly where the controller, master, and slave drives connected, even defining colors to identify them. Take a look at the ATA/66 cable in Figure 10.19. The connector on the left is colored blue—and you must use that connector to plug into the controller. The connector in the middle is gray—that's for the slave drive. The connector on the right is black—that's for the master drive. Any ATA/66 controller connections are colored blue to let you know it is an ATA/66 controller.

• **Figure 10.19** ATA/66 cable

> Ultra DMA mode 4, the most popular of the ATA-5 DMA modes, is also called ATA/66.

ATA/66 is backward compatible, so you may safely plug an earlier drive into an ATA/66 cable and controller. If you plug an ATA/66 drive into an older controller, it will work—just not in ATA/66 mode. The only risky action is to use an ATA/66 controller and hard drive with a non-ATA/66 cable. Doing so will almost certainly cause nasty data losses!

ATA-6

Hard drive size exploded in the early 21st century, and the seemingly impossible-to-fill 137-GB limit created by INT13 extensions became a barrier earlier

than most people had anticipated. When drives started hitting the 120-GB mark, the T13 committee adopted an industry proposal pushed by Maxtor (a major hard drive maker) called *Big Drive* that increased the limit to more than 144 petabytes (approximately 144,000,000 GB). Thankfully, T13 also gave the new standard a less-silly name, calling it **ATA/ATAPI-6** or simply ATA-6. Big Drive was basically just a 48-bit LBA, supplanting the older 24-bit addressing of LBA and INT13 extensions. Plus, the standard defined an enhanced block mode, enabling drives to transfer up to 65,536 sectors in one chunk, up from the measly 256 sectors of lesser drive technologies.

ATA-6 also introduced Ultra DMA mode 5, kicking the data transfer rate up to 100 MBps. Ultra DMA mode 5 is more commonly referred to as ATA/100 and requires the same 80-wire cable as ATA/66.

ATA-7

ATA-7 brought two new innovations to the ATA world: one evolutionary and the other revolutionary. The evolutionary innovation came with the last of the parallel ATA Ultra DMA modes; the revolutionary was a new form of ATA called serial ATA (SATA).

ATA/133

ATA-7 introduced the fastest and probably least adopted of all of the ATA speeds, Ultra DMA mode 6 (**ATA/133**). Even though it runs at a speed of 133 MBps, the fact that it came out with SATA kept many hard drive manufacturers away. ATA/133 uses the same cables as Ultra DMA 66 and 100.

While you won't find many ATA/133 hard drives, you will find plenty of ATA/133 controllers. There's a trend in the industry to color the controller connections on the hard drive red, although this is not part of the ATA-7 standard.

Serial ATA

The real story of ATA-7 is SATA. For all its longevity as the mass storage interface of choice for the PC, parallel ATA has problems. First, the flat ribbon cables impede airflow and can be a pain to insert properly. Second, the cables have a limited length, only 18 inches. Third, you can't hot-swap PATA drives. You have to shut down completely before installing or replacing a drive. Finally, the technology has simply reached the limits of what it can do in terms of throughput.

Serial ATA addresses these issues. SATA creates a point-to-point connection between the SATA device—hard disk, CD-ROM, CD-RW, DVD-ROM, DVD-RW, BD-R, BD-RE, and so on—and the SATA controller, the **host bus adapter (HBA)**. At a glance, SATA devices look identical to standard PATA devices. Take a closer look at the cable and power connectors, however, and you'll see significant differences (see Figure 10.20).

• **Figure 10.20** SATA hard disk power (left) and data (right) cables

Each SATA variety is named for the revision to the SATA specification that introduced it:
SATA 1.0: 1.5 Gbps
SATA 2.0: 3 Gbps
SATA 3.0: 6 Gbps

Because SATA devices send data serially instead of in parallel, the SATA interface needs far fewer physical wires—seven instead of the eighty wires that is typical of PATA—resulting in much thinner cabling. This might not seem significant, but the benefit is that thinner cabling means better cable control and better airflow through the PC case, resulting in better cooling.

Further, the maximum SATA-device cable length is more than twice that of an IDE cable—about 40 inches (1 meter) instead of 18 inches. Again, this might not seem like a big deal unless you've struggled to connect a PATA hard disk installed into the top bay of a full-tower case to an IDE connector located all the way at the bottom of the motherboard.

SATA does away with the entire master/slave concept. Each drive connects to one port, so no more daisy-chaining drives. Further, there's no maximum number of drives—many motherboards are now available that support up to eight SATA drives. Want more? Snap in a SATA HBA and load 'em up!

The big news, however, is in data throughput. As the name implies, SATA devices transfer data in serial bursts instead of parallel, as PATA devices do. Typically, you might not think of serial devices as being faster than parallel, but in this case, a SATA device's single stream of data moves much faster than the multiple streams of data coming from a parallel IDE device—theoretically, up to 30 times faster. SATA drives come in three common varieties: 1.5 Gbps, 3 Gbps, and 6 Gbps, which have a maximum throughput of 150 MBps, 300 MBps, and 600 MBps, respectively.

SATA is backward compatible with current PATA standards and enables you to install a parallel ATA device, including a hard drive, optical drive, and other devices, to a serial ATA controller by using a **SATA bridge**. A SATA bridge manifests as a tiny card that you plug directly into the 40-pin connector on a PATA drive. As you can see in Figure 10.21, the controller chip on the bridge requires separate power; you plug a Molex connector into the PATA drive as normal. When you boot the system, the PATA drive shows up to the system as a SATA drive.

SATA's ease of use has made it the choice for desktop system storage, and its success is already showing in the fact that more than 90 percent of all hard drives sold today are SATA drives.

• **Figure 10.21** SATA bridge

AHCI Windows Vista and later operating systems support the *Advanced Host Controller Interface (AHCI)*, a more efficient way to work with SATA HBAs. Using AHCI unlocks some of the advanced features of SATA, such as hot-swapping and native command queuing.

When you plug in a SATA drive to a running Windows computer that does not have AHCI enabled, the drive doesn't appear automatically. In Windows XP/Vista, you need to go to the Control Panel and run the Add New Hardware to make the drive appear, and in Windows 7, you need to run hdwwiz.exe from the Start menu Search bar. With AHCI, the drive should appear in My Computer/Computer immediately, just what you'd expect from a hot-swappable device.

Native command queuing (NCQ) is a disk-optimization feature for SATA drives. It enables faster read and write speeds.

AHCI is implemented at the CMOS level (see "BIOS Support: Configuring CMOS and Installing Drivers," later in this chapter) and generally needs to be enabled before you install the operating system. Enabling it after installation will cause Windows Vista and 7 to Blue Screen. How nice.

eSATA **External SATA (eSATA)** extends the SATA bus to external devices, as the name would imply. The eSATA drives use connectors similar to internal SATA, but they're keyed differently so you can't mistake one for the other. Figure 10.22 shows eSATA connectors on the back of a motherboard.

External SATA uses shielded cable lengths up to 2 meters outside the PC and is hot-swappable. The beauty of eSATA is that it extends the SATA bus at full speed, which tops out at a theoretical 6 Gbps, whereas the fastest USB connection (USB 3.0, also called SuperSpeed USB) maxes out at 5 Gbps. It's not that big of a speed gap, especially when you consider that neither connection type fully utilizes its bandwidth yet, but even in real-world tests, eSATA still holds its own.

If a desktop system doesn't have an eSATA external connector, or if you need more external SATA devices, you can install an eSATA HBA PCIe card

Tech Tip

Enabling AHCI After the Fact

If you want to enable AHCI but you've already installed Windows Vista or Windows 7, don't worry! Microsoft has developed a procedure (http://support.microsoft.com/kb/922976) that will have you enjoying all that AHCI fun in no time. Before you jump in, note that this procedure requires you to edit your Registry, so remember to always make a backup before you start editing.

For the scoop on PC Cards and ExpressCards—both technologies designed to add expansion options for portable computers—see Chapter 18.

• **Figure 10.22** eSATA connectors

• **Figure 10.23** eSATA ExpressCard

In addition to eSATA ports, you'll also run into eSATAp ports on some laptops. This port physically combines a powered USB connection with a speedy eSATA connection; you can connect a USB, eSATA, or special eSATAp cable into the port. eSATAp enables you to connect an internal drive (HDD, SSD, or optical drive) to your laptop without an enclosure, using a single cable to power it and send/receive data.

SCSI is pronounced "scuzzy."

• **Figure 10.24** SCSI host adapter

or eSATA internal-to-external slot plate. You can similarly upgrade laptop systems to support external SATA devices by inserting an eSATA ExpressCard (see Figure 10.23). There are also USB-to-eSATA adapter plugs. Install eSATA PCIe, PC Card, or ExpressCard following the same rules and precautions for installing any expansion device.

■ SCSI: Still Around

Many specialized server machines and enthusiasts' systems use the **small computer system interface (SCSI)** technologies for various pieces of core hardware and peripherals, from hard drives to printers to high-end tape-backup machines. SCSI is different from ATA in that SCSI devices connect together in a string of devices called a *chain*. Each device in the chain gets a SCSI ID to distinguish it from other devices on the chain. Last, the ends of a SCSI chain must be terminated. Let's dive into SCSI now, and see how SCSI chains, SCSI IDs, and termination all work.

SCSI is an old technology dating from the late 1970s, but it has been updated continually. SCSI is faster than ATA (though the gap is closing fast), and until SATA arrived, SCSI was the only good choice for anyone using RAID (see the "RAID" section a little later). SCSI is arguably fading away, but it deserves some mention.

SCSI Chains

SCSI manifests itself through a **SCSI chain**, a series of SCSI devices working together through a host adapter. The host adapter provides the interface between the SCSI chain and the PC. Figure 10.24 shows a typical SCSI PCI host adapter. Many techs refer to the host adapter as the *SCSI controller*, so you should be comfortable with both terms.

All SCSI devices can be divided into two groups: internal and external. Internal SCSI devices are attached inside the PC and connect to the host adapter through the latter's internal connector. Figure 10.25 shows an internal SCSI device, in this case a CD-ROM drive. External devices hook to the external connector of the host adapter. Figure 10.26 is an example of an external SCSI device.

Internal SCSI devices connect to the host adapter with a 68-pin ribbon cable (see Figure 10.27). This flat, flexible cable functions precisely like a PATA cable. Many external devices connect to the host adapter with a 50-pin high-density (HD) connector. Figure 10.28 shows a host adapter external port. Higher-end SCSI devices use a 68-pin HD connector.

Some early versions of SCSI used a 25-pin connector. This connector was much more popular on Apple devices, though it did see use on PCs with the old SCSI Zip drives. While the connector is now obsolete, you need to know about it for the CompTIA A+ 801 exam.

• **Figure 10.25** Internal SCSI CD-ROM

Multiple internal devices can be connected simply by using a cable with enough connectors (see Figure 10.29). The 68-pin ribbon cable shown in Figure 10.27, for example, can support up to four SCSI devices, including the host adapter.

Assuming the SCSI host adapter has a standard external port (some controllers don't have external connections at all), plugging in an external SCSI device is as simple as running a cable from device to controller. The external SCSI connectors are D-shaped so you can't plug them in backward. As an added bonus, some external SCSI devices have two ports, one to connect to the host adapter and a second to connect to another SCSI device. The

• **Figure 10.26** Back of external SCSI device

process of connecting a device directly to another device is called *daisy-chaining*. You can daisy-chain as many as 15 devices to one host adapter. SCSI chains can be internal, external, or both (see Figure 10.30).

• **Figure 10.27** Typical 68-pin ribbon cable

• **Figure 10.28** 50-pin HD port on SCSI host adapter

• **Figure 10.29** Internal SCSI chain with two devices

Internal SCSI devices

SCSI host adapter

• **Figure 10.30** Internal and external devices on one SCSI chain

Internal SCSI devices

External SCSI devices

SCSI host adapter

Old SCSI equipment allowed SCSI IDs from 0 to 7 only.

SCSI IDs

If you're going to connect a number of devices on the same SCSI chain, you must provide some way for the host adapter to tell one device from another. To differentiate devices, SCSI uses a unique identifier called the **SCSI ID**. The SCSI ID number can range from 0 to 15. SCSI IDs are similar to many other PC hardware settings in that a SCSI device can theoretically have any SCSI ID as long as that ID is not already taken by another device connected to the same host adapter.

Some conventions should be followed when setting SCSI IDs. Typically, most people set the host adapter to 7 or 15, but you can change this setting. Note that there is no order for the use of SCSI IDs. It does not matter which device gets which number, and you can skip numbers. Restrictions on IDs apply only within a single chain. Two devices can have the same ID, in other words, as long as they are on different chains (see Figure 10.31).

Every SCSI device has some method of setting its SCSI ID. The trick is to figure out how as you're holding the device in your hand. A SCSI device may use jumpers, dip switches, or even tiny dials; every new SCSI device is a new adventure as you try to determine how to set its SCSI ID.

SCSI device SCSI ID 6

SCSI device SCSI ID 1

SCSI host adapter SCSI ID 7

SCSI host adapter SCSI ID 7

• **Figure 10.31** IDs don't conflict between separate SCSI chains.

Termination

Whenever you send a signal down a wire, some of that signal reflects back up the wire, creating an echo and causing electronic chaos. SCSI chains use **termination** to prevent this problem. Termination simply means putting something on the ends of the wire to prevent this echo. Terminators are usually pull-down resistors and can manifest themselves in many different ways. Most of the devices within a PC have the appropriate termination built in. On other devices, including SCSI chains and some network cables, you have to set termination during installation.

The rule with SCSI is that you *must* terminate *only* the ends of the SCSI chain. You have to terminate the ends of the cable, which usually means that you need to terminate the two devices at the ends of the cable. Do *not* terminate devices that are not on the ends of the cable. Figure 10.32 shows some examples of where to terminate SCSI devices.

• **Figure 10.32** Location of the terminated devices

Because any SCSI device might be on the end of a chain, most manufacturers build SCSI devices that can self-terminate. Some devices can detect that they are on the end of the SCSI chain and automatically terminate themselves. Most devices, however, require you to set a jumper or switch to enable termination (see Figure 10.33).

• **Figure 10.33** Setting termination

■ Protecting Data with RAID

Ask experienced techs "What is the most expensive part of a PC?" and they'll all answer in the same way: "It's the data." You can replace any single part of your PC for a few hundred dollars at most, but if you lose critical data—well, let's just say I know of two small companies that went out of business because they lost a hard drive full of data.

Data is king; data is your PC's *raison d'être*. Losing data is a bad thing, so you need some method to prevent data loss. Of course, you can do backups, but if a hard drive dies, you have to shut down the computer, reinstall a new hard drive, reinstall the operating system, and then restore the backup. There's nothing wrong with this as long as you can afford the time and cost of shutting down the system.

A better solution, though, would save your data if a hard drive died and enable you to continue working throughout the process. This is possible if you stop relying on a single hard drive and instead use two or more drives

to store your data. Sounds good, but how do you do this? Well, first of all, you could install some fancy hard drive controller that reads and writes data to two hard drives simultaneously (see Figure 10.34). The data on each drive would always be identical. One drive would be the primary drive and the other drive, called the *mirror* drive, would not be used unless the primary drive failed. This process of reading and writing data at the same time to two drives is called **disk mirroring**.

If you really want to make data safe, you can use a separate controller for each drive. With two drives, each on a separate controller, the system will continue to operate even if the primary drive's controller stops working. This super-drive mirroring technique is called **disk duplexing** (see Figure 10.35). Disk duplexing is also much faster than disk mirroring because one controller does not write each piece of data twice.

Even though duplexing is faster than mirroring, they both are slower than the classic one-drive, one-controller setup. You can use multiple drives to increase your hard drive access speed. **Disk striping** (without parity) means spreading the data among multiple (at least two) drives. Disk striping by itself provides no redundancy. If you save a small Microsoft Word file, for example, the file is split into multiple pieces; half of the pieces go on one drive and half on the other (see Figure 10.36).

The one and only advantage of disk striping is speed—it is a fast way to read and write to hard drives. But if either drive fails, *all* data is lost. You should not do disk striping—unless you're willing to increase the risk of losing data to increase the speed at which your hard drives save and restore data.

RAID 1 (mirroring)
• Exactly two (redundant) drives
• Safe but slow
• Both drives are assigned the same drive letter.

SATA RAID Controller

• **Figure 10.34** Mirrored drives

RAID 1 (duplexing)
• Exactly two (redundant) drives
• Faster and safer
• Both drives are assigned the
 same drive letter.

SATA
RAID
Controller

• **Figure 10.35** Duplexing drives

RAID 0 (striping)
• Two or more (non-redundant) drives
• Fast, but not really safe
• Both drives are assigned the
 same drive letter.

SATA
RAID
Controller

• **Figure 10.36** Disk striping

Disk striping with parity, in contrast, protects data by adding extra information, called *parity data*, that can be used to rebuild data if one of the drives fails. Disk striping with parity requires at least three drives, but it is common to use more than three. Disk striping with parity combines the best of disk mirroring and plain disk striping. It protects data and is quite fast. The majority of network servers use a type of disk striping with parity.

RAID

A couple of sharp guys in Berkeley back in the 1980s organized the many techniques for using multiple drives for data protection and increasing speeds as the **redundant array of independent (or inexpensive) disks (RAID)**. They outlined seven levels of RAID, numbered 0 through 6:

- **RAID 0—Disk Striping** Disk striping requires at least two drives. It does not provide redundancy to data. If any one drive fails, all data is lost.

- **RAID 1—Disk Mirroring/Duplexing** RAID 1 arrays require at least two hard drives, although they also work with any even number of drives. RAID 1 is the ultimate in safety, but you lose storage space because the data is duplicated; you need two 100-GB drives to store 100 GB of data.

- **RAID 2—Disk Striping with Multiple Parity Drives** RAID 2 was a weird RAID idea that never saw practical use. Ignore it.

- **RAID 3 and 4—Disk Striping with Dedicated Parity** RAID 3 and 4 combined dedicated data drives with dedicated parity drives. The differences between the two are trivial. Unlike RAID 2, these versions did see some use in the real world but were quickly replaced by RAID 5.

- **RAID 5—Disk Striping with Distributed Parity** Instead of dedicated data and parity drives, RAID 5 distributes data and parity information evenly across all drives. This is the fastest way to provide data redundancy. RAID 5 is by far the most common RAID implementation and requires at least three drives. RAID 5 arrays effectively use one drive's worth of space for parity. If, for example, you have three 200-GB drives, your total storage capacity is 400 GB. If you have four 200-GB drives, your total capacity is 600 GB.

- **RAID 6—Disk Striping with Extra Parity** If you lose a hard drive in a RAID 5 array, your data is at great risk until you replace the bad hard drive and rebuild the array. RAID 6 is RAID 5 with extra parity information. RAID 6 needs at least five drives, but in exchange you can lose up to two drives at the same time. RAID 6 is gaining in popularity for those willing to use larger arrays.

After these first RAID levels were defined, some manufacturers came up with ways to combine different RAIDs. For example, what if you took two pairs of striped drives and mirrored the pairs? You would get what is called RAID 0+1. Or what if (read this carefully now) you took two pairs of mirrored drives and striped the pairs? You then get what we call RAID 1+0

Tech Tip

RAID Lingo

No tech worth her salt says such things as "We're implementing disk striping with parity." Use the RAID level. Say, "We're implementing RAID 5." It's more accurate and very impressive to the folks in the accounting department!

An *array* in the context of RAID refers to a collection of two or more hard drives.

or what is often called RAID 10. Combinations of different types of single RAID are called *multiple RAID* or *nested RAID* solutions.

 There is actually a term for a storage system composed of multiple independent disks rather than disks organized by using RAID: *JBOD*, which stands for *just a bunch of disks* (or *drives*).

Implementing RAID

RAID levels describe different methods of providing data redundancy or enhancing the speed of data throughput to and from groups of hard drives. They do not say *how* to implement these methods. Literally thousands of methods can be used to set up RAID. The method you use depends largely on the level of RAID you desire, the operating system you use, and the thickness of your wallet.

The obvious starting place for RAID is to connect at least two hard drives in some fashion to create a RAID array. For many years, if you wanted to do RAID beyond RAID 0 and RAID 1, the only technology you could use was good-old SCSI. SCSI's chaining of multiple devices to a single controller made it a natural for RAID. SCSI drives make superb RAID arrays, but the high cost of SCSI drives and RAID-capable host adapters kept RAID away from all but the most critical systems—usually big file servers.

In the past few years, substantial leaps in ATA technology have made ATA a viable alternative to SCSI drive technology for RAID arrays. Specialized ATA RAID controller cards support ATA RAID arrays of up to 15 drives—plenty to support even the most complex RAID needs. In addition, the inherent hot-swap capabilities of serial ATA have virtually guaranteed that serial ATA will quickly take over the lower end of the RAID business. Personally, I think the price and performance of serial ATA mean SCSI's days are numbered.

Once you have a number of hard drives, the next question is whether to use hardware or software to control the array. Let's look at both options.

 Try This!

Managing Heat with Multiple Drives

Adding three or more fast hard drives into a cramped PC case can be a recipe for disaster to the unwary tech. All those disks spinning constantly create a phenomenal amount of heat. Heat kills PCs! You have to manage the heat inside a RAID-enabled system or risk losing your data, drives, and basic system stability. The easiest way to do this is to add fans, so Try This!

Open up your PC case and look for built-in places to mount fans. How many case fans do you have installed now? What size are they? What sizes can you use? (Most cases use 80-mm fans, but 60- and 120-mm fans are common as well.) Jot down the particulars of your system and take a trip to the local PC store to check out the fans.

Before you get all fan-happy and grab the biggest and baddest fans to throw in your case, don't forget to think about the added noise level. Try to get a compromise between keeping your case cool enough and avoiding early deafness.

Hardware Versus Software

All RAID implementations break down into either hardware or software methods. Software is often used when price takes priority over performance. Hardware is used when you need speed along with data redundancy. Software RAID does not require special controllers; you can use the regular ATA controllers, SATA controllers, or SCSI host adapters to make a software RAID array. But you do need "smart" software. The most common software implementation of RAID is the built-in RAID software

that comes with Windows 2008 Server and Windows Server 2008 R2. The Disk Management program in these Windows Server versions can configure drives for RAID 0, 1, or 5, and it works with PATA, SATA, and/or SCSI (see Figure 10.37). Disk Management in Windows XP and Windows Vista can only do RAID 0, while Windows 7's Disk Management can do RAID 0 and 1.

Windows Disk Management is not the only software RAID game in town. A number of third-party software programs work with Windows or other operating systems.

Software RAID means the operating system is in charge of all RAID functions. It works for small RAID solutions but tends to overwork your operating system easily, creating slowdowns. When you *really* need to keep going, when you need RAID that doesn't even let the users know a problem has occurred, hardware RAID is the answer.

Hardware RAID centers on an *intelligent* controller—either a SCSI host adapter or a PATA/SATA controller that handles all of the RAID functions (see Figure 10.38). Unlike a regular PATA/SATA controller or SCSI host adapter, these controllers have chips that have their own processor and memory. This allows the card, instead of the operating system, to handle all of the work of implementing RAID.

Most RAID setups in the real world are hardware-based. Almost all of the many hardware RAID solutions provide *hot-swapping*—the ability to replace a bad drive without disturbing the operating system. Hot-swapping is common in hardware RAID.

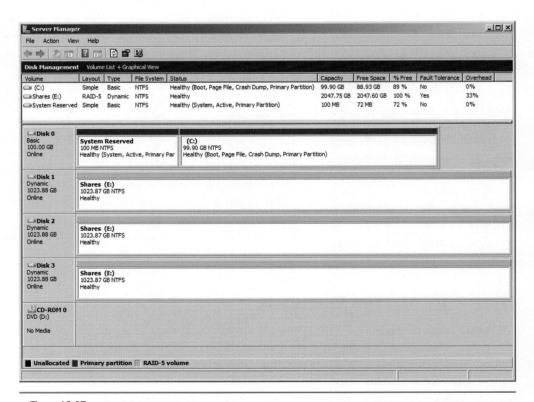

• **Figure 10.37** Disk Management tool of Computer Management in Windows Server 2008 R2

Hardware-based RAID is invisible to the operating system and is configured in several ways, depending on the specific chips involved. Most RAID systems have a special configuration utility in Flash ROM that you access after CMOS but before the OS loads. Figure 10.39 shows a typical firmware program used to configure a hardware RAID solution.

Personal RAID

Due to drastic reductions in the cost of ATA RAID controller chips, in the past few years we've seen an explosion of ATA-based hardware RAID solutions built into mainstream motherboards. While this "ATA RAID on the motherboard" began with parallel ATA, the introduction of serial ATA made motherboards with built-in RAID extremely common.

These personal RAID motherboards might be common, but they're not used too terribly often given that these RAID solutions usually provide only RAID 0 or RAID 1. If you want to use RAID, spend a few extra dollars and buy a RAID 5–capable controller.

The Future Is RAID

RAID has been with us for about 20 years, but until only recently it was the domain of big systems and deep pockets. During those 20 years, however, a number of factors have come together to make RAID a reality for both big servers and common desktop systems. Imagine a world where dirt-cheap RAID on every computer means no one ever again losing critical data. I get goose bumps just thinking about it!

• **Figure 10.38** Serial ATA RAID controller

RAID controllers aren't just for internal drives; some models can handle multiple eSATA drives configured at any of the RAID levels. If you're feeling lucky, you can create a RAID array using both internal and external SATA drives.

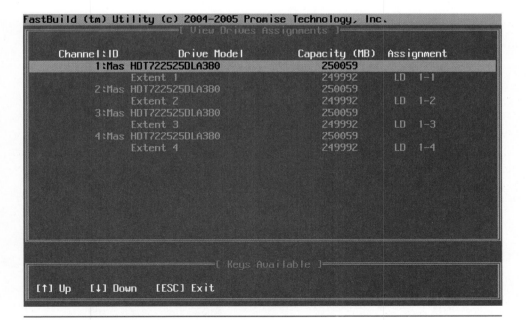

```
FastBuild (tm) Utility (c) 2004-2005 Promise Technology, Inc.
                    [ View Drives Assignments ]

   Channel:ID        Drive Model      Capacity (MB)   Assignment
         1:Mas  HDT722525DLA380          250059
                Extent 1                 249992       LD  1-1
         2:Mas  HDT722525DLA380          250059
                Extent 2                 249992       LD  1-2
         3:Mas  HDT722525DLA380          250059
                Extent 3                 249992       LD  1-3
         4:Mas  HDT722525DLA380          250059
                Extent 4                 249992       LD  1-4

                        [ Keys Available ]

   [↑] Up   [↓] Down   [ESC] Exit
```

• **Figure 10.39** RAID configuration utility

■ Installing Drives

Installing a drive is a fairly simple process if you take the time to make sure you have the right drive for your system, configure the drive properly, and do a few quick tests to see if it's running properly. Since PATA, SATA, and SCSI have different cabling requirements, we'll look at each separately.

Choosing Your Drive

First, decide where you're going to put the drive. Look for an open ATA connection. Is it PATA or SATA? Is it a dedicated RAID controller? Many motherboards with built-in RAID controllers have a CMOS setting that enables you to turn the RAID on or off (see Figure 10.40).

Second, make sure you have room for the drive in the case. Where will you place it? Do you have a spare power connector? Will the data and power cables reach the drive? A quick test fit is always a good idea.

Jumpers and Cabling on PATA Drives

If you have only one hard drive, set the drive's jumpers to master or stand-alone. If you have two drives, set one to master and the other to slave. See Figure 10.41 for a close-up of a PATA hard drive, showing the jumpers.

At first glance, you might notice that the jumpers aren't actually labeled *master* and *slave*. So how do you know how to set them properly? The easiest way is to read the front of the drive; most drives have a diagram on the housing that explains how to set the jumpers properly. Figure 10.42 shows the label of one of these drives, so you can see how to set the drive to master or slave.

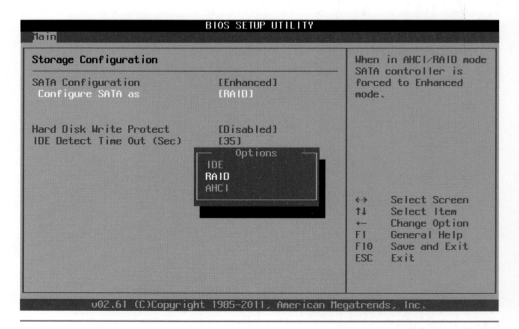

• **Figure 10.40** Settings for RAID in CMOS

Mike Meyers' CompTIA A+ Guide to 801: Managing and Troubleshooting PCs

• **Figure 10.42** Drive label showing master/slave settings

• **Figure 10.41** Master/slave jumpers on a hard drive

Hard disk drives may have other jumpers that may or may not concern you during installation. One common set of jumpers is used for diagnostics at the manufacturing plant or for special settings in other kinds of devices that use hard drives. Ignore them; they have no bearing in the PC world. Second, many drives provide a third setting to be used if only one drive connects to a controller. Often, master and single drive are the same setting on the hard drive, although some hard drives require separate settings. Note that the name for the single drive setting varies among manufacturers. Some use Single; others use 1 Drive or Standalone.

Many PATA hard drives use a jumper setting called *cable select* rather than master or slave. As the name implies, the position on the cable determines which drive will be master or slave: master on the end, slave in the middle. For cable select to work properly with two drives, you must set both drives as cable select and the cable itself must be a special cable-select cable. If you see a ribbon cable with a pinhole through one wire, watch out! That's a cable-select cable.

If you don't see a label on the drive that tells you how to set the jumpers, you have several options. First, look at the drive maker's Web site. Every drive manufacturer lists its drive jumper settings on the Web, although finding the information you want can take a while. Second, try phoning the hard drive maker directly. Unlike many other PC parts manufacturers, hard drive producers tend to stay in business for a long time and offer great technical support.

Hard drive cables have a colored stripe that corresponds to the number-one pin—called *pin 1*—on the connector. You need to make certain that pin 1 on the controller is on the same wire as pin 1 on the hard drive. Failing to plug in the drive properly will also prevent the PC from recognizing the drive. If you incorrectly set the master/slave jumpers or cable to the hard drives, you won't break anything; it just won't work.

Finally, you need to plug a Molex connector from the power supply into the drive. All modern PATA drives use a Molex connector.

Most of the high-speed ATA 66/100/133 cables support cable select—try one and see!

Cabling SATA Drives

Installing SATA hard disk drives is even easier than installing PATA devices because there's no master, slave, or cable select configuration to mess with. In fact, there are no jumper settings to worry about at all, as SATA supports only a single device per controller channel. Simply connect the power and plug in the controller cable as shown in Figure 10.43—the OS automatically detects the drive and it's ready to go. The keying on SATA controller and power cables makes it impossible to install either incorrectly.

The biggest problem with SATA drives is that many motherboards come with four or more. Sure, the cabling is easy enough, but what do you do when it comes time to start the computer and the system is trying to find the right hard drive to boot up? That's where CMOS comes into play (which you'll read about a little later).

Connecting Solid-State Drives

You install a solid-state drive as you would any PATA or SATA drive. Just as with earlier hard drive types, you either connect SSDs correctly and they work, or you connect them incorrectly and they don't. If they fail, nine times out of ten they will need to be replaced.

• **Figure 10.43** Properly connected SATA cable

You're most likely to run into solid-state drives today in portable computers. SSDs are expensive and offer a lot less storage capacity compared to traditional hard drives. Because they require a lot less electricity to run, on the other hand, they make a lot of sense in portable computers where battery life is essential. You can often use solid-state drives to replace existing platter-based drives in laptops.

Keep in mind the following considerations before installing or replacing an existing HDD with an SSD:

- Does the system currently use a PATA or SATA interface? You need to make sure your solid-state drive can connect properly.

- Do you have the appropriate drivers and firmware for the SSD? This is especially important if you run Windows XP. Windows Vista and 7, on the other hand, are likely to load most currently implemented SSD drivers. As always, check the manufacturer's specifications before you do anything.

- Do you have everything important backed up? Good! You are ready to turn the system off, unplug the battery, ground yourself, and join the wonderful world of solid state.

SSDs address the many shortcomings of traditional HDDs. With solid-state technology, there are no moving metal parts, less energy is used, they come in smaller form factors, and you can access that fancy PowerPoint presentation you created and saved almost instantaneously. In geek terms, little or no latency is involved in accessing fragmented data with solid-state devices.

Connecting SCSI Drives

Connecting SCSI drives requires three things. You must use a controller that works with your drive. You need to set unique SCSI IDs on the controller and the drive. You also need to connect the ribbon cable and power connections properly.

With SCSI, you need to attach the data cable correctly. You can reverse a PATA cable, for example, and nothing happens except the drive doesn't work. If you reverse a SCSI cable, however, you can seriously damage the drive. Just as with PATA cables, pin 1 on the SCSI data cable must go to pin 1 on both the drive and the host adapter.

■ BIOS Support: Configuring CMOS and Installing Drivers

Every device in your PC needs BIOS support, and the hard drive controllers are no exception. Motherboards provide support for the ATA hard drive controllers via the system BIOS, but they require configuration in CMOS for the specific hard drives attached. SCSI drives require software drivers or firmware on the host adapter.

In the old days, you had to fire up CMOS and manually enter CHS information whenever you installed a new ATA drive to ensure the system

Installing solid-state removable media such as USB thumb drives and flash memory cards (such as SD cards) is covered in Chapter 11.

SSDs are more dependable as well as more expensive than traditional hard drives. They use less energy overall, have smaller form factors, are noiseless, and use NAND (nonvolatile flash memory) technology to store and retrieve data. They can retrieve (read) data much faster than typical HDDs.

Tech Tip

Don't Defragment SSDs

Don't defragment an SSD! Because solid-state drives access data without having to find that data on the surface of a physical disk first, there's never any reason to defrag one. What's more, SSDs have a limited (albeit massive) number of read/write operations before they turn into expensive paperweights, and the defragmentation process uses those up greedily.

Don't let your hard drive flop around inside your case. Remember to grab a screwdriver and screw the hard drive to a slot in your case.

saw the drive. Today, this process is automated. In fact, if you just plug in a hard drive and turn on your computer, there's a 99 percent chance that your BIOS and OS will figure everything out for you.

Configuring Controllers

As a first step in configuring controllers, make certain they're enabled. Most controllers remain active, ready to automatically detect new drives, but you can disable them. Scan through your CMOS settings to locate the controller on/off options (see Figure 10.44 for typical settings). This is also the time to check whether your onboard RAID controllers work in both RAID and non-RAID settings.

Autodetection

If the controllers are enabled and the drive is properly connected, the drive should appear in CMOS through a process called *autodetection*. Autodetection is a powerful and handy feature that takes almost all of the work out of configuring hard drives. Here's how it works.

One of your hard drives stores the operating system needed when you boot your computer, and your system needs a way to know where to look for this operating system. Older BIOS supported a maximum of only four ATA drives on two controllers, called the *primary controller* and the *secondary controller*. The BIOS looked for the master drive on the primary controller when the system booted up. If you used only one controller, you used the primary controller. The secondary controller was used for CD-ROMs, DVDs, or other nonbootable drives.

Older CMOS made this clear and easy, as shown in Figure 10.45. When you booted up, the CMOS queried the drives through autodetection, and whatever drives the CMOS saw showed up here. In some even older

• **Figure 10.44** Typical controller settings in CMOS

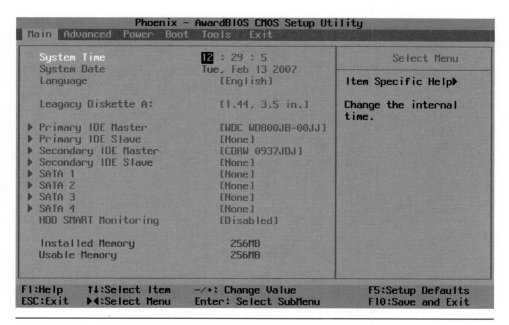

```
         Phoenix - AwardBIOS CMOS Setup Utility
  Main  Advanced  Power  Boot  Tools  Exit

    System Time            12 : 29 : 5              Select Menu
    System Date            Tue, Feb 13 2007
    Language               [English]          Item Specific Help▶

    Leagacy Diskette A:    [1.44, 3.5 in.]    Change the internal
                                              time.
  ▶ Primary IDE Master     [WDC WD800JB-00JJ]
  ▶ Primary IDE Slave      [None]
  ▶ Secondary IDE Master   [CDRW 0937JDJ]
  ▶ Secondary IDE Slave    [None]
  ▶ SATA 1                 [None]
  ▶ SATA 2                 [None]
  ▶ SATA 3                 [None]
  ▶ SATA 4                 [None]
    HDD SMART Monitoring   [Disabled]

    Installed Memory       256MB
    Usable Memory          256MB

  F1:Help      ↑↓:Select Item   -/+: Change Value    F5:Setup Defaults
  ESC:Exit     ▶◀:Select Menu   Enter: Select SubMenu  F10:Save and Exit
```

• **Figure 10.45** Old standard CMOS settings

CMOS, you had to run a special menu option called Autodetect to see the drives in this screen. There are places for up to four devices; notice that not all of them actually have a device.

The autodetection screen indicated that you installed a PATA drive correctly. If you installed a hard drive on the primary controller as master but messed up the jumper and set it to slave, it showed up in the autodetection screen as the slave. If you had two drives and set them both to master, one drive or the other (or sometimes both) didn't appear, telling you that something was messed up in the physical installation. If you forgot to plug in the ribbon cable or the power, the drives wouldn't autodetect.

SATA changed the autodetection happiness. The SATA world has no such thing as master, slave, or even primary and secondary controller. To get around this, motherboards with SATA use a numbering system—and every motherboard uses its own numbering system! One common numbering method uses the term *channels* for each controller. The first boot device is channel 1, the second is channel 2, and so on. (PATA channels may have a master and a slave, but a SATA channel has only a master, because SATA controllers support only one drive.) So instead of names of drives, you see numbers. Take a look at Figure 10.46.

Whew! Lots of hard drives! This motherboard supports six SATA connections. Each connection has a number, with hard drives on SATA 1 and SATA 2, and the optical drive on SATA 6. Each was autodetected and configured by the BIOS without any input from me. Oh, to live in the future!

Boot Order

If you want your computer to run, it's going to need an operating system to boot. While the PCs of our forefathers (those of the 1980s and early 1990s) absolutely required you to put the operating system on the primary master,

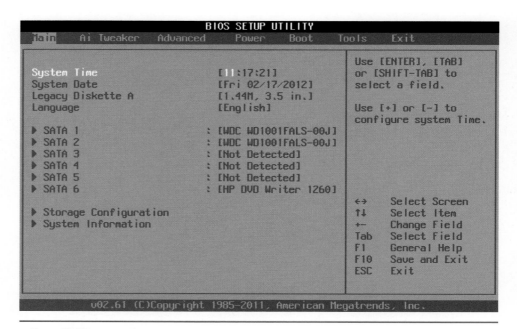

• Figure 10.46 New standard CMOS features

BIOS makers eventually enabled you to put the OS on any of the four drives and then tell the system through CMOS which hard drive to boot. With the many SATA drives available on modern systems, you're not even limited to a mere four choices. Additionally, you may need to boot from an optical disc, a USB thumb drive, or even a floppy disk (if you're feeling retro). CMOS takes care of this by enabling you to set a *boot order*.

Figure 10.47 shows a typical boot-order screen, with a first, second, and third boot option. Many users like to boot first from the optical drive and then from a hard drive. This enables them to put in a bootable optical disc

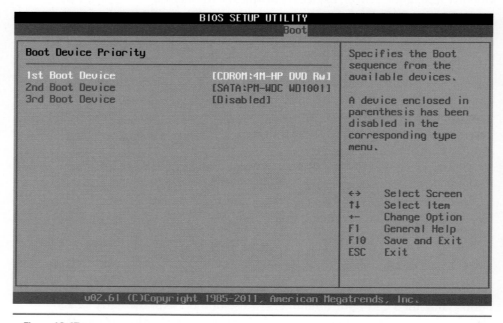

• Figure 10.47 Boot order

Mike Meyers' CompTIA A+ Guide to 801: Managing and Troubleshooting PCs

if they're having problems with the system. Of course, you can set it to boot first from your hard drive and then go into CMOS and change it when you need to—it's your choice.

Most modern CMOS setup utilities include a second screen for determining the boot order of your hard drives. You might want to set up a boot order that goes optical drive, followed by hard drive, and then USB thumb drive, but what if you have more than one hard drive? This screen enables you to set which hard drive goes first. If you have a different operating system on each hard drive, this can be very helpful.

Enabling AHCI

On motherboards that support AHCI, you implement it in CMOS. You'll generally have up to three options: IDE or compatibility mode, AHCI, or RAID. Use compatibility mode to install older operating systems, such as Windows XP. Going to AHCI or RAID enables the AHCI option for the HBA.

Beyond A+

Hybrid Hard Drives

Windows Vista and Windows 7 support hybrid hard drives (HHDs), drives that combine flash memory and spinning platters to provide fast and reliable storage, and offer ReadyBoost for faster caching and booting. Samsung has drives with 128-MB and 256-MB flash cache, for example, that shave boot times in half and, because the platters don't have to spin all of the time, add 20–30 minutes more of battery life for portable computers. Adding that much more run time with only a tiny price premium and no extra weight is the Holy Grail of portable computing.

Chapter 10 Review

■ Chapter Summary

After reading this chapter and completing the exercises, you should understand the following about hard drive technologies.

Explain how hard drives work

■ Traditional hard drives contain aluminum platters coated with a magnetic medium and read/write heads that float on a cushion of air. Hard drives store data in a tiny magnetic field called a flux that defines a zero or a one. The switching back and forth of the field is called flux reversal. The incredible storage capacity of today's drives results from Partial Response Maximum Likelihood (PRML) encoding that includes intelligent circuitry to analyze each flux reversal.

■ Two technologies have been used to move read/write heads across the platters: stepper motors and voice coil. Very susceptible to physical deterioration and temperature changes, the now obsolete stepper motors moved the actuator arm in fixed increments or steps, often resulting in data-transfer errors or the inability to access data on a cold drive. The heads had to be parked to a non-data area when not in use to prevent possible damage to the disk surface. Today's drives use a linear or voice coil motor consisting of a permanent magnet surrounding a coil on the actuator arm. Electrical current causes the coil to generate a magnetic field that moves the actuator arm and thus the read/write heads. Containing no data, one side of one platter is used as a map to position the heads directly over the data. Voice coil technology automatically parks the heads when the drive loses power.

■ Disk geometry for a particular hard drive consists of three primary values: heads, cylinders, and sectors per track (sectors/track). There are two read/write heads per platter. A hard drive can have either an even or an odd number of heads. A cylinder defines a group of tracks of the same diameter. Each track is sliced into tiny slivers called sectors, each of which stores 512 bytes of data. Disk geometry uses the number of sectors per track. Combining cylinders, heads, and sectors/track is

referred to as CHS. Write precompensation and landing zone, two other geometric values, have no relevance in today's PCs, but most CMOS utilities still support them.

■ Hard drives run at a set spindle speed, measured in *revolutions per minute* (*RPM*). Older drives ran at a speed of 3600 RPM, but new drives are hitting 15,000 RPM. The faster the spindle speed, the faster the controller can store and retrieve data. Common speeds include 5400, 7200, 10,000 and 15,000 RPM.

■ Solid-state drives use memory chips to store data and don't have any metal spinning parts. They require less electricity than platter-based drives and offer faster reads and writes. At the time of this writing, they cost substantially more than traditional drives.

Identify and explain the PATA and SATA hard drive interfaces

■ Today's hard drives have either an ATA interface or a SCSI interface. ATA drives may be parallel ATA (PATA) or serial ATA (SATA). A specification of the American National Standards Institute (ANSI), the AT Attachment (ATA) interface (commonly but incorrectly referred to as IDE) used a 40-pin ribbon cable, had a built-in controller, and did not require a low-level format. By 1995, EIDE was the dominant interface. Its features included higher capacities, support for non–hard drive storage devices, a four-device maximum, and improved throughput. The terms ATA, IDE, and EIDE are used interchangeably to describe all PATA devices.

■ PATA drives use a 40-pin plug and a controller that connects them to the external data bus. Although the real controller is built into the hard drive itself, the 40-pin connector on the motherboard is called the controller.

■ The advanced technology attachment packet interface (ATAPI) enables non–hard drive devices to use a PATA controller. ATAPI devices, such as CD-ROM drives, use the same 40-pin interface and follow the same rules of master, slave, and cable select jumper settings.

- Originally, IDE drives used the same BIOS command set introduced years earlier. Maximum values of 1024 cylinders, 16 heads, and 63 sectors per track limited an IDE drive's capacity to 528 million bytes (504 MB). Western Digital developed the LBA sector translation method to accommodate larger EIDE drives. LBA supports drives with up to 256 heads, for a storage capacity limit of 8.4 GB.

- As drive capacity neared the 8.4-GB maximum, Phoenix Technologies broke the limit by coming up with a new set of BIOS commands called Interrupt 13 extensions (INT13). Completely ignoring the CHS values, INT13 supports drives up to 137 GB by reporting a stream of addressable sectors to LBA.

- As drive capacity neared the 137-GB limit, the ANSI ATA committee adopted ATA/ATAPI-6, a new standard that increased the limit to more than 144 petabytes (144,000,000 GB). It uses a 48-bit addressing scheme and an enhanced block mode that transfers up to 65,536 sectors at a time.

- PATA hard drives use direct memory access (DMA) mode to send data directly to RAM, bypassing the CPU. Instead of using the slow DMA controller chip, today's DMA transfers use bus mastering to transfer 32 bits of data. Hard drives typically use one of the following modes: Ultra DMA mode 4 (ATA/66), Ultra DMA mode 5 (ATA/100), and Ultra DMA mode 6 (ATA/133). To use Ultra DMA, you must have a controller and an 80-wire ribbon cable. Some motherboards combine different speeds of ATA controllers, with the higher-speed controller indicated with a bright color. The 80-wire ribbon cable indicates where to connect the master and slave drives. High-end PATA devices can use lower-end controllers, but they will operate at the slower speed. Ultra DMA was the fastest data transfer method until Serial ATA.

- Serial ATA (SATA) devices look identical to standard PATA devices (except their data and power connectors), but their thinner seven-wire cables provide better airflow and may be up to 1 meter (39.4 inches) long. SATA does away with the entire master/slave concept. Each drive connects to one port, so no more daisy-chaining drives.

- SATA devices are hot-swappable, great for RAID technology. SATA transfers data in serial bursts for up to 30 times the throughput of PATA. SATA drives come in three varieties: 1.5 Gbps, 3 Gbps, and 6 Gbps, which have a maximum throughput of 150 MBps, 300 MBps, and 600 MBps, respectively.

Identify and explain the SCSI hard drive interfaces

- All SCSI chains, which support either 8 or 16 devices including the controller, require proper termination to prevent signal echo. Additionally, each device on a chain requires a unique SCSI ID, which can be set by jumpers, switches, or dials.

- All SCSI devices can be divided into two groups: internal and external. Internal SCSI devices connect to the host adapter with a 68-pin ribbon cable. External devices connect to the host adapter with either a 50-pin HD connector or a 68-pin HD connector. SCSI enables you to daisy-chain devices together to form longer SCSI chains.

- Improper termination or incorrect SCSI ID settings are the two most common causes of SCSI devices not working. The key factor here is that you must terminate only the ends of the SCSI chain.

Describe how to protect data with RAID

- Drive mirroring writes data simultaneously to two hard drives, enabling the system to continue to work if one hard drive dies. A faster and even more effective technique is drive duplexing, which performs mirroring by using separate controllers for each drive. A third way to create redundant data is disk striping with parity. This technique, requiring at least three drives, combines the redundancy of disk mirroring with the speed of disk striping. Although disk striping without parity works very fast, splitting the data across two drives means you'll lose *all* data if either drive fails.

- Numbered 0 through 6, there are seven official levels of RAID, but the most commonly used ones are RAID 0 (disk striping), RAID 1 (disk mirroring or duplexing), and RAID 5 (disk striping with distributed parity).

- RAID may be implemented through hardware or software methods. Although software implementation is cheaper, hardware techniques provide better performance. Windows Server 2008 and Windows Server 2008 R2 include built-in RAID software for RAID 0, RAID 1, and RAID 5 for either ATA or SCSI. Windows XP and Windows Vista include support for RAID 0, while Windows 7 supports RAID 0 and 1. RAID software solutions tend to overwork your operating system, resulting in slowdowns. Hardware RAID is invisible to the

OS and is usually hot-swappable. A hardware ATA RAID controller usually requires CMOS configuration. Many motherboards include built-in ATA-based hardware RAID 0 and RAID 1 capabilities.

- SCSI drives were a natural for the multiple-disk RAID. Specialized ATA RAID controller cards support ATA RAID arrays of up to 15 drives. With its hot-swap capabilities, SATA has for the most part taken over lower-end RAID from SCSI.

Install hard drives

- Older PATA drives use a 40-wire cable, while the newer Ultra DMA drives use an 80-wire cable. Either round or flat and containing no twists, each ribbon cable supports two drives. A diagram on the hard drive's housing shows how to set its jumpers to identify it as master, slave, standalone (on some drives), or cable select (cable position determines whether the drive will be master or slave). Two devices on one cable must both be set to cable select, and the cable itself must also be cable select, as indicated with a pinhole through one wire. Align the colored stripe on the cable with pin 1 on the controller and the drive. Use a Molex connector to provide power to the drive.

- SATA supports only a single device per controller channel, so there are no master, slave, or cable select jumpers. SATA controller and power cables are keyed to prevent incorrect insertion. You can connect a PATA device to a SATA motherboard controller by way of a SATA bridge.

- Solid-state drives are PATA, SATA, eSATA, SCSI, or USB. Before upgrading or installing an SSD, you should verify that the new drive uses the same interface as the old drive or that you have the proper connection type available. As for any hardware device, it is also important to ensure you have the appropriate SSD drivers and firmware before installation.

Configure CMOS and install drivers

- When plugging in a new hard drive to your motherboard, most BIOS can autodetect and properly configure your drive for you. You may need to enable a SATA channel in CMOS so that BIOS knows to look for a new drive, but this usually is not necessary.

- If the autodetection feature of the CMOS utility does not detect a drive, it is installed incorrectly or the drive itself is bad. On a PATA drive, check the master/slave jumper settings. Make sure that the ribbon cable aligns pin 1 with pin 1, and that the Molex connector is supplying power to the drive. On a SATA drive, check that the SATA data and power cables are properly connected.

■ Key Terms

sector *(250)*
sectors per track (sectors/track) *(250)*
sector translation *(256)*
serial ATA (SATA) *(253)*
Self-Monitoring, Analysis, and Reporting Technology (S.M.A.R.T.) *(259)*
small computer system interface (SCSI) *(264)*

solid-state drive (SSD) *(252)*
stepper motor *(249)*
termination *(267)*
track *(250)*
Ultra DMA *(259)*
voice coil *(249)*

■ Key Term Quiz

Use the Key Terms list to complete the sentences that follow. Not all terms will be used.

1. An ATA hard drive connects to the controller with a(n) _____, while an Ultra DMA mode 4 drive uses a(n) _____.

2. A(n) _____ is composed of a group of tracks of the same diameter that the read/write heads can access without moving.

3. To install a parallel ATA device to a serial ATA controller, use a tiny card called a(n) _____.

4. LBA, developed by Western Digital, uses _____ to get around the limits of 1024 cylinders, 16 heads, and 63 sectors/track.

5. Seen in RAID 5, _____ uses at least three drives and combines the best features of disk mirroring and disk striping.

6. A CD-ROM drive that is _____-compliant installs and cables just like an EIDE drive.

7. The ANSI ATA committee adopted the _____ standard, called "Big Drive" by Maxtor, that allows drives with more than 144 petabytes.

8. Drives known as _____ transfer data at 133 MBps.

9. Drives that use _____ bypass the CPU and send data directly to memory.

10. Devices known as _____ devices require termination at both ends of a chain.

■ Multiple-Choice Quiz

1. Which of the following is *not* used to compute storage capacity in CHS disk geometry?

 A. Sectors per track

 B. Tracks

 C. Heads

 D. Cylinders

2. Which level of RAID is disk striping with distributed parity?

 A. RAID 0

 B. RAID 1

 C. RAID 5

 D. RAID 6

3. Counting both channels, what is the maximum number of drives/devices that EIDE can support?

 A. One

 B. Two

 C. Seven

 D. Four

4. Which of the following is *not* true about cable select?

 A. Both drives/devices should be set for cable select.

 B. Cable select requires a special cable with a pinhole through one wire.

 C. The colored stripe on the ribbon cable should align with pin 1 on the controller and drive.

 D. Position of the drives on the cable does not matter.

5. If you install two IDE drives on the same cable, how will the computer differentiate them?

 A. The CMOS setup allows you to configure them.

 B. You must set jumpers to determine which drive functions as master and which functions as slave.

 C. You will set jumpers so each drive has a unique ID number.

 D. The drives will be differentiated by whether you place them before or after the twist in the ribbon cable.

6. What was the maximum hard drive size allowed by BIOS routines for the original AT command set?

 A. 528 MB

 B. 1024 MB

 C. 504 MB

 D. 1028 MB

7. Which of the following terms does *not* describe parallel ATA devices?

 A. IDE

 B. EIDE

 C. SCSI

 D. ATA

8. Shelby wants to add a 500-GB hard drive to her computer. Which of the following will allow her to do so?

 A. CHS

 B. LBA

 C. ECHS

 D. INT13

9. Which of the following techniques provides redundancy by using two disks and two controllers?

 A. Drive mirroring

 B. Drive duplexing

 C. Disk striping

 D. Disk striping with parity

10. How many wires does an Ultra DMA ATA cable have?

 A. 24

 B. 34

 C. 40

 D. 80

11. Billy just installed a second hard drive, but the autodetection utility in CMOS does not detect it. Sara told him he probably has the jumpers set incorrectly or forgot to connect the Molex power connector. John told him his new hard drive is probably bad and he should return it. Who is probably correct, Sara or John?

 A. Sara is correct.

 B. John is correct.

 C. Neither is correct.

 D. Either John or Sara may be correct.

12. Which of the following is *not* an advantage of serial ATA (SATA)?

 A. It is hot-swappable.

 B. Thinner cables provide better airflow inside the case.

 C. SATA provides faster data throughput than PATA.

 D. SATA cables must be shorter than PATA cables.

13. What standard did the ANSI ATA committee adopt that increased disk storage capacity to more than 144 petabytes?

 A. ATA/ATAPI-6

 B. LBA

 C. INT13

 D. ECHS

14. Which of the following can SSDs use to retain data integrity when a system loses power or is turned off?

 A. DRAM

 B. RAM drive

 C. NAND

 D. SDRAM

15. Which of the following represent common solid-state drive form factors?

 A. AT, ATX, and BTX

 B. 8-inch, 2.5-inch, and 5.25-inch

 C. 1.8-inch, 2.5-inch, and 3.5-inch

 D. IEEE 1394, USB, and SCSI

■ Essay Quiz

1. Discuss at least three advantages of serial ATA over parallel ATA.

2. Compare and contrast hardware and software RAID implementations.

3. Your friend Blaine has a Core i5 computer with a great video card. Currently, it has only a 320-GB hard drive and a CD-RW drive. Because he's interested in video, he knows he needs more storage capacity and wants to add a second hard drive. What advice will you give him about selecting a new hard drive?

4. Hard drives include other features and characteristics not included in this chapter. Choose one of the following topics and use the Internet to define and explain it to the class.

 - Zone bit recording
 - "Pixie dust" hard drives

5. Your office is about to purchase ten new portable computers for the sales force and needs a recommendation. Prepare a short essay that compares and contrasts platter-based and solid-state drives so your boss can pick what's best for the staff.

Lab Projects

• Lab Project 10.1

Access the CMOS setup for your computer and examine the settings that apply to your hard drive(s). In particular, look at the initial screen to see if it is set to autodetect the kind of hard drive. Is the mode set to LBA or something else? Try to find a screen that includes PIO modes and examine this setting. What other screens apply to the hard drive? When you finish, be sure to choose Quit without saving.

• Lab Project 10.2

Visit your local computer store or use the Internet to discover what kinds of hard drives and hard drive interfaces are commonly offered with new computers. Try to determine whether the motherboards offer parallel ATA interfaces or offer only serial ATA interfaces, either onboard or through an expansion card. If you were purchasing a new computer, would you select PATA or SATA? Why?

• Lab Project 10.3

Your supervisor has decided to implement RAID on the old company server machine, where everyone stores their work-related data. Come up with two competing RAID setups, one that maximizes security of data at the lowest cost possible and another that maximizes speed but retains some security. Cost is not a factor for the second RAID plan.

• Lab Project 10.4

If your lab has the equipment, install a second hard drive in your system. Reboot, enter CMOS, and verify that both drives are detected. Boot into your operating system and verify that both drives are accessible. (You may need to partition and format the second drive before it is actually usable.)

Removable Media

"Bring my screwdriver and my special CD of town-saving music."

—JIMMY NEUTRON, *JIMMY NEUTRON: BOY GENIUS*

In this chapter, you will learn how to

- **Describe and install floppy disk drives**
- **Demonstrate the variations among flash drives and other tiny drives**
- **Identify and install optical-media technology**

Removable media refers to any type of mass storage device that you may use in one system and then physically remove from that system and use in another. Removable media has been a part of the PC since its introduction back in 1980. Back then, the only removable media available was floppy disks, but being able to move programs and data easily from one machine to another was quickly established as one of the strongest points of the PC. Over time, higher-capacity removable media technologies were introduced. Some technologies—CDs, DVDs, Blu-ray Discs, and thumb drives, for example—have become very common. Other technologies (which you may or may not have heard of), such as Iomega Zip drives or HD DVDs, were popular for a time but faded away or were discontinued. The history of PCs has also left a trash heap of removable media technologies that were trumpeted in with fanfare and a lot of money but never really saw any adoption.

Today's highly internetworked computers have reduced the need for removable media as a method of sharing programs and data, but removable media has so many other uses that it's still going strong. Removable media is the perfect tool for software distribution, data archiving, and system backup. Figure 11.1 shows my software toolbox. As a PC technician, you'll not only need to install, maintain, and troubleshoot removable media on systems for users, but also find yourself turning to removable media as a way to store and run software tools to perform all types of PC support.

This chapter covers the most common types of removable media used today and the forsaken floppy drive. For the sake of organization, the removable media types are broken down into these groups:

● **Figure 11.1** Author's toolbox

- **Floppy drives** The traditional floppy drive
- **Flash memory** From USB thumb drives to flash memory cards
- **Optical discs** Any shiny disc technology, from CD-ROMs and DVDs to Blu-ray Discs
- **External drives** Any hard drive or optical drive that connects to a PC via an external cable

If you go by the earlier description of removable memory, two other technologies, PC Cards and tape backups, also fit as removable media. PC Cards are a laptop-centric technology and are covered in Chapter 18.

Historical/Conceptual

■ Floppy Drives

Good old floppies! These little disks, storing a whopping 1.44 MB of data per disk, were a part of PCs from the beginning and made it all the way to the first decade of the 21st century. For decades, the PC industry made one attempt after another to replace the floppy with some higher-capacity removable media, only to keep falling back to the floppy disk. Floppy drive technology was well entrenched: motherboard makers found floppies easy to add, all BIOS supported them, and they were almost always the first boot device, so techs loved floppies when they helped boot a system.

Over the past several years, floppy drives have disappeared from mass-produced PCs thanks to an industry push called *legacy-free computing*: an initiative forwarded by Microsoft and Intel back in 2001 to rid computers of old technologies such as PS/2 ports, serial ports, parallel ports—and

> You might notice that I speak about floppy drives as if they don't exist anymore. That's because no one really uses them these days, and even if you wanted to, most modern motherboards don't have the required connections to install a floppy drive. But the CompTIA A+ 220-801 exam wants you to know about them on the off chance you run into one while hunkered down in an abandoned building during the apocalypse.

• **Figure 11.2** Floppy drive and floppy disk

The term "floppy" comes from the fact that early floppy disks were actually floppy. You could easily bend one. Newer floppy disks came in much more robust, rigid plastic casings, but the term has stuck—we still call them floppies.

floppy drives (interesting how long it took to start being adopted by PC makers). Thus, the venerable floppy drive, without enough capacity to hold even a single MP3 or digital photo, died.

Floppy Drive Basics

When you insert a **floppy disk** into a **floppy drive**, the protective slide on the disk opens, revealing the magnetic media inside the plastic casing. A motor-driven spindle snaps into the center of the drive to make it spin. A set of read/write heads then moves back and forth across the disk, reading or writing tracks on the disk as needed. The 3½-inch-wide floppy disk arrived in 1987 and stored 1.44 MB (see Figure 11.2). You use a **3½-inch floppy drive** to access the contents of the disk.

Whenever a system accesses a floppy disk in its floppy drive, a read/write LED on the outside front of the drive flashes on. Don't try to remove the floppy disk from the drive when this light is lit! That light means that the read/write heads are accessing the floppy drive, so pulling the disk out while the light is on can damage the floppy disk. When the light is off, you can push in the small release button on the front of the drive to eject the floppy disk.

801

Installing Floppy Drives

All Windows systems reserve the drive letters A: and B: for floppy drives. You cannot name them anything other than A: or B:, but you can configure a floppy to get either drive letter. However, convention dictates that if you have only one floppy drive, you should call it A:. The second floppy drive is then called B:.

Floppy drives connect to the computer via a **34-pin ribbon cable**. If the cable supports two floppy drives, it has a seven-wire twist in the middle to differentiate electronically between the A: and B: drives. Given that the majority of users do not want two floppy drives (or one, for that matter), many system makers have dropped the twist and saved a couple of pennies on a simpler cable (see Figure 11.3).

By default, almost all PCs that still support floppy drives first try to boot to a floppy before any other boot device, looking for an operating system. This process enables technicians to insert a floppy disk into a sick

• **Figure 11.3** Floppy cable for only one drive

computer to run programs when the hard drives fail. It also means hackers can insert bootable floppy disks into servers and do bad things. You do have a choice, however, because most systems have special CMOS settings with which you can change this default boot order to something other than the default drive A: and then C:; I'll show you how in a minute.

Inserting Ribbon Cables

Look at the floppy cable in Figure 11.3. Notice the connector on the left side. This connector, identical to the other connector on the same cable, plugs into the floppy controller on the motherboard, as shown in Figure 11.4. Notice how clearly the motherboard has **pin 1** marked in Figure 11.4. Not all motherboards are so clear. Make sure to orient the cable so that the colored stripe on the side of the cable is aligned with pin 1.

Here are a few tips on cable orientation. (By the way, these rules work for all ribbon cables, not just floppy cables.) Ribbon cable connectors usually have a distinct orientation notch in the middle. If your cable connector has an orientation notch and the controller socket has a slot in which the orientation notch fits, your job is easy (see Figure 11.5).

Unfortunately, not all connectors use the orientation notch. Try looking in the motherboard book. All motherboard books provide a graphic of the motherboard showing the proper orientation position. Look at other ribbon cables on the motherboard. In almost all motherboards, all plugs orient the same way. Last of all, just guess! You will not destroy anything by inserting the cable backward. When you boot up, the floppy drive will not work. This is not a big deal; turn off the system and try again.

After you insert the floppy ribbon cable into the floppy controller, you need to insert the ribbon cable into the floppy drive. Watch out here! You still need to orient the cable by pin 1—all the rules of ribbon cable insertion apply here, too. Before you plug in the floppy ribbon cable to the floppy drive, you need to know which connector on the cable to use; it makes a big difference. The specific connector that you insert into the floppy drive determines its drive letter.

If the floppy drive is installed on the end connector, it becomes the A: drive; if the drive is installed on the middle connector, it is the B: drive (see Figure 11.6). If you're installing only one floppy, make sure you install it in the A: drive position.

• **Figure 11.4** Plugging a floppy cable into a controller, pin 1 labeled at left

• **Figure 11.5** Floppy controller with notch

In the past, the CompTIA A+ certification exams have been very focused on the pins on cables! Know the number (34) and orientation (pin 1 to pin 1) for the pins on the floppy drive ribbon cable.

Drive A Drive B To Controller

• **Figure 11.6** Cable placement determines the drive letter.

Power

Floppy drives need electricity to work, just like every other device in the PC. Modern 3½-inch floppy drives use the small **mini power connector**. Be careful! Inserting a mini connector incorrectly is easy, and if you install it incorrectly, you'll destroy the floppy drive and make what we call "The Nasty Smell." Look at Figure 11.7, a bottom view of a properly installed mini power connector—note the chamfers (beveled edges) that show correct orientation. The problem lies in the plastic used to make the connector. The plastic connector bends easily, so even the least brawny techs can put the plug in a mini backward or hit only three of the four pins.

Great! You have installed a floppy drive! Once you have physically installed the floppy drive, it's time to go into CMOS.

CMOS

After the floppy drive is installed, you need to configure the CMOS settings, which must correspond to the capacities of the drives. Look in your CMOS for a menu called "Standard CMOS Features" (or something similar to that) to see your floppy settings. Most CMOS setups configure the A: drive by default as a 3½-inch, 1.44-MB drive, so in most cases the floppy is already configured. Simply double-check the setting in CMOS; if it's okay, exit without changing anything. Figure 11.8 shows a typical CMOS setting for a single floppy drive. On the rare occasion that you require a setting other than the typical 3½-inch, 1.44-MB A: drive, simply select the drive (A: or B:) and enter the correct capacity.

• **Figure 11.7** Properly installed mini power connector

Disabling the Boot Up Floppy Seek option tells the PC not to check the floppy disk during the POST, which isn't very handy except for slightly speeding up the boot process (see Figure 11.9).

Many CMOS setup utilities have an option called Floppy 3 Mode Support. Refer to Figure 11.8 to see an example of a CMOS with this option. A Mode 3 floppy is a special 1.2-MB format used outside the United States, primarily in Japan. Unless you live in Japan and use Mode 3 floppy disks, ignore this option.

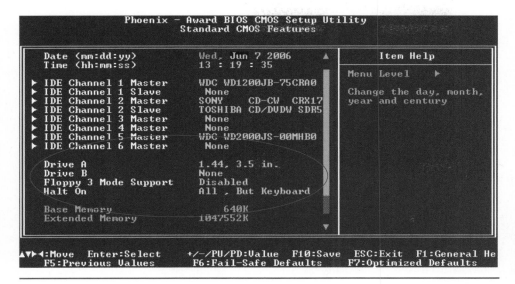

• **Figure 11.8** CMOS setting for one standard floppy drive

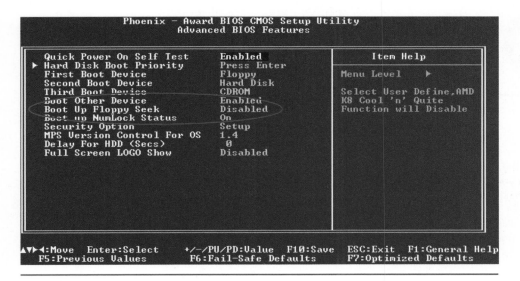

• **Figure 11.9** CMOS Boot Up Floppy Seek option

■ Flash Memory

Flash memory, the same flash memory that replaced CMOS technology for your system BIOS, found another home in PCs in the form of removable mass storage devices. Flash memory comes in two families: USB thumb drives and memory cards. USB thumb drives are flash devices that contain a standard USB connection. "Memory card" is a generic term for a number of tiny cards that are used in cameras, smartphones, and other devices. Both of these families can manifest themselves as drives in Windows, but they usually perform different jobs. USB thumb drives have replaced virtually all other rewritable removable media as the way people transfer files or keep copies of important programs. My thumb drives (yes, I have two on me at all times) keep backups of my current work, important photos, and a

stack of utilities I need to fix computers. Memory cards are very small and make a great way to store data on small devices and then transfer that data to your PC.

USB Thumb Drives

Moving data between computers is always a pain, but USB flash memory drives, also known as **USB thumb drives**, jump drives, and flash drives, are an incredibly popular solution (see Figure 11.10). For a low price, you can get a 32-GB thumb drive that holds as much data as 22,000 standard 3½-inch floppy disks.

The smallest thumb drives are slightly larger than an adult thumbnail; others are larger and more rounded. The drives are hot-swappable in all modern editions of Windows. You simply plug one into any USB port and it appears as a removable storage device in My Computer or Computer. After you plug the drive into a USB port, you can copy or move data to or from your hard disk and then unplug the unit and take it with you. You can read, write, and delete files directly from the drive. Because these are USB devices, they don't need an external power source. The nonvolatile flash memory is solid-state, so it's shock resistant and is supposed to retain data safely for a decade.

• Figure 11.10 USB thumb drives

Remember to change the boot order in CMOS when you want to boot from a USB flash drive. If you use the wrong boot order, your BIOS will skip straight to your hard drive and load your OS.

The latest systems enable you to boot to a thumb drive. With a bootable thumb drive, you can replace bootable floppies, CDs, and DVDs with fast flash drives. Making a thumb drive bootable is a bit of a challenge, so most of the classic bootable-utility CD makers have created USB versions that seek out your thumb drive and add an operating system with the utilities you wish to use. Most of these are simply versions of Linux-based live CDs. If you want to try it, check out GParted Live at http://gparted.sourceforge.net and click on the Live CD/USB link.

Flash Cards

Flash cards are the way people store data on small appliances. Digital cameras, smartphones, and MP3 players often come with slots for some type of memory card. Memory cards come in a number of incompatible formats, so let's start by making sure you know the more common ones.

CompactFlash

CompactFlash (CF) is the oldest, most complex, and physically largest of all removable flash media cards (see Figure 11.11). Roughly one inch wide, CF cards use a simplified PCMCIA bus (see Chapter 18 for details) for interconnection. CF cards come in two sizes: CF I (3.3 mm thick) and CF II (5 mm thick). CF II cards are too thick to fit into CF I slots.

Clever manufacturers have repurposed the CF form factor to create the microdrive (see Figure 11.12). **Microdrives** are true hard drives, using platters

• Figure 11.11 CF card

and read/write heads that fit into the tiny CF form factor. Microdrives are slower and use more power than flash drives and, when they were first introduced, cost much less than an equivalent CF flash card. From the user's standpoint, CF flash cards and microdrives look and act exactly the same way, although the greater power consumption of microdrives makes them incompatible with some devices. These days, microdrives have been surpassed in size, speed, and cost by their flash cousins and have become more difficult to find.

SmartMedia

SmartMedia came out as a competitor to CF cards and for a few years was quite popular in digital cameras (see Figure 11.13). The introduction of SD media reduced SmartMedia's popularity, and no new devices use this media.

• **Figure 11.12** Microdrive

Secure Digital

Secure Digital (SD) cards are arguably the most common flash media format today. About the size of a small postage stamp, you'll see SD cards in just about any type of device that uses flash media.

SD cards come in two smaller forms called *Mini Secure Digital* (*MiniSD*) cards and *Micro Secure Digital* (*MicroSD*) cards. They're extremely popular in cellular phones that use flash memory, but they see little use in other devices. Figure 11.14 shows the three forms of SD cards.

SD cards come in three storage capacities. *Standard SD* cards store from 4 MB to 4 GB, *Secure Digital High Capacity* (*SDHC*) cards store 4 GB to 32 GB, and *Secure Digital Extended Capacity* (*SDXC*) cards have a storage capacity of 32 GB to 2 TB. Early SD card readers and devices cannot read the SDHC or SDXC cards, though the latter standards provide backward compatibility.

• **Figure 11.13** SmartMedia

SD cards developed out of an older, slower flash memory technology called *MultiMediaCard* (*MMC*). If you happen to have an MMC card lying around, you can use it in almost any SD card slot. SD cards are a little thicker than MMC cards, though, so the reverse is not true.

Memory Stick

Sony always likes to use proprietary formats, and their **Memory Stick** flash memory is no exception. If you own something from Sony and it uses flash memory, you'll need a Memory Stick, though not all Memory Sticks are manufactured by Sony (see Figure 11.15). There are several Memory Stick formats, including Standard, Pro, Duo, Pro Duo, and Micro.

• **Figure 11.14** SD, MiniSD, and MicroSD cards

• **Figure 11.15** Memory Stick

• **Figure 11.16** xD card

xD Picture Card

The proprietary **Extreme Digital (xD) Picture Cards** (see Figure 11.16) are about half the size of an SD card. They're almost exclusively used in Olympus and Fujifilm digital cameras, although Olympus (the developer of the xD technology) produces a USB housing so you can use an xD Picture Card like any other USB flash memory drive. The xD Picture Cards come in three flavors: original, Standard (Type M), and Hi-Speed (Type H). The Standard cards are slower than the original cards but offer greater storage capacity. The Hi-Speed cards are two to three times faster than the others and enable you to capture full-motion video—assuming the camera has that capability, naturally!

Card Readers

Whichever type of flash memory you use, your PC must have a **card reader** to access the data on the card directly. A number of inexpensive USB card readers are available today (see Figure 11.17), and some PCs come with built-in readers—handy to have when someone pulls out an SD card and says "Let's look at the pictures I just took!" Of course, if the person just happened to bring her camera and USB cable along, you could connect the camera to the PC and pull pictures in that way. Just make sure you have spare batteries, too! Wouldn't a card reader be a more elegant solution?

Whichever type of flash memory you have, understand that it acts exactly like a hard drive. If you wish, you can format a memory card and copy, paste, and rename files.

• **Figure 11.17** USB card reader

■ Optical Drives

CD, DVD, and Blu-ray Disc drives and discs come in a variety of flavors and formats, enabling you to back up data, record music, master home videos, and much, much more. **Optical disc** is the generic term for all those different types of shiny, 12-centimeter-wide discs that, if you're a slob like me, collect around your computer like pizza boxes. The drives that support them are called **optical drives**. This section examines optical discs, finishing with the details about installing optical drives.

CD stands for **compact disc**, a medium that was originally designed more than 25 years ago as a replacement for vinyl records. The **digital versatile disc (DVD)** first eliminated VHS cassette tapes from the commercial home movie market, and has also grown into a contender for backups and high-capacity storage. **Blu-ray Disc (BD)** eliminated the High-Definition DVD (HD DVD) format to become the only high-definition and high-capacity optical format.

Going beyond those big three household names, the term "optical disc" refers to technologies such as CD-ROM, CD-R, CD-RW, DVD, DVD+RW, HD DVD, BD-R, BD-RE, and so on. Each of these technologies will be discussed in detail in this chapter—for now, understand that although "optical disc" describes a variety of exciting formats, they all basically boil down to the same physical object: that little shiny disc.

CD-Media

The best way to understand the world of optical discs is to sort out the many types of technologies available, starting with the first: the compact disc. All you're about to read is relevant and fair game for the CompTIA A+ 220-801 exam. Let's begin by looking at how CDs work.

How CDs Work

CDs—the discs that you buy in music stores or may find in software boxes—store data via microscopic pits. CD producers use a power laser to burn these pits into a glass master CD. Once the CD producer creates a master, expensive machines create plastic copies, using a very high-tolerance injection molding process. The copies are coated with a reflective metallic covering and then finished with lacquer for protection. CDs store data on only one side of the disc—we don't flip a CD as we used to flip vinyl records. Did I just sound really old? The data on a CD is near the top of the CD, where the label is located (see Figure 11.18).

• **Figure 11.18** Location of the data

Many people believe that scratching a CD on the bottom makes it unreadable. This is untrue. If you scratch a CD on the bottom (the shiny side), just polish out the scratches—assuming that they aren't too deep—and reread the CD. A number of companies sell inexpensive CD-polishing kits. It's the scratches on the *top* of the disc that wreak havoc on CDs. Avoid writing on the top with anything other than a soft-tipped pen, and certainly don't scratch the top!

CD readers (such as the one in your car or the one in your PC) use a laser and mirrors to read the data from the CD. The metallic covering of the CD makes a highly reflective surface; the pits create interruptions in that surface, while the non-pitted spots, called *lands*, leave it intact. The laser picks up on the reflected pattern that the pits and lands create, and the CD drive converts this pattern into binary ones and zeros. Because the pits are so densely packed on the CD, a vast amount of data can be stored: a standard CD holds up to 5.2 billion bits, or 650 million bytes, of data.

CD Formats

The first CDs were designed for playing music and organized the music in a special format called **CD-Digital Audio (CDDA)**, which we usually just call CD-audio. CD-audio divides the CD's data into variable-length tracks; on music CDs, each song gets one track. CD-audio is an excellent way to store music, but it lacks any error checking, file support, or directory structure, making it a terrible way to store data. For this reason, The Powers That Be created a special method for storing data on a CD, called—are you ready—**CD-ROM**. The CD-ROM format divides the CD into fixed sectors, each holding 2353 bytes.

Most CD-ROM drives also support a number of older, less well-known formats. You may never come across these formats—CD Text, CD+G, and so forth—although you may see them listed among compatible formats on the packaging for a new drive or with a program like Nero InfoTool (see Figure 11.19). Don't let these oddball formats throw you—with few exceptions, they've pretty much fallen by the wayside. All CD-ROM drives read all of these formats, assuming that the system is loaded with the proper software.

The CD-ROM format is something like a partition in the hard drive world. CD-ROM may define the sectors (and some other information), but it doesn't enable a CD-ROM disc to act like a hard drive, with a file structure, directories, and such. To make a CD-ROM act like a hard drive, there's another layer of formatting that defines the file system used on the drive.

At first glance you might think "Why don't CD-ROMs just use a FAT or an NTFS format like hard drives?" Well, first of all, they could. There's no law of physics that prevented the CD-ROM world from adopting any file system. The problem is that the CD makers did not want CD-ROM to

Try This!

Repairing a CD-ROM

To revive scratched CD-ROMs and other CD-media in the comfort of your home or office, get a CD polishing kit, familiarize yourself with its operation, and then Try This!

1. Take a CD-ROM *that you don't mind potentially ruining* and make light scratches on the bottom of the disc. Be sure not to scratch too heavily! Just try to replicate the everyday wear and tear that you've probably seen on CD-ROMs. If you have a disc that's already lightly scratched, that's even better.

2. Use the CD-polishing kit, following the provided instructions exactly.

be tied to Microsoft's or Apple's or anyone else's file format. In addition, they wanted non-PC devices to read CDs, so they invented their own file system just for CD-ROMs called **ISO-9660**. This format is sometimes referred by the more generic term, **CD File System (CDFS)**. The vast majority of data CD-ROMs today use this format.

Over the years, extensions of the ISO-9660 have addressed certain limitations, such as the characters used in file and directory names, filename length, and directory depth.

CD-ROM Speeds

The first CD-ROM drives processed data at roughly 150,000 bytes per second (150 KBps), copying the speed from the original CD-audio format. Although this speed is excellent for listening to music, the CD-ROM industry quickly recognized that installing programs or transferring files from a CD-ROM at 150 KBps was the electronic equivalent of watching paint dry. Since the day the first CD-ROM drives for PCs hit the market, there has been a desire to speed them up to increase their data throughput. Each increase in speed is measured in multiples of the original 150-KBps

• **Figure 11.19** Crazy CD formats

drives and given an × to show speed relative to the first (1×) drives. Here's a list of the common CD-ROM speeds, including most of the early speeds that are no longer produced:

1× 150 KBps	10× 1500 KBps	40× 6000 KBps
2× 300 KBps	12× 1800 KBps	48× 7200 KBps
3× 450 KBps	16× 2400 KBps	52× 7800 KBps
4× 600 KBps	24× 3600 KBps	60× 9000 KBps
6× 900 KBps	32× 4800 KBps	72× 10800 KBps
8× 1200 KBps	36× 5400 KBps	

Keep in mind that these are maximum speeds that are rarely met in real-life operation. You can, however, count on a 32× drive to read data faster than an 8× drive. As multipliers continue to increase, so many other factors come into play that telling the difference between a 48× drive and a 52× drive, for example, becomes difficult. High-speed CD-ROM drives are so inexpensive, however, that most folks buy the fastest drive possible—at least installations go faster!

• **Figure 11.20** A CD-R disc, with its capacity clearly labeled

Some music CD players can't handle CD-R discs.

CD-R

Making CD-ROMs requires specialized, expensive equipment and substantial expertise, so a relatively small number of CD-ROM production companies do it. Yet, since the day the first CD-ROMs came to market, demand has been terrific for a way that ordinary PC users could make their own CDs. The CD industry made a number of attempts to create a technology that would let users record, or *burn*, their own CDs.

In the mid-1990s, the CD industry introduced the **CD-recordable (CD-R)** standard, which enables affordable CD-R drives, often referred to as *CD burners*, to add data to special CD-R discs. Any CD-ROM drive can then read the data stored on the CD-R, and all CD-R drives can read regular CD-ROMs. CD-R discs come in two varieties: a 74-minute disc that holds approximately 650 MB, and an 80-minute variety that holds approximately 700 MB (see Figure 11.20). A CD-R burner must be specifically designed to support the longer, 80-minute CD-R format, but most drives you'll encounter can do this.

CD-R discs function similarly to regular CD-ROMs, although the chemicals used to make them produce a brightly colored recording side on almost all CD-R discs. CD-ROM discs, in contrast, have a silver recording side. CD-R technology records data by using special organic dyes embedded into the disc. This dye is what gives the CD-R its distinctive bottom color. CD-R burners have a second burn laser, roughly ten times as powerful as the read laser, that heats the organic dye. This causes a change in the reflectivity of the surface, creating the functional equivalent of a CD-ROM's pits.

Once the CD-R drive burns data onto a CD-R, the data cannot be erased or changed short of destroying the disc itself. Early CD-R drives required that the entire disc be burned in one burn session, wasting any unused part of the CD-R disc. These were called single-session drives. All modern CD-R drives are **multisession drives**, so you can go back and burn additional data onto the CD-R disc until the disc is full. Multisession drives also have the capability to "close" a partially filled CD-R so that no more data can be burned onto that disc.

CD-R drives have two speeds that matter: the record speed and the read speed, both expressed as multiples of the 150-KBps speed of the original CD-ROM drives. The record speed, which is listed first, is always equal to or slower than the read speed. For example, a CD-R drive with a specification of 8×24× would burn at 8× and read at 24×.

CD-RW

For all their usefulness, CD-R drives have disappeared from the market. Notice that I didn't say CD-R *discs* have disappeared. Just as CD-R drives could both burn CD-R discs and read CD-ROMs, a newer type of drive called **CD-rewritable (CD-RW)** took over the burning market from CD-R drives. Although this drive has its own type of CD-RW discs, it also can burn to CD-R discs, which are much cheaper.

CD-RW technology enables you not only to burn a disc, but to *burn over* existing data on a CD-RW disc. This is not something you need for every disc. For example, I create CD-R archives of my completed books to store the text and graphics for posterity—this is data I want to access later but do not need to modify. While I'm still working on this book, however, I might make a backup copy. As I work on it, I'll update the backup. I couldn't do that with a CD-R. The CD-RW format, on the other hand, essentially takes CD-media to the functional equivalent of a 650-MB floppy disk. Once again, CD-RW discs look exactly like CD-ROM discs with the exception of a colored bottom side. Figure 11.21 shows all three formats.

A CD-RW drive works by using a laser to heat an amorphous (noncrystalline) substance that, when cooled, slowly becomes crystalline. The crystalline areas are reflective, whereas the amorphous areas are not. Because both CD-R and CD-RW drives require a powerful laser, making a drive that could burn CD-Rs and CD-RWs was a simple process, and plain CD-R drives disappeared almost overnight. Why buy a CD-R drive when a comparably priced CD-RW drive could burn both CD-R and CD-RW discs?

CD-RW drive specs have three multiplier values. The first shows the CD-R write speed, the second shows the CD-RW rewrite speed, and the third shows the read speed. Write, rewrite, and read speeds vary tremendously among the various brands of CD-RW drives; here are just a few representative samples: 8×4×32×, 12×10×32×, and 48×24×48×.

One of the goals with the introduction of CD-RWs was the idea of making a CD-RW act like a hard drive so you could simply drag a file onto the CD-RW (or CD-R) and just as easily drag it off again. This goal was difficult for two reasons: first, the different file formats made on-the-fly conversion risky; second, CD-RWs don't store data exactly the same way as hard drives and would quickly wear out if data were copied in the same manner.

Two developments, UDF and packet writing, enable you to treat a CD-RW just like a hard drive—with a few gotchas. The not-so-new kid in town with CD-media file formats is the **universal data format (UDF)**. UDF is a replacement for ISO-9660 and all of its various extensions, resulting in a single file format that any drive and operating system can read. UDF has taken over the DVD world (all movie DVDs use this format) and is poised to also become the CD-media file format in the near future. UDF handles very large files and is excellent for all rewritable CD-media. UDF has been available for quite a while, but until Windows Vista came out, no version of Windows could write to UDF-formatted discs. They could *read* the discs, but if you wanted to *write* to them in Windows you had to use one of a number of third-party UDF tools such as Roxio's DirectCD and Nero's InCD. UDF also supports a feature called Mount Rainier—better known as packet writing—that works with UDF so you can copy individual files back and forth like a hard drive. With UDF and packet writing, rewritable CD-media is as easy to use as a hard drive.

• **Figure 11.21** CD-ROM, CD-R, and CD-RW discs

You can rewrite CD-RW discs a limited number of times. The number varies according to the source, but expect a maximum life of about 1000 rewrites, although in real life you'll get considerably fewer.

• **Figure 11.22** Optical drive in Windows

I cover more on installation and ATAPI compliance later in this chapter.

Windows and CD-Media

Virtually all optical drives are **ATAPI-compliant**, meaning they plug into the ATA controllers on the motherboard, just like a hard drive, so you don't need to install drivers. You just plug in the drive and, assuming you didn't make any physical installation mistakes, the drive appears in Windows (see Figure 11.22).

Windows displays an optical drive in My Computer or Computer with the typical optical drive icon and assigns it a drive letter. Every modern edition of Windows enables you to burn music or files to a CD using Windows Media Player or Windows Explorer, respectively. Almost every new CD-RW drive comes with some type of burner software, as well, and other third-party developers also create software that burns music and data to CD—you might have heard of Apple's iTunes software? Figure 11.23 shows the opening menu of one that I like, the popular Nero optical disc–burning program.

When I buy a new program on CD, the first thing I do is make a backup copy; then I stash the original under lock and key. If I break, melt, or otherwise destroy the backup, I quickly create a new one from the original. I can easily copy the disc, because my system, like many, has both a regular CD-ROM and a CD-RW drive (even though CD-RW drives read CD-ROM discs). I can place a CD in the CD-ROM drive and a CD-R or CD-RW disc in the CD-RW drive. Then I use a disk-copy application to create an exact replica of the CD quickly. CD-RW drives work great for another, bigger type of backup: not the archival "put it on the disc and stash it in the closet" type of backup but rather the daily/weekly backups that most of us do (or should do!) on our systems. Using CD-R discs for these backups is wasteful; once

• **Figure 11.23** Nero optical disc–burning program

a disc fills up, you throw it away at the next backup. But with CD-RW, you can use the same set of CD-RW discs time and again to perform backups.

Music CDs

Computers do not hold a monopoly on CD burning. Many companies offer consumer CD burners that work with your stereo system. These come in a wide variety of formats, but they're usually dual-deck player/recorder combinations. These recorders do not use regular CD-R or CD-RW discs. Instead, under U.S. law, these home recorders must use a slightly different disc called a **music CD-R**. Makers of music CDs pay a small royalty for each CD (and add it to your price). You can record *to* a music CD-R or CD-RW, but you cannot record *from* one—the idea being to restrict duplication. If you decide to buy one of these burners, make sure to buy the special music CD-Rs. Music CD-Rs are designed specifically for these types of devices and may not work well in a PC.

DVD-Media

For years, the video industry tried to create an optical-media replacement for videotape. The 12-inch-diameter *laserdisc* format originally introduced by Philips gained some ground in the 1980s and 1990s. But the high cost of both the discs and the players, plus various marketing factors, meant there was never a very large laserdisc market. You may still find one of them sitting around, however, or you may know someone who invested in a small collection during the laserdisc's heyday.

The DVD was developed by a large consortium of electronics and entertainment firms during the early 1990s and released as digital *video* discs in 1995. The transformation of DVD to a data storage medium required a name change to digital *versatile* discs. You'll still hear both terms used. The industry also uses the term **DVD-video** to distinguish the movie format from the data formats.

With the exception of the DVD logo stamped on all commercial DVDs (see Figure 11.24), DVDs look exactly like CD-media discs; but that's pretty much where the similarities end. DVD has become the fastest growing media format in history and has completely overtaken VHS as the preferred media for video. Additionally, one variant of DVD called DVD-RAM has enjoyed some success as a mass storage medium.

The single best word to describe DVD is *capacity*. All previous optical discs stored a maximum of 700 MB of data or 80 minutes of video. The lowest capacity DVD holds 4.37 GB of data, or two hours of standard-definition video. The highest capacity version DVDs store roughly 16 GB of data, or more than eight hours of video! DVD achieves these amazing capacities by using a number of technologies, but three are most important. First, DVD uses smaller pits than CD-media, and packs them much more densely. Second, DVD comes in both *single-sided* (*SS*) and *double-sided* (*DS*) formats. As the name implies, a DS disc holds twice the data of an SS disc, but it also requires you to flip the disc to read the other side. Third, DVDs come in *single-layer* (*SL*) and *dual-layer* (*DL*) formats. DL formats use two pitted layers on each side, each with a slightly different reflectivity index. Table 11.1 shows the common DVD capacities.

• **Figure 11.24** Typical DVD-video

The CompTIA A+ 801 exam refers to dual-layer DVDs as **DL DVD**, while a rewritable DVD is called a **Dual Layer DVD-RW**.

Table 11.1	DVD Versions/Capacities
DVD Version	**Capacity**
DVD-5 (12 cm, SS/SL)	4.37 GB, more than two hours of video
DVD-9 (12 cm, SS/DL)	7.95 GB, about four hours of video
DVD-10 (12 cm, DS/SL)	8.74 GB, about four and a half hours of video
DVD-18 (12 cm, DS/DL)	15.90 GB, more than eight hours of video

Tech Tip

MPEG Standards

Reproducing video and sound on the PC provides interesting challenges for developers. How do you take a motion picture from film, translate it into ones and zeros that the CPU understands, process those bits, and then send high-quality video and sound to the monitor and speakers for the pleasure of the computer user? How much data do you think is required to display even a two-minute clip of a car racing through a city street, in all the minute detail of the shops, people, screeching tires, road debris, and so on? For that matter, how do you store the obviously huge amount of data required to do this?

To handle these chores, the Moving Picture Experts Group (MPEG) has released coding standards such as MPEG-1, MPEG-2, and MPEG-4. Each standard provides a different compression algorithm, *which makes the files manageable. The standards also implement various technologies to handle movement, called motion compensation. The details of the standards matter a lot to the folks producing the movies and other video and audio content, but here's the short answer that should suffice for the purposes of a PC tech.*

MPEG-1 is the standard on which video and MP3, among other technologies, are based. The most common implementations of this standard provide a resolution of 352 × 240 at 30 fps. This video quality falls just below that of a conventional VHS video.

One very well-known subset of MPEG-1 is better known for audio than video. MPEG-1 Layer 3, better known as MP3 format, dominates the world of audio. MP3 takes an uncompressed audio file and compresses it dramatically, but the algorithm is so tight that the music that comes out of the speakers remains almost completely faithful to the original audio file. To paraphrase a catchphrase from the 1980s—I want my MP3s!

MPEG-2 provides resolutions of 720 × 480 and 1280 × 720 at 60 fps (as well as others), plus CD-quality audio, making it adequate for all major TV standards, even HDTV. MPEG-2 is the standard that covers DVD-ROM technology—it can compress two hours of video into a file no larger than a few gigabytes. Although encoding video into MPEG-2 format requires a computer with some serious firepower, even a modest PC can decompress and play such a video.

*The **MPEG-4** standard is based on MPEG-1, MPEG-2, and Apple's QuickTime technology. MPEG-4 graphics and video files use what's known as wavelet compression to create files that are more compact than either JPEG or QuickTime files. This superior compression makes MPEG-4 popular for delivering video and images over the Web. MPEG-4 higher-efficiency standards such as advanced video coding are included with MPEG-4 and used for Blu-ray Discs. And notably, MPEG-4 provides Intellectual Property Management and Protection (IPMP), which supports digital rights management.*

MPEG-7 is designed to complement the previous standards as a fast and efficient multimedia content searching tool.

MPEG-21 is concerned with and focuses on coding and digital rights. MPEG-21 uses a Rights Expression Language (REL) and a Rights Data Dictionary to protect digital material from illicit file sharing.

DVD-Video

The most beautiful trait of DVD-video is its capability to store two hours of video on one side. You drop in a DVD-video and get to watch an entire movie without flipping it over. DVD-video supports TV-style 4:3 aspect-ratio screens as well as 16:9 theater screens, but it is up to the producer to decide which to use. Many DVD-video producers used to distribute DVD movies on DS media with a 4:3 ratio on one side and 16:9 ratio on the other, though that isn't as common anymore. DVD-video relies on the **MPEG-2** standard of video and audio compression to reach the magic of two hours of video per side. *Moving Picture Experts Group (MPEG)* is a group of compression standards for both audio and video. The MPEG-2 standard offers resolutions of up to 1280 × 720 at 60 frames per second (fps), with full CD-quality audio (standard DVDs only offer 480 vertical resolution, the same as regular television).

DVD-ROM

DVD-ROM is the DVD equivalent of the standard CD-ROM data format except that it's capable of storing up to almost 16 GB of data. Almost all DVD-ROM drives also fully support DVD-video, as well as most CD-ROM formats. Most DVD drives sold with PCs are DVD-ROM drives.

Recordable DVD

The IT industry has no fewer than *six* distinct standards of recordable DVD-media: DVD-ROM for general use, DVD-R for authoring, **DVD-RW**, DVD+R, **DVD+RW**, and DVD-RAM. Both DVD-R standard discs and DVD+R discs work like CD-Rs. You can write to them but not erase or alter what's written. DVD-RW, DVD+RW, and DVD-RAM discs can be written and rewritten, just like CD-RW discs. Most DVD drives can read all formats with the exception of DVD-RAM. DVD-RAM is the only DVD format that uses a cartridge, so it requires a special drive (see Figure 11.25). DVD-RAM is still around, but fading away.

Although there is little if any difference in quality among the standards, the competition between corporations pushing their preferred standards has raged for years. Sony and Phillips, for example, pushed the + series, whereas other manufacturers pushed the – series. Worse, no recordable DVD drive manufactured before 2003 could write any format except its own. You could plop down US$250 on a brand-new DVD+RW drive and still find yourself unable to edit a disc from your friend who used the DVD-RW format! Half of the time, the drive couldn't even *read* the competing format disc.

The situation is much better today, as DVD±RW combo drives in PCs play just about anyone else's DVDs. The challenge is DVD players. If you want to make a DVD of your family picnic and then play it on the DVD player hooked to your television, take the time to read the documentation for your player to make sure it reads that particular DVD format—not all players read all formats.

• **Figure 11.25** DVD-RAM disc

Blu-ray Disc-Media

Blu-ray Disc is considered the next generation in optical disc formatting and storage technology after CD and DVD. Because of its near-perfect audio and video quality; mass acceptance by industry-leading computer, electronics, game, music, retail, and motion picture companies; and huge storage capacities of up to 25 GB (single-layer disc) and 50 GB (dual-layer disc), Blu-ray Disc technology is expected to eventually make CD- and DVD-media and devices obsolete.

Blu-ray Discs come in two physical sizes, standard and mini. The standard size matches that of earlier optical discs, such as CD-R and DVD-RW, and is what you'll see used in computers and for movies (see Figure 11.26). The mini-size discs are a lot smaller and, naturally, offer less storage. You'll find mini Blu-ray Discs in very high-end camcorders. Table 11.2 shows the details of the two formats.

There was a brief battle for supremacy in the high-definition digital war between Blu-ray Disc and a competing high-definition optical disc standard called HD DVD. Major content manufacturers and developers leaned toward Blu-ray Disc, and in early 2008, Toshiba—the primary company behind HD DVD—threw in the towel. HD DVD is no longer being developed or supported.

If you own a PlayStation 3, you already have a Blu-ray Disc player. That's the optical format the game system uses.

Table 11.2	Standard and Mini Blu-ray Disc Comparison Chart		
Type	**Size**	**Capacity (single layer)**	**Capacity (dual layer)**
Standard disc	12 cm	25 GB	50 GB
Mini disc	8 cm	7.8 GB	15.6 GB

● **Figure 11.26** Standard Blu-ray Disc

● **Figure 11.27** A combination CD/DVD/Blu-ray Disc drive

Blu-ray Disc technology offers several advantages over DVD aside from raw capacity. First, Blu-ray Disc uses a blue-violet laser (hence the Blu in the name) with a wavelength of 405 nanometers (nm). (DVD uses a red-laser technology with a wavelength of 650 nm.) The 405-nm wavelength is smaller and much more precise, enabling better use of space during the creation process and ultimately resulting in a sharper image. Second, Blu-ray Disc can handle high-definition (HD) video in resolutions far higher than DVD. Finally, Blu-ray Disc supports many more video compression schemes, giving producers more options for putting content on discs.

BD-ROM

BD-ROM (read only) is the Blu-ray Disc equivalent of the standard DVD-ROM data format except, as noted earlier, it can store much more data and produces superior audio and video results. Almost all BD-ROM drives are fully backward compatible and support DVD-video as well as most CD-ROM formats. If you want to display the best possible movie picture quality on your HDTV, you should get a Blu-ray Disc player and use Blu-ray Discs in place of DVDs. Most new computer systems still don't come standard with Blu-ray Disc drives installed. You can often custom-order a system with a Blu-ray Disc drive or you can simply install one yourself. Figure 11.27 shows a Blu-ray Disc drive.

BD-R and BD-RE

Blu-ray Discs come in two writable formats, BD-R (for recordable) and BD-RE (for rewritable). You can write to a **BD-R** disc one time. You can write to and erase a **BD-RE** disc several times. There are also BD-R and BD-RE versions of mini Blu-ray Discs.

Blu-ray Disc Burners

Blu-ray Disc burners cost more than a standard optical drive but will eventually be as common as the average CD-RW or DVD-RW. Blu-ray Disc burners and other Blu-ray Disc drives can be connected internally or externally to a system. It is common for them to be connected externally via USB (3.0 usually) or eSATA or internally through SATA. Operating systems such as Windows, XP, Windows Vista, and Windows 7 all support Blu-ray Disc burners and software. The software you use for burning is totally up to you; however, as always, you should follow the manufacturer's specifications for the best results. Most multidrive Blu-ray Disc burners offer the following support features.

- **Media support** BD-R, BD-RE, DVD-ROM, DVD-RAM, DVD-video, DVD+/-R DL, DVD+/-R, DVD+/-RW, CD-DA, CD-ROM, CD-R, and CD-RW

- **Write speed (max)** 2× BD-R, 4× DVD+/-R DL, 8× DVD+/-R(8×), and 24× CD-R

- **Rewrite speed (max)** 2× BD-RE, 8× DVD+RW, 6× DVD-RW, 5× DVD-RAM, and 16× CD-RW

- **Read speed (max)** 2× BD-ROM, 8× DVD-ROM, and 32× CD-ROM

- **Compatibility** Most Blu-ray Disc drives are backward compatible, meaning they can read and play CDs and DVDs. CD and DVD drives and players cannot read or play Blu-ray Discs.

Installing Optical Drives

From ten feet away, optical drives of all flavors look absolutely identical. Figure 11.28 shows a CD-RW drive, a DVD drive, and a BD-R drive. Can you tell them apart just by a glance? In case you were wondering, the CD-RW drive is on the bottom, the DVD drive is next, and finally the BD-R drive is on the top. If you look closely at an optical drive, you will normally see its function either stamped on the front of the case or printed on a label somewhere less obvious (see Figure 11.29).

Connections

Most internal optical drives use SATA connections (though you'll find some drives still use a PATA cable) and support the ATAPI standard. (Other connections, such as SCSI and USB, are possible but less common.) External optical drives often use USB, FireWire, or eSATA connections. ATAPI treats an optical drive exactly as though it were an ATA drive. PATA optical drives have regular 40-pin IDE connectors and master/slave jumpers. SATA optical drives use standard SATA or eSATA cables. You install them as you would install any ATA hard drive. Figure 11.30 shows a typical DVD installation using SATA.

- **Figure 11.28** CD-RW, DVD, and BD-R drives

- **Figure 11.29** Label on optical drive indicating its type

• **Figure 11.30** Typical DVD installation

ATAPI drives require no CMOS changes as part of the installation process. When the industry first introduced ATAPI drives, techs familiar with hard-drive installations swamped the CD-ROM makers' service departments asking how to set up the drives in CMOS. To reduce these calls, BIOS makers added a CD-ROM option in many CMOS setup utilities, just to give the techs something to do! You can find this option in many older CMOS setup utilities. This setting actually didn't do anything at all; it just kept users from bothering the CD-ROM makers with silly support calls. Modern motherboards report the actual model numbers of optical drives,

Cross Check

Master/Slave Settings

You normally set up a PATA optical drive as a slave to a hard drive master. You learned about master and slave settings for PATA drives in Chapter 10, so cross-check your memory!

1. What are the various ways you can determine which drive on an IDE controller acts as slave and which acts as master?

2. What factors should you consider when deciding where to install an optical drive, either as a master or as a slave? Is there any difference in your answer for a system with one hard drive versus one with two hard drives?

giving techs a degree of assurance that they configured and installed the drive correctly (see Figure 11.31).

Device Manager

When you install a new optical drive, such as a DVD drive, into an existing system, the first question to ask is "Does Windows recognize my DVD drive?" You can determine this by opening My Computer/Computer and verifying that a DVD drive is present (see Figure 11.32). When you want to know more, go to Device Manager.

• **Figure 11.31** Autodetect settings for two optical drives

Device Manager contains most of the information about optical drives. Open Device Manager and find your drive in the list of devices. Right-click on the drive and select Properties to see more information. The General tab tells you about the current status of the DVD drive, basically saying whether the device is working properly or not—rather less useful than actually trying the device. Other tabs, such as the Driver tab, provide other pertinent information about the drive.

Auto Insert Notification

Another setting of note is the Auto Insert Notification option, often referred to as **AutoPlay**. This setting enables Windows to detect automatically the presence of audio or data optical discs when they are placed in the drive. Windows XP and Windows Vista/7 deal with AutoPlay in different ways.

Windows XP provides a simple approach to AutoPlay. By default, when you insert a CD- or DVD-media disc that doesn't have an **autorun.inf** file, Windows XP asks you what you want to do (see Figure 11.33). You can change the default behavior simply by accessing the Properties dialog box

• **Figure 11.32** DVD drive letter in Computer

Tech Tip

External Optical Drives

Almost all new PCs have one, two, or three external expansion buses—USB, FireWire, or eSATA—and the makers of optical drives have quickly taken this fact to heart. Many manufacturers have released external versions of CD, DVD, and Blu-ray Disc drives, both readers and burners. Of the three, eSATA is fastest, with USB 3.0 close behind and FireWire a distant third.

Many ultra-light laptops don't have an optical drive built in; the only way to load an OS on them is through an external drive.

You won't find many CD or DVD drives with eSATA—they just can't take advantage of the blazing speed offered by the best of the external ports. Blu-ray Disc drive manufacturers, on the other hand, have released several drives with both eSATA and USB 3.0 connections. Since both connections offer almost the same speed (in practical usage, at least), feel free to use either connection.

• **Figure 11.33** Windows XP prompting user for action

• **Figure 11.34** AutoPlay tab for a CD-RW drive

for a particular drive in My Computer and making your selection on the AutoPlay tab. Figure 11.34 shows some of the options for a typical Windows XP machine.

AutoPlay in Windows Vista and Windows 7 is much more robust and offers many more options than in Windows XP. For example, you can choose to enable or disable AutoPlay for all media and devices. (Using AutoPlay for all media and devices is the default.) But what's more interesting is that you can enable very specific actions for Windows to take when digital media or devices are inserted or detected. For an audio CD, for example, you can specify that Windows should use Windows Media Player. If a DVD or Blu-ray movie is detected, you can tell AutoPlay to play the disc by using PowerDVD 12 or some other program. You can adjust AutoPlay options in Windows Vista/7 through Control Panel | Hardware and Sound | AutoPlay.

You can also change the drive letter for an optical drive, just as you can change the letter of a hard drive. You'll find that option in Disk Management (see Figure 11.35).

Applications

A regular CD-ROM drive installation involves no applications. You install it, Windows sees it, and you're finished. CD-R and CD-RW drives, in contrast, require applications to enable their burning features. Windows Media Player, included with most copies of Windows, is capable of burning music to CDs, while Windows Explorer can burn data to your CDs.

DVD and Blu-ray Disc drives need software to enable you to watch movies and burn DVD and Blu-ray video, though burning your data to DVD is still handled by Windows Explorer. (Burning to Blu-ray media requires third-party software.) Windows Media Player makes an excellent DVD-watching application, but to burn DVD-videos, you'll need to turn to Windows DVD Maker (Vista/7) or a third-party tool like Nero or Roxio Creator.

Ever wanted to make a perfect copy of a CD so you can keep your original in a safe place? You can do so by using a special file type called an ISO file. An **ISO file** is a complete copy—an ISO image as we say—of an optical disc. As you might imagine, they are huge files, but they are also very important to techs. Techs use ISO images to send each other copies of bootable utility discs. For example, if you want a copy of the Ultimate Boot CD, you go to their Web site and download an ISO image. With Windows XP and Windows Vista, you'll need a third-party burning program (Windows 7 can burn ISO images) and go through a special process called burning an ISO image. Learn how to burn ISO images with your burning program; you'll use it all the time.

• **Figure 11.35** Change CD drive letter option in Disk Management

Blu-ray Disc Drive Considerations

Physically installing, attaching, and maintaining optical drives is pretty straightforward, but a Blu-ray Disc drive installation requires some special considerations. If you plan to use your Blu-ray Disc drive primarily for storage purposes, for example, system requirements are minimal. If you plan on watching Blu-ray Disc movies in HD resolution (720p, 1080i, or 1080p), on the other hand, the requirements are quite hefty. Here's a list of recommended minimum specs.

- **Processor** At the very least, a Pentium 4, Pentium D, or dual or multicore processor; or an AMD Athlon 64 X2 or Phenom multicore processor.

- **System memory** At least 1 GB RAM for Windows XP; 2 GB RAM for Windows Vista/7.

- **Video** You need an HDCP-compliant (either DVI or HDMI) video card and drivers. That's a lot of initials in one sentence! Here's the scoop. The High-Bandwidth Digital Content Protection (HDCP) is a standard developed by Intel to ensure copyright protection on behalf of the Motion Picture Association of America. The digital visual interface (DVI) and High-Definition Multimedia Interface (HDMI) standards enable fast, uncompressed connections between an HDTV, PC, and any other DVI/HDMI component. HDMI, which transmits both video and audio signals, has all but replaced the older DVI standard that only supports video. AMD and NVIDIA both offer Blu-ray Disc–compliant PCIe video cards with enough horsepower to get the job done.

Burning Digital Music Files to a CD

Almost all computers and many portable CD players now can play recordable CDs loaded with MP3 files. This enables you to mix songs from your music collection and fit a lot of songs on a disc (MP3s are smaller than CD-audio files). That's a great feature—but where do digital audio files come from and how do you put them on a CD?

You can create MP3s from your favorite CDs by using a *ripper*. A ripper is a piece of software that takes standard CD-audio files and compresses them, using specialized algorithms, into much smaller files while maintaining most of the audio qualities of the original file. One legal note, however: you should only make MP3s from CDs that you have purchased. Borrowing a CD from a friend and ripping MP3s from it is illegal! Likewise, downloading MP3s from unauthorized sources on the Internet is also illegal. You don't want to go to jail because you just had to listen to the latest, greatest single from your favorite artist, right?

Now that I've taken care of the legal disclaimer, get ready to burn your MP3s. You need three things: a recordable/rewritable optical drive, some CD authoring software, and, of course, a blank disc. I recommend a CD-R. (Audio-only devices stand a much better chance of playing a CD-R successfully rather than a CD-RW.)

1. Confirm that you have a CD-R/RW drive installed in your computer. You don't have to have a drive like this to rip audio files *from* a CD, but you must have one to burn digital audio to a CD-R.

2. Launch your favorite CD authoring software. Popular titles in this category include Nero Burning ROM and Roxio Creator.

3. Most CD authoring programs use a simple drag-and-drop interface, similar to the Windows Explorer interface. Browse to the location of the audio files and select them. Then drag them into the appropriate area—this is often called the *queue*.

4. After you've selected all the files you want to have on your CD, it's time to burn. The procedure for initiating the CD-burning sequence is different for each program. You should always make sure to *close* the CD after you've burned it. Most standalone CD players (even ones that play MP3s) won't play CD-Rs that haven't been closed.

Once you've keyed in all of the configuration information, just sit back and watch the fireworks. Always be sure to use CD-media that is rated appropriately for your drive, for both speed and media type. In no time at all, you'll be listening to MP3s while jogging around the park.

CyberLink provides an awesome tool called BD & 3D Advisor that will tell you if your system meets the requirements to play Blu-ray Discs. You can get it at www.cyberlink.com/prog/bd-support/diagnosis.do.

Region Codes

Production movies on DVD and Blu-ray Disc can feature a **region code**, encoding that enables you to play those movies only on a player that shares the same region code. This was instituted to try to stop piracy of movies, though it didn't manage to accomplish that goal.

Can you play a DVD or Blu-ray Disc encoded to play in the geographical region location of Somalia on your system manufactured in the U.S.A.? Why sure you can. To do so, however, you have to change the region code on your DVD or Blu-ray Disc player to match Somalia (5 or B, respectively, in case you're curious). You can only change the region code on your player four times. After that, you get stuck with whatever was the last-used region code.

Most optical devices are set to play only discs encoded for the region in which they were sold or manufactured. You can easily check and set your device's current region code under the hardware properties of your optical device in any version of Windows. As either a technician or home enthusiast, you should be familiar with the following optical device and media region codes.

 Be sure you are familiar with the Blu-ray Disc requirements discussed in this section, especially the stringent requirements for supporting high-definition video and audio. Also, be aware that CompTIA expects you to be somewhat knowledgeable of DVD/BD region codes, so pay attention to those as well.

DVD Region Codes:

- **REGION 0** All regions
- **REGION 1** United States, Canada
- **REGION 2** Europe, Japan, Middle East, South Africa, Greenland
- **REGION 3** South Korea, Taiwan, Hong Kong, areas of Southeast Asia
- **REGION 4** Australia, New Zealand, Central and South America
- **REGION 5** Eastern Europe, Russia, India, Africa
- **REGION 6** China
- **REGION 7** Reserved for special and future use
- **REGION 8** Reserved for cruise ships and airlines

Blu-ray Disc Region Codes:

- **A** East Asia (China and Mongolia excluded), Southeast Asia, Americas, and their dependencies
- **B** Africa, Southwest Asia, Europe (except Russia), Oceania, and their dependencies
- **C** Central Asia, East Asia (China and Mongolia only), South Asia, central Eurasia (including Russia), and their dependencies

Beyond A+

Color Books

The term *color books* is often used in the world of CD-media. Color books are—well, books! In this case, they're the standards developed in the industry to describe various media. For example, the Red book describes the

original audio CD format. If you have a lot of money—say, US$3000—you may purchase copies of these books, and yes, their covers really match the colors of the standards. You might hear a fellow computer support person using these terms. Instead of saying, "Does your CD-ROM read CD-RWs?" they will say, "Is that CD-ROM of yours Orange book?" Technical specifications also use these terms. I personally don't like the way many people refer to these book colors, but the terms are used enough that you should memorize the meanings of at least three book colors: Red, Yellow, and Orange. Table 11.3 shows a complete list of CD-media book colors.

Table 11.3	CD-Media Book Colors
Application	**Book**
Audio CDs	Red book
Data CDs	Yellow book
CD-I	Green book
Recordable CDs	Orange book
Video CD	White book
CD Extra	Blue book

BDXL

If you think Blu-ray Disc's 50-GB capacity is limiting, check out *BDXL* discs. The BDXL format was introduced in June 2010, although drives capable of reading and writing to the discs didn't start appearing until late 2011. That's right: you can't use BDXL discs in that standard Blu-ray Disc drive you just bought. You'll need a drive that specifically supports the new format. So why would you want one? In a word: capacity.

BDXL discs come in two flavors: a triple-layer BDXL disc supports a capacity of 100 GB, and a quadruple-layer disc has a capacity of 128 GB. That's a lot of room, but it comes at a high price. As of early 2012, a single disc cost US$100—that's a dollar per gigabyte for a triple-layer disc! At those prices, you could go out and get yourself a nice solid-state drive, which is much more flexible as a storage device. Needless to say, BDXL isn't quite ready for the spotlight, but as prices come down, this could become a great option for optical disc storage.

Chapter 11 Review

■ Chapter Summary

After reading this chapter and completing the exercises, you should understand the following about floppy disk drives, flash memory, and optical media technology.

Explain and install floppy disk drives

- Floppy disk drives are a thing of the past. The small, 1.44-MB capacity floppy disks have been replaced by higher-capacity removable media.

- Floppy disks are constructed of a flexible magnetic disc housed inside a square plastic case. The case has a sliding protective cover that opens to reveal a portion of the magnetic media when inside a floppy drive. Read/write heads inside the floppy disk drive move back and forth across the media, reading or writing data as necessary.

- During disk access, an LED on the front of the drive lights up. Never eject a floppy disk when this light is on.

- Floppy disks appeared around 1986 and are 3½ inches.

- You may have a maximum of two floppy disk drives in a system, and they must use either the drive letter A: or B:; however, a single floppy disk drive can be configured to use either drive letter. By convention, if your system has only one floppy disk drive, you should configure it as drive A:.

- A 34-pin ribbon data cable is used to connect the floppy disk drive to the motherboard; a 4-pin mini connector supplies power. Attaching the data cable backward won't damage anything, but the drive won't work. If you attach the power connector incorrectly, you risk damaging the drive.

- Most floppy ribbon cables have three connectors and a twist. The end without the twist connects to the motherboard, matching the red stripe on the cable with pin 1 of the motherboard connector. The drive attached to the middle connector on the cable receives the drive letter B:. The drive attached to the other end of the cable (after the twist) is assigned the drive letter A:.

- After connecting a floppy disk drive, configure the CMOS settings. Make sure the CMOS settings match your floppy disk drive size/capacity; for example, 3½ inches and 1.44 MB.

Demonstrate the variations among flash drives and other tiny drives

- Flash memory includes USB thumb drives and memory cards. USB thumb drives contain a standard USB connection and have replaced many other forms of removable media as the way to transfer files. Memory cards, a generic term, are used in digital cameras, smartphones, and other devices.

- Thumb drives store much more data than floppies—sometimes up to the equivalent of thousands of floppy disks. They are hot-swappable in Windows and don't require an external power source, as they are powered directly from the USB. Most new PCs enable you to boot from a USB thumb drive.

- Flash cards, which are used in portable devices such as digital cameras, smartphones, and MP3 players, come in many varieties. The most common types are CompactFlash, Secure Digital, Memory Stick, and Extreme Digital (xD) Picture Card.

- CompactFlash cards are the oldest of the common types of flash cards. At about 1 inch wide, they use the PCMCIA bus and come in two thicknesses: CF I at 3.3 mm thick and CF II at 5 mm thick.

- Secure Digital is perhaps the most popular flash card today. Smaller versions of Secure Digital cards, MiniSD and MicroSD, are also available.

- Memory Stick, a proprietary format from Sony, comes in several formats, including Standard, Pro, Duo, Pro Duo, and Micro.

- xD Picture Cards, developed by Olympus, are about half the size of Secure Digital cards and are used almost exclusively in digital cameras.

- No matter what type of flash card you have, you need a card reader to access it. Some PCs have built-in card readers. External USB card readers are also available. Sometimes a device such as a digital camera or smartphone can double as a card reader.

Identify and install optical-media technology

- CDs store data by using microscopic pits burned into a glass master CD with a powerful laser. Expensive machines create plastic copies of the glass master that are then coated with a reflective metallic coating. CDs store data on one side of the disc only. The CD drive reads the pits and the non-pitted areas (lands) and converts the pattern into ones and zeros.

- CDs come in many varieties. CD-Digital Audio is for playing music, but it lacks error checking, file support, and directory structure. CD-ROM discs are for storing data. They use the ISO-9660 file system, also known as CDFS. Extensions of ISO-9660 have offered improvements to file and directory naming, filename length, and directory depth.

- CD-ROM speeds have increased substantially from the original 150 KBps. Increased speeds are measured in multiples of 150 KBps, so a 10× CD-ROM has a maximum speed of 1500 KBps.

- CD-recordable (CD-R) discs hold either 650 MB or 700 MB and can store either audio or data. Special organic dyes that give the CD-Rs their distinctive bottom color aid in the burning process. A strong laser in the CD drive heats the dye and changes the reflectivity of the CD-R's surface, resulting in a reflective/less-reflective pattern that is converted to ones and zeros. Once data is burned to a CD-R, the data cannot be erased. With multisession drives, you can burn data to a portion of a disc and then go back later and burn more data to the disc. CD-R discs are rated with two speeds: a write speed followed by a read speed.

- CD-rewritable (CD-RW) discs, unlike CD-Rs, enable you to erase data and burn new data. CD-RWs are rated with three speeds: write speed followed by rewrite speed followed by read speed. The UDF file format (the replacement for ISO-9660) handles large files better than CDFS. Packet writing, a feature used by UDF, allows you to copy files back and forth to a CD-RW like a hard drive.

- Most CD drives are ATAPI-compliant and do not need drivers installed for them to work.

- Windows can burn CD-Rs, CD-RWs, and all forms of burnable DVDs without additional software, but it cannot burn to Blu-ray Discs. If you need to burn to Blu-ray Disc, you need a third-party application.

- Many companies offer standalone CD burners that attach to your stereo system instead of your PC; however, these machines use a different type of CD called a music CD-R and are not compatible with standard CD-R or CD-RW discs.

- DVDs were released as digital video discs in 1995, but as usage evolved to include data storage, the name was changed to digital versatile disc. The lowest capacity DVD holds 4.37 GB of data. DVDs offer much higher capacities than CDs, because DVDs use smaller and more densely packed pits, can be burned on both sides of the disc, and can burn two layers of pits per side for a total of four layers. DVD-video uses the MPEG-2 video standard and can store two hours of video on a single side.

- DVD-ROM, the DVD equivalent of CD-ROM, can store up to 16 GB of data. Recordable DVD-media comes in many varieties: DVD-R for general purpose, DVD-R for authoring, DVD+R, DVD-RW, DVD+RW, and DVD-RAM. You can write to DVD-R and DVD+R but not erase them. You can both burn and erase DVD-RW, DVD+RW, and DVD-RAM.

- Standard Blu-ray Discs have storage capacities of up to 25 GB (single-layer disc) and 50 GB (dual-layer disc) and provide near-perfect picture quality.

- You can write to a BD-R (recordable) disc one time. You can erase and write to a BD-RE (rewritable) disc several times.

- Blu-ray Disc external devices are connected via USB, FireWire, or eSATA and internally via PATA, SATA, SCSI, or USB connections.

- Most Blu-ray Disc burners support BD-R, BD-RE, DVD-ROM, DVD-RAM, DVD-video, DVD+/-R

DL, DVD+/-R, DVD+/-RW, CD-DA, CD-ROM, CD-R, and CD-RW formats. CD and DVD drives do not support Blu-ray Disc technologies. Most optical drives use SATA connections and support the ATAPI standard. PATA drives use a regular 40-pin IDE connector; SATA drives use a standard SATA or eSATA (for external use) connector. You install them just as you would any ATA hard drive. After installing a new optical drive, check My Computer/Computer or Device Manager to confirm that Windows sees the drive.

■ The Windows feature Auto Insert Notification (or AutoPlay) causes Windows to automatically begin an action when an optical disc is inserted in the drive. Windows XP's AutoPlay can be configured by accessing the AutoPlay tab in the drive's Properties dialog box. AutoPlay options in Windows Vista and Windows 7 can be adjusted through Control Panel | Hardware and Sound | AutoPlay.

■ An ISO file is a complete copy of an entire CD, DVD, or Blu-ray Disc. Windows XP and Windows Vista can't burn an ISO image back to disc, though Windows 7 and third-party programs such as Nero or Roxio Creator can.

■ Key Terms

3½-inch floppy drive *(290)*
34-pin ribbon cable *(290)*
ATAPI-compliant *(302)*
AutoPlay *(309)*
autorun.inf *(309)*
BD-ROM *(306)*
Blu-ray Disc (BD) *(297)*
card reader *(296)*
CD-Digital Audio (CDDA) *(298)*
CD File System (CDFS) *(299)*
CD-recordable (CD-R) *(300)*
CD-rewritable (CDRW) *(300)*
CD-ROM *(298)*
compact disc (CD) *(297)*
CompactFlash (CF) *(294)*
digital versatile disc (DVD) *(297)*
DL DVD *(303)*
Dual Layer DVD-RW *(303)*
DVD-ROM *(304)*
DVD-RW *(305)*
DVD+RW *(305)*
DVD-video *(303)*

Extreme Digital (xD) Picture Card *(296)*
floppy disk *(290)*
floppy drive *(290)*
ISO file *(310)*
ISO-9660 *(299)*
Memory Stick *(295)*
microdrive *(294)*
mini power connector *(292)*
MPEG-2 *(304)*
MPEG-4 *(304)*
multisession drives *(300)*
music CD-R *(303)*
optical disc *(297)*
optical drive *(297)*
pin 1 *(291)*
region code *(313)*
removable media *(288)*
Secure Digital (SD) *(295)*
SmartMedia *(295)*
universal data format (UDF) *(301)*
USB thumb drive *(294)*

■ Key Term Quiz

Use the Key Terms list to complete the sentences that follow. Not all terms will be used.

1. If you want to burn part of a disc and finish burning it at a later time, you need to select a(n) _____ .

2. Drives with BURN-Proof technology were designed to eliminate the problem of

 _____ .

3. The first kind of CD disc was the _____ that is still used for music but is inappropriate for data because it lacks any error correction techniques.

4. While a CD-ROM disc holds about 650 MB of data, a(n) _____ stores from 4.37 GB to 15.9 GB, depending on the number of sides and layers used.

5. Floppy drives use a(n) _____ to connect the floppy drive to the motherboard.

6. The red stripe on a floppy drive cable must be oriented to _____ on the controller.

7. Currently, the most popular flash memory cards are _____.

8. The floppy disk has been replaced by the _____ because of its large capacity and portability.

9. DVD-video uses the _____ standard of video.

10. DVDs use the _____ file structure.

■ Multiple-Choice Quiz

1. You just installed a floppy drive and you notice that the floppy drive LED stays on. What is most likely the problem?

 A. You attached the floppy drive to the wrong connector on the ribbon cable.

 B. You forgot to configure the floppy drive through the CMOS setup.

 C. You did not attach the colored stripe on the ribbon cable to pin 1 at the drive or at the controller.

 D. You forgot to attach the power cable to the floppy drive.

2. If the floppy disk you used last week will not work today in your floppy drive, what should you do first to determine if the problem is the drive or the disk?

 A. Try another disk in the drive or try the disk in another drive.

 B. Open the computer and check the ribbon cable.

 C. Replace the floppy drive.

 D. Check the CMOS settings.

3. What kind of disc must you use in a non-PC CD burner that works with your stereo system?

 A. CDDA

 B. CD-RW

 C. CD-UDF

 D. Music CD-R

4. What is the minimum capacity of a DVD?

 A. 650 MB

 B. 3.47 GB

 C. 4.37 GB

 D. 7.34 GB

5. If you have two floppy disc drives in your system, which one receives the drive letter A:?

 A. The drive jumpered for master

 B. The drive connected to the primary floppy drive controller

 C. The drive in the middle of the floppy cable

 D. The drive at the end of the floppy cable

6. Which type of flash memory card is currently the oldest?

 A. CompactFlash

 B. Memory Stick

 C. Secure Digital

 D. SmartMedia

7. Which device allows your computer to read flash memory cards?

 A. Scanner

 B. Card reader

 C. Floppy drive

 D. ZIP drive

8. AutoPlay reads which of the following files when an optical disc is inserted?

 A. autoplay.inf

 B. autorun.inf

 C. autorun.ini

 D. autorun.exe

9. The contents of an optical disc can be saved as what kind of file?

 A. ISO

 B. ISO-9660

 C. INF

 D. CDDA

10. Both CD and DVD drive speeds are based on multiples of the original CD-ROM drive speed. What is that speed?

 A. 100 KBps

 B. 150 KBps

 C. 100 MBps

 D. 150 MBps

11. You are looking for a CD-RW drive that can write CD-Rs at 48×, read CDs at 52×, and write CD-RWs at 32×. Which of the following answers meets your specifications?

 A. 52×48×32×

 B. 32×48×52×

 C. 48×32×52×

 D. 48×52×32×

12. What settings in the CMOS setup must you change to install an optical drive?

A. Number of heads and cylinders the drive has

B. Whether the drive is installed on the primary or secondary IDE channel

C. Whether the jumpers on the drive are set to master or slave

D. None, because an optical drive is not configured through the CMOS setup

13. What type of DVD can store 15.9 GB of data or more than eight hours of video?

 A. Double-sided, single-layered

 B. Single-sided, single-layered

 C. Single-sided, dual-layered

 D. Double-sided, dual-layered

14. Which of the following kinds of discs is the best choice for performing regular backups?

 A. CD-ROM/XA

 B. CD-Interactive (CD-I)

 C. CD-R

 D. CD-RW

15. While studying abroad, you purchased brand-new Blu-ray Discs produced in China. After returning to the United States, you find they will not work in your Blu-ray Disc player. What is most likely the problem?

 A. The Blu-ray Discs have a C region code.

 B. The Blu-ray Discs have a 6 region code.

 C. The Blu-ray Discs have a B region code.

 D. The Blu-ray Discs have an A region code.

■ Essay Quiz

1. Why do many manufacturers build computers without floppy drives? If you bought a new computer, would you still want a floppy disk drive in it? Write a short essay defending or attacking the floppy drive.

2. You have been tasked to provide removable media for each of the technicians in your department. One tech wants a card reader and SD cards, and another wants a USB thumb drive.

Write a memo outlining the advantages of each technology and make a recommendation.

3. Your friend Jack's hard drive died last week, so he bought a new hard drive and installed it. Now he's trying to install Windows XP, but his computer will not boot to the CD-ROM drive. He's called you for help. What does he need to do to get his computer to recognize and boot to the CD-ROM drive so he can install the OS?

4. Your department is getting ready to replace the old computers, and your boss Mrs. Turner has asked you to investigate what kind of optical drives the new computers should have. Write a memo to your boss listing the device(s) you have selected and justifying your choice(s).

5. Your friend Dudley wants to burn high-definition movies on his desktop system, which currently only has a CD-RW drive. He eventually wants to play back the movies with the highest possible picture quality on his brand-new HDTV. What kind of technology and other considerations would you suggest to Dudley to achieve his goal?

Lab Projects

• Lab Project 11.1

If your lab PC has a floppy disk drive, install a second floppy disk drive. How does your system determine which is drive A: and which is drive B:? Reverse the ribbon cable on the A: drive so the red stripe no longer aligns with pin 1. What happens when you boot the system back up? Can the drive read disks in this condition?

• Lab Project 11.2

Flash media comes in a bunch of different forms. Take a trip to your local computer store—or even to a drugstore that has digital picture processing—and see what sort of media or flash devices they have available. What are some of the advantages or disadvantages of one form factor over another?

• Lab Project 11.3

Use the Internet to check these sites: www.compaq.com, www.dell.com, and www.gateway.com. What kinds of optical drives do these companies offer with their new computers? Do any of the companies offer multiple optical drives? If so, which ones and what devices? What upgrades for optical drives do the companies offer and how expensive are the upgrades? If you were buying a new PC, which optical drive(s) would you want on your computer? Why?

• Lab Project 11.4

Adding a second optical drive to a PC enables you to do some fun things, from making your own music CDs to watching movies. Assuming you want to install a PATA drive, you then need to face some issues. Which controller should you use, primary or secondary? Should both optical drives be on the same controller or on different controllers? Why?

Most techs would install a burner as secondary master and put a read-only drive on the primary as slave, but different drives require different considerations. If you don't plan to copy CD to CD, there's no reason the read-only CD shouldn't be secondary slave. The key is you have to experiment.

Install a second optical drive—preferably a burner—and run it through its paces. Copy files and burn discs to and from the optical and hard drives. Then change the configuration of your drives (such as having both optical drives on the same controller) and run through the testing process again. Do you notice any differences?

Lab Projects

• Lab Project 11.5

Use a map of the world, an atlas, or a globe. See if you can identify the three assigned Blu-ray region code areas. (Hint: The codes are A, B, and C.) Next, see if you can identify the specifically assigned DVD region code areas. (Hint: The codes are 1, 2, 3, 4, 5, and 6.) Next, using Windows XP, Vista, or 7, look under the hardware properties of your DVD or Blu-ray Disc player to identify your region code.

Chapter 12 Input Devices

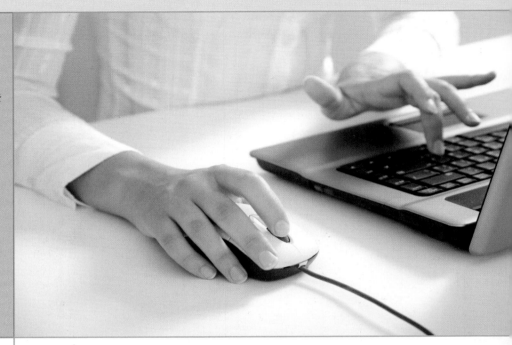

"The Macintosh uses an experimental pointing device called a 'mouse'. There is no evidence that people want to use these things. I don't want one of these new-fangled devices."

—John C. Dvorak, 1984

In this chapter, you will learn how to

- Explain how to support common input/output ports
- Identify certain standard input devices on a PC
- Describe how certain multimedia input devices work on a PC

In Chapter 3, you learned how to recognize and connect a number of common devices and the ports they use. Because these devices and their ports sometimes fail, it is important that you learn how they work and how to recognize them. This chapter reviews some of the major types of input ports and discusses a number of common and not-so-common input devices.

The CompTIA A+ 220-801 exam separates standard input devices and multimedia devices. Standard input devices, such as keyboards and mice, are found on virtually every PC. Multimedia input devices support video and sound functions. This chapter concentrates on both of these categories. You'll learn how to identify and support both the most common and some of the most unusual input devices used in today's PCs.

■ Supporting Common Ports

Whenever you're dealing with a device that isn't playing nicely, you need to remember that you're never dealing with just a device—you're dealing with a device and the port to which it is connected. Before you start troubleshooting the device, you need to take a look at the issues and technologies of some of the more common input/output (I/O) ports and see what needs to be done to keep them running well.

Serial Ports

Finding a new PC with a real serial port is difficult because devices that traditionally used serial ports have for the most part moved on to better interfaces like USB. Physical serial ports may be hard to find on new PC cases, but many devices—in particular, the modems many people still use to access the Internet—continue to use built-in serial ports.

While the physical connection is called a serial port, Windows refers to it as a COM port, usually COM1. Open Device Manager on a system and see if you have an icon for Ports (COM and LPT). If you do, click the plus (+) sign to the left of the icon to open it and see the ports on your system—don't be surprised if you have COM ports on your PC. Even if you don't see any physical serial ports on your PC, the serial ports are there; they're simply built into some other device, probably a modem.

Your PC's expansion bus uses parallel communication: multiple data wires, each one sending one bit of data at a time between your devices. Many I/O devices use serial communication: one wire to send data and another wire to receive data. The job of a **serial port** is to convert data moving between parallel and serial devices. A traditional serial port consists of two pieces: the physical, 9-pin DB connector (see Figure 12.1) and a chip that actually does the conversion between the serial data and parallel data, called the **universal asynchronous receiver/transmitter (UART)** chip. If you want to be completely accurate, the UART *is* the serial port. The port on the back of your PC is nothing more than a standardized connector that enables different serial devices to use the serial port. The UART holds all of the smarts that make the true serial port.

RS-232 is a very old standard that defines everything about serial ports: how fast they communicate, the language they use, even how the connectors should look. The RS-232 standard specifies that two serial devices must talk to each other in 8-bit chunks of data, but it also allows flexibility in other areas, such as speed and error-checking. Serial came out back in the days when devices were configured manually, and the RS-232 standard has never been updated for automatic configuration. Serial ports are a throwback to the old days of computer maintenance

Having trouble finding a PC with serial ports? Try a laptop—almost all laptops come with built-in modems.

 Tech Tip

UARTs and COM Ports

Every UART in a system is assigned a COM port value. An internal modem snaps right into your expansion bus, so every internal modem has a built-in UART. Therefore, even though a modem doesn't have a physical serial connection, it most certainly has a serial port—a built-in one.

● **Figure 12.1**　Serial port

● **Figure 12.2** Serial port settings

Tech Tip

Add-on Serial Ports

If you need a serial port to support some older device but have a motherboard that doesn't have one, don't fret. You can always get a PCI expansion card with classic, 9-pin serial ports.

(though they're still very prevalent in some hardware, such as in high-end routers) and are the last manually configured port you'll find on a PC.

So what type of settings do you need to configure on a serial port? Find a PC with a real serial port (a real 9-pin connector on the back of the PC). Right-click the COM port and choose Properties to see the properties of that port in Device Manager. Open the Port Settings tab and click the Advanced button to see a dialog box that looks like Figure 12.2.

Devices such as modems that have built-in serial ports don't have COM port icons in Device Manager because there's nothing to change. Can you see why? Even though these devices are using a COM port, that port is never going to connect to anything other than the device it's soldered onto, so all of the settings are fixed and unchangeable—thank goodness!

When you are configuring a serial port, you will have a lot of different settings to configure, many of which may or may not make sense. The convenient part about all this is that when you get a new serial device to plug into your serial port, the instructions will tell you what settings to use. Figure 12.3 shows an instruction sheet for a Cisco switch.

USB Ports

You should be familiar with the concept of USB, USB connectors, and USB hubs from the discussion of those concepts in Chapter 3. Here's a more in-depth look at USB and some of the issues involved with using USB devices.

Understanding USB

The cornerstone of a USB connection is the **USB host controller**, an integrated circuit that is usually built into the chipset and controls every USB device that connects to it. Inside the host controller is a **USB root hub**: the part of the host controller that makes the physical connection to the USB ports. Every USB root hub is really just a bus—similar in many ways to an expansion bus. Figure 12.4 shows a diagram of the relationship between the host controller, root hub, and USB ports.

A single host controller can theoretically support up to 127 devices, though real-life circumstances severely limit that. Even if a host adapter supports a certain number of ports, there's no guarantee that the motherboard maker will supply that many ports. To give a common example, a host

Connecting a PC or Terminal to the Console Port

To connect a PC to the console port, use the supplied RJ-45-to-DB-9 adapter cable. To connect the switch console port to a terminal, you need to provide a RJ-45-to-DB-25 female DTE adapter. You can order a kit (part number ACS-DSBUASYN=) containing that adapter from Cisco. For console port and adapter pinout information, see the "Cable and Adapter Specifications" section.

The PC or terminal must support VT100 terminal emulation. The terminal-emulation software—frequently a PC application such as Hyperterminal or Procomm Plus—makes communication between the switch and your PC or terminal possible during the setup program.

Follow these steps to connect the PC or terminal to the switch:

Step 1 Configure the baud rate and character format of the PC or terminal to match these console port default characteristics:

- 9600 baud

- 8 data bits

- 1 stop bit

- No parity

After you have gained access to the switch, you can change the console baud rate through the **Administration > Console Baud Rate** window in the Cluster Management Suite (CMS).

Step 2 Using the supplied RJ-45-to-DB-9 adapter cable, insert the RJ-45 connector into the console port, as shown in Figure 2-1.

Step 3 Attach the DB-9 female DTE adapter of the RJ-45-to-DB-9 adapter cable to a PC, or attach an appropriate adapter to the terminal.

Step 4 Start the terminal-emulation program if you are using a PC or terminal.

Figure 2-1: Connecting to the Console Port

RJ-45
console
port

• **Figure 12.3** Serial port instructions

adapter might support eight ports while the motherboard maker only supplies four adapters.

The most important point to remember about this is that every USB device connected to a single host adapter/root hub *shares* that USB bus with every other device connected to it. The more devices you place on a single host adapter, the more the total USB bus slows down and the more power they use. These issues are two of the biggest headaches that take place with USB devices in the real world.

• **Figure 12.4** Host controller, root hub, and USB ports

USB devices, like any electrical device, need power to run, but not all take care of their own power needs. A powered USB device comes with its own electrical cord that is usually connected in turn to an AC adapter. *Bus-powered* USB devices take power from the USB bus itself; they don't bring

any AC or DC power with them. When too many bus-powered devices take too much power from the USB bus, bad things happen—some devices won't work; other devices will lock up. You'll also often get a simple message from Windows saying that the hub power has been exceeded, and it just won't work.

USB Standards and Compatibility

The USB standard has gone through several revisions, but you'll run into only three different versions in the real world:

- USB 1.1 was the first widely adopted standard and defined two speeds: **Low-Speed USB**, running at a maximum of 1.5 Mbps (plenty for keyboards and mice), and **Full-Speed USB**, running at up to 12 Mbps.

- The USB 2.0 standard introduced **Hi-Speed USB** running at a whopping 480 Mbps.

- USB 3.0 is capable of speeds of up to 5 Gbps—ten times faster than USB 2.0! USB 3.0 is commonly referred to as **SuperSpeed USB**.

If you think all of those names and numbers are confusing, you're right. Table 12.1 provides a quick reference to help you sort it all out.

Table 12.1	USB Standards	
Name	**Standard**	**Maximum Speed**
Low-Speed USB	USB 1.1	1.5 Mbps
Full-Speed USB	USB 1.1	12 Mbps
Hi-Speed USB	USB 2.0	480 Mbps
SuperSpeed USB	USB 3.0	5 Gbps

Hi-Speed USB is fully backward compatible with USB 1.1 devices, while USB 3.0 is backward compatible with USB 2.0 devices. Those old devices won't run any faster than they used to, however. To take advantage of the fastest USB speeds, you must connect Hi-Speed USB devices to Hi-Speed USB ports by using Hi-Speed USB cables (or connect SuperSpeed USB devices to SuperSpeed USB ports with SuperSpeed USB cables). Although backward compatibility at least enables you to use the newer USB device with an older port, a quick bit of math tells you how much time you're sacrificing when you're transferring a 2-GB file at 480 Mbps instead of 5 Gbps!

Most people want to take advantage of these amazing speeds, but what do you do if your motherboard doesn't have built-in Hi-Speed or SuperSpeed USB ports? One option is to add a USB 2.0 or USB 3.0 adapter card like the one shown in Figure 12.5.

Motherboards capable of both USB 1.1 and USB 2.0 usually share the available USB ports (see Figure 12.6). For every USB port on your computer, plugging in a Low-Speed or Full-Speed device uses the USB 1.1 host controller, and plugging in a Hi-Speed device uses the USB 2.0 host controller.

> Each standard defines more than just the speed. Because they were incorporated into the newer standard, many Low-Speed and Full-Speed USB devices are also USB 2.0 devices.

> The USB Implementers Forum (USB-IF) does not officially use "Low-Speed" and "Full-Speed" to describe 1.5-Mbps and 12-Mbps devices, calling both of them simply "USB." On the CompTIA A+ 220-801 exam, though, you'll see the marketplace-standard nomenclature used here.

• **Figure 12.5** USB adapter card

USB 3.0, on the other hand, is different enough from USB 2.0 that it uses separate and clearly marked ports. The USB 3.0 standard suggests that these ports be colored blue to differentiate them. You can still plug older USB devices into a USB 3.0 port, but they will run at the slower speeds. The only ports that work at 5 Gbps are the blue USB 3.0 ports (see Figure 12.7).

• **Figure 12.6** Shared USB ports

USB Cables and Connectors

You learned about USB connectors in Chapter 3, but here's a quick refresher. USB connectors and ports come in multiple sizes: A, B, mini-A, mini-B, micro-A, and micro-B. USB A ports and connectors are for interfacing with the PC. Most peripherals use B, mini-B, or micro-B connectors and ports. Micro connections are especially popular on smartphones.

Almost any USB device can use any USB standard's cable, though you won't always get the best possible speeds. USB 1.1 and USB 2.0 cables look and work the same. Your connection speed will change primarily based on the quality of the cable.

There is one big exception to this cross-compatibility, however: to achieve SuperSpeed speeds with USB 3.0, you'll need a USB 3.0 cable (see Figure 12.8). Because the USB 3.0 B connector is larger than other B connectors, a USB 3.0 cable will only work with USB 3.0 devices.

Cable length is an important limitation to keep in mind with USB. USB 1.1 and USB 2.0 specifications allow for a maximum cable length of 5 meters, although you may add a powered USB hub every 5 meters to extend this distance. Although most USB devices never get near this maximum, some

On USB 1.1 and 2.0 cables, the A and B ports and connectors use four pins, while the rest use five pins. USB 3.0 A and B ports and connectors use nine pins. A larger, 11-pin USB 3.0 B connector that can supply extra power to a device also exists.

In general, your connection will operate at the speed of the slowest device involved. If you have a USB 2.0 device connected to a USB 3.0 port on your PC, it will operate at USB 2.0 speeds.

• **Figure 12.7** USB 3.0 ports

• **Figure 12.8** USB 3.0 cable

• Figure 12.9 USB cable

Try This!

What Speed Is Your USB?

Open Device Manager and locate two or three controllers under the Universal Serial Bus icon. The Standard Enhanced Host Controller is the Hi-Speed controller. The Standard OpenHCD Host Controller is the Low- and Full-Speed controller. You might also have a third controller named the Extensible Host Controller Interface (xHCI). This controller, as you might have guessed, is for USB 3.0 SuperSpeed connections.

devices, such as digital cameras, can come with cables at or near the maximum 5-meter cable length. The USB 3.0 standard doesn't define a maximum cable length, but to reach the fastest speeds possible, you shouldn't use a cable longer than 3 meters. Because USB is a two-way (bi-directional) connection, as the cable grows longer, even a standard, well-shielded, 20-gauge, twisted-pair USB cable begins to suffer from electrical interference. To avoid these problems, I stick to cables that are no more than about 2 meters long.

If you really want to play it safe, spend a few extra dollars and get a high-quality USB cable like the one shown in Figure 12.9. These cables come with extra shielding and improved electrical performance to make sure your USB data gets from the device to your computer safely.

USB Hubs

Each USB host controller supports up to 127 USB devices, but as mentioned earlier, most motherboard makers provide only six to eight real USB ports. So what do you do when you need to add more USB devices than the motherboard provides ports? You can add more host controllers (in the form of internal cards), or you can use a USB hub. A **USB hub** is a device that extends a single USB connection to two or more USB ports, almost always directly from one of the USB ports connected to the root hub. Figure 12.10 shows a typical USB hub. USB hubs are sometime embedded into peripherals. The keyboard in Figure 12.11 comes with a built-in USB hub—very handy!

USB hubs are one of those parts of a PC that tend not to work nearly as well in the real world as they do on paper. (Sorry, USB folks, but it's true!) USB hubs have a speed just like any other USB device; for example, the hub in the keyboard in Figure 12.11 runs at Full-Speed. This becomes a problem when someone decides to insert a Hi-Speed USB device into one of those

• Figure 12.10 USB hub

• Figure 12.11 USB keyboard with built-in hub

ports, as it forces the Hi-Speed device to crawl along at only 12 Mbps. Windows is nice enough to warn you of this problem with a bubble over the system tray like the one shown in Figure 12.12.

Hubs also come in powered and bus-powered versions. If you choose to use a general-purpose USB hub like the one shown in Figure 12.10, try to find a powered one, as too many devices on a single USB root hub will draw too much power and create problems.

• **Figure 12.12** Windows XP speed warning

USB Configuration

The biggest troubleshooting challenge you encounter with USB is a direct result of its widespread adoption and ease of use. Pretty much every modern PC comes with multiple USB ports, and anyone can easily pick up a cool new USB device at the local computer store. The problems arise when all of this USB installation activity gets out of control, with too many devices using the wrong types of ports or pulling too much power. Happily, by following a few easy steps, you can avoid or eliminate these issues.

The first and often-ignored rule of USB installation is this: Always install the device driver for a new USB device *before* you plug it into the USB port. Once you've installed the device driver and you know the ports are active (running properly in Device Manager), feel free to plug in the new device and hot-swap to your heart's content. USB device installation really is a breeze as long as you follow this rule!

Windows includes a large number of built-in drivers for USB devices. You can count on Windows to recognize keyboards, mice, and other basic devices with their built-in drivers. Just be aware that if your new mouse or keyboard has some extra buttons, the default USB drivers will probably not support them. To be sure I'm not missing any added functionality, I always install the driver that comes with the device or an updated one downloaded from the manufacturer's Web site.

When you're looking to add a new USB device to a system, first make sure your machine has a USB port that supports the speed you need for the USB device. On more modern PCs, this is likely to be a nonissue. Even then, if you start adding hubs and such, you can end up with devices that either won't run at all or, worse yet, exhibit strange behaviors.

The last and toughest issue is power. A mismatch between available and required power for USB devices can result in nonfunctioning or malfunctioning USB devices. If you're pulling too much power, you must take devices off that root hub until the error goes away. Buy an add-in USB hub card if you need to use more devices than your current USB hub supports.

To check the USB power usage in Windows, open Device Manager and locate any USB hub under the Universal Serial Bus Controller icon. Right-click the hub and select Properties, and then select the Power tab. This shows you the current use for each of the devices connected to that root hub (see Figure 12.13).

Most root hubs provide 500 mA per port—more than enough for any USB device. Most power problems take place when you start adding hubs, especially bus-powered hubs, and then you add too many devices to them. Figure 12.14 shows the Power tab for a bus-powered hub; note that it provides a maximum of 100 mA per port.

There are exceptions to the "install the driver first" rule. USB thumb drives, for example, don't need extra drivers at all. Just plug them in and Windows picks them up. (Technically speaking, though, that means the drivers came *preinstalled* with the operating system!)

Tech Tip

Refresh the Tab
The Power tab of the USB Root Hub Properties dialog box shows you the power usage only for a given moment, so to ensure you keep getting accurate readings, you must click the Refresh button to update its display. Make sure your USB device works, and then refresh to see the maximum power used.

• Figure 12.13 USB hub Power tab

• Figure 12.14 General purpose bus-powered hub

• Figure 12.15 Power Management tab

There's one more problem with USB power: sometimes USB devices go to sleep and don't wake up. Actually, the system is telling them to sleep to save power. You can suspect this problem if you try to access a USB device that was working earlier but that suddenly no longer appears in Device Manager. To fix this, head back in to Device Manager to inspect the hub's Properties, but this time open the Power Management tab and uncheck the *Allow the computer to turn off this device to save power* checkbox, as shown in Figure 12.15.

FireWire Ports

At first glance, **FireWire**, also known as IEEE 1394, looks and acts much like USB. FireWire has all of the features of USB, but it uses different connectors and is actually the older of the two technologies. For years, FireWire had the upper hand when it came to moving data quickly to and from external devices. The onset of Hi-Speed and SuperSpeed USB, along with the introduction of eSATA for external hard drives, changed that, and FireWire has lost ground to USB in many areas.

Understanding FireWire

FireWire has three distinct types of connects, all of which are becoming increasingly uncommon on PCs. The first is a 6-pin *powered* connector, the type you see on some desktop PCs. Like USB, a FireWire port is capable of

Mike Meyers' CompTIA A+ Guide to 801: Managing and Troubleshooting PCs

providing power to a device. The second type of connector is a 4-pin connector, which you see on portable computers and such FireWire devices as cameras. This type of connector does not provide power to a device, so you need to find another method of powering the external device. The third connector is an uncommon 9-pin powered connector for higher-speed devices.

FireWire comes in two speeds: **IEEE 1394a**, which runs at 400 Mbps, and **IEEE 1394b**, which runs at 800 Mbps. FireWire devices can also take advantage of bus mastering, enabling two FireWire devices—such as a digital video camera and an external FireWire hard drive—to communicate directly with each other. When it comes to raw speed, FireWire 800—that would be 1394b, naturally—is faster than Hi-Speed USB but not SuperSpeed USB.

FireWire does have differences from USB other than just speed and a different-looking connector. First, a USB device must connect directly to a hub, but a FireWire device may use either a hub or daisy chaining. Figure 12.16 shows the difference between hubbed connections and daisy chaining. Second, FireWire supports a maximum of 63 devices, compared to USB's 127. Third, each cable in a FireWire 400 daisy chain has a maximum length of 4.5 meters, as opposed to USB's 5 meters.

• **Figure 12.16** Hubbed versus daisy chain connections

Configuring FireWire

In a Windows environment, FireWire is subject to many of the same issues as USB, such as the need to preinstall drivers, verify that onboard devices are active, and so on. But none of these issues are nearly as crucial with a FireWire connection. For example, as with USB, you really should install a FireWire device driver before attaching the device, but given that 95 percent of the FireWire devices used in PCs are either external hard drives or digital video connections, the preinstalled Windows drivers almost always work perfectly. FireWire devices do use much more power than USB devices, but the FireWire controllers are designed to handle higher voltages, and they'll warn you on the rare chance that your FireWire devices pull too much power.

Like USB and serial ports (or any other ports, for that matter), you can always add more FireWire ports using a PCI expansion card. Standard installation procedures apply.

General Port Issues

No matter what type of port you use, if it's not working, you should always check out a few issues. First of all, make sure you can tell a port problem from a device problem. Your best bet here is to try a second "known good"

device in the same port to see if that device works. If it does *not*, you can assume the port is the problem. It's not a bad idea to reverse this and plug the device into a known good port.

If you're pretty sure the port's not working, you can check three things: First, make sure the port is turned on. Almost any I/O port on a motherboard can be turned off in CMOS. Reboot the system and find the device and see if the port's been turned off. You can also use Windows Device Manager to disable most ports. Figure 12.17 shows a disabled parallel port in Device Manager—you'll see a small down-pointing arrow in Windows Vista/7 or a red *X* over the device icon in Windows XP. To turn the port back on, right-click the device's icon and choose Enable.

Being able to turn off a port in Device Manager points to another not-so-obvious fact: ports need drivers just as devices need drivers. Windows has excellent built-in drivers for all common ports, so if you fail to see a port in Device Manager (and you know the port is turned on in CMOS), you can bet the port itself has a physical problem.

Because ports have connectors inserted and removed from them repeatedly, eventually they can physically break. Figure 12.18 shows the back of a USB port that's been pushed on too hard for too long and has physically separated from the motherboard. Unless you're an expert solderer, you either must stop using those ports or replace the entire motherboard.

Many ports (or the plugs that fit into those ports) use tiny pins or relatively delicate metal casings that are susceptible to damage. PS/2 plugs are some of the worst for bent pins or misshaped casings. Figure 12.19 shows

A "known good" device is simply a device that you know is in good working order. All techs count heavily on the use of known good devices to check other devices. For example, if you think a PC has a bad keyboard, borrow one from the PC next door and see if that keyboard works on the broken machine.

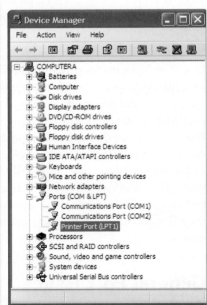

• **Figure 12.17** Disabled parallel port in Device Manager in both Vista and XP

what happened to a PS/2 plug when I was in a hurry and thought that force was an alternative to lining up the plug properly. Replacement plugs are available—but again, unless you're excellent at soldering, they're not a viable alternative. Still, if you're patient, you might be able to save the plug. Using needle-nose pliers and a pair of scissors, I was able to reshape the plug so that it once again fit in the PS/2 port.

Standard Input Devices

So what is a "standard" input device? I'm hoping you immediately thought of the mouse and the keyboard, two of the most basic, necessary, and abused input devices on a computer. But those aren't the only things the CompTIA A+ 220-801 exam considers as standard. The full list of standard input devices includes:

- Keyboards
- Mice
- Scanners
- Biometric devices
- Bar code readers
- Touch screens
- KVM switches
- Gamepads and joysticks
- Digitizers

You probably don't use most of these "standard" devices every day, so I'll cover each of them in detail.

• **Figure 12.18** Broken USB port

• **Figure 12.19** Badly bent PS/2 plug

Keyboards

Keyboards are both the oldest and still the primary way you input data into a PC. Windows comes with perfectly good drivers for any keyboard, although some fancier keyboards may come with specialized keys that require a special driver be installed to operate properly. About the only issue that might affect keyboard installation is if you're using a USB keyboard: make sure that the USB Keyboard Support option is enabled in CMOS (see Figure 12.20). Other than that, any keyboard installation issue you're likely to encounter is covered in the "Supporting Common Ports" sections at the beginning of this chapter.

There's not much to do to configure a standard keyboard. The only configuration tool you might need is the Keyboard Control Panel applet. This tool enables you to change the repeat delay (the amount of time you must hold down a key before the keyboard starts repeating the character), the repeat rate (how quickly the character is repeated after the repeat delay), and the default cursor blink rate. Figure 12.21 shows the default Windows Keyboard Properties window—some keyboard makers provide drivers that add extra tabs.

> **Tech Tip**
>
> **Wireless Keyboards and Batteries**
> *Wireless keyboards are a wonderful convenience because they remove the cable between you and the PC, but make sure you keep a complete set of spare batteries around.*

```
OnChip USB              V1.1+2.0
 - USB Keyboard Support    Enabled
 - USB Mouse Support       Enabled
```

• **Figure 12.20** CMOS USB Keyboard Support option

• Figure 12.21 Keyboard Control Panel applet

Keyboards might be easy to install, but they do fail occasionally. Given their location—right in front of you—the three issues that cause the most keyboard problems stem from spills, physical damage, and dirt.

Spilling a soda onto your keyboard can make for a really bad day. If you're quick and unplug the keyboard from the PC before the liquid hits the electrical components, you might be able to save the keyboard. It'll take some cleaning, though (keep reading for cleaning tips). More often than not, you'll get a sticky, ill-performing keyboard that is not worth the hassle—just replace it!

Other common physical damage comes from dropping objects onto the keyboard, such as a heavy book (like the one in your hands). This can have bad results! Most keyboards are pretty resilient, though, and can bounce back from the hit.

Clean dirt and grime off the keys by using a cloth dampened with a little water, or if the water alone doesn't do the job, use a bit of isopropyl alcohol on a cloth (see Figure 12.22).

Dirty keys might be unsightly, but dirt under the keys might cause the keyboard to stop working completely. When your keys start to stick, grab a bottle of compressed air and shoot some air under the keys. Do this outside or over a trash can—you'll be amazed how much junk gets caught under the keys! If you really mess up a keyboard by dumping a chocolate milkshake on the keys, you're probably going to need to dismantle the keyboard to clean it. This is pretty easy as long as you keep track of where all of the parts go. Keyboards are made of layers of plastic that create the electrical connections when you press a key. Unscrew the keyboard (keep track of the screws!) and gently peel away the plastic layers, using a damp cloth to clean each layer (see Figure 12.23). Allow the sheets to dry and then reassemble the keyboard.

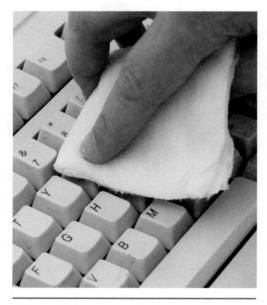

• Figure 12.22 Cleaning keys

• Figure 12.23 Serious keyboard surgery

Mike Meyers' CompTIA A+ Guide to 801: Managing and Troubleshooting PCs

Sometimes dirt or foreign objects get under individual keys, requiring you to remove the key to get to the dirt or object. Removing individual keys from a keyboard is risky business, because keyboards are set up in many different ways. Most manufacturers use a process in which keys are placed on a single plastic post. In that case, you may use a screwdriver or other flat tool to safely pop off the key (see Figure 12.24). Be careful! You'll need to use a good amount of force and the key will fly across the room. Other keyboard makers (mainly on laptops) use tiny plastic pins shaped like scissors. In that case, beware—if you try prying one of these off, you'll permanently break the key!

The bottom line when it comes to stuck keys is that the keyboard's probably useless with the stuck key, so you might as well try to clean it. Worse comes to worst, you can always buy another keyboard.

• **Figure 12.24** Prying off a key

Mice

Have you ever tried to use Windows without a mouse? It's not fun, but it can be done. All techs eventually learn the Windows navigation hot keys for those times when mice fail, but all in all we do love our mice. Like keyboards, Windows comes with excellent drivers for all standard mice; the exception you're likely to encounter is the more advanced mice that come with extra buttons.

You can adjust mouse settings through the Mouse Control Panel applet. Figure 12.25 shows the Windows 7 version.

All of the settings you need for adjusting a mouse can be found in the Mouse Properties window. In particular, make sure to adjust the mouse speed and double-click speed to fit your preferences.

• **Figure 12.25** Mouse Control Panel applet

● **Figure 12.26** Removing the collar on a ball mouse

● **Figure 12.27** Cleaning the rollers on a ball mouse

Two types of mouse technologies used to battle it out on the market: ball mice and optical mice. These days you'll only see the latter. **Ball mice** use a small round ball, while **optical mice** use LED or lasers and a camera to track their movements and thus move the mouse pointer across the screen. The problem with ball mice is that the ball inside the mouse picks up dirt over time and deposits the dirt on internal rollers that contact the ball. Dirt builds up to the point that the mouse stops responding smoothly. If you are struggling with your ball mouse to point at objects on your screen, you need to clean the mouse. Few mice manufacturers still make ball mice, as they tend to require far more maintenance than optical mice.

To access the internals of a ball mouse, turn it over and remove the protective cover over the mouse ball. The process of removing the cover varies, but it usually involves rotating the collar that surrounds the ball until the collar pops out (see Figure 12.26). Be careful—without the collar, the mouse ball will drop out the instant you turn the mouse upright.

Use any nonmetallic tool to scrape the dirt from the roller without scratching or gouging the device. Although you could use a commercial "mouse cleaning kit," I find that a fingernail or a pencil eraser cleans the rollers quite nicely and at much less expense (see Figure 12.27). Clean a ball mouse in this way at least every two or three months.

Optical mice require little maintenance and almost never need cleaning, as the optics that make them work are never in contact with the grimy outside world. On the rare occasion where an optical mouse begins to act erratically, try using a cloth or damp cotton swab to clean out any bits of dirt that may be blocking the optics (see Figure 12.28).

Scanners

You can use a scanner to make digital copies of existing paper photos, documents, drawings, and more. Better scanners give you the

● **Figure 12.28** Cleaning an optical mouse

option of copying directly from a photographic negative or slide, providing images of stunning visual quality—assuming the original photo was halfway decent, of course! In this section, you'll look at how scanners work and then turn to what you need to know to select the correct scanner for you or your clients.

How Scanners Work

All **flatbed scanners**, the most common variety of scanner, work the same way. You place a photo or other object face down on the glass, close the lid, and then use software to initiate the scan. The scanner runs a bright light along the length of the glass tray once or more to capture the image. Figure 12.29 shows an open scanner.

The scanning software that controls the hardware can be manifested in a variety of ways. Nearly every manufacturer has some sort of drivers and other software to create an interface between your computer and the scanner. When you push the front button on the Epson Perfection scanner in Figure 12.30, for example, the Epson software opens the Photoshop program as well as its own interface.

You can also open your favorite image-editing software first and choose to acquire a file from a scanner. Figure 12.31 shows the process of acquiring an image from a scanner in the popular free image-editing software, GNU Image Manipulation Program (otherwise known

• **Figure 12.29** Scanner open with photograph face down

• **Figure 12.30** Epson software with Photoshop open in the background

• **Figure 12.31** Acquiring an image in GNU Image Manipulation Program

Tech Tip

Optical Character Recognition

In addition to loading pictures into your computer, many scanners offer a feature called optical character recognition (OCR), a way to scan a document and have the computer turn the picture into text that you can manipulate by using a word processing program. Many scanners come with OCR software, such as ABBYY FineReader.

as GIMP). As in most such software, you choose File | Create and then select Scanner. In this case, the scanner uses the traditional TWAIN drivers. **TWAIN** stands for *Technology Without an Interesting Name*—I'm not making this up!—and has been the default driver type for scanners for a long time.

At this point, the drivers and other software controlling the scanner pop up, providing an interface with the scanner (as shown in Figure 12.31). Here you can set the resolution of the image as well as many other options.

How to Choose a Scanner

You must consider five primary variables when choosing a scanner: resolution, color depth, grayscale depth, connection, and scan speed. You can and will adjust the first three during the scanning process, although probably only down from their maximum. You need to decide on the connection before you buy. The scan speed relates to all four of the other variables, and the maximum speed is hard-coded into the scanner.

Configurable Variables Scanners convert the scanned image into a grid of dots. The maximum number of dots determines how well you can capture an image and how the image will look when scaled up in size. Most folks use the term *resolution* to define the grid size. As you might imagine, the higher the resolution, the better the scanned image will look and scale.

Older scanners can create images of only 600 × 600 dots per inch (dpi), while newer models commonly achieve four times that density, and high-end machines do much more. Manufacturers cite *two* sets of numbers for a scanner's resolution: the resolution it achieves mechanically—called the **optical resolution**—and the enhanced resolution it can achieve with assistance from some onboard software.

The enhanced resolution numbers are useless. I recommend at least 2400 × 2400 dpi optical resolution or better, although you can get by with a lower resolution for purely Web-destined images.

The **color depth** of a scan defines the number of bits of information the scanner can use to describe each individual dot. This number determines color, shade, hue, and so forth, so a higher number makes a dramatic difference in your picture quality. With binary numbers, each extra bit of information *doubles* the quality. An 8-bit scan, for example, can save up to 256 color variations per dot. A 16-bit scan, in contrast, can save up to 65,536 variations, not the 512 that you might expect!

Modern scanners come in 24-bit, 36-bit, and 48-bit variations. These days, 48-bit scanners are common enough that you shouldn't have to settle for less, even on a budget. Figures 12.32, 12.33, and 12.34 show pretty clearly the difference resolution makes when scanning.

Scanners differ a lot in **grayscale depth**, a number that defines how many shades of gray the scanner can save per dot. This matters if you work with black-and-white images in any significant way, because grayscale depth is usually a much lower number than color depth. Current consumer-level scanners come in 8-bit, 12-bit, and 16-bit grayscale varieties. I recommend 16-bit or better.

Connection Almost all modern scanners plug into the USB port on your PC, although some high-end models offer FireWire as well. Older scanners come in SCSI and parallel varieties.

Scanning Speed Scanners have a maximum scanning speed defined by the manufacturer. The time required to complete a scan is also affected by the parameters you set; the time increases as you increase the amount of detail captured. A typical low-end scanner, for example, takes upwards of 30 seconds to scan a 4 × 6 photo at 300 dpi. A faster scanner, in contrast, can crank out the same scan in 10 seconds.

Raise the resolution of the scan to 600 dpi at 48-bit resolution, and that faster scanner can take a full minute to complete the scan. Adjust your scanning settings to optimize for your project. Don't always go for the highest possible scan if you don't need the resolution.

Connections matter as well. A good Hi-Speed USB scanner can scan an 8 × 10 image in about 12 seconds at 300 dpi. I made the mistake of taking the scanner to a friend's house to scan some of her jewelry, but she had only a Full-Speed USB port. I plugged the scanner into her PC and it took about 45 seconds to scan each 8 × 10 image. We were up all night finishing the project!

Installation and Scanning Tips

Most USB and FireWire devices require you to install the software drivers before you plug in the device for the first time. I have run into exceptions,

• **Figure 12.32** Earring scanned at 72 dpi and 24-bit color

• **Figure 12.33** Same earring, scanned at 300 dpi and 24-bit color

• **Figure 12.34** Same earring, scanned at 1200 dpi and 24-bit color

As of early 2012, USB 3.0 scanners hadn't really caught on. Scanners are now limited by their own scanning speed, not their connection to the PC.

though, so I strongly suggest you read the scanner's documentation before you install.

As a general rule, you should obtain the highest quality scan you can manage, and then play with the size and image quality when it's time to include it in a Web site or an e-mail. The amount of RAM in your system—and to a lesser extent, the processor speed—dictates how big a file you can handle.

If you travel a lot, you'll want to make sure to use the locking mechanism for the scanner light assembly. Just be sure to unlock before you try to use it or you'll get a light that's stuck in one position. That won't make for very good scans!

Biometric Devices

If you look up *biometrics* on the popular Wikipedia Web site, you'll get the following definition: "Biometric identifiers are the distinctive, measurable characteristics used to label and describe individuals." The field of biometrics also encompasses a number of security devices, such as door locks and security cameras, that don't really fit into the world of PCs. This section concentrates on the types of biometrics that you can actually buy and use on your PC. Within the realm of computers, biometrics includes a huge number of technologies, from thumb drives that read fingerprints to software that does voice recognition.

PCs use biometrics for security. **Biometric devices** scan and remember unique aspects of various body parts such as your retina, iris, head image, or fingerprint, using some form of sensing device such as a retinal scanner. This information is used as a key to prevent unauthorized people from accessing whatever the biometric device is securing. Most biometric devices currently used in PCs secure only themselves. The USB thumb drive in Figure 12.35 has a tiny fingerprint scanner. You slide your finger (any finger you choose) over the drive to unlock the contents of the thumb drive.

• **Figure 12.35** USB thumb drive with fingerprint scanner (photo courtesy of Lexar Media, Inc.)

Less common are biometric security devices that secure entire computers. The Microsoft fingerprint scanner is a USB device that replaces standard user name and password security. Figure 12.36 shows the scanner built into a keyboard. When a program or Web site asks for a user name and password, you simply press your finger against the fingerprint scanner. It confirms your identity (assuming your fingerprint matches), and then special software that comes with the scanner supplies the program or Web site with your stored user name and password.

Biometric devices are also used for recognition. Recognition is different from security in that the biometric device doesn't care who you are; it just wants to know what you're doing. The best example of this is voice recognition. Voice recognition programs convert human voice input into commands or text. Voice recognition for PCs has been around for some time. Although it has never achieved enough accuracy to replace a keyboard completely, voice recognition is common in devices that have a limited number of commands to

• **Figure 12.36** Microsoft fingerprint scanner on a keyboard

interpret, such as smartphones. If you speak the words "Call Mike Meyers" into your smartphone, your phone knows what to do—at least, *my* phone does!

No matter what biometric device you use, you use the same steps to make it work:

1. Install the device.

2. Register your identity with the device by sticking your eye, finger, or other unique body part (Why are you snickering?) into or onto the device so it can scan you.

3. Configure its software to tell the device what to do when it recognizes your scanned identity.

Bar Code Readers

Bar code readers are designed to read standard **Universal Product Code (UPC)** bar codes (see Figure 12.37). We read bar codes for only one reason—to track inventory. Bar code readers enable easy updating of inventory databases stored on PCs.

• Figure 12.37 Typical UPC code

Two types of bar code readers are commonly found with PCs: pen scanners and hand scanners. Pen scanners look like an ink pen and must be swiped across the bar code (see Figure 12.38). Hand scanners are held in front of the UPC code while a button is pressed to scan. All bar code readers emit a tone to let you know the scan was successful.

Older bar code readers used serial ports, but all of the newer readers use either PS/2 or USB ports. No configuration is usually necessary, other than making sure that the particular bar code reader works with whatever database/point of sale software you use. When in doubt, most people find the PS/2-style bar code readers work best, as they simply act like a keyboard. You plug the reader into your keyboard port and then plug your keyboard into the reader. Then all you need is software that accepts keyboard input (and what one doesn't!), and it will work.

• Figure 12.38 Pen scanner (photo courtesy of Wasp Barcode Technologies)

Touch Screens

A **touch screen** is a monitor with some type of sensing device across its face that detects the location and duration of contact, usually by a finger or stylus. All touch screens then supply this contact information to the PC as though it were a click event from a mouse. Touch screens are used in situations for which conventional mouse/keyboard input is either impossible or impractical. Here are a few places you'll see touch screens at work:

- Smartphones
- Information kiosks
- Point of sale systems
- Tablets

Touch screens can be separated into two groups: built-in screens like the ones in smartphones, and standalone touch screen monitors like those used in many point of sale systems. From a technician's standpoint, you can think of a standalone touch screen as a monitor with a built-in mouse. All touch screens have a separate USB or PS/2 port for the "mouse" part of the device, along with drivers you install just as you would for any USB mouse.

Windows Vista and Windows 7 include Control Panel applets for configuring the touch screens on Tablet PCs. Windows Vista comes with Pen and Input Devices and Tablet PC Settings. Windows 7 combines the tools into the Tablet PC Settings applet. (Note that the Tablet PC Settings applet will only appear on Windows 7 Tablet PCs—you won't find it on laptops or desktops.) You can use these applets to adjust how you interact with the touch screen just as you would with the Mouse or Keyboard applets. The applets enable you to configure what happens when you tap, double-tap, use gestures called "flicks," and more.

KVM Switches

A **keyboard, video, mouse (KVM) switch** is a hardware device that most commonly enables multiple computers to be viewed and controlled by a single mouse, keyboard, and screen. Some KVMs reverse that capability, enabling a single computer to be controlled by multiple keyboards, mice, or other devices. KVMs are especially useful in data centers where multiple servers are rack mounted, space is limited, and power is a concern. An administrator can use a single KVM to control multiple server systems from a single keyboard, mouse, and monitor.

There are many brands and types of KVM switches. Some enable you to connect to only two systems, and some support hundreds. Some even come with audio output jacks to support speakers. Typical KVMs come with two or more sets of wires that are used for input devices such as PS/2 and/or USB mice and video output (see Figure 12.39).

To use a KVM, you simply connect a keyboard, mouse, and monitor to the KVM and then connect the KVM to the desired computers. Once connected and properly configured, assigned keyboard hotkeys—a combination of keys typically assigned by the KVM manufacturer—enable you to toggle between the computers connected to the KVM. In most cases, you simply tap the SCROLL LOCK key twice to switch between sessions.

Installing a KVM is not difficult; the most important point to remember is to connect the individual sets of cables between the KVM ports and each computer one at a time, keeping track of which keyboard, mouse, and video cable go to which computers. (I highly recommend labeling and using twist or zip ties.)

If you get the connections wrong, the KVM won't function as desired. If you connect a mouse and keyboard wires to the correct KVM port, for example, but attach the same computer's video cable to a different port on the KVM, you won't get the correct video when you try to switch to that computer.

● **Figure 12.39** A typical KVM switch

The same holds true for the mouse and keyboard cables. Don't cross the cables!

Gamepads and Joysticks

Whether you're racing through tight turns at top speeds or flying a state-of-the-art jet fighter, having the right controller for the job is important for an enjoyable gaming experience. Two peripherals are commonly used for controlling PC games: joysticks and gamepads.

Over the past decade, flight simulator programs have declined in popularity, and so have joysticks (see Figure 12.40). Once a required component of a gamer's arsenal, you only need joysticks now if you are a *serious* flight simulator fan. Most modern PC games are controlled by mouse and keyboard.

Some PC games, especially those that were designed to played on consoles like the Microsoft Xbox 360 or Sony PlayStation 3, are best enjoyed when using a gamepad. A *gamepad* looks more like your standard video game controller, usually covered in an array of buttons and triggers (see Figure 12.41).

Joysticks and gamepads have used plenty of connectors over the years, including the eponymous joystick connector. These days, they all connect to your PC via USB. Depending on the complexity of the controller, you may need to install drivers to get a joystick or gamepad working. Simpler controllers, however, can probably get by using the default gamepad drivers included in Windows.

You'll need to configure your joystick or gamepad to make sure all the buttons and controls work properly. In Windows XP and Vista, open the Game Controllers Control Panel applet. In Windows 7, open the Start menu and select Devices and Printers. Right-click on the controller and select *Game controller settings*. Select your device from the list of controllers and click Properties. Depending on your gamepad or joystick, you'll be able

Older KVMs are said to be *passive*, meaning they don't continuously communicate with all connected systems. This can cause problems if the connected systems automatically reboot after a power surge or loss. Modern-day active KVMs resolve this issue through *peripheral emulation*, meaning they communicate with and monitor all systems connected to the KVM.

• **Figure 12.40** A joystick

• **Figure 12.41** A gamepad

to configure the buttons, sticks, triggers, and more (see Figure 12.42). You can calibrate the analog sticks so they accurately register your movements. You can even adjust the amount of vibration used by the controller's force feedback (if available).

Once you've set up your controller, you should be ready to take to the skies, or the streets, or wherever else you go to game.

Digitizers

PCs and Macs have quickly become the most powerful and flexible tools available for visual artists. Given the number of applications dedicated to producing various visual styles, including painting, sketching, animation, and more, digital art stands toe-to-toe with its more traditional counterpart. It's only reasonable that a category of hardware would appear to help users take advantage of these tools.

A **digitizer** (otherwise known as a *pen tablet*) enables users to paint, ink, pencil, or otherwise draw on a computer (see Figure 12.43). Now, don't get carried away and start taking watercolors to your monitor. The digitizer receives input using a special surface. When a user presses against the surface, usually using a stylus, the surface transforms (or digitizes) the analog movements into digital information. The drawing application receives the information from the digitizer and

• **Figure 12.42** Game controller properties

You might also need to configure your controller from within the game you want to play. Most games are set to use keyboard and mouse controls by default. You'll need to play around with the settings to enable your game controller.

Not all digitizers are designed for digital art. Some are used for handwriting, technical drawings, writing complex characters, or even as a replacement mouse.

• **Figure 12.43** A type of digitizer known as the Wacom pen tablet

turns it into an image onscreen (see Figure 12.44). If you draw a line on the digitizer, for example, that line should appear onscreen.

Most digitizers connect to your PC via a USB connection. You'll need to install drivers before you connect the device, although they should be included in the box. The digitizer should also include a configuration utility. Here you can adjust the pressure sensitivity of the stylus, configure buttons on the tablet, and set the portion of the screen to which the tablet can draw.

You might also find an option to calibrate the digitizer. To ensure that where you press on the digitizer matches up with where you want it to appear on your monitor,

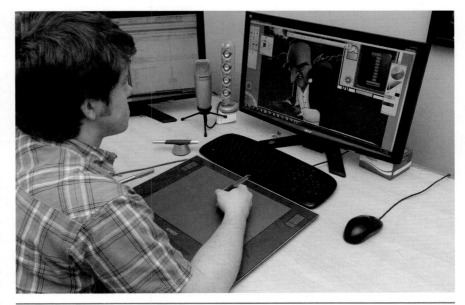

• **Figure 12.44** Drawing with a digitizer

you'll need to use the digitizer to click on a series of marks that appear on your monitor. If your digitizer is incorrectly calibrated, your inputs won't appear correctly when you are drawing.

Multimedia Devices

The CompTIA A+ 220-801 exam separates standard input devices from multimedia input devices. I don't think this makes much sense, since many people use joysticks, scanners, and digitizers for multimedia purposes. A better distinction might be non-audio/video input devices versus audio/video input devices, since that is the most obvious way to distinguish them here.

Popular multimedia devices like digital cameras and digital camcorders have found their way into almost every home. Their affordability and ease of use make them a no-brainer for families looking to capture every moment of their (cats') lives. Some people also use webcams to enable video chats with friends and family around the world. You'll learn about all three multimedia devices in this section.

Digital Cameras and Camcorders

Digital cameras and camcorders electronically simulate older film and tape technology and provide a wonderful tool for capturing a moment and then sending it to friends and relatives. Because digital cameras and camcorders interface with computers, CompTIA A+ certified techs need to know the basics.

In addition to drivers, most digitizers require specific software to use their advanced functions. With digital art digitizers, for example, you'll need a graphic arts program like Adobe Illustrator or Autodesk SketchBook, which know how to use several brands and varieties of pen tablets.

The CompTIA A+ 220-801 objectives also list MIDI devices and microphones as multimedia input devices. You'll learn more about these when I cover sound devices in Chapter 17.

While digital cameras and digital camcorders can be considered distinct products, their features have become nearly identical. Both take pictures. Both take videos. In fact, a lot of high-end digital cameras take better video than digital camcorders. Because of this feature and function overlap, I'm presenting them here together.

Many digital camcorders include built-in hard drives for storing large amounts of high-definition video. This removes the need to constantly switch out memory cards.

Cross Check

Flash Media

You learned all about the many types of flash media and micro drives back in Chapter 11, so go there now and answer these questions. What's the difference between a thumb drive and an SD card? Can you make a bootable flash-media drive?

• **Figure 12.45** Secure Digital card

Storage Media—Digital Film

Digital cameras and camcorders save the pictures and videos they take onto some type of *removable storage media*. Think of it as digital film. Probably the most common removable storage media used in modern digital cameras (and probably your best choice) is the Secure Digital (SD) card (see Figure 12.45). About the size of a Wheat Thin (roughly an inch square), you can find these tiny cards with capacities ranging from 1 GB to 32 GB. They are among the fastest of the various media types at transferring data to and from a PC, and they're quite sturdy.

Connection

These days, digital cameras plug directly into a USB port (see Figure 12.46). Another common option, though, is to connect only the camera's storage media to the computer, using one of the many digital media readers available.

You can find readers designed specifically for SD cards, as well as other types. Plenty of readers can handle multiple media formats. Many computers come with a decent built-in digital media reader (see Figure 12.47).

Many digital camcorders use USB connections, although you'll find FireWire connections on slightly older models.

• **Figure 12.46** Camera connecting to USB port

Quality

As with scanners, you should consider the amount of information a particular model of camera or camcorder can capture, which in the digital world is expressed as some number of **megapixels**. Instead of light-sensitive film, digital cameras and camcorders have one CCD (charged coupled device) or CMOS (complementary metal-oxide semiconductor) sensor covered with photosensitive pixels (called *photosites*) to capture the still image or video; the more pixels on the sensor, the higher the resolution of the images it captures.

• **Figure 12.47** Digital media reader built into computer

Not so long ago, a 1-megapixel digital camera was the bleeding edge of digital photographic technology, but now you can find cameras with ten times that resolution for a hundred dollars. As a basis of reference, a 5-megapixel camera produces snapshot-sized (4 × 6 inch) pictures with print photograph quality, whereas a 10-megapixel unit can produce a high-quality 8 × 10 inch print.

Another feature of most digital cameras and camcorders is the capability to zoom in on your subject. The way you ideally want to do this is the

way film cameras do it, by using the camera's optics—that's the lens. Most cameras above the basic level have some **optical zoom**—meaning the zoom is built into the lens of the camera—but almost all models include multiple levels of **digital zoom**, accomplished by some very clever software in the camera. Choose your camera based on optical zoom: 3× at a minimum or better if you can afford it. Digital zoom is useless.

Camcorder optical zoom ranges are often much larger. You can find digital cameras with an optical zoom of 30× or more.

Form Factor

As was the case with film cameras, size matters on digital cameras and camcorders. These devices come in several form factors. They range from tiny, ultra-compact models that readily fit in a shirt pocket to monster cameras with huge lenses. Although it's not universally true, the bigger the camera/camcorder, the more features and sensors it can have. Thus bigger is usually better in terms of quality.

In shape, digital cameras come in a rectangular package, in which the lens retracts into the body, or as an SLR-type, with a lens that sticks out of the body. Figure 12.48 shows both styles.

Camcorders also come in multiple shapes (see Figure 12.49). Some are arranged vertically; others are more horizontal. Some are large enough that you need to use two hands to hold them. The latest form factors include two lenses so they can capture 3-D videos. Now your cat can fly right off the screen.

• **Figure 12.48** Typical digital cameras

• **Figure 12.49** Digital camcorders

Web Cameras

PC cameras, often called **webcams** because their most common use is for Internet video communication, are fairly new to the world of input devices. Too many people run out and buy the cheapest one, not appreciating the vast difference between a discount webcam and more expensive models; nor do they take the time to configure the webcam properly. Let's consider some of the features you should look for when buying webcams and some of the problems you can run into when using them.

The biggest issue with webcams is the image quality. Webcams measure their resolution in pixels. You can find webcams with resolutions of as few as 100,000 pixels and webcams with millions of pixels. Most people who use webcams agree that 1.3 million pixels (megapixels) is pretty much the highest resolution quality you can use before your video becomes so large it will bog down even a broadband connection.

The next issue with webcams is the frame rate, that is, the number of times the camera "takes your picture" each second. Higher frame rates make for smoother video; 30 frames per second is considered the best. A good camera with a high megapixel resolution and fast frame rate will provide you with excellent video conferencing capabilities. Figure 12.50 shows the author chatting via webcam using Skype software.

Most people who use online video also want a microphone. Many cameras come with microphones, or you can use your own. Those who do a lot of video chatting may prefer to get a camera without a microphone and then buy a good quality headset with which to speak and listen.

Many cameras now can track you when you move, to keep your face in the picture—a handy feature for fidgety folks using video conferencing! This interesting technology recognizes a human face with little or no "training" and rotates its position to keep your face in the picture. Some companies even add funny extras, which, although not very productive, are good for a laugh (see Figure 12.51).

> Read more about pixels and frame rates in Chapter 13.

• **Figure 12.50** Video chatting by webcam with Skype

Almost all webcams use USB connections. Windows comes with a limited set of webcam drivers, so always make sure to install the drivers supplied with the camera before you plug it in. Most webcams use Hi-Speed USB, so make sure you're plugging your webcam into a Hi-Speed USB port.

Once the camera is plugged in, you'll need to test it. All cameras come with some type of program, but finding the program can be a challenge. Some brands put the program in the system tray, some place it in My Computer/Computer, others put it in the Control Panel—and some do all three! Figure 12.52 shows the Control Panel applet that appeared when I installed the webcam driver.

The biggest challenge to using webcams is getting your webcam applications to recognize that your webcam is available and configured for use. Every program does this differently, but conceptually the steps are basically the same (with plenty of exceptions):

1. Tell the program you want to use a camera.

2. Tell the program whether you want the camera to turn on automatically when you chat.

3. Configure the image quality.

4. Test the camera.

If you're having problems with a camera, always go through the general I/O problems first, as this will clear up most problems. If you're still having trouble getting the camera to work in a program, be sure to turn off all other programs that may be using the camera. Windows allows only one program at a time to use a webcam.

• **Figure 12.51** This webcam program's animated character mirrors your movements as you conference with friends or coworkers.

• **Figure 12.52** Camera Settings applet

Chapter 12 Review

■ Chapter Summary

After reading this chapter and completing the exercises, you should understand the following about input devices.

Explain how to support common input/output ports

- Many new computers do not come with serial ports as other high-speed ports such as USB have replaced them. You can tell if you have serial ports by checking for the COM port icon in Device Manager.

- The UART chip that comprises the serial port converts data moving between the parallel expansion bus on a PC and the serial bus used by many I/O devices. Most serial port connectors consist of a 9-pin DB connector. The connector on the PC or device itself (not the cable) is male. Serial ports are also known as RS-232, which is the standard that describes how serial ports work.

- The USB host controller (sometimes called a host adapter) controls every USB device connected to it. The host controller includes a root hub that provides the physical connection for devices. Host controllers support many ports, but the number of USB ports a system has is usually dependent on what the motherboard manufacturer decided to supply. The host controller is shared by every device plugged into it, so speed and power are reduced with each new device.

- Powered USB devices require their own power cord, in which case they do not pull power from the USB bus itself. Bus-powered devices draw their power directly from the USB bus and do not require a separate power cord. Too many bus-powered devices may result in system lockups, device lockups, or devices that just don't work. To solve the power problem, unplugging a device or two will lower the demand for bus power. Alternatively, you can purchase and install a USB expansion card, which will provide another USB host controller with its own set of connection ports.

- Multiple USB standards are in use today: USB 1.1 defines Low-Speed USB, which runs at 1.5 Mbps, and Full-Speed USB, which runs at 12 Mbps. USB 2.0 defines Hi-Speed USB, which runs at 480 Mbps.

USB 3.0 defines SuperSpeed USB, which runs at 5 Gbps.

- Devices of any speed can connect to any port, though they will run at the speed of the slowest device. A USB 3.0 device connected to a USB 2.0 port will run at 480 Mbps.

- In theory, the USB interface can support up to 127 devices on a single USB port; in reality, too many devices on a single USB chain will overtax its power capabilities. USB specifications allow for a maximum cable length of 5 meters, although you may add a powered USB hub every 5 meters to extend this distance.

- USB hubs extend the number of USB devices you can connect to a single port. Make sure you get a powered Hi-Speed USB hub so it will support the fastest speed and not draw power away from other devices.

- Normally, you will install the device driver before connecting the USB device to the system. Although this is the norm, it is not carved in stone. Be sure to read the manual that came with your device for instructions on installation. For example, many USB devices, such as flash drives, do not need a separate driver installed and work fine if simply plugged in.

- FireWire has three distinct types of connectors: 6- and 9-pin powered connectors and a 4-pin connector that doesn't provide power. IEEE 1394a runs at 400 Mbps and IEEE 1394b runs at 800 Mbps.

- FireWire devices must connect directly to a root hub but may be daisy chained to support up to 63 devices. Similar to USB devices, you should install the drivers before connecting the FireWire device, but most devices can use the generic Windows driver and thus can be plugged in immediately.

- When troubleshooting problems, first determine if the issue is a port problem or a device problem. Swap out the troubled device for a known good device (one that works in another computer). If a known good device fails, you can safely assume you have a port problem. If a known good device functions properly, you most likely have a device

problem. For device problems, replace the device. For port problems, verify that the port is enabled, make sure you have the drive installed for the port itself, and check the condition of the cables and physical connectors.

Identify certain standard input devices on a PC

- Keyboards are the oldest type of input device and still the primary way users input data. Although a keyboard works without the installation of additional drivers, you need to install drivers for specialty keyboards, such as keyboards with fancy buttons or other programmable features. If you're using a USB keyboard, make sure to enable USB keyboard support in CMOS Setup.

- Configure basic keyboard settings in the Keyboard Control Panel applet. You can change the repeat delay, repeat rate, and cursor blink rate. Clean dirty keys with a damp cloth or isopropyl alcohol. Compressed air works well to dislodge hair, dust, and other small objects from the keys. With most keyboards you can pop off individual keys to do some deep cleaning. Some keyboards (such as those on laptops) are not meant to have keys removed, and doing so might permanently damage the keyboard.

- Mice work with the generic Windows drivers. You need to install mouse drivers only if your mouse has special programmable features, such as additional buttons. Various mouse settings can be configured via the Mouse Control Panel applet. Configurable settings include mouse speed, double-click speed, and acceleration.

- The internal rubber ball on a ball mouse should be cleaned every few months. Rotate the collar on the underside of the mouse to release the rubber ball. Optical mice, which use LEDs or lasers to track movement, may occasionally need their lenses wiped free of grime, but overall outperform and outlive ball mice.

- Flatbed scanners have a hinged lid and flat glass surface on which you can place material to be scanned. Most scanners come with software to control the hardware and to control the scanning process itself. The scan software enables you to select the color mode and resolution of the scanned document. Scanners use a traditional TWAIN driver to transfer digital images to the PC. Some scanners offer additional features, such as OCR capabilities.

- When choosing a scanner, consider the scanner's optical resolution (ignore the enhanced resolution), color depth, grayscale depth, connection type, and scan speed. The higher these numbers, the better quality the scanned images will be. Shoot for a minimum 2400 × 2400 dpi optical resolution, 48-bit color depth, 16-bit grayscale depth, and a Hi-Speed USB or FireWire connection.

- Biometric devices scan various body parts, such as fingerprints or retinas, for authentication, security, and recognition. Some biometric devices control access to an entire PC, while some small devices, such as USB thumb drives, have biometric fingerprint scanners built in to control access to the single device. Voice recognition allows users to speak commands to the computer, such as "Call Mike Meyers" to dial the phone via a modem.

- Bar code readers read the standard Universal Product Code (UPC) bar code. The two types of bar code readers are pen scanners and hand scanners. Pen scanners look like ink pens and must be swiped across the bar code. Hand scanners are aimed at the bar code and when a button or trigger is pressed, the reader scans the bar code. All bar code scanners produce an audible tone to verify that the bar code has been read. Old bar code readers used serial ports, but newer ones use either USB or PS/2 connections.

- Tablets feature touch screens, as do information kiosks, smartphones, and point of sale systems. Touch screens can be operated with either a finger or a stylus. Some devices, such as smartphones, have built-in touch screens, while a point of sale system may use a standalone touch screen monitor. Use the Pen and Input Device applet in Windows Vista or the Tablet PC Settings applet in Windows Vista or 7 to configure the touch screens on Tablet PCs.

- KVM switches are hardware devices with which multiple systems can be monitored and controlled by a single mouse, keyboard, and monitor. KVMs are most commonly used in data centers, enabling administrators to control multiple rack-mounted servers from a single keyboard, mouse, and monitor station.

- When keyboard and mouse aren't sufficient, gamepads and joysticks enable you to control your PC games. Most game controllers connect via USB. You can use the Game Controllers applet in Windows XP/Vista or Devices and Printers in Windows 7 to configure your devices.

- Digitizers enable you to write, draw, or paint onto your PC. Using a stylus and special surface, the digitizer translates your analog movements into digital information understood by graphic arts applications. Popular digitizers like the Wacom series of pen tablets include configuration screens that enable you to set properties like pressure sensitivity and custom hot keys.

Describe how certain multimedia input devices work on a PC

- Most digital cameras and camcorders store images on removable media, such as SD cards. Photos and videos can be transferred to a PC by connecting the camera directly to a USB or FireWire port. Alternatively, if the PC is equipped with a media card reader, the flash memory card can be removed from the camera and inserted directly to the PC's card reader.

- A 5-megapixel camera will produce 4 × 6 pictures with print photograph quality, while a 10-megapixel camera will produce 8 × 10 pictures with print photograph quality. The more sensors a camera has, the better the image quality, so you'll find that physically larger cameras take better pictures than the tiny ones. Look for a camera with at least 3× optical zoom and ignore the digital zoom that is advertised.

- Webcams are often used for Internet video communication. A 1.3-megapixel webcam delivers a decent resolution video without bogging down a broadband connection. Look for a webcam that has a frame rate of about 30 frames per second. Some webcams come with built-in microphones, but if you want high-quality audio without feedback or echo, invest in a microphone headset. After installing the driver and connecting a webcam, be sure to configure it properly so your Internet chat software knows to use the webcam.

■ Key Terms

Ball mouse *(336)*
bar code reader *(341)*
biometric device *(340)*
color depth *(339)*
digital camera *(345)*
digital zoom *(347)*
digitizer *(344)*
FireWire *(330)*
flatbed scanner *(337)*
Full-Speed USB *(326)*
grayscale depth *(339)*
Hi-Speed USB *(326)*
IEEE 1394a *(331)*
IEEE 1394b *(331)*
keyboard, video, mouse switch (KVM) *(342)*
Low-Speed USB *(326)*

megapixels *(346)*
optical mouse *(336)*
optical resolution *(339)*
optical zoom *(347)*
RS-232 *(323)*
serial port *(323)*
SuperSpeed USB *(326)*
touch screen *(341)*
TWAIN *(338)*
universal asynchronous receiver/transmitter (UART) *(323)*
Universal Product Code (UPC) *(341)*
USB host controller *(324)*
USB hub *(328)*
USB root hub *(324)*
webcam *(348)*

■ Key Term Quiz

Use the Key Terms list to complete the sentences that follow. Not all terms will be used.

1. Serial ports are defined by the _____ standard.

2. A(n) _____ is useful when scanning a page from a book; a(n) _____ is useful when scanning the price of retail items at a store.

3. A(n) _____ device transfers data at up to 12 Mbps on the universal serial bus.

4. A(n) _____ FireWire device transfers data at up to 800 Mbps.

5. A(n) _____ captures digital images on removable media; a(n) _____ transmits digital images across the Internet for video communication.

6. The amount of information a digital camera can capture is measured in _____.

7. A scanner's ability to produce color, hue, and shade is defined by its _____.

8. The _____ contains the logic to convert data moving between parallel and serial devices.

9. When comparing digital cameras and their zoom capabilities, pay attention to the _____ and ignore the _____.

10. For moving the mouse pointer, most people prefer a(n) _____ over a(n) _____ because the former is much easier to keep clean.

■ Multiple-Choice Quiz

1. How many devices can a single USB host controller support?

 A. 2

 B. 4

 C. 63

 D. 127

2. What is the maximum USB cable length as defined by the USB 2.0 specification?

 A. 4.5 feet

 B. 4.5 meters

 C. 5 feet

 D. 5 meters

3. Malfunctioning USB devices may be caused by which of the following?

 A. Too many USB devices attached to the host controller

 B. Improper IRQ settings for the device

 C. Device plugged in upside-down

 D. USB 1.1 device plugged into USB 2.0 port

4. What do digitizers enable people to do on a PC?

 A. Capture video

 B. Draw, paint, and write

 C. Secure using fingerprints

 D. Switch between multiple computers using the same keyboard, mouse, and monitor

5. Which FireWire standard is properly matched with its speed?

 A. IEEE 1394a, 400 Mbps

 B. IEEE 1394 a, 480 Mbps

 C. IEEE 1394b, 400 Mbps

 D. IEEE 1394b, 480 Mbps

6. FireWire supports a maximum of how many devices?

 A. 2

 B. 4

 C. 63

 D. 127

7. What icon does Windows XP's Device Manager display over disabled devices?

 A. Yellow triangle

 B. Red X

 C. Blue I

 D. Green D

8. A user reports that his mouse is jittery. What is the most likely cause?

 A. His optical mouse has the wrong driver installed.

 B. His wireless mouse has a dead battery.

 C. His ball mouse has acquired dirt in the rollers.

 D. He had one too many cups of coffee that morning.

9. Which specifications describe a high-quality webcam that won't bog down an Internet connection?

 A. 5 megapixels at 15 frames per second

 B. 1.3 megapixels at 15 frames per second

 C. 5 megapixels at 40 frames per second

 D. 1.3 megapixels at 30 frames per second

10. Which device is a biometric device?

 A. Bar code reader

 B. Optical mouse

 C. Retinal scanner

 D. Flatbed scanner

11. The number that defines how many shades of gray per dot a scanner can save is referred to as what?

 A. Resolution

 B. DPI

 C. Color depth

 D. Grayscale depth

12. A color depth of 16-bits can store how many color variations per dot?

 A. 16

 B. 32

 C. 512

 D. 65,536

13. Which of the following lists the technologies in order from slowest to fastest?

 A. SuperSpeed USB, Full-Speed USB, Hi-Speed USB, IEEE 1394a, IEEE 1394b

 B. Full-Speed USB, IEEE 1394a, Hi-Speed USB, IEEE 1394b, SuperSpeed USB

 C. Full-Speed USB, SuperSpeed USB, Hi-Speed USB, IEEE 1394a, IEEE 1394b

 D. Low-Speed USB, SuperSpeed USB, IEEE 1394a, Hi-Speed USB, IEEE 1394b

14. In Windows 7, which Control Panel applet enables you to configure a game controller, such as a joystick or gamepad?

 A. Devices and Printers

 B. Joysticks and Gamepads

 C. Input Devices

 D. Game controllers are only configured within a PC game.

15. While testing a newly installed KVM switch, you can't display the second connected system while tapping the SCROLL LOCK key. What is most likely the problem?

 A. Incorrect KVM UPC code

 B. Crossed video cable

 C. Locked SCROLL LOCK key

 D. Active KVM

■ Essay Quiz

1. A friend at the local film school needs a new keyboard and external hard drive. What advice can you give her about the connection style for each of these devices?

2. Dylan is excited because he just got a new USB digital camera. He tried to install it on his laptop, but the computer doesn't recognize it. He's called you for help. What will you tell him?

3. Ken asks for your help because he is always forgetting his Windows password. What can you recommend to make logons easier for him?

4. Sandra's always trying new video games. She usually plays role-playing games like *World of Warcraft*, but a friend bought her a new flight simulator. She wants to get the most out of the experience. What device should she get to enhance her experience? How should she set it up?

5. The new head of sales is frustrated because when she tries to use her keyboard, letters continue to print across the screen even if she quickly taps a key, resulting in messages that lllloooooooookkkk lllliiiikkkkeeee tttthhhhiiiissss. How can you walk her through fixing this problem over the phone?

Lab Projects

• Lab Project 12.1

Many personal computers do not normally include FireWire ports. Check the following three Web sites: www.dell.com, www.hp.com, and www.apple.com. Is a FireWire port standard built-in equipment on their new computers? If so, how many FireWire ports are included? If not, do the sites offer FireWire as an optional add-on?

• Lab Project 12.2

Explore the Keyboard and Mouse Control Panel applets. Change the settings and try to use the devices. Which settings caused the most frustration? Were there any changes you made that you preferred over the original settings?

• Lab Project 12.3

Grab a lab partner, a pen and pad of paper, and a stop watch. How many input devices can you two name in 30 seconds? Reset the timer. How many output devices can you two name in 30 seconds? Are any devices considered both input and output?

Video

chapter

13

*"Video killed the radio star
Video killed the radio star
In my mind and in my car
We can't rewind, we've gone
too far."*

—The Buggles, "Video Killed the
Radio Star," *The Age of Plastic*

**In this chapter, you will learn
how to**

- **Explain how video displays work**
- **Select the proper video card**
- **Install and configure video**

The term *video* encompasses a complex interaction among numerous parts of the PC, all designed to put a picture on the screen. The **monitor** or **video display** shows you what's going on with your programs and operating system. It's the primary output device for the PC. The video card or **display adapter** handles all of the communication between the CPU and the monitor (see Figure 13.1). The operating system needs to know how to handle communication between the CPU and the display adapter, which requires drivers specific for each card and proper setup within Windows. Finally, each application needs to be able to interact with the rest of the video system.

Let's look at monitors and display adapters individually. I'll bring them back together as a team later in the chapter so you can understand the many nuances that make video so challenging. Let's begin with the video display and then move to the display adapter.

● **Figure 13.1** Typical monitor and video card

■ Video Displays

To understand displays, you need a good grasp of each component and how they work together to make a beautiful (or not so beautiful) picture on the screen. Different types of displays use different methods and technologies to accomplish this task. Video displays for PCs come in three varieties: CRT, LCD, and projectors. The first two you'll see on the desktop or laptop; the last you'll find in boardrooms and classrooms, splashing a picture onto a screen.

Historical/Conceptual

CRT Monitors

Cathode ray tube (CRT) monitors were the original computer monitors—those heavy, boxy monitors that take up half your desk. Although for the most part they've been replaced by LCD technology on new systems, plenty of CRT monitors are still chugging away in the field. As the name implies, this type of display contains a large cathode ray tube, a type of airtight vacuum tube. One end of this tube is a slender cylinder that contains three electron guns. The other end of the tube, which is fatter and wider, is the display screen.

 CRT monitors are so heavy that you have to be careful when placing them on monitor stands. All monitor stands have weight limitations, so don't place a heavy monitor on a light stand!

Before we begin in earnest, I want to give you a note of warning about the inside of a traditional monitor. I will discuss what can be repaired and what requires more specialized expertise. Make no mistake—the interior of a monitor might appear similar to the interior of a PC because of the printed circuit boards and related components, but the similarity ends there. No PC has voltages exceeding 15,000 to 30,000 V, but most monitors do. So let's get one thing perfectly clear: Opening up a monitor can kill you! Even when the power is disconnected, certain components retain a substantial voltage for an extended period of time. You can inadvertently short one of the components and fry yourself—to death. Given this risk, certain aspects of monitor repair lie outside the necessary skill set for a normal PC support person, and definitely outside the CompTIA A+ certification exam domains! I will

Electron stream

Phosphor coating

Yoke

Electron guns

Vacuum tube

● **Figure 13.2** Electron stream in the CRT

⚠ The inside of a CRT has very high voltage components. These can kill you. Be careful!

show you how to address the problems you can fix safely and make sure you understand the ones you need to hand over to a monitor shop.

The inside of the display screen has a phosphor coating. When power is applied to one or more of the electron guns, a stream of electrons shoots towards the display end of the CRT (see Figure 13.2). Along the way, this stream is subjected to magnetic fields generated by a ring of electromagnets called a *yoke* that controls the electron beam's point of impact. When the phosphor coating is struck by the electron beam, it releases its energy as visible light.

When struck by a stream of electrons, a phosphor quickly releases a burst of energy. This happens far too quickly for the human eye and brain connection to register. Fortunately, the phosphors on the display screen have a quality called **persistence**, which means the phosphors continue to glow after being struck by the electron beam. Too much persistence and the image is smeary; too little and the image appears to flicker. The perfect combination of beam and persistence creates the illusion of a solid picture.

801

Refresh Rate

The monitor displays video data as the electron guns make a series of horizontal sweeps across the screen, energizing the appropriate areas of the phosphorous coating. The sweeps start at the upper-left corner of the monitor and move across and down to the lower-right corner. The screen is "painted" only in one direction; then the electron guns turn and retrace their path across the screen, to be ready for the next sweep. These sweeps are called **raster lines** (see Figure 13.3).

One raster line

• Figure 13.3 Electron guns sweep from left to right.

The time it takes to draw one line across the screen and be ready for the next is called the horizontal refresh rate (HRR). This is measured in KHz (thousands of lines per second).

• Figure 13.4 Horizontal refresh rate

The speed at which the electron beam moves across the screen is known as the **horizontal refresh rate (HRR),** as shown in Figure 13.4. The monitor draws a number of lines across the screen, eventually covering the screen with glowing phosphors. The number of lines is not fixed, unlike television screens, which have a set number of lines. After the guns reach the lower-right corner of the screen, they turn off and point back to the upper-left corner. The amount of time it takes to draw the entire screen and get the electron guns back to the upper-left corner is called the **vertical refresh rate (VRR),** shown in Figure 13.5.

The monitor does not determine the HRR or VRR; the video card "pushes" the monitor at a certain VRR and then the monitor sets the corresponding HRR. If the video card is set to push at too low a VRR, the monitor produces a noticeable flicker, causing eyestrain and headaches for users. Pushing the monitor at too high a VRR, however, causes a definite distortion of the screen image and will damage the circuitry of the monitor and eventually destroy it. The number one killer of monitors is improper VRR settings, and the number one reason your office is filled with crabby workers is that the VRR is set too low. All good PC support techs understand this and take substantial time tweaking the VRR to ensure that the video card pushes the monitor at the highest VRR without damaging the monitor—this is the Holy Grail of monitor support!

The number of times per second the electron guns can draw the entire screen and then return to the uppper left-corner is called the vertical refresh rate (VRR). This is measured in Hz (screens per second).

• Figure 13.5 Vertical refresh rate

Try This!

Discovering Your Refresh Rate

You should know the refresh rate for all CRTs you service. Setting up monitors incorrectly can cause havoc in the workplace, so Try This!

1. Most PCs have two places where you can discover the current refresh rate of the monitor. Many monitors offer a menu button for adjusting the display. Often it shows the refresh rate when you push it once.

2. If that doesn't work, go to the Control Panel and open the Display applet (Windows XP/7) or Personalization applet (Windows Vista). Select the Settings tab (XP), Display Settings option (Vista), or *Change display settings* link (7) and then click on Advanced or Advanced settings. Select the Monitor tab in the Monitor Properties dialog box.

3. Write down your refresh rate. How does it compare with that of your classmates?

• **Figure 13.6** A monitor is a grid of red, green, and blue phosphors.

• **Figure 13.7** Shadow mask

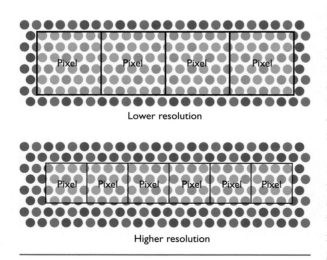

• **Figure 13.8** Resolution versus pixel size

Phosphors and Shadow Mask

All CRT monitors contain dots of phosphorous or some other light-sensitive compound that glows *red*, *green*, or *blue* (RGB) when an electron gun sweeps over it. These **phosphors** are evenly distributed across the front of the monitor (see Figure 13.6).

A normal CRT has three electron guns: one for the red phosphors, one for the blue phosphors, and one for the green phosphors. It is important to understand that the electron guns do not fire colored light; they simply fire electrons at different intensities, which then make the phosphors glow. The higher the intensity of the electron stream, the brighter the color produced by the glowing phosphor.

Directly behind the phosphors in a CRT is the **shadow mask**, a screen that allows only the proper electron gun to light the proper phosphors (see Figure 13.7). This prevents, for example, the red electron beam from "bleeding over" and lighting neighboring blue and green dots.

The electron guns sweep across the phosphors as a group, turning rapidly on and off as they move across the screen. When the group reaches the end of the screen, it moves to the next line. It is crucial to understand that turning the guns on and off, combined with moving the guns to new lines, creates a mosaic that is the image you see on the screen. The number of times the guns turn on and off, combined with the number of lines drawn on the screen, determines the number of mosaic pieces used to create the image. These individual pieces are called **pixels**, from the term *picture elements*. You can't hold a pixel in your hand; it's just the area of phosphors lit at one instant when the group of guns is turned on. The size of pixels can change depending on the number of times the group of guns is turned on and off and the number of lines drawn.

Resolution

Monitor **resolution** is always shown as the number of horizontal pixels times the number of vertical pixels. A resolution of 640 × 480, therefore, indicates a horizontal resolution of 640 pixels and a vertical resolution of 480 pixels. If you multiply the values together, you can see how many pixels are on each screen: 640 × 480 = 307,200 pixels per screen. An example of resolution affecting the pixel size is shown in Figure 13.8.

Some common resolutions are 640 × 480, 800 × 600, 1024 × 768, 1280 × 960, 1280 × 1024, and 1600 × 1200. Notice that most of these resolutions match a 4:3 ratio. This is called the **aspect ratio**. Many monitors are shaped like television screens, with a 4:3 aspect ratio, so most resolutions are designed to match—or at least be close to—that shape. Other monitors, generically called *wide-screen monitors*, have a 16:9 or 16:10 ratio. Two of the common resolutions you'll see with these monitors are 1366 × 768 and 1920 × 1080.

The last important issue is to determine the maximum possible resolution for a monitor. In other words, how small can one pixel be? Well, the answer lies in the phosphors. A pixel must be made up of at least one red, one green, and one blue phosphor to make any color, so the smallest theoretical pixel would consist of one group of red, green, and blue phosphors: a **triad** (see Figure 13.9). Various limitations in screens, controlling electronics, and electron gun technology make the maximum resolution much bigger than one triad.

Great! Now that you have the basics of CRT monitors, let's turn to LCD monitors. Although the technology differs dramatically between the monitor types, most of the terms used for CRTs also apply to LCD functions.

See the "Modes" section later in this chapter for the names of each resolution.

• **Figure 13.9** One triad

LCD Monitors

Liquid crystal displays (LCDs) are the most common type of display technology for PCs. LCD monitors have many advantages over CRTs. They are thinner and lighter, use much less power, are virtually flicker-free, and don't emit potentially harmful radiation. LCDs still have resolution, refresh rates, and bandwidth, but LCDs also come with their own family of abbreviations, jargon, and terms you need to understand so you can install, maintain, and support LCDs.

How LCDs Work

The secret to understanding the most common type of LCD panels is to understand the concept of the polarity of light. Anyone who played with a prism in sixth grade or has looked at a rainbow knows that light travels in waves (no quantum mechanics here, please!), and the wavelength of the light determines the color. What you might not appreciate is the fact that light waves emanate from a light source in three dimensions. It's impossible to draw a clear diagram of three-dimensional waves, so instead, let's use an analogy. To visualize this, think of light emanating from a flashlight. Now think of the light emanating from that flashlight as though someone was shaking a jump rope. This is not a rhythmic shaking, back and forth or up and down; it's more as if a person went crazy and was shaking the jump rope all over the place—up, down, left, right—constantly changing the speed.

That's how light really acts. Well, I guess we could take the analogy one step further by saying the person has an infinite number of arms, each holding a jump rope shooting out in every direction to show the three-dimensionality of light waves, but (a) I can't draw that and (b) one jump rope will suffice to explain the typical LCD panels. The varying speeds create wavelengths, from very short to very long. When light comes into your eyes at many different wavelengths, you see white light. If the light came in only one wavelength, you would see only that color. Light flowing through a polarized filter (like sunglasses) is like putting a picket fence between you and the people shaking the ropes. You see all of the wavelengths, but only the waves of similar orientation. You would still see all of the colors, just fewer of them because you only see the waves of the same orientation, making the image darker. That's why many sunglasses use polarizing filters.

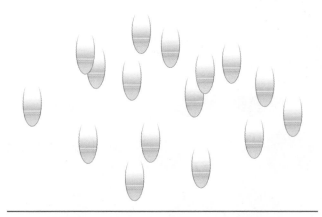

• **Figure 13.10** Waves of similar orientation

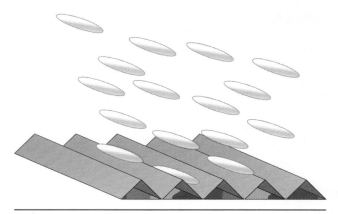

• **Figure 13.11** Liquid crystal molecules tend to line up together.

Now, what would happen if you added another picket fence but put the slats in a horizontal direction? This would effectively cancel out all of the waves. This is what happens when two polarizing filters are combined at a 90-degree angle—no light passes through.

Now, what would happen if you added a third fence between the two fences with the slats at a 45-degree angle? Well, it would sort of "twist" some of the shakes in the rope so that the waves could then get through. The same thing is true with the polarizing filters. The third filter twists some of the light so that it gets through. If you're really feeling scientific, go to any educational supply store and pick up three polarizing filters for about (US)$3 each and try it. It works.

Liquid crystals take advantage of the property of polarization. Liquid crystals are composed of a specially formulated liquid full of long, thin crystals that always want to orient themselves in the same direction, as shown in Figure 13.10. This substance acts exactly like a liquid polarized filter. If you poured a thin film of this stuff between two sheets of glass, you'd get a darn good pair of sunglasses.

Imagine cutting extremely fine grooves on one side of one of those sheets of glass. When you place this liquid in contact with a finely grooved surface, the molecules naturally line up with the grooves in the surface (see Figure 13.11).

If you place another finely grooved surface, with the grooves at a 90-degree orientation to the other surface, opposite of the first one, the molecules in contact with that side will attempt to line up with it. The molecules in between, in trying to line up with both sides, will immediately line up in a nice twist (see Figure 13.12). If two perpendicular polarizing filters are then placed on either

• **Figure 13.12** Liquid crystal molecules twisting

Polarizing filter

Polarizing filter

• **Figure 13.13** No charge, enabling light to pass

side of the liquid crystal, the liquid crystal will twist the light and enable it to pass (see Figure 13.13).

If you expose the liquid crystal to an electrical potential, however, the crystals will change their orientation to match the direction of the electrical field. The twist goes away and no light passes through (see Figure 13.14).

A color LCD screen is composed of a large number of tiny liquid crystal molecules (called **sub-pixels**) arranged in rows and columns between polarizing filters. A translucent sheet above the sub-pixels is colored red, green, or blue. Each tiny distinct group of three sub-pixels—one red, one green, and one blue—forms a physical pixel, as shown in Figure 13.15.

Polarizing filter

Polarizing filter

• **Figure 13.14** Electrical charge, no light is able to pass

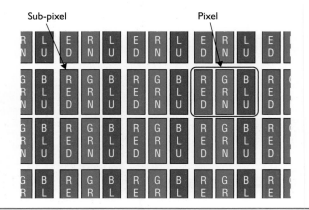

• **Figure 13.15** LCD pixels

LCD pixels are very different from the pixels in a CRT. A CRT pixel's size changes depending on the resolution. The pixels in an LCD panel are fixed and cannot be changed. See the section "LCD Resolution" later in the chapter for the scoop.

• **Figure 13.16** Single character for static LCD numeric display

Tech Tip

TN and IPS

The most common TFT displays use a technology called twisted nematic (TN)*, which produces a decent display for a modest price. Most TN displays use only 6 bits for each color—red, green, and blue—and that 18-bit display will not reproduce the full 24-bit true color that video cards can send to it. This means the panel fudges a little bit when asked to do something it can't do, and this can produce noticeable problems with reproduction.*

Better TFT displays use a technology called In-Plane Switching (IPS) *to create a wider viewing angle and far better color re-creation than TN panels can provide. Graphics professionals use IPS monitors, for example, because they can display what might print more faithfully than TN screens. Manufacturers use many types of IPS technology to find the right mix of price-to-performance.*

Once all of the pixels are laid out, how do you charge the right spots to make an image? Early LCDs didn't use rectangular pixels. Instead, images were composed of different-shaped elements, each electrically separate from the others. To create an image, each area was charged at the same time. Figure 13.16 shows the number zero, a display made possible by charging six areas to make an ellipse of sorts. This process, called *static charging*, is still quite popular in more basic numeric displays such as calculators.

The static method would not work in PCs due to its inherent inflexibility. Instead, early LCD screens used a matrix of wires (see Figure 13.17). The vertical wires, the Y wires, ran to every sub-pixel in the column. The horizontal wires, the X wires, ran along an entire row of sub-pixels. There had to be a charge on both the X wires and the Y wires to make enough voltage to light a single sub-pixel.

If you wanted color, you had to have three matrices. The three matrices intersected very close together. Above the intersections, the glass was covered with tiny red, green, and blue dots. Varying the amount of voltage on the wires made different levels of red, green, and blue, creating colors (see Figure 13.18).

We call this usage of LCD technology **passive matrix**. All LCD displays on PCs used only passive matrix for many years. Unfortunately, passive matrix is slow and tends to create a little overlap between individual pixels. This gives a slightly blurred effect to the image displayed. Manufacturers eventually came up with a speedier method of display, called **dual-scan passive matrix**, in which the screen refreshed two lines at a time.

Thin Film Transistor

Current LCD monitors use some form of **thin film transistor (TFT)** or **active matrix** technology (see Figure 13.19). Instead of using X and Y wires, one or more tiny transistors control each color dot, providing faster picture display, crisp definition, and much tighter color control than passive or dual-scan technologies could provide.

LCD Components

The typical LCD monitor is composed of three main components: the LCD panel, the backlight(s), and the inverters. The LCD panel creates the image,

• **Figure 13.17** An LCD matrix of wires

• **Figure 13.18** Passive matrix display

• **Figure 13.19** Active matrix display

• **Figure 13.20** LCD internals

the **backlights** illuminate the image so you can see it, and the **inverters** send power to the backlights. Figure 13.20 shows a typical layout for the internal components of an LCD monitor.

LCD Monitors with CCFL Backlights One of the great challenges to LCD power stems from the fact that the backlights need AC power while the electronics need DC power. Figure 13.20 shows one of the many ways that LCD monitor makers handle this issue. The AC power from your wall socket goes into an AC/DC transformer that changes the power to DC. The LCD panel uses this DC power.

Note in Figure 13.20 that this monitor has two backlights: one at the top and one at the bottom. Most LCDs have two backlights, although some have only one. Most LCD backlights use **cold cathode fluorescent lamp (CCFL)** technology, popular for its low power use, even brightness, and long life. Figure 13.21 shows a CCFL from an LCD panel.

CCFLs need AC power to operate, but given that the transformer converts the incoming AC power to DC, each CCFL backlight needs a device called an inverter to convert the DC power back into AC. Figure 13.22 shows a typical inverter used in an LCD.

Looking once again at Figure 13.20, note the two input connectors, DVI and VGA. DVI is a digital signal, so it connects directly to the LCD's logic circuitry. The VGA goes to an analog-to-digital converter before reaching the LCD logic board.

Keep in mind that Figure 13.20 is a generic illustration. The actual location and interconnections of the components are as variable as the number of LCD panels available today!

• **Figure 13.21** CCFL backlight

• **Figure 13.22** Inverter

> The CompTIA A+ 801 exam refers to LEDs as a display type, but such displays don't exist aside from marketing terms. LEDs manifest only as one form of backlighting for LCD monitors. Even so-called "LED monitors" and "LED televisions" are simply LCDs with LED backlights. The terms are merely marketing speak.

> Be sure you understand the features of CRT, LCD, LED, plasma, projector, and OLED display types.

> Two LCD panels that have the same physical size may have different native resolutions.

LED Monitors Manufacturers also use several types of **light-emitting diode (LED)** light for backlighting, either directly illuminating pixels from behind or flooding the panel from the edges of the bezel. The former produces outstanding contrast and color, but costs a lot more than the edge types. The edge types function similarly to a CCFL-style display, so they produce similar contrast and colors to the older technology. Manufacturers have rebranded LCD monitors that use LEDs for backlighting as **LED monitors**.

Using LEDs for backlighting reduces the thickness of the panels and reduces the overall electricity usage. LEDs don't need AC power, so there's no inverter to get involved in lighting the panel. Many smaller devices, such as smartphones and tablets, use LED backlights to save battery use. The better panels are also in high demand from graphics professionals.

LCD Resolution

All LCD monitors have a **native resolution**, such as 1680 × 1050, that enables them to display the sharpest picture possible. As mentioned earlier, the pixels are fixed. You simply cannot run an LCD monitor at a resolution higher than the native one. Worse, because LCDs have no equivalent to a shadow mask, they can't run at a *lower* than native resolution without severely degrading image quality. A CRT can simply use more dots and the filtering and smoothing of the shadow mask to make a picture at a lower resolution look as good and crisp as the same picture at a higher resolution, but an LCD cannot. The LCD has to use an edge-blurring technique called **anti-aliasing** to soften the jagged corners of the pixels when running at lower than native resolution, which simply does not look as good. The bottom line? Always set the LCD at native resolution!

Brightness

The strength of an LCD monitor's backlights determines the brightness of the monitor. The brightness is measured in **nits**. LCD panels vary from 100 nits on the low end to over 1000 nits or more on the high end. Average LCD panels are around 300 nits, which most monitor authorities consider excellent brightness.

Response Rate

An LCD panel's **response rate** is the amount of time it takes for all of the sub-pixels on the panel to go from pure black to pure white and back again. This is roughly the same concept as the CRT refresh rate, but with one important difference. Once the electron gun on a CRT lights a phosphor, that phosphor begins to fade until it is lit again. An individual LCD sub-pixel holds its intensity until the LCD circuitry changes that sub-pixel, making the problem of flicker nonexistent on LCDs.

Manufacturers measure LCD response rates in milliseconds, with lower being better. A typical lower-end or older LCD has a response rate of 20–25 ms. The screens look fine, but you'll get some ghosting if you try to watch a movie or play a fast-paced video game. In recent years, manufacturers have figured out how to overcome this issue, and you can find many LCD monitors with a response rate of 2–4 ms.

Refresh Rate

The refresh rate for an LCD monitor is described using numbers similar to those used to describe the refresh rate for a CRT monitor, such as 60 Hz, but the terms mean slightly different things between the two technologies. With CRTs, as you'll recall, the phosphors on the screen start to lose their glow and need to be hit again by the electron guns many times per second to achieve an unwavering or flicker-free image. Each dot on an active matrix LCD, in contrast, has its own transistor to light it up. There's no need to freshen up the dot; it's on or off. Regardless of the refresh rate for the LCD, therefore, there's never any flicker at all caused by refresh rate.

The refresh rate for an LCD monitor refers to how often a screen can change or update completely. Think of the refresh rate as a metronome or timer and you'll be closer to how it works in an LCD. For most computing issues, 60 Hz is fine and that's been the standard for the industry. Humans see things that change as infrequently as 24 times per second—the standard for motion pictures at the cinema, for example, and the best high-definition (HD) signal—as a full motion video. To be able to change almost three times faster is perfectly acceptable, even in higher-end applications such as fast-moving games.

Monitor manufacturers have released 120-Hz LCD monitors in a response to the convergence of LCDs, televisions, and computers to enable you to see HD movies or standard-definition (SD) content without any problems or visual artifacts on an LCD monitor. The easiest number that provides a whole-number division for both 24 frames per second and 30 frames per second was 120 Hz. The latter is the standard for SD content.

Tech Tip

Dealing with High-Resolution LCDs

The hard-wired nature of LCD resolution creates a problem for techs and consumers when dealing with bigger, better-quality monitors. A typical 17-inch LCD usually has 1280 × 1024 or higher resolution, for example, and the larger 20+-inch LCDs can go up to 1920 × 1080 or more. These high resolutions make the menus and fonts on a monitor super tiny, a problem for people with less-than-stellar vision. Many folks throw in the towel and run these high-end LCDs at lower resolution and just live with the lower-quality picture, but that's not the best way to resolve this problem.

Microsoft enables incredible customizing of the interface. You can change the font size, shape, and color. You can resize the icons, toolbars, and more. You can even change the number of dots per inch (DPI) for the full screen, making everything bigger or smaller!

For basic customizing, start at the Control Panel | Display applet | Appearance tab or Control Panel | Personalization applet. To change the DPI for the display, go to the Settings tab and click the Advanced button in Windows XP; in Windows Vista, just click the Adjust font size (DPI) option in the Tasks list. In Windows 7, click Display and the select one of the preset font sizes or a custom size. Your clients will thank you!

One nit equals one candela/m². One candela is roughly equal to the amount of light created by a candle.

A video card needs to be able to support Dual-Link DVI to run a 120-Hz monitor or television. See the discussion on DVI later in this chapter for details.

The CompTIA A+ 801 exam expects you to understand the refresh rate, resolution, and native resolution of a monitor.

Contrast Ratio

A big drawback of LCD monitors is that they don't have nearly the color saturation or richness of contrast of a good CRT monitor—although LCD technology continues to improve every year. A good contrast ratio—the difference between the darkest and lightest spots that the monitor can display—is 450:1, although a quick trip to a computer store will reveal LCDs with lower levels (250:1) and higher levels (1000:1).

LCD monitor manufacturers market a *dynamic contrast ratio* number for their monitors, which measures the difference between a full-on, all-white screen, and a full-off, or all-black screen. This yields a much higher number than the standard contrast ratio. My Samsung panels have a 1000:1 contrast ratio, for example, but a 20,000:1 dynamic contrast ratio. Sounds awesome, right? In general, the dynamic contrast ratio doesn't affect viewing on computer monitors. Focus on the standard contrast ratio when making decisions on LCD screens.

Projectors

Projectors are a third option for displaying your computer images, and the best choice when displaying to an audience or in a classroom. There are two ways to project an image on a screen: rearview and front-view. As the name would suggest, a **rearview projector** (see Figure 13.23) shoots an image onto a screen from the rear. Rearview projectors are always self-enclosed and are very popular for televisions, but are virtually unheard of in the PC world.

A **front-view projector** shoots the image out the front and counts on you to put a screen in front at the proper distance. Front-view projectors connected to PCs running Microsoft PowerPoint have been the cornerstone of every meeting almost everywhere for at least the past ten years (see Figure 13.24). This section deals exclusively with front-view projectors that connect to PCs.

Projector Technologies

Projectors that connect to PCs have been in existence for almost as long as PCs themselves. Given all that time, a number of technologies have been used in projectors. The first generation of projectors used CRTs. Each color used a separate CRT that projected the image onto a

● **Figure 13.23** Rearview projector (photo courtesy of Samsung)

● **Figure 13.24** Front-view projector (photo courtesy of Dell Inc.)

screen (see Figure 13.25). CRT projectors create beautiful images, but are expensive, large, and very heavy, and have for the most part been abandoned for more recent technologies.

Given that light shines through an LCD panel, LCD projectors are a natural fit for front projection. LCD projectors are light and very inexpensive compared to CRTs but lack the image quality. LCD projectors are so light that almost all portable projectors use LCD (see Figure 13.26).

All projectors share the same issues as their equivalent-technology monitors. LCD projectors have a specific native resolution, for example. In addition, you need to understand three concepts specific to projectors: lumens, throw, and lamps.

Lumens

The brightness of a projector is measured in lumens. A **lumen** is the amount of light given off by a light source from a certain angle that is perceived by the human eye. The greater the lumen rating of a projector, the brighter the projector will be. The best lumen rating depends on the size of the room and the amount of light in the room. There's no single answer for "the right lumen rating" for a projector, but use this as a rough guide. If you use a projector in a small, darkened room, 1000 to 1500 lumens will work well. If you use a projector in a mid-sized room with typical lighting, you'll need at least 2000 lumens. Projectors for large rooms have ratings over 10,000 lumens and are very expensive.

Throw

A projector's **throw** is the size of the image at a certain distance from the screen. All projectors have a recommended minimum and maximum throw distance that you need to take into consideration. A typical throw would be expressed as follows. A projector with a 16:9 image aspect ratio needs to be 11 to 12 feet away from the projection surface to create a 100-inch diagonal screen. A *long throw lens* has about a 1:2 ratio of screen size to distance, so to display a 4-foot screen, you'd have to put the projector 8 feet away. Some *short throw lenses* drop that ratio down as low as 1:1!

Lamps

The bane of every projector is the lamp. Lamps work hard in your projector, as they must generate a tremendous amount of light. As a result, they generate quite a bit of heat, and all projectors come with a fan to keep the lamp from overheating. When you turn off a projector, the fan continues to run until the lamp is fully cooled. Lamps are also expensive, usually in

• **Figure 13.25** CRT projector

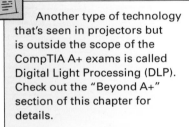
 Another type of technology that's seen in projectors but is outside the scope of the CompTIA A+ exams is called Digital Light Processing (DLP). Check out the "Beyond A+" section of this chapter for details.

• **Figure 13.26** LCD projector (photo courtesy of ViewSonic)

the range of a few hundred dollars (U.S.), which comes as a nasty shock to someone who's not prepared for that price when the lamp dies!

Plasma Displays

Plasma display panels (*PDP*) are a popular technology for displaying movies, competing directly with LCD screens for the flat-panel space. They offer a wider viewing angle and richer picture than the typical LCD and cost less. They weigh a lot more and consume much more electricity, though, compared to LCDs.

Unfortunately, plasma TVs have two issues that make them a bad choice for PC use. First is *burn-in*—the tendency for a screen to leave a "ghost" image even after the image is off the screen. Plasma TV makers have virtually eliminated burn-in, but even the latest plasma displays are subject to burn-in when used as PC displays.

The second issue is *overscan*, a problem that can affect LCD-based TVs as well. Overscan is when the TV blows up the image, cropping off the edges of the picture. TVs do this for historical reasons, but the side effect is that when used with a PC, things like your taskbar get cut off. Some manufacturers have a setting to disable this feature, but not all do. Because media center PCs are becoming more common, CompTIA included the plasma display device in the 220-801 exam objectives. I would advise against using a plasma screen with a media center PC.

Common Features

CRT or LCD, all monitors share a number of characteristics that you need to know for purchase, installation, maintenance, and troubleshooting.

Size

CRT monitors come in a large number of sizes, all measured in inches (although most metric countries provide the metric equivalent value). All monitors provide two numbers: the monitor size and the actual size of the screen. The monitor size measures from two opposite diagonal corners. The actual screen is measured from one edge of the screen to the opposite diagonal side. This latter measurement is often referred to as the **viewable image size (VIS)**, as shown in Figure 13.27. You will commonly see a size

Monitor size Viewable image size

• **Figure 13.27** Viewable image size of a CRT

difference of one to two inches between the two measurements. A 17-inch CRT monitor, for example, might have a 15.5-inch VIS.

LCD monitors dispense with the two values and simply express the VIS value. A 15-inch LCD monitor will have about the same viewing area as a 17-inch CRT.

Connections

CRT monitors for PCs all use the famous 15-pin, three-row, DB-type connector (see Figure 13.28) and a power plug. The DB connector is also called a *D-shell* or *D-subminiature* connector or simply a *VGA connector*. Larger or multipurpose monitors may have a few other connectors, but as far as the CRT is concerned, these are the only two you need for video.

Controlling a CRT requires an *analog signal* from the video card, meaning a signal that rises and falls in waves like a series of *S*s on their side. LCDs and computers, on the other hand, use digital signals, on or off, one or zero. There's no one-half signal in digital!

The video information stored on a video card's RAM is clearly digital. Video cards include a special chip (or function embedded into a chip that does several other jobs) called the **random access memory digital-to-analog converter (RAMDAC)**. As the name implies, the RAMDAC takes the digital signal from the video card and turns it into an analog signal for the analog CRT (see Figure 13.29).

Well, RAMDACs certainly make sense for analog CRT monitors. If you want to plug your LCD monitor into a regular video card, however, you need circuitry on the LCD monitor to convert the signal from analog to digital (see Figure 13.30).

Many LCD monitors use exactly this process. These are called *analog LCD monitors*. The monitor really isn't analog; it's digital, but it takes a standard VGA input. These monitors have one advantage: You may use any standard VGA video card. But these monitors require adjustment of the analog timing signal to the digital clock inside the monitor. This used to be a fairly painful process, but most analog LCD monitors now include intelligent circuitry to make this process either automatic or very easy.

You'll often hear the terms *flat-panel display*, *LCD panel*, or *LED monitor* to describe LCD monitors. I prefer the term *LCD monitor*, but you should be prepared to hear it a few different ways.

• **Figure 13.28** A traditional CRT connector

The RAMDAC translates the digital signal to an analog signal.

Digital data in RAM

Analog signal to monitor

• **Figure 13.29** An analog signal sent to a CRT monitor

The RAMDAC in the LCD converts the analog signal back to digital.

Digital data in RAM

Converts to analog

• Figure 13.30 Converting analog back to digital on the LCD

Why convert the signal from digital to analog and then back to digital? Well, many monitor and video card people agree that it just doesn't make much sense. We now see quite a few digital LCD monitors and digital video cards. They use a completely different connector than the old 15-pin DB connector used on analog video cards and monitors. After a few false starts with connection standards, under names such as P&D and DFP, the digital LCD world, with a few holdouts, moved to the **digital visual interface (DVI)** standard. DVI is actually three different connectors that look very much alike: DVI-D is for digital, DVI-A is for analog (for backward compatibility if the monitor maker so desires), and the DVI-A/D or DVI-I (interchangeable) accepts either a DVI-D or DVI-A. DVI-D and DVI-A are keyed so that they will not connect.

DVI-D and DVI-I connectors come in two varieties, single-link and dual-link. *Single-link DVI* has a maximum bandwidth of 165 MHz, which, translated into practical terms, limits the maximum resolution of a monitor to 1920 × 1080 at 60 Hz or 1280 × 1024 at 85 Hz. *Dual-link DVI* uses more pins to double throughput and thus grant higher resolutions (see Figure 13.31). With dual-link DVI, you can have displays up to a whopping 2048 × 1536 at 60 Hz!

Digital connectors are quickly replacing analog in the monitor world. Digital makes both the monitor and the video card cheaper, provides a clearer signal because no conversion is necessary, and makes installation easy. Many monitors and video cards these days only support digital signals, but there are still quite a few of each that provide both digital and analog connections.

The video card people have it easy. They either include both a VGA and a DVI-D connector or they use a DVI-I connector. The advantage to DVI-I is that you can add a cheap DVI-I-to-VGA adapter (one usually comes with

• Figure 13.31 Dual-link DVI-I connector

You can plug a single-link DVI monitor into a dual-link DVI connector and it'll work just fine.

• **Figure 13.32** DVI-to-VGA adapter

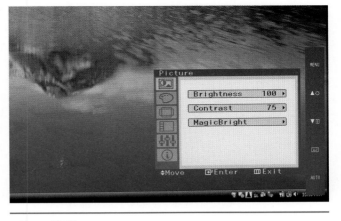

• **Figure 13.33** Typical menu controls

the video card) like the one shown in Figure 13.32 and connect an analog monitor just fine.

Monitor makers have it tougher. Most LCD monitor makers have made the jump to DVI, but many include a VGA connector for those machines that still need it.

Unless you're buying a complete new system, you'll rarely buy a video card at the same time you buy a monitor. When you're buying a monitor or a video card, make sure that the new device will connect to the other!

Adjustments

Most adjustments to the monitor take place at installation, but for now, let's just make sure you know what they are and where they are located. Clearly, all monitors have an On/Off button or switch. Also, see if you can locate the Brightness and Contrast buttons. Beyond that, most monitors (at least the only ones you should buy) have an onboard menu system, enabling a number of adjustments. Every monitor maker provides a different way to access these menus, but they all provide two main functions: physical screen adjustment (bigger, smaller, move to the left, right, up, down, and others) and color adjustment. The color adjustment lets you adjust the red, green, and blue levels to give you the best color tones. All of these settings are a matter of personal taste. Make sure the person who will use the computer understands how to adjust these settings (see Figure 13.33).

Power Conservation

CRT and LCD monitors differ greatly in the amount of electricity they require. The bottom line is that CRTs use a lot and LCDs use a lot less. Here's the scoop.

Approximately half the power required to run a desktop PC is consumed by the CRT monitor. Monitors that meet the Video Electronics Standards Association (VESA) specification for **Display Power Management Signaling (DPMS)** can reduce monitor power consumption by roughly 75 percent. This is accomplished by reducing or eliminating the signals sent by the video card to the monitor during idle periods. By eliminating these pulses, the monitor essentially takes catnaps. The advantage over simply shutting the monitor off is in the time it takes to restore the display.

Tech Tip

Power Switch Versus DPMS

Turning off the monitor with the power switch is the most basic form of power management. The downside to this is the wear and tear on the cathode ray tube itself. The cathode ray tube is the most expensive component of a CRT monitor, and frequently turning the monitor on and off can damage the tube. When using a non-DPMS monitor or video card, it is best to turn the monitor on once during the day and then turn it off only when you are finished for the day. This on-off cycle must be balanced against the life of the CRT display phosphors. The typical monitor loses about half its original brightness after roughly 10,000 to 15,000 hours of display time. Leaving the monitor on all of the time brings a noticeable decrease in brightness in just over a year (8766 hours). The only way around this is enabling the DPMS features of the monitor or taking care to turn the monitor off.

A typical CRT monitor consumes approximately 120 watts. During a catnap or power-down mode, the energy consumption is reduced to below 25 watts, while enabling the screen to return to use in less than ten seconds. Full shutoff is accomplished by eliminating all clocking pulses to the monitor. Although this reduces power consumption to below 15 watts, it also requires anywhere from 15 to 30 seconds to restore a usable display.

A typical LCD monitor, in contrast, uses less than half the electricity that a CRT uses. A 19-inch, 4:3 aspect-ratio flat panel, for example, uses around 33 watts at peak usage and less than 2 watts in DPMS mode. Larger LCDs use more power at peak usage than smaller ones. A 21-inch wide-screen model, for example, might draw ~75 watts at peak but drop down to less than 2 watts in DPMS mode. Swapping out CRTs with LCDs is a great way to save on your electric bill!

■ Display Adapters

The display adapter, or video card, handles the video chores within the PC, processing information from the CPU and sending it out to the monitor.

The display adapter is a complex set of devices. A graphics processor of some type processes data from the CPU and outputs commands to the display. Like any other processor, the graphics processor needs RAM. The graphics processor needs fast connectivity between it, the CPU, and system RAM. The display adapter must have a connection compatible with the monitor.

Traditionally, and still quite commonly, the display adapter was an expansion card that plugged into the motherboard (see Figure 13.34). Although many new systems have the display adapter circuitry built into the motherboard, most techs still call it the video card, so we'll start there. This section looks at five aspects that define a video card: display modes, motherboard connection, graphics processor circuitry, video memory, and connections.

• **Figure 13.34** Typical video card

Modes

The trick to understanding video cards is to appreciate the beginnings and evolution of video. Video output to computers was around long before PCs were created. At the time PCs became popular, video was almost exclusively text-based, meaning that the only image the video card could place on the monitor was one of the 256 ASCII characters. These characters were made up of patterns of pixels that were stored in the system BIOS. When a program wanted to make a character, it talked to DOS or to the BIOS, which stored the image of that character in the video memory. The character then appeared on the screen.

The beauty of text video cards was that they were simple to use and cheap to make. The simplicity was based on the fact that only 256 characters existed, and no color choices were available—just monochrome text.

You could, however, choose to make the character bright, dim, normal, underlined, or blinking. Positioning the characters was easy, as space on the screen allowed for only 80 characters per row and 24 rows of characters.

Long ago, RAM was very expensive, so video card makers were interested in using the absolute least amount of RAM possible. Making a monochrome text video card was a great way to keep down RAM costs. Let's consider this for a minute. First, the video RAM is where the contents of the screen are located. You need enough video RAM to hold all of the necessary information for a completely full screen. Each ASCII character needs 8 bits (by definition), so a monitor with 80 characters/row and 24 rows will need

80 characters × 24 rows = 1920 characters = 15,360 bits or 1920 bytes

The video card would need less than 2000 bytes of memory, which isn't much, not even in 1981 when the PC first came out. Now, be warned that I'm glossing over a few things—where you store the information about underlines, blinking, and so on. The bottom line is that the tiny amount of necessary RAM kept monochrome text video cards cheap.

Very early on in the life of PCs, a new type of video, called a *graphics video card*, was invented. It was quite similar to a text card. The text card, however, was limited to the 256 ASCII characters, whereas a graphics video card enabled programs to turn any pixel on the screen on or off. It was still monochrome, but programs could access any individual pixel, enabling much more creative control of the screen. Of course, it took more video RAM. The first graphics cards ran at 320 × 200 pixels. One bit was needed for each pixel (on or off), so

320 × 200 = 64,000 bits or 8000 bytes

That's a lot more RAM than was needed for text, but it was still a pretty low amount of RAM—even in the old days. As resolutions increased, however, the amount of video RAM needed to store this information also increased.

After monochrome video was invented, moving into color for both text and graphics video cards was a relatively easy step. The only question was how to store color information for each character (text cards) or pixel (graphics cards). This was easy—just set aside a few more bits for each pixel or character. So now the question becomes, "How many bits do you set aside?" Well, that depends on how many colors you want. Basically, the number of colors determines the number of bits. For example, if you want four colors, you need 2 bits (2 bits per pixel). Then, you could do something like this

00 = black	01 = cyan (blue)
10 = magenta (reddish pink)	11 = white

So if you set aside 2 bits, you could get 4 colors. If you want 16 colors, set aside 4 bits, which would make 16 different combinations. Nobody ever invented a text mode that used more than 16 colors, so let's start thinking in terms of only graphics mode and bits per pixels. To get 256 colors, each pixel would have to be represented with 8 bits. In PCs, the number of colors—called the **color depth**—is always a power of 2: 4, 16, 256, 64 K, and so on. Note that as more colors are added, more video RAM is needed to store

• Figure 13.35 Adjusting color settings in Windows XP

the information. Here are the most common color depths and the number of bits necessary to store the color information per pixel:

2 colors = 1 bit (mono)

4 colors = 2 bits

16 colors = 4 bits

256 colors = 8 bits

64 K colors = 16 bits

16.7 million colors = 24 bits

Most technicians won't say, for example, "I set my video card to show over 16 million colors." Instead, they'll say, "I set my color depth to 24 bits." Talk in terms of bits, not colors. It is assumed that you know the number of colors for any color depth.

You can set the color depth for a Windows XP computer in the Display Properties dialog box on the Settings tab (see Figure 13.35). If you set up a typical Windows XP computer, you'll notice that Windows offers you 32-bit color quality, which might make you assume you're about to crank out more than 4 billion colors, but that's simply not the case. The 32-bit color setting offers 24-bit color plus an 8-bit alpha channel. An alpha channel controls the opacity of a particular color. By using an alpha channel, Windows can more effectively blend colors to create the effect of semi-transparent images. In Windows XP, you see this in the drop shadow under a menu; in Windows Vista and Windows 7, almost every screen element can be semi-transparent (see Figure 13.36).

• Figure 13.36 Semi-transparency in Windows Vista

Your video card and monitor are capable of showing Windows in a fixed number of different resolutions and color depths. The choices depend on the resolutions and color depths the video card can push to the monitor and the amount of bandwidth your monitor can support. Any single combination of resolution and color depth you set for your system is called a **mode**. For standardization, VESA defines a certain number of resolutions, all derived from the granddaddy of video modes: VGA.

VGA

With the introduction of the PS/2, IBM introduced the **video graphics array (VGA)** standard. This standard offered 16 colors at a resolution of 640 × 480 pixels. VGA supported such an amazing variety of colors by using an analog video signal instead of a digital one, as was the case prior to the VGA standard. A digital signal is either all on or all off. By using an analog signal, the VGA standard can provide 64 distinct levels for the three colors (RGB)—that is, 64^3 or 262,144 possible colors—although only 16 or 256 can be seen at a time. For most purposes, 640 × 480 and 16 colors defines VGA mode. This is typically the display resolution and color depth referred to on many software packages as a minimum display requirement. Every video card made in the past 15 years can output as VGA, but VGA-only cards are now obsolete.

> To accommodate rotated LCD monitors in portrait view, the video resolution numbers might be reversed. Rather than 1280 × 1024, for example, you might see 1024 × 1280. The amount of RAM needed remains the same regardless.

Beyond VGA

The 1980s were a strange time for video. Until the very late 1980s, VGA was the highest mode defined by VESA, but demand grew for modes that went beyond VGA. This motivated VESA to introduce (over time) a number of new modes with names such as SVGA, XGA, and many others. Even today, new modes are being released! Table 13.1 shows the more common modes.

The video card must have sufficient RAM to support each combination of color depth and resolution. Many years ago this mattered, when video cards had scant megabytes of memory. A video card with only 2 MB of RAM, for example, could handle a high color (16-bit) display at 1024 × 768, but not the same resolution with true color (24-bit). Table 13.2 shows common modes and the minimum video memory needed. All modern video cards can handle true color at any resolution.

Table 13.1	Typical Display Modes		
Video Mode	**Resolution**	**Aspect Ratio**	**Typical Device**
SVGA	800 × 600	4:3	Small monitors
HDTV 720p	1280 × 720	16:9	Lowest resolution that can be called HDTV
SXGA	1280 × 1024	5:4	Native resolution for many desktop LCD monitors
WXGA	1366 × 768	16:9	Widescreen laptops
WSXGA	1440 × 900	16:10	Widescreen laptops
SXGA+	1400 × 1050	4:3	Laptop monitors and high-end projectors
UXGA	1600 × 1200	4:3	Larger CRT monitors
HDTV 1080p	1920 × 1080	16:9	Full HDTV resolution
WUXGA	1920 × 1200	16:10	For 24"+ widescreen monitors
QWXGA	2048 × 1152	16:9	For smaller, fine monitors
WQXGA	2560 × 1600	16:10	For 27"+ widescreen monitors
WQUXGA	3840 × 2400	16:10	For smaller, fine monitors

Table 13.2	Common Modes and the Minimum Video Memory Required	
Resolution	**16-bit (High Color)**	**24-bit (True Color)**
640 × 480	1 MB	1 MB
800 × 600	1 MB	2 MB
1024 × 768	2 MB	4 MB
1280 × 1024	4 MB	4 MB
1600 × 1200	4 MB	6 MB

Motherboard Connection

Techs will encounter four ways that display adapters connect to a motherboard. The oldest connector type, PCI, is used today only for an additional card to support extra monitors. Slightly newer but still quite old in computer terms is AGP. Every current discrete video card plugs into the PCIe slot on a motherboard. Finally, many motherboards have the display adapter built-in. I'll discuss integrated graphics after talking about graphics processors and memory types, at which point the topic will make more sense. For now, let's look at PCI, AGP, and PCIe.

PCI

Using more color depth slows down video functions. Data moving from the video card to the display has to go through the video card's memory chips and the expansion bus, and this can happen only so quickly. The standard PCI slots used in almost all systems for many years are limited to 32-bit transfers at roughly 33 MHz, yielding a maximum bandwidth of 132 MBps. This sounds like a lot until you start using higher resolutions, high color depths, and higher refresh rates. (The refresh rates mattered because we only had CRTs when video cards used the PCI bus.)

For example, take a typical display at 800 × 600 with a fairly low refresh of 70 Hz. The 70 Hz means the display screen is being redrawn 70 times per second. If you use a low color depth of 256 colors, which is 8 bits ($2^8 = 256$), you can multiply all of the values together to see how much data per second has to be sent to the display:

$$800 \times 600 \times 1 \text{ byte} \times 70 = 33.6 \text{ MBps}$$

If you use the same example at 16 million (24-bit) colors, the figure jumps to 100.8 MBps. You might say, "Well, if PCI runs at 132 MBps, it can handle that!" That statement would be true if the PCI bus had nothing else to do but tend to the video card, but almost every system has more than one PCI device, each requiring part of that throughput. The PCI bus simply cannot handle the needs of any current systems and is therefore used only for adding a second (or third) video card to a system to support an extra monitor.

• **Figure 13.37** AGP

AGP

Intel answered the desire for video bandwidth even higher than PCI with the **Accelerated Graphics Port (AGP)**. AGP is a single, special port, similar to a PCI slot, that is dedicated to video. You will never see a motherboard with two AGP slots. Figure 13.37 shows an early-generation AGP. AGP is derived from the 66-MHz, 32-bit PCI 2.1 specification. AGP uses a function called *strobing* that increases the signals two, four, and eight times for each clock cycle.

Simply describing AGP as a faster PCI would seriously misrepresent the power of AGP. AGP has several technological advantages over PCI, including the bus, the internal operations, and the capability to handle 3-D texturing (discussed later in the chapter).

First, AGP currently resides alone, on its own personal data bus, connected directly to the Northbridge (see Figure 13.38). This is important because more advanced versions of AGP outperform every bus on the system except the frontside bus!

Second, AGP takes advantage of pipelining commands, similar to the way CPUs pipeline. Third, AGP has a feature called **sidebanding**—basically a second data bus that enables the video card to send more commands to the Northbridge while receiving other commands at the same time.

Video cards do all kinds of neat stuff with their RAM; for example, video cards store copies of individual windows so they can display the windows at different points on the screen very quickly. A demanding application can quickly max out the onboard RAM on a video card, so AGP provides a pathway so the AGP card can "steal" chunks of the regular system memory to store video information, especially textures. This is generically called a *system memory access* and is quite popular.

AGP has gone through three sets of specifications (AGP 1.0, AGP 2.0, and AGP 3.0), but the official names tend to be ignored. Most techs and consumers refer to the various cards by their strobe multiplier, such as AGP 1×, 2×, 4×, and 8×. The only problem with blurring the distinctions between the specifications comes from the fact that many new motherboards simply don't support the older AGP cards because the older cards require a different physical connection than the new ones.

• **Figure 13.38** An AGP bus

• **Figure 13.39** AGP 8× slot

• **Figure 13.40** PCIe video card connected in PCIe slot

Some motherboards support multiple types of AGP. Figure 13.39 shows an AGP slot that accommodates everything up to 8×, even the very rare AGP Pro cards. Note that the tab on the slot covers the extra pins required for AGP Pro.

Because many AGP cards will run on older AGP motherboards, you can get away with mixing AGP specifications. To get the best, most stable performance possible, you should use an AGP card that's fully supported by the motherboard.

The only significant downside to AGP lies in the close connection tolerances required by the cards themselves. It's very common to snap in a new AGP card and power up just to get a no-video-card beep or a system that doesn't boot. Always take the time to ensure that an AGP card is snapped down securely and screwed in before starting the system.

PCIe

AGP is a great way to get video information to and from video cards very quickly, but it has the downside of being a unique connector in a world where saving money is important. AGP, being based on PCI, also uses a parallel interface. When the **PCI Express (PCIe)** interface was developed to replace PCI, the PCIe designers worked hard to make sure it would also replace AGP. PCIe is a natural evolution for video because it is incredibly fast, using a serial communication method. Also, because PCIe is a true expansion bus designed to talk to the CPU and RAM, it also supports all of the little extras found in AGP, such as sidebanding and system memory access. All PCIe video cards use the PCIe ×16 connector (see Figure 13.40). PCIe replaced AGP as the primary video interface almost overnight.

> **✓ Cross Check**
>
> **PCIe Versions**
>
> You first encountered PCIe way back in Chapter 8, so check your memory now. What's the significance of PCIe 1.0 versus 2.0? What kind of data transfers can PCIe 3.0 devices attain?

Graphics Processor

The graphics processor handles the heavy lifting of taking commands from the CPU and translating them into coordinates and color information that the monitor understands and displays. Most techs today refer to the device that processes video as a **graphics processing unit (GPU)**.

Video card discussion, at least among techs, almost always revolves around the graphics processor the video card uses and the amount of RAM onboard. A typical video card might be called an XFX Radeon HD7970 3-GB 384-bit GDDR5 PCI Express 3.0, so let's break that down. XFX is the

manufacturer of the video card; Radeon HD7970 is the graphics processor; 3-GB 384-bit GDDR5 describes the dedicated video RAM and the connection between the video RAM and the graphics processor; and PCI Express 3.0 describes the motherboard expansion slot the card requires.

Many companies make the hundreds of different video cards on the market, but only three companies produce the vast majority of graphics processors found on video cards: NVIDIA, AMD, and Intel. NVIDIA and AMD make and sell graphics processors to third-party manufacturers who then design, build, and sell video cards under their own branding. Intel made its own line of cards, but now concentrates on graphics processors built into motherboards. Figure 13.41 shows an NVIDIA GeForce GTX 570 on a board made by EVGA.

Your choice of graphics processor is your single most important decision in buying a video card. Low-end graphics processors usually work fine for the run-of-the-mill user who wants to write letters or run a Web browser. High-end graphics processors are designed to support the beautiful 3-D games that are so popular today, and they provide excellent video playback for high-definition video. We'll look at 3-D issues a little later in this chapter, but we'll save HD video for Chapter 17.

• **Figure 13.41** NVIDIA GeForce GTX 570

Video Memory

Video memory is crucial to the operation of a PC. It is probably the hardest-working set of electronics on the PC. Video RAM constantly updates to reflect every change that takes place on the screen. When you're working with heavy-duty applications (such as games), video memory can prove to be a serious bottleneck in three ways: data throughput speed, access speed, and simple capacity.

Manufacturers have overcome these bottlenecks by upping the width of the bus between the video RAM and video processor; using specialized, super-fast RAM; and adding more and more total RAM.

First, manufacturers reorganized the video display memory on cards from the typical 32-bit-wide structure to 64, 128, 256, and 384 bits wide. Because the system bus is limited to 32 or 64 bits, this would not be of much benefit if video display cards weren't really coprocessor boards. Most of the graphics rendering and processing is handled on the card by the video processor chip rather than by the CPU. The main system simply provides the input data to the processor on the video card. Because the memory bus on the video card is as much as eight times wider than the standard 32-bit pathway (256 bits), data can be manipulated and then sent to the monitor much more quickly (see Figure 13.42).

• **Figure 13.42** Wide path between video processor and video RAM

Specialized types of video RAM have been developed for graphics cards, and many offer substantial improvements in video speeds. The single most important feature that separates DRAM from video RAM is that video RAM can read and write data at the same time. Table 13.3 shows a list of common video memory technologies used yesterday and today—make sure you know these for the exams!

Table 13.3	Video RAM Technologies	
Acronym	**Name**	**Purpose**
VRAM	Video RAM	The original graphics RAM
WRAM	Window RAM	Designed to replace VRAM; never caught on
SGRAM	Synchronous Graphics RAM	A version of SDRAM with features to speed up access for graphics
DDR SDRAM	Double Data Rate Synchronous DRAM	Used on budget graphics cards and very common on laptop video cards
DDR2 SDRAM	Double Data Rate version 2, Synchronous DRAM	Popular on video cards until GDDR3; lower voltage than DDR memory
GDDR3 SDRAM	Graphics Double Data Rate, version 3	Similar to DDR2 but runs at faster speeds; different cooling requirements
GDDR4 SDRAM	Graphics Double Data Rate, version 4	Upgrade of GDDR3; faster clock
GDDR5 SDRAM	Graphics Double Data Rate, version 5	Successor to GDDR4; double the input/output rate of GDDR4

Finally, many advanced 3-D video cards come with huge amounts of video RAM. It's very common to see cards with 64, 128, 256, or 512 MB of RAM, or even 1, 2, or 3 GB of RAM! Why so much? Even with PCI Express, accessing data in system RAM always takes a lot longer than accessing data stored in local RAM on the video card. The huge amount of video RAM enables game developers to optimize their games and store more essential data on the local video RAM.

Integrated GPUs

A lot of current motherboards have integrated GPUs or are ready for a CPU with an integrated GPU. The motherboard GPU can be a separate chip attached to the motherboard or can be built into the Northbridge chip. You might run into AMD Radeon chips or NVIDIA nForce chips powering the GPU. Intel has long integrated the Intel Graphics Media Accelerator (GMA) into its chipsets.

AMD, Intel, and NVIDIA make CPUs with integrated GPUs that vary a lot in graphical performance. Some of AMD's Fusion processors, for example, have a CPU/GPU combination that rivals any CPU/discrete graphics card combination, though only at a level seen in portable computers. They're good enough for casual gaming and even some medium-duty games. Intel's graphics support is geared to desktop performance, not gaming at all. NVIDIA's Tegra line is focused on gaming on mobile devices such as tablets and smartphones.

With an integrated GPU, the CPU circuitry is getting pretty crowded. A single AMD Fusion chip, for example, integrates two to four CPU cores, a memory controller that supports DDR3, cache memory, and a GPU that can handle advanced 3-D graphics. Wow! One of the best parts of all this integration is that the chip requires far less electricity than comparable discrete components. Many techs and companies call current integrated GPUs *accelerated processing units* (*APUs*), though that term can be applied to other chips that integrate multiple processing functions.

Connector Types and Associated Cables

You can find many different connectors on video cards, plus variations within those connector types. CompTIA also makes a distinction between the names of the ports on the cards and the cables associated with them, though most techs will refer to the connectors and cables by multiple names interchangeably. Here's the scoop.

Standard monitors connect through one of three connectors:

- DVI
- DB-15
- DisplayPort

Video cards offer other connector types for connecting to things like television sets, camcorders, and other multimedia devices, although these are mostly associated with older cards:

- RCA
- BNC
- Mini-DIN
- HDMI

The video card shown in Figure 13.43 has three connectors: DB-15, DVI-I, and S-video. Other connectors enable the video card to connect to composite, component, and even high-definition devices.

For Standard Monitors

You know about the standard monitor connectors, the DB-15 that most people call VGA and DVI, from the monitor discussion earlier. About the only thing to add is that most DVI connections on video cards these days natively support analog signals. You can use a simple DVI-to-VGA adapter, for example, for connecting a VGA cable to a video card.

Apple Mac desktop models use a **DisplayPort** connection rather than VGA or DVI for connecting to a monitor. Dell offers support for DisplayPort as well at the time of this writing. Figure 13.44 shows a DisplayPort jack on a Dell portable.

> The CompTIA A+ competencies mention *RJ-45* as a video connector type and Ethernet as a video cable type. The only place you'll find both used in video is with SP Controls' *CatLinc* system. CatLinc uses adapters to connect your VGA, DVI, HDMI, and component devices to a CAT5 cable (commonly associated with Ethernet networks). CAT5 cables enable the video signal to be transmitted across greater distances more clearly at a lower cost.

• **Figure 13.43** Video card connectors: VGA, S-video, and DVI-I

> The CompTIA A+ 801 exam might make a distinction between the VGA cable and the DB-15 connector into which it plugs.

• **Figure 13.44** DisplayPort jack

S-video Proprietary

• **Figure 13.45** S-video and proprietary round connectors

• **Figure 13.46** Composite and component connection options

CompTIA has pulled out all the stops on adding extra acronyms to your plate with connector types. The 220-801 exam objectives refer to the mini-DIN used with S-video as a *Din-6* (yes, with the weird initial capping of Din rather than DIN to refer to the acronym). Most techs refer to the port as an *S-video port*, but CompTIA seems to reserve the S-video label only to the cable.

Some video cards with built-in TV tuners that enable the PC to be a TV as well as a computer have a standard coaxial jack for connecting a cable or antenna. See Chapter 17 for the scoop on TV tuners.

For Multimedia Devices

Video cards can have one or more standard connections plus non-standard connections for hooking the PC to a multimedia device, such as a television, DVD or Blu-ray Disc player, or video camera. The earliest type of connector commonly found is the mini-DIN for attaching an S-video cable. This provides decent-quality video output or, in some cases, input. You'll sometimes find a proprietary round connector that supports S-video and a proprietary dongle that adds support for video through either component connection or composite connections. Figure 13.45 shows the similar round ports.

A composite connector provides a video signal through a single cable that plugs into a standard RCA jack, whereas a component adapter provides a split signal: red, green, and blue (RGB). Figure 13.46 shows the two connector dongles. Note that all are RCA connectors.

The best connections for outputting to television are the **High Definition Multimedia Interface (HDMI)** connectors. Some devices offer HDMI output directly (such as the portable pictured in Figure 13.47), while other video cards support HDMI through a special cable that connects to a dual-link DVI port. Figure 13.48 shows an example of such a cable.

HDMI comes in three standard sizes, Standard, Mini, and Micro. (Plus there's the Type E connector used exclusively for automobile video systems—and don't we all need video while driving?) Standard HDMI is what you'll find on video cards and televisions and some portable devices. Most tablet devices out today use Mini HDMI (see Figure 13.49).

• **Figure 13.47** HDMI port between two USB ports on Lenovo laptop

• **Figure 13.48** DVI-to-HDMI cable

• **Figure 13.49** Mini HDMI port

■ Installing and Configuring Video

Once you've decided on the features and price for your new video card and monitor, you need to install them into your system. As long as you have the right connection to your video card, installing a monitor is straightforward. The challenge comes when installing the video card.

During the physical installation of a video card, watch out for two possible issues: long cards and proximity of the nearest expansion card. Some high-end video cards simply won't fit in certain cases or block access to needed motherboard connectors such as the SATA sockets. There's no clean fix for such a problem—you simply have to change at least one of the components (video card, motherboard, or case). Because high-end video cards run very hot, you don't want them sitting right next to another card; make sure the fan on the video card has plenty of ventilation space. A good practice is to leave the slot next to the video card empty to allow better airflow (see Figure 13.50). (Many high-end video cards come as double-wide cards with built-in air vents, so you don't have any choice but to take up double the space.)

Try This!

Install a Video Card

You know how to install an expansion card from your reading in earlier chapters. Installing a video card is pretty much the same, so Try This!

1. Refer to Chapter 8 for the steps on installing a new card.

2. Plug the monitor cable into the video card port on the back of the PC and power up the system. If your PC seems dead after you install a video card, or if the screen is blank but you hear fans whirring and the internal speaker sounding off *long-short-short-short*, your video card likely did not get properly seated. Unplug the PC and try again.

• **Figure 13.50**　Installing a video card

Once you've properly installed the video card and connected it to the monitor, you've conquered half the territory for making the video process work properly. You're ready to tackle the drivers and tweak the operating system, so let's go!

Software

Configuring your video software is usually a two-step process. First you need to load drivers for the video card. Then you need to open the Control Panel and go to the Display applet (Windows XP/7) or Personalization applet (Windows Vista) to make your adjustments. Let's explore how to make the video card and monitor work in Windows.

Drivers

Just like any other piece of hardware, your video card needs a driver to function. Video card drivers install pretty much the same way as all of the other drivers we've discussed thus far: either the driver is already built into Windows or you must use the installation media that comes with the video card.

Video card makers are constantly updating their drivers. Odds are good that any video card more than a few months old has at least one driver update. If possible, check the manufacturer's Web site and use the driver located there if there is one. If the Web site doesn't offer a driver, it's usually best to use the installation media. Always avoid using the built-in Windows driver as it tends to be the most dated.

We'll explore driver issues in more detail after we discuss the Display and Personalization applets. Like so many things about video, you can't fully understand one topic without understanding at least one other!

Using the Display and Personalization Applets

With the driver installed, you're ready to configure your display settings. The Display applet or Personalization applet on the Control Panel is your next stop. The **Display applet** and **Personalization applet** provide convenient, central locations for all of your display settings, including resolution, refresh rate, driver information, and color depth.

The default Display applet window in Windows XP, called the Display Properties dialog box (see Figure 13.51), has five tabs: Themes, Desktop, Screen Saver, Appearance, and Settings. The first four tabs have options you can choose to change the look and feel of Windows and set up a screensaver; the fifth tab is where you make adjustments that relate directly to your monitor and video card.

• **Figure 13.51**　Display Properties dialog box in Windows XP

The Personalization applet in Windows Vista offers functions similar to the Display applet, but each function manifests as a clickable option rather than as a separate tab (see Figure 13.52). Four of the seven options mirror the look and feel options of earlier versions of Windows, such as Window Color and Appearance, Desktop Background, Screen Saver, and Theme. The last option, Display Settings, is where you make adjustments to your monitor and video card. Two options, Sounds and Mouse Pointers, don't concern us at all at this time.

With Windows 7, Microsoft created a more visually oriented Personalization applet (see Figure 13.53). Most users typically want to change only their background or theme rather than anything else, so those options are front and center. Other options are in the Tasks panel on the left or in the Display applet, which is different than Windows XP's display applet.

Whether discussing tabs or options, the functions on all three applets are pretty much the same, so let's do this in one discussion. I'll point out any serious differences among the versions.

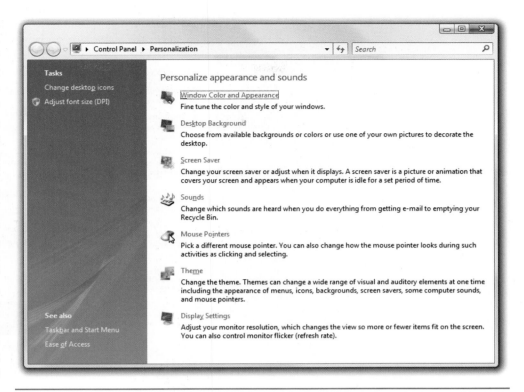

• **Figure 13.52** Personalization applet in Windows Vista

• **Figure 13.53** Personalization applet in Windows 7

• **Figure 13.54** Theme option in the Windows Vista Personalization applet

Making the Screen Pretty

Three tabs/options in the Display/Personalization applet have the job of adjusting the appearance of the screen: Themes/Theme, Desktop/Desktop Background, and Appearance/Window Color and Appearance. Windows 7 simplifies this process by making those adjustments available on the Personalization screen, as you saw in Figure 13.53. Windows themes are preset configurations of the look and feel of the entire Windows environment (see Figure 13.54).

The Desktop tab in Windows XP (see Figure 13.55) or Desktop Background link in Windows Vista/7 defines the background color or image. In Windows XP, it also includes the handy Customize Desktop button that enables you to define the icons as well as any Web pages you want to appear on the desktop. Windows Vista/7 give you the option to position the image on the screen (see Figure 13.56), and the *Change desktop icons* option in the Tasks list in the Personalization applet enables you to choose which system icons (such as Computer, Recycle Bin, and Network) show up on your desktop, as well as which graphical icons they use.

The last of the tabs for the look and feel of the desktop in Windows XP is the Appearance tab. Think of the Appearance tab as the way to fine-tune the theme to your liking. The main screen gives only a few options—the real power is when you click the Advanced button to open the Advanced Appearance dialog box (see Figure 13.57). Using this dialog box, you may adjust almost

• **Figure 13.55** Desktop tab on Display Properties dialog box

• Figure 13.56 Desktop Background options in Windows 7

• Figure 13.57 Advanced Appearance dialog box in Windows XP

Figure 13.58 Window Color and Appearance options in Windows 7

Figure 13.59 Screen Saver Settings in Windows 7

everything about the desktop, including the types of fonts and colors of every part of a window.

The Window Color and Appearance option in Windows Vista is a little simpler on the surface, enabling you to change the color scheme, intensity, and transparency. Windows 7 shows similar controls following the Windows Color link (see Figure 13.58). You can unlock the full gamut of options, though, by clicking the *Open classic appearance properties for more color options* link in Windows Vista or *Advanced appearance settings* in Windows 7.

Screen Saver

At first glance, the Screen Saver tab/option seems to do nothing but set the Windows screensaver—no big deal, just about everyone has set a screensaver (see Figure 13.59). But another option on the Screen Saver tab gets you to one of the most important settings of your system: power management. Click on the Power button or *Change power settings* option to get to the Power Options Properties dialog box or Power Options applet (see Figure 13.60).

Figure 13.60 Power Options applet in Windows 7

The tabs and options define all of the power management of the system. Power management is a fairly involved process, so we'll save the big discussion for where we need to save power the most: Chapter 18.

Settings Tab/Display Settings Applet/Display Applet

The Settings tab in Windows XP and the Display Settings applet in Windows Vista (see Figure 13.61) are the centralized location for configuring all of your video settings in Windows XP/Vista. From the main screen you can adjust both the resolution and the color depth. Windows only displays resolutions and color depths that your video card/monitor combination can accept and that are suitable for most situations. Everyone has a favorite resolution, and higher isn't always better. Especially for those with trouble seeing small screen elements, higher resolutions can present a difficulty—already small icons are *much* smaller at 1280 × 1024 than at 800 × 600. Try

Figure 13.61 Display Settings applet and Settings tab

all of the resolutions to see which you like—just remember that LCD monitors look sharpest at their native resolution (usually the highest listed).

Clicking the Display link in the Tasks list of the Personalization applet in Windows 7 takes you to a simpler interface, again designed to give you quick access to only features you might commonly want to change. Changing the font size is centrally featured, but links in the top left of the task pane enable you to drill down to more advanced options, such as setting the color depth (see Figure 13.62).

Another option you may see in the Settings tab/ Display Settings applet is multiple monitors. To see the same feature options in Windows 7, click the *Change display settings* link in the Display applet. Windows supports the use of two (or more) monitors. These monitors may work together like two halves of one large monitor, or the second monitor might simply show a duplicate of what's happening on the first monitor. Multiple monitors are handy if you need lots of screen space but don't want to buy a really large, expensive monitor (see Figure 13.63).

• **Figure 13.62** Display applet in Windows 7

• **Figure 13.63** My editor hard at work with dual monitors

There are two ways to set up multiple monitors: plug in two or more video cards or use a single video card that supports multiple monitors. Both methods are quite common and work well. Multiple monitors are easy to configure: just plug in the monitors and Windows should detect them. Windows will show the monitors in the applet, as shown in Figure 13.64 for Windows 7. By default, the second monitor is not enabled. To use the second monitor, just select *Extend my Windows desktop onto this monitor* in Windows XP, *Extend the desktop onto this monitor* in Windows Vista, or use the Multiple displays dropdown box and select *Extend these displays* in Windows 7.

If you need to see more advanced settings, click on...that's right, the Advanced or Advanced Settings button in Windows XP/Vista, or on the Advanced settings link in the Screen Resolution dialog box in Windows 7. The title of the dialog

• **Figure 13.64** Enabling multiple monitors

box that opens reflects the monitor and video card. As you can see in Figure 13.65, this particular computer uses a pair of Samsung SyncMaster T220 monitors running off of an ATI Radeon 5750 video card.

The two tabs you're most likely to use are the Adapter and Monitor tabs. The Adapter tab gives detailed information about the video card, including the amount of video memory, the graphics processor, and the BIOS information (yup, your video card has a BIOS, too!). You can also click on the List All Modes button to change the current mode of the video card, although any mode you may set here, you can also set in the sliders on the main screen.

If you're still using a CRT, you'll find the Monitor tab a handy place. This is where you can set the refresh rate (see Figure 13.66). Windows only shows refresh rates that the monitor says it can handle, but many monitors can take a faster—and therefore easier on the eyes—refresh rate. To see all of the modes the video card can support, uncheck the *Hide modes that this monitor cannot display* option.

If you try this, always increase the refresh rate in small increments. If the screen looks better, use it. If the screen seems distorted or disappears, wait a moment and Windows will reset to the original refresh rate. Be careful when using modes that Windows says the monitor cannot display. Pushing a CRT past its fastest refresh rate for more than a minute or two can damage it.

All LCD monitors have a fixed refresh rate.

• **Figure 13.65** Advanced video settings, Adapter tab

• **Figure 13.66** Advanced video settings, Monitor tab

• **Figure 13.67** Third-party video tab

Most video cards add their own tab to the Advanced dialog box. In the case of the tab shown in Figure 13.67, you'd need to click on the Catalyst Control Center button to see more settings for the video card. What you see here varies by model of card and version of driver, but here's a list of some of the more interesting settings you might see.

Color Correction Sometimes the colors on your monitor are not close enough for your tastes to the actual color you're trying to create. In this case you use color correction to fine-tune the colors on the screen to get the look you want.

Rotation All monitors are by default wider than they are tall. This is called *landscape mode*. Some LCD monitors can be physically rotated to facilitate users who like to see their desktops taller than they are wide (*portrait mode*). Figure 13.68 shows the author's LCD monitor rotated in portrait mode. If you want to rotate your screen, you must tell the system you're rotating it.

Modes Most video cards add very advanced settings to enable you to finely tweak your monitor. These very dangerous settings have names such as "sync polarity" or "front porch" and are outside the scope of both CompTIA A+ certification and the needs of all but the most geeky techs. These settings are mostly used to display a non-standard resolution. Stay out of those settings!

Working with Drivers

Now that you know the locations of the primary video tools within the operating system, it's time to learn about fine-tuning your video. You need to know how to work with video drivers from within the Display (Windows XP/7) and Personalization (Windows Vista) applets, including how to update them, roll back updates, and uninstall them.

Windows is very persnickety when it comes to video card drivers. You can crash Windows and force a reinstallation simply by installing a new video card and not uninstalling the old card's drivers. This doesn't happen every time but certainly can happen. As a basic rule, always uninstall the old card's drivers before you install drivers for a new card.

When you update the drivers for a card, you have a choice of uninstalling the outdated drivers and then installing new drivers—which makes the process the

same as for installing a new card—or you can let Windows flex some digital muscle and install the new ones right over the older drivers.

To update your drivers, go to the Control Panel and double-click the Display applet (Windows XP and Windows 7) or click the Personalization applet and click Display Settings (Windows Vista). In the Display Properties dialog box in Windows XP, select the Settings tab and click the Advanced button. In Windows Vista's Display Settings dialog box, select the Monitor tab and click the Advanced Settings button. In the Display applet for Windows 7, click *Change display settings* in the Tasks list and then click the *Advanced settings* link. In the dialog box that appears (all versions), click the Adapter tab and then click the Properties button. In the Properties dialog box for your adapter (see Figure 13.69), select the Driver tab and then click the Update Driver button to run the Hardware Update wizard.

3-D Graphics

No other area of the PC world reflects the amazing acceleration of technological improvements more than **3-D graphics**—in particular, 3-D gaming—which attempts to create images with the same depth and texture as objects seen in the real world. We are spectators to an amazing new world where software and hardware race to produce new levels of realism and complexity displayed on the computer screen. Powered by the wallets of tens of millions of PC gamers always demanding more and better, the video industry constantly introduces new video cards and new software titles that make today's games so incredibly realistic and fun. Although the gaming world certainly leads the PC industry in 3-D technologies, many other PC applications—such as *Computer Aided Design* (*CAD*) programs—quickly snatch up these technologies, making 3-D more useful in many ways other than just games. In this section, we'll add to the many bits and pieces of 3-D video encountered over previous chapters in the book and put together an understanding of the function and configuration of 3-D graphics.

Before the early 1990s, PCs did not mix well with 3-D graphics. Certainly, many 3-D applications existed, primarily 3-D design programs such as AutoCAD and Intergraph, but these applications would often run only on expensive, specialized hardware—not so great for casual users.

The big change took place in 1992 when a small company called id Software created a new game

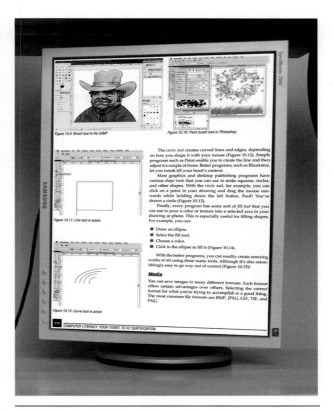

• **Figure 13.68**　Portrait mode

• **Figure 13.69**　Adapter Properties dialog box

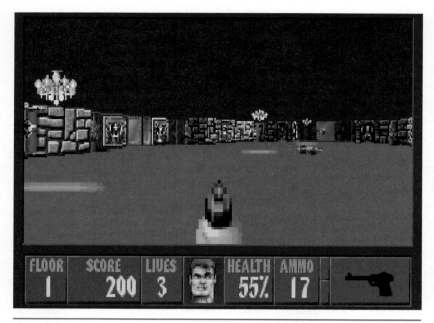

• **Figure 13.70** Wolfenstein 3D

• **Figure 13.71** Each figure had a limited number of sprites.

called *Wolfenstein 3D* (see Figure 13.70). They launched an entirely new genre of games, now called *first-person shooters* (FPSs), in which the player looks out into a 3-D world, interacting with walls, doors, and other items, and shoots whatever bad guys the game provides.

Wolfenstein 3D shook the PC gaming world to its foundations. That this innovative format came from an upstart little company made *Wolfenstein 3D* and id Software into overnight sensations. Even though their game was demanding on hardware, they gambled that enough people could run it to make it a success. The gamble paid off for John Carmack and John Romero, the creators of id Software, making them the fathers of 3-D gaming.

Early 3-D games used fixed 3-D images called **sprites** to create the 3-D world. A sprite is nothing more than a bitmapped graphic such as a BMP file. These early first-person shooters would calculate the position of an object from the player's perspective and place a sprite to represent the object. Any single object had only a fixed number of sprites—if you walked around an object, you noticed an obvious jerk as the game replaced the current sprite with a new one to represent the new position. Figure 13.71 shows different sprites for the same bad guy in *Wolfenstein 3D*. Sprites weren't pretty, but they worked without seriously taxing the 486s and early Pentiums of the time.

The second generation of 3-D games began to replace sprites with true 3-D objects, which are drastically more complex than sprites. A true 3-D object is composed of a group of points called **vertices**. Each vertex has a defined X, Y, and Z position in a 3-D world. Figure 13.72 shows the vertices for a video game character in a 3-D world.

The computer must track all of the vertices of all of the objects in the 3-D world, including the ones you cannot currently see. Keep in mind that objects may be motionless in the 3-D world (a wall, for example), may have animation (such as a door opening and closing), or may be moving (like bad monsters trying to spray you with evil alien goo). This calculation process is called *transformation* and, as you might imagine, is extremely taxing to most CPUs. Intel's SIMD and AMD's 3DNow! processor extensions were expressly designed to perform transformations.

Once the CPU has determined the positions of all vertices, the system begins to fill in the 3-D object. The process begins by drawing lines (the 3-D term is *edges*) between vertices to build the 3-D object into many triangles. Why triangles? Well, mainly by consensus of game developers. Any shape works, but triangles make the most sense from a mathematical standpoint. I could go into more depth here, but that would require talking about trigonometry, and I'm gambling you'd rather not read that detailed a description! All 3-D games use triangles to connect vertices. The 3-D process then

groups triangles into various shapes called **polygons**. Figure 13.73 shows the same model as Figure 13.72, now displaying all of the connected vertices to create a large number of polygons.

Originally, the CPU handled these calculations to create triangles, but now special 3-D video cards do the job, greatly speeding up the process.

The last step in second-generation games was texturing. Every 3-D game stores a number of image files called **textures**. The program wraps textures around an object to give it a surface. Textures work well to provide dramatic detail without using a lot of triangles. A single object may take one texture or many textures, applied to single triangles or groups of triangles (polygons). Figure 13.74 shows the finished warrior.

True 3-D objects, more often referred to as *rendered*, immediately created the need for massively powerful video cards and much wider data buses. Intel's primary motivation for creating AGP was to provide a big enough pipe for massive data pumping between the video card and the CPU. Intel gave AGP the ability to read system RAM to support textures. If it weren't for 3-D games, AGP (and probably even PCIe) would almost certainly not exist.

3-D Video Cards

No CPU of the mid-1990s could ever hope to handle the massive processes required to render 3-D worlds. Keep in mind that to create realistic movement, the 3-D world must refresh at least 24 times per second. That means that this entire process, from transformation to texturing, must repeat once every 1/24th of a second! Furthermore, although the game re-creates each screen, it must also keep score, track the positions of

• **Figure 13.72** Vertices for a video game warrior

• **Figure 13.73** Connected vertices forming polygons on a 3-D character

• **Figure 13.74** Video game warrior with textures added

all of the objects in the game, provide some type of intelligence to the bad guys, and so on. Something had to happen to take the workload off the CPU. The answer came from video cards.

Video cards were developed with smart onboard GPUs. The GPU helped the CPU by taking over some, and eventually all, of the 3-D rendering duties. These video cards not only have GPUs but also have massive amounts of RAM to store textures.

But a problem exists with this setup: How do we talk to these cards? This is done by means of a device driver, of course, but wouldn't it be great if we could create standard commands to speed up the process? The best thing to do would be to create a standardized set of instructions that any 3-D program could send to a video card to do all of the basic work, such as "make a cone" or "lay texture 237 on the cone you just made."

The video card instructions standards manifested themselves into a series of **application programming interfaces (APIs)**. In essence, an API is a library of commands that people who make 3-D games must use in their programs. The program currently using the video card sends API commands directly to the device driver. Device drivers must know how to understand the API commands. If you were to picture the graphics system of your computer as a layer cake, the top layer would be the program making a call to the video card driver that then directs the graphics hardware.

Several APIs have been developed over the years, with two clear winners among all of them: OpenGL and DirectX. The **OpenGL** standard was developed for UNIX systems but has since been *ported*, or made compatible with, a wide variety of computer systems, including Windows and Apple computers. As the demand for 3-D video became increasingly strong, Microsoft decided to throw its hat into the 3-D graphics ring with its own API, called DirectX. We look at DirectX in depth in the next section.

Although they might accomplish the same task (for instance, translating instructions and passing them on to the video driver), every API handles things just a little bit differently. In some 3-D games, the OpenGL standard might produce more precise images with less CPU overhead than the DirectX standard. In general, however, you won't notice a large difference between the images produced by OpenGL and DirectX.

DirectX and Video Cards

In the old days, many applications communicated directly with much of the PC hardware and, as a result, could crash your computer if not written well enough. Microsoft tried to fix this problem by placing all hardware under the control of Windows, but programmers balked because Windows added too much work for the video process and slowed down everything. For the most demanding programs, such as games, only direct access of hardware would work.

This need to "get around Windows" motivated Microsoft to unveil a new set of protocols called **DirectX**. Programmers use DirectX to take control of certain pieces of hardware and to talk directly to that hardware; it provides the speed necessary to play the advanced games so popular today. The primary impetus for DirectX was to build a series of products to enable Windows to run 3-D games. That's not to say that you couldn't run 3-D games in Windows *before* DirectX; rather, it's just that Microsoft wasn't involved in the API rat race at the time and wanted to be. Microsoft's goal

in developing DirectX was to create a 100-percent stable environment, with direct hardware access, for running 3-D applications and games within Windows.

DirectX is not only for video; it also supports sound, network connections, input devices, and other parts of your PC. Each of these subsets of DirectX has a name, such as DirectDraw, Direct3D, or DirectSound.

- **DirectDraw** Supports direct access to the hardware for 2-D graphics
- **Direct3D** Supports direct access to the hardware for 3-D graphics—the most important part of DirectX
- **DirectInput** Supports direct access to the hardware for joysticks and other game controllers
- **DirectSound** Supports direct access to the hardware for waveforms
- **DirectMusic** Supports direct access to the hardware for MIDI devices
- **DirectPlay** Supports direct access to network devices for multiplayer games
- **DirectShow** Supports direct access to video and presentation devices

Microsoft constantly adds to and tweaks this list. As almost all games need DirectX and all video cards have drivers to support DirectX, you need to verify that DirectX is installed and working properly on your system. To do this, use the **DirectX Diagnostic Tool (dxdiag)**, as shown in Figure 13.75.

• **Figure 13.75** The DirectX Diagnostic Tool

In Windows XP, you can find it in the System Information program. After you open System Information (it usually lives in the Accessories | System Tools area of the Start menu), click the Tools menu and select DirectX Diagnostic Tool.

For Windows Vista/7, go to Start and type **dxdiag** in the Search bar. Press ENTER to run the program.

The System tab gives the version of DirectX. The system pictured in Figure 13.75 runs DirectX 10.

So, what does DirectX do for video cards? Back in the bad old days before DirectX became popular with the game makers, many GPU makers created their own chip-specific APIs. 3dfx had Glide, for example, and S3 had ViRGE. This made buying 3-D games a mess. There would often be multiple versions of the same game for each card. Even worse, many games never used 3-D acceleration because it was just too much work to support all of the different cards.

That all changed when Microsoft beefed up DirectX and got more GPU makers to support it. That in turn enabled the game companies to write games by using DirectX and have them run on any card out there. The bottom line: When Microsoft comes out with a new version of DirectX, all of the GPU companies hurry to support it or they will be left behind.

Trying to decide what video card to buy gives me the shakes—too many options! One good way to narrow down your buying decision is to see what GPU is hot at the moment. I make a point to check out these Web sites whenever I'm getting ready to buy, so I can see what everyone says is the best.

- http://arstechnica.com
- www.hardocp.com
- www.tomshardware.com
- www.sharkyextreme.com

Beyond A+

DLP

Digital Light Processing (*DLP*) displays use a chip covered in microscopically small mirrors (see Figure 13.76).

These individual mirrors move thousands of times per second toward and away from a light source. The more times per second they move toward a light source, the whiter the image; the fewer times they move, the grayer the image. See Figure 13.77 for a diagram of how the mirrors would appear in a microscopic close-up of the chip. The lamp projects through a color wheel onto the DLP chip. The DLP chip creates the image by moving the tiny mirrors, which in turn reflect onto the screen.

● **Figure 13.76** DLP chip (photo courtesy of Texas Instruments)

DLP was very popular for a time in home theater systems, as it makes an amazingly rich image. DLP has had very little impact on PC monitors, but has had great success in projectors. DLP projectors are much more expensive than LCD projectors, but many customers feel the extra expense is worth the image quality.

● **Figure 13.77** Microscopic close-up of DLP showing tiny mirrors—note that some are tilted.

Chapter 13 Review

■ Chapter Summary

After reading this chapter and completing the exercises, you should understand the following about video.

Explain how video displays work

- The term *video* encompasses a complex interaction among numerous parts of the PC, all designed to put a picture on the screen. The monitor is the primary output device for the PC and shows you what's going on with your programs and operating system. The video card or display adapter handles all of the communication between the CPU and the monitor. Video displays come in three varieties: CRT, LCD, and projectors.

- CRT monitors have a tube that contains three electron guns at the slender end and a display screen coated with phosphor at the wide end. The speed of the electron beam across the screen is the horizontal refresh rate (HRR), more commonly referred to as the refresh rate. The vertical refresh rate (VRR) is the time it takes to draw the entire screen and return the electron guns to the upper-left corner.

- Monitors do not determine the HRR or VRR. The video card "pushes" the monitor at a certain VRR that, in turn, determines the HRR. Setting the VRR too low results in screen flicker, which causes headaches and eyestrain. Setting the VRR too high results in image distortion and damage to the monitor's circuitry.

- A monitor is a grid of red, green, and blue light-sensitive dots called phosphors. Normal CRT monitors have three electron guns that fire electrons of different intensities (not colors) at the colored phosphors. A shadow mask prevents electron bleed-over so electrons from any of the three guns hit only their own colored phosphors. The area of phosphors lit at one instant is a pixel and must consist of at least one red, one green, and one blue phosphor; therefore, the smallest pixel, a triad, would consist of three phosphors.

- Resolution is the number of horizontal pixels times the number of vertical pixels. A resolution of 640 × 480 means 640 pixels across and 480 pixels down, for a total of 307,200 pixels total. Many monitors have a resolution that matches a 4:3 aspect ratio. Widescreen monitors have an aspect ratio of 16:9 or 16:10.

- Liquid crystal displays are the most common type of display for PCs. They offer many advantages over CRTs. An LCD monitor is thinner, lighter, uses less power, is virtually flicker-free, and does not emit potentially harmful radiation.

- An LCD screen is composed of tiny liquid crystal molecules called sub-pixels. Although you may find dual-scan passive matrix on some low-end LCD panels, most of today's LCD panels use active matrix or thin film transistor (TFT) technology.

- The typical LCD monitor is composed of the LCD panel, backlights, and inverters. Most backlights require AC power and the electronics require DC. The AC/DC transformer changes the AC wall current into DC that the LCD panel can use. Most LCD backlights use cold cathode fluorescent lamp (CCFL) technology. CCFLs require AC power, so inverters convert the DC back to AC. Newer and better LCDs use LED backlights. These use DC, so they require no inverter. Manufacturers refer to these types of displays as LED monitors.

- LCD monitors, unlike CRTs, have a native resolution and a fixed pixel size. LCDs cannot run at a resolution higher than their native resolution, and running a lower resolution results in degraded image quality. Anti-aliasing softens the edges of jagged pixel corners when running at lower resolutions, but as the image quality degrades, you should use the native resolution.

- LCD monitor brightness is determined by its backlights and is measured in nits. An average LCD measures around 300 nits, with higher numbers being brighter and better.

- The time it takes for sub-pixels to go from pure black to pure white and back again is the LCD's response rate. Response rate is measured in milliseconds, with lower numbers being faster and better. An excellent LCD monitor has a response rate somewhere between 2 and 4 ms.

- LCD monitors lack the color saturation and contrast of a CRT, making CRT the choice for graphics artists. Look for an LCD monitor with a contrast ratio of 450:1 or higher.

- Projectors come in two main varieties: rearview and front-view. Rearview projectors shoot an

image onto the screen from the back and are almost always self-enclosed. They are a popular choice for televisions, but not for PCs. Front-view projectors shoot an image from the front and are widely used during computer presentations.

- LCD projectors, like LCD monitors, have a native resolution and are lightweight, but lack the image quality of a CRT. Projector brightness is measured in *lumens*. Larger numbers are brighter and better, with 1500 lumens being sufficient for a small, dark room. The size of the projected image at a certain distance from the screen is the projector's *throw*. LCD projectors come with internal fans that cool the lamp. Lamps are costly to replace and are considered consumable (meaning you can expect to replace them periodically).

- Measured from two opposite diagonal corners, size for CRT monitors is not usually the same as the viewable image size. A 17-inch CRT monitor might have only a 15.5-inch VIS. Because LCD monitors report only VIS, a 15-inch LCD monitor may have approximately the same viewing area as a 17-inch CRT.

- CRT monitors require two connectors: a 15-pin, three-row, DB-type connector and a power plug. Video cards use a RAMDAC, which takes the digital signal from the video card and turns it into an analog signal for the CRT. LCD monitors require a digital signal. Analog LCD monitors reverse the effects of the RAMDAC so you can plug your LCD monitor into the 15-pin VGA connector on the video card.

- The DVI standard allows the digital signal from the PC to be used by the LCD monitor without any digital-to-analog-and-back-to-digital conversion. The DVI standard includes DVI-D, DVI-A, and DVI-I. Both DVI-D and DVI-I come in single-link and dual-link varieties, with dual-link offering significantly higher resolutions.

- Monitors have adjustment controls for brightness, contrast, image size and position, and color adjustment. These controls are usually accessed via an onboard menu system rather than with hardware knobs or dials.

- A CRT monitor accounts for about half of the power consumption of a desktop PC. Monitors using the VESA standard for Display Power Management Signaling (DPMS) can cut monitor power consumption by about 75 percent. An LCD monitor uses less than half the electricity a CRT uses.

Select the proper video card

- The display adapter, or video card, handles the video chores within the PC, processing information from the CPU and sending it out to the monitor. The display adapter is a complex set of devices. The video card has two major pieces: the video RAM and the video processing circuitry. The video RAM stores the video image, and the processing circuitry is similar to that of your computer's CPU.

- The combination of a specific resolution and color depth is referred to as a mode. The VGA mode is defined by a resolution of 640 × 480 and 4-bit color depth (16 colors). Modern video cards and monitors are capable of supporting many modes.

- Using more color depth slows down video functions. PCI slots maxed out at a bandwidth of 132 MBps. The Accelerated Graphics Port (AGP) is better suited for video than PCI because it resides alone on its own bus, pipelines commands, and supports sidebanding and system memory access.

- AGP has undergone several specification upgrades, and the cards are normally referred to by their strobe multiplier. Although you can mix some AGP specifications, it is best to use an AGP card that is fully supported by your motherboard. Make sure AGP cards are properly and fully inserted in the AGP port, as they require a close connection between card and port.

- PCI Express video cards currently dominate the market for all recent systems. Like AGP, PCI Express supports sidebanding and system memory access, but it uses a faster serial communication method than that of the parallel communication method used by AGP.

- Video cards are identified by their manufacturer, model number, graphics processor, amount of video RAM, and the slot to which they connect. Although a number of companies produce video cards, the three major manufacturers of graphics processors are NVIDIA, AMD, and Intel. The most important decision when buying a video card is the graphics processor, especially if you play 3-D games.

- To overcome the bottlenecks of data throughput speed, access speed, and capacity of video RAM, manufacturers use specialized fast RAM and more and more total RAM. Video memory technologies include VRAM, WRAM, SGRAM, DDR SDRAM, DDR2 SDRAM, GDDR3 SDRAM, GDDR4 SDRAM, and GDDR5 SDRAM.

- A lot of current motherboards have integrated GPUs or are ready for a CPU with an integrated GPU. The motherboard GPU can be a separate chip attached to the motherboard or can be built into the Northbridge chip. You might run into AMD Radeon chips or NVIDIA nForce chips powering the GPU. Intel has long integrated the Intel Graphics Media Accelerator (GMA) into its chipsets.

- You can find many different types of connector types on video cards, plus variations within those types. CompTIA also makes a distinction between the names of the ports on the cards and the cables associated with them, though most techs will refer to the connectors and cables by multiple names interchangeably.

- Common connectors and cables include VGA (DB-15), DVI, DisplayPort, and HDMI. Other less-common connectors and cables include BNC (used with coaxial cable), Din-6 (used with S-video), and RCA (used with component and composite cables).

Install and configure video

- During the physical install of a video card, be conscious of long cards and proximity to other PCI cards. Long cards simply don't fit in some cases, and close proximity to other expansion cards can cause overheating.

- Video card drivers install pretty much the same as all other drivers: either the driver is already built into Windows or you must use the installation media that comes with the video card.

- As a basic rule, always uninstall an old video card's drivers before you install drivers for a new card.

- The Display applet (Windows XP) or Personalization applet (Windows Vista) provides a convenient, central location for adjusting all of your display settings, including resolution, refresh rate, driver information, and color depth. Windows 7 splits its display controls across both the Display applet and the Personalization applet.

- In Windows XP's Display applet, the Screen Saver tab provides access to the power-management settings. In Windows Vista and Windows 7, this is an option in the Personalization applet.

- The Settings tab in Windows XP's Display applet provides access for configuring all of your video settings, such as resolution, color depth, and dual monitor configuration. The Settings tab also provides an Advanced button for access to the Monitor tab. The Monitor tab enables you to set the refresh rate for your CRT monitor. Most video cards add their own tabs to the Advanced section. In Windows Vista, all of these controls are contained within the Personalization | Display Settings option. In Windows 7, these controls are found within the Display | Change display settings option.

- You can configure dual monitors by using a video card with two monitor connectors or by using two video cards. Either way, once both monitors are connected, you can enable the second monitor in Windows XP from the Display applet's Settings tab, in Windows Vista from the Personalization | Display Settings option, and in Windows 7 from the Display | Change display settings option.

- Early 3-D games used sprites to create a 3-D world. Later games replaced sprites with true 3-D objects composed of vertices. Bitmap textures are used to tile a section of the screen to provide a surface in the 3-D world.

- Video cards use a series of APIs to translate instructions for the video device driver. If you were to picture the graphics system of your computer as a layer cake, the top layer would be the program making a call to the graphics hardware. The next layer is the API. The device driver comes next, and way down at the base of the cake is the actual graphics hardware: RAM, graphics processor, and RAMDAC. OpenGL and DirectX are the most popular APIs.

- DirectX includes several subsets, including DirectDraw, Direct3D, DirectInput, Direct Sound, DirectMusic, DirectPlay, and DirectShow. You can verify your DirectX installation via the DirectX Diagnostics Tool, which is found in Windows XP under the Tools menu of the System Information utility and in Windows Vista/7 by typing **dxdiag** in the Start | Search bar.

■ Key Terms

3-D graphics (395)
Accelerated Graphics Port (AGP) (378)

active matrix (364)
anti-aliasing (366)

application programming interface (API) *(398)*
aspect ratio *(360)*
backlight *(365)*
cathode ray tube (CRT) *(357)*
cold cathode fluorescent lamp (CCFL) *(365)*
color depth *(375)*
digital visual interface (DVI) *(372)*
DirectX *(398)*
DirectX Diagnostic Tool (dxdiag) *(399)*
display adapter *(356)*
Display applet *(386)*
DisplayPort *(383)*
Display Power-Management Signaling (DPMS) *(373)*
dual-scan passive matrix *(364)*
front-view projector *(368)*
graphics processing unit (GPU) *(380)*
High Definition Multimedia Interface (HDMI) *(384)*
horizontal refresh rate (HRR) *(359)*
inverter *(365)*
light-emitting diode (LED) *(366)*
liquid crystal display (LCD) *(361)*
lumen *(369)*
mode *(377)*
monitor *(356)*
native resolution *(366)*
nit *(367)*
OpenGL *(398)*

passive matrix *(364)*
PCI Express (PCIe) *(380)*
persistence *(358)*
Personalization applet *(386)*
phosphors *(360)*
pixel *(360)*
polygons *(397)*
projector *(368)*
random access memory digital-to-analog converter (RAMDAC) *(371)*
raster line *(358)*
rearview projector *(368)*
resolution *(360)*
response rate *(367)*
shadow mask *(360)*
sidebanding *(379)*
sprite *(396)*
sub-pixel *(363)*
texture *(397)*
thin film transistor (TFT) *(364)*
throw *(369)*
triad *(361)*
vertical refresh rate (VRR) *(359)*
vertices *(396)*
video display *(356)*
video graphics array (VGA) *(377)*
viewable image size (VIS) *(370)*

■ Key Term Quiz

Use the Key Terms list to complete the sentences that follow. Not all terms will be used.

1. To provide the optimal display for an LCD monitor, always set it to its _____.

2. On a CRT screen, a(n) _____ consists of one red, one green, and one blue phosphor; in theory, the smallest pixel a monitor can display.

3. DirectX is a(n) _____, a program that translates instructions for the video device driver.

4. Using an aspect ratio of 4:3, the _____ refers to the number of horizontal pixels times the number of vertical pixels.

5. The _____ bus, designed specifically for video cards, connects directly to the Northbridge, but has for the most part been phased out in favor of the _____ bus.

6. The actual screen size of a CRT monitor is known as the _____.

7. The number of sweeps or raster lines that the electron guns make across the screen is called the _____ while the time it takes to draw the entire screen is called the _____.

8. Apple Macs primarily use the _____ display connector type.

9. A(n) _____ handles the video processing chores in modern systems.

10. The size of the projected image at a specific distance from the screen is defined as the projector's _____.

■ Multiple-Choice Quiz

1. What are 3-D objects made of at the most basic level?

 A. Sprites

 B. Textures

 C. Vertices

 D. Nurbs

2. Which of the following resolutions will produce the best quality picture on the monitor (assuming the monitor is capable of displaying the resolutions well)?

 A. 640 × 480

 B. 800 × 600

 C. 1024 × 768

 D. 1280 × 1024

3. The typical LCD monitor is composed of the LCD panel, backlights, and what else?

 A. Yoke coil

 B. Inverter

 C. Shadow mask

 D. Electromagnet

4. CRT monitors attach to the video card by using a(n) _____ connector.

 A. 9-pin, 2-row, DB

 B. 36-pin Centronics

 C. 15-pin, 3-row, DB

 D. 25-pin, 2-row, DB

5. Which of the following statements best describes the electron guns in a CRT monitor?

 A. A single gun shoots electrons at the phosphors on the screen.

 B. Three electron guns, one each for red, green, and blue phosphors, paint the screen.

 C. The electron guns stay on all of the time to shoot electrons that produce the solid image on the screen.

 D. One electron gun shoots red phosphors, another shoots green phosphors, and the third shoots blue phosphors at the screen.

6. Many cheaper computers and laptops use what kind of video card?

 A. Integrated

 B. PCIe

 C. AGP

 D. PCI

7. What advantages do LCD monitors offer over CRT monitors?

 A. Better color and more contrast

 B. Energy efficiency and no emission of potentially harmful radiation

 C. Electron guns fire CMYK instead of RGB

 D. Both A and B

8. Which projector produces the brightest image?

 A. One with the longest throw lens

 B. One with the largest lamp

 C. One with the largest degaussing coil

 D. One with the highest lumen rating

9. Which statement best describes pixels?

 A. Pixels consist of exactly one red, one green, and one blue phosphor.

 B. Pixels on a CRT are always the same size.

 C. Higher resolutions result in more pixels per row.

 D. LCDs don't use pixels.

10. A user wishes to display millions of colors. What is the minimum color depth the user must set in the adapter settings?

 A. 4-bit

 B. 8-bit

 C. 16-bit

 D. 24-bit

11. What is the most popular API used by 3-D game developers?

 A. DirectX

 B. OpenGL

 C. DigitalDirector

 D. RAMDAC

12. A Windows XP user calls in complaining that her monitor is too small. Upon further questioning, you find out that it's not the monitor that's small, but the font and icon size that are too small! What would you do to help the user fix the problem?

 A. In the Control Panel, open the Display applet. Select the Settings tab and increase the screen resolution.

B. In the Control Panel, open the Display applet. Select the Settings tab and decrease the screen resolution.

C. In the Control Panel, open the Monitor applet. Select the Settings tab and increase the screen resolution.

D. In the Control Panel, open the Monitor applet. Select the Settings tab and decrease the screen resolution.

13. Which two technologies are used for backlights in LCD monitors?

A. CCFL and LED

B. CCFL and LCD

C. CCFL and AC

D. HDMI and DisplayPort

14. What tool enables you to test 3-D video in a modern PC?

A. DirectX

B. dxdiag

C. OpenGL

D. NVIDIA

15. Which Control Panel applet in Windows 7 enables you to change settings involving how the monitor shows text and the Windows theme that determines the colors of boxes and other visual items?

A. Display

B. Personalization

C. System

D. Visualization

■ Essay Quiz

1. Your company is getting ready to replace their computers and monitors. You would like to see all of the new PCs come with LCD monitors. Write a memo to your boss that talks about the advantages of LCD monitors over CRT monitors, but also discusses some of the variations among LCD technologies that she should take into consideration.

2. You've been tasked to write a guide for new users of Windows 7, specifically how to tailor their screens to suit their eyes and sensibilities. Write a short essay discussing the appropriate Control Panel applets and the various things they can do.

Lab Projects

• Lab Project 13.1

If you just received a $500 bonus and decided to buy a new video system for your computer, what would you select? Go to the local computer store or to Web sites such as www.newegg.com and pick out the best combination of monitor and video card that you can buy with your bonus. Now imagine that you also received a $200 birthday gift and have decided to purchase an even better graphics card and monitor. Which ones will you select now that you have $700 to spend?

• Lab Project 13.2

Monitors are not the only output device for the computer. Research one of the following devices and prepare a short essay for the class about how the device works and its features, cost, and connections.

■ Rearview projectors

■ Plasma monitors

■ Touch screens

Local Area Networking

chapter
14

"I'm interested in upgrading my 28.8 kilobaud Internet connection to a 1.5 megabit fiber optic T1 line. Will you be able to provide an IP router that's compatible with my token ring Ethernet LAN configuration?"

—COMIC BOOK GUY, *THE SIMPSONS*

In this chapter, you will learn how to

- **Install and troubleshoot structured cabling**
- **Explain the basics of TCP/IP**
- **Install and configure wired networks**

Networks dominate the modern computing environment. A vast percentage of businesses have PCs connected in a small local area network (LAN), and big businesses simply can't survive without connecting their many offices into a single wide area network (WAN). Even the operating systems of today demand networks. Windows XP, Vista, and 7, for example, come out of the box *assuming* you'll attach them to the Internet just to make them work past 30 days (product activation), and they get all indignant if you don't.

Because networks are so common today, every good tech needs to know the basics of networking technology, operating systems, implementation, and troubleshooting. Accordingly, this chapter teaches you how to build and troubleshoot a basic network. First, let's move beyond the basic switch and UTP cable with RJ-45 connectors you saw in Chapter 4 and discover how real-world networks connect using alternatives to RJ-45, such as fiber. You'll see how professionals use a concept called "structured cabling" with wired networks to ensure their reliability and ease of use. I'll even show you the tools needed to make your own structured cable system.

The second part of this chapter gets down and dirty into TCP/IP and how Windows uses it in a typical network. I'll break down the TCP/IP protocol so you can appreciate how it works.

Next, we'll go through the process of setting up a small network from start to finish. This includes details on planning a network, installing and configuring NICs, setting up switches, configuring TCP/IP—everything you need so that Windows will enable you to share folders, printers, libraries, and so on.

The chapter closes with a popular topic: troubleshooting a network. Windows comes with plenty of powerful tools to help you when the network stops functioning. I'll show you the tools and combine that with a troubleshooting process that helps you get a network up and running again.

 This chapter only covers local area networks, such as a group of computers in a single office. We'll save connecting to the Internet for Chapter 16. But be ready! You need to understand everything in this chapter before you can take the next step and connect to the Internet.

■ Beyond Basic Ethernet Cabling

Ethernet is the dominant networking technology, and unshielded twisted-pair (UTP) wired Ethernet networks using RJ-45 connectors are the most dominant form of Ethernet. Back in Chapter 4, you got a very basic exposure to an Ethernet network, so now we can take things a bit deeper and look at more network technologies, starting with alternatives to UTP, touring some of the more unique devices you might see in a network, and learning about proper cabling.

Know your cable types for the CompTIA A+ 220-801 exam: STP, UTP, CAT 3, CAT 5, CAT 5e, and CAT 6. Recall the differences between plenum-grade cable and PVC-sheathed cables.

Alternative Connections

UTP is very popular, but Ethernet, as well as other types of networks, can use alternative cabling that you need to be able to identify. Every CompTIA A+ certified tech needs to know about fiber optic cabling and coaxial cable, so let's start there.

Fiber Optic

Fiber optic cable is a very attractive way to transmit Ethernet network frames. First, because it uses light instead of electricity, fiber optic cable is immune to electrical problems such as lightning, short circuits, and static. Second, fiber optic signals travel much farther, 2000 meters or more (compared with 100 meters on UTP). Most fiber Ethernet networks use *62.5/125 multimode* fiber optic cable. All fiber Ethernet networks that use this type of cabling require two cables. Figure 14.1 shows three of the more common connectors used in fiber optic networks. Square *SC* connectors are shown in the middle and on the right, and the round *ST* connector is on the left.

Like many other fiber optic connectors, the SC and ST connectors are half-duplex, meaning data flows only one way—hence the need for two cables in a fiber installation. Newer and higher-end fiber installations use connectors with names like LC or MT-RJ.

 Tech Tip

Crossover Cables
You can hook two network cards directly together using a special UTP cable called a **crossover cable**. *A crossover cable is a standard UTP cable with one RJ-45 connector using the 568A standard and the other using the 568B standard. This reverses the signal between sending and receiving wires and thus does the job of a hub or switch. Crossover cables work great as a quick way to network two PCs. You can purchase a crossover cable at any computer store.*

Figure 14.1 Typical fiber optic cables with connectors

Multimode and Single-Mode Light can be sent down a fiber optic cable as regular light or as laser light. Each type of light requires totally different fiber optic cables. Most network technologies that use fiber optics use light-emitting diodes (LEDs) to send light signals. These use *multimode* fiber optic cabling. Multimode fiber transmits multiple light signals at the same time, each using a different reflection angle within the core of the cable. The multiple reflection angles tend to disperse over long distances, so multimode fiber optic cables are used for relatively short distances.

Network technologies that use laser light use *single-mode* fiber optic cabling. Using laser light and single-mode fiber optic cables allows for phenomenally high transfer rates over long distances. Except for long-distance links, single-mode is currently quite rare; if you see fiber optic cabling, you can be relatively sure it is multimode.

There are close to 100 different Ethernet fiber optic cabling standards, with names like 1000BaseSX and 10GBaseSR. The major difference is the speed of the network (there are also some important differences in the way systems interconnect, and so on). If you want to use fiber optic cabling, you need a fiber optic switch and fiber optic network cards, and they're not cheap. The fiber optic cabling itself is delicate, expensive, and difficult to use, so it is usually reserved for use in data centers and is rarely used to connect desktop PCs.

Fiber networks follow the speed and distance limitations of their networking standard, so it's hard to pin down precise numbers on true limitations. Multimode overall is slower and has a shorter range than single-mode. A typical multimode network runs at 10, 100, or 1000 Mbps, though some can go to 10,000 Mbps. Distances for multimode runs generally top out at ~600 meters. With single-mode, speed and distance—depending on the standard—can blow multimode away. The record transmission speed in 2011, for example, was 100 *terabits* per second and that was over 100 *miles*!

> Know fiber connector types and the difference between multimode and single-mode fiber.

> There are a number of Ethernet standards that use fiber optic cable instead of UTP.

Coax/BNC

Early versions of Ethernet ran on **coaxial cable** instead of UTP. While the Ethernet standards using coax are long gone, coax lives on in the networking world, primarily for cable modems and satellite connections. Coax cable consists of a center cable (core) surrounded by insulation. This in turn is covered with a *shield* of braided cable (see Figure 14.2). The center core actually carries the signal. The shield effectively eliminates outside interference. The entire cable is then surrounded by a protective insulating cover.

Coax cables are rated using an RG name. There are hundreds of RG ratings for coax, but the only two you need to know for the CompTIA A+ exams are RG-59 and RG-6. Both standards are rated by impedance, which is measured in ohms. Both RG-6 and RG-59 have a 75-ohm impedance. Both of these coax cables are used by your cable television, but RG-59 is thinner and doesn't carry data quite as far as RG-6. The RG rating is clearly marked on the cable.

Figure 14.2 Typical coax cable

• **Figure 14.3** BNC connector

• **Figure 14.4** F-type connector

Coax most commonly uses two different types of connectors. A BNC connector (see Figure 14.3) uses a quarter twist connector, and an F-type connector uses a screw connector. BNC is uncommon, but F-type is on the back of all cable modems and most televisions (see Figure 14.4).

> There is no hard limit to how fast coaxial cable can transmit data. Most cable broadband Internet implementations, however, top out at around 50 Mbps.

Network Devices

Back in Chapter 4 you read about hubs, switches, and routers. Let's do a quick review and add a few other devices.

Hubs

Hubs were the main interconnection for older Ethernet networks (see Figure 14.5). Any incoming signal on any port on a hub is re-created (repeated) and sent out on every connected port on the hub. The downside to hubs is that all connected devices have to share the total bandwidth. Hubs are extremely rare today, having been replaced by switches.

• **Figure 14.5** Typical hubs

Switches

Switches are the current most common interconnection for Ethernet networks (see Figure 14.6). A **switch** looks like a hub, but a switch automatically creates point-to-point connections between any two computers. By separating every connection, each computer can use the full bandwidth of the switch.

Bridges

If someone knows Morse code, it doesn't matter what medium you use to communicate the patterns of a coded method. You can blink a flashlight in his or her face, beat on a bongo drum, or tap into a telegraph machine: the person will understand the code. Ethernet functions

• **Figure 14.6** Typical switch

similarly. The code for Ethernet is the same no matter what medium transfers that message. That means you can easily connect two Ethernet networks that use completely different media internally, such as UTP to fiber or maybe UTP to wireless. In these cases you need a device called a bridge. A **bridge** will always have two interfaces, one interface for each of the different media (see Figure 14.7).

Networked Attached Storage (NAS)

You already know that networks enable you to share files and services with multiple PCs. In most cases, network administrators store files on a server system. This server might be a dedicated file server—a machine running Windows Server 2008 R2, for example—or it might just be someone's regular Windows machine with a shared folder. You can also use a *networked attached storage (NAS)* system. A NAS is basically a headless system (no monitor, no keyboard, and no mouse) that you plug into a network (Figure 14.8). A NAS is almost totally self-configuring, requiring only a name and network type (domain/workgroup).

Understand that a NAS only does one thing: share its hard drives. Almost all NAS devices use some form of Web interface for configuration, enabling you to control the NAS from a Web browser on any PC in the network.

There are hundreds of different NAS solutions to choose from. For most people, the big criteria are storage capacity, RAID options, and ease of configuration.

> We tend to use the term *network appliance* for any headless computer (that is, one with no direct interface) designed to do very specific duties. A NAS box is a perfect example of a network appliance.

• **Figure 14.7** Typical bridge

• **Figure 14.8** Typical NAS

Routers

A **router** connects LANs together using the TCP/IP protocol. By definition, a router must have at least two connections—one into a network, and one out to another network. Some more powerful routers have many more connections. Figure 14.9 shows a typical home router.

• **Figure 14.9** Typical home router

The CompTIA A+ 220-801 exam assumes you have a basic understanding of how routers work. To detail the process, I'll need to dive a bit deeper into TCP/IP. Check out the "TCP/IP" section later in this chapter.

The CompTIA A+ 220-801 exam expects you to know the differences between hubs, routers, switches, bridges, and access points.

Structured Cabling

If you want a functioning, dependable, real-world network, you need a solid understanding of a set of standards collectively called **structured cabling**. These standards, defined by the Telecommunications Industry Association/Electronic Industries Alliance (TIA/EIA)—yes, the same folks who tell you how to crimp an RJ-45 onto the end of a UTP cable—give professional cable installers detailed standards on every aspect of a cabled network, from the type of cabling to use to standards on running cable in walls, even the position of wall outlets.

The CompTIA A+ 801 exam requires you to understand the basic concepts involved in installing network cabling and to recognize the components used in a network. The CompTIA A+ 801 exam does not, however, expect you to be as knowledgeable as a professional network designer or cable installer. Your goal should be to understand enough about real-world cabling systems to communicate knowledgeably with cable installers and to perform basic troubleshooting. Granted, by the end of this section, you'll know enough to try running your own cable (I certainly run my own cable), but consider that knowledge extra credit.

The idea of structured cabling is to create a safe, reliable cabling infrastructure for all of the devices that may need interconnection. Certainly this applies to computer networks, but also to telephone, video—anything that might need low-power, distributed cabling.

You should understand three issues with structured cabling. Cable basics start the picture, with switches, cabling, and PCs. You'll then look at the components of a network, such as how the cable runs through the walls and where it ends up. This section wraps up with an assessment of connections leading outside your network.

A structured cabling system is useful for more than just computer networks. You'll find structured cabling defining telephone networks and video conferencing setups, for example.

Cable Basics—A Star Is Born

Back in Chapter 4 we developed the idea of a LAN in its most basic configurations: a switch, some UTP cable, and a few PCs—in other words, a typical physical star network (see Figure 14.10).

• **Figure 14.10** A switch connected by UTP cable to two PCs

No law of physics prevents you from placing a switch in the middle of your office and running cables on the floor to all the computers in your network. This setup works, but it falls apart spectacularly when applied to a real-world environment. Three problems present themselves to the network tech. First, the exposed cables running along the floor are just waiting for someone to trip over them, giving that person a wonderful lawsuit opportunity. Simply moving and stepping on the cabling will, over time, cause a cable to fail due to wires breaking or RJ-45 connectors ripping off cable ends. Second, the presence of other electrical devices close to the cable can create interference that confuses the signals going through the wire. Third, this type of setup limits your ability to make any changes to the network. Before you can change anything, you have to figure out which cables in the huge rat's nest of cables connected to the switch go to which machines. Imagine *that* troubleshooting nightmare!

"Gosh," you're thinking (okay, I'm thinking it, but you should be, too), "there must be a better way to install a physical network." A better installation would provide safety, protecting the star from vacuum cleaners, clumsy coworkers, and electrical interference. It would have extra hardware to organize and protect the cabling.

Cross Check

TIA/EIA Standards

You should remember the TIA/EIA 568 wiring standards from Chapter 4, but do you remember how to tell the difference between 568A and 568B?

Finally, the new and improved star network installation would feature a cabling standard with the flexibility to enable the network to grow according to its needs and then to upgrade when the next great network technology comes along. That is the definition of structured cabling.

Structured Cable Network Components

Successful implementation of a basic structured cabling network requires three essential ingredients: a telecommunications room, horizontal cabling, and a work area. Let's zero in on one floor of a typical office. All the cabling runs from individual PCs to a central location, the **telecommunications room** (see Figure 14.11). What equipment goes in there—a switch or a telephone system—is not the important thing. What matters is that all the cables concentrate in this one area.

All cables run horizontally (for the most part) from the telecommunications room to the PCs. This cabling is called, appropriately, **horizontal cabling**. A single piece of installed horizontal cabling is called a **run**. At the opposite end of the horizontal cabling from the telecommunications room is the work area. The **work area** is often simply an office or cubicle that potentially contains a PC and

Telecommunications room

• **Figure 14.11** Telecommunications room

a telephone. Figure 14.12 shows both the horizontal cabling and work areas.

Each of the three parts of a basic star network—the telecommunications room, the horizontal cabling, and the work area(s)—must follow a series of strict standards designed to ensure that the cabling system is reliable and easy to manage. The cabling standards set by TIA/EIA enable techs to make sensible decisions on equipment installed in the telecommunications room, so let's tackle horizontal cabling first, and then return to the telecommunications room. We'll finish up with the work area.

Horizontal Cabling A horizontal cabling run is the cabling that goes more or less horizontally from a work area to the telecommunications room. In most networks, this cable is a CAT 5e or better UTP, but when you move into structured cabling, the TIA/EIA standards define a number of other aspects of the cable, such as the type of wires, number of pairs of wires, and fire ratings.

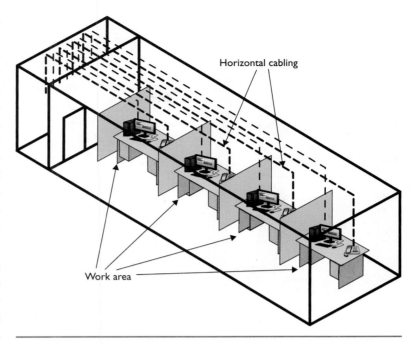

• **Figure 14.12** Horizontal cabling and work area

A single piece of cable that runs from a work area to a telecommunications room is called a *run*. In most networks, this cable is CAT 5e or better UTP.

Solid Core Versus Stranded Core All UTP cables come in one of two types: solid core or stranded core. Each wire in **solid core** UTP uses a single solid wire. With **stranded core**, each wire is actually a bundle of tiny wire strands. Each of these cable types has its benefits and downsides. Solid core is a better conductor, but it is stiff and will break if handled too often or too roughly. Stranded core is not quite as good a conductor, but it will stand up to substantial handling without breaking. Figure 14.13 shows a close-up of solid and stranded core UTP.

TIA/EIA specifies that horizontal cabling should always be solid core. Remember, this cabling is going into your walls and ceilings, safe from the harmful effects of shoes and vacuum cleaners. The ceilings and walls enable you to take advantage of the better conductivity of solid core without the

• **Figure 14.13** Solid and stranded core UTP

• Figure 14.14 A short equipment rack

Equipment racks evolved out of the railroad signaling racks from the 19th century. The components in a rack today obviously differ a lot from railroad signaling, but the 19-inch width has remained the standard for well over 100 years.

• Figure 14.15 A floor-to-ceiling rack

risk of cable damage. Stranded cable also has an important function in a structured cabling network, but I need to discuss a few more parts of the network before I talk about where to use stranded UTP cable.

The Telecommunications Room

The telecommunications room is the heart of the basic star. This room is where all the horizontal runs from all the work areas come together. The concentration of all this gear in one place makes the telecommunications room potentially one of the messiest parts of the basic star. Even if you do a nice, neat job of organizing the cables when they are first installed, networks change over time. People move computers, new work areas are added, network topologies are added or improved, and so on. Unless you impose some type of organization, this conglomeration of equipment and cables decays into a nightmarish mess.

Fortunately, the TIA/EIA structured cabling standards define the use of specialized components in the telecommunications room that make organizing a snap. In fact, it might be fair to say that there are too many options! To keep it simple, we're going to stay with the most common telecommunications room setup and then take a short peek at some other fairly common options.

Equipment Racks The central component of every telecommunications room is one or more equipment racks. An **equipment rack** provides a safe, stable platform for all the different hardware components. All equipment racks are 19 inches wide, but they vary in height from two- to three-foot-high models that bolt onto a wall (see Figure 14.14) to the more popular floor-to-ceiling models (see Figure 14.15).

You can mount almost any network hardware component into a rack. All manufacturers make rack-mounted switches that mount into a rack with a few screws. These switches are available with a wide assortment of ports and capabilities. There are even rack-mounted servers, complete with slide-out keyboards, and rack-mounted uninterruptible power supplies (UPSs) to power the equipment (see Figure 14.16).

All rack-mounted equipment uses a height measurement known simply as a **U**. A U is 1.75 inches. A device that fits in a 1.75-inch space is called a 1U; a device designed for a 3.5-inch space is a 2U; and a device that goes into a 7-inch space is called a 4U. Most rack-mounted devices are 1U, 2U, or 4U. The rack in Figure 14.15 is called a 42U rack to reflect the total number of Us it can hold.

Patch Panels and Cables Ideally, once you install horizontal cabling, you should never move it. As you know, UTP horizontal cabling has a solid core, making it pretty stiff. Solid core cables can handle some rearranging,

• Figure 14.16 A rack-mounted UPS

but if you insert a wad of solid core cables directly into your switches, every time you move a cable to a different port on the switch, or move the switch itself, you will jostle the cable. You don't have to move a solid core cable many times before one of the solid copper wires breaks, and there goes a network connection!

Luckily for you, you can easily avoid this problem by using a patch panel. A **patch panel** is simply a box with a row of female connectors (ports) in the front and permanent connections in the back, to which you connect the horizontal cables (see Figure 14.17).

• **Figure 14.17** Typical patch panels

The most common type of patch panel today uses a special type of connecter called a **110 block**, or sometimes a *110-punchdown block*. UTP cables connect to a 110 block using a **punchdown tool**. Figure 14.18 shows a typical punchdown tool, and Figure 14.19 shows the punchdown tool punching down individual strands.

The punchdown block has small metal-lined grooves for the individual wires. The punchdown tool has a blunt end that forces the wire into the groove. The metal in the groove slices the cladding enough to make contact.

Not only do patch panels prevent the horizontal cabling from being moved, but they are also your first line of defense in organizing the cables. All patch panels have space in the front for labels, and these labels are the network tech's best friend! Simply place a tiny label on the patch panel to identify each cable, and you will never have to experience that sinking feeling of standing in the telecommunications room of your nonfunctioning network, wondering which cable is which. If you want to be a purist, there is an official, and rather confusing, TIA/EIA labeling methodology called TIA/EIA 606, but a number of real-world network techs simply use their own internal codes (see Figure 14.20).

The CompTIA A+ 801 exam expects you to know that a punchdown tool is used for securing UTP connections to a punchdown block. It's not until you go for CompTIA Network+ certification that you'll be expected to know how to use these tools.

• **Figure 14.18** Punchdown tool

• **Figure 14.19** Punching down a 110 block

• **Figure 14.20** Typical patch panels with labels

Patch panels are available in a wide variety of configurations that include different types of ports and numbers of ports. You can get UTP, STP, or fiber ports, and some manufacturers combine several different types on the same patch panel. Panels are available with 8, 12, 24, 48, or even more ports.

UTP patch panels, like UTP cables, come with CAT ratings, which you should be sure to check. Don't blow a good CAT 6 cable installation by buying a cheap patch panel—get a CAT 6 patch panel! A higher-rated panel supports earlier standards, so you can use a CAT 6 or even CAT 6a rack with CAT 5e cabling. Most manufacturers proudly display the CAT level right on the patch panel (see Figure 14.21).

Once you have installed the patch panel, you need to connect the ports to the switch through **patch cables**. Patch cables are short (typically two- to five-foot) UTP cables. Patch cables use stranded rather than solid cable, so they can tolerate much more handling. Even though you can make your own patch cables, most people buy premade ones. Buying patch cables enables you to use different-colored cables to facilitate organization (yellow for accounting, blue for sales, or whatever scheme works for you). Most prefabricated patch cables also come with a reinforced (booted) connector specially designed to handle multiple insertions and removals (see Figure 14.22).

Making Your Own Patch Cables Although most people prefer simply to purchase premade patch cables, making your own is fairly easy. To make your own, use stranded UTP cable that matches the CAT level of your horizontal cabling. Stranded cable also requires specific crimps, so don't use crimps designed for solid cable. Crimping is simple enough, although getting it right takes some practice.

Figure 14.23 shows the two main tools of the crimping trade: an RJ-45 crimper with built-in wire stripper and a pair of wire snips. Professional cable installers naturally have a wide variety of other tools as well.

Here are the steps for properly crimping an RJ-45 onto a UTP cable. If you have some crimps, cable, and a crimping tool handy, follow along!

> The CompTIA A+ 801 exam expects you to know that a cable tech uses a crimper or crimping tool to attach an RJ-45 to the end of a UTP cable.

• **Figure 14.21** CAT level on patch panel

• **Figure 14.22** Typical patch cable

• **Figure 14.23** Crimper and snips

1. Cut the cable square using RJ-45 crimpers or scissors.

2. Strip off one-half inch of plastic jacket from the end of the cable (see Figure 14.24).

3. Slowly and carefully insert each individual wire into the correct location according to either TIA/EIA 568A or B (see Figure 14.25). Unravel as little as possible.

4. Insert the crimp into the crimper and press (see Figure 14.26). Don't worry about pressing too hard; the crimper has a stop to prevent you from using too much pressure.

Figure 14.27 shows a nicely crimped cable. Note how the plastic jacket goes into the crimp.

• **Figure 14.24** Properly stripped cable

• **Figure 14.25** Inserting the individual strands

• **Figure 14.26** Crimping the cable

• **Figure 14.27** Properly crimped cable

● **Figure 14.28** Adding a boot

A good patch cable should include a boot. Figure 14.28 shows a boot being slid onto a newly crimped cable. Don't forget to slide each boot onto the patch cable *before* you crimp both ends!

After making a cable, you need to test it to make sure it's properly crimped. We use a handy cable tester (a kind of multimeter), available in any good electronics store, to verify all the individual wires are properly connected and in the correct location (see Figure 14.29).

The Work Area

From a cabling standpoint, a work area is nothing more than a wall outlet that serves as the termination point for horizontal network cables: a convenient insertion point for a PC and a telephone. (In practice, of course, the term "work area" includes the office or cubicle.) A wall outlet itself consists of one or two female jacks to accept the cable, a mounting bracket, and a faceplate. You connect the PC to the wall outlet with a patch cable (see Figure 14.30).

The female RJ-45 jacks in these wall outlets also have CAT ratings. You must buy CAT-rated jacks for wall outlets to go along with the CAT rating of the cabling in your network. In fact, many network connector manufacturers use the same connectors, often 110 punchdowns, in the wall outlets that they use on the patch panels (see Figure 14.31). These modular outlets significantly increase the ease of installation.

The last step is connecting the PC to the wall outlet. Here again, most folks use a patch cable. Its stranded cabling stands up to the abuse caused by moving PCs, not to mention the occasional kick.

The work area may be the simplest part of the structured cabling system, but it is also the source of most network failures. When a user can't access the network and you suspect a broken cable, the first place to look is the work area.

● **Figure 14.29** Typical tester

● **Figure 14.30** Typical work area outlet

• **Figure 14.31** Punching down a modular jack

■ TCP/IP

The **Transmission Control Protocol/Internet Protocol (TCP/IP)** is the primary protocol of most modern networks, including the Internet. For a PC to access the Internet, it must have TCP/IP loaded and configured properly. TCP/IP has become so predominant that most network folks use it even on networks that do not connect to the Internet. Although TCP/IP is powerful, it is also a bit of a challenge to set up. So whether you are installing a modem for a dial-up connection to the Internet or setting up 500 computers on their own private *intranet*, you must understand some TCP/IP basics. You'll go through the following basic sections of the protocol and then you'll look at specific steps to install and configure TCP/IP.

Network Addressing

Any network address must provide two pieces of information: it must uniquely identify the machine and it must locate that machine within the larger network. In a TCP/IP network, the IP address identifies the PC and the network on which it resides. If you look at an IP address, it's not apparent which part of the address identifies the network and which part is the unique identifier of the computer. Let's review IP addresses and then see how they identify PCs and networks.

IP Addresses

In Chapter 4, you learned that TCP/IP networks don't identify PCs by name but by IP address. The **IP address** is the unique identification number for your system on the network. IP addresses consist of four sets of eight binary numbers (octets), each set separated by a period. This is called *dotted-decimal notation*. So, instead of a computer being called SERVER1, it gets an address like so:

202.34.16.11

Written in binary form, the address would look like this:

```
11001010.00100010.00010000.00001011
```

To make the addresses more comprehensible to users, the TCP/IP folks decided to write the decimal equivalents:

```
00000000 = 0
00000001 = 1
00000010 = 2
...
11111111 = 255
```

Subnet Mask

Part of every IP address identifies the network (the network ID), and another part identifies the local computer (the host ID, or host) on the network. A NIC uses a value called the **subnet mask** to distinguish which part of the IP address identifies the network ID and which part of the address identifies the host. The subnet mask blocks out (or masks) the network portion of an IP address.

Let's look at a typical subnet mask: 255.255.255.0. When you compare the subnet mask to the IP address, any part that's all 255s is the network ID. Any part that's all zeros is the host ID. Look at the following example:

IP address: 192.168.4.33

Subnet mask: 255.255.255.0

Because the first thee octets are 255, the network ID is 192.168.4 and the host ID is 33.

Every computer on a single LAN must have the same network ID and a unique host ID. That means every computer on the preceding network must have an IP address that starts with 192.168.4. Every computer on the network must have a unique IP address. If two computers have the same IP address, they won't be able to talk to each other, and other computers won't know where to send data. This is called an *IP conflict*.

You can never have an IP address that ends with a 0 or a 255, so for the preceding example, we can have addresses starting at 192.168.4.1 and ending at 192.168.4.254: a total of 254 addresses. But what if you have more than 254 computers? Well, you just take a 255 out of the subnet mask like this:

255.255.0.0

If the IP address is 192.168.4.33, then we now have a network ID of 192.168 and a host of 4.33. We can have addresses ranging from 192.168.0.1

to 192.168.255.254. (Notice the 0 and the 255? You can have 0s and 255s in an IP address, just not at the end of the IP address.)

So how many addresses can you have now? Well, let's count them out:

192.168.0.1

192.168.0.2

…

192.168.0.254

192.168.1.1

192.168.1.2

…

192.168.255.253

192.168.255.254

You would have a total of 65,534 addresses on your network. So with a subnet mask of 255.255.255.0, you get 254 addresses and a network ID of 192.168.4; and with a subnet mask of 255.255.0.0, you get 65,534 addresses and a network ID of 192.168. That just leaves one big question: who picks the network ID?

Class Licenses

The folks who organized IP addressing way back in the 1970s came up with a way to pass out network IDs using something called *class licenses*. IP addresses are divided into class licenses that correspond with the potential size of the network: Class A, Class B, and Class C. Class A licenses were intended for huge companies and organizations, such as major multinational corporations, universities, and governmental agencies. Class B licenses were assigned to medium-size companies, and Class C licenses were designated for smaller LANs.

Class A networks use the first octet to identify the network address and the remaining three octets to identify the host. Class B networks use the first two octets to identify the network address and the remaining two octets to identify the host. Class C networks use the first three octets to identify the network address and the last octet to identify the host. Table 14.1 lists range (class) assignments.

You'll note that the IP address ranges listed in Table 14.1 skip from 126.x.x.x to 128.x.x.x. That's because the 127 address range (i.e., 127.0.0.0–127.255.255.255) is reserved for network testing (loopback) operations. (We usually just use the address 127.0.0.1 for loopback purposes and call it the *localhost* address, but any address that starts with *127* will work just as well.) That's not the only reserved range, either! Each network class has a specific IP address range reserved for *private* networks—traffic from these networks doesn't get routed to the Internet at large. Class A's private range goes from 10.0.0.0 to 10.255.255.255. Class B has two private address ranges: 172.16.0.0 up to 172.31.255.254 for private

Table 14.1	Class A, B, and C Addresses		
Network Class	Address Range	No. of Network Addresses Available	No. of Host Nodes (Computers) Supported
A	1–126	129	16,777,214
B	128–191	16,384	65,534
C	192–223	2,097,152	254

addresses and 169.254.0.0 to 169.254.255.254 to accommodate the **Automatic Private IP Addressing (APIPA)** function (discussed later in the chapter). Class C's private addresses range from 192.168.0.0 to 192.168.255.254.

The default subnet mask for Class A addresses is 255.0.0.0; for Class B, it's 255.255.0.0; and for Class C, 255.255.255.0. For example, in the Class B IP address 131.190.4.121 with a subnet mask of 255.255.0.0, the first two octets (131.190) make up the network ID, and the last two (4.121) make up the host ID.

Interconnecting Networks with Routers

Now that you have a basic understanding of IP addressing, let's go back and watch a router in action. Let's take a look at a typical network: four computers and a networked printer all connected to a single switch (see Figure 14.32).

When network nerds draw out a network, they tend not to draw every device. Instead, they make a circle with the network ID and the subnet mask, as shown in Figure 14.33.

If you have two networks, just make two circles. Routers read IP addresses of incoming traffic and forward the traffic to the proper port. Since routers interconnect network IDs, we draw routers as boxes between networks, as shown in Figure 14.34

To make a router connect two networks requires a configuration process. There are a lot of different routers out there, from cheap home routers to multimillion-dollar routers that connect the big pipes of the Internet. The CompTIA A+ 220-801 exam only tests on a few basic settings on simple home routers. While we'll save the real configuration of routers for Chapter 16, there's one thing that's very important to understand now: every port

• **Figure 14.32**　Typical network

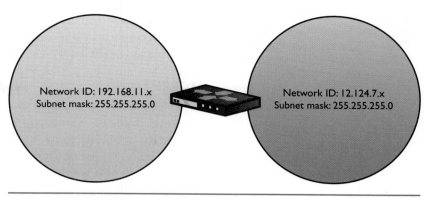

• **Figure 14.33** Same network shown as a circle

• **Figure 14.34** Router between two networks

on a router is a member of a different network ID. Let's zoom in on the router in Figure 14.34 and see how the ports are set up, as shown in Figure 14.35. Note that each router gets the first address in the network ID. This isn't a law of physics, just good manners. Keep in mind that the IP address for the router is usually the default gateway for all the computers for that network.

TCP/UDP

• **Figure 14.35** Router graphic in detail

When moving data from one system to another, the TCP/IP protocol suite needs to know if the communication is connection-oriented or connectionless. When you want to be positive that the data moving between two systems gets there in good order, use a connection-oriented application. If it's not a big deal for data to miss a bit or two, then connectionless is the way to go. The connection-oriented protocol used with TCP/IP is called the *Transmission Control Protocol* (*TCP*). The connectionless one is called the *User Datagram Protocol* (*UDP*).

Let me be clear: you don't *choose* TCP or UDP. The people who developed the applications decide which protocol to use. When you fire up your Web browser, for example, you're using TCP because Web browsers use a protocol called HTTP. HTTP is built on TCP.

Over 95 percent of all TCP/IP applications use TCP—that's why we call the protocol suite "TCP/IP" and not "UDP/IP." TCP gets an application's data from one machine to another reliably and completely. As a result, TCP comes with communication rules that require both the sending and receiving machines to acknowledge the other's presence and readiness to send and receive data.

UDP is the "fire and forget" missile of the TCP/IP protocol suite. UDP doesn't possess any of the extras you see in TCP to make sure the data is received intact. UDP works best when you have a lot of data to send that doesn't need to be perfect or when the systems are so close to each other that the chances of a problem occurring are too small to bother worrying about.

> Besides the physical ports on your computer and router, a networking *port* is also a 16-bit number (between 0 and 65,535) assigned to a TCP/IP session (or connection). The port number determines the software protocol used and how to handle the data packet. You'll learn more about ports in Chapter 16.

 The CompTIA A+ 220-801 exam expects you to know about other TCP/IP protocols for accomplishing other goals. They're all covered in Chapter 16.

A few dropped frames on a Voice over IP call, for example, won't make much difference in the communication between two people. So there's a good reason to use UDP: it's smoking fast compared to TCP.

TCP/IP Services

TCP/IP is a different type of protocol. Although it supports File and Printer Sharing, it adds a number of unique sharing functions, lumped together under the umbrella term **TCP/IP services**. The most famous TCP/IP service is called *Hypertext Transfer Protocol* (*HTTP*), the language of the World Wide Web. If you want to surf the Web, you must have TCP/IP. But TCP/IP supplies many other services beyond just HTTP. By using a service called Telnet, for example, you can access a remote system as though you were actually in front of that machine.

• **Figure 14.36** The ping command in action

Another example is a handy utility called ping. The **ping** command enables one machine to check whether it can communicate with another machine. Figure 14.36 shows an example of ping running on a Windows 7 system. Isn't it interesting that many TCP/IP services run from a command prompt? Good thing you know how to access one! I'll show you other services in a moment.

The goal of TCP/IP is to link any two hosts (remember, a *host* is just a computer in TCP/IP lingo), whether the two computers are on the same LAN or on some other network within the WAN. The LANs within the WAN are linked together with a variety of connections, ranging from basic dial-ups to dedicated high-speed (and expensive) data lines (see Figure 14.37). To move traffic between networks, you use routers (see Figure 14.38). Each host sends traffic to the router only when that data is destined for a remote network, cutting down on traffic across the more expensive WAN links. The host makes these decisions based on the destination IP address of each packet.

• **Figure 14.37** WAN concept

TCP/IP Settings

TCP/IP has a number of unique settings that you must configure correctly to ensure proper network

functionality. Unfortunately, these settings can be quite confusing, and there are several of them. Not all settings are used for every type of TCP/IP network, and it's not always obvious where you go to set them.

In Windows, you can configure network settings from the appropriate networking applet. To open Network Connections in Windows XP, either right-click on My Network Places and select Properties or open the Control Panel and select Network Connections (see Figure 14.39). In Windows Vista and Windows 7, either right-click on Network and select Properties or open the Control Panel and select Network and Sharing Center. In Windows Vista, you'll also need to click the *Manage network connections* link, and in Windows 7, you'll need to click *Change adapter settings*.

• **Figure 14.38** Typical router

The CompTIA A+ 801 exam assumes that someone else, such as a tech support person or some network guru, will tell you the correct TCP/IP settings for the network. Your only job is to understand roughly what those settings do and to know where to enter them so the system works. I already discussed default gateways and DNS back in Chapter 4, so the last big thing to cover is DHCP.

The CompTIA A+ 220-801 exam has a rather strange view of what you should know about networking. Take a lot of time practicing how to get to certain network configuration screens. Be ready for questions that ask, "Which of the following steps will enable you to change a particular value?"

DHCP To understand the **Dynamic Host Configuration Protocol (DHCP),** you must first remember that every machine must be assigned an IP address, a subnet mask, a default gateway, and at least one DNS server. These settings can be added manually by using the TCP/IP Properties dialog box. When you set the IP address manually, the IP address will not change and is called a **static IP address** (see Figure 14.40).

DHCP enables you to create a pool of IP addresses that are given temporarily to machines. DHCP is especially handy for networks of a lot of laptops that join and leave the network on a regular basis. Why give a machine that is on the network for only a few hours a day a static IP address? For that reason, DHCP is quite popular. If you add a NIC to a Windows system, the default TCP/IP settings are set to use DHCP. When you accept those

• **Figure 14.39** Network Connections showing dial-up and LAN connections

• **Figure 14.40** Setting a static IP address

● **Figure 14.41** Automatically obtaining an IP address

automatic settings, you're really telling the machine to use DHCP (see Figure 14.41).

To use DHCP you need a DHCP server. A DHCP server can be a program running on any computer in your network, but most commonly it's a feature added to routers.

TCP/IP Tools

All versions of Windows come with handy tools to test and configure TCP/IP. Those you're most likely to use in the field are ping, ipconfig, nslookup, and tracert. All of these programs are command-line utilities. Open a command prompt to run them; if you just place these commands in the Run or Search dialog box, you'll see the Command Prompt window open for a moment and then quickly close!

ping You've already encountered ping, a really great way to see if you can talk to another system. Here's how it works. Get to a command prompt and type **ping** followed by an IP address or by a DNS name, such as **ping www.chivalry.com**. Press the ENTER key on your keyboard and away it goes! Figure 14.42 shows the common syntax for ping.

The ping command has a few useful options beyond the basics. The first option is the –t switch. If you use the –t switch, ping continuously sends ping packets until you stop it with the break command (CTRL-C). The second option is the –l switch, which enables you to specify how big a ping packet to send. This helps in diagnosing specific problems with the routers between your computer and the computer you ping.

● **Figure 14.42** The ping command's syntax

> You can do some cool stuff with nslookup, and consequently some techs absolutely love the tool. It's way outside the scope of CompTIA A+ certification, but if you want to play with it, type **help** at the nslookup prompt and press ENTER to see a list of common commands and syntax.

ipconfig Windows offers the command-line tool **ipconfig** for a quick glance at your network settings. From a command prompt, type **ipconfig/ all** to see all of your TCP/IP settings (see Figure 14.43).

When you have a static IP address, ipconfig does little beyond reporting your current IP settings, including your IP address, subnet mask, default gateway, DNS servers, and WINS servers. When using DHCP, however, ipconfig is also the primary tool for releasing and renewing your IP address. Just type **ipconfig /renew** to get a new IP address or **ipconfig /release** to give up the IP address you currently have.

nslookup The **nslookup** command is a powerful command-line program that enables you to determine exactly what information the DNS server is

```
C:\Windows\system32\cmd.exe

C:\>ipconfig /all

Windows IP Configuration

    Host Name . . . . . . . . . . . . : Windows7
    Primary Dns Suffix  . . . . . . . :
    Node Type . . . . . . . . . . . . : Hybrid
    IP Routing Enabled. . . . . . . . : No
    WINS Proxy Enabled. . . . . . . . : No
    DNS Suffix Search List. . . . . . : totalhome

Ethernet adapter Local Area Connection:

    Connection-specific DNS Suffix  . : totalhome
    Description . . . . . . . . . . . : Intel(R) PRO/1000 MT Network Connection
    Physical Address. . . . . . . . . : 00-0C-29-04-A5-F7
    DHCP Enabled. . . . . . . . . . . : Yes
    Autoconfiguration Enabled . . . . : Yes
    Link-local IPv6 Address . . . . . : fe80::5d74:16a0:f201:2f37%10(Preferred)
    IPv4 Address. . . . . . . . . . . : 192.168.4.23(Preferred)
    Subnet Mask . . . . . . . . . . . : 255.255.255.0
    Lease Obtained. . . . . . . . . . : Thursday, April 26, 2012 11:19:24 AM
    Lease Expires . . . . . . . . . . : Wednesday, May 02, 2012 11:19:24 AM
    Default Gateway . . . . . . . . . : 192.168.4.1
    DHCP Server . . . . . . . . . . . : 192.168.4.12
    DHCPv6 IAID . . . . . . . . . . . : 234884137
    DHCPv6 Client DUID. . . . . . . . : 00-01-00-01-12-0E-1C-C7-00-0C-29-04-A5-F7
    DNS Servers . . . . . . . . . . . : 192.168.4.12
    NetBIOS over Tcpip. . . . . . . . : Enabled

Tunnel adapter isatap.totalhome:

    Media State . . . . . . . . . . . : Media disconnected
    Connection-specific DNS Suffix  . : totalhome
    Description . . . . . . . . . . . : Microsoft ISATAP Adapter
    Physical Address. . . . . . . . . : 00-00-00-00-00-00-00-E0
    DHCP Enabled. . . . . . . . . . . : No
    Autoconfiguration Enabled . . . . : Yes

Tunnel adapter Local Area Connection* 11:

    Connection-specific DNS Suffix  . :
    Description . . . . . . . . . . . : Teredo Tunneling Pseudo-Interface
    Physical Address. . . . . . . . . : 00-00-00-00-00-00-00-E0
    DHCP Enabled. . . . . . . . . . . : No
    Autoconfiguration Enabled . . . . : Yes
    IPv6 Address. . . . . . . . . . . : 2001:0:5ef5:79fd:8cd:348:3f57:fbe8(Preferred)
    Link-local IPv6 Address . . . . . : fe80::8cd:348:3f57:fbe8%12(Preferred)
    Default Gateway . . . . . . . . . : ::
    NetBIOS over Tcpip. . . . . . . . : Disabled

C:\>
```

• **Figure 14.43** An ipconfig /all command on Windows 7

giving you about a specific host name. Every version of Windows makes nslookup available when you install TCP/IP. To run the program, type **nslookup** from the command prompt and press the ENTER key (see Figure 14.44). Note that this gives you a little information and that the prompt has changed. That's because you're running the application. Type **exit** and press the ENTER key to return to the command prompt.

tracert The **tracert** utility shows the route that a packet takes to get to its destination. From a command line, type **tracert** followed by a space and an IP address or URL. The output describes the route from your machine to the destination machine, including all devices the packet passes through and how long each hop between devices takes (see Figure 14.45). The tracert command can come in handy when you have to troubleshoot bottlenecks. When users complain of difficulty reaching a particular

```
C:\Windows\system32\cmd.exe - nslookup

C:\>nslookup
Default Server:  totalhomedc2.totalhome
Address:  192.168.4.12

> totalsem.com
Server:  totalhomedc2.totalhome
Address:  192.168.4.12

Non-authoritative answer:
Name:    totalsem.com
Address:  216.40.231.195

>
```

• **Figure 14.44** The nslookup command in action

```
C:\Windows\system32\cmd.exe

C:\>tracert chivalry.com

Tracing route to chivalry.com [69.94.71.175]
over a maximum of 30 hops:

  1    <1 ms    <1 ms    <1 ms  Router.totalhome [192.168.4.1]
  2   122 ms   116 ms   116 ms  adsl-208-190-121-38.dsl.hstntx.swbell.net [208.190.121.38]

  3   120 ms   125 ms    43 ms  12.83.37.149
  4    48 ms    48 ms    49 ms  gar25.dlstx.ip.att.net [12.122.85.233]
  5    48 ms    48 ms    48 ms  192.205.34.142
  6    89 ms    89 ms    89 ms  OLM-LLC.Ulan495.asr1.JFK1.gblx.net [64.212.32.166]
  7    91 ms    90 ms    90 ms  gi1-1.corea.trum.fastdns.net [69.94.1.69]
  8    88 ms    88 ms    88 ms  chivalry.com [69.94.71.175]

Trace complete.

C:\>
```

• **Figure 14.45** The tracert command in action

Try This!

Running tracert

Ever wonder why your e-mail takes *years* to get to some people but arrives instantly for others? Or why some Web sites are slower to load than others? Part of the blame could lie with how many hops away your connection is from the target server. You can use tracert to run a quick check of how many hops it takes to get to somewhere on a network, so Try This!

1. Run tracert on some known source, such as www.microsoft.com or www.totalsem.com. How many hops did it take? Did your tracert time out or make it all of the way to the server?

2. Try a tracert to a local address. If you're in a university town, run a tracert on the campus Web site, such as www.rice.edu for folks in Houston, or www.ucla.edu for those of you in Los Angeles. Did you get fewer hops with a local site?

destination by using TCP/IP, you can run this utility to determine whether the problem exists on a machine or connection over which you have control, or if it is a problem on another machine or router. Similarly, if a destination is completely unreachable, tracert can again determine whether the problem is on a machine or router over which you have control.

Configuring TCP/IP

By default, TCP/IP is configured to receive an IP address automatically from a DHCP server on the network (and automatically assign a corresponding subnet mask). As far as the CompTIA A+ 801 exam is concerned, Network+ techs and administrators give you the IP address, subnet mask, and default gateway information and you plug them into the PC. That's about it, so here's how to do it manually:

1. In Windows XP, open the Control Panel and double-click the Network Connections applet. Double-click the Local Area Connection icon. In Windows Vista/7, open the Control Panel and go to the Network and Sharing Center applet. In Windows Vista, click the *Manage network connections* link, and in Windows 7, click *Change adapter settings*. After that, double-click the Local Area Network icon.

2. Click the Properties button, highlight Internet Protocol (TCP/IP), and click the Properties button. In Windows Vista/7, you should highlight Internet Protocol Version 4 (TCP/IPv4), as opposed to

Mike Meyers' CompTIA A+ Guide to 801: Managing and Troubleshooting PCs

IPv6, which you'll learn about later in this chapter.

3. In the Properties dialog box (see Figure 14.46), click the radio button next to *Use the following IP address*.

4. Enter the IP address in the appropriate fields.

5. Press the TAB key to skip down to the Subnet mask field. Note that the subnet mask is entered automatically, although you can type over this if you want to enter a different subnet mask.

6. Optionally, enter the IP address for a default gateway.

7. Optionally, enter the IP addresses of a primary DNS server and a secondary DNS server. (Figure 14.46 uses the Google DNS servers.)

8. Click the OK button to close the Properties dialog box.

9. Click the Close button to exit the Local Area Connection Status dialog box.

• **Figure 14.46** Setting up IP

Automatic Private IP Addressing

Windows supports a feature called Automatic Private IP Addressing (APIPA) that automatically assigns an IP address to the system when the client cannot obtain an IP address automatically. The Internet Assigned Numbers Authority, the nonprofit corporation responsible for assigning IP addresses and managing root servers, has set aside the range of addresses from 169.254.0.1 to 169.254.255.254 for this purpose.

If the computer system cannot contact a DHCP server, the computer randomly chooses an address in the form of 169.254.$x.y$ (where $x.y$ is the computer's identifier) and a 16-bit subnet mask (255.255.0.0) and broadcasts it on the network segment (subnet). If no other computer responds to the address, the system assigns this address to itself. When using APIPA, the system can communicate only with other computers on the same subnet that also use the 169.254.$x.y$ range with a 16-bit mask. APIPA is enabled by default if your system is configured to obtain an IP address automatically.

A computer system on a network with an active DHCP server that has an IP address in this range usually indicates a problem connecting to the DHCP server.

IPv6

When the early developers of the Internet set out to create an addressing or naming scheme for devices on the Internet, they faced several issues. Of course they needed to determine how the numbers or names worked, and for that they developed the Internet Protocol and IP addresses. But beyond that, they had to determine how many computers might exist in the future, and then make the IP address space even bigger to give Internet naming longevity. But how many computers would exist in the future?

Keep in mind that TCP/IP development took place back in the early 1970s. There were fewer than 1000 computers in the entire *world* at the time,

but that didn't keep the IP developers from thinking big! They decided to go absolutely crazy (as many people considered it at the time) and, in 1979, created the **Internet Protocol version 4 (IPv4)** 32-bit IP address space, creating approximately 4 billion IP addresses. That should have been fine for the foreseeable future!

It wasn't. First, the TCP/IP folks wasted huge chunks of IP addresses due to classful addressing and an easygoing method of parceling out IP addresses. Second, the Internet reached a level of popularity far beyond the original developers' imaginations. By the mid-1980s, the rate of consumption for IP addresses started to worry the Internet people and the writing was on the wall for IPv4's 32-bit addressing.

As a result, the Internet Engineering Task Force (IETF) developed a new IP addressing scheme called **Internet Protocol version 6 (IPv6)** that is slowly replacing IPv4. IPv6 extends the 32-bit IP address space to 128 bits, allowing up to 2^{128} addresses! That should hold us for the foreseeable future! This number—close to 3.4×10^{38} addresses—is something like all the grains of sand on Earth or 1/8 of all the molecules in the atmosphere.

Although they achieve the same function—enabling computers on IP networks to send packets to each other—IPv6 and IPv4 differ a lot when it comes to implementation. This section provides you with a quick overview to get you up to speed with IPv6 and show you how it differs from IPv4.

IPv6 Address Notation

The familiar 32-bit IPv4 addresses are written as 197.169.94.82, using four octets. The 128-bit IPv6 addresses are written like this:

2001:0000:0000:3210:0800:200C:00CF:1234

IPv6 uses a colon as a separator, instead of the period used in IPv4's dotted-decimal format. Each "group" is a hexadecimal number between 0000 and FFFF called, unofficially, a *field* or *hextet*.

A complete IPv6 address always has eight groups of four hexadecimal characters. If this sounds like you're going to type in really long IP addresses, don't worry, IPv6 offers a number of ways to shorten the address in written form.

First, leading zeros can be dropped from any group, so 00CF becomes CF and 0000 becomes 0. Let's rewrite the previous IPv6 address using this shortening method:

2001:0:0:3210:800:200C:CF:1234

Second, you can remove one or more consecutive groups of all zeros, leaving the two colons together. For example, using the :: rule, you can write the IPv6 address

2001:0:0:3210:800:200C:CF:1234

as

2001::3210:800:200C:CF:1234

You can remove any number of consecutive groups of zeros to leave a double colon, but you can only use this trick *once* in an IPv6 address.

Take a look at this IPv6 address:

FEDC:0000:0000:0000:00CF:0000:BA98:1234

If you really want to know how many IP addresses IPv6 provides, here's your number: 340,282,366,920,938,463,463,374, 607,431,768,211,456.

For those who don't play with hex regularly, one hexadecimal character (for example, *F*) represents 4 bits, so four hexadecimal characters make a 16-bit group. For some reason, the IPv6 developers didn't provide a name for the "group of four hexadecimal characters," so many techs and writers have taken to calling them fields or "hextets" to distinguish them from IPv4 "octets."

IPv4 addresses use 32 bits, and IPv6 addresses use 128 bits. Be sure you can identify their address length differences and address conventions.

Using the double-colon rule, you can reduce four groups of zeros; three of them follow the FEDC and the fourth comes after 00CF. Because of the "only use once" stipulation, the best and shortest option is to convert the address to

FEDC::CF:0:BA98:1234

You may not use a second :: to represent the fourth groups of zeros—only one :: is allowed per address! This rule exists for a good reason. If more than one :: was used, how could you tell how many groups of zeros were in each group? Answer: you couldn't.

Here's an example of a very special IPv6 address that takes full advantage of the double-colon rule, the IPv6 loopback address:

::1

Without using the double-colon nomenclature, this IPv6 address would look like this:

0000:0000:0000:0000:0000:0000:0000:0001

IPv6 still uses subnets, but you won't find a place to type in 255s anywhere. IPv6 uses the "/x" *Classless Inter-Domain Routing* (*CIDR*) nomenclature, where the /x refers to the number of bits in the subnet mask, just like in IPv4. Here's how to write an IP address and subnet for a typical IPv6 host:

FEDC::CF:0:BA98:1234/64

The unspecified address (all zeros) can never be used, and neither can an address that contains all ones (in binary) or all *F*s (in hex notation).

Where Do IPv6 Addresses Come From?

With IPv4, IP addresses come from one of two places: either you type in the IP address yourself (*static IP addressing*) or you use DHCP (also called *dynamic IP addressing*). With IPv6, addressing works very differently. Instead of one IP address, you can have up to three IP addresses on a single network card.

When a computer running IPv6 first boots up, it gives itself a *link-local address*, IPv6's equivalent to IPv4's APIPA address. Although an APIPA address can indicate a loss of network connectivity or a problem with the DHCP server, computers running IPv6 always have a link-local address. The first 64 bits of a link-local address are always FE80::. That means every address always begins with FE80:0000:0000:0000. If your operating system supports IPv6 and IPv6 is enabled, you can see this address. Figure 14.47 shows the link-local address for a typical system running the ipconfig utility.

Every computer running IPv6 will always have at least a link-local address.

If you want to force Windows to use the MAC address, just go to a command prompt and type this:

```
netsh interface ipv6
set global randomize
identifiers= disabled
```

The folks who designed IPv6 gave operating system makers a choice on how to make the last 64 bits of an IPv6 address. The first method uses a random value—and this is the way Windows does it. When you activate a NIC, Windows simply makes a random value for the last 64 bits of the IPv6 address. Once created, this unique 64-bit value will never change.

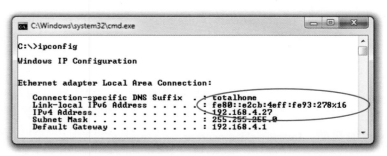

• **Figure 14.47** Link-local address in ipconfig

The alternative method to create the IPv6 address uses the MAC address of the network card (called the *Extended Unique Identifier, 64-bit*, or *EUI-64*). Be warned! The CompTIA A+ exams are Windows-centric, and Windows does not use this second method by default. Even though Windows does not currently use this method by default, understanding this is critical to understanding IPv6.

IPv6 Subnet Masks

IPv6 subnets function the same as IPv4 subnets, but you need to know two new rules:

- The last 64 bits of an IPv6 address are generated randomly or using the MAC address, leaving a maximum of 64 bits for the network ID. Therefore, no subnet is ever longer than /64.

- The IANA passes out /32 subnets to big ISPs and end users who need large allotments. ISPs and others may pass out /48 and /64 subnets to end users.

Therefore, the vast majority of IPv6 subnets are between /48 and /64. Subnet masks are just as important in IPv6 networks as they are in IPv4 networks. Unlike with IPv4 networks, however, all IPv6 networks with computers have a /64 subnet mask, so you'll rarely if ever need to make any changes manually.

Global Addresses

To get on the Internet, a system needs a second IPv6 address called a *global address*. The most common way to get a global address is to request it from the default gateway router, which must be configured to pass out global IPv6 addresses. When you plug a computer into a network, it sends out a very special packet called a *router solicitation* (*RS*) message, looking for a router (see Figure 14.48). The router hears this message and responds with a *router advertisement* (*RA*). This RA tells the computer its network ID and subnet (together called the *prefix*) and DNS server (if configured).

Once the computer gets a prefix, it generates the rest of the address just like with the link-local address. The computer ends up with a legitimate, 128-bit public IPv6 address as well as a link-local address. Figure 14.49 shows the IPv6 information in Windows 7.

Let's look at this process in detail with an example:

1. An IPv6-capable computer boots up. As it boots, it sends out a router solicitation message (FF02::2).

2. An IPv6-configured router hears the request and then sends to the computer a router advertisement containing the prefix and DNS. In this example, let's say it is 2001:470:ABCD:1/64.

3. The computer takes the prefix and adds the EUI-64 or a random value to the end of the prefix. If the MAC address is 00-0C-29-53-45-CA, then the address is 20C:29FF:FE53:45CA.

4. Putting the prefix with the last half of the address, you get the global address: 2001:470:ABCD:1:20C:29FF:FE53:45CA.

Hey everyone, is there a router out there?

Yeah, your network ID is 1080:: and your subnet is 2001:218:420::/64.

• **Figure 14.48** Getting a global address

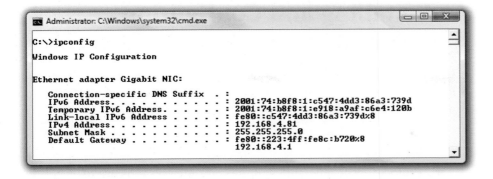

```
Administrator: C:\Windows\system32\cmd.exe

C:\>ipconfig

Windows IP Configuration

Ethernet adapter Gigabit NIC:

   Connection-specific DNS Suffix  . :
   IPv6 Address. . . . . . . . . . . : 2001:74:b8f8:1:c547:4dd3:86a3:739d
   Temporary IPv6 Address. . . . . . : 2001:74:b8f8:1:e918:a9af:c6e4:120b
   Link-local IPv6 Address . . . . . : fe80::c547:4dd3:86a3:739d%8
   IPv4 Address. . . . . . . . . . . : 192.168.4.81
   Subnet Mask . . . . . . . . . . . : 255.255.255.0
   Default Gateway . . . . . . . . . : fe80::223:4ff:fe8c:b720%8
                                       192.168.4.1
```

● **Figure 14.49** Windows system with a global IPv6 address

A global address is a true Internet address. If another computer is running IPv6 and also has a global address, it can access your system unless you have some form of firewall.

The addition of IPv6 makes programs such as ipconfig fairly complex. Take a look at Figure 14.50. With multiple NICs and both IPv4 and IPv6, the output is vast—too big to even put on a single screen.

> Computers using IPv6 need a *global* address to access the Internet.

```
C:\Windows\system32\cmd.exe

C:\>ipconfig /all

Windows IP Configuration

   Host Name . . . . . . . . . . . . : michaels-ws
   Primary Dns Suffix  . . . . . . . : totalhome
   Node Type . . . . . . . . . . . . : Hybrid
   IP Routing Enabled. . . . . . . . : No
   WINS Proxy Enabled. . . . . . . . : No
   DNS Suffix Search List. . . . . . : totalhome

Ethernet adapter Local Area Connection:

   Connection-specific DNS Suffix  . : totalhome
   Description . . . . . . . . . . . : Realtek PCIe GBE Family Controller
   Physical Address. . . . . . . . . : E0-CB-4E-93-02-78
   DHCP Enabled. . . . . . . . . . . : Yes
   Autoconfiguration Enabled . . . . : Yes
   IPv6 Address. . . . . . . . . . . : 2001:470:baf9:1::200(Preferred)
   Link-local IPv6 Address . . . . . : fe80::e2cb:4eff:fe93:278%16(Preferred)
   IPv4 Address. . . . . . . . . . . : 192.168.4.27(Preferred)
   Subnet Mask . . . . . . . . . . . : 255.255.255.0
   Lease Obtained. . . . . . . . . . : Thursday, April 26, 2012 8:37:26 AM
   Lease Expires . . . . . . . . . . : Wednesday, May 02, 2012 8:37:25 AM
   Default Gateway . . . . . . . . . : 2001:470:baf9:1::1
                                       192.168.4.1
   DHCP Server . . . . . . . . . . . : 192.168.4.12
   DHCPv6 IAID . . . . . . . . . . . : 400608078
   DHCPv6 Client DUID. . . . . . . . : 00-01-00-01-13-57-F6-2D-E0-CB-4E-93-02-78

   DNS Servers . . . . . . . . . . . : 192.168.4.12
   NetBIOS over Tcpip. . . . . . . . : Enabled

Ethernet adapter VMware Network Adapter VMnet1:

   Connection-specific DNS Suffix  . :
   Description . . . . . . . . . . . : VMware Virtual Ethernet Adapter for VMnet
1
   Physical Address. . . . . . . . . : 00-50-56-C0-00-01
   DHCP Enabled. . . . . . . . . . . : No
   Autoconfiguration Enabled . . . . : Yes
   Link-local IPv6 Address . . . . . : fe80::250:56ff:fec0:1%19(Preferred)
   IPv4 Address. . . . . . . . . . . : 192.168.22.1(Preferred)
   Subnet Mask . . . . . . . . . . . : 255.255.255.0
   Default Gateway . . . . . . . . . :
   DHCPv6 IAID . . . . . . . . . . . : 436228182
   DHCPv6 Client DUID. . . . . . . . : 00-01-00-01-13-57-F6-2D-E0-CB-4E-93-02-78

   DNS Servers . . . . . . . . . . . : fec0:0:0:ffff::1%1
```

● **Figure 14.50** The ipconfig command with IPv6 and IPv4

■ Installing and Configuring a Wired Network

Halfway through the chapter and we're finally getting to the good stuff: installing and configuring a network! To have network connectivity, you need to have three things in place:

- **NIC** The physical hardware that connects the computer system to the network media
- **Protocol** The language that the computer systems use to communicate
- **Network client** The interface that allows the computer system to speak to the protocol

If you want to share resources on your PC with other network users, you also need to enable Microsoft's File and Printer Sharing. Plus, of course, you need to connect the PC to the network switch via some sort of cable (preferably CAT 6 with Gigabit Ethernet cranking through the wires, but that's just me!). When you install a NIC, by default Windows installs upon setup the TCP/IP protocol, the Client for Microsoft Networks, and File and Printer Sharing for Microsoft Networks.

Installing a NIC

The NIC is your computer system's link to the network, and installing one is the first step required to connect to a network. NICs are manufactured to operate on specific media and network types, such as 1000BaseT Ethernet. Follow the manufacturer's instructions for installation. If your NIC is of recent vintage, it will be detected, installed, and configured automatically by Windows. You might need a driver disc or a driver download from the manufacturer's Web site.

The Add Hardware Wizard in Windows XP automates installation of non–plug-and-play devices or plug-and-play devices that were not detected correctly. Start the wizard by clicking Start | Control Panel and then double-clicking the icon for the Add Hardware applet. Click the Next button to select the hardware task you wish to perform, and follow the prompts to complete the wizard. If, for some reason, Windows Vista or Windows 7 doesn't automatically detect a new NIC after you turn the PC back on, go to Start | Control Panel | Add Hardware in Windows Vista or Start | Devices and Printers and click on *Add a device* in Windows 7 to install it.

Duplex and Half-Duplex

All modern NICs can run in **full-duplex** mode, meaning they can send and receive data at the same time. The vast majority of NICs and switches use a feature called *auto-sensing* to accommodate very old devices that might attach to the network and need to run in half-duplex mode. Half-duplex means that the device can send and receive, but not at the same time. An obvious example of a half-duplex device is the walkie-talkies you played with as a kid that required you to press and hold the orange button to transmit—at which time you couldn't hear anything. Half-duplex devices are

exceedingly rare in modern computers, but you need to understand this option. Some NICs just can't handle full-duplex communication when you connect them directly to another NIC by using a crossover cable—that is, no switch. Dropping both NICs down from full-duplex or auto-sensing can sometimes enable these odd NICs to communicate.

Link Lights

NICs made today have some type of light-emitting diode (LED) *status indicator* that gives information about the state of the NIC's link to whatever is on the other end of the connection. Even though you know the lights are actually LEDs, get used to calling them **link lights**, because that's the term all network techs use. NICs can have between one and four different link lights, and the LEDs can be any color. These lights give you clues about what's happening with the link and are one of the first items to check whenever you think a system is disconnected from the network (see Figure 14.51).

• **Figure 14.51** Mmmm, pretty lights!

Switches also have link lights, enabling you to check the connectivity at both ends of the cable. If a PC can't access a network, always check the link lights first. Multispeed devices usually have a link light that tells you the speed of the connection. In Figure 14.52, the light for port 2 on the top photo is orange, for example, signifying that the other end of the cable is plugged into either a 10BaseT or 100BaseT NIC. The same port connected to a Gigabit NIC—that's the lower picture—displays a green LED.

A properly functioning link light is steady on when the NIC is connected to another device. No flickering, no on and off, just on. A link light that is off or flickering shows a connection problem.

Another light is the **activity light**. This little guy turns on when the card detects network traffic, so it makes an intermittent flickering when operating properly. The activity light is a lifesaver for detecting problems, because in the real world, the connection light sometimes lies to you. If the connection light says the connection is good, the next step is to try to copy a file or do something else to create network traffic. If the activity light does not flicker, you have a problem.

Though no real standard exists for NIC LEDs, the CompTIA A+ exam will test you on some more-or-less *de facto* LED meanings. You should know that a solid green light means connectivity, a flashing green light means intermittent connectivity, no green light means no connectivity, and a flashing amber light means there are collisions on the network (which is sometimes okay). Also, know that the first things you should check when having connectivity issues are the NIC's LEDs.

• **Figure 14.52** Multispeed lights

No standard governs how NIC manufacturers use their lights; as a result, LEDs in NICs come in an amazing array of colors and layouts. When you encounter a NIC with a number of LEDs, take a moment to try to figure out what each one means. Although different NICs have different ways of arranging and using their LEDs, the functions are always the same: link, activity, and speed.

Wake-on-LAN

A popular feature of most NICs is the ability to turn on or wake up a powered-down or sleeping PC. You'll learn more about power management in Chapter 18, but for now, know that *Wake-on-LAN* is handy when you want to wake up one or multiple computers that you aren't physically near. To wake up a PC with Wake-on-LAN, you'll need to use a second PC to send either a special pattern or a *magic packet* (a broadcast packet that essentially repeats the destination MAC address many times).

A powered-down or sleeping PC knows to look for this special pattern or packet, at least after configured to do so. In Windows XP, go to the Control Panel and open Network Connections. In Windows Vista/7, go to the Control Panel and open Network and Sharing Center. Click *Manage network connections* (Vista) or *Change adapter settings* (7) on the left. For all versions of Windows, right-click on the adapter and select Properties. Click the Configure button in the Properties dialog box and then select the Power Management tab (see Figure 14.53). To enable Wake-on-LAN, make sure the checkbox next to *Allow this device to wake the computer* is checked. Optionally, you can select *Only allow a magic packet to wake the computer*, which will instruct the NIC to ignore everything but magic packets.

• **Figure 14.53** Wake-on-LAN settings on the Power Management tab

Wake-on-LAN is very convenient, but it has one nasty downside. As noted in the Properties dialog box, Wake-on-LAN can wake up or turn on laptops using wireless connections, even when they aren't plugged in or are inside a carrying case. Don't let your laptop's battery die or overheat—unless you know that you'll need it, turn off Wake-on-LAN on your laptop.

Your BIOS might also have settings for controlling Wake-on-LAN functions. Check your CMOS System Configuration tool to find out.

Configuring a Network Client

To establish network connectivity, you need a network client installed and configured properly. Let's look at Microsoft's client.

Installed as part of the OS installation, the Client for Microsoft Networks rarely needs configuration, and, in fact, few configuration options are available. To start it in Windows Vista/7, click Start, right-click Network, and select Properties. Then click *Manage network connections* (Vista) or *Change*

adapter settings (7) on the left. In Windows XP, click Start, right-click My Network Places, and select Properties.

In all versions of Windows, the next step is to double-click the Local Area Connection icon, click the Properties button, and highlight Client for Microsoft Networks. In Windows XP/Vista, click the Properties button. Windows 7 disables this option. Note, however, that there's not much to do here. Unless told to do something by a network administrator, just leave this alone.

Sharing and Security

Windows systems can share all kinds of **resources**: files, folders, entire drives, printers, faxes, Internet connections, and much more. Conveniently for you, the scope of the CompTIA A+ 220-801 exam is limited to folders, printers, and Internet connections. You'll see how to share folders and printers now; Internet connection sharing is discussed in Chapter 16.

Sharing Drives and Folders

All versions of Windows share drives and folders in basically the same manner. Right-click any drive or folder and choose Properties. Select the Sharing tab (see Figure 14.54). In Windows Vista/7, click the Advanced Sharing button. Select *Share this folder*, add something in the Comment or User limit fields if you wish (they're not required), and click Permissions (see Figure 14.55).

Hey! Doesn't NTFS have all those wild permissions such as Read, Execute, Take Ownership, and all that? Yes, it does, but NTFS permissions and network permissions are totally separate beasties. Microsoft wanted Windows to support many different file systems (NTFS, FAT16, FAT32), old and

• **Figure 14.54** Windows XP Sharing tab on NTFS volume

• **Figure 14.55** Network permissions

new. Network permissions are Microsoft's way of enabling you to administer file sharing on any type of partition supported by Windows, no matter how ancient. Sure, your options will be pretty limited if you are working with an older file system, but you *can* do it.

If you share a folder on an NTFS drive, as you normally do these days, you must set *both* the network permissions and the NTFS permissions to let others access your shared resources. Some good news: This is actually no big deal! Just set the network permissions to give everyone full control, and then use the NTFS permissions to exercise more precise control over *who* accesses the shared resources and *how* they access them. Open the Security tab to set the NTFS permissions.

> Windows offers two types of sharing: share-level and NTFS permissions.

Accessing Shared Drives/Directories

Once you have set up a drive or directory to be shared, the final step is to access that shared drive or directory from another machine. Windows XP uses My Network Places and Windows Vista and Windows 7 use Network, although you'll need to do a little clicking to get to the shared resources (see Figure 14.56).

You can also map network resources to a local resource name. For example, the FREDC share can be mapped to be a local hard drive such as E: or F:. From within any Explorer window (such as My Documents or Documents),

• **Figure 14.56** Shared resources in Network

choose Tools | Map Network Drive to open the Map Network Drive dialog box (see Figure 14.57). In Windows Vista/7, you might need to press the ALT key once to see the menu bar. Click the Browse button to check out the neighborhood and find a shared drive (see Figure 14.58).

Windows 2000 had the handy Add Network Place icon in My Network Places to add network locations you frequently access without using up drive letters. Windows XP removed the icon but added the menu option in its context bar on the left. Windows Vista and Windows 7 have removed it altogether but have added the ability to add links to network locations to your Favorites in Windows Explorer. Simply drag the network share, or

• **Figure 14.57** Map Network Drive dialog box in Windows 7

• **Figure 14.58** Browsing for shared folders

any folder for that matter, to the Favorites list in the Navigation pane on the left. Figure 14.59 shows how it looks on a Windows 7 system.

Mapping shared network drives is a common practice, as it makes a remote network share look like just another drive on the local system. The only downside to drive mapping stems from the fact that users tend to forget they are on a network. A classic example is the user who always accesses a particular folder or file on the network and then suddenly gets a "file not found" error when the workstation is disconnected from the network. Instead of recognizing this as a network error, the user often imagines the problem is a missing or corrupted file.

UNC

All computers that share must have a network name, and all of the resources they share must also have network names. Any resource on a network can be described by combining the name of the resource being shared and the name of the system sharing it. If a machine called SERVER1 is sharing its C: drive as FREDC, for example, the complete name would look like this:

```
\\SERVER1\FREDC
```

• **Figure 14.59** Adding a network location to the Windows 7 Navigation pane

This is called the **universal naming convention (UNC)**. The UNC is distinguished by its use of double backslashes in front of the sharing system's name and a single backslash in front of the shared resource's name. A UNC name can also point directly to a specific file or folder:

```
\\SERVER1\FREDC\INSTALL-FILES\SETUP.EXE
```

In this example, INSTALL-FILES is a subdirectory in the shared folder FREDC (which may or may not be called FREDC on the server), and SETUP .EXE is a specific file.

net

Windows enables you to view a network quickly from the command line through the **net command**. This works great when you plug into a network for the first time and, naturally, don't know the names of the other computers on that network. To see the many options that net offers, type **net** at a command prompt and press ENTER. The view and use options offer excellent network tools.

You can think of net view as the command-line version of My Network Places/Network. When run, net view returns a list of Windows computers on the network:

```
C:\Users\Mike>net view
Server Name              Remark
-------------------------------------------------
\\SABERTOOTH
\\UBERBOX
\\SERVER1

The command completed successfully.

C:\Users\Mike>
```

Once you know the names of the computers, you type **net view** followed by the computer name. The net view command will show any shares on that machine and whether they are mapped drives:

```
C:\>net view server1
Shared resources at SERVER1
Share name  Type  Used as  Comment
-----------------------------------------------------------
FREDC       Disk
Research    Disk  W:
The command completed successfully.
```

The net use command is a command-line method for mapping network shares. For example, if you wanted to map the Research share shown in the previous example to the X: drive, you simply type

```
C:\>net use x: \\server1\research
```

This will map drive X: to the Research share on the SERVER1 computer.

nbtstat

The nbtstat command is an old command-line utility that goes back to before Windows. It stands for NetBIOS over TCP/IP Statistics. Even though Net-BIOS is long gone, it's still a great tool for learning anything "Windowsy" you want to know about your network, such as "What other workgroups or domains are on this network?" It's also is a great tool to answer the question, "Who am I connected to right now?" Try running **nbtstat –s** to see all your connections:

```
C:\>nbtstat -s
Local Area Connection:
Node IpAddress: [192.168.15.102] Scope Id: []
                  NetBIOS Connection Table

    Local Name        State      In/Out  Remote Host          Input Output
    ---------------------------------------------------------------------
    UBERBOX   <00>  Connected    Out     SABERTOOTH  <20>      1KB   769B
    UBERBOX   <00>  Connected    Out     AARONV      <20>      760B  606B
    UBERBOX   <00>  Connected    Out     AARONV      <20>      950B  695B
    UBERBOX   <00>  Connected    Out     THEATER     <20>      620B  659B
    UBERBOX         Connected    In      SABERTOOTH  <00>      649KB 791KB
C:\>
```

Note that nbtstat –s shows every connection, even if two computers have multiple connections. You can also use nbtstat with the –c command for a more abbreviated list:

```
C:\>nbtstat -c
Local Area Connection:
Node IpAddress: [192.168.15.102] Scope Id: []

                  NetBIOS Remote Cache Name Table
        Name           Type         Host Address       Life [sec]
    ---------------------------------------------------------------
        AARONV    <20>  UNIQUE     192.168.15.100        327
        SABERTOOTH <20> UNIQUE     192.168.15.101        485
        THEATER   <20>  UNIQUE     192.168.15.201        380
C:\>
```

Sharing Printers

To learn about accessing shared printers in Windows, check out Chapter 19 for more information.

Sharing printers in Windows follows the same process as sharing drives and folders. Assuming that the system has printer sharing services loaded, in Windows XP and Vista go to the Printers folder in the Control Panel or Start menu and right-click the printer you wish to share. Select Sharing, and then click *Share this printer* and give it a name (see Figure 14.60). In Windows 7, choose Start | Devices and Printers, right-click on the printer you wish to share, select Printer properties, and then select the Sharing tab. From here it's just like XP and Vista—click *Share this printer* and you're done.

One of the most pleasant aspects of configuring a system for networking under all versions of Microsoft Windows is the amazing amount of the

process that is automated. For example, if Windows detects a NIC in a system, it automatically installs the NIC driver, a network protocol (TCP/IP), and Client for Microsoft Networks. So if you want to share a resource, everything you need is automatically installed. Note that although File and Printer Sharing is also automatically installed, you still must activate it by clicking the appropriate checkbox in the Local Area Connection Properties dialog box.

■ Troubleshooting Networks

Once you go beyond a single PC and enter the realm of networked computers, your troubleshooting skills need to take a giant leap up in quality. The secret to finding the right answer to networking problems on the CompTIA A+ 220-801 exam is to remember that the exam only asks about the skills to get a single computer back on the network. Granted, this might mean you'll need to check a switch or verify another system's connectivity, but in general, always focus your network troubleshooting answers on getting a single system up and running.

CompTIA likes to ask questions that deal with "no connectivity" or "intermittent connectivity." There are two ways to look at connectivity issues and CompTIA A+ exam objectives don't specify which type is covered on the exams. The first type of connectivity issue (and probably the one CompTIA means) is when your computer loses physical connectivity. The second type is when you're on the network and can't access a particular resource (you can access other resources, just not the one you want right now). Let's consider both.

● **Figure 14.60** Giving a name to a shared printer on Windows XP

The troubleshooting issues discussed here apply only to a LAN, and do not cover issues related to troubleshooting Internet access.

Repairing Physical Cabling

"The network's down!" is one of the most terrifying phrases a network tech will ever hear. Networks fail for many reasons, and the first thing to know is that good-quality, professionally installed cabling rarely goes bad, but when it does, you need to know what to do. Let's take a moment now to discuss what to do when you think you've got a problem with your physical network.

Symptoms

Losing physical connectivity is pretty obvious in Windows. Windows XP gives you a nice pop-up message warning you that you have lost a

• **Figure 14.61** Windows XP pop-up message and red X error icon

• **Figure 14.62** Windows 7 red X error icon

connection, along with a red X over the network icon (see Figure 14.61). Windows Vista and Windows 7 aren't quite as obvious, displaying only the red X over the network icon in the system tray to show you're not connected (see Figure 14.62).

If you encounter this problem, first check the obvious: Is the cable unplugged at your system? At the wall outlet? Then go for the less obvious: Is the NIC disabled in Device Manager? If these checks don't solve the problem, take a peek on the other side of the cable. If you're not connected to a running switch, you're going to get the disconnect errors.

Intermittent connectivity is often the same issue but typically is harder to figure out. Either way, read the next section to see how to get serious about testing for these pesky connectivity problems.

Diagnosing Physical Problems

Look for errors that point to physical disconnection. A key clue that the computer may have a physical problem is that a user gets a "No server is found" error, or tries to use the operating system's network explorer utility (like Network in Windows 7) and doesn't see any systems besides his or her own.

Multiple systems failing to access the network often points to hardware problems. This is where knowledge of your network cabling helps. If all the systems connected to one switch suddenly no longer see the network, but all the other systems in your network still function, you not only have a probable hardware problem, but also have a suspect—the switch.

Check the Lights

If you suspect a hardware problem, first check the link lights on the NIC and switch. If they're not lit, you know the cable isn't connected somewhere. If you're not physically at the system in question (if you're on a tech call, for example), you can have the user check his or her connection status through the link lights or through software.

If the problem system clearly cannot connect, eliminate the possibility of a failed switch or other larger problem by checking to make sure other people can access the network, and that other systems can access the shared resource (server) that the problem system can't see. Inspect the cable running from the back of the PC to the outlet. Finally, if you can, plug the system into a known good outlet and see if it works. A veteran network tech keeps a long patch cable for just this purpose. If you get connectivity with the second outlet, you should begin to suspect the structured cable running from the first outlet to the switch. Assuming the cable is installed properly and has been working correctly before this event, a simple continuity test will confirm your suspicion in most cases.

Check the NIC

Be warned that a bad NIC can also generate a "can't see the network" problem. Use the utility provided by the OS to verify that the NIC works. If you've got a NIC with diagnostic software, run it—this software will check the NIC's circuitry. The NIC's female connector is a common failure point, so NICs that come with diagnostic software often include a special test called a **loopback test**. A loopback test sends data out of the NIC and checks to see if it comes back. Some NICs perform only an internal loopback, which tests the circuitry that sends and receives, but not the actual connecting pins. A true external loopback requires a **loopback plug** inserted into the NIC's port (see Figure 14.63). If a NIC is bad, replace it.

Onboard NICs on laptops are especially notorious for breaking due to frequent plugging and unplugging. On some laptops, the NICs are easy to replace; others require a motherboard replacement.

• **Figure 14.63** Loopback plug

Cable Testing

The vast majority of network disconnection problems occur at the work area. If you've tested those connections, though, and the work area seems fine, it's time to consider deeper issues.

With the right equipment, diagnosing a bad horizontal cabling run is easy. Anyone with a network should own a midrange time-domain reflectometer (TDR) tester such as the Fluke MicroScanner. A TDR measures impedance in network cabling. If the tester measures any impedance, something is wrong with the cable. With a little practice, you can easily determine not only whether a cable is disconnected but also where the disconnection takes place. Sometimes patience is required, especially if you've failed to label your cable runs, but you will find the problem.

When you're testing a cable run, always include the patch cables as you test. This means unplugging the patch cable from the PC, attaching a tester, and then going to the telecommunications room. Here you'll want to unplug the patch cable from the switch and plug the tester into that patch cable, making a complete test, as shown in Figure 14.64.

• **Figure 14.64** Cable tester in action

Testing in this manner gives you a complete test from the switch to the system. In general, a broken cable must be replaced. A bad patch cable is an easy fix, but what happens if the horizontal cable is to blame? In these cases, I get on the phone and call my local installer. If a cable is bad in one spot, the risk of it being bad in another is simply too great to try anything other than total replacement.

Toners

It would be nice to say that all cable installations are perfect and that over the years they won't tend to grow into horrific piles of spaghetti-like, unlabeled cables. In the real world, though, you might eventually find yourself having to locate or *trace* cables. Even in the best-planned networks, labels fall off ports and outlets, mystery cables appear behind walls, new cable runs are added, and mistakes are made counting rows and columns on patch panels. Sooner or later, most network techs will have to be able to pick out one particular cable or port from a stack.

When the time comes to trace cables, network techs turn to a device called a toner for help. **Toner** is the generic term for two separate devices that are used together: a tone generator and a tone probe. The **tone generator** connects to the cable using alligator clips, tiny hooks, or a network jack, and it sends an electrical signal along the wire at a certain frequency. The **tone probe** emits a sound when it is placed near a cable connected to the tone generator. These two devices are often referred to by the brand-name Fox and Hound, a popular model of toner made by the Triplett Corporation (see Figure 14.65).

To trace a cable, connect the tone generator to the known end of the cable in question, and then position the tone probe next to the other end of each of the cables that might be the right one. The tone probe makes a sound when it's placed next to the right cable. Some toners have one tone probe that works with multiple tone generators. Each generator emits a separate frequency, and the probe sounds a different tone for each one. Even good toners are relatively inexpensive ($75); although inexpensive toners can cost less than $25, they don't tend to work well, so spending a little more is worthwhile. Just keep in mind that if you have to support a network, you'd do best to own a decent toner.

Fixing Common Problems

Let's go back and look at the second possible meaning for a loss in connectivity. It's very common to try to connect to a shared resource and either fail or find that a shared resource you've used time and again has suddenly disappeared.

Failing to Connect to a New Resource

When you can't connect to a resource on the first try, it often points to a configuration issue. In most cases, a quick double-check of the sharing system will reveal one of the following problems (and call for the associated solution).

You'll see a tone probe referred to on the CompTIA A+ exam as a *toner probe*.

• Figure 14.65

- You don't have the right share name? Go check at the serving system.

- You don't have the required user name/password? Ask someone who might have this knowledge, or double-check that your account has access.

- You don't have permission to use/access/connect to the shared resource? Make sure you have the correct permissions.

- You're not on the right homegroup/domain/workgroup? Check your system and the sharing system to verify which workgroup/domain name to use. On a homegroup, make sure you've used the proper password.

- The folder or printer isn't shared? Share it!

- The folder or printer doesn't exist? Make sure the serving system still hosts the folder you want. Install the network printer if you haven't yet.

Failing to Connect to a Previously Used Resource

If you suddenly can't connect to a resource that you've used many times before, go with the easy answers first:

- Verify that you are not already connected by using **nbtstat –s**.

- Check that you can see the resource using My Network Places/Network or **net view**.

- Check that the serving system is on.

- Check that the computer is physically connected to the serving system.

Chapter 14 Review

■ Chapter Summary

After reading this chapter and completing the exercises, you should understand the following about networking.

Install and troubleshoot structured cabling

■ Fiber optic Ethernet transmits light instead of electricity, achieving much greater maximum distances than other forms of Ethernet. Most fiber networks use LEDs to send light signals and use multimode fiber optic cabling. Networks that use laser light use single-mode fiber optic cabling. Laser light and single-mode cabling are used most often for very long-distance connections.

■ Most fiber optic cables use one of two connectors: the square SC type or the round ST type.

■ Early versions of Ethernet ran on coaxial cable instead of UTP. Coax cable consists of a center cable, or core, surrounded by insulation, covered by a shield of braided cable. Coaxial cables are rated using an RG name, with the two most popular standards being RG-6 and RG-59.

■ The two common coaxial cable connectors are the BNC twist connector and the F-type screw connector.

■ Hubs connected older Ethernet networks. They repeat data to every connected port.

■ Switches have replaced hubs as the modern interconnection point for Ethernet networks. They create point-to-point connections between two computers.

■ A bridge enables two devices with different connector types, such as UTP and fiber optic, to connect and communicate with one another.

■ A network attached storage (NAS) device is a simple box that supports one or more hard drives for sharing data across a network. These are often self-configuring. A NAS is a type of network appliance.

■ A router connects multiple LANs together. By definition, a router must have at least two connections: one into the network, and one out to another network.

■ Structured cabling refers to a set of standards for installing wired networks, including the type of cables to be used, where to place them, how to connect them, and so on. The idea is to create a safe and reliable cabling infrastructure. Structured cabling requires three ingredients: a telecommunications room, horizontal cabling, and a work area.

■ All UTP cables use either solid core or stranded core. Each wire in solid core UTP uses a single solid wire. With stranded core, each wire is actually a bundle of tiny wire strands. Each of these cable types has its benefits and downsides.

■ A patch panel is a box with a row of female connectors (or ports) in the front and permanent connections in the back, where you connect your horizontal cables. Most patch panels use a 110 block.

Explain the basics of TCP/IP

■ TCP/IP is the primary protocol of most modern networks, including the Internet. For a PC to access the Internet, it must have TCP/IP loaded and configured properly.

■ Any network address must provide two pieces of information: it must uniquely identify the machine and it must locate that machine within the larger network. In a TCP/IP network, the IP address identifies the PC and the network on which it resides.

■ Part of every IP address identifies the network (the network ID), and another part identifies the local computer (the host ID, or host) on the network. The subnet mask is a value that a NIC uses to distinguish which part of the IP address identifies the network ID and which part of the address identifies the host.

■ IP addresses are divided into class licenses that correspond with the potential size of the network: Class A, Class B, and Class C. Class A licenses were intended for huge companies and organizations, such as major multinational corporations, universities, and governmental agencies. Class B licenses were assigned to medium-size companies, and Class C licenses were designated for smaller LANs.

- When you want to be positive that the data moving between two systems gets there in good order, use a connection-oriented application. If it's not a big deal for data to miss a bit or two, then connectionless is the way to go. The connection-oriented protocol used with TCP/IP is called the Transmission Control Protocol (TCP). The connectionless one is called the User Datagram Protocol (UDP).

- TCP/IP provides sharing functions called services. Well-known TCP/IP services include HTTP, the language of the World Wide Web, Telnet, and ping.

- TCP/IP requires that several settings are properly configured before you can connect to a network. A network administrator should configure these for you. These settings include your IP address, default gateway, DNS settings, and DHCP settings.

- Windows includes several tools for testing and managing TCP/IP, including ping, ipconfig, nslookup, and tracert.

- By default, TCP/IP is configured to receive an IP address automatically from a DHCP server on the network (and automatically assign a corresponding subnet mask).

- Windows supports a feature called Automatic Private IP Addressing (APIPA) that automatically assigns an IP address to the system when the client cannot obtain an IP address automatically.

- IPv6 extends the 32-bit IP address space to 128 bits, allowing up to 2^{128} (that's close to 3.4×10^{38}) addresses. The familiar 32-bit IPv4 addresses are written as 197.169.94.82, using four octets. The 128-bit IPv6 addresses are written like this: 2001:0000:0000:3210:0800:200C:00CF:1234. A complete IPv6 address always has eight groups of four hexadecimal characters.

- You may have up to three IPv6 addresses on your PC at one time: a link-local address and two global addresses.

Install and configure wired networks

- When you install a NIC, by default, Windows installs upon setup the TCP/IP protocol (configured for DHCP), the Client for Microsoft Networks, and File and Printer Sharing for Microsoft Networks.

- To establish network connectivity, you need a network client installed and configured properly.

The Client for Microsoft Networks is installed as part of the OS installation.

- All versions of Windows share drives and folders in basically the same manner. Right-click any drive or folder, choose Properties, and then select the Sharing tab. In Windows Vista/7 click the Advanced Sharing button. Click the *Share this folder* radio button and type a share name.

- When sharing a folder on an NTFS drive, you must set the network permissions to give everyone full control, and then use the NTFS permissions (on the Security tab) to exercise more precise control over who accesses the shared resources and how they access them.

- Network resources can be mapped to a local resource name. This can be done from Windows Explorer or by right-clicking a share in My Network Places/Network and choosing Map Network Drive.

- All computers that share must have a share name, and all the resources they share must also have names. Any resource on a network can be described by combining the name of the resource being shared and the name of the system sharing it. The complete UNC name of the FREDC share on SERVER1, for example, would be \\SERVER1\FREDC.

- The nbtstat command shows you information about your network, including the workgroups or domains on the network.

- Windows provides the net utility to help you explore and diagnose a Windows network. One of the more popular options is net view, which lists other Windows systems on the network. Another popular option is the net use command to map a remote share as a network drive.

- To share a printer in Windows, open the Printers folder in the Control Panel or Start menu and right-click the printer you wish to share. Select Sharing, and then click *Share this printer* and give it a name.

Troubleshoot wired networks

- Look for errors that point to physical disconnection. A key clue that you may have a physical problem is that a user gets a "No server is found" error, or tries to use the operating system's network explorer utility (like Network in Windows 7) and doesn't see any systems besides his or her own.

- If you suspect a hardware problem, first check the link lights on the NIC and switch. If they're not lit, you know the cable isn't connected somewhere. If you're not physically at the system in question (if you're on a tech call, for example), you can have the user check his or her connection status through the link lights or through software.

- Be warned that a bad NIC can also generate a "can't see the network" problem. Use the utility provided by your OS to verify that the NIC works. If you've got a NIC with diagnostic software, run it—this software will check the NIC's circuitry.

- A loopback test sends data out of the NIC and checks to see if it comes back. Some NICs perform only an internal loopback, which tests the circuitry that sends and receives, but not the actual connecting pins. A true external loopback requires a loopback plug inserted into the NIC's port.

- A TDR measures impedance in network cabling. If the tester measures any impedance, something is wrong with the cable.

- When you're testing a cable run, always include the patch cables as you test. This means unplugging the patch cable from the PC, attaching a tester, and then going to the telecommunications room.

- When the time comes to trace cables, network techs turn to a device called a toner for help. The tone generator connects to the cable using alligator clips, tiny hooks, or a network jack, and it sends an electrical signal along the wire at a certain frequency. The tone probe emits a sound when it is placed near a cable connected to the tone generator. These two devices are often referred to by the brand-name Fox and Hound, a popular model of toner.

■ Key Terms

110 block *(417)*
activity light *(437)*
Automatic Private IP Addressing (APIPA) *(424)*
bridge *(412)*
coaxial cable *(410)*
crossover cable *(409)*
Dynamic Host Configuration Protocol (DHCP) *(427)*
equipment rack *(416)*
fiber optic cable *(409)*
full-duplex *(436)*
horizontal cabling *(414)*
Internet Protocol version 4 (IPv4) *(432)*
Internet Protocol version 6 (IPv6) *(432)*
IP address *(422)*
ipconfig *(428)*
link lights *(437)*
loopback plug *(447)*
loopback test *(447)*
net command *(443)*
nslookup *(428)*
patch cable *(418)*
patch panel *(417)*

ping *(426)*
punchdown tool *(417)*
resources *(439)*
run *(414)*
solid core *(415)*
static IP address *(427)*
stranded core *(415)*
structured cabling *(413)*
subnet mask *(422)*
switch *(411)*
TCP/IP services *(426)*
telecommunications room *(414)*
tone generator *(448)*
tone probe *(448)*
toner *(448)*
tracert *(429)*
Transmission Control Protocol/Internet Protocol (TCP/IP) *(421)*
U *(416)*
universal naming convention (UNC) *(443)*
work area *(414)*

Key Term Quiz

Use the Key Terms list to complete the sentences that follow. Not all terms will be used.

1. HTTP and Telnet are both examples of special sharing functions called _____.

2. The command-line utility called _____ enables one machine to check whether it can communicate with another machine.

3. A center cable surrounded by insulation and covered with a shield of braided cable is called _____.

4. A computer on a(n) _____ network gets a 32-bit address.

5. A computer on a(n) _____ network gets a 128-bit address.

6. The set of standards established by the TIA/EIA regarding network cabling is called _____.

7. _____ uses light, instead of electricity, to transmit data.

8. You can use a(n) _____ to connect two different types of network media, such as coaxial and UTP.

9. When troubleshooting a NIC, you'll need to crawl behind your computer and look for the _____, which should be on or blinking.

10. To test a possibly broken Ethernet port, plug in a(n) _____.

Multiple-Choice Quiz

1. Everything worked fine on your 1000BaseT network yesterday, but today no one can connect to the server. The server seems to be in good running order. Which of the following is the most likely problem?

 A. Someone changed all of the passwords for server access.

 B. A switch is malfunctioning.

 C. Someone's T connector has come loose on the bus.

 D. The server's cable is wired as TIA/EIA 568A and all of the others are wired as TIA/EIA 568B.

2. Simon's system can't contact a DHCP server to obtain an IP address automatically, but he can still communicate with other systems on his subnet. What feature of Windows makes this possible?

 A. Subnet masking

 B. Default gateway

 C. APIPA

 D. Client for Microsoft Networks

3. Which of the following is the correct net syntax for discovering which network shares on a particular server are mapped on your computer?

 A. net view \\fileserver

 B. net \\fileserver

 C. net map \\fileserver

 D. net share \\fileserver

4. A small device that enables you to test a NIC's circuitry is called?

 A. Loopback plug

 B. Port tester

 C. Multimeter

 D. Integrated network and logic probe

5. What is the term used to describe where the network hardware and patch panels are kept?

 A. Drop room

 B. Telecommunications room

 C. Routing room

 D. Telecloset room

6. You are down under your desk organizing some wires when you notice that the activity light on your NIC is blinking erratically. Is there a problem?

 A. Yes, the activity light should be on steadily when the computer is running.

 B. Yes, the activity light should be blinking steadily, not randomly.

 C. No, the light blinks when there is network traffic.

 D. No, the light blinks to show bus activity.

7. What is a common symptom of a bad network cable?

 A. Rapidly blinking link lights

 B. No link lights

 C. Solid on link lights

 D. Steady blinking link lights

8. What command-line utility would you run to show a list of network computers?

 A. net send

 B. show net_servers

 C. net use

 D. net view

9. When connecting a cable run onto a patch panel, which tool should you use?

 A. 110-punchdown tool

 B. Crimper

 C. TDR

 D. Tone generator

10. What is the structured cabling name for the end user's office space where network computers are set up?

 A. Backbone

 B. Building entrance

 C. Cable drop

 D. Work area

11. You are trying to locate which patch cable in the main switch traces back to a particular computer. Which tool should you use?

 A. Tone probe

 B. Cable tester

 C. Punchdown tool

 D. Butt set

12. Which of the following describes an IPv4 address? (Select three.)

 A. Uses decimal, not hexadecimal numbers

 B. Uses periods, not colons, as separators

 C. Uses four octets

 D. Uses eight sets of characters

13. Which of the following are fiber connector types? (Select three.)

 A. LC

 B. LS

 C. MT-RJ

 D. ST

14. What benefit does full-duplex offer?

 A. It enables NICs to send and receive signals at the same time.

 B. It enables NICs to send data twice as fast.

 C. It enables NICs to receive data twice as fast.

 D. It enables a switch to connect to both coaxial and fiber optic cables.

15. What do most techs call a toner or tone generator?

 A. TDR

 B. UTP

 C. UDP

 D. Fox and Hound

■ Essay Quiz

1. You are a tech for a small company and you get a call from Jessica, who cannot access the network anymore from her workstation. What techniques would you use to help troubleshoot her system and get her back working?

2. There are different classifications of IP addresses and different ways to assign them. Write a short essay on the difference between Class A, B, and C addresses, and how to choose either static or dynamic addressing.

3. Which types of computer network cable connections are you familiar with already? Write a short paragraph describing your experience.

4. Prepare a list of questions you would ask a large organization's network administrator regarding cabling, connections, hubs, switches, and even routers.

Lab Projects

• Lab Project 14.1

This chapter described how Windows automatically generates an IP address if there is no DHCP server. Experiment with this idea. If you have a network of Windows PCs that you can play with, make sure there is no DHCP server on the network. Use ipconfig and see what your IP address is, and try sharing it and pinging other systems. Try to share resources and access shared resources on other machines in the lab.

• Lab Project 14.2

The PC is not the only device that can connect to an Ethernet network. Do an Internet search or make a run to your local computer store and create a list of network devices. What did you find? How would they be used?

• Lab Project 14.3

Nearly every hardware manufacturer wants you to upgrade to their latest networking gear and they keep adding new features to entice you. Do a search through the bigger companies' product lists and compare the Linksys, Netgear, Microsoft, and D-Link devices:

www.linksys.com

www.netgear.com

www.microsoft.com

www.dlink.com

• Lab Project 14.4

The Internet is a big, sprawling place with big routers that move packets from place to place around the world. Using the tracert command, see how many hops it takes to get to various Web sites around the world.

Wireless Networking

In this chapter, you will learn how to

- **Discuss wireless networking components**
- **Analyze and explain wireless networking standards**

Wireless networks have been popular for many years now, but unlike wired networks, so much of how wireless works continues to elude people. Part of the problem might be that a simple wireless network is so inexpensive and easy to configure that most users and techs never really get into the *hows* of wireless. The chance to get away from all the cables and mess and just *connect* has a phenomenal appeal. Well, let's change all that and dive deeply into wireless networking.

Historical/Conceptual

■ Wireless Networking Components

Instead of a physical set of wires running between network nodes, wireless networks use either radio waves or beams of infrared light to communicate with each other. Various kinds of wireless networking solutions have come and gone in the past. The wireless radio wave networks you'll find yourself supporting these days are based on the **IEEE 802.11** wireless Ethernet standard—marketed as Wi-Fi—and on Bluetooth technology. Wireless networks using infrared light are limited to those that use the Infrared Data Association (IrDA) protocol. Finally, the cell phone companies have gotten into the mix and offer access to the Internet through cellular networks.

Wireless networking capabilities of one form or another are built into many modern computing devices. Infrared *transceiver* ports have been standard issue on portable computers, personal digital assistants (PDAs), and high-end printers for years, although they're absent from most of the latest PCs and portable computers. Figure 15.1 shows the infrared transceiver ports on an older laptop and PDA. Wireless Ethernet and often Bluetooth capabilities are now ubiquitous as integrated components, or you can easily add them by using PCI, PCI Express, or PC Card adapters. Figure 15.2 shows a desktop PCI Wi-Fi adapter. You can also add wireless network capabilities by using external USB wireless network adapters, as shown in Figure 15.3.

• Figure 15.1 Infrared transceiver ports on a laptop and PDA

• Figure 15.2 Wireless PCI add-on card

• Figure 15.3 External USB wireless NIC

Wireless networking is not limited to PCs. Most smartphones and tablets have wireless capabilities built-in or available as add-on options. Figure 15.4 shows a smartphone accessing the Internet over a Wi-Fi connection.

801

To extend the capabilities of a wireless Ethernet network, such as connecting to a wired network or sharing a high-speed Internet connection, you need a **wireless access point (WAP)**. A WAP centrally connects wireless network nodes in the same way that a hub connects wired Ethernet PCs. Many WAPs also act as switches and Internet routers, such as the Linksys device shown in Figure 15.5.

Most WAPs draw their power from a wall outlet, like any other electronic device. More advanced WAPs, especially those used in corporate settings, can also use a feature called **Power over Ethernet (PoE)**. Using PoE, you only need to plug a single Ethernet cable into the WAP to provide both power and a network connection.

Wireless communication via Bluetooth comes as a built-in option on newer PCs and peripheral devices, or you can add it to an older PC via an external USB Bluetooth adapter. Figure 15.6 shows a Bluetooth adapter with a Bluetooth-enabled mouse and keyboard.

Wireless Networking Software

Wireless devices use the same networking protocols and client that their wired counterparts use, and they operate by using the **carrier sense multiple access/collision avoidance (CSMA/CA)** networking scheme. The *collision avoidance* aspect differs slightly from the *collision detection* standard used in wired Ethernet. A wireless node listens in on the wireless medium to

• **Figure 15.4** Smartphone with wireless capability

PoE is often used with WAPs, but other network devices take advantage of this feature, too.

Wireless access points are commonly known as WAPs, APs, access points, or simply wireless routers.

• **Figure 15.5** Linksys device that acts as wireless access point, switch, and router

• **Figure 15.6** External USB Bluetooth adapter, keyboard, and mouse

see if another node is currently broadcasting data. If so, it waits a random amount of time before retrying. So far, this method is exactly the same as the method used by wired Ethernet networks. Because wireless nodes have a more difficult time detecting data collisions, however, they offer the option of using the *Request to Send/Clear to Send* (*RTS/CTS*) protocol. When enabled, a transmitting node that determines that the wireless medium is clear to use sends an RTS frame to the receiving node. The receiving node responds with a CTS frame, telling the sending node that it's okay to transmit. Then, once the data is sent, the transmitting node waits for an acknowledgment (ACK) from the receiving node before sending the next data packet. This option is very elegant, but keep in mind that using RTS/CTS introduces significant overhead to the process and can impede performance.

In terms of configuring wireless networking software, you need to do very little. Wireless network adapters are plug and play, so any modern version of Windows immediately recognizes one when it is installed, prompting you to load any needed hardware drivers. You will, however, need a utility to set parameters such as the network name.

Windows XP and later include built-in tools for configuring these settings, but some wireless adapters also come with configuration tools provided by the wireless network adapter vendor (see Figure 15.7). Using this utility, you can determine your link state and signal strength, configure your wireless networking *mode* (discussed next), and set security encryption, power saving options, and so on.

> Wireless networks use the carrier sense multiple access/collision avoidance (CSMA/CA) standard, while wired Ethernet networks use carrier sense multiple access/collision detection (CSMA/CD).

• **Figure 15.7** Wireless configuration utility

Wireless Network Modes

The simplest wireless network consists of two or more PCs communicating directly with each other without cabling or any other intermediary hardware. More complicated wireless networks use a WAP to centralize wireless communication and bridge wireless network segments to wired network segments. These two methods are called ad hoc mode and infrastructure mode.

Ad hoc Mode

Ad hoc mode is sometimes called *peer-to-peer mode*, with each wireless node in direct contact with every other node in a decentralized free-for-all, as shown in Figure 15.8. Two or more wireless nodes communicating in ad hoc mode form what's called an *Independent Basic Service Set* (*IBSS*). Ad hoc mode networks are suited for small groups of computers (less than a dozen or so) that need to transfer files or share printers. Ad hoc mode networks are also good for temporary networks such as study groups or business meetings.

Infrastructure Mode

Wireless networks running in **infrastructure mode** use one or more WAPs to connect the wireless network nodes to a wired network segment, as shown in Figure 15.9. A single WAP servicing a given area is called a *Basic Service Set* (*BSS*). This service area can be extended by adding more WAPs. This is called, appropriately, an *Extended Basic Service Set* (*EBSS*).

Wireless networks running in infrastructure mode require more planning and are more complicated to configure than ad hoc mode networks, but they also give you finer control over how the network operates. Infrastructure mode is better suited to networks that need to share dedicated resources such as Internet connections and centralized databases.

Wireless Networking Security

One of the major complaints against wireless networking is that it offers weak security. In many cases, all you need to do to access a wireless network is walk into a WAP's coverage area, turn on your wireless device, and connect! Furthermore, data packets are floating through the air instead of safely wrapped up inside network cabling. What's to stop an unscrupulous PC tech with the right equipment from grabbing those packets out of the air and reading that data himself?

Wireless networks use three methods to secure access to the network itself and secure the data that's being transferred. The **service set identifier (SSID)** parameter—also called the *network name*—is used to define the wireless network. This is very handy when you have a number of wireless networks in the same area.

SSID

One of the main security weaknesses with wireless networks is that, out of the box, *no* security is configured at all. Wireless devices *want* to be heard, and WAPs are usually configured to broadcast their presence to their maximum range and welcome all other wireless devices that respond.

Always change the default SSID to something unique, and change the password right away. Configuring a unique SSID name and password is the very least that you should do to secure a wireless network. The default SSID names and passwords are well known and widely available online. This is intended to make setting up a wireless network as easy as possible but can cause problems in places with a lot of overlapping wireless networks. Each wireless network node and access point needs to be configured with the same unique SSID name. This SSID name is then included in the header of every data packet broadcast in the wireless network's coverage area. Data packets that lack the correct SSID name in the header are rejected.

Another trick often seen in wireless networks is to tell the wireless device not to broadcast the SSID. People not authorized to access the network will have a harder time knowing it's there.

Changing the default SSID for the WAP is the first step in setting up a new wireless network.

MAC Address Filtering

Most WAPs also support **MAC address filtering**, a method that enables you to limit access to your wireless network based on the physical, hard-wired address of the units' wireless NIC. MAC address filtering is a handy way of creating a type of "accepted users" list to limit access to your wireless network, but it works best when you have a small number of users. A table stored in the WAP lists the MAC addresses that are permitted to participate in the wireless network. Any data packets that don't contain the MAC address of a node listed in the table are rejected.

Many techs shorten the term "MAC address filtering" to simply "MAC filtering." Either way works.

WEP

Early on, Wi-Fi developers introduced the **Wired Equivalent Privacy (WEP)** protocol to attempt to ensure that data is secured while in transit over the airwaves. WEP encryption uses a standard 40-bit encryption to scramble data packets. Many vendors also support 104-bit encryption. Note that some vendors advertise 128-bit encryption, but they actually use a 104-bit encryption key. Unfortunately, WEP encryption includes a flaw that makes it extremely vulnerable to attack. Although WEP is better than no encryption at all, keep in mind that WEP will not protect you from knowledgeable intruders.

WEP doesn't provide complete end-to-end encryption. WEP provides encryption only between the WAP and the wireless device. Encryption is stripped from the data packet as it travels "up" through the subsequent network layers. For true end-to-end encryption, you need to upgrade to WPA or WPA2.

WPA

The **Wi-Fi Protected Access (WPA)** protocol addresses the weaknesses of WEP and acts as a security protocol upgrade to WEP. WPA uses the **Temporal Key Integrity Protocol (TKIP)**, which provides a new encryption key for every sent packet. This protects WPA from many of the attacks that make

WEP vulnerable, though TKIP has since been deprecated, as it has flaws of its own. WPA also offers security enhancements over WEP such as an encryption key integrity-checking feature and user authentication through the industry-standard **Extensible Authentication Protocol (EAP)**. EAP provides a huge security improvement over WEP encryption. After all, MAC addresses are fairly easy to "sniff" out, because they're transmitted in unencrypted, clear text format. User names and passwords are encrypted and therefore much more secure. Even with these enhancements, WPA was intended only as an interim security solution until the IEEE 802.11i security standard was finalized and implemented.

WPA2

Today, Mac OS X and Windows support the full IEEE 802.11i standard, more commonly known as **Wi-Fi Protected Access 2 (WPA2)**, to lock down wireless networks. WPA2 uses the **Advanced Encryption Standard (AES)**, among other improvements, to provide a secure wireless environment. If you haven't upgraded to WPA2, you should.

WPS

While most techs can configure wireless networks blindfolded, the thought of passwords and encryption might intimidate the average user. If anything, most people plug in their wireless router and go on their merry way. Because everyone should secure their wireless network, the developers of Wi-Fi created **Wi-Fi Protected Setup (WPS)**, a standard included on most WAPs and clients to make secure connections easier to configure.

WPS works in one of two ways. Some devices use a push button, such as the one shown in Figure 15.10, and others use a password or code.

Let's say you want to connect a WPS-capable wireless printer to a WPS-capable WAP. First, you would press the button on the printer for a short moment (usually two seconds). You then have a set time (usually two minutes) to press the button on the WAP. This should automatically configure a secure connection.

• **Figure 15.10** WPS button on an e2500 Router

Some devices enable you to use a code. A WPS-capable WAP will have an eight-digit numeric code printed on the device. To access the WAP, just enter the code in Windows as you would a WPA/WPA2 password. Now you're on the network.

Sadly, WPS has a security flaw. A hacker can use a program to repeatedly guess the eight-digit code. Because of how the code is set up, it's very easy to guess. As long you have WPS enabled on your WAP, you are vulnerable. The only way to stop this hack is to shut down WPS. Check the WAP manufacturer's Web site for instructions on turning off WPS.

Access Point Placement and Radio Power

When setting up your wireless network, keep your space in mind. While encryption can protect your network from intruders, you can also limit your risk by hiding your network from outsiders altogether. When using

an omni-directional antenna, keep it near the center of your home or office. The closer you place it to a wall, the further away someone outside your home or office can be and still detect your wireless network.

Your wireless access point might also enable you to adjust the radio power levels of your antenna. Decrease the radio power until you can get reception at the furthest point *inside* your home or office, but not outside. This will take some trial and error.

Speed and Range Issues

Wireless networking data throughput speeds depend on several factors. Foremost is the standard that the wireless devices use. Depending on the standard used, wireless throughput speeds range from a measly 2 Mbps to a snappy 100+ Mbps. One of the other factors affecting speed is the distance between wireless nodes (or between wireless nodes and central- ized access points). Wireless devices dynamically negotiate the top speed at which they can communicate without dropping too many data packets. Speed decreases as distance increases, so the maximum throughput speed is achieved only at extremely close range (less than 25 feet or so). At the outer reaches of a device's effective range, speed may decrease to around 1 Mbps before it drops out altogether.

Speed is also affected by interference from other wireless devices operating in the same frequency range—such as cordless phones or baby monitors—and by solid objects. So-called *dead spots* occur when something capable of blocking the radio signal comes between the wireless network nodes. Large electrical appliances such as refrigerators are *very* effective at blocking a wireless network signal. Other culprits include electrical fuse boxes, metal plumbing, air conditioning units, and similar objects.

Wireless networking range is difficult to define, and you'll see most descriptions listed with qualifiers, such as "*around* 150 feet" and "*about* 300 feet." This is simply because, like throughput speed, range is greatly affected by outside factors. Interference from other wireless devices affects range, as does interference from solid objects. The maximum ranges listed in the next section are those presented by wireless manufacturers as the the- oretical maximum ranges. In the real world, you'll experience these ranges only under the most ideal circumstances. True effective range is probably about half what you see listed.

You can increase range in a couple of ways. You can install mul- tiple WAPs to permit "roaming" between one WAP's coverage area and another's—an EBSS, described earlier in this chapter. Or you can install a replacement that increases a single WAP's signal strength, thus increasing its range. If that is still not enough, signal boosters are available that can give you even more power.

■ Wireless Networking Standards

Today's wireless world is dominated by *radio frequency* (*RF*) technologies, in particular the 802.11 (Wi-Fi) standards. Other standards, such as infrared, Bluetooth, and cellular, have a place in today's market. To help you gain

Don't forget to physically protect the WAP, too. Most WAPs have physical Ethernet ports in addition to their wireless capabilities. These ports are not password-protected or encrypted. Keep the WAP in a location where unscrupulous folk can't get to it.

Tech Tip

Checking Signal Strength
You can see the speed and signal strength on your wireless network by looking at the wireless NIC's properties. In Windows XP, open the Network Connections applet in Control Panel, right-click your wireless NIC, and select Properties. In Vista/7, open the Network and Sharing Center, select Change Adapter Settings, then right-click your wireless NIC and select Properties.

Look for basic troubleshooting questions on the CompTIA A+ 220-801 exam dealing with factors that affect wireless connectivity, range, and speed.

a better understanding of wireless network technologies, this section provides a brief look at the standards they use.

IEEE 802.11-Based Wireless Networking

The IEEE 802.11 wireless Ethernet standard, more commonly known as **Wi-Fi**, defines methods by which devices may communicate by using *spread-spectrum* radio waves. Spread-spectrum broadcasts data in small, discrete chunks over the frequencies available within a certain frequency range.

The 802.11-based wireless technologies broadcast and receive on one of two license-free industrial, scientific, and medical (ISM) radio bands: 2.4 GHz and 5.8 GHz. Even though the ISM band is 5.8 GHz, we just say "5 GHz" for reasons I can't answer. Over the years, the original 802.11 standard has been extended to 802.11*a*, 802.11*b*, 802.11*g*, and 802.11*n* variations used in Wi-Fi wireless networks. Each of these versions of 802.11 uses one of the two ISM bands, with the exception of 802.11n, which uses one but may use both. Don't worry; I'll break this down for you in a moment.

Newer wireless devices can communicate with older wireless devices, so if you are using an 802.11n WAP, all of your 802.11g devices can use it. The exception to this is 802.11a, which requires that all of the equipment directly support it. The following paragraphs describe the important specifications of each of the popular 802.11-based wireless networking standards.

802.11a Despite the "a" designation for this extension to the 802.11 standard, **802.11a** was actually on the market *after* 802.11b. The 802.11a standard differs from the other 802.11-based standards in significant ways. Foremost is that it operates in the 5-GHz frequency range. This means that devices that use this standard are less prone to interference from other devices that use the same frequency range. 802.11a also offers considerably greater throughput than 802.11 and 802.11b at speeds up to 54 Mbps, though its actual throughput is no more than 25 Mbps in normal traffic conditions. Although its theoretical range tops out at about 150 feet, its maximum range will be lower in a typical office environment. Despite the superior speed of 802.11a, it isn't as widely adopted in the PC world as some of the following 802.11 versions.

802.11b **802.11b** was the first standard to take off and become ubiquitous in wireless networking. The 802.11b standard supports data throughput of up to 11 Mbps (with actual throughput averaging 4 to 6 Mbps)—on par with older wired 10BaseT networks—and a maximum range of 300 feet under ideal conditions. In a typical office environment, its maximum range is lower. The main downside to using 802.11b is, in fact, that it uses a very popular frequency. The 2.4-GHz ISM band is already crowded with baby monitors, garage door openers, microwaves, and wireless phones, so you're likely to run into interference from other wireless devices.

802.11g **802.11g** came out in 2003, taking the best of 802.11a and b and rolling them into a single standard. 802.11g offers data transfer speeds equivalent to 802.11a, up to 54 Mbps, with the wider 300-foot range of 802.11b. More important, 802.11g runs in the 2.4-GHz ISM band, so it is backward compatible with 802.11b, meaning that the same 802.11g WAP can service

In the early days of wireless networking, many techs and marketing people assumed Wi-Fi stood for *Wireless Fidelity*, a sort of play on the common sound signal of high fidelity. It might have at one time, but the Wi-Fi Alliance, the governing standards body for 802.11-based networking, just uses the term Wi-Fi today.

Wi-Fi is by far the most widely adopted wireless networking type today. Not only do millions of private businesses and homes have wireless networks, but many public places such as coffee shops and libraries also offer Internet access through wireless networks.

Devices that use the original 802.11 (with no letter) standard are obsolete these days. You're likeliest to find them in service on some brave early wireless adopter's network—or in a museum. The original 802.11 standard was hampered by both slow speeds (2 Mbps maximum) and limited range (about 150 feet). The 802.11 standard employed some of the same features that are in use in the current wireless standards; 802.11 uses the 2.4-GHz broadcast range.

both 802.11b and 802.11g wireless nodes. 802.11g was incredibly popular but has pretty much lost out to the newest version of 802.11, 802.11n.

802.11n The **802.11n** standard brings several improvements to Wi-Fi networking, including faster speeds and new antenna technology implementations.

The 802.11n specification requires all but hand-held devices to use multiple antennas to implement a feature called **multiple in/multiple out (MIMO)**, which enables the devices to make multiple simultaneous connections. With up to four antennas, 802.11n devices can achieve amazing speeds. (The official standard supports throughput of up to 600 Mbps, although practical implementation drops that down substantially.)

Many 802.11n WAPs employ *transmit beamforming*, a multiple-antenna technology that helps get rid of dead spots—or at least make them not so bad. The antennas adjust the signal once the WAP discovers a client to optimize the radio signal.

Like 802.11g, 802.11n WAPs can run in the 2.4-GHz ISM band, supporting earlier, slower 802.11b/g devices. However, 802.11n also has a more powerful, so-called *dual-band*. To use dual-band 802.11n, you need a more advanced (and more expensive) WAP that runs at both 5 GHz and 2.4 GHz simultaneously; some support 802.11a devices as well as 802.11b/g devices. Nice!

Know the differences among 802.11a, 802.11b, 802.11g, and 802.11n.

Table 15.1 compares the important differences among the versions of 802.11.

Table 15.1	Comparison of 802.11 Standards			
Standard	**802.11a**	**802.11b**	**802.11g**	**802.11n**
Max. throughput	54 Mbps	11 Mbps	54 Mbps	100+ Mbps
Max. range	150 feet	300 feet	300 feet	300+ feet
Frequency	5 GHz	2.4 GHz	2.4 GHz	2.4 and 5 GHz
Security	SSID, MAC filtering, industry-standard WEP, WPA	SSID, MAC filtering, industry-standard WEP, WPA	SSID, MAC filtering, industry-standard WEP, WPA	SSID, MAC filtering, industry-standard WEP, WPA
Compatibility	802.11a	802.11b	802.11b, 802.11g	802.11b, 802.11g, 802.11n (802.11a in some cases)
Communication mode	Ad hoc or infrastructure	Ad hoc or infrastructure	Ad hoc or infrastructure	Ad hoc or infrastructure
Description	Eight available channels. Less prone to interference than 802.11b and 802.11g.	Fourteen channels available in the 2.4-GHz band (only eleven of which can be used in the U.S. due to FCC regulations). Three non-overlapping channels.	Improved security enhancements. Fourteen channels available in the 2.4-GHz band (only eleven of which can be used in the U.S. due to FCC regulations). Three non-overlapping channels.	Same as 802.11g but adds the 5-GHz band that 802.11a uses. 802.11n can also make use of multiple antennas (MIMO) to increase its range and speed.

Other Wireless Standards

While Wi-Fi dominates the wireless networking market, it isn't the only standard. A lot of smaller networks (we're talking two computers small) use infrared or Bluetooth to connect devices. Mobile devices, such as smartphones and some tablets, connect wirelessly via cellular networks.

Infrared Wireless Networking

Wireless networking using infrared technology is largely overlooked these days, probably because of the explosion of interest for newer and faster wireless standards. But it is still a viable method to transfer files on some older devices.

Apple computers also support IrDA, as do Linux PCs.

Communication through infrared devices is enabled via the **Infrared Data Association (IrDA)** protocol. The IrDA protocol stack is a widely supported industry standard and has been included in all versions of Windows since Windows 95.

In speed and range, infrared isn't very impressive. Infrared devices are capable of transferring data up to 4 Mbps—not too shabby, but hardly stellar. The maximum distance between infrared devices is 1 meter. Infrared links are direct line-of-sight and are susceptible to interference. Anything that breaks the beam of light can disrupt an infrared link: a badly placed can of Mountain Dew, a coworker passing between desks, or even bright sunlight hitting the infrared transceiver can cause interference.

Many modern laptops still come with a little infrared window, but don't let that fool you into thinking the laptop has IrDA networking. These IR receivers are for use with remotes so you can use the laptop just like a TV or DVD player.

Infrared is designed to make a point-to-point connection between two devices only in ad hoc mode. No infrastructure mode is available. You can, however, use an infrared access point device to enable Ethernet network communication using IrDA. Infrared devices operate at half-duplex, meaning that while one is talking, the other is listening—they can't talk and listen at the same time. IrDA has a mode that emulates full-duplex communication, but it's really half-duplex. The IrDA protocol offers exactly nothing in the way of encryption or authentication. Infrared's main security feature is the fact that you have to be literally within arm's reach to establish a link. Clearly, infrared is not the best solution for a dedicated network connection, but for a quick file transfer or print job without getting your hands dirty, it'll do in a pinch.

Table 15.2 lists infrared's important specifications.

Table 15.2	Infrared Specs
Standard	**Infrared (IrDA)**
Max. throughput	Up to 4 Mbps
Max. range	1 meter (39 inches)
Security	None
Compatibility	IrDA
Communication mode	Point-to-point ad hoc

Bluetooth

Bluetooth wireless technology (named for ninth-century Danish king Harald Bluetooth) is designed to create small wireless networks preconfigured to do very specific jobs. Some great examples are audio devices such as headsets that connect to your smartphones, **personal area networks (PANs)** that link two PCs for a quick-and-dirty wireless network, and input devices such as keyboards and mice. Bluetooth is *not* designed to be a full-function networking solution, nor is it meant to compete with Wi-Fi. If anything, Bluetooth has replaced infrared as a means to connect PCs to peripherals.

Bluetooth, like any technology, has been upgraded over the years to make it faster and more secure. Two major versions of Bluetooth are widespread today. The first generation (versions 1.1 and 1.2) supports speeds around 1 Mbps. The second generation (2.0 and 2.1) is backward compatible with its first-generation cousins and adds support for more speed by introducing Enhanced Data Rate (EDR), which pushes top speeds to around 3 Mbps.

 The Bluetooth 3.0 and 4.0 standards were released several years ago, though neither has seen the same level of adoption as earlier standards.

The IEEE organization has made first-generation Bluetooth the basis for its 802.15 standard for wireless PANs. Bluetooth uses a broadcasting method that switches among any of the 79 frequencies available in the 2.45-GHz range. Bluetooth hops frequencies some 1600 times per second, making it highly resistant to interference.

Generally, the faster and further a device sends data, the more power it needs to do so, and the Bluetooth designers understood a long time ago that some devices (such as a Bluetooth headset) could save power by not sending data as quickly or as far as other Bluetooth devices may need. To address this, all Bluetooth devices are configured for one of three classes that define maximum power usage in milliwatts (mW) and maximum distance:

Class 1	100 mW	100 meters
Class 2	2.5 mW	10 meters
Class 3	1 mW	1 meter

Bluetooth is made to replace the snake's nest of cables that currently connects most PCs to their various peripheral devices—keyboard, mouse, printer, speakers, scanner, and the like—but you won't be swapping out your 802.11-based networking devices with Bluetooth-based replacements anytime soon.

Having said that, Bluetooth-enabled wireless networking is comparable to other wireless technologies in a few ways:

- Like infrared, Bluetooth is acceptable for quick file transfers where a wired connection (or a faster wireless connection) is unavailable.
- Almost all wireless headsets are now Bluetooth.
- Bluetooth's speed and range make it a good match for wireless print server solutions.

Bluetooth hardware comes either integrated into many newer portable electronic gadgets such as smartphones or as an adapter added to an internal or external expansion bus. Bluetooth networking is enabled through ad hoc–styled device-to-device connections, or in an infrastructure-like mode through Bluetooth access points. Bluetooth access points are very similar to 802.11-based access points, bridging wireless Bluetooth PAN segments to wired LAN segments.

Cellular

A **cellular wireless network** enables you to connect to the Internet through a network-aware smartphone, tablet, or other mobile device. To learn more about cellular data networks, check out Chapter 16.

■ Chapter Summary

After reading this chapter and completing the exercises, you should understand the following about wireless networking.

Discuss wireless networking components

■ The wireless radio wave networks you'll find yourself supporting these days are those based on the IEEE 802.11 wireless Ethernet standard Wi-Fi and on the newer Bluetooth technology. Many cellular phone providers also provide Internet access through their networks. Wireless networks using infrared light use the IrDA protocol.

■ Wireless networking capabilities of one form or another are built into many modern computing devices. Wireless Ethernet and Bluetooth are almost ubiquitous as integrated components or can easily be added by using USB, PCI, PCI Express, or PC Card adapters. Many smartphones and tablets have wireless capabilities built in or available as add-on options.

■ To extend the capabilities of a wireless Ethernet network, such as connecting to a wired network or sharing a high-speed Internet connection, you need a WAP. A WAP centrally connects wireless network nodes in the same way that a hub connects wired Ethernet PCs.

Analyze and explain wireless networking standards

■ Wireless devices use the same networking protocols and client that their wired counterparts use, and they operate by using the CSMA/CA networking scheme, where nodes check before broadcasting. Wireless nodes also use the RTS/CTS protocol. When enabled, a transmitting node that determines that the wireless medium is clear to use sends an RTS frame to the receiving node. The receiving node responds with a CTS frame, telling the sending node that it's okay to transmit. Then, once the data is sent, the transmitting node waits for an acknowledgment (ACK) from the receiving node before sending the next data packet.

■ You will need a utility to set parameters such as your SSID. Windows XP and up have built-in tools for this, but many adapters come with configuration tools provided by the wireless network adapter vendor.

■ The simplest wireless network consists of two or more PCs communicating directly with each other without cabling or any other intermediary hardware (ad hoc mode). More complicated (and more common) wireless networks use a WAP to centralize wireless communication and bridge wireless network segments to wired network segments (infrastructure mode).

■ Ad hoc networks are also good for temporary networks such as study groups or business meetings.

■ Infrastructure mode is better suited to business networks or networks that need to share dedicated resources such as Internet connections and centralized databases.

■ Out of the box, wireless networks have no security configured at all. Wireless devices want to be heard, and WAPs are usually configured to broadcast their presence to their maximum range and welcome all other wireless devices that respond. Further, data packets are floating through the air instead of safely wrapped up inside network cabling.

■ Most WAPs support MAC address filtering, a method that enables you to limit access to your wireless network based on the physical, hard-wired address of the unit's wireless network adapter.

■ Enabling WEP encrypts your data to secure it while in transit over the airwaves, but the WEP encryption standard itself is flawed and cannot be relied upon to protect your data against a knowledgeable and motivated attacker.

■ WPA and WPA2 address the weaknesses of WEP and act as a sort of security protocol upgrade to WEP-enabled devices. WPA and WPA2 offer security enhancements such as an encryption key integrity-checking feature and user authentication through the industry-standard EAP.

■ Wi-Fi Protected Setup (WPS) was designed to make connecting wireless devices as easy as pushing a button. Because of its security flaws, however, you should avoid using WPS and disable it entirely.

- Depending on the standard used, wireless throughput speeds range from a measly 2 Mbps to a snappy 100+ Mbps. Wireless devices dynamically negotiate the top speed at which they can communicate without dropping too many data packets.

- Wireless networking speed and range are greatly affected by outside factors, such as interference from other wireless devices or solid objects. A wireless device's true effective range is probably about half the theoretical maximum listed by the manufacturer.

- 802.11a differs from the other 802.11-based standards in significant ways. Foremost, it operates in a different frequency range, 5 GHz, so 802.11a devices are less prone to interference. 802.11a also offers considerably greater throughput than 802.11 and 802.11b at speeds up to 54 Mbps, but its range tops out at only about 150 feet. 802.11a isn't widely adopted in the PC world.

- The 802.11b standard supports data throughput of up to 11 Mbps—on par with older wired 10BaseT networks—and a range of up to 300 feet under ideal conditions.

- The 802.11g standard offers data transfer speeds equivalent to 802.11a, up to 54 Mbps, with the wider 300-foot range of 802.11b. Because 802.11g is backward compatible with 802.11b, the same 802.11g WAP can service both 802.11g and 802.11b wireless nodes.

- 802.11n ups the speed even more to 100+ Mbps and extends the range to greater than 300 feet by using MIMO (multiple in/multiple out) with extra antennas. You can also configure it to use the less crowded 5-GHz band if you are using a dual-mode WAP.

- Wireless networking using infrared (IR) technology is enabled via the Infrared Data Association—IrDA—protocol stack, a widely supported industry standard, and has been included in all versions of Windows since Windows 95. IR is designed to make only a point-to-point connection between two devices in ad hoc mode of up to 4 Mbps, at a maximum distance of 1 meter.

- Bluetooth wireless technology is designed to create small wireless personal area networks (PANs) that link PCs to peripheral devices such as PDAs and printers, input devices such as keyboards and mice, and even consumer electronics such as cell phones, home stereos, televisions, home security systems, and so on. Bluetooth is not designed to be a full-function networking solution.

- Cellular wireless networks enable you to connect to the Internet through a smartphone or portable device with an access card.

■ Key Terms

802.11a *(464)*
802.11b *(464)*
802.11g *(464)*
802.11n *(465)*
ad hoc mode *(460)*
Advanced Encryption Standard (AES) *(462)*
Bluetooth *(467)*
carrier sense multiple access/collision avoidance (CSMA/CA) *(458)*
cellular wireless network *(468)*
Extensible Authentication Protocol (EAP) *(462)*
IEEE 802.11 *(457)*
Infrared Data Association (IrDA) *(466)*

infrastructure mode *(460)*
MAC address filtering *(461)*
multiple in/multiple out (MIMO) *(465)*
personal area network (PAN) *(467)*
Power over Ethernet (PoE) *(458)*
service set identifier (SSID) *(460)*
Temporal Key Integrity Protocol (TKIP) *(461)*
Wi-Fi *(464)*
Wi-Fi Protected Access (WPA) *(461)*
Wi-Fi Protected Access 2 (WPA2) *(462)*
Wi-Fi Protected Setup (WPS) *(462)*
Wired Equivalent Privacy (WEP) *(461)*
wireless access point (WAP) *(458)*

Key Term Quiz

Use the Key Terms list to complete the sentences that follow. Not all terms will be used.

1. A technology for setting up wireless PANs and connecting to some peripherals is called _____.

2. Establishing a unique _____ or network name helps ensure that only wireless network devices configured similarly are permitted access to the network.

3. The wireless Ethernet standard that operates at a maximum of 54 Mbps on the 2.4-GHz frequency is _____.

4. Computers are in _____ when they connect directly together without using a WAP.

5. The 802.11 protocol is more commonly known as _____.

6. Of the three common wireless encryption protocols, _____ is the *least* secure.

7. The wireless Ethernet standard that runs at speeds up to 54 Mbps but has limited range because it uses the 5-GHz frequency is _____.

8. If you need to share an Internet connection or connect to a wired network through your wireless network, you would use _____.

9. The _____ feature enables devices on 802.11n networks to make multiple simultaneous connections, allowing for a theoretical throughput of 600 Mbps.

10. 802.11 implements _____, which proactively avoids network packet collisions rather than simply detecting them when they occur.

Multiple-Choice Quiz

1. Two wireless nodes that are communicating directly with each other, without any intermediary systems or hardware, are using what wireless mode?
 A. Ad hoc
 B. Bluetooth
 C. Infrastructure
 D. 802.11

2. What device centrally connects wireless network nodes in the same way that a hub or switch connects wired Ethernet PCs?
 A. Bluetooth adapter
 B. Wireless NIC
 C. SSID
 D. WAP

3. What is the approximate range of an 802.11b/g network?
 A. ~1000 ft
 B. ~300 ft
 C. ~150 ft
 D. ~500 ft

4. Which encryption method used on wireless networks is the most secure?
 A. WEP
 B. Wi-Fi
 C. WINS
 D. WPA2

5. What can limit wireless connectivity to a list of accepted users based on the hard-wired address of their wireless NIC?
 A. Encryption
 B. MAC filtering
 C. NWLink
 D. WEP

6. Which wireless standard combines the longest range with the most throughput?
 A. 802.11a
 B. 802.11b
 C. 802.11g
 D. 802.11n

7. Personal area networks are created by what wireless technology?

 A. Bluetooth

 B. IrDA

 C. Wi-Fi

 D. Cellular wireless

8. What is the best technology if you need Internet access from anywhere in the country?

 A. Bluetooth

 B. IrDA

 C. Wi-Fi

 D. Cellular wireless

9. What standard gained a speed boost in its second version with Enhanced Data Rate technology?

 A. Bluetooth

 B. IrDA

 C. Wi-Fi

 D. Cellular wireless

10. Which of these Wi-Fi security protocols is the least secure and is easily hacked?

 A. WEP

 B. WAP

 C. WINS

 D. WPA2

11. What is a cheap and easy way to extend the range of a WAP?

 A. Upgrade the antenna.

 B. Buy a WAP that advertises a longer range.

 C. You can't easily boost range.

 D. Upgrade the wireless NICs.

12. What is the technical name of a wireless network?

 A. SSID

 B. BSSID

 C. SSD

 D. WPA

13. What is the approximate range of a Bluetooth PAN?

 A. ~100 ft

 B. ~30 ft

 C. ~5 ft

 D. ~50 ft

14. Which of the following 802.11 standards can make use of both the 2.4- and 5-GHz bands?

 A. 802.11a

 B. 802.11b

 C. 802.11g

 D. 802.11n

15. Which of the following devices is a major source of interference for Wi-Fi networks?

 A. Cell phones

 B. Small FM radio transmitters

 C. Microwaves

 D. Fluorescent lights

■ Essay Quiz

1. Some friends of yours insist that wireless network standard 802.11a was available before 802.11b. They also say 802.11a is "better" than 802.11b. Find the pages in this chapter that discuss these standards, and jot down some notes to explain the facts.

2. You are enrolled in a writing class at the local community college. This week's assignment is to write on a technical subject. Write a short paragraph about each of the wireless standards that can reach theoretical speeds of 54 Mbps.

3. Prepare a short memo to your instructor (or friend) that outlines the basic differences between WEP and WPA encryption methods. Use any standard memo format you are familiar with. Include a company or school logo on the top of the page to make the memo appear to be printed on company stationery (or "letterhead").

4. Write a few paragraphs describing the pros and cons of both wired and wireless networks. Specifically, compare 100BaseT to the 802.11n standard. Then conclude with a statement of your own personal preference. You'll need to draw on information you found in this chapter and in Chapter 14.

Lab Projects

• Lab Project 15.1

You just received a nice tax return and want to expand your home network. Your current wired home network setup consists of two Intel Core 2 Duo desktop PCs with 10/100-Mbps NICs and a relative's older laptop with both an RJ-45 port and 802.11b wireless built in. The main Internet connection coming into your home enters your more powerful desktop system first and then spreads out to a 100-Mbps switch from there. With your own money to be spent buying equipment, you seek a solution that will satisfy your needs for a long time.

You want to buy your new equipment locally so you can set it up right away. Use the Internet to explore prices and equipment in local stores. Also check out reviews of the items you are interested in obtaining. After you have done sufficient research, prepare an itemized price list with your choices arranged like the following table:

ITEM	STORE/MODEL	PRICE	QUANTITY	TOTAL
Wireless NICs, PCI\PCIe				
Wireless NICs, PC Card				
Wireless Access Point				
Other				
TOTALS				

• Lab Project 15.2

You have been tasked with expanding your company's wireless network. Your IT manager asked you to create a presentation that explains wireless routers and their functions. She specifically said to focus on the 802.11g and 802.11n wireless network standards. Create a brief but informative PowerPoint presentation that includes comparisons of these two technologies. You may include images of actual wireless bridges from vendor Web sites as needed, being sure to cite your sources. Include any up-to-date prices from your research as well.

The Internet

chapter
16

"The Internet is a great way to get on the Net."

—BOB DOLE

In this chapter, you will learn how to

- **Explain how the Internet works**
- **Connect to the Internet**
- **Use Internet application protocols**

Imagine coming home from a long day at work building and fixing PCs, sitting down in front of your shiny new computer, double-clicking the single icon that sits dead center on your monitor...and suddenly you're enveloped in an otherworldly scene, where 200-foot trees slope smoothly into snow-white beaches and rich blue ocean. Overhead, pterodactyls soar through the air while you talk to a small chap with pointy ears and a long robe about heading up the mountain in search of a giant monster... A TV show from the Syfy channel? Spielberg's latest film offering? How about an interactive game played by millions of people all over the planet on a daily basis by connecting to the Internet? If you guessed the last one, you're right.

This chapter covers the skills you need as a PC tech to help people connect to the Internet. It starts with a brief section on how the Internet works, along with the concepts of connectivity, and then it goes into the specifics on hardware, protocols, and software that you use to make the Internet work for you (or for your client). Let's get started!

Historical/Conceptual

■ How the Internet Works

Thanks to the Internet, people can communicate with one another over vast distances, often in the blink of an eye. As a PC tech, you need to know how PCs communicate with the larger world for two reasons. First, knowing the process and pieces involved in the communication enables you to troubleshoot effectively when that communication goes away. Second, you need to be able to communicate knowledgeably with a network technician who comes in to solve a more complex issue.

Internet Tiers

You probably know that the Internet is millions and millions of computers all joined together to form the largest network on earth, but not many folks know much about how these computers are organized. To keep everything running smoothly, the Internet is broken down into groups called **tiers**. The main tier, called *Tier 1*, consists of nine companies called *Tier 1 providers*. The Tier 1 providers own long-distance, high-speed fiber-optic networks called *backbones*. These backbones span the major cities of the earth (not all Tier 1 backbones go to all cities) and interconnect at special locations called *network access points* (*NAPs*). Anyone wishing to connect to any of the Tier 1 providers must pay large sums of money. The Tier 1 providers do not charge each other to connect.

Tier 2 providers own smaller, regional networks and must pay the Tier 1 providers. Most of the famous companies that provide Internet access to the general public are Tier 2 providers. *Tier 3 providers* are even more regional and connect to Tier 2 providers.

The piece of equipment that makes this tiered Internet concept work is called a backbone router. *Backbone routers* connect to more than one other backbone router, creating a big, interwoven framework for communication. Figure 16.1 illustrates the decentralized and interwoven nature of the Internet. The key reason for interweaving the backbones of the Internet was to provide alternative pathways for data if one or more of the routers went down. If Jane in Houston sends a message to her friend Polly in New York City, for example, the shortest path between Jane and Polly in this hypothetical situation is this: Jane's message originates at Rice University in Houston, bounces to Emory University in Atlanta, flits through Virginia Commonwealth University in Richmond, and then zips into SUNY

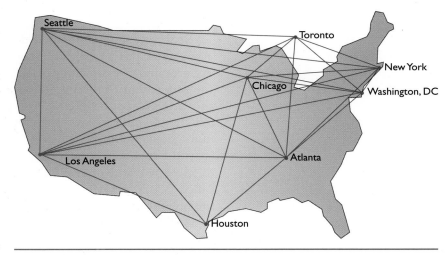

• **Figure 16.1** Internet Tier 1 connections

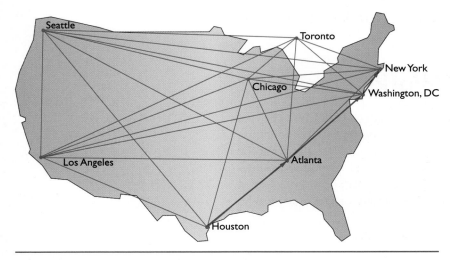

• **Figure 16.2** Message traveling from Houston to NYC

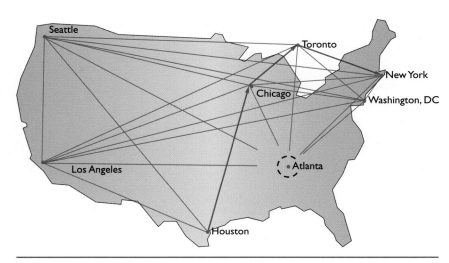

• **Figure 16.3** Rerouted message from Houston to NYC

in New York City (see Figure 16.2). Polly happily reads the message and life is great. The Internet functions as planned.

But what happens if the entire southeastern United States experiences a huge power outage and Internet backbones in every state from Virginia to Florida go down? Jane's message would bounce back to Rice and the Rice computers. Being smart cookies, the routers would reroute the message to nodes that still functioned—say, Rice to University of Chicago, to University of Toronto, and then to SUNY (see Figure 16.3). It's all in a day's work for the highly redundant and adaptable Internet. At this point in the game, the Internet simply cannot go down fully—barring, of course, a catastrophe of Biblical proportions.

TCP/IP—The Common Language of the Internet

As you know from all the earlier chapters in this book, hardware alone doesn't cut it in the world of computing. You need software to make the machines run and create an interface for humans. The Internet is no exception. TCP/IP provides the basic software structure for communication on the Internet.

Because you spent a good deal of Chapter 14 working with TCP/IP, you should have an appreciation for its adaptability and, perhaps more importantly, its extendibility. TCP/IP provides the addressing scheme for computers that communicate on the Internet through IP addresses, such as 192.168.4.1 or 16.45.123.7. As a protocol, though, TCP/IP is much more than just an addressing system. TCP/IP provides the framework and common language for the Internet. And it offers a phenomenally wide-open structure for creative purposes. Programmers can write applications built to take advantage of the TCP/IP structure and features, creating what are called TCP/IP services. The cool thing about TCP/IP services is that they're limited only by the imagination of the programmers.

At this point, you have an enormous, beautifully functioning network. All the backbone routers connect with fiber and thick copper cabling backbones, and TCP/IP enables communication and services for building applications for humans to interface across the distances. What's left?

Oh, that's right: how do you tap into this great network and partake of its goodness?

Internet Service Providers

Every Tier 1 and Tier 2 provider leases connections to the Internet to companies called **Internet service providers (ISPs)**. ISPs essentially sit along the edges of the Tier 1 and Tier 2 Internet and tap into the flow. You can, in turn, lease some of the connections from the ISP and thus get on the Internet.

ISPs come in all sizes. Comcast, the cable television provider, has multiple, huge-capacity connections into the Internet, enabling its millions of customers to connect from their local machines and surf the Web. Contrast Comcast with Unisono, an ISP in San Miguel de Allende, Mexico (see Figure 16.4). Billed as the "the fastest Internet service" in San Miguel de

• **Figure 16.4** Unisono homepage

Allende, it services only a small (but delightful) community and the busy tourist crowd.

Connection Concepts

Connecting to an ISP requires two things to work perfectly: hardware for connectivity, such as a modem and a working cable line; and software, such as protocols to govern the connections and the data flow (all configured in Windows) and applications to take advantage of the various TCP/IP services. Once you have a contract with an ISP to grant you access to the Internet, a technician will often install your Internet connection device and any software you need. With most ISPs, a DHCP server will provide your PC with the proper TCP/IP information. As you know, the router to which you connect at the ISP is often referred to as the **default gateway**. Once your PC is configured, you can connect to the ISP and get to the greater Internet. Figure 16.5 shows a standard PC-to-ISP-to-Internet connection. Note that various protocols and other software manage the connectivity between your PC and the default gateway.

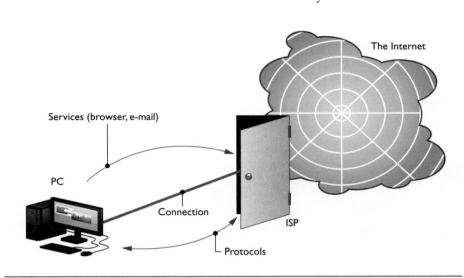

• **Figure 16.5** Simplified Internet connectivity

801

■ Connecting to the Internet

PCs commonly connect to an ISP by using one of nine technologies that fit into four categories: dial-up, both analog and ISDN; dedicated, such as DSL, cable, fiber, and LAN; wireless, including cellular and WiMAX; and satellite. Analog dial-up is the slowest of the bunch and requires a telephone line and a special networking device called a modem. ISDN uses digital dial-up and has much greater speed. Dedicated connections (cable and DSL) most often use a box that connects to a regular Ethernet NIC like you played with in Chapter 14. Wireless connections are a mixed bag, depending on the device and service you have. Some are built-in, while others use a box you attach to your LAN. Satellite is the odd one out here; it may use either a modem or a NIC, depending on the particular configuration you have, although most folks will use a NIC. Let's take a look at all these various connection options, and then finish this section by discussing basic router configuration and Internet Connection Sharing in Windows.

Dial-up

A dial-up connection to the Internet requires two pieces to work: hardware to dial the ISP, such as a modem or ISDN terminal adapter; and software to govern the connection, such as Microsoft's **Dial-up Networking (DUN)**. Let's look at the hardware first, and then we'll explore software configuration.

Modems

At some point in the early days of computing, some bright guy or gal noticed a colleague talking on a telephone, glanced down at a PC, and then put two and two together: why not use telephone lines for data communication? The basic problem with this idea is that traditional telephone lines use analog signals, while computers use digital signals (see Figure 16.6). Creating a dial-up network required equipment that could turn digital data into an analog signal to send it over the telephone line, and then turn it back into digital data when it reached the other end of the connection. A device called a modem solved this dilemma.

Modems enable computers to talk to each other via standard commercial telephone lines by converting analog signals to digital signals, and vice versa. The term *modem* is short for modulator/demodulator, a description of transforming the signals. Telephone wires transfer data via analog signals that continuously change voltages on a wire. Computers hate analog signals. Instead, they need digital signals, voltages that are either on or off, meaning the wire has voltage present or it does not. Computers, being binary by nature, use only two states of voltage: zero volts and positive volts. Modems take analog signals from telephone lines and turn them into digital signals that the PC can understand (see Figure 16.7). Modems also take digital signals from the PC and convert them into analog signals for the outgoing telephone line.

A modem does what is called *serial communication*: It transmits data as a series of individual ones and zeros. The CPU can't process data this way. It needs parallel communication, transmitting and receiving data in discrete 8-bit chunks (see Figure 16.8). The individual serial bits of data are converted into 8-bit parallel data that the PC can understand through the **universal asynchronous receiver/transmitter (UART)** chip (see Figure 16.9).

There are many types of UARTs, each with different functions. All serial communication devices are really

Analog: Increasing and decreasing waves of electricity

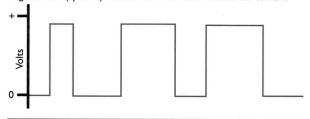

Digital: A set (specific) increase and decrease in electrical current

• **Figure 16.6** Analog signals used by a telephone line versus digital signals used by the computer

• **Figure 16.7** Modem converting analog signal to digital signal

• **Figure 16.8** CPUs can't read serial data.

• Figure 16.9 The UART chip converts serial data to parallel data that the CPU can read.

② It uses a serial port's UART.

① An external modem has no UART.

• Figure 16.10 An external modem uses the PC's serial port.

UART

• Figure 16.11 An internal modem has UART built in.

AMR, ACR, and CNR slots have gone away, though you'll still find them on older systems. Current systems use built-in components or PCIe ×1 slots for modems, sound, and NICs.

little more than UARTs. *External* modems can convert analog signals to digital ones and vice versa, but they must rely on the serial ports to which they're connected for the job of converting between serial and parallel data (see Figure 16.10). Internal modems can handle both jobs because they have their own UART built in (see Figure 16.11).

Phone lines have a speed based on a unit called a **baud**, which is one cycle per second. The fastest rate that a phone line can achieve is 2400 baud. Modems can pack multiple bits of data into each baud; a 33.6 kilobits per second (Kbps) modem, for example, packs 14 bits into every baud: 2400 × 14 = 33.6 Kbps. Thus, it is technically incorrect to say, "I have a 56-K baud modem." The correct statement is, "I have a 56-Kbps modem." But don't bother; people have used the term "baud" instead of **bits per second (bps)** so often for so long that the terms have become functionally synonymous.

Modem Connections Internal modems connect to the PC very differently from how external modems connect. Almost all internal modems connect to a PCI or PCI Express expansion bus slot inside the PC, although cost-conscious manufacturers may use smaller modems that fit in special expansion slots designed to support multiple communications features such as modems, NICs, and sound cards (see Figure 16.12). Older AMD motherboards used Audio/Modem Riser (AMR) or Advanced Communication Riser (ACR) slots, while Intel motherboards used Communication and Networking Riser (CNR) slots.

External modems connect to the PC through an available serial port (the old way) or USB port (see Figure 16.13). USB offers simple plug and play and easy portability between machines, plus such modems require no external electrical source, getting all the power they need from the USB connection.

Cross Check

Installing a PCI\PCIe Modem

Installing a PCI or PCIe modem card involves pretty much the same process as installing any other PCI\PCIe card. Refer to Chapter 8 and cross check your knowledge of the process.

1. What do you need to guard against when installing a PCI\ PCIe card?

2. Any issues involving drivers, plug and play, or other hardware topics?

Dial-up Networking

The software side of dial-up networks requires configuration within Windows to include information provided by your ISP. The ISP provides a dial-up telephone number or numbers, as well as your user name and initial password. In addition, the ISP will tell you about any special configuration options you need to specify in the software setup. The full configuration of dial-up networking is beyond the scope of this book, but you should at least know where to go to follow instructions from your ISP. Let's take a look at the Network and Internet Connections applet in Windows XP.

• **Figure 16.12** A CNR modem

• **Figure 16.13** A USB modem

• **Figure 16.14** The Connections tab in the Internet
Properties dialog box

Configuring Dial-up To start configuring a dial-up connection in
Windows XP, open the Control Panel. Select Network and Inter-
net Connections from the Pick a category menu and then choose
Set up or change your Internet connection from the Pick a task menu.
The Internet Properties dialog box opens with the Connections
tab displayed (see Figure 16.14). All your work will proceed
from here.

Click the Setup button to run the New Connection Wizard (see
Figure 16.15), and then work through the screens. At this point,
you're going to need information provided by your ISP to config-
ure your connection properly. When you finish the configuration,
you'll see a new Connect To option on the Start menu if your sys-
tem is set up that way. If not, open up Network Connections, and
your new dial-up connection will be available. Figure 16.16 shows
the option to connect to a fictitious ISP, Cool-Rides.com.

Windows Vista and 7 handle dial-up connections in the same
way. Open the Network and Sharing Center and click on *Set up a
new connection or network* (see Figure 16.17).

Select *Set up a dial-up connection* on the next screen and then
enter your dial-up information, as shown in Figure 16.18.

PPP Dial-up links to the Internet have their own special hard-
ware protocol called **Point-to-Point Protocol (PPP)**. PPP is a stream-
ing protocol developed especially for dial-up Internet access. To
Windows, a modem is nothing more than a special type of network adapter.
You can configure a new dial-up connection in the Network and Sharing
Center in Vista/7 or the Network Connections applet in XP.

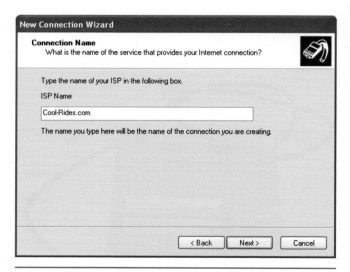

• **Figure 16.15** The New Connection Wizard

• **Figure 16.16** Connection options in Network Connections

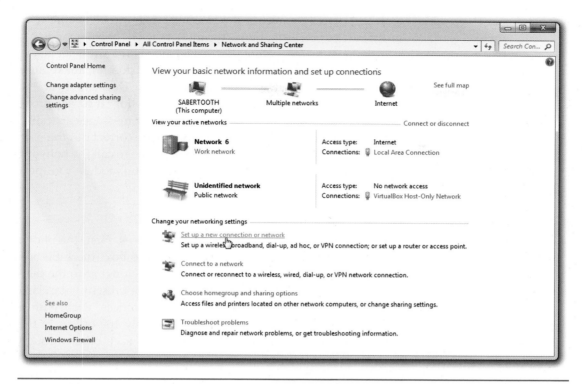

• **Figure 16.17** Set up a connection or network in Windows 7

• **Figure 16.18** Creating a dial-up connection in Windows 7

Most dial-up "I can't connect to the Internet"–type problems are user errors. Your first area of investigation is the modem itself. Use the modem's properties to make sure the volume is turned up. Have the user listen to the connection. Does she hear a dial tone? If she doesn't, make sure the modem's line is plugged into a good phone jack. Does she hear the modem dial and then hear someone saying, "Hello? Hello?" If so, she probably dialed the wrong number! Wrong password error messages are fairly straightforward—remember that the password may be correct but the user name may be wrong. If she still fails to connect, it's time to call the network folks to see what is not properly configured in her dial-up modem's Properties dialog box.

ISDN

A standard telephone connection comprises many pieces. First, the phone line runs from your phone out to a network interface box (the little box on the side of your house) and into a central switch belonging to the telephone company. (In some cases, intermediary steps are present.) Standard metropolitan areas have a large number of central offices, each with a central switch. Houston, Texas, for example, has nearly 100 offices in the general metro area. These central switches connect to each other through high-capacity *trunk lines*. Before 1970, the entire phone system was analog; over time, however, phone companies began to upgrade their trunk lines to digital systems. Today, the entire telephone system, with the exception of the line from your phone to the central office, and sometimes even that, is digital.

During this upgrade period, customers continued to demand higher throughput from their phone lines. The old telephone line was not expected to produce more than 28.8 Kbps (56-K modems, which were a *big* surprise to the phone companies, didn't appear until 1995). Needless to say, the phone companies were very motivated to come up with a way to generate higher capacities. Their answer was actually fairly straightforward: make the entire phone system digital. By adding special equipment at the central office and the user's location, phone companies can now achieve a throughput of up to 64 K per line (see the paragraphs following) over the same copper wires already used by telephone lines. This process of sending telephone transmission across fully digital lines end-to-end is called **integrated services digital network (ISDN)** service.

ISDN service consists of two types of channels: Bearer, or B, channels and Delta, or D, channels. B channels carry data and voice information at 64 Kbps. D channels carry setup and configuration information and carry data at 16 Kbps. Most providers of ISDN allow the user to choose either one or two B channels. The more common setup is two B/one D, usually called a *basic rate interface* (*BRI*) setup. A BRI setup uses only one physical line, but each B channel sends 64 Kbps, doubling the throughput total to 128 Kbps. ISDN also connects much faster than modems, eliminating that long, annoying, mating call you get with phone modems. The monthly cost per B channel is slightly more than a regular phone line, and usually a fairly steep initial fee is levied for the installation and equipment. The big limitation is that you usually need to be within about 18,000 feet of a central office to use ISDN.

Another type of ISDN, called a primary rate interface (PRI), is composed of twenty-three 64-Kbps B channels and one 64-Kbps D channel, giving it a total throughput of 1.544 megabits per second. PRI ISDN lines are also known as T1 lines.

The physical connections for ISDN bear some similarity to analog modems. An ISDN wall socket usually looks something like a standard RJ-45 network jack. The most common interface for your computer is a device called a *terminal adapter* (*TA*). TAs look much like regular modems, and like modems, they come in external and internal variants. You can even get TAs that connect directly to your LAN.

DSL

Digital subscriber line (DSL) connections to ISPs use a standard telephone line but special equipment on each end to create always-on Internet connections at blindingly fast speeds, especially when compared with analog dial-up connections. Service levels vary around the United States, but the typical upload speed is ~768 Kbps, while download speed comes in at ~3+ Mbps.

DSL requires little setup from a user standpoint. A tech comes to the house to install the DSL receiver, often called a DSL modem (see Figure 16.19), and possibly hook up a wireless router. The receiver connects to the telephone line and the PC (see Figure 16.20). The tech (or the user, if knowledgeable) then configures the DSL modem and router (if there is one) with the settings provided by the ISP, and that's about it! Within moments, you're surfing the Web. You don't need a second telephone line. You don't need to wear a special propeller hat or anything. The only kicker is that your house has to be within a fairly short distance from a main phone service switching center (central office), something like 18,000 feet.

Cable

Cable offers a different approach to high-speed Internet access, using regular cable TV cables to serve up lightning-fast speeds. It offers faster service than most DSL connections, with a 1–10 Mbps upload and 6–100+ Mbps download. Cable Internet connections are theoretically available anywhere you can get cable TV.

The two most common forms of DSL you'll find are *asynchronous* (*ADSL*) and *synchronous* (*SDSL*). ADSL lines differ between slow upload speed (such as 384 Kbps, 768 Kbps, and 1 Mbps) and faster download speed (usually 3–15 Mbps). SDSL has the same upload and download speeds, but telecom companies charge a lot more for the privilege. DSL encompasses many such variations, so you'll often see it referred to as *x*DSL.

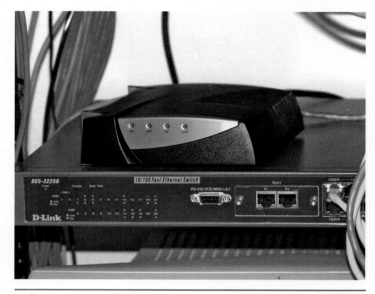

• **Figure 16.19** A DSL receiver

• **Figure 16.20** DSL connections

The term *modem* has been warped and changed beyond recognition in modern networking. Both DSL and cable—fully digital Internet connections—use the term *modem* to describe the box that takes the incoming signal from the Internet and translates it into something the PC can understand.

• **Figure 16.21** Cable connections

Cable Internet connections start with an RG-6 or RG-59 cable coming into your house. The cable connects to a cable modem that then connects to a small home router or your NIC via Ethernet. Figure 16.21 shows a typical cable setup using a router.

LAN

Most businesses connect their internal local area network (LAN) to an ISP-supplied Ethernet network. Figure 16.22 shows a typical small-business wiring closet with routers that connect the LAN to the ISP's Ethernet. You learned all about wiring up a LAN in Chapter 14, so there's no need to go through any basics here. To complete a LAN connection to the Internet, you need a router to connect the ISP's network to your network. Most office buildings come with preinstalled Ethernet at varying speeds.

802.11 Wireless

802.11 Wireless is so prevalent that for many of us it's the way we get to the Internet. Wireless access points (WAPs) designed to serve the public abound in coffee shops, airports, fast-food chains, and bars. Even some cities provide partial to full 802.11 coverage.

We covered 802.11 in detail in Chapter 15, so there's no reason to repeat the process of connecting to a hotspot. However, do remember that most hotspots do not provide any level of encryption, meaning it's a trivial task for a bad guy to monitor your connection and read everything you send or receive.

802.11 works well as an Internet access option for densely populated areas, but 802.11's short range makes it impractical in areas where it's not easy to place new access points.

• **Figure 16.22** A wiring closet

An 802.11 network that covers a single city is an excellent example of a Metropolitan Area Network (MAN).

Fiber

Until recently, high costs meant that only those with money to burn could enjoy the super-fast speeds of a fiber connection. Now DSL providers have developed very popular fiber-to-the-node (FTTN) and fiber-to-the-premises (FTTP) services that provide Internet (and more), making them head-to-head competitors with the cable companies. With FTTN, the fiber connection runs from the provider to a box somewhere in your neighborhood. This box is connected to your home or office using

Mike Meyers' CompTIA A+ Guide to 801: Managing and Troubleshooting PCs

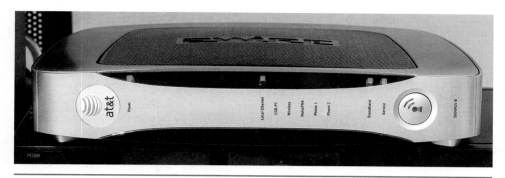

• **Figure 16.23** U-verse gateway

normal coaxial or Ethernet cabling. FTTP runs from the provider straight to a home or office, using fiber the whole way. Once inside the home or office, you can use any standard cabling (or wireless) to connect your PCs to the Internet. One popular FTTN service is AT&T's U-verse, which offers speeds up to 24 Mbps for downloads and 3 Mbps for uploads (see Figure 16.23). Verizon's FiOS service is the most popular and widely available FTTP service in the United States, providing download speeds up to 150 Mbps and upload speeds up to 50 Mbps (if you can afford it, of course).

Cellular

Who needs computers when you can get online with any number of mobile devices? Okay, there are plenty of things a smartphone or tablet can't do, but with the latest advances in cellular data services, your mobile Internet experience will feel a lot more like your home Internet experience than it ever has before.

Cellular data services have gone through a number of names over the years, so many that trying to keep track of them and place them in any order is extremely challenging. In an attempt to make organization somewhat clearer, the cellular industry developed a string of marketing terms using the idea of generations: first generation devices are called 1G, second generation are 2G, followed by 3G and 4G. On top of that, many technologies use G-names such as 2.5G to show they're not 2G but not quite 3G. You'll see these terms all over the place, especially on your phones (see Figure 16.24). Marketing folks tend to bend and flex the definition of these terms in advertisements, so you should always read more about the device and not just its generation.

The first generation (1G) of cell phone data services was analog and not at all designed to carry packetized data. It wasn't until the early 1990s that two fully digital technologies called the Global System for Mobile Communications (GSM) and code division multiple access (CDMA) came into wide acceptance. GSM evolved into GPRS and EDGE, while CDMA introduced EV-DO. GPRS and EDGE were 2.5G technologies, while EV-DO was true 3G. Current standards, with names like UTMS, HSPA+, and HSDPA, have brought GSM-based networks into the world of 3G and 3.5G. Current mobile data services provide real-world download speeds around 3 or 4 Mbps.

• **Figure 16.24** iPhone with 4G showing

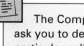 The CompTIA A+ will not ask you to define a G-level for a particular cellular technology.

 You can share your smartphone's or tablet's connection to a cellular network using a process called *tethering*. You'll need to turn on the service on your device, then connect your phone to your computer, either wirelessly as a *mobile hotspot* or directly using a USB connection. Most carriers charge extra to enable tethering on your smartphone or tablet. Check with your carrier to see if your service plan supports tethering.

Just like LANs and WANs, we also have WLANs and WWANs. A wireless wide area network (WWAN) works similar to a WLAN, except it connects multiple networks like a WAN. WiMAX is an excellent example of a WWAN.

The current cutting-edge set of cellular technologies use the term 4G. The two biggest 4G technologies currently available are called **Worldwide Interoperability for Microwave Access (WiMAX)** and 3GPP **Long Term Evolution (LTE)**. With these networks, you'll see download speeds closer to 10 Mbps, though WiMAX lags behind LTE in the speed department. In fact, while the CompTIA A+ 220-801 exam objectives specifically cover WiMAX, the wireless technology has already been replaced as the 4G frontrunner. The only major U.S. WiMAX carrier, Clearwire, Inc., has declared their intentions to adopt LTE, along with every other major mobile phone network in the United States. But since CompTIA asked, and there are plenty of WiMAX users (for now), I'm more than happy to tell you a little more about WiMAX.

WiMAX runs at (depending on distance from a tower) a maximum speed of around 10 Mbps. The maximum range is 30 miles. There are two versions of WiMAX. Line-of-sight (LoS) WiMAX uses fixed antennas that point directly at a WiMAX transceiver. Non-LoS WiMAX (currently far more popular) uses base stations that are not visible to the WiMAX tower. As you might imagine, LoS WiMAX is far faster than non-LoS WiMAX.

Satellite

Satellite connections to the Internet get the data beamed to a satellite dish on your house or office; a receiver handles the flow of data, eventually sending it through an Ethernet cable to the NIC in your PC. I can already sense people's eyebrows raising. "Yeah, that's the download connection. But what about the upload connection?" Very astute, me hearties! The early days of satellite required you to connect via a modem. You would upload at the slow 26- to 48-Kbps modem speed, but then get super-fast downloads from the dish. It worked, so why complain? You really can move to that shack on the side of the Himalayas to write the great Tibetan novel and still have DSL-speed Internet connectivity. Sweet!

Satellite might be the most intriguing of all the technologies used to connect to the Internet today. As with satellite television, though, you need to have the satellite dish point at the satellites (toward the south if you live in the United States). The only significant issue to satellite is that the distance the signal must travel creates a small delay called the *satellite latency*. This latency is usually unnoticeable unless the signal degrades in foul weather such as rain and snow.

Satellite setup consists of a dish, professionally installed with line-of-sight to the satellite. A coax cable runs from the dish to your satellite modem. The satellite modem has an RJ-45 connection, which you may then connect directly to your computer or to a router.

Connection to the Internet

So you went out and signed up for an Internet connection. Well, now it's time to get connected. You basically have two choices:

1. Connect a single computer to your Internet connection
2. Connect a network of computers to your Internet connection

Connecting a single computer to the Internet is easy. If you're using wireless, you connect to the wireless box using the provided information, although a good tech will always go through the proper steps to protect the wireless network. If you choose to go wired, you run a cable from whatever type of box is provided to the PC.

If you want to connect a number of computers using wired connections, you'll need to grab a router. Several manufacturers offer robust, easy-to-configure routers that enable multiple computers to connect to a single Internet connection. These boxes require very little configuration and provide firewall protection between the primary computer and the Internet, which you'll learn more about in Chapter 20. All it takes to install one of these routers is simply to plug your computer into any of the LAN ports on the back, and then to plug the cable from your Internet connection into the port labeled Internet or WAN.

There are hundreds of perfectly fine choices for SOHO (small office/home office) routers, but the author's current favorite is the Cisco E2500 (see Figure 16.25). This little router has four 10/100 Ethernet ports for the LAN computers, and a Wi-Fi radio for any wireless computers you may have. The Cisco E2500, like all home routers, uses a technology called **Network Address Translation (NAT)**. NAT performs a little network subterfuge: It presents an entire LAN of computers to the Internet as a single machine. It effectively hides all of your computers and makes them appear invisible to other computers on the Internet. All anyone on the Internet sees is your *public* IP address. This is the address your ISP gives you, while all the computers in your LAN use private addresses that are invisible to the world. NAT therefore acts as a firewall, protecting your internal network from probing or malicious users from the outside.

• **Figure 16.25** Common home router with Wi-Fi

Basic Router Configuration

SOHO routers require very little in the way of configuration and in many cases will work perfectly (if incredibly unsafely) right out of the box. In some cases, though, you may have to deal with a more complex network that requires changing the router's settings. The vast majority of these routers have built-in configuration Web pages that you access by typing the router's IP address into a browser. The address varies by manufacturer, so check the router's documentation. If you typed in the correct address, you should then receive a prompt for a user name and password, as in Figure 16.26. As with the IP address, the default user name and password change depending on the model/manufacturer. Once you enter the

• **Figure 16.26** Router asking for user name and password

correct credentials, you will be greeted by the router's configuration pages (see Figure 16.27). From these pages, you can change any of the router's settings. Now look at a few of the basic settings that CompTIA wants you to be familiar with.

Changing User Name and Password All routers have a user name and password that gives you access to the configuration screen. One of the first changes you should make to your router after you have it working is to change the user name and password to something other than the default. This is especially important if you have open wireless turned on, which you'll recall from Chapter 15. If you leave the default user name and password, anyone who has access to your LAN can easily gain access to the router and change its settings. Fortunately, router manufacturers make it

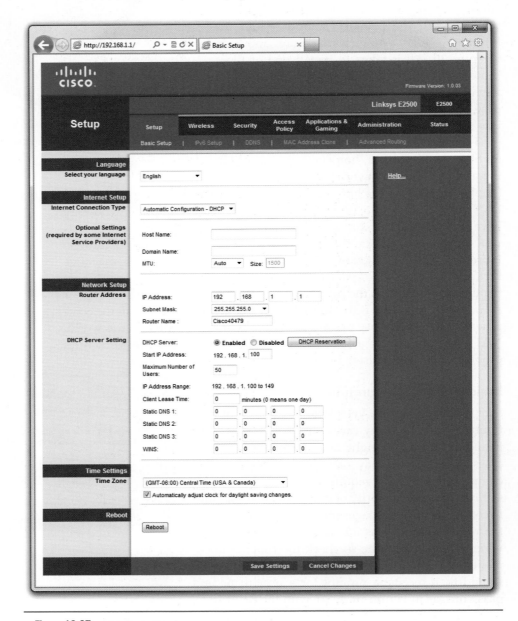

• **Figure 16.27** Configuration home page

Mike Meyers' CompTIA A+ Guide to 801: Managing and Troubleshooting PCs

● **Figure 16.28** Changing the password

easy to change a router's login credentials. On my E2500, for example, I just click on the Administration tab and fill in the appropriate boxes as shown in Figure 16.28.

Setting Static IP Addresses With the user name and password taken care of, let's look at setting up the router to use a static IP address for the Internet or WAN connection. In most cases, when you plug in the router's Internet connection, it receives an IP address using DHCP just like any other computer. Of course, this means that your Internet IP address will change from time to time, which can be a bit of a downside. This does not affect most people, but for some home users and businesses, it can present a problem. To solve this problem, most ISPs enable you to order a static IP (for an extra monthly charge). Once your ISP has allocated you a static IP address, you must manually enter it into your router. You do this the same way as the previous change you've just looked at. My router has an Internet Setup configuration section where I can enter all the settings that my ISP has provided me (see Figure 16.29). Remember, you must change your connection type from Automatic/DHCP to Static IP to enter the new addresses.

● **Figure 16.29** Entering a static IP address

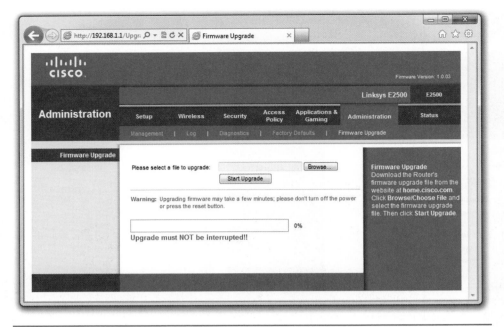

• **Figure 16.30** Firmware update page

Updating Firmware

Routers are just like any other computer in that they run software—and software has bugs, vulnerabilities, and other issues that sometimes require updating. The router manufacturers call these "firmware updates" and make them available on their Web sites for easy download. To update a modern router, download the latest firmware from the manufacturer's Web site to your computer. Then you enter the router's configuration Web page and find the firmware update screen. On my router, it looks like Figure 16.30. From here, just follow the directions and click Upgrade (or your router's equivalent). A quick word of caution: Unlike a Windows update, a firmware update gone bad can *brick* your router. In other words, it can destroy the hardware and make it as useful as a brick sitting on your desk. This rarely happens, but you should keep it in mind when doing a firmware update.

Windows Internet Connection Sharing

Internet Connection Sharing (ICS) enables one system to share its Internet connection with other systems on the network, just like your router at home. Figure 16.31 shows a typical setup for ICS. Note the terminology used here. The PC that connects to the Internet and then shares that connection via ICS with other machines on a LAN is called the *ICS host* computer. PCs that connect via a LAN to the ICS host computer are simply called client computers.

• **Figure 16.31** Typical ICS setup

To connect multiple computers to a single ICS host computer requires several things in place. First, the ICS host computer has to have a NIC dedicated to the internal connections. If you connect via dial-up, for example, the ICS host computer uses a modem to connect to the Internet. It also has a NIC that plugs into a switch. Other PCs on the LAN likewise connect to the switch. If you connect via some faster service, such as DSL that uses a NIC cabled to the DSL receiver, you'll need a second NIC in the ICS host machine to connect to the LAN and the client computers.

Setting up ICS in Windows is very simple. If you are using Windows XP, right-click on My Network Places and select Properties. If you are using Windows Vista or 7, open the Network and Sharing Center and click on *Manage network connections* (Vista) or *Change adapter settings* (7) in the Task list. Then access the Properties dialog box of the connection you wish to share.

Click the the Advanced tab (Windows XP) or Sharing tab (Vista and 7) and select *Allow other network users to connect through this computer's Internet connection* (see Figure 16.32). Clients don't need any special configuration but should simply be set to DHCP for their IP address and other configurations.

● **Figure 16.32** Enabling Internet Connection Sharing in Windows Vista

■ Internet Application Protocols

Once you've established a connection to the Internet, you need applications to get anything done. If you want to surf the Web, you need an application called a **Web browser**, such as Mozilla Firefox or Google Chrome. If you want to make a VoIP phone call, you need an application like Skype or Google Voice. These applications in turn use very clearly designed application protocols. All Web browsers use the **Hypertext Transfer Protocol (HTTP)**. All e-mail clients use Post Office Protocol 3 (POP3) or Internet Message Access Protocol 4 (IMAP4) to receive e-mail. All e-mail applications use Simple Mail Transfer Protocol (SMTP) to send their e-mails. Every Internet protocol has its own rules and its own port numbers. Though there are tens of thousands of application protocols in existence, lucky for you, CompTIA only wants you to understand the following commonly used application protocols:

- World Wide Web (HTTP and HTTPS)
- E-mail (POP3, IMAP4, and SMTP)
- Telnet
- SSH
- FTP/SFTP
- Remote Desktop (RDP)
- VoIP (SIP)

In addition to the application protocols we see and use daily, there are hundreds, maybe thousands, of application protocols that run behind the scenes, taking care of important jobs to ensure that the application protocols we do see run well. You've encountered a number of these hidden application protocols back in Chapter 14. Take DNS. Without DNS, you couldn't

Windows XP provides a tool called the *Network Setup Wizard* that enables you to configure computers on a LAN to share folders and printers. This tool is especially useful on networks that use Internet Connection Sharing with a Windows XP machine as the default gateway.

To run the Wizard, go to Start | Control Panel | Network and Internet Connections | Network Connections. Under Common Tasks, click Network Setup Wizard. Follow the steps in the Wizard to create a floppy disk with a small setup program used to configure other computers to share resources (folders, printers, and so on).

type www.google.com in your Web browser. DHCP is another great example. You don't see DHCP do its job, but without it, any computers relying on DHCP won't receive IP addresses.

Here's another one: People don't like to send credit card information, home phone numbers, or other personal information over the Web for fear this information might be intercepted by hackers. Fortunately, there are methods for encrypting this information, the most common being **Hypertext Transfer Protocol Secure (HTTPS)**. Although HTTPS looks a lot like HTTP from the point of view of a Web browser, HTTPS uses port 443. It's easy to tell if a Web site is using HTTPS because the Web address starts with *https*, as shown in Figure 16.33, instead of just *http*. But you don't deal with HTTPS directly; it just works in your browser automatically.

In order to differentiate the application protocols you see from the application protocols you don't see, I'm going to coin the term "utility protocol" to define any of the hidden application protocols. So, using your author's definition, HTTP is an application protocol and DNS is a utility protocol. All TCP/IP protocols use defined ports, require an application to run, and have special settings unique to that application. You'll look at several of these services and learn how to configure them. As a quick reference, Table 16.1 lists the names, functions, and port numbers of the application protocols CompTIA would like you to know. Table 16.2 does the same for utility protocols.

After you've read about these protocols, you'll learn about Virtual Private Networks and the protocols they use. I'll also tell you about a few more Internet support utilities that don't quite fit anywhere else.

• **Figure 16.33** A secure Web page

Table 16.1	Application Protocol Port Numbers	
Application Protocol	**Function**	**Port Number**
HTTP	Web pages	80
FTP	File transfer	20, 21
SFTP	Secure file transfer	22
IMAP4	Incoming e-mail	143
POP3	Incoming e-mail	110
SMTP	Outgoing e-mail	25
Telnet	Terminal emulation	23
SSH	Encrypted terminal emulation	22
RDP	Remote Desktop	3389
SIP	Voice over IP	5060

Table 16.2	Utility Protocol Port Numbers		
HTTPS	Secure web pages	TCP	43
DNS	Allows the use of DNS naming	UDP	53
DHCP	Automatic IP addressing	UDP	67, 68
LDAP	Querying directories	TCP	389
SNMP	Remote management of network devices	UDP	161
SMB	Windows naming/folder sharing	TCP	445
		UDP	137, 138, 139

The World Wide Web

The Web provides a graphical face for the Internet. *Web servers* (servers running specialized software) provide Web sites that you access by using the HTTP protocol on port 80 and thus get more or less useful information. Using Web-browser software, such as Internet Explorer or Mozilla Firefox, you can click a link on a Web page and be instantly transported—not just to some Web server in your home town—to anywhere in the world. Figure 16.34 shows Firefox at the home page of my company's Web site, www.totalsem.com. Where is the server located? Does it matter? It could be in a closet in my office or in a huge data center in Houston. The great part about the Web is that you can get from here to there and access the information you need with a click or two of the mouse.

Although the Web is the most popular part of the Internet, setting up a Web browser takes almost no effort. As long as the Internet connection is working, Web browsers work automatically. This is not to say you can't make plenty of custom settings, but the default browser settings work almost every time. If you type in a Web address, such as that of the best search engine on the planet—www.google.com—and it doesn't work, check the line and your network settings and you'll figure out where the problem is.

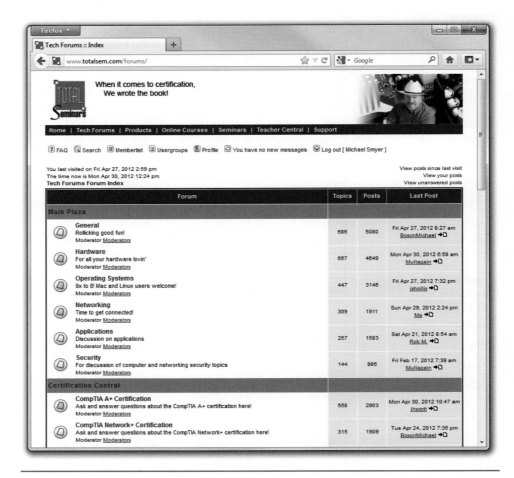

• **Figure 16.34** Mozilla Firefox showing a Web page

Configuring Internet Explorer

The Internet Options Control Panel applet is only for the Internet Explorer Web browser. If you use any other browser (Firefox, Chrome, and so on), Internet Options has no effect.

Web browsers are highly configurable. On most Web browsers, you can set the default font size, choose whether to display graphics, and adjust several other settings. Although all Web browsers support these settings, where you go to make these changes varies dramatically. If you are using the popular Internet Explorer that comes with Windows, you will find configuration tools in the Internet Options Control Panel applet or under the Tools menu in Internet Explorer (see Figure 16.35). Note that the applet is called Internet Options, but the window it launches is labeled Internet Properties.

There are obviously more browsers than just Internet Explorer, so I'll begin by explaining the options available to you in Internet Explorer, and then show you some of the common options found in other browsers, too.

When you open the Internet Options applet, you'll see seven tabs along the top. The first tab is the General tab. These settings control the most basic features of Internet Explorer: the home page, your browsing history, searching, and other appearance controls. If you want to delete or change how Internet Explorer stores the Web sites you've visited, use this tab.

The Security tab enables you to set how severely Internet Explorer safeguards your Web browsing (see Figure 16.36). Each setting can be adjusted for a particular zone, such as the Internet, your local intranet, trusted sites,

● **Figure 16.35** Internet Options applet

● **Figure 16.36** The Security tab in Internet Options

and restricted sites. You can configure which Web sites fall into which zones. Once you've picked a zone to control, you can set Internet Explorer's security level. The High security level blocks more Web sites and disables some plug-ins, while Medium-high and Medium allow less-secure Web sites and features to display and operate.

The Privacy tab works a lot like the Security tab, except it controls privacy matters, such as cookies and pop-ups. There is a slider that enables you to control what is blocked—everything is blocked on the highest setting; nothing is blocked on the lowest. Go here if you don't like the idea of Web sites tracking your browsing history (though cookies do other things, too, like authenticate users).

The Content tab also controls what your browser will and will not display. This time, however, it filters content using certificates and a tool called the Content Advisor, which uses ratings that consider language, gambling, substance abuse, and more. The Content tab also enables you to adjust the AutoComplete feature that fills in Web addresses for you, as well as control settings for RSS feeds and Web Slices.

The Connections tab enables you to do a lot of things. You can set up your connection to the Internet, via broadband or dial-up, connect to a VPN, configure a proxy server connection, or adjust some LAN settings (which you probably won't need to deal with). Because they're a little complicated, and CompTIA wants you to know about them, let's quickly talk about proxy servers.

• **Figure 16.37** The Advanced tab in Internet Options

Many corporations use a proxy server to filter employee Internet access, and when you're on their corporate network, you need to set your proxy settings within the Web browser (and any other Internet software you want to use). A **proxy server** is software that enables multiple connections to the Internet to go through one protected PC. Applications that want to access Internet resources send requests to the proxy server instead of trying to access the Internet directly, which both protects the client PCs and enables the network administrator to monitor and restrict Internet access. Each application must therefore be configured to use the proxy server.

Moving on, the Programs tab in Internet Options contains settings for your default Web browser, any add-ons you use (like Java), and how other programs deal with HTML files and e-mail messages.

The Advanced tab does exactly what it sounds like: lists a bunch of advanced options that you can turn on and off with the check of a box (see Figure 16.37). The available options include accessibility, browsing, international, and, most importantly, security settings. From here, you can control how Internet Explorer checks Web site certificates, among many other settings.

Configuring Other Web Browsers

I don't want to stomp all over Internet Explorer and tell you how bad it is—okay, yes I do. You can download several other Web browsers that run faster and support more Web standards. Two of the big browser heavyweights that fit this description are Mozilla Firefox and Google Chrome.

You control their settings just like you do in Internet Explorer, though you won't find an applet tucked away in Control Panel. In Google Chrome, you can click on the wrench icon in the upper-right corner of the browser and select Settings. In Mozilla Firefox, click on the Firefox button in the upper-left corner and click on Options.

In these menus, you'll find a lot of settings very similar to the ones you find in Internet Options. In fact, Firefox's controls are laid out almost exactly the same, though you won't find everything in the same place (see Figure 16.38). Google Chrome's controls look more like a Web page, but it still controls the same features: home page, security, font size, cookies, and all your old favorites (see Figure 16.39). Take some time to use these browsers and explore their settings. You'll be surprised how your knowledge of one browser helps you set up another.

• **Figure 16.38** Mozilla Firefox options

• **Figure 16.39** Google Chrome settings

E-mail

You can use a desktop program to access e-mail. The most popular client by far is Microsoft Outlook. E-mail clients need a little more setup. First, you must provide your e-mail address and password. All e-mail addresses come in the now-famous *accountname@Internet domain* format. Figure 16.40 shows e-mail information entered into the Windows Live Mail account setup wizard.

Next you must add the names of the **Post Office Protocol version 3 (POP3)** or **Internet Message Access Protocol version 4 (IMAP4)** server and the **Simple Mail Transfer Protocol (SMTP)** server. The POP3 or IMAP4 server is the computer that handles incoming (to you) e-mail. POP3 is by far the most widely used standard, although IMAP4 supports some features POP3 doesn't. For example, IMAP4 enables you to search through messages on the mail server to find specific keywords and select the messages you want to download onto your machine. Even with the advantages of IMAP4 over POP3, the vast majority of incoming mail servers use POP3.

The SMTP server handles your outgoing e-mail. These two systems may often have the same name, or close to the same name, as shown in Figure 16.41. Your ISP should provide you with all these settings. If not, you should be comfortable knowing what to ask for. If one of these names is incorrect, you will either not get your e-mail or not be able to send e-mail. If an e-mail setup that has been working well for a while suddenly gives you

The term *Internet appliance* enjoyed some popularity in the 1990s to describe the first wave of consumer devices accessible via TCP/IP. You could use a Web browser to check on the status of an Internet-connected refrigerator, for example, or check to see if you'd left the stove on (and if so, shut it off remotely). Although the term is no longer in use, it might show up on the 220-801 exam.

Make sure you know your port numbers for these e-mail protocols! POP3 uses port 110, IMAP4 uses port 143, and SMTP uses port 25.

• **Figure 16.40** Adding an e-mail account to Windows Live Mail

• **Figure 16.41** Adding POP3 and SMTP information in Windows Live Mail

errors, it is likely that either the POP3 or SMTP server is down or that the DNS server has quit working.

When I'm given the name of a POP3 or SMTP server, I use ping to determine the IP address for the device, as shown in Figure 16.42. I make a point to write this down. If I ever have a problem getting mail, I'll go into my SMTP or POP3 settings and type in the IP address (see Figure 16.43). If my mail starts to work, I know the DNS server is not working.

 Microsoft provides a special type of e-mail server called an Exchange server. This is used mainly in large businesses so that employees can access their e-mail, calendars, and instant messages from a variety of locations. To set up an Exchange e-mail client, go to the Control Panel and run the Mail applet. Then click E-mail Accounts and then New. After that, click Next and fill in your e-mail address and password.

• **Figure 16.42** Using ping to determine the IP address

Some e-mail servers use SSL encryption for extra security. Every major e-mail client will have a setting called Connection security, or Security, or something like that. If your e-mail server uses encryption, change this setting to SSL.

• **Figure 16.43** Entering IP addresses into POP3 and SMTP settings

File Transfer Protocol (FTP)

File transfer protocol (FTP), using ports 20 and 21, is a great way to share files between systems. FTP server software exists for most operating systems, so you can use FTP to transfer data between any two systems regardless of the operating system. To access an FTP site, you must use an FTP client such as FileZilla, although most Web browsers provide at least download support for FTP. Just type in the name of the FTP site. Figure 16.44 shows Firefox accessing ftp.kernel.org.

Although you can use a Web browser, all FTP sites require you to log on. Your Web browser will assume that you want to log on as "anonymous." If you want to log on as a specific user, you have to add your user name to the URL. (Instead of typing **ftp://ftp.example.com**, you would type **ftp://mikem@ftp.example.com**.) An anonymous logon works fine for most public FTP sites. Many techs prefer to use third-party programs such as the robust FileZilla (see Figure 16.45) for FTP access because these third-party applications can store user name and password settings. This enables you to access the FTP site more easily later. Keep in mind that FTP was developed during a more trusting time, and that whatever user name and password you send over the network is sent in clear text. Don't use the same password for an FTP site that you use for your domain logon at the office!

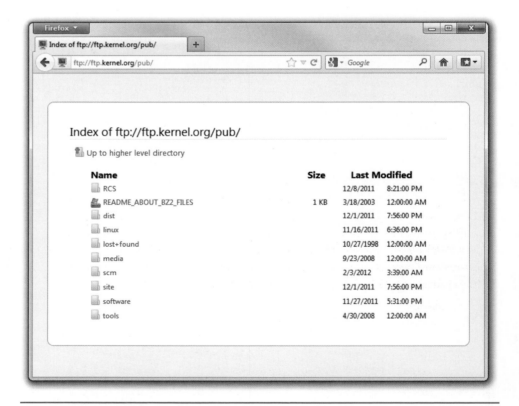

• **Figure 16.44** Accessing an FTP site in Firefox

• **Figure 16.45** The FileZilla FTP program

Telnet and SSH

Telnet is a terminal emulation program for TCP/IP networks that uses port 23 and enables you to connect to a server or fancy router and run commands on that machine as if you were sitting in front of it. This way, you can remotely administer a server and communicate with other servers on your network. As you can imagine, this is rather risky. If *you* can remotely control a computer, what's to stop others from doing the same? Of course, Telnet does not allow just *anyone* to log on and wreak havoc with your network. You must enter a special user name and password to run Telnet. Unfortunately, Telnet shares FTP's bad habit of sending passwords and user names as clear text, so you should generally use it only within your own LAN.

If you need a remote terminal that works securely across the Internet, you need **Secure Shell (SSH)**. In fact, today SSH has replaced Telnet in almost all places Telnet used to be popular. To the user, SSH works just like Telnet. Behind the scenes, SSH uses port 22, and the entire connection is encrypted, preventing any eavesdroppers from reading your data. SSH has one other trick up its sleeve: it can move files or any type of TCP/IP network traffic through its secure connection. In networking parlance, this is called **tunneling**, and it is the core of most secure versions of Internet technologies such as SFTP (discussed next) and VPN, which I will discuss in more depth later in the chapter.

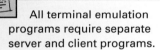
All terminal emulation programs require separate server and client programs.

The CompTIA A+ 220-801 exam tests your knowledge of a few networking tools, such as Telnet, but only enough to let you support a CompTIA Network+ tech or network administrator. If you need to run Telnet (or its more secure cousin, SSH), you will get the details from a network administrator. Implementation of Telnet falls well beyond CompTIA A+.

SFTP

Secure FTP is nothing more than FTP running through an SSH tunnel. This can be done in a number of ways. You can, for example, start an SSH session between two computers. Then, through a moderately painful process, start an FTP server on one machine and an FTP client on the other and redirect the input and output of the FTP data to go through the tunnel. You can also get a dedicated SFTP server and client. Figure 16.46 shows OpenSSH, a popular SSH server with a built-in SFTP feature as well.

Voice over IP

You can use **Voice over IP (VoIP)** to make voice calls over your computer network. Why have two sets of wires, one for voice and one for data, going to every desk? Why not just use the extra capacity on the data network for your phone calls? That's exactly what VoIP does for you. VoIP works with every type of high-speed Internet connection, from DSL to cable to satellite.

VoIP doesn't refer to a single protocol but rather to a collection of protocols that make phone calls over the data network possible. The most common VoIP application protocol is Session Initiation Protocol (SIP), but some popular VoIP applications like Skype are completely proprietary.

• **Figure 16.46** OpenSSH

Try This!

Checking Latency with ping

Latency is the bane of any VoIP call because of all the problems it causes if it is too high. A quick way to check your current latency is to use the ever-handy ping, so Try This!

1. Run ping on some known source, such as www.microsoft.com or www.totalsem.com.

2. When the ping finishes, take note of the average round-trip time at the bottom of the screen. This is your current latency to that site.

Venders such as Skype, Cisco, Vonage, and Comcast offer popular VoIP solutions, and many corporations use VoIP for their internal phone networks. A key to remember when installing and troubleshooting VoIP is that low network latency is more important than high network speed. **Latency** is the amount of time a packet takes to get to its destination and is measured in milliseconds. The higher the latency, the more problems, such as noticeable delays during a VoIP call.

VoIP isn't confined to your computer, either. It can completely replace your old copper phone line. Two popular ways to set up a VoIP system are to either use dedicated **VoIP phones**, like the ones that Cisco makes, or use a small VoIP phone adapter (see Figure 16.47) that can interface with your existing analog phones.

True VoIP phones have RJ-45 connections that plug directly into the network and offer advanced features such as HD-quality audio and video calling. Unfortunately, these phones require a complex and expensive network to function, which puts them out of reach of most home users.

• **Figure 16.47** Vonage Box VoIP phone adapter

For home users, it's much more common to use a VoIP phone adapter to connect your old-school analog phones. These little boxes are very simple to set up: just connect it to your network, plug in a phone, and then check for a dial tone. With the VoIP service provided by cable companies, the adapter is often built right into the cable modem itself, making setup a breeze.

Remote Desktop

In Microsoft networking, we primarily share folders and printers. At times, it would be convenient to be "transported" to another computer—to feel as if your hands were actually on its keyboard. There are plenty of programs that do exactly this, generically called remote desktops.

Like so many other Windows applications, remote desktops originally came from third-party companies. Microsoft bought the companies and

• **Figure 16.48** TightVNC in action

absorbed their code into the Windows operating system. Many third-party remote desktop applications are available. One of the most popular is Tight-VNC. TightVNC is totally cross-platform, enabling you to run and control a Windows system remotely from your Mac or vice versa, for example. Figure 16.48 shows TightVNC in action.

Windows offers an alternative to VNC: Remote Desktop. **Remote Desktop** provides control over a remote server with a fully graphical interface. Your desktop *becomes* the server desktop (see Figure 16.49).

Wouldn't it be cool if, when called about a technical support issue, you could simply see what the client sees? (I'm not talking voyeur cam, here.) When the client says that something doesn't work, it would be great if you could transfer yourself from your desk to your client's desk to see precisely what the client sees. This would dramatically cut down on the miscommunication that can make a tech's life so tedious. Windows Remote Assistance does just that. **Remote Assistance** enables you to give anyone control of your desktop. If a user has a problem, that user can request support directly from you. Upon receiving the support-request e-mail, you can then log on to the user's system and, with permission, take the driver's seat. Figure 16.50 shows Remote Assistance in action.

With Remote Assistance, you can do anything you would do from the actual computer. You can troubleshoot some hardware configuration or driver problem. You can install drivers, roll back drivers, download

• **Figure 16.49** Windows Remote Desktop Connection dialog box

• Figure 16.50 Remote Assistance in action

new ones, and so forth. You're in command of the remote machine as long as the client allows you to be. The client sees everything you do, by the way, and can stop you cold if you get out of line or do something that makes the client nervous! Remote Assistance can help you teach someone how to use a particular application. You can log on to a user's PC and fire up Outlook, for example, and then walk through the steps to configure it while the user watches. The user can then take over the machine and walk through the steps while you watch, chatting with one another the whole time. Sweet!

Remote desktop applications provide everything you need to access one system from another. They are common, especially now that Microsoft provides Remote Desktop for free. Whichever application you use, remember that you will always need both a server and a client program. The server goes on the system you want to access and the client goes on the system you use to access the server. On many solutions, the server and client software are integrated into a single product.

In Windows, you can turn Remote Assistance and Remote Desktop on and off and configure other settings. Go to the System Control Panel applet. In Windows XP, click on the Remote tab. In Windows Vista and Windows 7, click *Remote settings*. You will see checkboxes for both Remote Assistance and Remote Desktop, along with buttons to configure more detailed settings. (In Windows XP, you'll only see Remote Desktop controls if you installed the Remote Desktop client, which is not installed by default.)

The Remote Desktop executable file is mstsc.exe. You can also open Remote Desktop from a command-line interface by typing **mstsc** and pressing ENTER.

Windows 7 (and Windows Vista with the appropriate update) is capable of running specific applications hosted on a Windows Server 2008/2008 R2 machine. Think of it as Remote Desktop without the desktop—a single application run on one machine (a server) and appearing on another desktop (a client). You can set up your connection to the Windows Server machine using the RemoteApp and Desktop Connections applet in Control Panel.

• **Figure 16.51** VPN connecting computers across the United States

• **Figure 16.52** Typical tunnel

• **Figure 16.53** Endpoints must have their own IP addresses.

Virtual Private Networks

Remote connections have been around for a long time, long before the Internet existed. The biggest drawback about remote connections was the cost to connect. If you were on one side of the continent and had to connect to your LAN on the other side of the continent, the only connection option was a telephone. Or, if you needed to connect two LANs across the continent, you ended up paying outrageous monthly charges for a private connection. The introduction of the Internet gave people wishing to connect to their home networks a very cheap connection option, but with one problem: the whole Internet is open to the public. People wanted to stop using dial-up and expensive private connections and use the Internet instead, but they wanted to do it securely.

Those clever network engineers worked long and hard and came up with several solutions to this problem. Standards have been created that use encrypted tunnels between a computer (or a remote network) to create a private network through the Internet (see Figure 16.51), resulting in what is called a **Virtual Private Network (VPN)**.

An encrypted tunnel requires endpoints—the ends of the tunnel where the data is encrypted and decrypted. In the SSH tunnel you've seen thus far, the client for the application sits on one end and the server sits on the other. VPNs do the same thing. Either some software running on a computer or, in some cases, a dedicated box must act as an endpoint for a VPN (see Figure 16.52).

To make VPNs work requires a protocol that uses one of the many tunneling protocols available and adds the capability to ask for an IP address from a local DHCP server to give the tunnel an IP address that matches the subnet of the local LAN. The connection keeps the IP address to connect to the Internet, but the tunnel endpoints must act like NICs (see Figure 16.53). Let's look at one of the protocols, PPTP.

PPTP VPNs

So how do we make IP addresses appear out of thin air? Microsoft got the ball rolling with the **Point-to-Point Tunneling Protocol (PPTP)**, an advanced version of a protocol used for dial-up Internet called PPP that handles all of this right out of the box. The only trick is the endpoints. In Microsoft's view, a VPN is intended for individual clients (think employees on the road) to connect back to the office network, so Microsoft places the PPTP endpoints on the client and a special remote access server program called Routing and Remote Access Service (RRAS), available on Server versions of Windows, on the server (see Figure 16.54).

On the Windows client side, you right-click on My Network Places and click on Create a New Connection (Windows XP) or type **VPN** into the Start Search bar (Windows Vista and 7) and press ENTER. This presents you with a dialog box where you can enter all your VPN server information. Your network administrator will most likely provide this to you. The result is a virtual network card that, like any other NIC, gets an IP address from the DHCP server back at the office (see Figure 16.55).

When your computer connects to the RRAS server on the private network, PPTP creates a secure tunnel through the Internet back to the private LAN. Your client takes on an IP address of that network, as if your computer were plugged into the LAN back at the office. Even your Internet traffic will go through your office first. If you open your Web browser, your client will go across the Internet to the office LAN and then use the LAN's Internet connection! Because of this, Web browsing is very slow over a VPN.

A system connected to a VPN looks as though it's on the local network but often performs much slower than if the system were connected directly back at the office.

• **Figure 16.54** RRAS in action

● **Figure 16.55** VPN connection in Windows

Support Applications (Internet Utilities)

The CompTIA A+ 220-801 objectives list three rather unique protocols. Personally, I doubt you'll ever deal directly with two of them, and the other is more common to LANs, not the Internet, but you should know a little bit about all three anyway.

LDAP

The **Lightweight Directory Access Protocol (LDAP)** enables operating systems and applications to access directories. If you've got a Windows Server system running Active Directory, for example, Windows uses LDAP to do anything with Active Directory. If you're sitting at a computer and add it to an Active Directory domain, Windows uses LDAP commands to update the Active Directory with the computer's information. You don't see LDAP, but it works hard to keep networks running smoothly.

SNMP

The **Simple Network Management Protocol (SNMP)** enables remote query and remote configuration of just about anything on a network. Assuming all your computers, switches, routers, and so on are SNMP-capable, you can use programs to query the network for an unimaginable amount of data. SNMP is a popular tool to check on your network, but you'll need to take the CompTIA Network+ exam to see SNMP in action.

SMB

The **Server Message Block (SMB)** protocol isn't even an application but rather proof of the power of Microsoft. SMBs date back to the old Net-BIOS naming service and were the tools that tossed a PC's name around a network. NetBIOS names are gone, but SMBs are the reason that tools like Network can show you all the computers on your network. SMB is so powerful that other operating systems copy SMB using a popular program called SAMBA. SAMBA emulates SMB—it makes non-SMB operating systems on a network look like Windows.

Beyond A+

The areas covered by the CompTIA A+ 220-801 exam does a great job on the more common issues of dealing with the Internet, but a few hot topics (although beyond the scope of the CompTIA A+ 801 exam) are so common and important that you need to know them: online gaming, chatting, and file sharing.

Online Gaming

One of the more exciting and certainly more fun aspects of the Internet is online gaming. Competing online against a real person or people makes for some pleasant gaming. Enjoying classics such as Hearts and Backgammon with another human can be challenging and fun. Another popular genre of online gaming is the "first-person shooter." These games place you in a small world with up to 32 other players. A great example is Valve Software's *Counter-Strike: Source* (see Figure 16.56).

No discussion of online gaming is complete without talking about the most amazing game type of all: the massively multiplayer online role-playing game (MMORPG). Imagine being an elfin wizard, joined by a band of friends, all going on adventures together in a world so large that it would take a real 24-hour day to journey across it! Imagine that in this same world, 2000 to 3000 other players, as well as thousands of game-controlled characters, are participating! Plenty of MMORPGs are out there, but the most popular today is *World of Warcraft* (see Figure 16.57).

Each of these games employs good old TCP/IP to send information, using ports reserved by the game. For instance, the Quake series of games uses port 26000, while DirectX uses ports 47624 and 2300–2400.

Chat

If there's one thing we human beings love to do, it's chat. The Internet provides a multitude of ways to do so, whether by typing or actual talking. Keep in mind that chatting occurs in real time. As fast as you can type or talk, whoever is at the other end hears or sees what you have to say. To chat, however, you need some form of chat software. The oldest family of chat programs is based on the Internet Relay Chat (IRC) protocol; a very common IRC chat program is mIRC. IRC protocols allow for a number of other little extras as well, such as being able to share files.

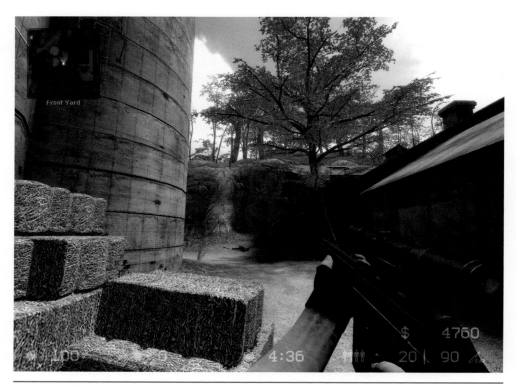

• **Figure 16.56** Counter-Strike: Source

Today, companies such as Google, AOL, Yahoo!, and Microsoft have made their own chat programs (otherwise known as instant messengers, or IMs) that not only provide text chat but also add features such as voice and

• **Figure 16.57** My editor playing World of Warcraft

video, turning your PC into a VoIP phone! Figure 16.58 shows the popular Microsoft Windows Live Messenger software.

File Sharing

The last extra Internet function to discuss is also probably the most controversial: file sharing. File sharing started over a decade ago and consisted of a whole bunch of computers with one program loaded, such as Napster or Kazaa. The file-sharing program enables each of the computers running that program to offer files to share, such as music and movies. Once all of the file-sharing programs connect to the Internet, any of them can download any file offered by any other in the group.

File sharing through such *distributed* sharing software becomes almost anonymous and free—and that's the problem. You can share *anything*, even copyright-protected music, movies, and more. The music industry in particular has come out swinging to try to stop file-sharing practices. As a result, the music industry is working on a way to shut down those persons who share lots of files. Software developers and file sharers haven't backed down, creating Internet protocols such as BitTorrent that can share files faster and more efficiently. Figure 16.59 shows one of the more popular BitTorrent protocol programs called µTorrent (the µ is the symbol for "micro," so you pronounce it "micro torrent"). BitTorrent has many legitimate uses as well—its protocol is extremely efficient for the distribution of large files

• **Figure 16.58** Windows Live Messenger in action

• **Fgure 16.59** μTorrent

and has become the method of choice for distributing Linux distributions and is even used to distribute and patch *World of Warcraft* and *Starcraft II*!

These example programs just scratch the surface of the many applications that use the Internet. One of the more amazing aspects of TCP/IP is that its basic design is around 40 years old. We use TCP/IP in ways completely outside the original concept of its designers, yet TCP/IP continues to show its power and flexibility. Pretty amazing!

Chapter 16 Review

■ Chapter Summary

After reading this chapter and completing the exercises, you should understand the following about the Internet.

Explain how the Internet works

- A PC tech needs to know how PCs communicate with the world for two reasons: to troubleshoot when a process or piece stops working, and to communicate knowledgeably with a network technician who comes in to solve a more complex issue.

- The Internet is broken down into three tiers. Tier 1 providers own the fiber-optic backbones that interconnect at network access points. Backbone routers create an interwoven framework for redundant communications. Tier 2 providers own smaller, regional networks. Tier 3 providers are even more regional and connect to Tier 2 providers.

- Internet service providers (ISPs) lease connections to the Internet from Tier 1 and Tier 2 providers. In turn, ISPs lease connections to allow individuals and companies to access the Internet. ISPs may serve customers nationwide, such as Comcast, or they may be limited to a small community of users.

- Connecting to the Internet requires hardware for connectivity and software to govern the connection and data flow. The router that connects you to your ISP is your default gateway.

Connect to the Internet

- Nine technologies are commonly used to connect a PC to an ISP. These technologies fit into four categories: (1) dial-up (analog and ISDN), (2) dedicated (DSL, cable, fiber, and LAN), (3) wireless (cellular and WiMAX), and (4) satellite. Analog dial-up, the slowest connection, uses a telephone line and a modem. ISDN is a much faster, digital dial-up method. With the exception of satellite, which may use either a modem or a NIC, all the other technologies use an Ethernet NIC.

- A dial-up connection needs hardware, such as a modem or ISDN terminal adapter, and software, such as Microsoft's DUN.

- A modem converts digital signals from the PC into analog signals that travel on telephone lines, and vice versa. An example of serial communication,

the modem transmits data as a series of ones and zeros. On the other hand, the computer processes data by using parallel communication of data in discrete 8-bit chunks. A UART chip converts serial to parallel and parallel to serial. An external modem uses the UART chip in the computer's serial port, while an internal modem has its own built-in UART.

- Modems may be internal or external. Many motherboards come with integrated modems. External modems attach to the PC's serial port or USB port.

- If you can't connect to the Internet, look at the modem's Properties dialog box to make sure the volume is turned up. Listen, too, for a befuddled voice on the other end that would indicate your modem is dialing the wrong number. Other things to check: Be sure the line is plugged into a good phone jack, and make sure the number and password are correct. If you still can't connect to the Internet, call the network technicians to check that the dial-up networking settings are correct.

- An ISDN consists of two types of channels: Bearer, or B, channels that carry data and voice at 64 Kbps, and Delta, or D, channels that transmit setup and configuration information at 16 Kbps. Users can use one or two B channels, but the most common setup is the BRI, consisting of two B channels and one D channel to provide a throughput total of 128 Kbps. Except for the steep cost of installation and equipment, ISDN lines are only slightly more expensive than regular phone lines, but this service is limited to an area within about 18,000 feet of a central office. ISDN uses a terminal adapter that looks like a regular modem and may be either external or internal.

- DSL modems connect to an ISP by using a standard telephone line and special connections on each end. Although service levels vary, typical upload speed is ~768 Kbps with a download speed of ~3+ Mbps. A tech usually comes to the house to install a DSL receiver (often called a DSL modem) as well as a NIC in the PC. DSL is usually limited to about 18,000 feet from a main phone service switching center.

- Cable TV companies offer high-speed Internet access, with an upload speed of about 1–10 Mbps and download transmission rates of 6–100+ Mbps.

- Wireless Internet service requires connecting to a LAN that's wired to an ISP.

- Fiber-to-the-node (FTTN) and fiber-to-the-premises (FTTP) enable super-fast Internet speeds using fiber cabling for most of the connection between the ISP's central office and your home. Fiber connections can provide download speeds up to 150+ Mbps and often provide Internet and telephone services over the same connection.

- Cellular data services have evolved over the past two decades through four loosely defined generations. Current and future technologies like WiMAX and LTE are considered 4G. WiMAX offers wireless speeds up to 10+ Mbps.

- The other wireless option is a satellite connection. Although early satellite technology required uploads through a slow modem (26–48 Kbps) and fast downloads through the dish, newer technology uses the modem only for the initial setup, sending both downloads and uploads through the dish.

- SOHO routers allow multiple users to easily share a broadband connection without having to leave a Windows computer running all the time. They provide NAT that allows you to share a single IP address while acting as an effective firewall. Configuration of SOHO routers is done through special Web pages built into the routers.

- ICS enables multiple systems to use one Internet connection. Included in all current Windows versions, ICS uses an ICS host computer connected to the Internet that then shares the connection via a LAN with client computers. The ICS host computer must have a NIC or modem to connect to the Internet and a NIC that plugs into a switch. The other PCs then connect to the switch.

Use Internet application protocols

- Applications provide TCP/IP services, including Web, e-mail, FTP, Telnet, and VoIP. Using Web browser software such as Internet Explorer or Mozilla Firefox, you can access Web sites and pages from Web servers throughout the world. If you are unsuccessful in connecting to a site, use the command-line tool ping to determine whether the server is up. Simply type **ping** followed by either the DNS name or the IP address.

- A proxy server is software that enables multiple connections to the Internet to go through one protected PC. Configure proxy settings from within your browser of choice. When using Internet Explorer, for example, set proxy settings on the Connections tab of Internet Options.

- You should also know how to adjust security settings in your Web browser. In IE, choose Tools | Internet Options and open the Security tab. You can set different security levels or manually select the features you want to enable or disable.

- Security also includes encrypting information such as credit card numbers, home phone numbers, or other personal information. The most common method of encrypting this information is HTTPS. You identify Web sites using HTTPS by the https that appears at the beginning of the Web address.

- You need an e-mail program such as Microsoft Outlook to receive e-mail. To set up an e-mail client, provide your e-mail address and password. E-mail addresses use the *accountname@Internet domain* format. You must also add the names of the POP3 or IMAP4 server for incoming mail and the SMTP server for outgoing mail.

- FTP enables you to send and receive files. You may use an FTP client such as FileZilla, although later versions of IE and other Web browsers provide support for FTP. You'll have to log on to an FTP site, but most public FTP sites allow anonymous logon.

- Telnet is a terminal emulation program for TCP/IP networks. It lets you connect to a server and run commands as if you were sitting in front of the server. Telnet requires a special user name and password. The user name and password will be sent over the network in clear text.

- SSH is the secure replacement for Telnet. SSH uses port 22, and the entire connection is encrypted, preventing any eavesdroppers from reading your data.

- Secure FTP (SFTP) is nothing more than FTP running through an SSH tunnel. You can either start an SSH session between two computers and configure your FTP client and server to run through the SSH tunnel, or use dedicated SFTP servers and clients.

- Voice over IP (VoIP) enables you to make voice calls over your computer network and refers to a collection of protocols. Venders such as Skype and Vonage offer VoIP solutions.

- Today, terminal emulation usually means graphical terminal emulation programs from third-party companies or in the Windows operating system. Terminal emulation programs require separate server and client programs. The modern Windows client is called Remote Desktop and is built into every version of Windows since XP.

- Remote Assistance, available with Windows XP and later, enables you to give anyone control of your desktop. Useful for giving a tech control of a computer to troubleshoot a hardware configuration or driver problem, you can also use Remote Assistance to install drivers or teach someone how to use a particular application.

- VPNs, or Virtual Private Networks, enable you to connect over the public Internet and access a remote network as if you were physically plugged into it. PPTP is the protocol used by Microsoft to provide this service. It works by creating virtual network cards that have their own IP address that match what the LAN uses.

- Other protocols include LDAP, SNMP, and SMB. The Lightweight Directory Access Protocol (LDAP) is used by many operating systems and applications to access directories. The Simple Network Management Protocol (SNMP) enables more query and configuration of just about anything on a network. The Server Message Block (SMB) protocol enables your computer to see all the other computers on a network using tools like Network.

■ Key Terms

baud *(480)*
bits per second (bps) *(480)*
default gateway *(478)*
Dial-up Networking (DUN) *(479)*
digital subscriber line (DSL) *(485)*
file transfer protocol (FTP) *(502)*
Hypertext Transfer Protocol (HTTP) *(493)*
Hypertext Transfer Protocol Secure (HTTPS) *(494)*
integrated services digital network (ISDN) *(484)*
Internet Connection Sharing (ICS) *(492)*
Internet Message Access Protocol version 4 (IMAP4) *(499)*
Internet service provider (ISP) *(477)*
latency *(505)*
Lightweight Directory Access Protocol (LDAP) *(510)*
Long Term Evolution (LTE) *(488)*
modem *(479)*
Network Address Translation (NAT) *(489)*
Point-to-Point Protocol (PPP) *(482)*
Point-to-Point Tunneling Protocol (PPTP) *(509)*

Post Office Protocol version 3 (POP3) *(499)*
proxy server *(498)*
Remote Assistance *(506)*
Remote Desktop *(506)*
Secure Shell (SSH) *(503)*
Server Message Block (SMB) *(511)*
Simple Mail Transfer Protocol (SMTP) *(499)*
Simple Network Management Protocol (SNMP) *(510)*
Telnet *(503)*
tier *(475)*
tunneling *(503)*
universal asynchronous receiver/transmitter (UART) *(479)*
Virtual Private Network (VPN) *(508)*
Voice over IP (VoIP) *(504)*
VoIP phone *(505)*
Web browser *(493)*
Worldwide Interoperability for Microwave Access (WiMAX) *(488)*

Key Term Quiz

Use the Key Terms list to complete the sentences that follow. Not all terms will be used.

1. The time it takes for a packet to travel to its destination and back is called _____.

2. Internet Explorer is a(n) _____.

3. The most common method used to encrypt information, such as credit card numbers, on the Internet is _____.

4. A(n) _____ is software that enables multiple connections to go to the Internet through one protected PC.

5. Although some people use the term to refer to modem speed, _____ actually means the number of cycles per second,

while _____ is a more accurate measurement of actual data throughput.

6. By using an anonymous logon, _____ allows you to send and receive files from a public site.

7. The service that provides the structure for the World Wide Web, allowing documents to be sent across the Web, is _____.

8. Dial-up links to the Internet use a streaming hardware protocol called _____.

9. A(n) _____ enables you to access a remote network over the Internet securely.

10. While technically incorrect, most users refer to the box provided by their cable or DSL Internet providers as a(n) _____.

Multiple-Choice Quiz

1. Which statements about integrated services digital network (ISDN) are true? (Select three.)

 A. An ISDN connection uses either an internal or an external terminal adapter (TA).

 B. BRI has two B channels and one D channel for a throughput total of 128 Kbps.

 C. PRI has 23 B channels and 1 D channel for a total throughput of 1.544 Mbps.

 D. ISDN consists of end-to-end high-speed analog lines.

2. What is the name for the router that your PC uses to connect to your Internet service provider?

 A. Loopback address

 B. Backbone

 C. IP address

 D. Default gateway

3. To configure dial-up networks with Windows XP, which applet should you use?

 A. Network and Internet Connections

 B. Network

 C. Internet Connection Sharing

 D. Remote Assistance

4. A Virtual Private Network creates a(n) _____ through the Internet.

 A. Tunnel

 B. BRI

 C. Connection

 D. SSH session

5. To check to see if the Web server you are trying to reach is available or is down, which command-line utility should you use?

 A. ping

 B. ICS

 C. Telnet

 D. NAT

6. Which of the following Internet connection methods limit the distance you can be from a central office? (Select two.)

 A. DSL

 B. Satellite

 C. Cable

 D. ISDN

7. If your modem cannot connect to the Internet, which of the following can you eliminate as a cause of the problem?

A. The phone line is dead.

B. All lines on the Internet are busy.

C. You dialed the wrong number.

D. The modem is bad.

8. What port does POP3 use?

A. 22

B. 110

C. 212

D. 42

9. Liz can receive her e-mail, but she cannot send e-mail. Which of the following is most likely causing her problem?

A. POP3

B. SMTP

C. IMAP4

D. UART

10. What is the name for the extremely fast networking connections through which Internet transmissions take place?

A. Gateways

B. Tier 1 providers

C. Backbones

D. ISPs

11. Which technology enables you to make voice calls over your computer network?

A. Internet Voice Protocol

B. Voice over IP

C. Digital Telephony Subscriber Service

D. Universal Asynchronous Receiver Transmitter

12. A user on Windows 7 has asked you to teach her how to use a feature of Microsoft Word. What tool should you use?

A. Remote Assistance

B. Remote Desktop

C. Telnet

D. Secure Shell (SSH)

13. What technology enables several computers to share a single network connection?

A. PPTP

B. ICS

C. PHP

D. SSH

14. Where would you go first if you needed to configure a small Linksys router to use a static IP address?

A. The Router Configuration applet in the Control Panel.

B. The router's configuration Web page.

C. Plug in a Yost cable and start PuTTY.

D. There is no way to give the router a static IP.

15. A new client lives in a rural area, outside the connectivity radius of the local cable company and definitely more than 20,000 feet away from the nearest switching center for the phone company. Which Internet option offers the client the best performance?

A. Cable

B. Dial-up

C. DSL

D. Satellite

■ Essay Quiz

1. With the rash of worms and viruses that attack computers connected to the Internet, how can you protect your computer?

2. Andrew's wife, Talena, collects pottery. Andrew found a shop on the Internet that has a piece she's been wanting. He'd love to give it to her for her birthday next week, but the only way it can arrive by then is if he pays for it with his credit card. He's a bit apprehensive about giving his credit card number over the Internet. He wants you to tell him whether you think the site is safe or not. How can you evaluate the site to determine whether it uses encryption for credit card numbers?

3. Sean is planning to take some distance education courses next term. He currently uses a regular phone line and a modem to connect to the Internet. He's consulted you to figure out what his options are for a faster connection. Review his options, explaining the advantages and disadvantages, along with any restrictions that may prevent his receiving the service.

4. With a child in high school and another at a local college, it's always a struggle in Tom's house about who gets to use the computer to do Internet research. It's not feasible for Tom to have two DSL connections, but he does have a second computer. What solution can you offer to solve his problem?

5. You've become a regular columnist for your company's monthly newsletter. Everybody in the company uses e-mail and browses the Web, but you're convinced that the company would benefit if employees knew how to use some of the other Internet services. You've decided that this month's article will highlight three other Internet services. Which three will you discuss and what will you include about each?

Lab Projects

• Lab Project 16.1

Remote Desktop is a great feature of Windows. However, making it work when the computer you want to connect to is behind a router or firewall can be difficult. You need to consider and configure many things, such as the computer's public IP address and port forwarding or Network Address Translation on the router. Using the Internet, find a tutorial or a step-by-step "how-to" article that guides you through configuring a remote computer and router to make a Remote Desktop connection possible.

• Lab Project 16.2

Remote Desktop provides the same functionality as some third-party software and services, such as the open source VNC software, Symantec's commercial pcAnywhere software, and the online service GoToMyPC.com. Each has its own benefits, such as no cost, ease of configuration, or cross-platform use. Research two other solutions that offer remote control functionality similar to Remote Desktop and compare and contrast the three. What are the similarities? What are the unique benefits of each? Which one would you be more likely to use yourself? Why?

• Lab Project 16.3

Have you heard of WebDAV? Web Distributed Authoring and Versioning is a set of extensions added to the Hypertext Transfer Protocol to support collaborative authoring on the Web. While HTTP is a reading protocol, WebDAV is a writing protocol created by a working group of the Internet Engineering Task Force (IETF). WebDAV offers a faster, more secure method of file transfer than FTP, and some predict that it may make FTP obsolete. It's already incorporated into most current operating systems and applications. Some authors say that WebDAV will change the way we use the Web. Use the Internet to learn more about WebDAV and its features. Apple calls it "a whole new reason to love the Net." After learning about WebDAV, see if you agree.

• Lab Project 16.4

Are all high-speed Internet connections created equal? Test them to find out! Speakeasy.net hosts one of the best Internet sites for testing the speed of an Internet connection: www.speakeasy.net/speedtest/

Test three to five Internet connections that you can easily get to, such as your home, a friend's house, your school, a library, and an Internet café. How do the connections compare? If you can, find out which technology the connections use. Which one seems to offer the best connection in your area?

chapter 17 Multimedia

Emmett Bradley: "Sir, are you telling me that your only real flight time is at the controls of a video game?"

Troy: "No, see, it's not—it's not a video game, all right? It's a flight simulator."

—Emmett Bradley and Troy, *Snakes on a Plane*

In this chapter, you will learn how to

- **Describe how to implement sound in a PC**
- **Install and configure video capture hardware and software**
- **Set up a PC to view television signals**

The PC long ago went well beyond a simple device used to create office documents and crunch numbers efficiently. With modern PCs, you can experience content on many levels, from realistic video to scintillating three-dimensional sound. Plus, you can add the hardware and software to turn the computer into a multimedia creation machine, capable of making movies and more.

This chapter looks at the many aspects of multimedia available in a modern PC. First, the chapter discusses how sound works in a PC, both to record and play it back. Second, you'll dive into video capture concepts, hardware, and software. Finally, the chapter rolls through the essentials of setting up the computer to bridge the gap into the entertainment world fully by installing and configuring TV tuner hardware and software. Rolling...and...action!

■ Sound

You're racing down the virtual track, pixels flying across the screen, hearing the engine roar as you take another turn and press down the accelerator—or you're surfing the Web for lovely scenic nature photos, with the sweet, mellifluous music of Mozart filling the room. Sound has become an integral component of the computing experience. Setting up and optimizing sound for the PC has become an integral skill for all computer techs.

Correctly setting up sound for a PC requires that you know about quite a few things, because the sound process has many components. You need a properly installed sound card (or built-in sound device) with the correct drivers loaded, reasonably high-quality speakers, support software such as the API for a particular game correctly configured in Windows, and a properly set up application that can use the features of the sound card. And every great tech needs to know the troubleshooting techniques to handle both routine and uncommon problems with sound.

Historical/Conceptual

How Sound Works in a PC

Like the ripples that roll across a pond when you drop a rock in the center, sound flows from a source in invisible but measurable waves that cause the membranes in your ears to vibrate and create sound. The sophistication of the human ear enables most people to differentiate the melodious from the raucous, the loud from the soft. Computers aren't nearly as sophisticated as the human ear and brain, so clear standards are a must for converting music into a format that a PC can use to record and play sound. Computer folks use the terms *capture* and *output* instead of record and play.

Sound-Capture Basics

Virtually every PC today comes with four critical components for capturing and outputting sound: a sound card or sound device built into the motherboard, speakers, microphone, and recording/playback software. Computers capture (record) sound waves in electronic format through a process called **sampling**. In its simplest sense, sampling means capturing the state or quality of a particular sound wave a set number of times each second. The sampling rate is measured in units of thousands of cycles per second, or kilohertz (KHz). The more often a sound is sampled, the better the reproduction of that sound. Most sounds in the PC world are recorded with a sampling rate of from 11 KHz (very low quality, like a telephone) to 192 KHz (ultra-high quality, better than the human ear).

Sounds vary according to their loudness (**amplitude**), how high or low their tone (**frequency**), and the qualities that differentiate the same note played on different instruments (**timbre**). All the characteristics of a particular sound wave—amplitude, frequency, timbre—need to be recorded and translated into ones and zeros to reproduce that sound accurately within the computer and out to your speakers.

Tech Tip

Sound Terminology

Every modern motherboard comes with sound processing capabilities built in. By default, techs refer to built-in sound as either built-in sound or as a sound card, even when there's no expansion card for sound. I'll do the same in this chapter.

• **Figure 17.1** Sound Recorder settings

WAV and MP3 are only two among a large number of file formats for sound. Not all sound players can play all of these formats; however, many sound formats are nothing more than some type of compressed WAV file, so with the right codec loaded, you can play most sound formats.

Tech Tip

Compressing WAV Files to MP3 Format

Using MP3 compression, you can shrink a WAV file by a factor of 12 without losing much sound quality. When you compress a WAV file into an MP3 file, the key decision is the bit rate. The bit rate *is the amount of information (number of bits) transferred from the compressed file to the MP3 decoder in 1 second. The higher the bit rate of an MP3 file, the higher the sound quality. The bit rate of MP3 audio files is commonly measured in thousands of bits per second, abbreviated* Kbps. *Most MP3 encoders support a range of bit rates from 24 Kbps up to 320 Kbps (or 320,000 bits per second). A CD-quality MP3 bit rate is 128 Kbps.*

The number of characteristics of a particular sound captured during sampling is measured by the **bit depth** of the sample. The greater the bit depth used to capture a sample, the more characteristics of that sound can be stored and thus re-created. An 8-bit sample of a Jimi Hendrix guitar solo, for example, captures 2^8 (256) characteristics of that sound per sample. It would sound like a cheap recording of a recording, perhaps a little flat and thin. A 16-bit sample, in contrast, captures 2^{16} (65,536) different characteristics of his solo and reproduces all the fuzzy overtones and feedback that gave Hendrix his unique sound.

The last aspect of sound capture is the number of tracks of sound you capture. Most commonly, you can capture either a single track (**monaural**) or two tracks (**stereo**). More advanced captures record many more sound tracks, but that's a topic for a more advanced sound capture discussion and well beyond CompTIA A+.

The combination of sampling frequency and bit depth determines how faithfully a digital version of a sound captures what your ear would hear. A sound capture is considered **CD quality** when recorded at 44.1 KHz, with 16-bit depth and in stereo. Most recording programs let you set these values before you begin recording. Figure 17.1 shows the configuration settings for Windows Sound Recorder.

Hey, wait a minute! Did you notice the Format setting in Figure 17.1? What's that? You can save those sampled sounds in lots of different ways—and that's where the term *format* comes into play.

Recorded Sound Formats

The granddaddy of all sound formats is **pulse code modulation (PCM)**. PCM was developed in the 1960s to carry telephone calls over the first digital lines. With just a few minor changes to allow for use in PCs, the PCM format is still alive and well, although it's better known as the *WAV* format so common in the PC world. WAV files are great for storing faithfully recorded sounds and music, but they do so at a price. WAV files can be huge, especially when sampled at high frequency and depth. A 4-minute song at 44.1 KHz and 16-bit stereo, for example, weighs in at a whopping 40-plus MB!

What's interesting about sound quality is that the human ear cannot perceive anywhere near the subtle variations of sound recorded at 44.1 KHz and 16-bit stereo. Clever programmers have written algorithms to store full-quality WAV files as compressed files, discarding unnecessary audio qualities of that file. These algorithms—really nothing more than a series of instructions in code—are called compressor/decompressor programs or, more simply, **codecs**. The most famous of the codecs is the Fraunhoffer MPEG-1 Layer 3 codec, more often called by its file extension, **MP3**.

MIDI

Every sound card can produce sounds in addition to playing prerecorded sound files. Every sound card comes with a second processor designed to interpret standardized **musical instrument digital interface (MIDI)** files. It's important to note that a MIDI file is not an independent music file, unlike a WAV file that sounds more or less the same on many different PCs. A MIDI file is a text file that takes advantage of the sound processing hardware to enable the PC to produce sound. Programmers use these small files to tell the sound card which notes to play; how long, how loud, and on which

instruments to play them; and so forth. Think of a MIDI file as a piece of electronic sheet music, with the instruments built into your sound card.

The beauty of MIDI files is that they're tiny in comparison to equivalent WAV files. The first movement of Beethoven's Fifth Symphony, for example, weighs in at a whopping 78 MB as a high-quality WAV file. The same seven-minute piece as a MIDI file, in contrast, slips in at a svelte 60 KB.

MIDI is hardware dependent, meaning the capabilities and quality of the individual sound card make all the difference in the world on the sound produced. Sound cards play MIDI files by using one of two technologies: FM synthesis or wave table synthesis.

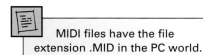

MIDI files have the file extension .MID in the PC world.

FM Synthesis Early processors used electronic emulation of various instruments—a technique often called **FM synthesis**—to produce music and other sound effects. Software developers could tell the sound processor to reproduce a piano playing certain notes, for example, and a sound resembling a piano would pour forth from the speakers. The problem with FM synthesis is that although the modulation sounds okay for a single note, such as middle C, it sounds increasingly electronic the farther up or down the scale you go from that prime note.

Wave Table Synthesis To address the odd techno-sound of early sound processors, manufacturers began embedding recordings of actual instruments or other sounds in the sound card. Modern sound cards use these recorded sounds to reproduce an instrument much more faithfully than with FM synthesis. When asked to play a C note on a piano or on a viola, for example, the sound processor grabs a prerecorded WAV file from its memory and adjusts it to match the specific sound and timing requested. This technique is called **wave table synthesis**. The number of instruments a sound card can play at once is called the **polyphony** of that card—typically 64 sounds on better cards. Most modern sound cards have samples of 128 instruments—a veritable symphony orchestra on a chip!

MIDI files are much less popular than other recorded formats on computers, but every Windows computer and every sound card still fully supports MIDI.

Other File Formats

The WAV, MP3, and MIDI formats may account for the majority of sound files, but plenty of other less common formats are out there. Here are the extensions of some other sound file formats you may run into in the PC world:

- **AAC** Advanced Audio Coding is the native format for songs downloaded into the Apple iTunes music library. The AAC format is part of the MPEG-4 standard, offers better compression algorithms than MP3, and is freely distributed.

- **AIFF** The Audio Interchange File Format is a popular sound format used on Mac computers. AIFF are often seen at Web sites, and you can use the well-known QuickTime Player to play them.

- **ASM** Assembly Language Source files are compressed sound files often seen on the Internet and used in streaming sound (streaming media is discussed later in this chapter).

- **ASX** Microsoft created the ASX format to facilitate streaming audio over the Internet through Windows Media Player. It's more than just a format, though; it acts like a super playlist and enables you to

play other sound file types as well. The full name of the format is Microsoft Advanced Streaming Redirector.

- **AU** Many players can play these files, including players on non-Windows systems, such as Sun, Next, UNIX, and Mac.

- **FLAC** The Free Lossless Audio Codec is an open format that can compress sound files without losing any data—it can even decompress a file back into an exact copy of the original. FLAC can reduce the size of audio files by up to 60 percent.

- **OGG** The Vorbis format is an open-source compression codec that competes well with the proprietary AAC and WMA codecs, as well as MP3. Vorbis files are saved with the .OGG filename extension, so you'll hear them (incorrectly) referred to as "Ogg" files.

- **RM** RealMedia files play either just audio or audio and video. They are proprietary to RealMedia, a popular player often used on the Internet. You must have RealMedia Player installed on your computer to play these files.

- **WMA** Windows Media Audio is Microsoft's proprietary compression format.

This list scratches the surface of the 100-plus sound file formats available, but it represents those you're most likely to encounter.

Playing Sounds

A large number of programs can play sounds on a typical Windows computer. First, virtually every Windows computer comes with Windows Media Player, possibly the most popular of all sound players. Figure 17.2 shows the default Media Player for Windows 7. You can download many

• **Figure 17.2** Windows Media Player

other players, of course, including iTunes, Apple's media program for Windows and Mac OS X. This is good, because not all sound players can play all sounds.

Many applications, especially games, play sounds too. In the not-too-distant past, a game or an application sometimes had its own sound format, but most applications and games today use standard WAV, MP3, or MIDI files.

Streaming media is a broadcast of data that is played on your computer and immediately discarded. Streaming media is incredibly popular on the Internet. Streaming media has spawned an entire industry of Internet radio stations and music databases. Two popular Internet radio players include Windows Media Player and Apple's iTunes. You can use streaming services like Spotify and Pandora to pick and choose the music you want to hear. With the spread of broadband Internet, the quality of streaming music has improved dramatically.

 Try This!

Play Sounds in Windows

The typical Windows PC comes with a number of applications for playing sound files. Take a tour of a typical Windows system to see these applications. This exercise uses Windows XP, but almost any version of Windows will also work. For this exercise, you need a Windows system with a functioning sound card, microphone, and speakers.

1. Using the file search feature in Windows, locate all of the files on your computer that have the extension *.wav*—all versions of Windows come with a number of WAV files. Double-click one of the files to play it. What program is associated with WAV files?

2. Repeat step 1, but this time look for files with the extension *.mid*. Not all versions of Windows have MIDI files. Double-click one of the files to play it. What program is associated with MIDI files?

3. From the Start button, search for any sound programs that may be on your system. You'll almost certainly run into Windows Media Player and Sound Recorder, but check to see whether any third-party programs are installed.

4. If possible, install a popular sound player such as Winamp or iTunes on your system. Both programs are free. You can get Winamp at www.winamp.com and iTunes at www.apple.com/itunes. Check Winamp's help files to see what types of file formats Winamp supports—a lot of formats!

5. If you have an Internet connection, try running some streaming audio. If you have Windows Media Player versions 7 through 10, go to the Radio Tuner. If you are running Windows Media Player 11 or later, go to the Media Guide. If you have Winamp, try going to www.shoutcast.com. With iTunes, just click the Radio link in the Library.

Getting the Right Sound Hardware

Modern motherboards come with built-in sound processing, plus you can buy a sound card that plugs into a PCI or PCIe expansion slot or into a USB port. Sound cards come with many features, including two separate sound processors (one for all of the recorded formats such as WAV and another for MIDI), recording capabilities, support for MIDI instruments, and more. All sound cards, from the cheapest to the most expensive, can play music and drive a pair of speakers, so techs need to delve a little deeper to understand the crucial differences among low-, mid-, and high-end sound cards. Sound cards differ in six basic areas: sound standard, processor capabilities, speaker support, recording quality, jacks, and extra features.

But the sound card itself is only one part of the equation. You also need good-quality speakers if you have any intention of listening to music or enjoying some of the more advanced features such as surround sound.

Sound Card Standards

Most sound cards follow one of two standards, AC'97 or Intel High Definition Audio, although no rule says manufacturers must follow these standards. This applies both to the sound processing hardware built into motherboards and to add-on sound cards.

The **AC'97** standard applies to lower-end audio devices, having been created when most folks listened to stereo sound at best. Both playback and recording capabilities of such sound cards offer adequate quality, certainly enough for the typical office PC. When you want to go beyond average, though, turn to a motherboard or add-on sound card that offers a newer standard.

Intel designed the **Intel High Definition Audio (HDA)** standard to support features such as true surround sound with many discrete speakers. Technically speaking, whereas AC'97 offers support for up to six channels at 48 KHz/20-bit quality, HDA cranks that up to eight channels at 192 KHz/32-bit quality, a substantial improvement. HDA also supports sending multiple streams of audio from one computer to different output devices, so you can enjoy Internet radio in one room, for example, and listen to a CD in another room, both played on the same computer.

Processor Capabilities

Sound processor capabilities differ dramatically from the low end to the high end, even though the prices don't reflect the great divide. The sound processor handles the communication among the application, operating system, and CPU and translates commands into sounds coming out of the speakers. Low-end sound processors do little more than translate, which means that the CPU has to do the heavy lifting on the processing front.

Better sound processors, in contrast, shoulder much of the processing burden and bring a series of extra features to the table. By handling a lot of the processing on board, these better sound processors free up the CPU for other duties and—in effect and in name—*accelerate* the sound process.

As they do with new microprocessor models, Intel gave the HDA standard a codename as well. Look for motherboards offering the *Azalia* sound option. That's Intel High Definition Audio.

Tech Tip

Azalia's Not Just for Intel Boards

Most chipset makers have adopted Intel High Definition Audio for their better motherboard offerings. That includes direct Intel competitors, such as NVIDIA. Everybody plays Azalia these days!

These decent sound processors also provide excellent sound reproduction, so your MP3s sound as awesome on your PC as they do on your stereo.

Most mid-range and all high-end sound processors offer support for various surround sound standards, enabling equally equipped games and other applications to provide positional audio effects and detailed sound modeling—features that make PC gaming take on a whole new dimension. You'll learn about the various standards in detail in the "Speakers" section of this chapter, but for now let an example suffice. With properly implemented positional audio, when you're sneaking down the hall, ready to steal the Pasha's treasure, you will hear behind you the sounds of the guards marching up to capture you. Such added realism has many potential benefits beyond games, but games are currently the primary beneficiary of this technology.

Speaker Support

Every sound card supports two speakers or a pair of headphones, but many better sound cards support five or more speakers in discrete channels. These multiple speakers provide surround sound—popular not only for games but also for those who enjoy watching movies on their PCs. The card shown in Figure 17.3, for example, has outputs for many speakers.

Another popular speaker addition is a subwoofer. A **subwoofer** provides the amazing low-frequency sounds that give an extra dimension to your movies, music, and games. Almost all modern sound cards support both surround sound and a subwoofer and advertise this with a nomenclature such as Dolby Digital or DTS. Figure 17.4 shows one type of surround speaker system. (You'll learn more about surround sound in the upcoming "Speakers" section.)

Recording Quality

Almost every sound card has an input for a powered microphone, but the high-end cards record with substantially lower amounts of noise or other audible artifacts. The measure that describes the relative quality of an input port is **signal-to-noise ratio** and is expressed in **decibels**. The smaller the number, the worse the card is for recording, because you're more likely to get noise. Most sound cards at the low end and in the mid range have a signal-to-noise ratio of 30 to 50 decibels, which makes them unacceptable for recording. High-end cards offer a 96 to 100+ signal-to-noise ratio, a level near what professional musicians use. Check the documentation before you buy or recommend a sound card for recording purposes (see Figure 17.5).

Jacks

Virtually every sound card comes with at least three connections: one for a stereo speaker system, one for a microphone, and one for a secondary input called line in. If you look at the back of a motherboard with a built-in sound card, you'll invariably see these three connections. On most systems, the

• **Figure 17.3** A sound card with multiple speaker connections

• **Figure 17.4** Surround speakers (photo courtesy of Klipsch Group, Inc.)

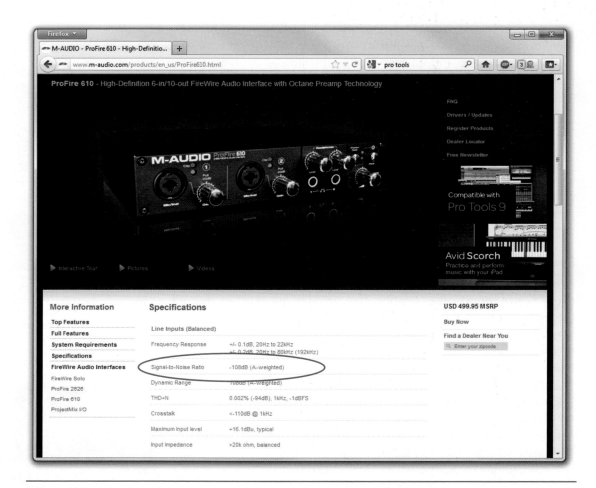

Figure 17.5 The M-AUDIO ProFire 610 advertises its excellent 108-decibel signal-to-noise ratio for recording.

main stereo speaker connector is green, the line in connector is blue, and the microphone connector is pink. You'll often find plenty of other connectors as well (see Figure 17.6).

Here's a list of some of the standard connectors:

Mini-audio connectors

Figure 17.6 Typical audio connections on a motherboard sound card

- **Main speaker out** Just what it sounds like, the main speaker output is where you plug in the standard speaker connector.

- **Line out** Some cards will have a separate line out connector that is often used to connect to an external device such as a CD or MP3 player. This enables you to output sounds from your computer.

- **Line in** The line in port connects to an external device such as a CD or MP3 player to allow you to import sounds into your computer.

- **Rear out** The rear out connector connects to the rear speakers for surround sound audio output.

- **Analog/digital out** The multifunction analog/digital out connection acts as a special digital connection to external digital devices or digital speaker systems, and it also acts as the analog connection to center and subwoofer channels. (See the "Speakers" section for a discussion of surround sound.)

- **Microphone** The microphone port connects to an external microphone for voice input.

- **Joystick** The now-obsolete joystick port connects a joystick or a MIDI device to the sound card. The joystick port is a two-row, DB-15 female connection, but few motherboards or sound cards include the port these days.

• **Figure 17.7** Breakout box for a SoundBlaster Live! Platinum sound card

Extra Features

With all motherboards including built-in sound these days, expansion sound card makers have responded by adding a host of extra goodies and capabilities to their cards that, for some folks, prove irresistibly tempting. These include a digital output to integrate the PC with a home entertainment unit and surround sound speaker setup; a breakout box that adds recording and output ports in a 5.25-inch bay; and a FireWire connection for direct gaming, file sharing, and immediate MP3 playing from a portable MP3 device. Figure 17.7 shows a version of the Creative Labs SoundBlaster breakout box. These features aren't for everyone, but they are compelling to many consumers.

• **Figure 17.8** High-quality speaker set (right) versus another manufacturer's low-end speaker set (left)

Speakers

It always blows me away when I walk into someone's study and hear tinny music whining from a $10 pair of speakers connected to a $2000 computer. If you listen to music or play games on your computer, a decent set of speakers can significantly improve the experience. Speakers come in a wide variety of sizes, shapes, technologies, and quality and can stump the uninformed tech who can't easily tell that the $50 set on the right sounds 100 times better than the $25 pair on the left (see Figure 17.8).

Speaker Standards

The advent of surround sound in the computing world has created a number of speaker standards. You should know these standards so you can choose the speakers that work best for you and your clients.

Stereo is the oldest speaker technology you'll see in the PC world. Stereo speakers are just what you might imagine: two speakers, a left and a right (see Figure 17.9). The two speakers share a single jack that connects to the sound card. Most cheap speakers are stereo speakers.

• **Figure 17.9** Stereo speakers

• **Figure 17.10** Typical 2.1 speakers

• **Figure 17.11** S/PDIF connectors

Only a few 5.1 PC speaker sets come with S/PDIF. In most cases, you'll have to use the regular audio outputs on the sound card. You'll find the connector more common on 6.1 and 7.1 sets.

A **2.1** speaker system consists of a pair of standard stereo speakers—called **satellites**—combined with a subwoofer (see Figure 17.10). The average 2.1 speaker system has a single jack that connects to the sound card and runs into the subwoofer. Another wire runs from the subwoofer to the two stereo speakers. If you want to enjoy great music and don't need surround sound, this is your speaker standard of choice.

Going beyond standard two-channel (stereo) sound has been a goal in the sound world since the 1970s. However, it wasn't until the advent of Dolby Laboratory's **Dolby Digital** sound standard in the early 1990s that surround sound began to take off. The Dolby Digital sound standard is designed to support five channels of sound: front-left, front-right, front-center, rear-left, and rear-right. Dolby Digital also supports a subwoofer—thus, the term **5.1**. Another company, **Digital Theatre Systems (DTS)**, created a competing standard that also supported a 5.1 speaker system. When DVDs were introduced, they included both Dolby Digital and DTS 5.1 standards, making 5.1 speakers an overnight requirement for home theater. If you want to enjoy your DVDs in full surround sound on your PC, you must purchase a full 5.1 speaker system. A number of 5.1 speaker systems are available for PCs. The choice you make is usually determined by what sounds best to you.

Many sound cards also come with a special **Sony/Philips Digital Interface (S/PDIF)** connector that enables you to connect your sound card directly to a 5.1 speaker system or receiver (see Figure 17.11). Using a single S/PDIF instead of a tangle of separate wires for each speaker greatly simplifies your sound setup. S/PIDF connections come in two types, optical and coaxial. The optical variety looks like a square with a small door (at right in Figure 17.11). The coaxial is a standard RCA connector (at left), the same type used to connect a CD player to your stereo. It doesn't matter which one you use; just make sure you have an open spot on your receiver or speakers.

Games can also take advantage of 5.1, 6.1, and 7.1 speakers, but they use the DirectX standard. **DirectX** offers numerous commands, also known as APIs, that issue instructions such as "make a sound on the right speaker" or "play music in both the right and left channels." DirectX simplifies the programming needed to create sound and video: rather than having to program sounds in different ways for each sound card option, games can talk DirectX. The hardware manufacturers simply have to ensure that their sound cards are DirectX compatible.

DirectX version 3 introduced **DirectSound3D (DS3D)**, which offered a range of commands to place a sound anywhere in 3-D space. Known as **positional audio**, it fundamentally changed the way most PC games were played. DS3D could not handle all sound information, but it supported extensions to its instructions for more advanced sound features. This challenged the sound card designers to develop more fully the concept of posi-

tional audio. Creative Labs responded by rolling out **environmental audio extensions (EAX)**, a set of audio presets that gave developers the capability to create a convincing sense of environment in entertainment titles and a realistic sense of distance between the player and audio events. Figure 17.12 shows an EAX setup screen.

In late 2000, a number of EAX effects were incorporated into the DirectX audio component of DirectX 8.0. This signaled the acceptance of EAX as the standard for audio effects in gaming. Shortly afterward, Creative Labs started releasing audio cards that were Dolby 5.1 compatible out of the box. This let you plug a 5.1 speaker system directly into your sound card. The sound card automatically decoded the Dolby/DTS sound track when you played a DVD and the EAX effects when you played a game that supported it. All current sound cards support DirectX and EAX.

Microsoft changed the way audio works in Windows Vista/7 from the way it works in previous versions of Windows. Most notably, Vista/7 doesn't support direct hardware access to sound, so DirectSound does not work. Third-party developers have created various workarounds for this lack of support to enable some older games and hardware to function in Windows Vista/7. Other developers have gotten behind the OpenAL API to provide environmental audio effects in Vista/7. Specific OpenAL drivers for games have to be included to provide that support.

Not all cards support Dolby Digital/DTS. Most software DVD players and some sound cards support Dolby Digital. DTS support is a little harder to come by. Check the manufacturer's Web site to determine whether your card will work with DTS.

Speaker Features

Speakers also come with a few other features that you should consider when choosing a set for yourself or your clients. Speakers offer a variety of power sources, controls accessibility, and headphone jacks.

Most speakers have volume controls as well as an on/off switch. Get a system that provides easy access to those controls by placing them on an easy-to-reach speaker or on a special control box.

• **Figure 17.12** EAX setup screen

The problem with headphones is that you need to plug them into the back of the sound card and then tell Windows to output to them from the Sound applet on the Control Panel. Save yourself a lot of hassle and get a speaker system that has a handy headphone jack on one of the speakers or on a control box.

Microphones

Speakers are great for listening to music, but what if you're a musician looking to record your own music? You'll need to plug a *microphone* into your sound card if you want to input audio into your PC (see Figure 17.13). A microphone records sound by detecting vibrations and turning them into an electronic signal. Microphones are most commonly used for recording voices, though you can easily record any other sounds. (Many musical instruments can be plugged into the line in port of your sound card, either directly or through a converter box.)

Microphones can also be used with speech-to-text programs that listen to what you say and then type it out on the screen. These programs can be finicky to use, but they're still fun to play around with. If you do use speech-to-text programs, look for a headset that has a built-in microphone (see Figure 17.14). The quality will be lower, but it will keep your hands free. (These headsets are also great for voice chatting while playing games on your PC.)

When searching for a microphone, you'll most likely be picking between *condenser* and *dynamic* microphones. I won't go too deeply into the science of recording sound, but here's a very quick rundown:

- Condenser microphones are often found in recording studios because they can record a wide range of sound at a high quality, but they are larger, more delicate, and must be powered.

- Dynamic microphones use a different technology to record sound, but are often found at live music events because they're much more rugged, don't need to be powered, and still sound great.

You can also buy microphones that connect via USB instead of the microphone port.

• **Figure 17.13** A standard microphone

• **Figure 17.14** Headsets are great for gaming.

Look for something that combines audio quality with affordability. The best condenser microphones can cost hundreds or thousands of dollars, but most people don't need a recording studio level of quality. A nice dynamic microphone or less-expensive condenser microphone will record great sound for about $100 to $200.

MIDI-enabled Devices

Music composition has changed dramatically over the past few decades. What used to be a painfully analog process of writing out music on paper, recording it to tape, and hoping for the best has become almost entirely digital. Hardware and software exist that enable you to record analog sounds to digital storage, and create entirely digital sound with special audio production software. One type of software, called a *digital audio workstation*, enables you to input MIDI information using an external **MIDI-enabled device** (see Figure 17.15). *Music notation* software also exists that enables you to write out notes on sheet music either by hand or with a MIDI device.

MIDI-enabled devices, also known as *MIDI controllers*, come in several form factors, but most look and feel like standard music keyboards (see Figure 17.16). Others use a grid or row of square buttons—the best ones light up, too! Keep in mind that these devices don't play music; they are incapable of making noise on their own. Only combined with the proper software will a MIDI device be able to make music. In the past, MIDI devices

External microphones are great for more than just your PC. Look for digital cameras and camcorders that include microphone ports. Built-in microphones are notoriously poor in quality and pick up all the noise made by the camera. Another way to increase your audio quality is via a pop filter, which you place between you and the microphone to minimize the poppy noise of *plosive* sounds (like the letters p and b).

• **Figure 17.15** Ableton Live, a digital audio workstation

used MIDI-to-serial or MIDI-to-joystick adapters, but almost all modern MIDI controllers use USB connections.

Many MIDI controllers can do more than just play music. More elaborate models include extra knobs, sliders, and buttons for controlling the digital audio workstation software. Your audio software should include options and instructions for configuring the MIDI device, but for many applications, you can just plug it in and start playing.

Installing Sound in a Windows System

You've got two choices for sound hardware on today's PCs: a separate sound card or onboard sound built into the motherboard. The installation process for a sound card is basically the same as the process for any other card. You snap the card into a slot, plug some speakers into the card, load a driver— and for the most part, you're finished. With onboard sound, you need to make sure the sound is enabled in your CMOS and then load the driver. As with most of the devices discussed in this book, sound card installation consists of three major parts: physical installation, device driver installation, and configuration.

Physical Installation

Physical installation is easy. Onboard sound is already physically installed, and most sound cards are run-of-the-mill PCI cards (see Figure 17.17), although you can find PCIe and USB versions too. The real trick to physical installation is deciding where to plug in the speakers, microphone, and so on. The surround sound devices so common today feature a variety of jacks, so you will probably want to refer to your sound card documentation for details, but here are a few guidelines:

• Figure 17.16 A MIDI keyboard

• Figure 17.17 Typical sound card

- The typical stereo or 2.1 speaker system will use only a single jack. Look for the jack labeled Speaker or Speaker 1.

- Surround speakers either use a single digital (S/PDIF) connection, which in most cases runs from the sound card to the subwoofer, or they need three separate cables: one for the front two speakers that runs to the Speaker 1 connector, one for the back two speakers that runs to the Speaker 2 connector, and a third cable for the center channel and subwoofer that runs to the digital/audio out or Speaker 3 connector.

Here's a quick look at sound card installation. As with any expansion card, you'll need a Phillips-head screwdriver to install a sound card, as well

as your electrostatic discharge (ESD) prevention equipment. Of course, you'll also need the sound card itself, a set of speakers, an audio cable if it's an older system, and a microphone if you want to be able to record sounds.

1. Shut down your computer, unplug it, and open the case.

2. Find an open PCI or PCIe slot and snap in the sound card. Remember to handle the card with tender loving care—especially if you're installing an expensive, high-end card! Make sure the card is securely seated, and secure it to the chassis with a hex screw.

Installing Drivers

Once the sound card is installed, start the system and let Windows install the card's drivers. This applies to expansion cards and onboard sound. As you might expect by now, you'll probably have a choice between the built-in Windows drivers and the driver that comes on an optical disc with your sound card. Just as with other cards, it's always best to install the driver that comes with the card. All sound devices have easy-to-use autorun-enabled installation discs that step you through the process (see Figure 17.18).

 Sound card drivers are updated occasionally. Take a moment to check the manufacturer's Web site to see whether your sound card has any driver updates.

You might run into one of the USB sound cards out on the market (see Figure 17.19), in which case the installation process is reversed. The only secret to these devices is to follow the important rule of all USB devices: *Install the drivers before you plug in the device.* Windows probably has basic drivers for these USB sound cards, but don't take a chance—always install the drivers first.

After your sound card and driver are installed, make a quick trip to Device Manager to ensure that the driver was installed correctly, and you're two-thirds of the way there. Installing the driver is never the last step for a sound card. Your final steps are to configure the sound card by using configuration programs and to test it by using an application. Most sound cards come with both special configuration programs and a few sound applications on the same installation disc that supplies the drivers. Take a look at these extra bits of software that I call *sound programs*.

• **Figure 17.18** Typical autorun screen for a sound card

• **Figure 17.19** USB sound card

Installing Sound Programs

You've already seen that you need a program to play sounds on your PC: Windows Media Player, Winamp, or something similar. But several other classes of sound programs also reside on your computer: programs for the configuration of your sound card—tools built into Windows as well as proprietary tools—and special applications that may or may not come with your sound card.

Windows Configuration Applications Every Windows computer comes with at least one important sound configuration program built right into the operating system: the Control Panel applet called Sound in Windows Vista/7 and Sounds and Audio Devices in Windows XP. Whatever the name, the applet performs the same job: it provides a location for performing most or all of the configuration you need for your sound card.

The Sounds and Audio Devices applet in Windows XP has five tabs: Volume, Sounds, Audio, Voice, and Hardware. The Volume tab is the most interesting. This tab adjusts the volume for the speakers, and it allows you to set up the type of speaker system you have, as shown in Figure 17.20.

• **Figure 17.20** Advanced Audio Properties dialog box

The Sounds tab allows you to add customized sounds to Windows events, such as the startup of a program or Windows shutdown. The Audio tab (see Figure 17.21) and Voice tab do roughly the same thing: they allow you to specify the device used for input and output of general sounds (Audio tab) and voice (Voice tab). These settings are handy for folks like me who have a regular microphone and speakers but also use a headset with microphone for voice recognition or Internet telephone software. By telling Windows to use the microphone for normal sounds and to use the headset for voice recognition, I don't have to make any manual changes when I switch from listening to an MP3 to listening to my brother when he calls me over the Internet.

The Hardware tab isn't used very often, but it does have one interesting feature: it shows you all of the audio and video codecs installed in your system. (See the section on "Missing Codecs" later in this chapter for more details on codecs.)

• **Figure 17.21** Audio tab

What you see in Windows Vista/7's Sound applet will vary depending on your installed audio devices. Don't be alarmed if your Sound applet looks a lot different than Figure 17.22.

Microsoft changed a few things between Windows XP and Windows Vista/7 when it comes to configuring sound. The Sound applet offers better support for multiple speaker setup, for example, and integration with televisions with HDMI configuration options.

To configure speakers, go to the Control Panel and click Hardware and Sound; then click Sound if in Category View or double-click the Sound applet if in Classic View/Icon View. Either route opens the Sound applet (see Figure 17.22).

Select the Speakers (Speakers/Headphones on some systems) option and click the Configure button to open the Speaker Setup dialog box (see Figure 17.23). Select the audio channel option that's appropriate for your

• **Figure 17.22** Sound applet in Windows Vista

• **Figure 17.23** Speaker Setup dialog box in Windows Vista

setup, such as the 5.1 system selected for my setup at the office and shown in Figure 17.23. You can click on individual speaker icons to test if the speakers are set up properly, or click the Test button to cycle through the whole range of speakers.

Proprietary Configuration Applications Many sound cards install proprietary software to support configuration features not provided by Windows. Figure 17.24 shows one such application. This special configuration application comes with Creative Labs sound cards to add a few tweaks to the speaker setup that the Sounds and Audio Devices applet doesn't support.

Most sound cards come with some form of configuration program that works with the Control Panel applet to tweak the sound the way you want it. Figure 17.25 shows the applet that came with my motherboard. One of its many interesting features is that it detects what types of devices are installed into the sound ports and adjusts the system to use them. In other words, I don't even have to look where I'm plugging in anything! If I plug a microphone into the front speaker port, the system just adjusts the outputs—very cool. Software and sound cards that can do this are called **autosensing**.

Take some time to experiment with the program that comes with your sound card—this is a great way to learn about some of the card's features that you might otherwise not even know are there!

• **Figure 17.24** Creative Labs Speakers and Headphone panel

• **Figure 17.25** Autosensing software detecting connected devices

Specialized Applications Some sound cards—Creative Labs sound cards are by far the most infamous for this—install one or more applications, ostensibly to improve your sound experience. These are not the configuration programs just described. These applications enable you to do anything from composing music to organizing your sound files. Personally, I don't have much use for an application such as the 3DMIDI Player (see Figure 17.26)—but you might be just the type of person who loves it. Be sure at least to install the applications that come with your card. If you don't like them, you can easily uninstall them.

Troubleshooting Sound

The problems you'll run into with sound seem to fall into one of two camps: those that are embarrassingly simple to repair and those that defy any possible logic and are seemingly impossible to fix. This section divides sound problems into three groups—hardware, configuration, and application problems—and gives you some ideas on how to fix these problems.

Hardware Problems

Hardware problems are by far the most common sound problems, especially if your sound card has worked for some amount of time already. Properly installed and configured sound cards almost never suddenly stop making sounds.

Volume The absolute first item to check when a sound dies is the volume controls. Remember that you can set the volume in two places: in software and on the speakers. I can't tell you the number of times I've lost sound only to discover that my wife turned down the volume on the speakers.

If your system tray (i.e., the *notification area*) is cluttered, making the little speaker icon hard to find, you can access the Play Control dialog box by opening the Sounds and Audio Devices applet in Windows XP's Control Panel. On the Volume tab—the one that's on top by default—click the Advanced button under Device volume. In Windows Vista/7, open the Sound applet and double-click on the playback device you want to adjust. Under the Levels tab in the Properties dialog box, use the slider to adjust the volume.

If you don't have a little speaker in your system tray at all in Windows XP, you can add it. Just check the box next to the *Place volume icon in the taskbar* option in the Sounds and Audio Devices Properties dialog box, Volume tab. In Windows Vista and Windows 7, right-click on the taskbar and select Properties. Click the Customize button under Notification area. Use the Notification Area Icons applet to enable the volume controls. Presto!

• **Figure 17.26** Creative Labs 3DMIDI Player program

If the speaker volume is okay, open the volume controls in Windows by clicking the little speaker icon on the system tray, and make sure that both the master volume and the volume of the other controls are turned up (see Figure 17.27).

Speakers The second place to look for sound problems is the speakers. Make sure the speakers are turned on and are getting good power. Then make sure the speakers are plugged into the proper connection on the back of the sound card. If this all checks out, try playing a sound, using any sound program. If the sound program *looks* like it is playing—maybe the application has an equalizer that is moving or a status marker that shows that the application is playing the sound—you may have blown speakers. Try another pair and see if the sound returns.

Configuration Problems

Configuration errors occur when the sound card is physically good but some setting hasn't been properly configured. I also include drive problems in this category. These errors happen almost exclusively at installation, but they can appear on a working system, too.

The first place to check is Device Manager. If the driver has a problem, you'll see it right there. Try reinstalling the driver. If the driver doesn't show any problems, again try playing a sound and see if the player acts as though the sound is playing. If that's the case, you need to start touring the Sound applet or Sounds and Audio Devices applet to see if you've made a configuration error—perhaps you have the system configured for 5.1 when you have a stereo setup, or maybe you set the default sound output device to some other device. Take your time and look—configuration errors always show themselves.

Application Problems

Application problems are always the hardest to fix and tend to occur on a system that was previously playing sounds without trouble.

First, look for an error message (see Figure 17.28). If an error code appears, write it down *exactly* as you see it and head to the program's support site. Odds are very good that if you have the error text, you'll get the fix right away from the support site. Of course, you can always hope the

Tech Tip

Sound Quality

Most of the time, speakers come in a matched set—whether it's a 2.1, 4.1, 5.1, or other system—and the manufacturer includes adequate connecting wires for the whole set. On occasion, you might run into a system in which the user has connected pairs of speakers from different sets or rigged a surround sound system by replacing the stock wires with much longer wires. Either option can create a perfectly functional surround sound system that works for a specific room, but you should make sure that all the speakers require the same wattage and that high-quality wire is used to connect them.

If you troubleshoot a system in which two of the speakers are very quiet and two are very loud, the wattages are probably different between the two pairs. A simple check of the labels should suffice to troubleshoot, or you can swap out one pair for a different pair and see if that affects the volume issues. Cheap wire, on the other hand, simply degrades the sound quality. If the speakers sounded good before being strung on long wires but they now have a lot of low-grade noise, blame the wires.

Technically speaking, turning down the volume in the volume control program isn't a configuration problem; it's just something I always check at the same time I check the volume on the speakers.

• **Figure 17.27** Volume controls in Windows XP

• **Figure 17.28** Sample error message

built-in help has some support, but help systems tend to be a little light in providing real fixes.

Don't always blame the sound application—remember that any sound file might be corrupted. Most sound players will display a clear error message, but not always. Try playing the sound file with a different application.

Last, a good approach almost always is to reinstall the application.

■ Video Capture

A microphone, sound card, and software enable you to capture audio, but with a camera capable of capturing full-motion video as well as sound, you can turn the PC into your very own movie studio. This is called **video capture**. To capture video from another source requires you to have the proper hardware installed to provide an interface with the camcorder or video player and, if the source is analog, provide translation of the signal as well; plus you need a properly configured application to do the capturing. Once captured, you can use an application to edit the video file and upload it to YouTube or save it to DVD or other removable media.

Hardware

You need the proper hardware installed to capture video. From a digital signal, such as a modern camcorder that records directly to its own internal solid state hard drive, you simply run a cable from the USB out port on the camcorder to the USB port on your computer. When capturing from an analog source, such as a VHS cassette player or a Hi-8 tape, you'll need some kind of connection and translation hardware.

> Some video capture devices are external, while others are internal PCI or PCIe cards. If you have an internal video capture card, install it into your PC as you would any other expansion card.

The Pinnacle Studio MovieBox Ultimate (pictured in Figure 17.29), for example, offers two different dedicated video connections (S-Video in the middle and the yellow RCA jack next to it) and stereo RCA audio jacks. The box uses a USB 2.0 connector to plug into the PC.

You need a decent-grade computer with lots of free hard drive space and a substantial amount of RAM to import the video and audio streams from an external source. And you'll certainly need a serious processor when it comes time to edit and compile a new video from the source material. There's no simple rule for how much of any resource you'll need. Different projects have different demands on the hardware. If you're setting up a new computer for video capture, the simple rule is to get as powerful a system as possible with as much hard drive and RAM capacity as you can afford.

Once you have the hardware in place, the true heavy lifting in video capture falls on the software.

• **Figure 17.29** A video capture device

Software

With video editing applications, such as Adobe Premiere Elements or Apple Final Cut, you can import video and then work with it directly. Figure 17.30 shows the former software capturing video and audio translated through the Pinnacle blueBox from a Hi-8 camcorder. Most webcams—even those built into portable computers—are analog rather than digital devices. Thus some software automatically creates break points in the import to make the editing process easier.

• **Figure 17.30** Importing video in Adobe Premiere Elements

The video editing software enables you to take video and audio from one or many sources and arrange clips into a time line. You can add and edit various transitions between clips, shorten clips, and so on. Figure 17.31 shows the storyboard from Final Cut Pro and a how-to video my team produced in-house.

• **Figure 17.31** Editing in Final Cut Pro

Once you've finished the editing process, you can export to a file for archiving, sending out on optical disc, or posting to a video sharing site. With an audio file, as discussed earlier, this is a simple process. You pick a format such as MP3 and save the file. Video is far more complicated.

A video is two or more separate tracks—moving picture and audio—that each go through a compression algorithm. Otherwise, the resulting files would be huge, even for short videos. The compressed tracks then get wrapped up into a **container file**, what's often called a **wrapper**. When you receive a file saved in a standard wrapper, such as .MOV for a QuickTime Movie file, you have no way to know for certain which codecs were used to compress the video or audio tracks inside that container file (see Figure 17.32).

• **Figure 17.32** A standard container file holds multiple tracks, each encoded separately.

Codecs

Video files use standard audio codecs for the audio tracks, such as WAV or MP3, but vary wildly in the type of video codecs used. Just as with audio codecs, video codecs take a video stream and compress it by using various algorithms. Here are some of the standard video codecs:

- MPEG-2 Part 2, used for DVDs

- MPEG-4 Part 2, a codec often used for Internet broadcasts; you'll find implementations of it with other names, such as DivX

- H.264, used for high-definition movies for Blu-ray Discs, among others

- Windows Media Video (WMV), the family of Microsoft-developed codecs

- Theora, an open-source codec developed to go with the Vorbis audio codec as part of the Ogg project

- TrueMotion VP6, used in Adobe Flash; and VP7, used for Skype video conferencing, among others

- VC-1 is a Microsoft-designed codec that competes with H.264 and other higher-end codecs for the hearts and minds of Blu-ray Disc developers. You'll usually find it wrapped in a WMV container file (see the following section).

Wrappers

When both the video and audio streams of your video file are compressed, the file is placed into some sort of container file or wrapper. The key thing to note here is that the wrapper file doesn't necessarily specify how the video or audio tracks were encoded. You can look at two seemingly identical movie files, for example, both saved with the .MOV file extension, and find that one will play audio and video just fine in Windows Media Player, but the other one might play only the audio and not the video because

Media Player lacks the specific codec needed to decode the video stream. (More on this in the "Troubleshooting Video Capture and Playback" section.) Here are some of the standard video wrappers:

- ASF, a container used mainly for WMA and WMV streams; note that you can also have a WMV wrapper for a WMV-format file.

- AVI, the standard container file for Windows

- Flash Video (.FLV) contains streams encoded with various codecs, such as H.263 or VP6; it can also handle H.264 codec. Flash Video has become the dominant standard for displaying video content on the Web through places such as YouTube and Hulu.

- MOV, the standard container file for Apple QuickTime for both Mac OS X and Windows

- MPEG-2 Transport Stream (MPEG-TS), a container for broadcasting that can handle many streams

- Ogg, a container file made for the open source Vorbis and Theora codecs

Troubleshooting Video Capture and Playback

Video capture and playback suffer from several quirks. On the capture side, you'll find dropped frames, problems synchronizing video and audio when capturing content from an analog device, and generally poor-quality captures. On the playback side, the only real issue is missing codecs.

Dropped Frames

Many things cause an initial capture to drop frames, the end result of which is loss of video information and choppy playback. This happens with both analog and digital sources, so it's not necessarily a conversion issue, and it's maddeningly common.

The most common fix for dropped frames is to *turn stuff off*. Some of this is obvious. If you're surfing the Web or doing instant messaging while trying to capture video, you'll drop frames with wild abandon. Don't do it. In fact, disconnect the computer completely from the Internet so no traffic happens in the background. Only do video capture on that machine and use another computer if you need to multitask.

Often the viewing of content you're capturing—while in the capture process—causes dropped frames. Best practice is to know what you're importing, turn off the playback or preview feature, and then start the capture. But the obvious programs aren't necessarily the primary cause of dropped frames.

Windows is a wildly extensible operating system, and programmers love to dump helper applications to run in the background to optimize their specific application. Install Apple's iTunes, for example, and you'll get more than you bargained for in programs installed. To go along with the iTunes player, the installation puts in automatic update-checking tools, iPod helpers, a quick-launch for QuickTime, and more.

The best solution is to have a machine dedicated to video capture. If you have a machine with multiple functions, however, you can turn off some of the automatically loading helper applications before you start the video capture process. You do this by stopping processes and services through Task Manager.

Sync Problems

There's also a common problem of video and audio going out of sync in the process of burning from a hard drive to a DVD, but that's a distinctly different problem than a lack of A/V sync in the capture process.

Capturing a video stream and an audio stream simultaneously can be tough, because it takes the computer a lot longer to encode the video stream than the audio stream. This can lead to significant disconnection between the video and audio streams, so they become desynchronized. It's surprisingly easy to create a movie that's very badly lip-synced! The process of synchronizing audio and video is called **A/V sync**.

You can fix this problem sometimes by changing software or even versions of software. Alternatively, if you're having problems with an analog capture, you can record the analog signal into a digital video camcorder and then try to capture from the digital device—a bit clunky, perhaps, but it can work. Finally, you do the last solution in processing, where you manually separate the audio and video streams and then put the whole thing back together synced properly.

Dealing with video capture can be difficult and time consuming, especially in the analog to digital process. A good resource to start learning the detailed ins and outs is with the folks at the Digital FAQ: www.digitalfaq.com.

Poor Capture Quality

A dedicated A/V computer should have a fast processor and a lot of RAM. You'll want plenty of hard drive storage space too.

Numerous factors can degrade the quality of a video capture, including background programs, marginal hardware for the job, and poor-quality source materials. For the background program issue, follow the same procedures as you did above with the dropped frames. If the computer or the capture components can't do the job, the only fix is to upgrade. The best things to upgrade are the capture hardware and the CPU. It goes almost without saying that you'll need gobs of RAM too.

There's very little you can do if your source material, such as an old video cassette, has degraded. You're simply not going to get a pristine capture from a damaged source. You can sometimes get better quality by having the heads on the camcorder or player cleaned or by using the camcorder on which the tape was initially recorded.

Missing Codecs

All versions of Windows come with some audio and video codecs installed. The default audio codecs will handle most common music formats, though you'll need to download the Vorbis codec if you want to use that format. Video codecs are a different animal.

The first clue you might have that your computer doesn't have the codec to process a video file properly is that the sound will play but no picture will appear. Occasionally, whatever media player you use will tell you that it's missing a video codec and attempt to go out onto the Internet to download a codec automatically. You can also download a codec or set of codecs manually.

• **Figure 17.33** Default audio codecs in Windows XP SP2

• **Figure 17.34** Default video codecs in Windows XP SP2

Windows XP makes it easy to see the installed codecs. In the Control Panel, open the Sounds and Audio Devices applet. Select the Hardware tab | Audio Codecs and click the Properties button. In the Audio Codecs Properties dialog box, select the Properties tab and you'll see all the installed audio codecs (see Figure 17.33).

Similarly, you can see the video codecs by choosing the Video Codecs option on the Hardware tab. Click through to the Properties tab. Figure 17.34 shows the default video codecs in Windows XP.

Microsoft made the codecs a bit more difficult to find in Windows Vista/7. In Vista/7, open Windows Media Player. Press CTRL-M to show the classic menus. Select Help | About Windows Media Player to open the About Windows Media Player dialog box (see Figure 17.35).

Click the link for Technical Support Information and Windows will open your default Web browser with a long page showing various multimedia settings. Scroll down the page and you'll find the audio and video codecs installed (see Figure 17.36).

If you don't have a codec that you need, you can download that specific codec. A great site for codec information is www.fourcc.org.

You can also download codec packs, such as the Vista Codec Package available at www.afreecodec.com. The packs contain just about everything you need to view and hear content found on the Internet.

• **Figure 17.35** About Windows Media Player dialog box in Windows Vista

Figure 17.36 Viewing audio and video codecs installed in Windows Vista

■ TV Tuners

TV tuners often include components for video capture, so you can get both devices on one card or expansion device.

With a **TV tuner**, you can have it all in one package: a computer and the latest TV show as well. Most local stations (in the United States, at least) broadcast high-definition signals, so with the proper TV tuner, you can watch your HDTV without any of the artifacting you see with both cable and satellite feeds. Plus you can make use of typical cable or satellite feeds to watch television as you would with a regular TV. To make it all happen requires four components: a tuner device, an antenna or cable connection, a tuning application, and some sort of program guide. We'll look at troubleshooting at the end.

Tuner Hardware

TV tuners come in just about every expansion option available for computers: expansion cards that plug into PCI or PCIe slots on the motherboard; PC Card or ExpressCard for portable computers; or Hi Speed USB for desktop and laptop computers. Figure 17.37 shows a PCIe version of an ATI tuner card.

To install a TV tuner, follow standard installation procedures.

To pick up a signal on the TV tuner, just as with a standalone television, you need some source. Most can handle a

Figure 17.37 ATI TV tuner card

Cross Check

Monitor Quality

The signal is not the only thing that affects your picture quality with a TV tuner. The quality and settings of the monitor itself matter a lot too. Viewing an HDTV signal on a 15-inch dim LCD won't quite do the content justice! Refer to Chapter 13 and see if you can answer these questions. What sort of response rate works for full-motion video without blurring? What does "native resolution" mean and what's the effect of using a non-native resolution? What tool do you use to change video settings in Windows XP? What about Windows Vista or Windows 7?

cable TV connection, for example, or an over-the-air antenna. Figure 17.38 shows a USB Hauppauge HDTV tuner card with retractable antenna. For such a small device, it picks up HDTV signals quite well. You'll get the best results for uncompressed HD signals by using a serious, mounted-on-the-rooftop metal antenna with lots of tines.

Tuner hardware comes with a standard coaxial connection. You can plug in a cable or satellite source just as you would with any regular television.

Tuner Software

Once you've installed the hardware, you need to load the specific application or applications that make the tuner work as a tuner. If you have a copy of Windows Media Center, that will often be the tool of choice. Tuner card distributors bundle third-party applications with their cards. Figure 17.39 shows the EyeTV software enabling the computer to show television shows.

• **Figure 17.38** Hauppauge TV tuner with retractable antenna

• **Figure 17.39** EyeTV tuner application

Tuner Troubleshooting

The two biggest issues with TV tuner devices are operating system compatibility and poor reception. Some cards simply don't work with Windows Vista or Windows 7, due to driver incompatibility or some other issue. The only fix for this problem is to use one that does work.

The antenna that comes with your tuner should enable you to pick up TV broadcasts in most places, certainly around cities. But a small sliver of metal can only do so well, so you'll experience stuttering, essentially lost frames that may or may not make the program you're viewing viewable. So an antenna used primarily for portable computing, such as the telescoping model pictured in Figure 17.38, is great, but if you install a tuner in a static computer, consider investing in a proper outdoor antenna.

Beyond A+

Publishing Multimedia

Created content needs an audience, whether that audience is close family, friends, or the general public. Once you've finished recording some original music or creating the new great video, the Internet today offers many venues for sharing with others. Any Web site can host video and sound files, but social media sites like Facebook make it easy to share multimedia files. The 800-pound gorilla in the virtual room, though, is Google's YouTube.

You can get a YouTube account for free and start uploading multimedia files within minutes. The files can be made available to the public or kept private according to your preferences. With ad revenue capabilities, you can make money off multimedia files you post to YouTube as well. Finally, you can post to YouTube and then embed files into your Web site with ease.

I embed the CompTIA A+ videos I make at my Web site:

www.totalsem.com/videos

You can also access them directly from Total Seminars' YouTube channel (see Figure 17.40).

When you want to publish your multimedia files, go to www.youtube.com and create a new account. Don't forget to send me a link!

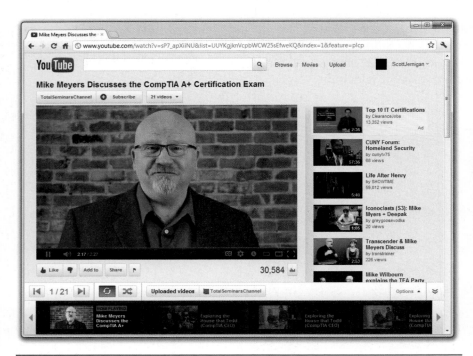

• **Figure 17.40** Hi!

Chapter 17 Review

■ Chapter Summary

After reading this chapter and completing the exercises, you should understand the following aspects of multimedia.

Describe how to implement sound in a PC

- The process by which sounds are stored in electronic format on your PC is called sampling. Sampling means capturing the state or quality of a particular sound wave a set number of times each second. All the characteristics of a particular sound wave—amplitude, frequency, timbre—need to be recorded and translated into ones and zeros to reproduce that sound accurately within the computer and out to your speakers. Sounds are sampled thousands of times per second. The amount of information stored at each sampling is called the bit depth, and the higher the bit depth, the better the recording.

- The popular WAV file format (as well as most other recorded sound formats) is based on PCM. WAV files can be huge, especially when sampled at high frequency and depth, so compression is a popular way to reduce the file size of recorded sounds. The most popular compressed file type is MP3.

- To play sounds, you must have some form of player software, such as Windows Media Player. Not all players can play all types of sound files. Some file formats, such as RealMedia, require their own proprietary players.

- MIDI files are not recordings like WAV files. A MIDI file is a text file that takes advantage of the sound processing hardware to enable the PC to produce sound. Programmers use these small files to tell the sound card which notes to play, how long, how loud, and on which instruments to play them, and so forth.

- Sound cards use either FM synthesis or wave table synthesis to store notes for MIDI. FM synthesis electronically simulates various instruments, whereas wave table synthesis uses pre-recorded instruments.

- A large number of other sound file formats are available, such as AAC and WMA. Sounds can also be found in video formats, applications, and streaming media, such as the Flash videos on YouTube.

- Low-end sound processors do little more than translate, which means that the CPU has to do the heavy lifting on the processing front. Better sound processors, in contrast, shoulder much of the processing burden and bring a series of extra features to the table. Most mid-range and all high-end sound processors offer support for various surround sound standards, enabling equally equipped games and other applications to provide positional audio effects and detailed sound modeling.

- Every sound card supports two speakers or a pair of headphones, but many better sound cards support five or more speakers in discrete channels. These multiple speakers provide surround sound and thumping bass through a subwoofer.

- Better sound cards have a lower signal-to-noise ratio and support for multiple audio connections, such as a microphone, line in, and S/PDIF. The latter is for high-end audio.

- Speaker standards include stereo (which uses a left speaker and a right speaker), 2.1 (stereo with an additional subwoofer), and surround sound. Do yourself or your client a favor and spend the extra money for good speakers. They don't cost that much more than cheap speakers and they make an enormous difference for the user experience.

- Surround sound is popular for games and DVD/Blu-ray movies. A number of surround sound standards exist, but the most common are Dolby Digital and DTS. The Dolby Digital and DTS standards both require at least five speakers and a subwoofer.

- You can use input devices such as microphones and MIDI-enabled devices to create music on your PC. You'll need software that can work with these devices.

- Sound card installation can be divided into three major steps: physical installation, device driver installation, and configuration.

- Although the physical installation of a sound card is straightforward, knowing where to plug in multiple speakers can be a bit of a challenge.

- It is preferable to use the driver that comes with the sound card as opposed to the Windows built-in drivers.

- Look for configuration programs in the Control Panel applet for audio, and in any proprietary applications that are installed with the sound card.

- You can divide sound problems into three groups: hardware, configuration, and application problems. The two first places to check when you suspect a hardware problem are the volume controls and speaker connectivity. Configuration errors almost always take place at installation of the sound card. Application problems are often the most challenging of all sound problems. Your best hope is an error message; you can then check the program's Web site for help.

Install and configure video capture hardware and software

- To capture video from a source requires you to have the proper hardware installed to provide an interface with the camcorder or video player and, if the source is analog, to provide translation of the signal as well. You also need a properly configured application to do the capturing.

- With a fully digital device, you can capture directly to the PC by using a FireWire or USB connection. With analog devices, you need some sort of translation hardware.

- A computer dedicated to video capture and editing needs to be a pretty stout machine, with lots of hard drive space and RAM. The capture and editing software has a major role in determining the quality of the capture and any subsequent video.

- A video is two or more separate tracks—moving picture and audio—that each go through a compression algorithm. The compressed tracks then get wrapped up into a container file or wrapper. A video can be compressed in one of the standard audio codecs, such as MP3, and one of many video codecs, such as H.264. The wrapper can likewise be one of many styles, such as AVI.

- Troubleshooting video capture generally falls into three categories: dropped frames, synchronization problems with audio and video, and general picture-quality issues. The simplest solution for dropped frames is to turn off any unnecessary program running, including processes and services. Sync problems generally require better software or additional hardware to solve. Poor-quality captures can be helped with better equipment or by turning off unnecessary programs, though a poor-quality source cannot be overcome.

- If you're missing a codec to play a video, you can download codec packs from a variety of sources. The place to start is www.fourcc.org.

Set up a PC to view television signals

- Setting up a PC to view television signals requires several components: a tuner device, an antenna or cable connection, a tuning application, and some sort of program guide. Tuner hardware comes in many forms, such as PCI or PCIe expansion cards and USB devices. Tuner devices come with a standard coaxial jack for connecting an exterior antenna or cable or satellite connection. Companies bundle specific tuner software and program guides with their cards.

- About the only issues you'll run into with tuner devices is software incompatibility (older cards, for example, might not have drivers for Windows Vista or Windows 7, or for any 64-bit operating system) and poor source. A small antenna simply can't capture the same quality or quantity of signal that a large, multi-tined traditional outdoor antenna can get.

■ Key Terms

2.1 *(532)*
5.1 *(532)*
AC'97 *(528)*
amplitude *(523)*
autosensing *(539)*

A/V sync *(546)*
bit depth *(524)*
CD quality *(524)*
codec *(524)*
container file *(544)*

decibels *(529)*
Digital Theatre Systems (DTS) *(532)*
DirectSound3D (DS3D) *(532)*
DirectX *(532)*
Dolby Digital *(532)*
environmental audio extensions (EAX) *(533)*
FM synthesis *(525)*
frequency *(523)*
Intel High Definition Audio (HDA) *(528)*
MIDI-enabled device *(535)*
monaural *(524)*
MP3 *(524)*
musical instrument digital interface (MIDI) *(524)*
polyphony *(525)*

positional audio *(532)*
pulse code modulation (PCM) *(524)*
sampling *(523)*
satellites *(532)*
signal-to-noise ratio *(529)*
Sony/Philips Digital Interface (S/PDIF) *(532)*
stereo *(524)*
streaming media *(527)*
subwoofer *(529)*
timbre *(523)*
TV tuner *(548)*
video capture *(542)*
wave table synthesis *(525)*
wrapper *(544)*

■ Key Term Quiz

Use the Key Terms list to complete the sentences that follow. Not all terms will be used.

1. A sound card can simulate a number of different instruments by using _____.

2. Unlike recorded sounds, _____ uses specialized text files that tell the sound card which sounds to play.

3. 44.1-KHz stereo is also known as _____ audio.

4. The process of capturing the state or quality of a particular sound wave a set number of times each second is called _____.

5. The most common compressed audio format is _____.

6. A series of instructions telling a computer how to read a compressed file is called a(n) _____.

7. You can view television channels on your computer by using a(n) _____.

8. To enable a computer to record full-motion video and sound, use _____.

9. The loudness of a sound is called its _____.

10. Better sound cards that can detect a device plugged into a port and adapt the features of that port are called _____ sound cards.

■ Multiple-Choice Quiz

1. CD-quality sound samples are recorded at 44 KHz, with 16-bit depth and what else?

 A. Monaural

 B. Stereo

 C. 5.1

 D. 2.1

2. What is the most common compressed sound format?

 A. MP3

 B. WAV

 C. VOC

 D. TXT

3. Almost all sound cards use which expansion bus?

 A. ISA

 B. AGP

 C. Internal

 D. PCI

4. Which audio file format can compress sound files without losing any data?

 A. MP3

 B. MIDI

 C. WAV

 D. FLAC

5. Which component of DirectX offered only a range of commands to place a sound anywhere in 3-D space?

 A. DirectSound

 B. DirectSound3D

 C. EAX

 D. A3D

6. What is the name of the direct competitor to Dolby Digital?

 A. DirectSound

 B. DirectSound3D

 C. DTS

 D. Surround Sound

7. To what does the *.1* in 5.1 or 2.1 refer?

 A. Volumetric sound positioning

 B. Subwoofer

 C. Subchannels

 D. Reverb positional matrices

8. Which version of DirectX introduced DirectSound3D?

 A. Version 8.0

 B. Version 3

 C. Version 2

 D. Version 1

9. Jane's sound card is suddenly not making any sound. She suspects that the volume is turned down. She checks the speaker volume and sees that it is turned up. What should she check next?

 A. The volume control program

 B. The application

 C. The speaker power

 D. Device Manager

10. What type of file is a MIDI file?

 A. Audio

 B. Binary

 C. MP3

 D. Text

11. Which company created the SoundBlaster sound card?

 A. Creative Audio

 B. Creative Labs

 C. EAX

 D. Microsoft

12. You want to copy audio from a CD player onto your computer. To which jack on the sound card should you connect your CD player?

 A. Line in

 B. Microphone

 C. Line out

 D. Digital out

13. Which term refers to recording sound on a PC?

 A. Import

 B. Capture

 C. Encode

 D. Compress/decompress

14. What does PCM stand for?

 A. Pulse code modulation

 B. Pulse code manipulation

 C. Peripheral component management

 D. Packaged codec management

15. If the first movement of Beethoven's Fifth Symphony were saved as a computer file, which file type would be the smallest in size?

 A. MP3

 B. WAV

 C. ASF

 D. MIDI

■ Essay Quiz

1. Detail in your own words how you think sound aided the evolution of the computer. What aspects of sound are necessary to computers? Why is sound needed?

2. Outline how you could use the connections provided on a modern sound card to create a multimedia home theater with your computer. Be sure to include hardware discussed in previous chapters, such as Blu-ray Disc and DVD-ROM drives.

3. Write an essay on the kind of TV tuner you would need for your computer. Detail what you personally would like to accomplish with your computer and how a TV tuner card would help you.

4. Your clients have been having trouble with dropped frames on video capture. Write a memo describing the things that they should check before calling for a technician.

5. Your boss has decided that all systems in the office need new speakers because the company that games together has more cohesion and happiness. Write a few paragraphs describing the speaker choices available and why one is better than the others.

Lab Projects

• Lab Project 17.1

Take a tour of the Web site for Creative Labs: www.creative.com. What sound-related products are currently featured there? Check out the specs for Creative's various SoundBlaster cards. Do you see sound cards that use an interface other than PCI? Which features are available only on high-end cards? Which model would you choose to upgrade your current system? Which would you choose if you were building a new system?

• Lab Project 17.2

Uninstall and reinstall the audio drivers on your system. First, check your sound card manufacturer's Web site for an updated driver. Reinstall, using the most recent driver you can find. Do any problems crop up during the process? After you get the new driver installed and working, do you notice an improvement in performance?

Portable Computing

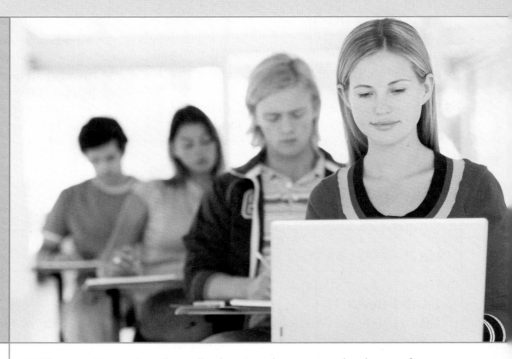

> *"The great thing about a computer notebook is that no matter how much you stuff into it, it doesn't get bigger or heavier."*
>
> —BILL GATES, *BUSINESS @ THE SPEED OF THOUGHT*

In this chapter, you will learn how to

- **Describe the many types of portable computing devices available**
- **Explain ways to expand portable computers**
- **Manage and maintain portable computers**
- **Upgrade and repair portable computers**
- **Troubleshoot portable computers**

There are times when the walls close in, when you need a change of scenery to get that elusive spark that inspires greatness... or sometimes you just need to get away from your coworkers for a few hours because they're driving you nuts! For many occupations, that's difficult to do. You need access to your documents and spreadsheets; you can't function without e-mail or the Internet. In short, you need a computer to get your job done.

Portable computing devices combine mobility with accessibility to bring you the best of both worlds; portables enable you to take some or even all of your computing capabilities with you when you go. Featuring all the bells and whistles of a desktop system, many portables offer a seamless transition from desk to café table.

This chapter looks at the classic portable computer, essentially a desktop PC transformed into a mobile format. Classic portables run Windows, Mac OS X, or some flavor of Linux.

Other portable devices, such as smartphones and tablets, run mobile operating systems designed to take advantage of small form factors and touch screens. In practice (and on the CompTIA A+ 220-801 exam), such mobile devices differ a lot from classic portable computers.

■ Portable Computing Devices

All portable devices share certain features. For output, they use LCD screens, although these vary from 20-inch behemoths to diminutive 10-inch displays. Portable computing devices employ sound of varying quality, from bland mono playback to fairly nice faux-surround reproductions. All of them run on DC electricity stored in batteries when not plugged into an AC outlet.

When asked about portable computing devices, most folks describe the traditional clamshell **notebook** computer, such as the one in Figure 18.1, with built-in LCD monitor, keyboard, and input device (a *touchpad*, in this case). The notebook is also called a portable or a **laptop**. All the terms are synonymous. A typical laptop computer functions as a fully standalone PC, potentially even replacing the desktop. The one in Figure 18.1, for example, has all of the features you expect the modern PC to have, such as a fast CPU, lots of RAM, a high-capacity hard drive, an optical drive, and an adequate sound system. Attach it to a network and you can browse the Internet and send e-mail.

• **Figure 18.1** A notebook PC

Input Devices

Portable computers come with a variety of input devices. Most have a fully functional keyboard and a device to control the mouse pointer.

Keyboard Quirks

Laptop keyboards differ somewhat from those of desktop PCs, primarily because manufacturers have to cram all the keys onto a smaller form factor. They use the QWERTY format, but manufacturers make choices with key size and placement of the non-alphabet characters. Almost every portable keyboard uses a **Function (FN) key** to enable some keys to perform a third duty. Figure 18.2 compares a standard desktop keyboard with a large portable keyboard. You'll note that the latter has no separate number pad on the right. To use the number pad, you press the FN key (lower left in this case) to transform the (7, 8, 9), (U, I, O), (J, K, L), and (M) keys into the (7, 8, 9), (4, 5, 6), (1, 2, 3), and (0) keys.

> The FN key also enables you to toggle other features specific to a portable, such as network connectivity and external displays. We'll examine these options in the next section of the chapter.

• **Figure 18.2** Keyboard comparison

Pointing Devices

Portables need a way to control your mouse pointer, but their smaller size requires manufacturers to come up with clever solutions. First, portables today have USB ports and can use every type of pointing device you'd see on a desktop. Second, early portables used *trackballs*, often plugged in like a mouse and clipped to the side of the case. Other models with trackballs placed them in front of the keyboard at the edge of the case nearest the user, or behind the keyboard at the edge nearest the screen.

The next wave to hit the laptop market was IBM's **TrackPoint** device, a joystick the size of a pencil eraser, situated in the center of the keyboard (see Figure 18.3). With the TrackPoint, you can move the pointer around without taking your fingers away from the "home" typing position. You use a forefinger to push the joystick around, and then click or right-click, using two buttons below the spacebar. This type of pointing device has since been licensed for use by other manufacturers, and it continues to appear on laptops today.

• **Figure 18.3** IBM TrackPoint

Mike Meyers' CompTIA A+ Guide to 801: Managing and Troubleshooting PCs

By far the most common laptop pointing device found today is the **touchpad** (see Figure 18.4)—a flat, touch-sensitive pad just in front of the keyboard. To operate a touchpad, you simply glide your finger across its surface to move the pointer, and tap the surface once or twice to single- or double-click. You can also click by using buttons just below the pad. Most people get the hang of this technique after just a few minutes of practice. The main advantage of the touchpad over previous laptop pointing devices is that it uses no moving parts—a fact that can really extend the life of a hard-working laptop.

Some manufacturers today include a **multitouch** touchpad that enables you to perform actions with multiple fingers, such as scrolling up and down or swiping to another screen or desktop.

• **Figure 18.4** Touchpad on a laptop

Display Types

Laptops come in a variety of sizes and at varying costs. One major contributor to the overall cost of a laptop is the size of the LCD screen. Most laptops offer a range between 10.1-inch to 17.3-inch screens (measured diagonally), while a few offer just over 20-inch screens.

Many manufacturers are phasing out the standard 4:3 aspect ratio screen in favor of the widescreen format. **Aspect ratio** is the comparison of the screen width to the screen height, as you'll recall from Chapter 13. Depending on screen resolution, widescreens can have varying aspect ratios of 10:6, 16:9, 16:9.5, or 16:10.

Laptop LCD screens come in a variety of supported resolutions, described with acronyms such as XGA, WXGA, WSXGA, and more. The *W* in front of the letters indicates widescreen. Table 18.1 lists commonly supported laptop display resolutions.

Laptop LCDs are the same in almost every way as desktop LCDs with a TFT screen, an inverter (if using a CCFL backlight), and a backlight (CCFL or LED). You know all about these screens from Chapter 13. Expect questions about laptop displays, but know that they're pretty much the same as desktop displays. The only major difference is that they contain an antenna, but we'll discuss this later in the chapter.

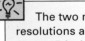 The two most common resolutions are WXGA for the 14- to 15-inch models and HD 1080 for the 17.3-inch models.

Table 18.1	Common Screen Resolutions	
Acronym	**Name**	**Native Resolution**
XGA	eXtended Graphics Array	1024 × 768
HD 720	HD 720	1280 × 720
WXGA (16:10)	Wide eXtended Graphics Array	1280 × 800
WXGA (16:9)	Wide eXtended Graphics Array	1366 × 768
SXGA	Super eXtended Graphics Array	1280 × 1024
SXGA+	Super eXtended Graphics Array Plus	1400 × 1050
HD 900	HD 900	1600 × 900
WSXGA+	Widescreen SXGA Plus	1680 × 1050
UXGA	Ultra eXtended Graphics Array	1600 × 1200
HD 1080	HD 1080	1920 × 1080
WUXGA	Widescreen UXGA	1920 × 1200

Laptop screens typically come with one of two types of finish: **matte** or **high-gloss**. The matte finish was the industry standard for many years and offered a good trade-off between richness of colors and the reduction of glare. The better screens have a wide viewing angle and decent response time. The major drawback for matte-finished laptop screens is that they wash out a lot in bright light. Using such a laptop at an outdoor café, for example, is almost hopeless during daylight.

Manufacturers released high-gloss laptop screens in 2006, and they rapidly took over many store shelves. The high-gloss finish offers sharper contrast, richer colors, and wider viewing angles when compared to the matte screens. Each manufacturer has a different name for high-gloss coatings. Dell calls theirs TrueLife, Acer calls theirs CrystalBrite, and HP calls theirs BrightView. The drawback to the high-gloss screens is that, contrary to what the manufacturers' claim, they pick up lots of reflection from nearby objects, including the user! So although they're usable outside during the day, you'll need to contend with increased reflection as well.

With the advent of LED backlighting for LCD panels, many manufacturers have switched back to an anti-glare screen, though they're not quite the matte screens of old. When the LED brightness is up high, these are lovely screens. (See the "Troubleshooting Portable Computers" section later in this chapter for issues specific to LED-backlit portables.)

As with other LCD technologies that you'll recall from Chapter 13, most LCD/LED screens use twisted nematic (TN) technology. Some laptop screens use In-Plane Switching (IPS) panels for the greater viewing angle and better color quality. You'll find IPS panels on expensive, professional-grade desktop-replacement portables.

What you will *not* find on portable PCs are two other display technologies, plasma and organic light-emitting diode (OLED). Plasma displays demand a lot more electricity than LCDs demand and are completely inappropriate for portable PCs. OLED screens sip energy when compared to LCDs, but they're still so expensive that you'll only find them on a few smartphones today.

The CompTIA A+ 801 exam objectives refer to plasma and OLED displays for laptops, but these don't exist. You'll find OLED displays on a few smartphones, but not on portable PCs, at least not at the time of this writing.

Desktop Replacements

A *desktop replacement* features a massive screen, a full-size keyboard, an optical drive (or maybe two), and plenty of hard drive space (see the portable on the left in Figure 18.5). Considering that it weighs almost as much as a mini-tower PC (or at least it feels like it does when I'm lugging it through the airport!), such a portable can be considered a **desktop replacement** because it does everything most people want to do with a desktop PC and doesn't compromise on performance just to make the laptop a few pounds lighter or the battery last an extra hour. Think power first, portability second.

The current sweet spot for desktop replacements is a 17.3-inch monitor with 16+ GB of DDR3 and either dual 1- to 2-TB HDDs or a single 512-GB to 1-TB SSD. Dedicated graphics are a must. Desktop replacements run the latest Intel high-end mobile processors and, of course, run Windows 7 64-bit edition. Such perfection in computing in a sub-8-pound format doesn't come cheap, so the question that immediately arises is, why buy a desktop replacement?

• **Figure 18.5** Desktop replacement (left) next to a standard portable computer (right)

Desktop replacements appeal to a diverse group of users. Most obviously, dedicated road warriors need to do everything on the plane, on the train, and in the hotel room. Second, having a computer that can work well on the road and in the office is convenient. Finally, some folks just prefer the compactness of a laptop. You can, after all, put it out of sight when you're finished with it and not have to dedicate space to an equally powerful desktop computer.

Netbooks

Netbooks offer a robust computing platform with low cost and long battery life. These machines usually have displays in the 10-inch range, small hard drives, and CPUs geared more for minimal power usage than raw speed.

A prime example of the netbook is the ASUS Eee PC, shown in Figure 18.6 sitting on a full-sized laptop. This netbook has a 9-inch screen, a 1.6-GHz Intel Atom CPU, and a small solid-state drive, and runs a customized Linux distribution. One distinguishing feature of these netbooks is the use of Intel's Atom processor. The Atom CPU is very useful for keeping power usage down but has much less computing power than its more power-hungry siblings. Therefore, most netbooks run either Windows 7 Starter edition or some form of Linux that is better suited for their limited resources.

• **Figure 18.6** ASUS Eee PC sitting on a normal laptop

Ultrabooks

Thin, light, and powerful, **Ultrabooks** are as much about power and portability as they are about looks. Ultrabooks are for people who can't give up the power of high-end computers but can afford to pay more for a smaller package. Intel set up the Ultrabook specifications in 2011, defining the form factor to use power-sipping Intel processors with integrated graphics. These Ultrabooks have maximum dimensions (18 to 23 mm thick, depending on the size of the screen) and a minimum battery life (5 hours). Several manufacturers are stepping into the Ultrabook market, mostly copying the thin-slice aesthetic of the MacBook Air. You won't find optical drives on these, and most use solid-state drives for storage. Some people find this limiting; those *in the know* (read: young people) won't care, as long as they can edit their HD movies while drinking at a coffee shop and looking good (see Figure 18.7).

Tablet PCs

Microsoft started the **Tablet PC** initiative way back in 2001, defining the devices as fully featured portables running a tablet-aware version of Windows and using a stylus to interact directly with the screen. Many Tablet PCs have come to market since then, fulfilling the needs of specific professions, notably medicine.

Instead of (or in addition to) a keyboard and mouse, Tablet PCs provide a screen that doubles as an input device. With a special pen, called a **stylus**, you can actually write on the screen (see Figure 18.8). Just make sure you don't grab your fancy Cross ballpoint pen accidentally and start writing on

Tablet PC is a Microsoft term and is *not* the equivalent of a tablet such as the Apple iPad or Samsung Galaxy Tab. The latter devices derive from the mobile phone market, as mentioned at the beginning of this chapter, so they're *not* PCs, but rather a unique class of mobile devices. According to Microsoft, a Tablet PC runs Windows.

• **Figure 18.7** Ultrabook (photo courtesy of Intel Free Press)

the screen! Unlike some touch screens, most Tablet PC screens are not pressure sensitive—you have to use the stylus to write on the screen. Tablet PCs come in two main form factors: *convertibles*, which include a keyboard that you can fold out of the way, and *slates*, which do away with the keyboard entirely. The convertible Tablet PC in Figure 18.8, for example, looks and functions just like the typical clamshell laptop shown back in Figure 18.1. But here it's shown with the screen rotated 180 degrees and snapped flat so it functions as a slate. Pretty slick!

• **Figure 18.8** A Tablet PC

Early Tablet PCs ran Windows XP Tablet edition. Windows Vista and Windows 7 support tablet features in all editions. You'll recall from Chapter 12 the dedicated Pen and Input Devices applet in Windows Vista. Windows Vista and 7 have a specific Tablet PC Settings applet (see Figure 18.9) that enables you to configure the tablet to recognize handwriting, place menus conveniently for right- or left-handed users, and more.

In applications that aren't "tablet-aware," the stylus acts just like a mouse, enabling you to select items, double-click, right-click, and so on. To input text with the stylus, you can either tap keys on a virtual keyboard (shown in Figure 18.10), write in the writing utility (shown in Figure 18.11), or use speech recognition software. With a little practice, most users find the computer's accuracy in recognizing their handwriting to be sufficient for most text input, although speedy touch-typists will probably still want to use a keyboard when typing longer documents.

Tablet PCs work well when you have limited space or have to walk around and use a laptop. Anyone who has ever tried to type with one hand while walking around the factory floor and holding the laptop with the other hand will immediately appreciate the beauty of a Tablet PC. In this scenario, Tablet PCs are most effective when combined with applications designed to be used with a stylus instead of a keyboard. An inventory control program, for example, might present drop-down lists and radio buttons to the user, making a stylus the perfect input tool. With the right custom application, Tablet PCs become indispensable tools.

Microsoft encourages software developers to take advantage of a feature they call *digital ink*, which allows applications to accept pen strokes as input without first converting the pen strokes into text or mouse-clicks. In Microsoft Journal, which comes with Tablet PCs, you can write on the screen just as though you were writing on

• **Figure 18.9** Tablet PC Settings applet

● **Figure 18.10** The virtual keyboard

a paper legal pad (see Figure 18.12). Many other applications, including Microsoft Office, allow you to add ink annotations. Imagine sitting on an airplane reviewing a Microsoft Word document and simply scribbling your comments on the screen (see Figure 18.13). No more printing out hard copy and breaking out the red pen for me! Imagine running a PowerPoint presentation and being able to annotate your presentation as you go.

Many useful third-party applications are designed specifically to take advantage of the Tablet PC form factor. In fields such as law and medicine,

● **Figure 18.11** The writing pad

• **Figure 18.12** Microsoft Journal preserves pen strokes as digital ink.

where Tablet PCs have been especially popular, the choices are endless. One handy free utility that anyone who spends time in front of an audience (teachers, salespeople, cult leaders, and so on) will appreciate is InkyBoard (www.cfcassidy.com/Inkyboard). InkyBoard provides a virtual dry-erase board, eliminating the need to find a real board when holding meetings. Ever wished you could have a record of everything that was written on the chalkboard in a class (or business meeting)? If the professor had used Inky-Board, creating and distributing a copy would be a snap.

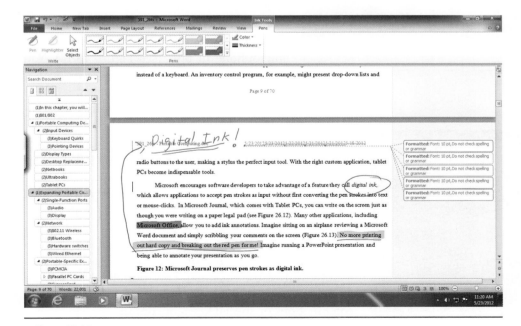

• **Figure 18.13** Microsoft Office supports digital ink.

■ Expanding Portable Computers

In the dark ages of mobile computing, you had to shell out top dollar for any device that would unplug, and what you purchased was what you got. Upgrade a laptop? Connect to external devices? You had few if any options, so you simply paid for a device that would be way behind the technology curve within a year and functionally obsolete within two.

Portable PCs today offer many ways to enhance their capabilities. Most feature external ports that enable you to add completely new functions to portables, such as attaching a scanner or mobile printer or both. You can take advantage of the latest wireless technology breakthrough simply by slipping a card into the appropriate slot on the laptop.

I'll first describe single-function ports, and then turn to networking options. Next, I'll cover card slots, and then finish with a discussion of general-purpose ports.

Single-Function Ports

All portable PCs come with one or more single-function ports. You'd have a hard time finding a portable computing device that doesn't have a speaker port, for example. Laptops invariably provide a video port such as a VGA or DVI connection for hooking up an external monitor.

Ports work the same way on portable PCs as they do on desktop models. You plug in a device to a particular port and, as long as Windows has the proper drivers, you will have a functioning device when you boot.

Audio

Portable PCs have a standard 3.5-mm audio out port and some have a similarly sized microphone in port (see Figure 18.14). You can plug in regular PC speakers or even a nice surround sound set to enable the laptop to play music just as well as a desktop computer can.

• **Figure 18.14** Standard audio ports

You control the sound (both out and in) through either the appropriate Control Panel applet in Windows or through some kind of switches on the laptop. The portable in Figure 18.15, for example, enables you to mute the speakers by pressing a special mute spot above the keyboard. Other portables use a combination of the FN key and another key to toggle mute on and off. You can also find many variations on how to control the volume coming out of the machine. Few portable PCs have a manual volume dial these days, instead relying on key combinations or special keys for control.

• **Figure 18.15** The mute spot on a laptop

Display

Most laptops support a second monitor via an analog VGA port or a digital port of some flavor, such as DVI, HDMI, Mini HDMI, Micro HDMI, or DisplayPort. With a second monitor attached, you can display Windows on only the laptop screen, on only the external monitor, or on both simultaneously. Not all portables can do all variations, but they're more common than not.

Most portables use the FN key plus another key on the keyboard to cycle through display options. Figure 18.16 shows a close-up of a typical keyboard with the Function key; note the other options you can access with the Function key, such as indicated on the F8 key. To engage the second monitor or to cycle through the modes, hold the Function key and press F8.

You can control how the external monitor displays through the Display applet in the Control Panel. Open Display and click on *Change display settings* (see Figure 18.17). Under the Screen Resolution panel, click the drop-down arrow next to Multiple displays (see Figure 18.18). You'll see several options. *Extend these displays* makes your desktop encompass both the laptop and the external monitor. *Duplicate these displays* places the

• **Figure 18.16** Laptop keyboard showing Function (FN) key that enables you to access additional key options, as on the F8 key

Although many laptops use the Function key method to cycle the monitor selections, that's not always the case. You might have to pop into the Display applet in the Control Panel to click a checkbox. Just be assured that if the laptop has a video output port, you can cycle through monitor choices!

• **Figure 18.17** Display applet

In Windows 7, the Windows key + P keyboard shortcut switches between multiple display modes.

• **Figure 18.18** Multiple display options menu

same thing on both displays. You'd use that for a presentation, for example, rather than for a work space. (The other two options shown in Figure 18.18 temporarily blank one or the other display.)

Network

It's a rare item to find a portable computer without at least one network connection option. Today's laptops come with 802.11, Bluetooth, and wired Ethernet connections. Some still have modems for connecting to older-style telephone jacks. Generally they work exactly as you've seen in previous chapters, but you may stumble into a few issues that are unique to laptops.

802.11 Wireless

Most portables today have Wi-Fi built directly into the chipset for connecting the device to a wireless access point (WAP) and from there to a bigger network, such as the Internet. The 802.11b standard is common on older laptops; newer ones use 802.11g or 802.11n.

Bluetooth

While not nearly as common as 802.11, plenty of laptops use Bluetooth as well. Bluetooth is really handy on a laptop because it gives you the ability to add wireless mice, keyboards, and headsets.

Hardware Switches

Laptops that come with 802.11 or Bluetooth have some form of on/off switch to toggle the antenna off or on so that you may use the laptop in areas where emissions aren't allowed (like a commercial aircraft). The switch may be hard wired, like the one shown in Figure 18.19, or it may be a toggle of the FN key plus another key on the keyboard. Also, if you're not using Wi-Fi or Bluetooth, turn them off to save electricity and lengthen the portable's battery life.

Wired Ethernet

Most laptops have an RJ-45 wired Ethernet connection like the one shown in Figure 18.20. These work exactly like any other Ethernet jack—they have link lights and connect via UTP cable.

There are two issues with RJ-45s on laptops. First, they do not have an on/off switch like the 802.11 and Bluetooth connections. You can turn them off just like you would turn off the NIC on a desktop: disable the NIC in Device Manager or turn the NIC off in BIOS. The other issue is the relative weakness of the physical connection. If you ever plug a laptop into a wired network and Windows doesn't see a connection, check the RJ-45 port.

Portable-Specific Expansion Slots

The makers of portable computers have developed methods for you to add features to a portable via specialized connections known generically as *expansion slots*. Once a common feature on laptops, these specialized expansion slots are quickly fading away due to the dominance of USB. Yet you'll still find laptops with these slots (and they're covered on the CompTIA A+ 220-801 exam), so let's take a look at expansion slots over the years.

PCMCIA

For many years, the *Personal Computer Memory Card International Association* (*PCMCIA*) established standards involving portable computers, especially when it came to expansion cards, which are generically called PC Cards. **PC Cards** are roughly credit card–sized devices that enhance and extend the functions of a portable PC. PC Cards are easy to use, inexpensive, and convenient. Figure 18.21 shows a typical PC Card.

Older portable PCs come with one or two PC Card slots, into which you insert a PC Card. Each card has at least one

• **Figure 18.19** Wireless switch

• **Figure 18.20** Ethernet port on laptop

• **Figure 18.21** PC Card

• **Figure 18.22** PC Card slots

Tech Tip

Keeping Your PC Cards Healthy

PC Cards typically come with a hard plastic storage case. Always be sure to use this case to store the cards when you're not using them. If dust, dirt, or grime gets into the array of contacts at the end of the card, the card won't work when you try to use it next. Also, be careful when using PC Cards that extend out of the PC Card slot past the edge of your laptop. One dark night, I set my laptop on the floor with a PC Card NIC sticking out of it while I went to get a drink of water. On my way back, I accidentally stepped on the card sticking out of my laptop and nearly snapped it in half. Luckily, my laptop wasn't damaged, but the card was toast!

function, but many have two, three, or more! You can buy a PC Card that offers connections for removable media, for example, such as combination SD and CF card readers. You can also find PC Cards that enable you to plug into multiple types of networks. All PC Cards are hot-swappable, meaning you can plug them in without powering down the PC.

The PCMCIA established two versions of PC Cards, one using a parallel bus and the other using a serial bus. Each version, in turn, offers two technology variations as well as several physical varieties. This might sound complicated at first, but here's the map to sort it all out.

Parallel PC Cards

Parallel PC Cards come in two flavors, **16-bit** and **CardBus**, and each flavor comes in three physical sizes, called Type I, Type II, and Type III. The 16-bit PC Cards, as the name suggests, are 16-bit, 5-V cards that can have up to two distinct functions or devices, such as a modem/network card combination. CardBus PC Cards are 32-bit, 3.3-V cards that can have up to eight (!) functions on a single card. Regular PC Cards fit into and work in CardBus slots, but the reverse is not true. CardBus totally dominates the current PC Card landscape, but you might still run into older 16-bit PC Cards.

Type I, II, and III cards differ only in the thickness of the card (Type I being the thinnest, and Type III the thickest). All PC Cards share the same 68-pin interface, so any PC Card will work in any slot that accepts that card type. Type II cards are by far the most common of PC Cards. Therefore, most older laptops have two Type II slots, one above the other, so the computer can accept two Type I or II cards or one Type III card (see Figure 18.22).

Although PCMCIA doesn't require that certain sizes perform certain functions, most PC Cards follow their recommendations. Table 18.2 lists the sizes and typical uses of each type of PC Card.

ExpressCard

Slots for **ExpressCard**, the high-performance serial version of the PC Card, have replaced PC Card slots on laptop PCs over the last decade. ExpressCard comes in two widths: 34 mm and 54 mm, called *ExpressCard/34* and *ExpressCard/54*. Figure 18.23 shows both ExpressCard varieties. Both cards are 75 mm long and 5 mm thick, which makes them shorter than all previous PC Cards and the same thickness as a Type II PC Card.

Table 18.2	PC Card Types and Their Typical Uses			
Type	**Length**	**Width**	**Thickness**	**Typical Use**
Type I	85.6 mm	54.0 mm	3.3 mm	Flash memory
Type II	85.6 mm	54.0 mm	5.0 mm	I/O (modem, NIC, and so on)
Type III	85.6 mm	54.0 mm	10.5 mm	Hard drives

ExpressCards connect to either the USB 2.0 bus or the PCI Express bus. These differ phenomenally in speed. The amazingly slow-in-comparison USB version has a maximum throughput of 480 Mbps. The PCIe version, in contrast, roars in at 2.5 Gbps in unidirectional communication.

Table 18.3 shows the throughput and variations for the parallel and serial PC Cards currently on the market.

PCMCIA announced ExpressCard 2.0 in 2009 with speeds up to 5 Gbps and support for SuperSpeed USB 3.0, and we expected to see devices roll out in 2010, but that's not what happened. PCMCIA has dissolved and shut its offices. The USB Implementer's Forum now manages all PC Card and ExpressCard standards, and there's not likely to be any further development.

Storage Card Slots

Many portable computers offer one or more flash-memory card slots to enable you to add storage to the portable. These slots also enable the fast transfer of data from the card to the portable, and vice versa. They come in the standard varieties that you already know from Chapter 11, such as SD, CompactFlash, and xD.

General-Purpose Ports

Laptops rarely come with all of the hardware you want. Today's laptops usually include at least USB ports to give you the option to add more hardware. Some laptops still provide legacy general-purpose expansion ports (PS/2, RS-232 serial ports, and so on) for installing peripheral hardware, while other portables focus on more modern ports like eSATA and FireWire. If you're lucky, you will have a docking station or port replicator so you don't have to plug in all of your peripheral devices one at a time.

USB, FireWire, and eSATA

Universal serial bus (USB), FireWire (or more properly, IEEE 1394), and eSATA enable users to connect a device while the PC is running—you won't have to reboot the system to install a new peripheral. With USB, FireWire, and eSATA, just plug the device in and go! Because portable PCs don't have a desktop's multiple internal expansion capabilities, USB, FireWire, and

• **Figure 18.23** 34-mm and 54-mm ExpressCards

You can find ExpressCards that supposedly support USB 3.0. While technically these cards have USB 3.0 ports, they connect to the PCIe bus and therefore aren't capable of true USB 3.0 speeds of up to 5 Gbps.

 The small device resting in a stand in Figure 18.24 is called a *personal digital assistant* (*PDA*), a precursor to modern smartphones and tablets such as the Apple iPhone and iPad. You could view pictures, take notes, check a calendar, listen to music, and more on these devices. Expect PDA as an answer choice in exam questions, but most likely as one of the wrong answers. PDAs are rarely used today.

Table 18.3	PC Card Speeds
Standard	**Maximum Theoretical Throughput**
PC Card using 16-bit bus	160 Mbps
CardBus PC Card using PCI bus	1056 Mbps
ExpressCard using USB 2.0 bus	480 Mbps
ExpressCard using PCIe bus	2.5 Gbps

Tech Tip

USB and Handheld Computing Devices

Almost all handheld computing devices—such as iPod music players—connect to PCs through USB ports. Most come with a USB cable that has a standard connector on one end and a proprietary connector on the other. Don't lose the cable!

Cross Check

Modern General-Purpose Ports

You learned about eSATA in Chapter 10. You explored USB and FireWire back in Chapter 3 and in Chapter 12. What kind of connectors do eSATA, USB, and FireWire use? What are the cable length limitations? How many devices can each technology support?

eSATA are three of the more popular methods for attaching peripherals to laptops (see Figure 18.24).

Port Replicators

A **port replicator** plugs into a single port on the portable computer—often a USB port but sometimes a proprietary port—and offers uncommon and common PC ports, such as serial, parallel, USB, network, and PS/2. By plugging the port replicator into your notebook computer, you can instantly connect the computer to nonportable components such as a printer, scanner, monitor, or a full-sized keyboard. Port replicators are typically used at home or in the office with the nonportable equipment already connected. Figure 18.25 shows a Dell Inspiron laptop connected to a port replicator.

The computer can access any devices attached to the port replicator; you don't need to connect each individual device to the PC. As a side bonus, port replicators enable you to attach legacy devices, such as parallel printers, to a new laptop

• **Figure 18.24** Devices attached to USB on a portable PC

Although portable PCs most often connect to port replicators via USB ports, some manufacturers have proprietary connections for proprietary port replicators. As long as such a portable PC has a USB port, you can use either the proprietary hardware or the more flexible USB devices.

• **Figure 18.25** Port replicator for a Dell portable computer

that only has modern multifunction ports such as USB and FireWire and not parallel or serial ports.

Docking Stations

Docking stations resemble port replicators in many ways, offering legacy and modern single- and multi-function ports (see Figure 18.26). The typical docking station uses a proprietary connection but has extra features built in, such as a DVD drive or PC Card slot for extra enhancements. You can find docking stations for many older small laptops. A docking station makes an excellent companion to such portables.

• **Figure 18.26** Docking station

■ Managing and Maintaining Portable Computers

Most portable PCs come from the factory solidly built and configured. Manufacturers know that few techs outside their factories know enough to work on them, so they don't cut corners. From a tech's standpoint, your most common work on managing and maintaining portables involves taking care of the batteries and extending the battery life through proper power management, keeping the machine clean, and avoiding excessive heat.

Everything you normally do to maintain a PC applies to portable PCs. You need to keep current on Windows patches and service packs and use stable, recent drivers. Run Check Disk with some frequency, and definitely defragment the hard drive. Disk Cleanup is a must if the laptop runs Windows. That said, let's look at issues specifically involving portables.

Batteries

Manufacturers have used three types of batteries for portable PCs: **Nickel-Cadmium (Ni-Cd)**, **Nickel-Metal Hydride (Ni-MH)**, and **Lithium-Ion (Li-Ion)**. Today, only Li-Ion is used because that battery chemistry provides the highest energy density for the weight and has few problems with external factors. Let's look at each battery type briefly.

Nickel-Cadmium

Ni-Cds were the first batteries commonly used in mobile PCs, which means the technology was full of little problems. Probably most irritating was a little thing called *battery memory*, or the tendency of a Ni-Cd battery to lose a significant amount of its rechargeability if it was charged repeatedly without being totally discharged. A battery that originally kept a laptop running for two hours would eventually only keep that same laptop going for 30 minutes or less. Figure 18.27 shows a typical Ni-Cd battery.

• **Figure 18.27** Ni-Cd battery

573

Nickel-Metal Hydride

Ni-MH batteries were the next generation of mobile PC batteries and are basically Ni-Cd batteries without most of the headaches. Ni-MH batteries are much less susceptible to memory problems, can tolerate overcharging better, can take more recharging, and can last longer between rechargings. Like Ni-Cds, Ni-MH batteries are susceptible to heat, but at least they are considered less toxic to the environment. Figure 18.28 shows a typical Ni-MH battery.

Lithium-Ion

The most common battery used today is Li-Ion. Li-Ion batteries are powerful, completely immune to memory problems, and last at least twice as long as comparable Ni-MH batteries on one charge. Sadly, they can't handle as many charges as Ni-MH types, but today's users are usually more than glad to give up total battery lifespan in return for longer periods between charges. Li-Ion batteries will explode if they are overcharged, so all Li-Ion batteries sold with PCs have built-in circuitry to prevent accidental overcharging. Lithium batteries can only be used on systems designed to use them. They can't be used as replacement batteries. Figure 18.29 shows a typical Li-Ion battery.

The Care and Feeding of Batteries

In general, keep in mind the following basics. First, always store batteries in a cool place. Although a freezer is in concept an excellent storage place, the moisture, metal racks, and food make it a bad idea. Second, keep the battery charged, at least to 70–80 percent. Third, never drain a battery all the way down unless required to do so as part of a *battery calibration* (where you, in essence, reset the battery according to steps provided by the manufacturer). Rechargeable batteries have only a limited number of charge-discharge cycles before overall battery performance is reduced. Fourth, *never* handle a battery that has ruptured or broken; battery chemicals are very dangerous. Finally, always recycle old batteries.

• **Figure 18.28** Ni-MH battery

> ### Tech Tip
>
> #### Lithium Polymer
> Lithium polymer (LiPO) *batteries are a variation of Li-Ion that places the heart of the battery—the electrolyte—into a solid polymer shape rather than an organic solvent. This enables the batteries to take on unusual forms beyond the simple cylinder or rectangle shapes. LiPO batteries haven't replaced Li-Ion in most portable PCs (with the Apple MacBook the obvious exception), but they are used heavily in smaller electronics such as tablets, smartphones, and portable media players.*

• **Figure 18.29** Li-Ion battery

Power Management

Many different parts are included in the typical laptop, and each part uses power. The problem with early laptops was that every one of these parts used power continuously, whether or not the system needed that device at that time. For example, the hard drive continued to spin even when it was not being accessed, and the LCD panel continued to display even when the user walked away from the machine.

The optimal situation would be a system where the user could instruct the PC to shut down unused devices selectively, preferably by defining a maximum period of inactivity that, when reached, would trigger the PC to shut down the inactive device. Longer periods of inactivity would eventually enable the entire system to shut itself down, leaving critical information loaded in RAM, ready to restart if a wake-up event (such as moving the mouse or pressing a key) told the system to restart. The system would have to be sensitive to potential hazards, such as shutting down in the middle of writing to a drive, and so on. Also, this feature could not add significantly to the cost of the PC. Clearly, a machine that could perform these functions would need specialized hardware and a specialized BIOS and operating system to operate properly. This process of cooperation among the hardware, the BIOS, and the OS to reduce power use is known generically as *power management*.

 Try This!

Recycling Old Portable PC Batteries

Got an old portable PC battery lying around? Well, you need to get rid of it, and there are some pretty nasty chemicals in that battery, so you can't just throw it in the trash. Sooner or later, you'll probably need to deal with such a battery, so Try This!

1. Do an online search to find the battery recycling center nearest to you.

2. Sometimes, you can take old laptop batteries to an auto parts store that disposes of old car batteries—I know it sounds odd, but it's true! See if you can find one in your area that will do this.

3. Many cities offer a hazardous materials disposal or recycling service. Check to see if and how your local government will help you dispose of your old batteries.

System Management Mode

Intel began the process of power management with a series of new features built into the 386SX CPU. These new features enabled the CPU to slow down or stop its clock without erasing the register information, as well as enabling power saving in peripherals. These features were collectively called **System Management Mode (SMM)**. All modern CPUs have SMM. Although a power-saving CPU was okay, power management was relegated to special "sleep" or "doze" buttons that would stop the CPU and all of the peripherals on the laptop. To take real advantage of SMM, the system needed a specialized BIOS and OS to go with the SMM CPU. To this end, Intel put forward the **Advanced Power Management (APM)** specification in 1992 and the **Advanced Configuration and Power Interface (ACPI)** standard in 1996.

Requirements for APM/ACPI

To function fully, APM and ACPI require a number of items. First, they require an SMM-capable CPU. As virtually all CPUs are SMM-capable, this is easy. Second, they need an APM-compliant BIOS that enables the CPU to shut off the peripherals when desired. The third requirement is devices

that will accept being shut off. These devices are usually called Energy Star devices, which signals their compliance with the EPA's Energy Star standard. To be an Energy Star device, a peripheral must be able to shut down without actually turning off and show that it uses much less power than the non–Energy Star equivalent. Last, the system's OS must know how to request that a particular device be shut down, and the CPU's clock must be slowed down or stopped.

ACPI goes beyond the APM standard by supplying support for hot-swappable devices—always a huge problem with APM. This feature aside, it is a challenge to tell the difference between an APM system and an ACPI system at first glance.

APM/ACPI Levels

APM defined four power-usage operating levels for a system. These levels are intentionally fuzzy to give manufacturers considerable leeway in their use; the only real difference among them is the amount of time each takes to return to normal usage. These levels are as follows:

- **Full On** Everything in the system is running at full power. There is no power management.

- **APM Enabled** CPU and RAM are running at full power. Power management is enabled. An unused device may or may not be shut down.

- **APM Standby** CPU is stopped. RAM still stores all programs. All peripherals are shut down, although configuration options are still stored. (In other words, to get back to APM Enabled, you won't have to reinitialize the devices.)

- **APM Suspend** Everything in the PC is shut down or at its lowest power-consumption setting. Many systems use a special type of Suspend called **hibernation**, where critical configuration information is written to the hard drive. Upon a wake-up event, the system is reinitialized, and the data is read from the drive to return the system to the APM Enabled mode. Clearly, the recovery time between Suspend and Enabled will be much longer than the time between Standby and Enabled.

ACPI, the successor to APM, handles all these levels plus a few more, such as "soft power on/off," that enables you to define the function of the power button. You should familiarize yourself with the following ACPI global (G) and sleeping (S) system power state specifications for both the CompTIA A+ 801 exam and your own practical application:

- **G0 (S0)** Working state
- **G1** Sleeping state mode. Further subdivided into four *S* states:
 - **S1** CPU stops processing. Power to CPU and memory (RAM) is maintained.
 - **S2** CPU is powered down.
 - **S3** Sleep or Standby mode. Power to RAM still on.
 - **S4** Hibernation mode. Information in RAM is stored to nonvolatile memory or drive and powered off.

Don't limit your perception of APM, ACPI, and Energy Star just to laptops. Virtually all desktop systems and many appliances also use the power management functions.

- **G2 (S5)** Soft power off mode. Certain devices used to wake a system—such as keyboard, LAN, USB, and other devices—remain on, while most other components are powered to a mechanical off state (G3).

- **G3** Mechanical off mode. The system and all components, with the exception of the real-time clock (RTC), are completely powered down.

Configuration of APM/ACPI

You configure APM/ACPI via CMOS settings or through Windows. Windows settings override CMOS settings. Although the APM/ACPI standards permit a great deal of flexibility, which can create some confusion among different implementations, certain settings apply generally to CMOS configuration. First is the ability to initialize power management; this enables the system to enter the APM Enabled mode. Often CMOS then presents time frames for entering Standby and Suspend modes, as well as settings to determine which events take place in each of these modes.

Many CMOS versions present settings to determine wake-up events, such as directing the system to monitor a modem or a NIC (see Figure 18.30). You'll see this feature as *Wake on LAN*,

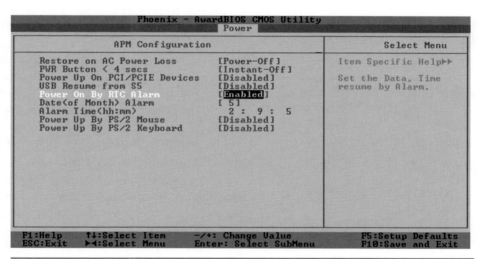

• **Figure 18.30** Setting a wake-up event in CMOS

or something similar. A true ACPI-compliant CMOS provides an ACPI setup option. Figure 18.31 shows a typical modern BIOS that provides this setting.

In Windows XP, you can also access your power options by right-clicking on the desktop, selecting Properties, and then clicking the Power button in the Monitor power section of the Screen Saver tab. In Windows Vista and 7, right-click the desktop, select Personalize, select Screen Saver, and then click on the *Change power settings* link.

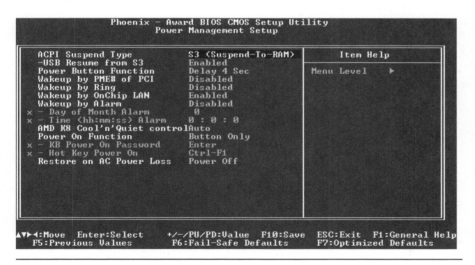

• **Figure 18.31** CMOS with ACPI setup option

● **Figure 18.32** The Windows XP Power Options applet's Power Schemes tab

APM/ACPI settings can be found in the Control Panel applet Power Options. In Windows XP, the Power Options applet has several built-in *power schemes* such as Home/Office and Max Battery that put the system into Standby or Suspend after a certain interval (see Figure 18.32). You can also require the system to go into Standby after a set period of time or to turn off the monitor or hard drive after a time, thus creating your own custom power scheme. This is technically called adjusting the **sleep timers**.

Windows Vista and Windows 7 offer **power plans** that enable better control over power use by customizing a balanced, power saver, or high performance power plan (see Figure 18.33). You can customize a power saver plan for your laptop, for example, and configure it to turn off the display at a certain time interval while on battery or plugged in and configure it to put the computer to sleep as desired (see Figure 18.34).

Another feature, Hibernate mode, takes everything in active memory and stores it on the hard drive just before the system powers down. When the PC comes out of hibernation, Windows reloads all the files and applications into RAM. Figure 18.35 shows the Power Options Properties applet in Windows XP.

Manual Control over Power Use

Most portable PCs give you several manual options for reducing battery use in certain circumstances. We've already discussed using the on/off switch or keyboard combination for disabling the Wi-Fi antenna, for example, and shutting off Bluetooth. Laptops with backlit

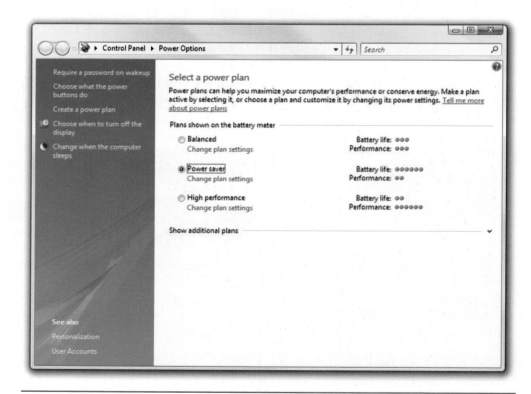

● **Figure 18.33** Windows Vista Balanced, Power saver, and High performance power plan options

• **Figure 18.34** Customizing a laptop power plan in Windows Vista

keyboards will have some way you can disable this feature when it's not needed, usually with a keyboard combination. You can also reduce the output of the LCD backlight using a combination of FN and another key to eke out a few more precious minutes of computing time before you have to shut

• **Figure 18.35** Windows XP hibernation settings in the Power Options applet

Try This!

Adjusting Your System's Power Management

Go into the Power Options applet and take a look at the various settings. What is the current power scheme for your computer? If you're using a laptop with Windows XP, is your system still using the Home/Office Desktop power scheme? If this is the case, change the power scheme to Portable/Laptop. If you're using a laptop with Windows Vista/7, check to see if you are running a balanced or high performance power plan. If you are, change the power plan to power saver and familiarize yourself with some of the advanced power settings (click on the *Change advanced power settings* link).

Try changing the individual settings for each power scheme. For instance, set a new value for the *System standby* setting—try making your computer go into standby after five minutes. Don't worry; you aren't going to hurt anything if you fiddle with these settings.

• **Figure 18.36** Keys for adjusting screen brightness

down. Figure 18.36 shows a close-up of the FN-activated keys for adjusting screen brightness.

One of the best ways to conserve battery use is to plan ahead for times when you'll be unplugged. When I travel, for example, and know that I'm going to need a certain set of files stored on my file server at the office, I put those files on my laptop before I leave, while it's still plugged into the AC. It's tempting to throw the files on a thumb drive so I don't have to break out my laptop at the office, right? Or to let Dropbox do my syncing for me when I get to a Wi-Fi hot-spot, but both USB and Wi-Fi use electricity.

Better than that even, Windows Vista and Windows 7 enable me to designate the files and folders I need as **offline files**, storing a local, duplicate copy of the files and folders on my hard drive. When I connect my laptop into my office network, those offline files are automatically synced with the files and folders on the file server. Anything I changed on the laptop gets written to the server. Anything anyone changed in those folders on the server gets written to my laptop. (If changes were made on both sides, a sync conflict pops up automatically, enabling you to resolve problems without fear of overwriting anything important.)

To designate a folder and its contents as offline files, right-click on the folder you want and select *Always available offline* from the menu (see Figure 18.37). The sync will occur and you're done. When you want to open the files offline, go to the Control Panel and open the Sync Center applet (see Figure 18.38). Click the *Manage offline files* link in the Tasks list to open the Offline Files dialog box (see Figure 18.39). Click the *View your offline files* button and you're in.

• **Figure 18.37** Setting up offline files

● **Figure 18.38** Sync Center applet

● **Figure 18.39** Offline Files dialog box

Cleaning

Most portable PCs take substantially more abuse than a corresponding desktop model. Constant handling, travel, airport food on the run, and so on can radically shorten the life of a portable if you don't take action. One of the most important things you should do is clean the laptop regularly. Use an appropriate screen cleaner (not a glass cleaner!) to remove fingerprints and dust from the fragile LCD panel.

If you've had the laptop in a smoky or dusty environment where the air quality alone causes problems, try cleaning it with compressed air. Compressed air works great for blowing out the dust and crumbs from the keyboard and for keeping PC Card sockets clear. Don't use water on your keyboard! Even a minor amount of moisture inside the portable can toast a component.

Heat

To manage and maintain a healthy portable PC, you need to deal with issues of heat. Every portable has a stack of electronic components crammed into a very small space. Unlike their desktop brethren, portables don't have lots of freely moving air space that enables fans to cool everything down. Even with lots of low-power-consumption devices inside, portable PCs crank out a good deal of heat. Excessive heat can cause system lockups and hardware failures, so you should handle the issue wisely. Try this as a starter guide:

- Use power management, even if you're plugged into the AC outlet. This is especially important if you're working in a warm (more than 80 degrees Fahrenheit) room.

- Keep air space between the bottom of the laptop and the surface on which it rests. Putting a laptop on a soft surface, such as a pillow on your lap, creates a great heat-retention system—not a good thing! Always use a hard, flat surface.

- Don't use a keyboard protector for extended amounts of time.

- Listen to your fan, assuming the laptop has one. If it's often running very fast—you can tell by the high-pitched whirring sound—examine your power management settings and your environment, and change whatever is causing heat retention.

- Speaking of fans, be alert to a fan that suddenly goes silent. Fans do fail on laptops, causing overheating and failure. All laptop fans can be replaced easily.

Protecting the Machine

Although prices continue to drop for basic laptops, a fully loaded system is still pricey. To protect your investment, you'll want to adhere to certain best practices. You've already read tips in this chapter to deal with cleaning and heat, so let's look at the "portable" part of portable computers.

Mike Meyers' CompTIA A+ Guide to 801: Managing and Troubleshooting PCs

Tripping

Pay attention to where you run the power cord when you plug in a laptop. One of the primary causes of laptop destruction is people tripping over the power cord and knocking the laptop off of a desk. This is especially true if you plug in at a public place such as a café or airport. Remember, the life you save could be your portable PC's!

Storage

If you aren't going to use your laptop for a while, storing it safely will go a long way toward keeping it operable when you do power it up again. Investing in a quality case is worth the extra few dollars—preferably one with ample padding. Not only will this protect your system on a daily basis when transporting it from home to office, but it will keep dust and pet hair away as well. Lastly, protect from battery leakage by removing the battery if you'll be storing your device for an extended time.

Travel

If you're traveling with a laptop, take care to guard against theft. If possible, use a case that doesn't look like a computer case. A well-padded backpack makes a great travel bag for a laptop and appears less tempting to would-be thieves. Don't forget to pack any accessories you might need, like modular devices, spare batteries, and AC adapters. Make sure to remove any disks, such as optical or floppies, from their drives. Most importantly—back up any important data before you leave!

Make sure to have at least a little battery power available. Heightened security at airports means you might have to power on your system to prove it's really a computer and not a transport case for questionable materials. And never let your laptop out of your sight. If going through an x-ray machine, request a manual search. The x-ray won't harm your computer like a metal detector would, but if the laptop gets through the line at security before you do, someone else might walk away with it. If flying, stow your laptop under the seat in front of you where you can keep an eye on it.

If you travel to a foreign country, be very careful about the electricity. North America uses ~115-V power outlets, but most of the world uses ~230-V outlets. Many portable computers have **auto-switching power supplies**, meaning they detect the voltage at the outlet and adjust accordingly. For these portables, a simple plug converter will do the trick. Other portable computers, however, have *fixed-input power supplies*, which means they run only on ~115-V or on ~230-V power. For these portables, you need a full-blown electricity converting device, either a step-down or step-up *transformer*. You can find converters and transformers at electrical parts stores, such as Radio Shack in the United States.

Shipping

Much of the storage and travel advice can be applied to shipping. Remove batteries and optical discs from their drives. Pack the laptop well and disguise the container as best you can. Back up any data and verify the warranty coverage. Ship with a reputable carrier and always request a tracking

• Figure 18.40 Cable lock

• Figure 18.41 LoJack (photo courtesy of Absolute Software Corporation)

number and, if possible, delivery signature. It's also worth the extra couple of bucks to pay for the shipping insurance. And when the clerk asks what's in the box, it's safer to say "electronics" rather than "a new 20-inch laptop computer."

Security

The fact is, if someone really wants to steal your laptop, they'll find a way. There are, however, some things you can do to make yourself, and your equipment, less desirable targets. As you've already learned, disguise is a good idea. Although you don't need to camouflage your laptop or carry it in a brown grocery bag on a daily basis, an inconspicuous carrying case will draw less attention.

Another physical deterrent is a laptop lock. Similar to a steel bicycle cable, there is a loop on one end and a lock on the other. The idea is to loop the cable around a solid object, such as a bed frame, and secure the lock to the small security hole on the side of the laptop (see Figure 18.40). Again, if someone really wants to steal your computer, they'll find a way. They'll dismantle the bed frame if they're desperate. The best protection is to be vigilant and not let the computer out of your sight.

An alternative to physically securing a laptop with a lock is to use a software tracking system. Software makers, such as Computer Security Products, Inc., at www.computersecurity.com, offer tracking software that transmits a signal to a central office if the computer is stolen and connected to a phone line or the Internet. Even LoJack, the company famous for recovering stolen automobiles via its tracking devices, lends its name to a tracking product sold by Absolute Software (see Figure 18.41). The location of the stolen PC can be tracked, and sensitive files can even be deleted automatically with the aid of the stealth signal.

■ Upgrading and Repairing Laptop Computers

A competent tech can upgrade and repair portable computers to a degree, though true laptop techs are specialists. Upgrading the basics usually means breaking out the trusty screwdriver and avoiding electrostatic discharge (ESD). *Repairing* portables successfully, on the other hand, requires research, patience, organization, special tools, and documentation. Plus you need a ridiculously steady hand. This section provides an overview of the upgrade and repair process.

Disassembly Process

Disassembling a portable PC is pretty easy. Putting it back together in working condition is the hard part! You need to follow a four-step process to succeed in disassembly/reassembly.

First, *document and label every cable and screw location*. Laptops don't use standard connectors or screws. Often you'll run into many tiny screws of varying threads. If you try to put a screw into the wrong hole, you could end up stripping the screw, stripping the hole, or getting the screw wedged into the wrong place.

Second, *organize any parts you extract from the laptop*. Seriously, put a big white piece of construction paper on your work surface, lay each extracted piece out in logical fashion, and clearly mark where each component connects and what it connects to as well.

Third, *refer to the manufacturer's documentation*. I can't stress this point enough. Unlike desktop PCs, portable PCs have no standardization of internal structure. Everything in the portable is designed according to the manufacturer's best engineering efforts. Two portables from the same manufacturer might have a similar layout inside, but it's far more likely that every model differs a lot.

Finally, you need to *use the appropriate hand tools*. A portable PC, especially on the inside, will have a remarkable variety of tiny screws that you can't remove/reinsert without tiny-headed Phillips or Torx drivers. You'll need tiny pry bars—metal and plastic—to open components. Figure 18.42 shows an entry-level toolkit for a laptop tech that you can order from iFixit.

• **Figure 18.42** Bare-minimum laptop repair tools

com (more on this site in a moment). Their professional version of the toolkit has 70 tools, plus there's an expansion kit! Like I said at the beginning of the chapter, portable techs are specialists.

Now that you have the official line on the disassembly process, let's get one thing clear: A lot of manufacturers don't provide documentation to just any tech, but only to authorized repair centers. So what do you do when faced with an unfamiliar laptop that a client brought in for repair?

You have essentially three options. First, you can find a dedicated laptop tech and refer your client to that person. If the problem is exceptionally complicated and the portable in question is mission critical, that's often the best option. If you want to tackle the problem or it looks like something you should be able to do, then you go to the sources: YouTube and iFixit.com.

Every portable computer has a specific make and model. Open up a Web browser and go to YouTube. Type in precisely what you want to do, such as "replace the keyboard on a Lenovo y530," and see what pops up (see Figure 18.43). You'll most likely be in shock and awe when you get the results back, especially if the laptop in question is a couple of years old. People all over the world have to deal with broken devices, so you're not alone.

• **Figure 18.43** YouTube search result

Once you've found the appropriate video or something that's close enough to enable the repair attempt, watch it. If it's too difficult for your skill level or requires a set of expensive tools, then fall back to step one and go find that dedicated tech. Otherwise, figure out what tools and parts you need. Parts specific to a laptop (as in that Lenovo keyboard in the preceding example) will need to be purchased from the manufacturer. More generic parts, like hard drives, CPUs, and so on, can be purchased from Newegg (my favorite tech store) or some other online retailer.

For general tools, parts, and a lot of very detailed step-by-step instructions, I highly recommend iFixit.com. Billed as a "free repair manual you can edit," iFixit is built by techs like you who conquer a problem, document the steps, and post the details (see Figure 18.44). This means the next tech along who runs into the same problem doesn't have to reinvent the wheel. Just go to iFixit.com. The proceeds from parts and tools they sell, by the way, go toward supporting the site. It's not a for-profit enterprise.

• **Figure 18.44** Some of the Dell laptop repair walkthroughs at iFixit.com

Standard Upgrades

Every CompTIA A+ tech should know how to perform the two standard upgrades to portable computers: adding RAM and replacing a hard drive. Let's go through the steps.

RAM

Stock factory portable PCs almost always come with a minimal amount of RAM, so one of the first laptop upgrades you'll be called on to do is to add more RAM. Economy laptops running Windows 7 Home Premium routinely sit on store shelves and go home to consumers with as little as 1 GB of RAM, an amount guaranteed to limit the use and performance of the laptop. The OS alone will consume more than half of the RAM! Luckily, every decent laptop has upgradeable RAM slots. Ancient laptops use either 72-pin or 144-pin SO-DIMMs with SDRAM technology. DDR, DDR2, and DDR3 systems primarily use 200-pin SO-DIMMs (see Figure 18.45), although some laptops use micro-DIMMs.

How to Add or Replace RAM Upgrading the RAM in a portable PC requires a couple of steps. First, you need to get the correct RAM. Many older portable PCs use proprietary RAM solutions, which means you need to order directly from Dell, HP, or Sony and pay exorbitant prices for the precious extra megabytes. Most manufacturers have taken pity on consumers in recent years and use standard SO-DIMMs or

> One of the most striking contrasts between portable PCs and tablets and smartphones is in upgradability. You can and should upgrade portable PCs. Mobile devices, on the other hand, offer almost no upgradability at all.

• **Figure 18.45** 200-pin SO-DIMM stick (front and back)

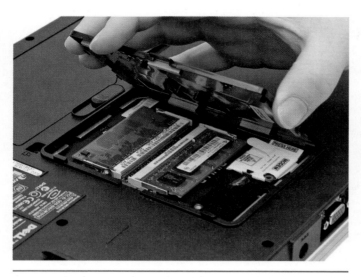

• **Figure 18.46** Removing a RAM panel

micro-DIMMs. Refer to the manufacturer's Web site or to the manual (if any) that came with the portable for the specific RAM needed.

Second, every portable PC offers a unique challenge to the tech who wants to upgrade the RAM, because there's no standard location for RAM placement in portables. More often than not, you need to unscrew or pop open a panel on the underside of the portable (see Figure 18.46). Then you press out on the restraining clips and the RAM stick pops up (see Figure 18.47). Gently remove the old stick of RAM and insert the new one by reversing the steps.

Always remove all electrical power from the laptop before removing or inserting memory. Disconnect the AC cord from the wall outlet. Take out the battery! Failure to disconnect from power can result in a fried laptop.

Shared Memory Some laptops (and desktops) support **shared memory**. Shared memory reduces the cost of video cards by reducing the amount of memory on the video card itself. Instead of having 256 MB of RAM, the video card might have only 64 MB of RAM but be able to borrow 192 MB of RAM from the system. This equates to a 256 MB video card. The video card uses regular system RAM to make up for the loss.

You cannot tell if a laptop is using shared memory in Windows. You have to go to CMOS to be sure.

The obvious benefit of shared memory is a less expensive video card (and a less expensive laptop!) with performance comparable to its mega-memory alternative. The downside is that your overall system performance will suffer because a portion of the system RAM is no longer available to programs. (The term *shared* is a bit misleading because the video card takes control of a portion of RAM. The video portion of system RAM is *not* shared back and forth between the video card processor and the CPU.) Shared memory technologies include TurboCache (developed by NVIDIA) and HyperMemory (developed by ATI).

Some systems give you control over the amount of shared memory, while others simply allow you to turn shared memory on or off. The settings are found in CMOS setup and only on systems that support shared memory. Shared memory is not reported to Windows, so don't panic if you have 1 GB of RAM in your laptop but Windows only sees 924 MB—the missing memory is used for video.

Adding more system RAM to a laptop with shared memory will improve laptop performance. Although it might appear to improve video performance, that doesn't tell the true story. It'll improve overall performance because the OS and CPU get more usable RAM. On some laptops, you can improve video performance as well, but that depends on the CMOS setup. If the shared memory is not set to maximum by default, increasing the overall memory and upping the portion reserved for video will improve video performance specifically.

• **Figure 18.47** Releasing the RAM

HDD/SSD

You can replace a hard disk drive (HDD) or solid-state drive (SSD) in a portable PC fairly easily, especially if the laptop is only a few years old. SATA drives in the 2.5-inch drive format now rule in all laptops. Although much smaller than regular 3.5-inch hard drives, they use all the same features and configurations. These smaller hard drives have suffered, however, from diminished storage capacity as compared to their 3.5-inch brothers. Currently, large 2.5-inch hard drives hold up to 1 TB, while the 3.5-inch hard drives can hold more than 3 TB of data!

If you have a much older laptop, it might have a PATA drive, which means you need to pay more attention to cabling and jumpers. Some PATA drive manufacturers may require you to set the drive to use a cable-select setting as opposed to master or slave, so check with the laptop maker for any special issues. Otherwise, no difference exists between 2.5-inch drives and their larger 3.5-inch brethren (see Figure 18.48).

• **Figure 18.48** The 2.5-inch and 3.5-inch drives are mostly the same.

One of the best upgrades you can make on a laptop is to go from an HDD to an SSD. Obviously, you'll get a lot less storage capacity for the money, but the trade-offs can be worth it. First, the SSD will use a lot less electricity than an HDD, thus extending battery life. Second, any SSD is rip-roaringly faster than an HDD and performance across the board will be boosted.

The process of replacing a hard drive mirrors that of replacing RAM. You find the hard drive hatch—either along one edge or in a compartment on the underside of the computer—and release the screws (see Figure 18.49). Remove the old drive and then slide the new drive into its place (see Figure 18.50). Reattach the hatch or cover and boot the computer. Grab a Windows disc and prepare to reinstall.

• **Figure 18.49** Removing the drive compartment cover

Comparing HDD with SSD Today

As I write this chapter, you can get roughly ten times the storage capacity on an HDD for the same cost as an SSD. In other words, $100 spent on an SSD would give me ~100 GB of storage, whereas I could purchase a 1-TB HDD for the same $100. So do some comparison shopping. What's the price point now? Are the trade-offs worth it for you or for your clients to make the switch from HDD to SSD?

• **Figure 18.50** Inserting a replacement drive

Hardware Replacement

Once you get beyond upgrading RAM and replacing a hard drive on a portable PC, you take the plunge into the laptop repair specialty. You can replace some components by lifting them out, detaching a ribbon cable, and then reversing the steps with the replacement part. Other parts require a full teardown of the laptop to the bare bones, which presents a much greater magnitude of difficulty. Because every portable PC differs from every other one, this section provides guidance, but not concrete steps, for replacement.

Components

Replaceable components require more work than the RAM or drive upgrades, but replacing them generally falls into the category of "doable." What I call *components* are the battery, keyboard, optical drive, internal speaker, and plastic parts.

Battery If a battery's performance falls below an acceptable level, you can replace it with a battery from the manufacturer or from an aftermarket vendor. Although this should be a simple swap replacement (and usually is), you might encounter a situation where the real problem wasn't the battery per se, but an inadequate or malfunctioning charging system. The new battery might not give you any better performance than the old one. Try it.

Keyboard Getting a keyboard off a laptop computer often requires little pry bars, but also look for screws, clips, and so on. Keyboards connect via a tiny, short, and very delicate cable, often held down by tape. Replacing one is tricky, but doable.

Optical Drive Replacing an optical drive can present a challenge. If the drive is part of a modular system, just pop out the old drive and pop in a new one. If the drive is part of the internal chassis of the portable, on the other hand, you're looking at a full dissection. (See the "Integral Parts" section for tips on dismantling the portable.)

Speaker Like the optical drive, replacing the internal speaker or speakers on a laptop can be simple or a total pain, depending on where the speakers connect. Some laptops have speakers mounted on the outside of the chassis. You pry off the covers, pull out the little speakers, disconnect the cable, and then reverse the process for replacement speakers. If the speakers are inside the chassis, on the other hand, you need to dismantle the portable to get to them. (See the "Integral Parts" section.)

• **Figure 18.51** ExpressCard blank

Plastic Parts Laptops have a few plastic parts that can get lost or broken. These are slot covers or card blanks designed to keep dust out of the memory card and expansion slots (see Figure 18.51). If you need to replace one of these, simply get a spare from the manufacturer or an aftermarket vendor and replace it.

Expansion Cards Not to be confused with PC Cards, many portable PCs have one or more true expansion slots for add-on cards. The more modular varieties will have a hatch on the bottom of the case that opens like the RAM hatch that gives you access to the slot(s). This enables you to change out an 802.11g wireless card, for example, for an 802.11n card, thus greatly enhancing the Wi-Fi experience on this device. Figure 18.52 shows a wide-open laptop with the expansion slot exposed.

• **Figure 18.52** Mini-PCIe expansion slot on laptop

Just like when installing RAM in a portable, you must avoid ESD and remove all electricity before you take out or put in an expansion card. Failure to remove the battery and the AC adapter can and probably will result in a shorted-out laptop motherboard, and that just makes for a bad day.

The only other consideration with expansion cards applies specifically to wireless. Not only will you need to connect the card to the slot properly, but you must reattach the antenna connection and often a separate power cable. Pay attention when you remove the card as to the placement of these vital connections.

You'll find one of two types of expansion slot in a portable. The older ones (think 2005 and earlier) use **Mini-PCI**, because PCI dominated that time period. Just about every portable since then uses PCI Express, so the laptops come with **Mini-PCIe** slots.

CPU Replacing a CPU on a modern portable takes a lot more work than replacing RAM or a Mini-PCIe expansion card, but follows the same general steps. Many CPUs mount facing the bottom of the portable, so that the venting goes away from your hands. When sitting properly on a flat surface, the heated air also goes to the back of the laptop and not toward the user. You access the CPU in this sort of system from the bottom of the portable.

As you can see in Figure 18.53, the CPU has an elaborate heat-sink and fan assembly that includes both the CPU and the chipset. Each of the pieces screws down in multiple places, plus the fan has a power connection. Aside from the tiny screws, there's no difference here in process between replacing a mobile CPU and a desktop CPU that you learned way back in Chapter 5.

First, remove all power from the laptop, including the battery. Remove the hatch to expose the CPU. Remove the heat-sink and fan assembly and lift out the CPU. Replace it with another CPU, apply thermal paste, and reattach the heat-sink and fan assembly. Reconnect the fan power connector and you're good to go.

• **Figure 18.53** CPU heat-sink and fan assembly exposed

Mike Meyers' CompTIA A+ Guide to 801: Managing and Troubleshooting PCs

Some older laptops use passive cooling and thus have the CPU pointed up rather than down. They have a heat sink beneath the keyboard that cools everything down. With that style laptop, you remove the keyboard and heat sink to expose the CPU.

Integral Parts

Some hardware replacements require you to get serious with the laptop, opening it fully to the outside, removing many delicate parts, and even stripping it down to the bare metal chassis. I leave these repairs to the professional laptop repair folks, simply because they have the specific tools and expertise to do the job efficiently. CompTIA expects you to understand the process, though, so I've outlined it here. This pertains to four components: screen, DC jack, touchpad, and system board.

Portables open in two different ways, depending on the manufacturer. You either peel away layers from the top down, through the keyboard, or from the bottom up, through the base. Either direction requires careful attention to detail, part connectivity, and locations. You'll need a system to keep track of the dozens of tiny screws.

Every one of the replacements here requires you to detach the screen from the main chassis of the portable. Aside from finding the connection points and removing the proper screws, you need to pay attention to the connection points for the data stream to the monitor and the antenna that's in the frame of the display.

Once you have the portable stripped down, you replace whichever component you're in there to replace and then begin the process of building it back up into a coherent unit. Pay incredibly careful attention to getting data cables connected properly as you rebuild. I can't imagine a worse tech experience than replacing a touchpad and rebuilding a laptop only to have missed a connection and having to do it all over again.

> The DC jack requires extra-special love when you need to replace one. The part is soldered to the main board, so to replace it means you'll need to not only strip the laptop to the bare metal, but also unsolder the old part and solder the new part. Then you'll rebuild the laptop and hope you got everything right. CompTIA cannot expect a CompTIA A+ technician to know how to do this stuff. Expect a question that explores whether it *can* be done. Rest assured, specialized techs can replace *any* component on a laptop, even the DC jack.

■ Troubleshooting Portable Computers

Many of the troubleshooting techniques you learned about for desktop systems can be applied to laptops. For example, take the proper precautions before and during disassembly. Use the proper hand tools, and document, label, and organize each plastic part and screw location for reassembly. Additionally, here are some laptop-specific procedures to try.

Laptop Won't Power On

- Verify AC power by plugging another electronic device into the wall outlet. If the other device receives power, the outlet is good.

- If the outlet is good, connect the laptop to the wall outlet and try to power on. If no LEDs light up, you may have a bad AC adapter. Swap it out with a known-good power adapter.

- A faulty peripheral device might keep the laptop from powering up. Remove any peripherals such as USB or FireWire devices.

Tech Tip

Battery Won't Charge

If you have a laptop with a battery that won't charge up, it could be one of two things: the battery might be cooked or the AC adapter isn't doing its job. To troubleshoot, replace the battery with a known-good battery. If the new battery works, you've found the problem. Just replace the battery. Alternatively, remove the battery and run the laptop on AC only. If that works, you know the AC adapter is good. If it doesn't, replace the AC adapter.

Screen Doesn't Come On Properly

- If the laptop is booting (you hear the beeps and the drives), first make sure the display is turned on. Press the FN key and the key to activate the screen a number of times until the laptop display comes on. If that doesn't work, check the LCD cutoff switch—on many laptops, this is the small nub somewhere near the screen hinge that shuts the monitor off when you close the laptop—and make sure it isn't stuck in the down position.

- If the laptop display is very dim, you may have lost an inverter. The clue here is that inverters never go quietly. They can make a nasty hum as they are about to die and an equally nasty popping noise when they actually fail. Failure often occurs when you plug in the laptop's AC adapter, as the inverters take power directly from the AC adapter. It's also possible that the backlights in the LCD panel have died, though this is much less common than a bad inverter.

- If the screen won't come on or is cracked, most laptops have a port for plugging in an external monitor, which you can use to log into your laptop.

- If you plug a laptop into an external monitor and that monitor does not display, remember that you have both a hardware and an OS component to making dual displays successful. There's usually a combination of FN and another key to toggle among only portable, only external, and both displays. Plus you have the Display applet in the Control Panel to mirror or extend the desktop to a second monitor.

- Many manufacturers have switched to LED displays on laptops, which has led to a phenomenon many techs thought long behind us: *flickering displays*. The LED backlights don't work quite the same as CCFL backlights, especially when you lower the brightness. This doesn't affect desktop LED displays, because they're usually so bright it doesn't matter. But portables need to be able to dim to save battery life. One technique for dimming LEDs is to have them turn on and off rapidly enough to keep the pixels lit, but slowly enough that there's a reduction in visible light and electricity use. With some of these panels, that flickering is not only noticeable, but headache and eyestrain inducing.

- There are two things you can do with a flickering LED display: crank up the brightness so that it goes away (and thus live with reduced battery life) or replace the laptop.

Wireless Doesn't Work or Works Intermittently

- If the wireless doesn't work at all, check along the front, rear, or side edges of the laptop for a physical switch that toggles the internal wireless adapter or Bluetooth adapter on and off.

- If a tech has recently replaced a component that required removal of the laptop display, dead wireless could mean simply a disconnected antenna. Most portables have the antenna built into the display panel, so check that connection.

- Try the special key combination for your laptop to toggle the wireless or Bluetooth adapter. You usually press the FN key in combination with another key.

- You might simply be out of range or, if the wireless works intermittently, then right at the edge of the range. Physically walk the laptop over to the wireless router or access point to ensure there are no out-of-range issues.

- With Bluetooth specifically, remember that the pairing process takes action or configuration on both devices to succeed. Turn on the Bluetooth device, actively seek it, and try again.

Input Problems

- If none of the keys work on your laptop, there's a good chance you've unseated the keypad connector. These connectors are quite fragile and are prone to unseating from any physical stress on the laptop. Check the manufacturer's disassembly procedures to locate and reseat the keypad.

- If you're getting numbers when you're expecting to get letters, the number lock (NUMLOCK) function key is turned on. The numlock LED should indicate the status. Turn it off.

- Laptop keyboards take far more abuse than the typical desktop keyboard, because of all those lunch meetings and café brainstorm sessions. Eating and drinking while over or around a keyboard just begs for problems. If you have a portable with sticking keys, look for the obvious debris in the keys. Use compressed air to clean them out. If you have serious goo and need to use a cleaning solution, disconnect the keyboard from the portable first. Make sure it's fully dried out before you reconnect it or you'll short it out.

- If the touchpad is having problems, a shot of compressed air does wonders for cleaning pet hair out of the touchpad sensors. You might get a cleaner shot if you remove the keyboard before using the compressed air. Remember to be gentle when lifting off the keyboard and make sure to follow the manufacturer's instructions.

- The touchpad driver might need to be reconfigured. Try the various options in the Control Panel | Mouse applet.

The troubleshooting issue known as a *ghost cursor* can mean one of two things. First, the display shows a trail of ghost cursors behind your real cursor as you move it. This might point to an aging display or an improperly configured refresh rate. Second, the cursor moves erratically, whether you are touching the touchpad or not. This probably means the touchpad has been damaged in some way and needs to be replaced.

Chapter 18 Review

■ Chapter Summary

After reading this chapter and completing the exercises, you should understand the following about portable computers.

Describe the many types of portable computing devices available

- All portable devices share certain features: video output using LCD screens, some kind of PC sound, and DC battery power. There's no industry standard for naming the vast majority of styles of portable computing devices.

- A portable PC refers in general to the clamshell, keyboard-on-the-bottom and LCD-screen-at-the-top design that is considered the shape of mobile PCs. The terms "laptop," "notebook," and "portable" all define the same form factor.

- Portable computers come with a variety of input devices. Most have a fully functional keyboard and a device to control the mouse pointer. The basic QUERTY format is followed, but manufacturers make choices with key size and placement of the non-alphabet characters. Almost every portable keyboard uses a Function (FN) key to enable some keys to perform a third duty.

- By far the most common laptop pointing device found today is the touchpad—a flat, touch-sensitive pad just in front of the keyboard. To operate a touchpad, you simply glide your finger across its surface to move the pointer, and tap the surface once or twice to single- or double-click.

- Laptop LCD screens come in a variety of supported resolutions, described with acronyms such as XGA, WXGA, WSXGA, and more. The *W* in front of the letters indicates widescreen. The two most common resolutions are WXGA for the 14- to 15-inch models and HD 1080 for the 17.3-inch models. The common finish is either matte or high-gloss.

- A portable PC can be considered a desktop replacement if it does everything most people want to do with a desktop PC. Desktop replacements appeal to road warriors and people who prefer to tuck computing devices out of sight when not in use.

- Netbook portables normally weigh less than three pounds and are less than an inch in thickness. These machines usually have smaller displays, lower-capacity hard drives, and CPUs that operate at lower speeds than their more full-sized brethren.

- Ultrabooks are for people who can't give up the power of high-end computers but can afford to pay more for a smaller package. Intel set up the Ultrabook specifications in 2011, defining the form factor to use power-sipping Intel processors with integrated graphics.

- Microsoft started the Tablet PC initiative way back in 2001, defining the devices as fully featured portables running a tablet-aware version of Windows and using a stylus to interact directly with the screen. Many Tablet PCs have come to market since then, fulfilling the needs of specific professions, notably medicine.

Explain ways to expand portable computers

- Every portable PC comes with one or more single-function ports. The most common of all is the ubiquitous USB port. Additionally, the single PS/2 port on some laptops supports both keyboards and pointing devices. Most portable computing devices have a speaker port, and some have line in and microphone jacks as well. Laptops invariably provide a video port such as a VGA, HDMI, DisplayPort, or DVI connection for hooking up an external monitor.

- Most laptops support a second monitor, giving the user the option to display Windows on the laptop only, the external monitor only, or both simultaneously. Usually a special Function (FN) key on the keyboard will cycle through the monitor configurations.

- All portables offer some kind of network connectivity, such as 802.11 Wi-Fi to connect to the Internet. Wired Ethernet ports are standard issue. Bluetooth is common for connecting peripherals. Portables have some way to toggle Wi-Fi and Bluetooth off and on to conserve battery life.

- PC Cards are roughly credit card–sized devices that enhance and extend the functions of a portable PC. Still commonly known by their older name, *PCMCIA cards*, PC Cards were standard on mobile computers for years but are slowly disappearing. All PC Cards are hot-swappable.

- Parallel PC Cards come in two flavors, 16-bit and CardBus, and each flavor comes in three different physical sizes, called Type I, Type II, and Type III. Type I, II, and III cards differ only in the thickness of the card (Type I being the thinnest and Type III the thickest). Type II cards are by far the most common. All parallel PC Cards share the same 68-pin interface. The 16-bit PC Cards are 16-bit, 5-V cards that can have up to two distinct functions or devices, such as a modem/network card combination. CardBus PC Cards are 32-bit, 3.3-V cards that can have up to eight different functions on a single card. The 16-bit PC Cards will fit into and work in CardBus slots, but the reverse is not true.

- The serial ExpressCard comes in two widths: 54 mm (ExpressCard/54) and 34 mm (ExpressCard/34). Both cards are 75 mm long and 5 mm thick, which makes them shorter than all previous PC Cards and the same thickness as a Type II PC Card. ExpressCards connect to either the Hi-Speed USB 2.0 bus (480 Mbps) or a PCI Express bus (2.5 Gbps).

- Most portable PCs have one or more general-purpose expansion ports that enable you to plug in many types of devices. Older portables sport RS-232 serial and IEEE 1284 parallel ports for mice, modems, printers, scanners, external CD-media drives, and more. USB, FireWire, and eSATA are popular and widespread methods for attaching peripherals to laptops. All have easy-to-use connectors and can be hot-swapped.

- Port replicators are devices that plug into a single port (usually USB but sometimes proprietary) and offer common PC ports, such as serial, parallel, USB, network, and PS/2. Docking stations resemble port replicators in many ways, offering legacy and modern single- and multi-function ports, but have extra features built in, such as optical drives or PC Card slots.

Manage and maintain portable computers

- Portable computers use three types of batteries: Nickel-Cadmium (Ni-Cd), Nickel-Metal Hydride (Ni-MH), and Lithium-Ion (Li-Ion). Today, only Li-Ion is used because that battery chemistry provides the highest energy density for the weight and has few problems with external factors.

- Batteries should be stored in a cool place and kept charged, at least to 70–80 percent. Never drain a battery all the way down unless required to do so as part of a battery calibration. Rechargeable batteries have only a limited number of charge-discharge cycles before overall battery performance is reduced. Because batteries contain dangerous chemicals, never handle one that has ruptured. Always recycle old batteries rather than disposing of them in the trash.

- The process of cooperation among the hardware, the BIOS, and the OS to reduce power use is known generically as power management. Early laptops used power continuously, regardless of whether the system was using the device at the time. With power management features, today's laptops can automatically turn off unused devices or can shut down the entire system, leaving the information in RAM ready for a restart. To perform these power management functions requires specialized hardware, BIOS, and an operating system that supports power management.

- Starting with the 386SX, Intel introduced System Management Mode (SMM), a power management system that would make the CPU and all peripherals go to "sleep." In 1992, Intel introduced the improved Advanced Power Management (APM) specification, followed by the Advanced Configuration and Power Interface (ACPI) standard in 1996.

- To use APM or ACPI, the computer must have an SMM-capable CPU, an APM-compliant BIOS, and devices that can be shut off. Referred to as Energy Star devices, these peripherals can shut down without actually turning off. The OS must also know how to request that a particular device be shut down. ACPI extends power-saving to include hot-swappable devices.

- Virtually all laptops and desktops use power management functions. APM defines four power-usage levels, including Full On, APM Enabled, APM Standby, and APM Suspend. ACPI, the successor to APM, handles all these levels plus a few more, totaling four Global (G) and six total (S) states. Support for APM was discontinued in Windows Vista, which uses ACPI.

- Configure APM/ACPI through CMOS or through the Power Options Control Panel applet in Windows, with Windows settings overriding CMOS settings. Many CMOS versions allow configuration of wake-up events.

- Hibernation writes information from RAM to the hard drive. Upon waking up, the data is returned to RAM, and programs and files are in the same state they were in when the computer entered hibernation.

- Laptops with backlit keyboards will have some way you can disable this feature when it's not needed, usually with a keyboard combination. You can also reduce the output of the LCD backlight using a combination of FN and another key to get a few more minutes of computing time before you have to shut down.

- Use an appropriate screen cleaner (not glass cleaner) to clean the LCD screen. Use compressed air around the keyboard and PC card sockets. Never use water around the keyboard.

- To combat the inevitable heat produced by a portable computer, always use power management, keep an air space between the bottom of the laptop and the surface on which it rests, don't use a keyboard protector for an extended period of time, and be aware of your fan.

- Store portable computers in quality cases when traveling. Well-padded backpacks not only keep a laptop protected but also make a system less appealing to would-be thieves. When traveling, don't forget accessories such as AC power cords, additional batteries, or modular devices. Remove all discs from drives and make sure you have enough battery power to boot up for security personnel. If shipping your computer, go with a reputable carrier, keep your tracking number, and request a delivery signature. Use a laptop lock or a software tracking system to protect your laptop when traveling.

Upgrade and repair portable computers

- You need to follow a four-step process to succeed in disassembly/reassembly. First, document and label every cable and screw location. Second, organize any parts you extract from the laptop. Third, refer to the manufacturer's documentation. Finally, you need to use the appropriate hand tools. If you can't get information directly from the manufacturer, try various online sites, such as YouTube or iFixit, for walkthroughs on fixing laptop problems.

- Every CompTIA A+ tech should know how to perform the two standard upgrades to portable computers: adding RAM and replacing a hard drive.

- Laptops use one of four types of RAM. Most older laptops use either 72-pin or 144-pin SO-DIMMs with SDRAM technology. DDR SDRAM systems primarily use 200-pin SO-DIMMs, although you'll also find 172-pin micro-DIMMs. Every decent laptop has upgradeable RAM slots. Get the correct RAM; many portable PC makers use proprietary RAM solutions. No standard exists for RAM placement in portables. More often than not, you need to unscrew or pop open a panel on the underside of the portable and press out on the restraining clips to make the RAM stick pop up so you can remove and replace it. Always disconnect from all electrical sources before removing or inserting RAM.

- Laptops that support shared memory benefit from more affordable video cards. The video card has less built-in RAM and uses a portion of the computer's system RAM to make up the difference. Although this results in a lower cost, system performance suffers because RAM that is shared with the video card is not available to programs. NVIDIA calls their shared memory technology TurboCache and ATI calls theirs HyperMemory.

- SATA drives in the 2.5-inch drive format now rule in all laptops. Currently, the larger 2.5-inch hard drives hold up to 500+ GB, while the larger 3.5-inch hard drives hold more than 3 TB. Upgrading from an HDD to an SSD can bring remarkable gains in battery life and performance.

- Once you get beyond upgrading RAM and replacing a hard drive on a portable PC, you take the plunge into the laptop repair specialty. You can replace some components by lifting them out, detaching a ribbon cable, and then reversing the steps with the replacement part. Other parts require a full teardown of the laptop to the bare bones, which presents a much greater level of difficulty.

- Standard tech-level repairs you should be able to do are replacing the battery, keyboard, and optical drive (usually—some are tough to get out). Others are replacing the small speakers and missing plastic parts.

- You can also open the hatch on the bottom of the case that opens like the RAM hatch to expose other parts for replacement. The same hatch might hold one or two Mini-PCIe slots, for example, and give you access to the CPU.

- Some hardware replacements require you to open a laptop, remove many delicate parts, and strip it down to the bare metal chassis. Dedicated laptop techs do these jobs, but you should know the process.

- Portables open in two different ways, depending on the manufacturer. You either peel away layers from the top down, through the keyboard, or from the bottom up, through the base. Either direction requires careful attention to detail, part connectivity, and locations. You'll need a system to keep track of the dozens of tiny screws.

Troubleshoot portable computers

- If your laptop won't power on, try a different wall outlet. If it still fails to power up, remove all peripheral devices and try again.

- If the screen doesn't come on properly, verify that the laptop is configured to use the built-in LCD screen by pressing the appropriate key to cycle through the internal and external monitors. If you hear a popping sound, you may have blown an inverter. If the screen is definitely broken, you may use an external monitor to access the laptop. One technique for dimming LEDs is to have them turn on and off rapidly enough to keep the pixels lit, but slowly enough that there's a reduction in visible light and electricity use. With some of these panels, that flickering is not only noticeable, but headache and eyestrain inducing.

- If wireless is not working, check for the physical switch on the side of the laptop that toggles power to the internal network card or Bluetooth adapter. If your laptop doesn't have a switch, check for a key combination or function key that toggles power. You also may be out of range. Physically walk the laptop closer to the wireless router or access point.

- If the keypad or touchpad doesn't work, try a shot of compressed air, reseat the physical internal connection, or reconfigure the driver settings through the Control Panel.

■ Key Terms

16-bit *(570)*
Advanced Configuration and Power Interface (ACPI) *(575)*
Advanced Power Management (APM) *(575)*
aspect ratio *(559)*
auto-switching power supply *(583)*
CardBus *(570)*
desktop replacement *(560)*
docking station *(573)*
ExpressCard *(570)*

Function (FN) key *(557)*
hibernation *(576)*
high-gloss *(560)*
laptop *(557)*
Lithium-Ion (Li-Ion) *(573)*
matte *(560)*
Mini-PCI *(592)*
Mini-PCIe *(592)*
multitouch *(559)*
netbook *(561)*

Nickel-Cadmium (Ni-Cd) *(573)*
Nickel-Metal Hydride (Ni-MH) *(573)*
notebook *(557)*
offline files *(580)*
PC Card *(569)*
PCMCIA card *(570)*
port replicator *(572)*
power plan *(578)*

shared memory *(588)*
sleep timer *(578)*
stylus *(562)*
System Management Mode (SMM) *(575)*
Tablet PC *(562)*
touchpad *(559)*
TrackPoint *(558)*
Ultrabook *(562)*

■ Key Term Quiz

Use the Key Terms list to complete the sentences that follow. Not all terms will be used.

1. A typical clamshell-style computer with built-in LCD monitor, keyboard, and input device is most commonly called a laptop or _____.

2. The _____ enables laptop keyboards to do more than two functions on a single key.

3. Many newer laptops feature _____ screens offering richer color, higher contrast, and wider viewing angles.

4. Intel set up the _____ specifications for super thin, super light, and super efficient laptops with integrated graphics and no optical drive.

5. The _____ replaced the PC Card as the external expansion slot of choice on laptops.

6. A(n) _____ plugs into a single port on the portable computer and offers uncommon and common PC ports, such as serial, parallel, USB, network, and PS/2.

7. Today's laptops use _____ for batteries because that battery chemistry provides the highest energy density for the weight.

8. Windows Vista and Windows 7 enable _____ for storing and automatically syncing files and folders between a portable and a file server.

9. Laptops using _____ are less expensive because the video card has less built-in memory, but the RAM it borrows from the system results in less memory available to programs.

10. Most laptops today have one or more _____ slots for internal expansion cards such as Wi-Fi NICs.

■ Multiple-Choice Quiz

1. Which of the following statements best describes hard drives typically found in laptops?

 A. They are 2.5-inch SATA drives, but they do not hold as much data as the 3.5-inch hard drives found in desktop PCs.

 B. They are 3.5-inch ATA drives just like those found in desktop PCs, but they usually require "cable select" settings rather than master or slave.

 C. They are 3.5-inch SATA drives that hold more data than the 2.5-inch hard drives found in desktop PCs.

 D. They are 2.5-inch PCMCIA drives, while desktops usually have 3.5-inch SCSI drives.

2. Which of the following APM power levels writes information from RAM to the hard drive and then copies the data back to RAM when the computer is activated again?

A. Full On

B. APM Enabled

C. APM Standby

D. Hibernation

3. Portable PCs typically use which of the following kinds of upgradeable RAM?

 A. 68-pin and 72-pin RIMMs

 B. 30-pin and 72-pin SIMMs

 C. 72-pin and 144-pin SO-DIMMs

 D. 30-pin and 72-pin SO-RIMMs

4. Where do you configure APM/ACPI in Windows?

 A. The Power Options applet in the Control Panel

 B. The Display applet in the Control Panel

 C. The Power Management applet in the Control Panel

 D. The Power and Devices applet in the Control Panel

5. Which of the following input devices will you most likely find on a portable PC?

 A. TrackPoint

 B. Touchpad

 C. Trackball

 D. Mouse

6. Which buses do ExpressCards use?

 A. Hi-Speed USB and FireWire

 B. Hi-Speed USB and PCI Express

 C. PCI and PCI Express

 D. Mini-PCI and Parallel

7. *Convertibles* and *slates* describe what type of device?

 A. Multicore processor

 B. Clamshell laptop computer

 C. PDA

 D. Tablet PC

8. If wireless networking is not working, what should you check?

 A. Check the switch on the side of the laptop that toggles power to the network card.

B. Make sure the Ethernet cable is plugged into the laptop.

C. Make sure the digitizer has been trained.

D. Make sure Power Management is enabled.

9. Erin has an older laptop with a switch on the back that says 115/230. What does this indicate?

 A. The laptop has an auto-switching power supply.

 B. The laptop has a fixed-input power supply.

 C. The laptop has a step-down transforming power supply.

 D. The laptop has a step-up transforming power supply.

10. Which of the following display types will you most commonly find on a portable PC today? (Select two.)

 A. LCD

 B. LED

 C. OLED

 D. Plasma

11. Jake has received two replacement memory sticks for his Dell laptop. What should he do first in the upgrade process?

 A. Disconnect the AC cord and remove the battery.

 B. Flip the laptop over and remove the RAM compartment cover.

 C. Remove the memory sticks from their antistatic bags and set them on the antistatic map next to the laptop.

 D. Remove the memory sticks from the laptop.

12. Steve complains that his Windows 7 laptop still isn't snappy enough after doubling the amount of RAM. What might improve system performance?

 A. Add more RAM.

 B. Replace the power supply.

 C. Replace the battery.

 D. Replace the HDD with an SSD.

13. Jim likes his laptop but complains that his wireless seems slow compared to all the new laptops. On further inspection, you determine his laptop runs 802.11g. What can be done to improve his network connection speed?

 A. Replace the regular RAM with 802.11n RAM.

 B. Replace the display with one with a better antenna.

 C. Replace the Mini-PCIe 802.11g card with an 802.11n card.

 D. Get a new laptop, because this one can't be upgraded.

14. Edgar successfully replaced the display on a laptop (a toddler had taken a ballpoint pen to it), but the customer called back almost immediately complaining that his wireless didn't work. What could the problem be?

 A. The problems are unrelated, so it could be anything.

 B. Edgar inadvertently disconnected the antenna from the Mini-PCIe 802.11 card.

 C. Edgar replaced the display with one without an internal antenna.

 D. Edgar failed to reconnect the antenna in the new display.

15. Rafael gets a tech call from a user with a brand new laptop complaining that working on it was causing headaches. What could the problem be?

 A. The laptop uses a plasma display.

 B. The laptop uses a CRT display.

 C. The laptop uses an LED display in power saving mode.

 D. The laptop uses an LED display in full power mode.

■ Essay Quiz

1. At the upcoming training seminar for new techs, your boss wants to make sure they understand and use power management settings. You've been asked to prepare a short presentation showing the range of power management settings available in Windows XP, Vista, and 7 and demonstrating how to set them. What will you include in your presentation?

2. You've been tasked to advise your group on current portable computer technology so they can purchase ten new laptops by the end of the quarter. In a short essay, weigh the pros and cons of getting desktop replacements versus smaller laptops that would come with docking stations.

3. Your boss has a new portable computer and is planning to take it with him on a business trip to Paris. He's not all that tech-savvy or much of a traveler, so write a memo that tells him what to do or avoid while traveling, especially overseas.

4. Norm wants to upgrade his laptop's hard drive, CPU, and RAM. Because he's upgraded all of these components on his desktop, he doesn't think he'll run into much trouble. What advice will you give him about selecting the components and upgrading the laptop?

Lab Projects

• Lab Project 18.1

This chapter mentioned that, although they are more expensive, portable PCs typically provide less processing power and smaller hard drives, and in general are not as full-featured as desktop computers. Use the Internet to check sites such as www.lenovo.com, www.toshiba.com, www .dell.com, and www.hp.com to compare the best equipped, most powerful laptop you can find with the best equipped, most powerful desktop computer you can find. How do their features and prices compare? Now find a less expensive laptop and try to find a desktop computer that is as similar as possible in terms of capabilities, and compare their prices.

• Lab Project 18.2

Continuing from the previous lab, go to the www .dell.com website and compare one of the better desktop-replacement laptops with one of the more basic laptops. List the features that are of interest to you personally, starting with the most important and continuing down. Then use the site to begin building the perfect laptop for you. Compare your results with others and discuss what's important to you.

Printer Technologies and Installation

"Faster! Faster! Faster would be better!"

—Capt. Malcolm Reynolds, *Serenity*

In this chapter, you will learn how to

- **Describe current printer technologies**
- **Explain the laser printing process**
- **Install a printer on a Windows PC**

Despite all of the talk about the "paperless office," printers continue to be a vital part of the typical office. In many cases, PCs are used exclusively for the purpose of producing paper documents. Many people simply prefer dealing with a hard copy. Programmers cater to this preference by using metaphors such as *page*, *workbook*, and *binder* in their applications. The CompTIA A+ certification strongly stresses the area of printing and expects a high degree of technical knowledge of the function, components, maintenance, and repair of all types of printers.

■ Printer Technologies

No other piece of your computer system is available in a wider range of styles, configurations, and feature sets than a printer, or at such a wide price variation. What a printer can and can't do is largely determined by the type of printer technology it uses—that is, how it gets the image onto the paper. Modern printers can be categorized into several broad types: impact, inkjet, dye-sublimation, thermal, laser, and solid ink.

Impact Printers

Printers that create an image on paper by physically striking an ink ribbon against the paper's surface are known as **impact printers**. Although *daisy-wheel* printers (essentially an electric typewriter attached to the PC instead of directly to a keyboard) have largely disappeared, their cousins, **dot-matrix printers**, still soldier on in many offices. Although dot-matrix printers don't deliver what most home users want—high quality and flexibility at a low cost—they're still widely found in businesses for two reasons: dot-matrix printers have a large installed base in businesses, and they can be used for multipart forms because they actually strike the paper. Impact printers tend to be relatively slow and noisy, but when speed, flexibility, and print quality are not critical, they provide acceptable results. PCs that print multipart forms, such as *point of sale* (POS) machines, use special *impact paper* that can print receipts in duplicate, triplicate, or more. These POS machines represent the major market for new impact printers, although many older dot-matrix printers remain in use.

Dot-matrix printers use a grid, or matrix, of tiny pins, also known as **printwires**, to strike an inked printer ribbon and produce images on paper (see Figure 19.1). The case that holds the printwires is called a **printhead**. Using either 9 or 24 pins, dot-matrix printers treat each page as a picture broken up into a dot-based raster image. The 9-pin dot-matrix printers are generically called *draft quality*, while the 24-pin printers are known as *letter quality* or **near-letter quality (NLQ)**. The BIOS for the printer (either built into the printer or a printer driver) interprets the raster image in the same way a monitor does, "painting" the image as individual dots. Naturally, the more pins, the higher the resolution. Figure 19.2 illustrates the components common to dot-matrix printers. Many dot-matrix printers use continuous-feed paper with holes on its sides that are engaged by metal sprockets to pull the paper through—this is known as *tractor-feed paper* because the sprockets are reminiscent of the wheels on a tractor.

● **Figure 19.1** An Epson FX-880+ dot-matrix printer (photo courtesy of Epson America, Inc.)

Inkjet Printers

Inkjet printers (also called *ink-dispersion printers*) like the one in Figure 19.3 are relatively simple devices. An inkjet printer uses a *printhead* connected to a *carriage* that contains the ink. A belt and motor move the carriage back and forth so the ink can cover the whole page. A *roller* grabs paper from a paper tray (usually under or inside the printer)

Platen Printhead Ribbon

Electronics Power supply Traverse assembly

Printers can also use *duplex assemblies*, which enable the printer to print automatically on both sides of the paper. Some printers include this feature built-in, while others require a piece of additional hardware that flips the paper for the printer.

• **Figure 19.2** Inside a dot-matrix printer

• **Figure 19.3** Typical inkjet printer

or feeder (usually on the back of the printer) and advances it through the printer (see Figure 19.4).

The ink is ejected through tiny tubes. Most inkjet printers use heat to move the ink, while a few use a mechanical method. The heat-method printers use tiny resistors or electroconductive plates at the end of each tube that literally boil the ink; this creates a tiny air bubble that ejects a droplet of ink onto the paper, thus creating a portion of the image (see Figure 19.5).

The ink is stored in special small containers called **ink cartridges**. Older inkjet printers had two cartridges: one for black ink and another for colored ink. The color cartridge had separate compartments for cyan (blue), magenta (red), and yellow ink, to print colors by using a method known as CMYK (you'll read more about CMYK later in this chapter). If your color cartridge ran out of one of the colors, you had to purchase a whole new color cartridge or deal with a messy refill kit.

Electronics Storage/cleaning/maintenance position

Traverse assembly Ink cartridges

Print area

Traverse guides Printhead and cartridge caddy Power supply

• **Figure 19.4** Inside an inkjet printer

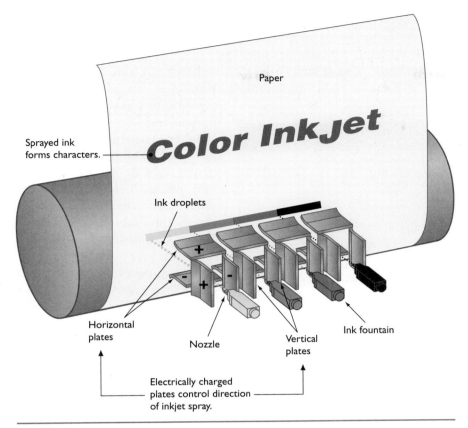

Sprayed ink
forms characters.

Paper

Color InkJet

Ink droplets

Horizontal
plates

Nozzle

Vertical
plates

Ink fountain

Electrically charged
plates control direction
of inkjet spray.

> If your impact printer isn't
> working right, first try replacing
> the paper and the ribbon. If
> it still won't work, you can
> find instructions for replacing
> the print head in the printer's
> manual.

• **Figure 19.5** Detail of the inkjet printhead

Printer manufacturers began to separate the ink colors into three separate cartridges so that printers came with four cartridges: one for each color and a fourth for black (see Figure 19.6). This not only was more cost-effective for the user, but it also resulted in higher quality printouts. Today you can find color inkjet printers with six, eight, or more color cartridges. In addition to the basic CMYK inks, the other cartridges provide for green, blue, gray, light cyan, dark cyan, and more. Typically, the more ink cartridges a printer uses, the higher the quality of the printed image—and the higher the cost of the printer.

The two key features of an inkjet printer are the **print resolution**—that is, the density of ink, which affects print quality—and the print speed. Resolution is measured in **dots per inch (dpi)**; higher numbers mean that the ink dots on the page are closer together, so your printed documents will look better. Resolution is most important when you're printing complex images such as full-color photos,

• **Figure 19.6** Inkjet ink cartridges

or when you're printing for duplication and you care that your printouts look good. Print speed is measured in **pages per minute (ppm)**, and this

 Print resolution is measured in dots per inch (dpi) and print speed is measured in pages per minute (ppm).

specification is normally indicated right on the printer's box. Most printers have one (faster) speed for monochrome printing—that is, using only black ink—and another for full-color printing.

Another feature of inkjet printers is that they can support a staggering array of print media. Using an inkjet printer, you can print on a variety of matte or glossy photo papers, iron-on transfers, and other specialty media; some printers can print directly onto specially coated optical discs, or even fabric. Imagine running a T-shirt through your printer with your own custom slogan (how about "I'm CompTIA A+ Certified!"). The inks have improved over the years, too, now delivering better quality and longevity than ever. Where older inks would smudge if the paper got wet or start to fade after a short time, modern inks are smudge proof and of archival quality—for example, some inks by Epson are projected to last up to 200 years.

Try This!

Pages per Minute Versus Price

Printer speed is a key determinant of a printer's price, and this is an easy assertion to prove, so Try This!

1. Fire up your browser and head over to the Web site for Hewlett-Packard (www.hp.com), Canon (www.usa.canon.com), Epson (www.epson.com), or Lexmark (www.lexmark.com). These four companies make most of the printers on the market today.

2. Pick a particular printer technology and check the price, from the cheapest to the most expensive. Then look for printers that have the same resolution but different ppm rates.

3. Check the prices and see how the ppm rate affects the price of two otherwise identical printers.

Dye-Sublimation Printers

The term *sublimation* means to cause something to change from a solid form into a vapor and then back into a solid. This is exactly the process behind *dye-sublimation printing*, sometimes called *thermal dye transfer* printing. **Dye-sublimation printers** are used mainly for photo printing, high-end desktop publishing, medical and scientific imaging, and other applications for which fine detail and rich color are more important than cost and speed. Smaller, specialized printers called *snapshot* printers use dye-sublimation specifically for printing photos at a reduced cost compared to their full-sized counterparts.

The dye-sublimation printing technique is an example of the so-called CMYK (**c**yan, **m**agenta, **y**ellow, blac**k**) method of color printing. It uses a roll of heat-sensitive plastic film embedded with page-sized sections of cyan (blue), magenta (red), and yellow dye; many also have a section of black dye. A printhead containing thousands of heating elements, capable of precise temperature control, moves across the film, vaporizing the dyes and causing them to soak into specially coated paper underneath before cooling and reverting to a solid form. This process requires one pass per page for each color. Some printers also use a final finishing pass that applies a protective laminate coating to the page. Figure 19.7 shows how a dye-sublimation printer works.

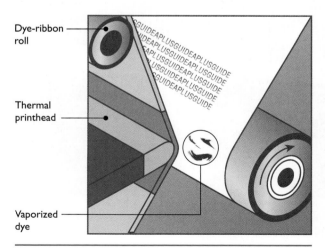

Dye-ribbon roll

Thermal printhead

Vaporized dye

• **Figure 19.7** The dye-sublimation printing process

Documents printed through the dye-sublimation process display *continuous-tone* images, meaning that the printed image is not constructed of pixel dots but a continuous blend of overlaid differing dye colors. This is in contrast to other print technologies' *dithered* images, which use closely packed, single-color dots to simulate blended colors. Dye-sublimation printers produce high-quality color output that rivals professional photo-lab processing.

Thermal Printers

Thermal printers use a heated printhead to create a high-quality image on special or plain paper. You'll see two kinds of thermal printers in use. The first is the *direct thermal* printer, and the other is the *thermal wax transfer* printer. Direct thermal printers use a heating element to burn dots into the surface of special heat-sensitive paper. If you remember the first generation of fax machines, you're already familiar with this type of printer. Many retail businesses still use it as a receipt printer, using large rolls of thermal paper housed in a feed assembly that automatically draws the paper past the heating element; some can even cut the paper off the roll for you.

Thermal wax printers work similarly to dye-sublimation printers, except that instead of using rolls of dye-embedded film, the film is coated with colored wax. The thermal printhead passes over the ribbon and melts the wax onto the paper. Thermal wax printers don't require special papers like dye-sublimation printers, so they're more flexible and somewhat cheaper to use, but their output isn't quite as good because they use color dithering.

Laser Printers

Using a process called *electro-photographic imaging*, **laser printers** produce high-quality and high-speed output of both text and graphics. Figure 19.8 shows a typical laser printer. Laser printers rely on the photoconductive properties of certain organic compounds. *Photoconductive* means that particles of these compounds, when exposed to light (that's the "photo" part), will *conduct* electricity. Laser printers usually use lasers as a light source because of their precision. Some lower-cost printers use LED arrays instead.

The first laser printers created only monochrome images. Today, you can also buy a color laser printer, although most laser printers produced today are monochrome. Although a color laser printer can produce complex full-color images such as photographs, they really shine for printing what's known as *spot color*—for example, eye-catching headings, lines, charts, or other graphical elements that dress up an otherwise plain printed presentation.

Tech Tip

Hidden Costs

Some printers use consumables—such as ink—at a much faster rate than others, prompting the industry to rank printers in terms of their cost per page. Using an inexpensive printer (laser or inkjet) costs around 4 cents per page, while an expensive printer can cost more than 20 cents per page—a huge difference if you do any volume of printing. This hidden cost is particularly pernicious in the sub-$100 inkjet printers on the market. Their low prices often entice buyers, who then discover that the cost of consumables is outrageous—these days, a single set of color and black inkjet cartridges can cost as much as the printer itself, if not more!

• **Figure 19.8** Typical laser printer

• **Figure 19.9** Components inside a laser printer

Color laser printers have four toner cartridges: black, cyan, magenta, and yellow.

Critical Components of the Laser Printer

The CompTIA A+ certification exams take a keen interest in the particulars of the laser printing process, so it pays to know your way around a laser printer (see Figure 19.9). Let's take a look at the many components of laser printers and their functions.

Toner Cartridge The **toner cartridge** in a laser printer is so named because of its most obvious activity: supplying the toner that creates the image on the page (see Figure 19.10). To reduce maintenance costs, however, many other laser printer parts, especially those that suffer the most wear and tear, have been incorporated into the toner cartridge. Although this makes replacement of individual parts nearly impossible, it greatly reduces the need for replacement; those parts that are most likely to break are replaced every time you replace the toner cartridge.

Photosensitive Drum The **photosensitive drum** (also called the *imaging drum*) is an aluminum cylinder coated with particles of photosensitive compounds. The drum itself is grounded to the power supply, but the coating is not. When light hits these particles, whatever electrical charge they may have "drains" out through the grounded cylinder.

Erase Lamp The **erase lamp** exposes the entire surface of the photosensitive drum to light, making the photosensitive coating conductive. Any electrical charge present in the particles bleeds away into the grounded drum, leaving the surface particles electrically neutral.

Primary Corona/Charge Roller The **primary corona** wire (or **primary charge roller**, in newer laser printers), located close to the photosensitive drum, never touches the drum. When the primary corona or primary charge roller is charged with an extremely high voltage, an electric field (or corona) forms, enabling voltage to pass to the drum and charge the photosensitive particles on its surface. The *primary grid* regulates the transfer of voltage, ensuring that the surface of the drum receives a uniform negative voltage of between ~600 and ~1000 volts.

Laser The **laser** acts as the writing mechanism of the printer. Any particle on the drum struck by the laser becomes conductive and its charge is drained away into the grounded core of the drum. The entire surface of the drum has a uniform negative charge of between ~600 and ~1000 volts following its charging by the primary corona wire or charge roller.

• **Figure 19.10** Laser printer's toner cartridge

When particles are struck by the laser, they are discharged and left with a ~100-volt negative charge. Using the laser, we can "write" an image onto the drum. Note that the laser writes a positive image to the drum.

Toner The **toner** in a laser printer is a fine powder made up of plastic particles bonded to iron particles. The *toner cylinder* charges the toner with a negative charge of between ~200 and ~500 volts. Because that charge falls between the original uniform negative charge of the photosensitive drum (~600 to ~1000 volts) and the charge of the particles on the drum's surface hit by the laser (~100 volts), particles of toner are attracted to the areas of the photosensitive drum that have been hit by the laser (that is, areas that have a *relatively* positive charge with reference to the toner particles).

 The toner used in laser printers is typically carbon particles mixed with a polyester resin.

Transfer Corona/Transfer Roller To transfer the image from the photosensitive drum to the paper, the paper must be given a charge that will attract the toner particles off of the drum and onto the paper. In older printers, the **transfer corona**, a thin wire, applied a positive charge to the paper, drawing the negatively charged toner particles to the paper. Newer printers accomplish the same feat using a **transfer roller** that draws the toner onto the paper. The paper, with its positive charge, is also attracted to the negatively charged drum. To prevent the paper from wrapping around the drum, a **static charge eliminator** removes the charge from the paper.

In most laser printers, the transfer corona/roller is outside the toner cartridge, especially in large, commercial-grade machines. The transfer corona/roller is prone to a build-up of dirt, toner, and debris through electrostatic attraction, and it must be cleaned. It is also quite fragile—usually finer than a human hair. Most printers with an exposed transfer corona/roller provide a special tool to clean it, but you can also—very delicately—use a cotton swab soaked in 90 percent denatured alcohol (don't use rubbing alcohol because it contains emollients). As always, never service any printer without first turning it off and unplugging it from its power source.

Fuser Assembly The **fuser assembly** is almost always separate from the toner cartridge. It is usually quite easy to locate, as it is close to the bottom of the toner cartridge and usually has two rollers to fuse the toner. Sometimes the fuser is somewhat enclosed and difficult to recognize because the rollers are hidden from view. To help you determine the location of the fuser, think about the data path of the paper and the fact that fusing is the final step of printing.

The toner is merely resting on top of the paper after the static charge eliminator has removed the paper's static charge. The toner must be permanently attached to the paper to make the image permanent. Two rollers, a pressure roller and a heated roller, are used to fuse the toner to the paper. The pressure roller presses against the bottom of the page, and the heated roller presses down on the top of the page, melting the toner into the paper. The heated roller has a nonstick coating such as Teflon to prevent the toner from sticking to the heated roller.

Power Supplies All laser printers have at least two separate power supplies. The first power supply is called the primary power supply or sometimes just the power supply. This power supply, which may actually be more than one power supply, provides power to the motors that move

the paper, the system electronics, the laser, and the transfer corona/roller. The high-voltage power supply usually provides power only to the primary corona/charge roller. The extremely high voltage of the high-voltage power supply makes it one of the most dangerous devices in the world of PCs! Before opening a printer to insert a new toner cartridge, it is imperative that you *always turn off* a laser printer!

To maintain a thermal printer, make sure to clean the heating element and remove debris from the rollers. Also remember to replace the paper when you get low!

Turning Gears A laser printer has many mechanical functions. First, the paper must be picked up. Next, the photosensitive roller must be turned and the laser, or a mirror, must be moved from left to right. The toner must be evenly distributed, and the fuser assembly must squish the toner into the paper. Finally, the paper must be kicked out of the printer and the assembly must be cleaned to prepare for the next page.

All of these functions are served by complex gear systems. In most laser printers, these gear systems are packed together in discrete units generically called *gear packs* or *gearboxes*. Most laser printers have two or three gearboxes that you can remove relatively easily in the rare case when one of them fails. Most gearboxes also have their own motor or solenoid to move the gears.

System Board Every laser printer contains at least one electronic board. On this board is the main processor, the printer's ROM, and the RAM used to store the image before it is printed. Many printers divide these functions among two or three boards dispersed around the printer (also known as sub-logic boards, as seen in Figure 19.9). An older printer may also have an extra ROM chip and/or a special slot where you can install an extra ROM chip, usually for special functions such as PostScript.

On some printer models, you can upgrade the contents of these ROM chips (the *firmware*) by performing a process called *flashing* the ROM. Flashing is a lot like upgrading the system BIOS, which you learned about in Chapter 7. Upgrading the firmware can help fix bugs, add new features, or update the fonts in the printer.

Of particular importance is the printer's RAM. When the printer doesn't have enough RAM to store the image before it prints, you get a memory overflow problem. Also, some printers store other information in the RAM, including fonts or special commands. Adding RAM is usually a simple job—just snapping in a SIMM or DIMM stick or two—but getting the *right* RAM is important. Call or check the printer manufacturer's Web site to see what type of RAM you need. Although most printer companies will happily sell you their expensive RAM, most printers can use generic DRAM like the kind you use in a PC.

Ozone Filter The coronas inside laser printers generate ozone (O_3). Although not harmful to humans in small amounts, even tiny concentrations of ozone will cause damage to printer components. To counter this

problem, most laser printers have a special ozone filter that needs to be vacuumed or replaced periodically.

Sensors and Switches Every laser printer has a large number of sensors and switches spread throughout the machine. The sensors are used to detect a broad range of conditions such as paper jams, empty paper trays, or low toner levels. Many of these sensors are really tiny switches that detect open doors and so on. Most of the time these sensors/switches work reliably, yet occasionally they become dirty or broken, sending a false signal to the printer. Simple inspection is usually sufficient to determine if a problem is real or just the result of a faulty sensor/switch.

If your laser printer is acting up, there are a few things to try. First, cleaning the printer with 90 percent alcohol and a cleaning towel and replacing the toner cartridge can solve a surprising number of problems. If that doesn't work, try running a calibration routine on your printer. Finally, if all else fails, you can buy a maintenance kit containing easily replaceable parts.

Solid Ink

Solid ink printers use just what you'd expect—solid inks. The technology was originally developed by Tektronix, whose printer division was acquired by Xerox. Solid ink printers use solid sticks of nontoxic "ink" that produce more vibrant color than other print methods. The solid ink is melted and absorbed into the paper fibers; it then solidifies, producing a continuous-tone output. Unlike dye-sublimation printers, all colors are applied to the media in a single pass, reducing the chances of misalignment. Solid ink sticks do not rely on containers like ink for inkjet printers and can be "topped off" midway through a print job by inserting additional color sticks without taking the printer offline.

These printers are fast, too! A full-color print job outputs the first page in about six seconds. Of course, all that speed and quality comes at a price. Xerox's base model starts at about twice the cost of a laser printer, with the expensive model selling for about six times the cost! Solid ink printers become a bit more affordable when you factor in the cost of consumables. A single stick of ink costs about as much as an inkjet cartridge, for example, but with a print capacity of 1000 pages, that completely beats the cost of inkjet cartridges over time.

Printer Languages

Now that you've learned about the different types of print devices and techniques, it's time to take a look at how they communicate with the PC. How do you tell a printer to make a letter *A* or to print a picture of your pet iguana? Printers are designed to accept predefined printer languages that handle both characters and graphics. Your software must use the proper language when communicating with your printer, so that your printer can output your documents onto a piece of paper. Following are the more common printer languages.

ASCII

You might think of the **American Standard Code for Information Interchange (ASCII)** language as nothing more than a standard set of characters, the basic alphabet in upper- and lowercase with a few strange symbols thrown in. ASCII actually contains a variety of control codes for transferring data, some of which can be used to control printers. For example, ASCII code 10 (or 0A in hex) means "Line Feed," and ASCII code 12 (0C) means "Form

Feed." These commands have been standard since before the creation of IBM PCs, and all printers respond to them. Being highly standardized has advantages, but the control codes are extremely limited. Printing high-end graphics and a wide variety of fonts requires more advanced languages.

PostScript

Adobe Systems developed the **PostScript** page description language in the early 1980s as a device-independent printer language capable of high-resolution graphics and scalable fonts. PostScript interpreters are embedded in the printing device. Because PostScript is understood by printers at a hardware level, the majority of the image processing is done by the printer and not the PC's CPU, so PostScript printers print faster. PostScript defines the page as a single raster image; this makes PostScript files extremely portable—they can be created on one machine or platform and reliably printed out on another machine or platform (including, for example, high-end typesetters).

Hewlett-Packard Printer Control Language (PCL)

Hewlett-Packard developed its **printer control language (PCL)** as a more advanced printer language to supersede simple ASCII codes. PCL features a set of printer commands greatly expanded from ASCII. Hewlett-Packard designed PCL with text-based output in mind; it does not support advanced graphical functions. The most recent version of PCL, PCL6, features scalable fonts and additional line drawing commands. Unlike PostScript, however, PCL is not a true page description language; it uses a series of commands to define the characters on the page. Those commands must be supported by each individual printer model, making PCL files less portable than PostScript files.

Windows GDI and XPS

Windows XP uses the **graphical device interface (GDI)** component of the operating system to handle print functions. Although you *can* use an external printer language such as PostScript, most users simply install printer drivers and let Windows do all the work. The GDI uses the CPU rather than the printer to process a print job and then sends the completed job to the printer. When you print a letter with a TrueType font in Windows, for example, the GDI processes the print job and then sends bitmapped images of each page to the printer. The printer sees a page of TrueType text, therefore, as a picture, not as text. As long as the printer has a capable enough raster image processor (explained later in this chapter) and plenty of RAM, you don't need to worry about the printer language in most situations. We'll revisit printing in Windows in more detail later in this chapter.

Windows Vista and Windows 7 support GDI printing, but they also include a printing subsystem called the **XML Paper Specification (XPS) print path**. XPS provides several improvements over GDI, including enhanced color management (which works with Windows Color System) and better print layout fidelity. The XPS print path requires a driver that supports XPS. Additionally, some printers natively support XPS, eliminating the

requirement that the output be converted to a device-specific printer control language before printing.

Printer Connectivity

Most printers connect to one of two ports on the PC: a DB-25 parallel port or a USB port. The parallel connection is the classic way to plug in a printer, but most printers today use USB. You'll need to know how to support the more obscure parallel ports, cables, and connections as well as the plug-and-play USB connections.

Parallel Communication and Ports

The **parallel port** was included in the original IBM PC as a faster alternative to serial communication. The IBM engineers considered serial communication, limited to 1 bit at a time, to be too slow for the "high-speed" devices of the day (for example, dot-matrix printers). The standard parallel port has been kept around for backward compatibility despite several obvious weaknesses.

Parallel ports may be far faster than serial ports, but they are slow by modern standards. The maximum data transfer rate of a standard parallel port is still only approximately 150 kilobytes per second (KBps). Standard parallel communication on the PC also relies heavily on software, eating up a considerable amount of CPU time that could be used better.

Parallel ports are hindered by their lack of true bidirectional capability. Although one-way communication was acceptable for simple line printers and dot-matrix printers, parallel communication also became popular for a wide range of external devices that required two-way communication. Although it is possible to get two-way communication out of a standard parallel port, the performance is not impressive.

 Many techs confuse the concept of duplex printing—a process that requires special printers capable of printing on both sides of a sheet of paper—with bidirectional printing. They are two different things!

IEEE 1284 Standard

In 1991, a group of printer manufacturers proposed to the *Institute of Electrical and Electronics Engineers* (*IEEE*) that a committee be formed to propose a standard for a backward-compatible, high-speed, bidirectional parallel port for the PC. The committee was the IEEE 1284 committee (hence the name of the standard).

The **IEEE 1284 standard** requires the following:

- Support for five distinct modes of operation: *compatibility mode*, *nibble mode*, *byte mode*, *EPP*, and *ECP*
- A standard method of negotiation for determining which modes are supported both by the host PC and by the peripheral device
- A standard physical interface (that is, the cables and connectors)
- A standard electrical interface (that is, termination, impedance, and so on)

Because only one set of data wires exists, all data transfer modes included in the IEEE 1284 standard are half-duplex: data is transferred in only one direction at a time.

 Tech Tip

IEEE 1284 Transfer Modes
The five modes of operation for parallel printing specified in the IEEE 1284 standard (compatibility, nibble, byte, EPP, ECP) are inching closer to obsolescence as USB printers take over the market. If you find yourself needing to optimize the performance of a legacy parallel printer, you can look up these modes by name, using various Web search tools.

Parallel Connections, Cabling, and Electricity

Although no true standard exists, *standard parallel cable* usually refers to a printer cable with the previously mentioned male **DB-25 connector** on one end and a 36-pin **Centronics connector** on the other (see Figure 19.11). The shielding (or lack thereof) of the internal wiring and other electrical characteristics of a standard parallel printer cable are largely undefined except by custom. In practice, these standard cables are acceptable for transferring data at 150 KBps, and for distances of less than 6 feet, but they would be dangerously unreliable for some transfer modes.

For more reliability at distances up to 32 feet (10 meters), use proper IEEE 1284–compliant cabling. The transfer speed drops with the longer cables, but it does work, and sometimes the trade-off between speed and distance is worth it.

• **Figure 19.11** Standard parallel cable with 36-pin Centronics connector on one end and DB-25 connector on the other

Installing a parallel cable is a snap. Just insert the DB-25 connector into the parallel port on the back of the PC and insert the Centronics connector into the printer's Centronics port and you're ready to go to press! If your PC didn't include a parallel port, you can always add one with a PCI or PCIe expansion card.

> Some printers come with both USB and parallel connections, but this, like the parallel port in general, has become very rare. If you need a parallel printer for a system, be sure to confirm that the particular model you want will work with your system!

USB Printers

New printers now use USB connections that you can plug into any USB port on your computer. USB printers don't usually come with a USB cable, so you need to purchase one when you purchase a printer. (It's quite a disappointment to come home with your new printer only to find you can't connect it because it didn't come with a USB cable.) Most printers use the standard USB type A connector on one end and the smaller USB type B connector on the other end, although some use two type A connectors. Whichever configuration your USB printer has, just plug in the USB cable—it's that easy!

> In almost all cases, you must install drivers before you plug a USB printer into your computer. You'll learn about installing printer drivers later in this chapter.

Network Printers

Connecting a printer to a network isn't just for offices anymore. More and more homes and home offices are enjoying the benefits of network printing. It used to be that to share a printer on a network—that is, to make it available to all network users—you would physically connect the printer to a single computer and then share the printer on the network. The downside to this was that the computer to which the printer was connected had to be left on for others to use the printer.

Today, the typical **network printer** comes with its own onboard network adapter that uses a standard RJ-45 Ethernet cable to connect the printer directly to the network by way of a router. Other printers include a built-in Wi-Fi adapter to enable wireless printing over the network. The printer

can typically be assigned a static IP address, or it can acquire one dynamically from a DHCP server. (Don't know what a router, IP address, or DHCP server is? Take a look back at Chapters 4 and 14.) Once connected to the network, the printer acts independently of any single PC. Some of the more costly network printers come with a built-in Wi-Fi adapter to connect to the network wirelessly. Alternatively, some printers offer Bluetooth or infrared (IR) interfaces for networking.

Even if a printer does not come with built-in Ethernet, Wi-Fi, or Bluetooth, you can purchase a standalone network device known as a *print server* to connect your printer to the network. These print servers, which can be Ethernet or Wi-Fi, enable one or several printers to attach via USB cable (or even parallel port, if you still have a printer that old). So take that ancient ImageWriter dot-matrix printer and network it—I dare you!

Other Printers

Plenty of other connection types are available for printers. We've focused mainly on parallel, USB, and networked connections. Be aware that you may run into an old serial port printer or a SCSI printer. Although this is unlikely, know that it's a possibility.

■ The Laser Printing Process

The laser printing process can be broken down into seven steps, and the CompTIA A+ 220-801 exam expects you to know them all. As a tech, you should be familiar with these phases, as this can help you troubleshoot printing problems. For example, if an odd line is printed down the middle of every page, you know there's a problem with the photosensitive drum or cleaning mechanism and the toner cartridge needs to be replaced.

The seven steps to the laser printing process may be performed in a different order, depending on the printer, but it usually goes like this:

1. Processing
2. Charging
3. Exposing
4. Developing
5. Transferring
6. Fusing
7. Cleaning

Processing

When you click the Print button in an application, several things happen. First, the CPU processes your request and sends a print job to an area of memory called the print spooler. The **print spooler** enables you to queue up multiple print jobs that the printer will handle sequentially. Next, Windows sends the first print job to the printer. That's your first potential bottleneck—if it's a big job, the OS has to dole out a piece at a time and you'll see the

 The CompTIA A+ 220-801 exam objectives refer to a wireless print connection called "802.11x." This is not a new Wi-Fi standard. It's a generic term used to describe all Wi-Fi standards, including 802.11a, 802.11b, 802.11g, and 802.11n.

 You'll find print servers outside standalone network devices. In fact, your Windows PC is capable of operating as a print server. Anytime you plug a printer into a PC and share the printer over the network, the sharing PC can be referred to as a print server. The CompTIA A+ 220-801 exam, however, will most likely stick to standalone print server boxes, as opposed to Windows print servers.

little printer icon in the notification area at the bottom right of your screen. Once the printer icon goes away, you know the print queue is empty—all jobs have gone to the printer.

Once the printer receives some or all of a print job, the hardware of the printer takes over and processes the image. That's your second potential bottleneck and has multiple components.

Raster Images

Impact printers transfer data to the printer one character or one line at a time, whereas laser printers transfer entire pages at a time to the printer. A laser printer generates a **raster image** (a pattern of dots) of the page, representing what the final product should look like. It uses a device (the laser) to "paint" a raster image on the photosensitive drum. Because a laser printer has to paint the entire surface of the photosensitive drum before it can begin to transfer the image to paper, it processes the image one page at a time.

A laser printer uses a chip called the **raster image processor (RIP)** to translate the raster image into commands to the laser. The RIP takes the digital information about fonts and graphics and converts it to a rasterized image made up of dots that can then be printed. An inkjet printer also has a RIP, but it's part of the software driver instead of onboard hardware circuitry. The RIP needs memory (RAM) to store the data that it must process.

A laser printer must have enough memory to process an entire page. Some images that require high resolutions require more memory. Insufficient memory to process the image will usually be indicated by a memory overflow ("MEM OVERFLOW") error. If you get a memory overflow error, try reducing the resolution, printing smaller graphics, or turning off RET (see the following section for the last option). Of course, the best solution to a memory overflow error is simply to add more RAM to the laser printer.

Do not assume that every error with the word *memory* in it can be fixed simply by adding more RAM to the printer. Just as adding more RAM chips will not solve every conventional PC memory problem, adding more RAM will not solve every laser printer memory problem. The message "21 ERROR" on an HP LaserJet, for example, indicates that "the printer is unable to process very complex data fast enough for the print engine." This means that the data is simply too complex for the RIP to handle. Adding more memory would *not* solve this problem; it would only make your wallet lighter. The only answer in this case is to reduce the complexity of the page image (that is, fewer fonts, less formatting, reduced graphics resolution, and so on).

Resolution

Laser printers can print at different resolutions, just as monitors can display different resolutions. The maximum resolution that a laser printer can handle is determined by its physical characteristics. Laser printer resolution is expressed in dots per inch (dpi). Common resolutions are 600 × 600 dpi or 1200 × 1200 dpi. The first number, the horizontal resolution, is determined by how fine a focus can be achieved by the laser. The second number is determined by the smallest increment by which the drum can be turned. Higher resolutions produce higher-quality output, but keep in mind that higher resolutions also require more memory. In some instances, complex images can be printed only at lower resolutions because of their

Tech Tip

Inkjet RIPs

Inkjet printers use RIPs as well, but they're written into the device drivers instead of the onboard programming. You can also buy third-party RIPs that can improve the image quality of your printouts; for an example, see www.colorbytesoftware.com.

high memory demands. Even printing at 300 dpi, laser printers produce far better quality than dot-matrix printers because of **resolution enhancement technology (RET)**.

RET enables the printer to insert smaller dots among the characters, smoothing out the jagged curves that are typical of printers that do not use RET (see Figure 19.12). Using RET enables laser printers to output high-quality print jobs, but it also requires a portion of the printer's RAM. If you get a MEM OVERFLOW error, sometimes disabling RET will free up enough memory to complete the print job.

Charging

Now we turn to the physical side of the printing process. To make the drum receptive to new images, it must be charged (see Figure 19.13). Using the primary corona wire or primary charge roller, a uniform negative charge is applied to the entire surface of the drum (usually between ~600 and ~1000 volts).

Exposing

A laser is used to create a positive image on the surface of the drum. Every particle on the drum hit by the laser releases most of its negative charge into the drum.

Developing

Those particles with a lesser negative charge are positively charged relative to the toner particles and attracts them, creating a developed image (see Figure 19.14).

• **Figure 19.12** RET fills in gaps with smaller dots to smooth out jagged characters.

• **Figure 19.13** Charging the drum with a uniform negative charge

• **Figure 19.14** Writing the image and applying the toner

Static eliminator

Fuser rollers

Transfer corona

• **Figure 19.15** Transferring the image to the paper and fusing the final image

The heated roller produces enough heat to melt some types of plastic media, particularly overhead transparency materials. This could damage your laser printer (and void your warranty), so make sure you're printing on transparencies designed for laser printers!

Transferring

The printer must transfer the image from the drum onto the paper. The transfer corona or transfer roller gives the paper a positive charge; then the negatively charged toner particles leap from the drum to the paper. At this point, the particles are merely resting on the paper and must still be permanently fused to the paper.

Fusing

The particles have been attracted to the paper because of the paper's positive charge, but if the process stopped here, the toner particles would fall off the page as soon as you lift it. Because the toner particles are mostly composed of plastic, they can be melted to the page. Two rollers—a heated roller coated in a nonstick material and a pressure roller—melt the toner to the paper, permanently affixing it. Finally, a static charge eliminator removes the paper's positive charge (see Figure 19.15). Once the page is complete, the printer ejects the printed copy and the process begins again with the physical and electrical cleaning of the printer.

Cleaning

The printing process ends with the physical and electrical cleaning of the photosensitive drum (see Figure 19.16). Before printing another new page, the drum must be returned to a clean, fresh condition. All residual toner left over from printing the previous page must be removed, usually by scraping the surface of the drum with a rubber cleaning blade. If residual particles remain on the drum, they will appear as random black spots and streaks on the next page. The physical cleaning mechanism either deposits the residual toner in a debris cavity or recycles it by returning it to the toner supply in the toner cartridge. The physical cleaning must be done carefully. Damage to the drum will cause a permanent mark to be printed on every page.

The printer must also be electrically cleaned. One or more erase lamps bombard the surface of the drum with the appropriate wavelengths of light, causing the surface particles to discharge into the grounded drum. After the cleaning process, the drum should be completely free of toner and have a neutral charge.

■ Installing a Printer in Windows

You need to take a moment to understand how Windows handles printing, and then you'll see how to install, configure, and troubleshoot printers in these operating systems.

To Windows, a printer is not a physical device; it is a *program* that controls one or more physical printers. The *physical* printer is called a print device by Windows (although I continue to use the term "printer" for most

• **Figure 19.16** Cleaning and erasing the drum

purposes, just like almost every tech on the planet). Printer drivers and a spooler are still present, but in Windows, they are integrated into the printer itself (see Figure 19.17). This arrangement gives Windows amazing flexibility. For example, one printer can support multiple print devices, enabling a system to act as a print server. If one print device goes down, the printer automatically redirects the output to a working print device.

The general installation, configuration, and troubleshooting issues are basically identical in all modern versions of Windows. Here's a review of a typical Windows printer installation. I'll mention the trivial differences among Windows XP, Vista, and 7 as I go along.

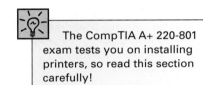
The CompTIA A+ 220-801 exam tests you on installing printers, so read this section carefully!

Setting Up Printers

Setting up a printer is so easy that it's almost scary. Most printers are plug and play, so installing a printer is reduced to simply plugging it in and loading the driver if needed. With USB printers (and infrared printers, for that matter), Windows won't even wait for you to do anything—once you connect a printer (or point the IR beam at a compatible PC), Windows immediately detects and installs the printer.

• **Figure 19.17** Printer driver and spooler in Windows

If the system does not detect the printer or if the printer is not plug and play, however, click Start | Printers and Faxes in Windows XP to open the Printers applet. In Windows Vista, you need to open the Control Panel and find the Printer menu item—it is either by itself or, in the categorized view, under Hardware. With Windows 7, go to Start | Devices and Printers. As you might guess, you install a new printer by clicking the Add a Printer icon/button (somehow Microsoft has managed to leave the name of this option unchanged through all Windows versions since 9x). This starts the Add Printer Wizard.

The Add Printer Wizard enables you to install a local printer or a network printer. This distinction is actually a little misleading. Windows divides printer installation into two scenarios: a printer connected directly to a PC (your local PC or another PC on a network), or a standalone printer directly connected to a switch or router. While you might think the local versus network installation options divide these scenarios nicely, they do not. Let's take a quick look at both local and network installations so you know when to use each.

Installing a Local Printer

At first glance, you might think the local printer installation option is used to install your standard USB printer, but don't forget that Windows will automatically detect and install USB printers (or any other plug-and-play printer). So what do you use it for? This option is most commonly used to install printers using a parallel connection or to install standalone network printers using an IP address. Using current versions of Windows and a modern printer, you shouldn't need to use the IP address to install a standalone network printer, but it can be a helpful alternative if Windows won't detect it any other way.

For parallel port printers, check the *Automatically detect and install my Plug and Play printer* option in Windows XP (see Figure 19.18). Windows won't automatically detect a new parallel device. When you check this box and click Next, Windows XP will run a search for any plug-and-play printers, including those connected via parallel cables. (Windows Vista and Windows 7 don't include this option; you'll need to configure parallel-connected printers manually by selecting a port and driver.)

If you need to install a standalone network printer using its IP address, uncheck the *Automatically detect and install my Plug and Play printer* option in Windows XP and click Next. In Windows Vista and Windows 7, click *Add a local printer*. In the *Create a new port* drop-down box, select Standard TCP/IP Port. Click Next. Type the IP address here.

> Confusingly, you can also get to the IP address entry screen in Windows Vista and Windows 7 via the network installation option, but not directly. Only after the network option fails to automatically detect a networked printer can you enter the IP address manually by clicking *The printer that I want isn't listed* and selecting *Add a printer using a TCP/IP address or hostname*.

> You will be unable to install a printer using the drivers that came with a disc unless you have administrative privileges.

• **Figure 19.18** Automatically detecting plug-and-play printers in Windows XP

Whether you use a parallel port or a TCP/IP port, you'll need to manually select the proper driver (see Figure 19.19). Windows includes a lot of printer drivers, but you can also use the handy Have Disk option to use the disc that came with the printer. If you use the driver included on the disc, Windows will require administrator privileges to proceed; otherwise, you won't be able to finish the installation. The Windows Update button enables you to grab the latest printer drivers via the Internet.

You'll be asked if the new local printer should be the default printer and whether or not you want to share it with other PCs on the network. And before you ask, yes, you can share a standalone network printer connected to your PC via a TCP/IP port using File and Printer Sharing, though the printer would be disabled for other users any time you turned off your PC. You'll be asked to print a test page to make sure everything works. Then you're done!

Installing a Network Printer

Surprisingly, setting up network printers doesn't require much more effort than setting up local printers, unless you're using Windows XP—but isn't that always the case? When you try to install a network printer in Windows Vista or Windows 7, the Add Printer Wizard will scan for any available printers on your local network. More often than not, the printer you are looking for will pop up in a list (see Figure 19.20). When you select that printer and click Next, Windows will search for drivers. If you need to, you

• **Figure 19.20** List of available shared printers on a network

• **Figure 19.19** Selecting drivers

> If you need to search for drivers online, make sure you download the driver designed for your operating system! If you have a 64-bit copy of Windows 7, the 32-bit Windows 7 drivers won't work.

> Remember printer sharing from Chapter 14? Here's the other side of the operation. Keep in mind that after you install a shared printer onto your PC, you can actually share that shared printer with others. Windows considers the shared printer *your* printer, so you can do what you want with it, including sharing it.

If a computer is a member of a Windows 7 homegroup and printer sharing is enabled, all printers connected to the homegroup are shared with that computer automatically.

Depending upon how your network shares printers, you can end up seeing the same printer shared multiple ways. Everyone who has a shared printer installed can share the same printer again as their own printer. This can lead to some confusing printer usage, especially once people start turning off their computers and breaking the connections to the shared printer. Avoid this web of print sharing.

In addition to the Devices and Printers applet, Windows 7 (excluding the Home Premium edition) also includes the Print Management console. This tool enables you to view and modify all the printers and drivers on your PC or connected to your network. You can also manage any Windows print servers connected to the network. Many of Print Management's advanced features go beyond the scope of the CompTIA A+ 220-801 exam, but know that it centralizes (and in a few cases, enhances) the standard printer controls in Windows 7. You can find Print Management in Control Panel | Administrative Tools | Print Management.

can pick from a list of available drivers or use the disc that came with the printer. Either way, you're already done.

Windows XP doesn't include this automatic discovery feature, and if Windows Vista or Windows 7 fails to find your printer, you'll need to configure the network printer manually. Every version of Windows includes multiple methods of doing this. These methods change depending on whether you are connected to a domain or a workgroup.

If you are on a workgroup, you can browse for a printer on your network, connect to a specific printer (using its name or URL), or use a TCP/IP address or hostname (Windows Vista/7 only), as you can see in Figure 19.21. In a domain, most of those options remain the same, except that instead of browsing the workgroup, you can search and browse the domain using several search parameters, including printer features, printer location, and more. Once you've found your printer, you might be prompted for drivers. Provide them using the usual methods described earlier and then you are finished!

Remember that Windows doesn't always see your network's printers exactly how they are physically arranged. Imagine you have a network with three PCs. Andy's computer has a printer connected via USB, whereas Beth's computer and Carol's computer have no printers. There is, however, a second printer connected directly to their router via Ethernet. Beth has configured her PC to connect directly to the network printer using an IP address. Now that she's done that, she can actually share that printer with the rest of her network, even though it's not attached to her computer—Windows doesn't care where it is. The process for sharing a local printer and a network printer is identical because Windows considers both printers to be installed on your PC and under your control. So now Andy and Beth both share printers. When Carol goes looking for shared printers to use,

• **Figure 19.21** Options for finding network printers

the network printer attached to the router will look like Beth's printer, as if it were directly connected to Beth's machine.

Figure 19.22 shows a typical Windows XP Printers and Faxes screen on a system with one printer installed. Note the small checkmark in the icon's corner; this shows that the device is the default printer. If you have multiple printers, you can change the default printer by right-clicking the printer's icon and selecting *Make Default Printer* in Windows XP or *Set as default printer* in Windows Vista/7.

In addition to the regular driver installation outlined previously, some installations use printer emulation. *Printer emulation* simply means using a substitute printer driver for a printer, as opposed to using one made exclusively for that printer. You'll run into printer emulation in two circumstances. First, some new printers do not come with their own drivers. They instead emulate a well-known printer (such as an HP LaserJet 4) and run perfectly well on that printer driver. Second, you may see emulation in the "I don't have the right driver!" scenario. I keep about three different HP LaserJet and Epson inkjet printers installed on my PC because I know that with these printer drivers, I can print to almost any printer. Some printers may require you to set them into an *emulation mode* to handle a driver other than their native one.

 Figure 19.22 Installed default printer in the Printers and Faxes applet

Optimizing Print Performance

Although a quality printer is the first step toward quality output, your output relies on factors other than the printer itself. What you see on the screen may not match what comes out of the printer, so calibration is important. Using the wrong type of paper can result in less than acceptable printed documents. Configuring the printer driver and spool settings can also affect your print jobs.

Calibration

If you've ever tweaked that digital photograph so it looks perfect on your screen, only to discover that the final printout was darker than you had hoped, consider calibrating your monitor. **Calibration** matches the print output of your printer to the visual output on your monitor and governs that through software. All three parts need to be set up properly for you to print what you see consistently.

Computer monitors output in RGB—that is, they compose colors using red, green, and blue pixels, as discussed in Chapter 13—while printers mix their colors differently to arrive at their output. As mentioned earlier, the

CMYK method composes colors from cyan (blue), magenta (red), yellow, and black.

The upshot of all this is that the printer tries to output—by using CMYK (or another technique)—what you see on the screen using RGB. Because the two color modes do not create color the same way, you see color shifts and not-so-subtle differences between the onscreen image and the printed image. By calibrating your monitor, you can adjust the setting to match the output of your printer. You can do this manually through "eyeballing" it or automatically by using calibration hardware.

To calibrate your monitor manually, obtain a test image from the Web (try sites such as www.DigitalDog.net) and print it out. If you have a good eye, you can compare this printout to what you see on the screen and make the adjustments manually through your monitor's controls or display settings.

Another option is to calibrate your printer by using an International Color Consortium (ICC) color profile, a preference file that instructs your printer to print colors a certain way—for example, to match what is on your screen. Loading a different color profile results in a different color output. Color profiles are sometimes included on the installation media with a printer, but you can create or purchase custom profiles as well. The use of ICC profiles is not limited to printers; you can also use them to control the output of monitors, scanners, or even digital cameras. Windows Vista/7 include *Windows Color System* (*WCS*) to help build color profiles for use across devices. WCS is based on a new standard Microsoft calls *color infrastructure and translation engine* (*CITE*).

Beyond A+

Multifunction Peripherals

It's a common theme in computing: why have two devices that do one thing each when you can have one device that does two things? In that spirit, manufacturers started gluing various peripherals together to create *multifunction peripherals*, or *MFPs* (see Figure 19.23). These devices can include printers, scanners, fax machines, photocopiers, and more. All of your standard connection options are available, including USB, parallel, Ethernet, Wi-Fi, and more.

One of the best parts of a multifunction device is that all of these functions are available using a single connection. On the other hand, because a multifunction device is much more complicated than a single-function device, you'll probably need to follow very specific instructions and use the manufacturer-supplied installation disc to get it all working. Many multifunction devices also include functions that don't require a PC at all, such as photocopying and faxing. You can even print files from a digital camera's memory card without plugging the MFP into a PC.

• **Figure 19.23** All-in-one printer/scanner/fax machine/copier/coffee maker/iPod dock

Chapter 19 Review

■ Chapter Summary

After reading this chapter and completing the exercises, you should understand the following aspects of printers.

Describe current printer technologies

- Impact printers create an image on paper by physically striking an ink ribbon against the paper's surface. The most commonly used impact printer technology is dot matrix. Dot-matrix printers have a large installed base in businesses, and they can be used for multipart forms because they actually strike the paper. Dot-matrix printers use a grid, or matrix, of tiny pins, also known as printwires, to strike an inked printer ribbon and produce images on paper. The case that holds the printwires is called a printhead. Dot-matrix printers come in two varieties: 9-pin (draft quality) and 24-pin (letter quality).

- Inkjet printers include a printhead mechanism, support electronics, a transfer mechanism to move the printhead back and forth, and a paper feed component to drag, move, and eject paper. They eject ink through tiny tubes. The heat or pressure used to move the ink is created by tiny resistors or electroconductive plates at the end of each tube.

- Ink is stored in ink cartridges. Older color printers used two cartridges: one for black and one for cyan, magenta, and yellow. Newer printers come with four, six, eight, or more cartridges.

- The quality of a print image is called the print resolution. The resolution is measured in dots per inch (dpi), which has two values: horizontal and vertical. An example of a resolution is 600 × 600 dpi. Printing speed is measured in pages per minute (ppm). Modern inkjet printers can print on a variety of media, including glossy photo paper, optical discs, or fabric.

- Dye-sublimation printers are used to achieve excellent print quality, especially in color, but they're expensive. Documents printed through the dye-sublimation process display continuous-tone images, meaning that each pixel dot is a blend of the dye colors. This is in contrast to other print technologies' dithered images, which use closely packed, single-color dots to simulate blended colors.

- Two kinds of thermal printers create either quick one-color printouts such as faxes or store receipts (direct thermal) or higher-quality color prints (thermal wax transfer).

- Using a process called electro-photographic imaging, laser printers produce high-quality and high-speed output. Laser printers usually use lasers as a light source because of their precision, but some lower-cost printers may use LED arrays instead. The toner cartridge in a laser printer supplies the toner that creates the image on the page; many other laser printer parts, especially those that suffer the most wear and tear, have been incorporated into the toner cartridge. Although the majority of laser printers are monochrome, you can find color laser printers capable of printing photographs.

- Be aware of the cost of consumables when purchasing a printer. Some less expensive printers may seem like a good deal, but ink or toner cartridge replacements can cost as much as the entire printer.

- The photosensitive drum (or imaging drum) in a laser printer is an aluminum cylinder coated with particles of photosensitive compounds. The erase lamp exposes the entire surface of the photosensitive drum to light, making the photosensitive coating conductive and leaving the surface particles electrically neutral. When the primary corona or charge roller is charged with an extremely high voltage, an electric field (or corona) forms, enabling voltage to pass to the drum and charge the photosensitive particles on its surface; the surface of the drum receives a uniform negative voltage of between ~600 and ~1000 volts.

- The laser acts as the writing mechanism of the printer. When particles are struck by the laser, they are discharged and left with a ~100 volt negative charge. The toner in a laser printer is a fine powder made up of plastic particles bonded to iron particles. The toner cylinder charges the toner with a negative charge of between ~200 and ~500 volts. Because that charge falls between the original

uniform negative charge of the photosensitive drum (~600 to ~1000 volts) and the charge of the particles on the drum's surface hit by the laser (~100 volts), particles of toner are attracted to the areas of the photosensitive drum that have been hit by the laser. The transfer corona or transfer roller applies a positive charge to the paper, drawing the negatively charged toner particles on the drum to the paper. The toner is merely resting on top of the paper after the static charge eliminator has removed the paper's static charge. Two rollers, a pressure roller and a heated roller, are used to fuse the toner to the paper.

- All laser printers have at least two separate power supplies. The primary power supply, which may actually be more than one power supply, provides power to the motors that move the paper, the system electronics, the laser, and the transfer corona. The high-voltage power supply usually only provides power to the primary corona/charge roller; it is one of the most dangerous devices in the world of PCs. Always turn off a laser printer before opening it up.

- A laser printer's mechanical functions are served by complex gear systems packed together in discrete units generically called gear packs or gearboxes. Most laser printers have two or three. Every laser printer has sensors that detect a broad range of conditions, such as paper jams, empty paper trays, or low toner levels.

- Every laser printer contains at least one electronic system board (many have two or three) that contains the main processor, the printer's ROM, and the RAM used to store the image before it is printed. When the printer doesn't have enough RAM to store the image before it prints, you get a memory overflow problem. Most printers can use generic DRAM like the kind you use in your PC, but check with the manufacturer to be sure.

- Because even tiny concentrations of ozone (O_3) will cause damage to printer components, most laser printers have a special ozone filter that needs to be vacuumed or replaced periodically.

- Solid ink printers use sticks of solid ink to produce extremely vibrant color. The inks are melted, absorbed into the paper fibers, and then solidify, producing continuous-tone output in a single pass. The solid ink sticks may be inserted midway through a print job if a certain color needs to be topped off.

- ASCII contains a variety of control codes for transferring data, some of which can be used to control printers; ASCII code 10 (or 0A in hex) means "Line Feed," and ASCII code 12 (0C) means "Form Feed." These commands have been standard since before the creation of IBM PCs, and all printers respond to them; however, the control codes are extremely limited. Utilizing high-end graphics and a wide variety of fonts requires more advanced languages.

- Adobe Systems' PostScript page description language is a device-independent printer language capable of high-resolution graphics and scalable fonts. Because PostScript is understood by printers at a hardware level, the majority of the image processing is done by the printer and not the PC's CPU, so PostScript printers print faster. PostScript defines the page as a single raster image; this makes PostScript files extremely portable.

- Hewlett-Packard's printer control language (PCL) features a set of printer commands greatly expanded from ASCII, but it does not support advanced graphical functions. PCL6 features scalable fonts and additional line drawing commands. PCL uses a series of commands to define the characters on the page, rather than defining the page as a single raster image like PostScript.

- Windows XP use the graphical device interface (GDI) component of the operating system to handle print functions. The GDI uses the CPU rather than the printer to process a print job and then sends the completed job to the printer. As long as the printer has a capable-enough raster image processor (RIP) and plenty of RAM, you don't need to worry about the printer language at all in most situations. Windows Vista/7 include support for the XML Paper Specification (XPS) print path, which requires an XPS-compatible driver. Some devices support XPS natively.

- Most printers connect to one of two ports on the PC: a DB-25 parallel port or a USB port. The parallel connection is the classic way to plug in a printer, but new printers use USB. The parallel port was included in the original IBM PC as a faster alternative to serial communication and has been kept around for backward compatibility. Parallel ports are slow by modern standards, with a maximum data transfer rate of 150 KBps. Parallel ports lack true bidirectional capability. A standard parallel connection normally

manifests as a female DB-25 connector on the PC and a corresponding male connector on the printer cable. The parallel connector on the printer side is called a Centronics connector.

- IEEE 1284 was developed as a standard for a backward-compatible, high-speed, bidirectional parallel port for the PC. It requires support for compatibility, nibble mode, byte mode, EPP, and ECP; a standard method of negotiating compatible modes between printer and PC; standard cables and connectors; and a standard electrical interface.

- USB is the most popular type of printer connection today. USB printers rarely come with the necessary USB cable, so you may need to purchase one at the same time you purchase the printer.

- Network printers come with their own network card and connect directly to a network. This can be an RJ-45 port for an actual cable, or it can be a wireless network card. Some printers offer Bluetooth or infrared adapters for networking.

Explain the laser printing process

- Laser printing is a seven-step process: processing, charging, exposing, developing, transferring, fusing, and cleaning.

- Laser printers generate a pattern of dots, called a raster image, representing what each page should look like. Laser printers use the laser to "paint" the raster image on the photosensitive drum. Laser printers use a chip called the RIP to translate the raster image sent to the printer into commands to the laser.

- Laser printer resolution is expressed in dots per inch (dpi). Common resolutions are 600 dpi × 600 dpi or 1200 dpi × 1200 dpi. The first number, the horizontal resolution, is determined by how fine a focus can be achieved by the laser. The second number is determined by the smallest increment by which the drum can be turned. Higher resolutions produce higher-quality output but also require more memory. Even printing at 300 dpi, laser printers produce far better quality than dot-matrix printers, because RET enables the printer to insert smaller dots among the characters, smoothing out the jagged curves that are typical of printers that do not use RET.

- Using the primary corona wire or primary charge roller, a uniform negative charge is applied to the entire surface of the drum (usually between ~600 and ~1000 volts) to make the drum receptive to new images.

- A laser is used to write a positive image relative to the toner particles on the surface of the drum, attracting them and creating a developed image.

- The transfer corona or transfer roller gives the paper a positive charge, making the negatively charged toner particles leap from the drum to the paper.

- The toner particles are mostly composed of plastic, so they can be melted to the page. Two rollers, a heated roller coated in a nonstick material and a pressure roller, melt the toner to the paper, permanently affixing it.

- The printing process ends with the physical and electrical cleaning of the photosensitive drum. All residual toner left over from printing the previous page must be removed, usually by scraping the surface of the drum with a rubber cleaning blade. One or more erase lamps bombard the surface of the drum with the appropriate wavelengths of light, causing the surface particles to discharge completely into the grounded drum.

Install a printer on a Windows PC

- In Windows, a printer is not a physical device; it is a program that controls one or more physical printers. The physical printer is called a print device. Print drivers and a spooler are still present, but they are integrated into the printer itself.

- To install a printer not automatically detected by Windows, select Start | Printers and Faxes in Windows XP to open the Printers and Faxes applet. In Windows Vista, select the Printers applet from the Control Panel. In Windows 7, go to Start | Devices and Printers. You install a new printer by clicking the Add a Printer icon to start the Add Printer Wizard. You must choose to install a local or a network printer; and you must select a port for a local printer. Windows automatically detects and installs USB printers. You must specify the printer type from the wizard's list, or use the Have Disk option. The wizard also features a Windows Update button you can use to get the latest printer driver via the Internet.

- One printer will always be the default printer. If you have more than one printer installed, you can make any printer the default printer. The icon for the default printer has a small checkmark in the corner. If you have multiple printers, you can change the default printer by right-clicking the printer's icon in the appropriate printer applet and selecting Make Default Printer (XP) or Set as default printer (Vista/7).

- Printer emulation means to use a substitute printer driver for a printer, as opposed to one made exclusively for that printer. Some printers are designed to emulate other, more widely supported models. If you don't have the specific driver for a printer, you can often use the driver from a similar model.
- Your monitor creates colors by using RGB, while a printer outputs in CMYK. This difference can lead to a printed page differing greatly in color and tone from what you see on the monitor. Calibrating your monitor to your printer is an important step in printing the colors you see on your screen. Manually calibrate your monitor by eyeballing it, by using ICC color profiles to instruct the printer to output colors a certain way, or by using calibration hardware and software to automate the process. Windows Vista/7 include Windows Color System to help build color profiles for use across devices.

■ Key Terms

American Standard Code for Information Interchange (ASCII) *(613)*

calibration *(625)*

Centronics connector *(616)*

DB-25 connector *(616)*

dot-matrix printer *(605)*

dots per inch (dpi) *(607)*

dye-sublimation printer *(608)*

erase lamp *(610)*

fuser assembly *(611)*

graphical device interface (GDI) *(614)*

IEEE 1284 standard *(615)*

impact printer *(605)*

ink cartridge *(606)*

Inkjet printer *(605)*

laser *(610)*

laser printer *(609)*

near-letter quality (NLQ) *(605)*

network printer *(616)*

pages per minute (ppm) *(607)*

parallel port *(615)*

photosensitive drum *(610)*

PostScript *(614)*

primary charge roller *(610)*

primary corona *(610)*

printer control language (PCL) *(614)*

printhead *(605)*

print resolution *(607)*

print spooler *(617)*

printwire *(605)*

raster image *(618)*

raster image processor (RIP) *(618)*

resolution enhancement technology (RET) *(619)*

solid ink printer *(613)*

static charge eliminator *(611)*

thermal printer *(609)*

toner *(611)*

toner cartridge *(610)*

transfer corona *(611)*

transfer roller *(611)*

XML Paper Specification (XPS) print path *(614)*

■ Key Term Quiz

Use the Key Terms list to complete the sentences that follow. Not all terms will be used.

1. The _____ requires support for compatibility mode, nibble mode, byte mode, EPP, and ECP.

2. A standard parallel printer cable normally has a male _____ on one end and a 36-pin _____ on the other.

3. A printer that creates an image on paper by physically striking an ink ribbon against the paper's surface is known as a(n) _____.

4. Laser printers use lasers to create the print image on a(n) _____.

5. The _____ on a standard laser printer contains a pressure roller and a heated roller.

6. Adobe Systems' _____ is a device-independent printer language capable of high-resolution graphics and scalable fonts.

7. Windows XP uses the _____ component of the operating system to handle print functions.

8. The resolution of a printer is measured in _____.

9. A printer's speed is rated in _____.

10. The _____ is responsible for cleaning the photosensitive drum of electrical charge.

■ Multiple-Choice Quiz

1. Which part of a laser printer applies a positive charge to the paper that attracts the toner particles to it?

 A. Erase lamp

 B. Transfer corona

 C. Laser

 D. Primary corona

2. What is the approximate maximum data transfer rate of a standard parallel port?

 A. 50 KBps

 B. 150 KBps

 C. 500 KBps

 D. 2 MBps

3. Janet just bought a new computer. She wants to install her three-year-old inkjet printer on the new system but has lost the driver disc. She can't get on the Internet to download the latest drivers. What should she do for drivers?

 A. Install a driver for a similar printer.

 B. She's stuck until she can get on the Internet.

 C. She can use the Mac drivers.

 D. She can install the printer without drivers.

4. John just installed a second printer on his system. When he prints in Microsoft Word, the job goes to the wrong printer. What does he need to do to get print jobs always to go to one printer or the other?

 A. He needs to set the primary printer.

 B. He needs to set the main printer.

 C. He needs to set the default printer.

 D. He needs to set the system printer.

5. What is laser printer resolution measured in?

 A. Dots per inch

 B. Pixels per inch

 C. Lasers per inch

 D. Dots per pixel

6. What type of printer physically strikes an ink ribbon on top of the paper to create a printout?

 A. Laser printer

 B. Inkjet

 C. Impact

 D. Dye-sublimation

7. What color method do printers use to put colors on a printout?

 A. RGB

 B. SSID

 C. DPI

 D. CMYK

8. Most current printers connect to a PC using what type of cable?

 A. Serial

 B. Parralel

 C. eSATA

 D. USB

9. Most inkjet printers use what to shoot ink at the paper?

 A. Pressure

 B. Heat

 C. Springs

 D. Gravity

10. The dye-sublimation printing technique is an example of what method of color printing?

 A. CMYK

 B. Thermal wax transfer

 C. RGB

 D. Direct thermal

11. The output from your inkjet printer appears much darker than what you see on your screen. What is the problem?

 A. You are using a paperweight that is not supported in the MSDS.

 B. The printer and monitor need to be calibrated.

 C. The color ink cartridges are almost empty.

 D. The black ink cartridge is almost empty.

12. What is the best way to make a printer available to everyone on your network and maintain the highest level of availability?

 A. Use a FireWire printer connected to a user's PC and share that printer on the network.

 B. Use a USB printer connected to a user's PC and share that printer on the network.

 C. Use a network printer connected directly to the network.

 D. Use a mechanical switch box with the printer.

13. Sheila in accounting needs to print receipts in duplicate. The white copy stays with accounting and the pink copy goes to the customer. What type of printer should you install?

 A. Inkjet

 B. Impact

 C. Laser jet

 D. Thermal wax transfer

14. Your laser printer fails to print your print jobs and instead displays a MEM OVERFLOW error. What can you do to rectify the problem? (Select two.)

 A. Install more printer RAM.

 B. Install more PC RAM.

 C. Upgrade the RIP.

 D. Disable RET.

15. What is the proper order of the laser printing process?

 A. Process, clean, charge, expose, develop, transfer, and fuse

 B. Process, charge, expose, develop, transfer, fuse, and clean

 C. Clean, expose, develop, transfer, fuse, process, and charge

 D. Clean, charge, expose, develop, process, fuse, and transfer

■ Essay Quiz

1. Your department needs a number of color inkjet printers. At your organization, though, all purchases are handled through professional buyers. Sadly, they know nothing about color inkjet printers. You need to submit a Criteria for Purchase form to your buyers. This is the standard form that your organization gives to buyers so they know what to look for in the products they buy. What are the top three purchasing criteria that you think they need to consider? Write the criteria as simply and clearly as possible.

2. Interview a person who uses a computer for work. Ask what the person does and then write a short description of the type of printer that would most suit that person's needs. Explain why this printer would be the best choice.

3. You have been tasked to make a recommendation for a printer purchase for a busy office of ten people. Make a case for purchasing either an inkjet or laser printer, providing enough information to compare the two technologies. You can choose the type of business, so recommend the appropriate printer, such as a laser printer to an office that primarily produces text documents. Make your recommendation opposite to the one you made for essay question #2.

4. Write a short essay comparing and contrasting inkjet printers with the three less-common print technologies: dye-sublimation, thermal, and solid ink.

5. Your boss is fascinated by the laser printing process. Write a short memo that outlines how it works, in the proper order.

Lab Projects

• Lab Project 19.1

Laser printers often have rather complex maintenance procedures and schedules. Select a laser printer—preferably one that you actually have on hand—and answer the following questions.

1. Using the user's guide or online sources, determine the exact cleaning procedures for your laser printer. How often should it be vacuumed? Do any parts need to be removed for cleaning? Does the manufacturer recommend any specialized cleaning steps? Does your printer come with any specialized cleaning tools? Does the manufacturer have any recommended cleaning tools you should purchase?

2. Based on the information you gathered, create a cleaning toolkit for your laser printer. Be sure to include a vacuum. Locate sources for these products and determine the cost of the toolkit.

3. Determine the model number of the toner cartridge. Locate an online company that sells name-brand (such as Hewlett-Packard) toner cartridges. Locate an equivalent third-party toner cartridge. Assuming that the printer uses a toner cartridge every three months, what is your per system annual cost savings using third-party toner cartridges?

4. All toner cartridges have a material safety data sheet (MSDS). Locate the MSDS for your model of toner cartridge and read it. Note any potential hazards of the toner cartridges.

5. Print out the description of the cleaning kit you created as well as the manufacturer's cleaning instructions.

• Lab Project 19.2

Using the same laser printer you used in the first project, locate and compile, on paper, all of the following information about your printer:

- User's guide
- List of error codes

- Troubleshooting guides
- Location of the latest drivers for Windows

Securing Computers

20

"Strategy without tactics is the slowest route to victory. Tactics without strategy is the noise before defeat."

—SUN TZU, *THE ART OF WAR*

In this chapter, you will learn how to

- **Explain the threats to your computers and data**
- **Describe key security concepts and technologies**

Your PC is under siege. Through your PC, a malicious person can gain valuable information about you and your habits. He can steal your files. He can run programs that log your keystrokes and thus gain account names and passwords, credit card information, and more. He can run software that takes over much of your computer processing time and use it to send spam or steal from others. The threat is real and right now. Worse, he's doing one or more of these things to your clients as I write these words. You need to secure your computer and your users' computers from these attacks.

But what does *computer security* mean? Is it an antivirus program? Is it big, complex passwords? Sure, it's both of these things, but what about the fact that your laptop can be stolen easily or that improper ventilation can cause hard drives and other components to die?

To secure computers, you need both a sound strategy and proper tactics. From a strategic sense, you need to understand the threat from unauthorized access to local machines as well as the big threats posed when computers go onto networks. Part of the big picture means to know what policies, software, and hardware to put in place to stop those threats. From a tactical in-the-trenches sense, you need to master the details, to know how to implement and maintain the proper tools. Not only do you need to install antivirus programs in your users' computers, for example, but you also need to update those programs regularly to keep up with the constant barrage of new viruses.

■ Analyzing Threats

Threats to your data and PC come from two directions: accidents and malicious people. All sorts of things can go wrong with your computer, from users getting access to folders they shouldn't see to a virus striking and deleting folders. Files can be deleted, renamed, or simply lost. Hard drives can die, and optical discs get scratched and rendered unreadable. Accidents happen and even well-meaning people can make mistakes.

Unfortunately, a lot of people out there intend to do you harm. Add that intent together with a talent for computers, and you have a deadly combination. Let's look at the following issues:

- Unauthorized access
- Data destruction, accidental or deliberate
- Administrative access
- Catastrophic hardware failures
- Malware
- Environmental threats

Unauthorized Access

Unauthorized access occurs when a person accesses resources without permission. Resources in this case mean data, applications, and hardware. A user can alter or delete data; access sensitive information, such as financial data, personnel files, or e-mail messages; or use a computer for purposes the owner did not intend.

Not all unauthorized access is malicious—often this problem arises when users who are randomly poking around in a computer discover that they can access resources in a fashion the primary user did not intend. Unauthorized access becomes malicious when outsiders knowingly and intentionally take advantage of weaknesses in your security to gain information, use resources, or destroy data!

One of the ways to gain unauthorized access is through intrusion. You might imagine someone kicking in a door and hacking into a computer, but more often than not it's someone sitting at a home computer, trying various passwords over the Internet. Not quite as glamorous, but still….

Dumpster diving is the generic term for anytime a hacker goes through your refuse, looking for information. This is also a form of intrusion. The amount of sensitive information that makes it into any organization's trash bin boggles the mind! Years ago, I worked with an IT security guru who gave me and a few other IT people a tour of our office's trash. In one 20-minute tour of the personal wastebaskets of one office area, we had enough information to access the network easily, as well as to embarrass seriously more than a few people. When it comes to getting information, the trash is the place to look!

Shoulder surfing is another technique for gaining unauthorized access. Shoulder surfing is simply observing someone's screen or keyboard to get information, often passwords. As the name implies, it usually requires the bad guy looking over your shoulder to see what you are doing.

Social Engineering

Although you're more likely to lose data through accident, the acts of malicious users get the vast majority of headlines. Most of these attacks come under the heading of **social engineering**—the process of using or manipulating people inside the networking environment to gain access to that network from the outside—which covers the many ways humans can use other humans to gain unauthorized information. This unauthorized information may be a network login, a credit card number, company customer data—almost anything you might imagine that one person or organization may not want a person outside of that organization to access.

Social engineering attacks aren't hacking—at least in the classic sense of the word—although the goals are the same. Social engineering means people attacking an organization through the people in the organization or physically accessing the organization to get the information they need. Following are a few of the more classic types of social engineering attacks.

> It's common for social engineering attacks to be used together, so if you discover one of them being used against your organization, it's a good idea to look for others.

Infiltration

Hackers can physically enter your building under the guise of someone who might have a legitimate reason for being there, such as cleaning personnel, repair technicians, or messengers. They then snoop around desks, looking for whatever they can find. They might talk with people inside the organization, gathering names, office numbers, department names—little things in and of themselves but powerful tools when combined later with other social engineering attacks.

Dressing the part of a legitimate user—with fake badge and everything—enables malicious people to gain access to locations and thus potentially your data. Following someone through the door, for example, as if you belong, is called **tailgating**. Tailgating is a common form of infiltration.

Telephone Scams

Telephone scams are probably the most common social engineering attack. In this case, the attacker makes a phone call to someone in the organization to gain information. The attacker attempts to come across as someone inside the organization and uses this to get the desired information. Probably the most famous of these scams is the "I forgot my user name and password" scam. In this gambit, the attacker first learns the account name of a legitimate person in the organization, usually using the infiltration method. The attacker then calls someone in the organization, usually the help desk, in an attempt to gather information, in this case a password.

> **Hacker:** "Hi, this is John Anderson in accounting. I forgot my password. Can you reset it, please?"
>
> **Help Desk:** "Sure, what's your user name?"
>
> **Hacker:** "j_w_Anderson"
>
> **Help Desk:** "OK, I reset it to e34rd3."

Certainly telephone scams aren't limited to attempts to get network access. There are documented telephone scams against organizations aimed at getting cash, blackmail material, or other valuables.

Phishing

Phishing is the act of trying to get people to give their user names, passwords, or other security information by pretending to be someone else electronically. A classic example is when a bad guy sends you an e-mail that's supposed to be from your local credit card company asking you to send them your user name and password. Phishing is by far the most common form of social engineering done today.

Data Destruction

Often an extension of unauthorized access, data destruction means more than just intentionally or accidentally erasing or corrupting data. It's easy to imagine some evil hacker accessing your network and deleting all your important files, but authorized users may also access certain data and then use that data beyond what they are authorized to do. A good example is the person who legitimately accesses a Microsoft Access product database to modify the product descriptions, only to discover that she can change the prices of the products, too.

This type of threat is particularly dangerous when users are not clearly informed about the extent to which they are authorized to make changes. A fellow tech once told me about a user who managed to mangle an important database when someone gave him incorrect access. When confronted, the user said: "If I wasn't allowed to change it, the system wouldn't let me do it!" Many users believe that systems are configured in a paternalistic way that wouldn't allow them to do anything inappropriate. As a result, users often assume they're authorized to make any changes they believe are necessary when working on a piece of data they know they're authorized to access.

Administrative Access

Every operating system enables you to create user accounts and grant those accounts a certain level of access to files and folders in that computer. As an administrator, supervisor, or root user, you have full control over just about every aspect of the computer. Windows XP, in particular, makes it entirely too easy to give users administrative access to the computer, especially Windows XP Home, which has only two kinds of users: administrators and limited users. Because you can't do much as a limited user, most home and small office systems simply use multiple administrator accounts. If you need to control access, you need to use non-Home versions of Windows.

System Crash/Hardware Failure

As with any technology, computers can and will fail—usually when you can least afford for it to happen. Hard drives crash, the power fails—it's all part of the joy of working in the computing business. You need to create redundancy in areas prone to failure (such as installing backup power in case of electrical failure) and perform those all-important data backups.

Physical Theft

A fellow network geek once challenged me to try to bring down his newly installed network. He had just installed a powerful and expensive firewall router and was convinced that I couldn't get to a test server he added to his network just for me to try to access. After a few attempts to hack in over the Internet, I saw that I wasn't going to get anywhere that way.

So I jumped in my car and drove to his office, having first outfitted myself in a techy-looking jumpsuit and an ancient ID badge I just happened to have in my sock drawer. I smiled sweetly at the receptionist and walked right by my friend's office (I noticed he was smugly monitoring incoming IP traffic by using some neato packet-sniffing program) to his new server.

I quickly pulled the wires out of the back of his precious server, picked it up, and walked out the door. The receptionist was too busy trying to figure out why her e-mail wasn't working to notice me as I whisked by her carrying the 65-pound server box. I stopped in the hall and called him from my cell phone.

Me (cheerily): "Dude, I got all your data!"

Him (not cheerily): "You rebooted my server! How did you do it?"

Me (smiling): "I didn't reboot it—go over and look at it!"

Him (really mad now): "YOU <EXPLETIVE> THIEF! YOU STOLE MY SERVER!"

Me (cordially): "Why, yes. Yes, I did. Give me two days to hack your password in the comfort of my home, and I'll see everything! Bye!"

I immediately walked back in and handed him the test server. It was fun. The moral here is simple: Never forget that the best network software security measures can be rendered useless if you fail to protect your systems physically!

Malware

Networks are without a doubt the fastest and most efficient vehicles for transferring computer viruses among systems. News reports focus attention on the many malicious software attacks from the Internet, but a huge number of such attacks still come from users who bring in programs on optical discs and USB drives.

Environmental Threats

Your computer is surrounded by a host of dangers all just waiting to wreak havoc: bad electricity from the power company, a host of chemicals that just by the nature of your business may or may not be near your computer, dust, heat, cold, wet…it's a jungle out there!

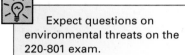
Expect questions on environmental threats on the 220-801 exam.

Power

We've covered power issues extensively back in Chapter 9. Don't ever fail to appreciate the importance of surge suppressors and uninterruptible power supplies (UPSs) to protect your electronics from surges, brownouts, and blackouts. Also remember that network devices need power protection as well. Figure 20.1 shows a typical UPS protecting a network rack.

• **Figure 20.1** UPS on rack

How's the Air in There?

Proper environmental controls help secure servers and workstations from the environmental impact of excessive heat, dust, and humidity. Such *environmental controls* include air conditioning, proper ventilation, air filtration, and monitors for temperature and humidity. A CompTIA A+ technician maintains an awareness of temperature, humidity level, and ventilation, so that he or she can tell very quickly when proper levels or settings are out of whack.

A PC works best in an environment where the air is clean, dry, and room temperature. CompTIA doesn't expect you to become an environmental engineer, but it does expect you to explain and deal with how dirty or humid or hot air can affect a computer. We've covered all of these topics to some extent throughout the book so let's just do a quick overview with security in mind.

Dirty Air Dust and debris aren't good for any electronic components. Your typical office air conditioning does a pretty good job of eliminating the worst offenders, but not all computers are in nice offices. No matter where the computers reside, you need to monitor your systems for dirt. The best way to do this is observation as part of your regular work. Dust and debris will show up all over the systems, but the best place to look are the fans. Fans will collect dust and dirt quickly (see Figure 20.2).

All electronic components get dirty over time. To clean them, you need to use either compressed air or a nonstatic vacuum. So which one do you use? The rule is simple: If you don't mind dust blowing all over the place, use compressed air. If you don't want dust blowing all over the place, use a vacuum.

• **Figure 20.2** Dirty fan

Equipment closets filled with racks of servers need proper airflow to keep things cool and to control dusty air. Make sure that the room is ventilated and air-conditioned (see Figure 20.3) and that the air filters are changed regularly.

If things are really bad, you can enclose a system in a dust shield. Dust shields come complete with their own filters to keep a computer clean and happy even in the worst of environments.

• **Figure 20.3** Air-conditioning vent in a small server closet

Temperature and Humidity Most computers are designed to operate at room temperature, which is somewhere in the area of 22°C (72°F) with the relative humidity in the 30–40 percent range. Colder and dryer is better for computers (but not for people), so the real challenge is when the temperature and the humidity go higher.

A modern office will usually have good air conditioning and heating, so your job as a tech is to make sure that things don't happen to prevent your air conditioning from doing its job. That means you're pretty much always on ventilation patrol. Watch for the following to make sure air is flowing:

- Make sure ducts are always clear of obstructions.

- Make sure ducts are adjusted (not too hot or too cold).

- Don't let equipment get too closed off from proper ventilation.

Toxic Materials

Every office is filled with chemicals, compositions that invariably get stored, spilled, or dumped. If something spills and it's not something you're familiar with, refer to the Material Safety Data Sheet (MSDS) for proper documentation for handling and disposal. Always comply with local government regulations when dealing with chemicals, including batteries and the metals on circuit boards.

■ Security Concepts and Technologies

Tech Tip

Recycling E-Waste

Most cities in the U.S. have one or more environmental services center that you can use to recycle electronic components. For your city, try a Google (or other search engine) search on the term "environmental services" and you'll almost certainly find a convenient place for e-waste disposal.

Once you've assessed the threats to your computers and networks, you need to take steps to protect those valuable resources. Depending on the complexity of your organization, this can be a small job encompassing some basic security concepts and procedures, or it can be exceedingly complex. The security needs for a three-person desktop publishing firm, for example, would differ wildly from those of a defense contractor supplying top-secret toys to the Pentagon.

From a CompTIA A+ certified technician's perspective, you need to understand the big picture (that's the strategic side), knowing the concepts and available technologies for security. At the implementation level (that's the tactical side), you're expected to know where to find such things as security policies in Windows. A CompTIA Network+ or CompTIA Security+ tech will give you the specific options to implement. So let's look at three concept and technology areas: access control, data classification and compliance, and reporting.

Access Control

Access is the key. If you can control access to the data, programs, and other computing resources, you've secured your systems. **Access control** is composed of four interlinked areas that a good security-minded tech should think about: physical security, authentication, users and groups, and security policies. Much of this you know from previous chapters, but this section should help tie it all together as a security topic.

Secure Physical Area and Lock Down Systems

The first order of security is to block access to the physical hardware from people who shouldn't have access. This isn't rocket science. Lock the door to your workspace. Don't leave a PC unattended when logged in. In fact, don't ever leave a system logged in, even as a limited user. God help you if you walk away from a server still logged in as an administrator. You're tempting fate.

Employee ID badges are now so common that even relatively small organizations use them. Badges are a great way not only to control building access but also to store authentication tools such as radio frequency identification (RFID) or smart cards (see "Authentication" later in this chapter). Figure 20.4 shows a typical badge.

Be aware of the risk of shoulder surfing. One handy tool to prevent this is a privacy filter. A privacy filter is little more than a framed sheet or film that you apply to the front of your monitor. Privacy filters reduce the viewing angle, making it impossible to see the contents on the screen for anyone except those directly in front of the screen (see Figure 20.5).

Security is more of an issue when users walk away from their computers, even for a moment. When you see a user's computer logged in and unattended, do the user and your company a huge favor and lock the computer. Just walk up and press WINDOWS LOGO KEY-L on the keyboard to lock the system. It works in all versions of Windows. Better yet, make a point to make users aware of this issue so they understand the risk and can take the precaution themselves. You should also instruct them how to password-protect their screensaver. When the password feature is enabled, a user won't be able to return to the desktop until they've entered the proper password. It's a little like locking the computer, and good for those who like using screensavers.

• **Figure 20.4** Typical employee badge/smart card

While you're looking at a user's monitor, examine around his or her desk. Is the user writing down passwords and putting them in plain sight? If so, tell the user to get rid of them! Teach users to create easy-to-remember passwords. Are critical, personal, or sensitive documents also lying about in plain sight? The user should put them in a closed, secure place. Documents no longer needed should be shredded immediately.

• **Figure 20.5** Privacy filter

Authentication

Security requires properly implemented **authentication**, which means in essence how the computer determines who can or should access it and, once accessed, what that user can do. A computer can authenticate users through software or hardware, or a combination of both.

You can categorize ways to authenticate into three broad areas: knowledge factors, ownership factors, and inherent factors. A *knowledge factor* is something the user knows, like a password or personal identification number (PIN). An *ownership factor* is something the user has, like an ID card or security token. An *inherent factor* (also called a biometric) is something that is part of the user, like a fingerprint or retinal pattern.

Multifactor authentication provides the best authentication, where a user must use two or more factors to prove his or her identity. Note that multifactor means more than one factor, not just more than one *thing*. Logging in with a user name and password is two things, for example, but because both fall into the category of what a user knows, it's not multifactor authentication.

Many organizations use *two-factor authentication*. An example is a key fob that generates a numeric key. A user authenticates by entering his or her user name and password (something you know) and is then prompted to enter the key (something you have).

Software Authentication: Proper Passwords It's still rather shocking to me to power up a friend's computer and go straight to his or her desktop, or with my married-with-kids friends, to click one of the parents' user account icons and not be prompted for a password. This is just wrong! I'm always tempted to assign passwords right then and there—and not tell them the passwords, of course—so they'll see the error of their ways when they try to log on next. I don't do it but always try to explain gently the importance of good passwords.

You must always require that your users have proper passwords. Don't let them write passwords down or tape them to the underside of their mouse pads either!

It's not just access to Windows that you need to think about. There's always the temptation for people to do other mean things, such as changing CMOS settings, opening up the case, and even stealing hard drives. Any of these actions renders the computer inoperable to the casual user until a tech can undo the damage or replace components. All modern CMOS setup utilities come with a number of tools to protect your computer, such as drive lock, intrusion detection, and of course system access passwords such as the one shown in Figure 20.6. Refer to Chapter 7 to refresh yourself on what you can do at a BIOS level to protect your computer.

Hardware Authentication Smart cards and biometric devices enable modern systems to authenticate users with more authority than mere passwords. **Smart cards** are credit card–sized cards with circuitry that can identify the bearer of the card. Smart cards are relatively common for such tasks as authenticating users for mass transit systems, for example, but are fairly uncommon in computers. Figure 20.7 shows a smart card and keyboard combination.

 A popular way to remember authentication factors is to think of them as something you know (passwords), something about you (biometric), and something you have (badge, key fob, or security token).

 Remember the concept of *single sign-on* from Chapter 4? You can log on to any computer in a domain using one set of credentials. In addition to being a time-saver, this is also a great security feature that helps network administrators better control who can gain access to the network.

 Some routers enable you to set up a demilitarized zone (DMZ), which enables all incoming traffic to your computers. This is dangerous, so don't do it!

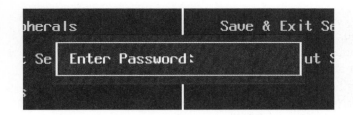

• **Figure 20.6** CMOS access password request

• **Figure 20.7** Keyboard-mounted smart card reader being used for a commercial application (photo courtesy of Cherry Corp.)

How's this for full disclosure? Microsoft does not claim that the keyboard in Figure 20.11 offers any security at all. In fact, the documentation specifically claims that the fingerprint reader is an accessibility tool, not a security device. Because it enables a person to log on to a local machine, though, I think it falls into the category of authentication devices.

Security tokens are devices that store some unique information that the user carries on their person. They may be digital certificates, passwords, or biometric data. They may also store an RSA token. *RSA tokens* are random-number generators that are used with user names and passwords to ensure extra security. Most security tokens come in the form of key fobs, as shown in Figure 20.8.

You can also get many types of security tokens as software. Anyone who plays *World of Warcraft* knows that there's an entire illegal industry known as "gold farmers" who like to hack accounts and steal all the hard-earned loot your character collects. It's a terrible feeling to log in to the game only to find your character cleaned out (see Figure 20.9).

To counter this problem, Blizzard Entertainment, the folks who own *World of Warcraft*, provide free security tokens. Most folks think "hardware" in the form of key fobs when they hear the words "security tokens," but you can also download a security token as software—Blizzard offers an app for your smartphone, as shown in Figure 20.10.

People can guess or discover passwords, but it's a lot harder to forge someone's fingerprints. The keyboard in Figure 20.11 authenticates users on a local machine by using fingerprints. Other devices that will do the trick are key fobs and retinal scanners. Devices that require some sort of physical, flesh-and-blood authentication are called **biometric devices**.

Clever manufacturers have developed key fobs and smart cards that use RFID to transmit authentication information so users don't have to insert something into a computer or card reader. The Privaris plusID combines, for example, a biometric fingerprint fob with an RFID tag that makes security as easy as opening a garage door remotely! Figure 20.12 shows a plusID device.

• **Figure 20.8** RSA key fob (photo courtesy of EMC Corp.)

• **Figure 20.9** I've been robbed! My fine armor is gone, my bags are empty, and my bank account only has a few copper pieces!

For some reason, CompTIA lists *retinal scanners* as a form of biometric security. While retinal scanners do exist, I have been in hundreds of high-security facilities and have only seen one retinal scanner in operation in almost 30 years as a tech. CompTIA should remove this silly objective, but until they do, Figure 20.13 shows about the only image of a retinal scanner in operation you'll ever encounter.

NTFS, not FAT32!

The file system on a hard drive matters a lot when it comes to security. On a Windows machine with multiple users, you simply must use NTFS or

• **Figure 20.10** Blizzard Entertainment security token for iPhone

• **Figure 20.11** Microsoft keyboard with fingerprint accessibility

plusID

PRIVARIS·

• Figure 20.12 plusID (photo courtesy of Privaris, Inc.)

you have no security at all. Not just primary drives but also any secondary drives in computers in your care should be formatted as NTFS, with the exception of removable drives such as the one you use to back up your system.

When you run into a multiple-drive system that has a second or third drive formatted as FAT32, you can use the **convert** command-line utility to go from FAT to NTFS. The syntax is pretty straightforward. To convert a D: drive from FAT or FAT32 to NTFS, for example, you'd type the following:

convert d: /fs:ntfs

You can substitute a mount name in place of the drive letter in case you have a mounted volume. The command has a few extra switches as well, so at the command prompt, type **/?** after the convert command to see all of your options.

Users and Groups

Windows uses user accounts and groups as the bedrock of access control. A user account is assigned to a group, such as Users, Power Users, or Administrators, and by association gets certain permissions on the computer. Using NTFS enables the highest level of control over data resources.

Assigning users to groups is a great first step in controlling a local machine, but this feature really shines once you go to a networked environment. Let's go there now.

User Account Management Through Groups

Access to user accounts should be restricted to the assigned individuals, and those who configure the permissions to those accounts must remember the *principle of least privilege*: Accounts should have permission to access

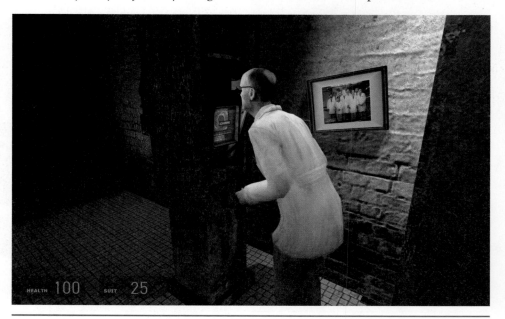

• Figure 20.13 Retinal scanner in *Half-Life 2*

only the resources they need and no more. Tight control of user accounts is critical to preventing unauthorized access. Disabling unused accounts is an important part of this strategy, but good user account management goes far deeper than that.

Groups are a great way to achieve increased complexity without increasing the administrative burden on network administrators, because all operating systems combine permissions. When a user is a member of more than one group, which permissions does that user have with respect to any particular resource? In all operating systems, the permissions of the groups are *combined*, and the result is what you call the **effective permissions** the user has to access the resource. As an example, if Rita is a member of the Sales group, which has List Folder Contents permission to a folder, and she is also a member of the Managers group, which has Read and Execute permissions to the same folder, Rita will have both List Folder Contents *and* Read and Execute permissions to that folder.

Watch out for *default* user accounts and groups—they can become secret backdoors to your network! All network operating systems have a default Everyone group that can be used to sneak into shared resources easily. This Everyone group, as its name implies, literally includes anyone who connects to that resource. Windows gives full control to the Everyone group by default, for example, so make sure you know to lock this down! The other scary one is the Guest account. The Guest account is the only way to access a system without a user name and password. Unless you have a compelling reason to provide guest access, you should always make sure the Guest account is disabled.

All of the default groups—Everyone, Guest, Users—define broad groups of users. Never use them unless you intend to permit all of those folks access to a resource. If you use one of the default groups, remember to configure them with the proper permissions to prevent users from doing things you don't want them to do with a shared resource!

Security Policies

Although permissions control how users access shared resources, there are other functions you should control that are outside the scope of resources. For example, do you want users to be able to access a command prompt on their Windows system? Do you want users to be able to install software? Would you like to control what systems a user can log on to or at what time of day a user can log on? All network operating systems provide you with some capability to control these and literally hundreds of other security parameters, under what Windows calls *policies*. I like to think of policies as permissions for activities, as opposed to true permissions, which control access to resources.

A policy is usually applied to a user account, a computer, or a group. Let's use the example of a network composed of Windows XP Professional systems with a Windows Server 2008 system. Every Windows XP system has its own local policies program, which enables policies to be placed on that system only. Figure 20.14 shows the tool you use to set local policies on an individual system, called **Local Security Policy**, being used to deny the user account Danar the capability to log on locally.

 When you open the Local Security Policy tool in Windows XP, note that the program is labeled "Local Security Settings," even though the icon is labeled "Local Security Policy." In Windows Vista and Windows 7, it is always called Local Security Policy.

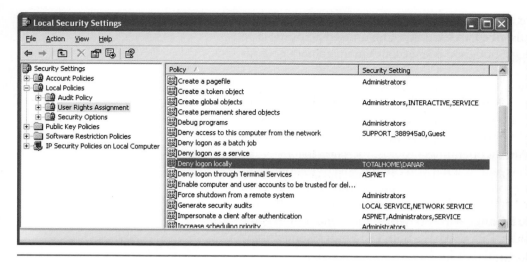

● **Figure 20.14** Local Security Policy

Local policies work great for individual systems, but they can be a pain to configure if you want to apply the same settings to more than one PC on your network. If you want to apply policy settings *en masse*, you need to step up to Windows Active Directory domain-based **Group Policy**. By using Group Policy, you can exercise deity-like—Microsoft prefers to use the term *granular*—control over your network clients.

Want to set default wallpaper for every PC in your domain? Group Policy can do that. Want to make certain tools inaccessible to everyone except authorized users? Group Policy can do that, too. Want to control access to the Internet, redirect home folders, run scripts, deploy software, or just remind folks that unauthorized access to the network will get them nowhere fast? Group Policy is the answer. Figure 20.15 shows Group Policy; I'm about to change the default title on every instance of Internet Explorer on every computer in my domain!

That's just one simple example of the settings you can configure by using Group Policy. You can apply literally hundreds of tweaks through Group Policy, from the great to the small, but don't worry too much about familiarizing yourself with each and every one. Group Policy settings are a big topic on most of the Microsoft certification tracks, but for the purposes of the CompTIA A+ 220-801 exam, you simply have to be comfortable with the concept behind Group Policy.

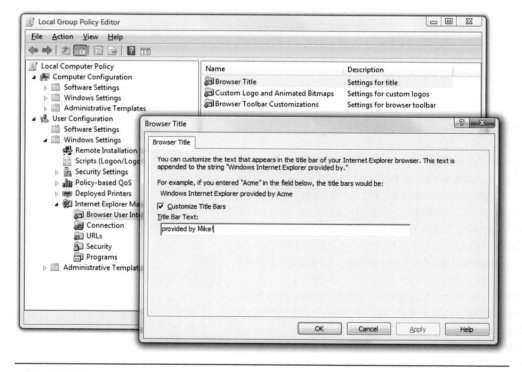

● **Figure 20.15** Using Group Policy to make IE title say "provided by Mike!"

Although I could never list every possible policy you can enable on a Windows system, here's a list of some commonly used ones:

- **Prevent Registry Edits** If you try to edit the Registry, you get a failure message.

- **Prevent Access to the Command Prompt** Keeps users from getting to the command prompt by turning off the Run command and the Command Prompt shortcut.

- **Log on Locally** Defines who may log on to the system locally.

- **Shut Down System** Defines who may shut down the system.

- **Minimum Password Length** Forces a minimum password length.

- **Account Lockout Threshold** Sets the maximum number of logon attempts a person can make before being locked out of the account.

- **Disable Windows Installer** Prevents users from installing software.

- **Printer Browsing** Enables users to browse for printers on the network, as opposed to using only assigned printers.

Although the CompTIA A+ 220-801 exam doesn't expect you to know how to implement policies on any type of network, you are expected to understand that policies exist, especially on Windows networks, and that they can do amazing things to control what users can do on their systems. If you ever try to get to a command prompt on a Windows system only to discover the Run command is dimmed, blame it on a policy, not the computer!

Data Classification and Compliance

Larger organizations, such as government entities, benefit greatly from organizing their data according to its sensitivity—what's called **data classification**—and making certain that computer hardware and software stay as uniform as possible. In addition, many government and internal regulations apply fairly rigorously to the organizations.

Data classification systems vary by the organization, but a common scheme classifies documents as public, internal use only, highly confidential, top secret, and so on. Using a classification scheme enables employees such as techs to know very quickly what to do with documents, the drives containing documents, and more. Your strategy for recycling a computer system left from a migrated user, for example, will differ a lot if the data on the drive was classified as internal use only or top secret.

Compliance means, in a nutshell, that members of an organization or company must abide by or comply with all of the rules that apply to the organization or company. Statutes with funny names such as Sarbanes-Oxley impose certain behaviors or prohibitions on what people can and cannot do in the workplace.

From a technician's point of view, the most common compliance issue revolves around software, such as what sort of software users can be allowed to install on their computers or, conversely, why you have to tell a user that he can't install the latest application that may help him do the job more effectively because that software isn't on the approved list. This can lead to some uncomfortable confrontations, but it's part of a tech's job.

The concepts behind compliance in IT are not, as some might imagine at first blush, to stop you from being able to work effectively. Rather they're designed to stop users with not quite enough technical skill or knowledge from installing malicious programs or applications that will destabilize their systems. This keeps technical support calls down and enables techs to focus on more serious problems.

Reporting

As a final weapon in your security arsenal, you need to report any security issues so a network administrator or technician can take steps to make them go away. You can set up auditing within Windows so that the OS reports problems to you. **Event Viewer** enables you to read the logs created by auditing. You can then do your work and report those problems. Let's take a look.

Auditing

The Security section of Event Viewer doesn't show you anything by default. To unlock the full potential of Event Viewer, you need to set up auditing. *Auditing* in the security sense means to tell Windows to create an entry in the Security Log when certain events happen, such as when a user logs on—called **event auditing**—or tries to access a certain file or folder—called **object access auditing**. Figure 20.16 shows Event Viewer tracking logon and logoff events.

• **Figure 20.16** Event Viewer displaying security alerts

The CompTIA A+ 220-801 exam doesn't test you on creating a brilliant auditing policy for your office—that's what network administrators do. You simply need to know what auditing does and how to turn it on or off so you can provide support for the network administrators in the field. To turn on auditing at a local level, go to Local Security Policy in Administrative Tools. Select Local Policies and then click Audit Policy. Double-click one of the policy options and select one or both of the checkboxes in the Properties dialog box that opens. Figure 20.17 shows the Audit object access Properties dialog box.

Event Viewer stores log files in %SystemRoot%\System32\ Config.

Incidence Reporting

Once you've gathered data about a particular system or you've dealt with a computer or network problem, you need to complete the mission by telling your supervisor. This is called **incidence reporting**. Many companies have pre-made forms that you simply fill out and submit. Other places are less formal. Regardless, you need to do this!

Incidence reporting does a couple of things for you. First, it provides a record of work you've accomplished. Second, it provides a piece of information that, when combined with other information you might or might not know, reveals a pattern or bigger problem to someone higher up the chain. A seemingly innocuous security audit report, for example, might match other such events in numerous places in the building at the same time and thus show that conscious, coordinated action rather than a glitch was at work.

Evidence Handling

As a tech, you'll need to deal with people who use company computers in prohibited ways. In most cases, you're not paid to be the police and should

• **Figure 20.17** Audit object access Properties dialog box, with Local Security Policy open in the background

not get involved. There are times, however, where something bad—really bad—takes place on one of the systems you support, and if you're the first tech person there, everyone is going to turn to you for action.

A technician should ignore personal information in and around a person's computer. As mentioned back in Chapter 2, you should treat anything said to you and anything you see as a personal confidence, not to be repeated to customers, coworkers, or bosses. Here's Mike's Rule of Confidentiality: "Unless it's a felony or an imminent physical danger, you didn't see nothin'." This includes any confidential customer materials. Try not to look at anything that isn't directly related to your job. (Sometimes that's impossible, but limit your exposure.) If you're waiting on a printout at a printer and suddenly there's a bunch of printed pages coming out of the printer with employee payroll information, set it to the side and pretend you never saw it.

But what about the scary stuff? Obvious espionage? Pornography? People passing out personal information? Hacking? In these cases, you've just become the first line of defense and you need to act accordingly. Let's address the objectives as listed by CompTIA for the 220-801 exam.

Identify the Action or Content as Prohibited Use common sense, but keep in mind that most organizations have an Acceptable Use Policy that employees must sign. The Acceptable Use Policy defines what actions employees may or may not perform on company equipment. Remember that these polices aren't just for obvious issues such as using a computer for personal use. These policies cover computers, phones, printers, and even the network itself. This policy will define the handling of passwords, e-mail, and many other issues.

Report Through Proper Channels In most cases, you'll report any prohibited actions or content directly to your supervisor. There's also a chance your company will have a security officer or incident response leader who you'll contact instead. Do *not* speak to the person committing the infraction unless your supervisor approves that contact.

Data/Device Preservation You might end up in a situation serious enough that a computer or other device becomes evidence. In these cases, the location of the system and who has touched it may come into question, so you need to establish a **chain of custody**: a documented history of who has been in possession of the system. You'll hopefully have a legal expert to guide you, but the following are fairly common rules:

1. Isolate the system. Shut down the system and store it in a place where no one else can access it.

2. Document when you took control of the system and the actions you took: shutting it down, unplugging it, moving it, and so on. Don't worry about too much detail, but you must track its location.

3. If another person takes control of the system, document the transfer of custody.

Chapter 20 Review

■ Chapter Summary

After reading this chapter and completing the exercises, you should understand the following about computer security.

Explain the threats to your computers and data

■ Threats to your data come from two sources: accidents and malicious people.

■ Unauthorized access occurs when a user accesses resources in an unauthorized way. Not all unauthorized access is malicious and some is even accidental. Authorized access can lead to data destruction by users who do not intend to be malicious. When users have access to a file or database, they typically believe the system won't let them make any changes they are not authorized to make.

■ Most computer attacks are accomplished through social engineering rather than hacking. Telephone scams are one of the most common social engineering tactics. Dumpster diving involves physically going through an organization's trash looking for documents that might reveal user names, passwords, or other sensitive information. Be sure to secure your computer equipment in a locked room to prevent physical theft.

■ Computers, hard drives, and power all fail. As a tech, you need to plan for redundancy in these areas. You also need to protect your computers against viruses distributed through the network and removable media. You should implement good access policies and implement methods for tracking computer usage.

■ Protect your PC from environmental dangers such as power surges, dirty or humid air, heat, or toxic hazards.

Describe key security concepts and technologies

■ Controlling access to programs, data, and other computing resources is the key to securing your system. Access control includes four interlinked areas requiring your attention: physical security, authentication, users and groups, and security policies.

■ Store computers with sensitive data in a locked room and never walk away from your computer while logged on. Log out or lock the computer by pressing WINDOWS LOGO KEY-L. Some companies lock down computer rooms with ID badges that act as key cards, using RFID or smart cards for authentication. Be aware of those around you in the space, and watch out for shoulder surfers looking at your monitor while you work.

■ The three forms of authentication include knowledge factors (something the user knows, like a password or PIN), ownership factors (something the user has, like a key or card), and inherent factors (something about the user, such as a fingerprint).

■ Accounts should be given permissions to access only what they need and no more. Unused accounts should be disabled.

■ When a user account is a member of several groups, and permissions have been granted to groups, the user account will have a set of combined permissions that may conflict. The resulting permissions that ultimately control access are referred to as the effective permissions.

■ Make sure to lock down the default Everyone group of which all users are automatically members. Never use the default Everyone or Users groups or the default Guest account unless you intend to permit all those accounts access to resources.

■ Policies control permissions for activities, such as installing software, accessing a command prompt, or logging on at a particular time of day. A policy is usually applied to a user account, computer account, or a group. Use the Local Security Policy tool to manage policies for an individual computer.

■ Group Policy enables you to control such things as deploying software or setting each computer in a domain to use the same wallpaper. Commonly used policies include Prevent Registry Edits, Prevent Access to the Command Prompt, Log On Locally, and Minimum Password Length.

- Data classification systems vary by the organization, but a common scheme classifies documents as public, internal use only, highly confidential, top secret, and so on. Using a classification scheme enables employees such as techs to know very quickly what to do with documents, drives containing documents, and more.

- Compliance means that members of an organization or company must abide by or comply with all of the rules that apply to the organization or company. From a technician's point of view, the most common compliance issue revolves around software, such as what sort of software users can be allowed to install on their computers. Compliance keeps technical support calls down and enables techs to focus on more serious problems.

- Use Event Viewer to track activity on your system. By default, the Security section doesn't show you everything, so it is good practice to enable event auditing and object access auditing. Event auditing creates an entry in the Security Log when certain events happen, such as a user logging on, while object access auditing creates entries in response to object access, such as someone trying to access a certain file or folder.

- Incidence reporting means telling your supervisor about the data you've gathered regarding a computer or network problem. This provides a record of what you've done and accomplished. It also provides information that, when combined with other information you may or may not know, may reveal a pattern or bigger problem to someone higher up the chain.

- Try to avoid any personal information on a PC. If you find something private (that isn't illegal), ignore it and forget about it. If you find something illegal, you must follow the proper procedures. If a device you work on becomes evidence in legal proceedings, isolate the system and document everything that happens going forward. Pay special attention to the chain of custody, or whoever is currently in control of the machine.

■ Key Terms

access control *(641)*

authentication *(643)*

biometric device *(644)*

chain of custody *(652)*

compliance *(649)*

convert *(646)*

data classification *(649)*

dumpster diving *(636)*

effective permissions *(647)*

event auditing *(650)*

Event Viewer *(650)*

Group Policy *(648)*

incidence reporting *(651)*

Local Security Policy *(647)*

object access auditing *(650)*

phishing *(637)*

shoulder surfing *(636)*

smart card *(643)*

social engineering *(636)*

tailgating *(636)*

telephone scam *(637)*

unauthorized access *(635)*

■ Key Term Quiz

Use the Key Terms list to complete the sentences that follow. Not all terms will be used.

1. Mary's company routinely labels data according to its sensitivity or potential danger to the company if someone outside accesses the data. This is an example of _____.

2. Once you've gathered data about a particular system or you've dealt with a computer or network problem, you need to complete the mission by telling your supervisor. This is called _____.

3. _____ is the act of trying to get people to give their usernames, passwords, or other security information by pretending to be someone else electronically.

4. Enable _____ to create Event Viewer entries when a specific file is accessed.

5. Although not all _____ is malicious, it can lead to data destruction.

6. Most attacks on computer data are accomplished through _____.

7. Going through someone's trash to uncover personal information is known as _____.

8. Many companies authenticate access to secure rooms using an ownership factor such as a(n) _____.

9. A _____ is an authentication device that uses your physical body in some way, such as a retinal or fingerprint scanner.

10. Following someone into a restriced area is known as _____.

■ Multiple-Choice Quiz

1. What is the process of using or manipulating people to gain access to network resources?

 A. Cracking

 B. Hacking

 C. Network engineering

 D. Social engineering

2. Which of the following might offer good hardware authentication?

 A. Strong password

 B. Encrypted password

 C. NTFS

 D. Smart card

3. Which of the following tools would enable you to stop a user from logging on to a local machine but still enable him to log on to the domain?

 A. AD Policy filter

 B. Group Policy Auditing

 C. Local Security Policy

 D. User Settings

4. John dressed up in a fake security guard uniform that matched the uniforms of a company and then walked in with some legitimate employees in an attempt to gain access to company resources. What kind of attack is this?

 A. Administrative access

 B. Data destruction

 C. Spoofing

 D. Tailgating

5. The first day on the job, Jill received a spreadsheet that listed approved software for users and clear instructions not to allow any unapproved software. What kind of policy must she follow?

 A. Classification

 B. Compliance

 C. Group

 D. Security

6. Which of the following would be considered an environmental threat? (Choose three.)

 A. Temperature

 B. Humidity

 C. Malware

 D. Power

7. A user account is a member of several groups, and the groups have conflicting rights and permissions to several network resources. The culminating permissions that ultimately affect the user's access are referred to as what?

 A. Effective permissions

 B. Culminating rights

 C. Last rights

 D. Persistent permissions

8. What type of authentication uses at least two different methods to determine the user's identity?

 A. Multiple authentication

 B. Multifactor authentication

 C. Plural authentication

 D. Enforced authentication

9. What system enables users to categorize documents by importance and privacy?

 A. NTFS

 B. Authentication

 C. Data classification

 D. Group policy

10. Which threats are categorized as social engineering? (Select all that apply.)

 A. Telephone scams

 B. Dumpster diving

 C. Trojan horses

 D. Spyware

11. What do you call the documented list of everyone who has had access to a computer?

 A. Access control list

 B. Ownership log

 C. User access list

 D. Chain of custody

12. A user calls and complains that the technician who fixed his computer removed some software he used to listen to music on the Internet. A check of approved software does not include the LimeWire application, so what should the supervisor do?

 A. Applaud the technician for proper compliance.

 B. Educate the user about the legal issues involved with music downloads.

 C. Add the LimeWire application to the approved software list and make the technician apologize and reinstall the software.

 D. Check with the user's supervisor about adding LimeWire to the approved software list.

■ Essay Quiz

1. Your boss is considering getting an Internet connection for the office so employees have access to e-mail, but she is concerned about hackers getting into the company server. What can you tell your boss about safeguards you will implement to keep the server safe?

Lab Project

• Lab Project 20.1

You have learned a little bit about the Local Security Policy in Windows. Fire up your Web browser and do a search for Local Security Policy. Make a list of at least five changes you might consider making to your personal computer by using the Local Security Policy tool. Be sure to include what the policy is, what it does, and where in the tool it can be configured.

The Right PC for You

chapter

21

"If you build it, he will come."

—FIELD OF DREAMS

In this chapter, you will learn how to

- **Research and build a standard thick client**
- **Customize a professional PC**
- **Build a specialized consumer PC**

Now that you've learned all about PCs, you have the great joy of being able to build the PC of your desire, choose your favorite video card or motherboard, and assemble, from the ground up, the perfect system for you or your client. People will turn to you for advice, too: Which parts do I need? Where should I buy them? What do you think about this?

There's nothing wrong with buying a prebuilt system from a local brick-and-mortar or online store. If you want solid warranties, repair agreements, and so on, Dell or HP can help you out. But off-the-shelf computers aren't for everyone. Your needs or your client's needs might be too specific. In that case, it's time for you to do one of the most fun things a PC tech can do: the custom PC build!

For the first time in the history of the CompTIA A+ exams, CompTIA requires you to understand how to build certain types of PCs. This chapter will help you define these PC types, understand the issues involved in building these computers, and, at the same time, have a little fun.

Because this is a first for CompTIA, the creative team at Total Seminars took extra time to understand what CompTIA was trying to say. In general, we agree with the definitions of the custom configurations with the exception of the following two types. From the 220-801 exam objectives:

1.9 Evaluate and select appropriate components for a custom configuration, to meet customer specifications or needs.

- Standard thick client
 - Desktop applications
 - Meets recommended requirements for running Windows
- Thin client
 - Basic applications
 - Meets minimum requirements for running Windows

I'm not a fan of the term "client." It's outdated. What CompTIA calls a *thick client*, I'd call a *basic desktop*, and instead of a *thin client*, I'd call it a *single-purpose machine* (because that's all a thin client can handle). To CompTIA, the only real separation between a thick client and a thin client is meeting the "recommended" or "minimum" requirements for Windows, respectively. It's oversimplified. Even *that* might be okay, except Microsoft no longer provides minimum requirements for Windows 7. Oh well. We can only guess what CompTIA was thinking.

This chapter begins by explaining how to find the parts for a custom PC—you'll be doing a lot of reading, that's for sure. The rest of the chapter discusses the components you need for each custom build: thick clients, thin clients, virtualization and media workstations, home theater and server PCs, and (best of all) gaming PCs.

Building Your First PC

There's almost no better feeling than when you realize you know enough about PCs that you can say: "I think I'm comfortable building my own PC!" If you don't feel ready, let the information in this chapter be that extra push that takes you over the edge.

Building your first PC is both fun and scary. This is the first time you bring together everything you know about hardware. You'll make mistakes, and some brand-new piece of equipment you buy won't work the first time. You'll mount the CPU wrong and the system won't boot. That huge tower case with 23 fans will make too much noise and you'll hate it. But for all these mistakes, don't lose track of the fact that you're building your own PC. Your computer . . . your . . . precious (see Figure 21.1)!

Evaluating Parts

The most difficult (and most fun) part of buying a PC is picking which parts you want. Knowing which parts to buy for each type of PC is the cornerstone of this entire chapter. Let's take a moment to consider the processes and steps you can use to discover and evaluate the right parts for specific system types.

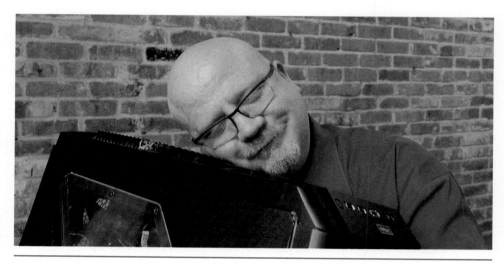

• Figure 21.1 Mike and "Precious," his favorite self-built PC

Read the Reviews

Every component has a review somewhere. Go to Google, type in the name and model number of a part, and add the word "review" at the end. There are two types of reviews: industry reviews written by professionals, and personal reviews written by people who purchased and use the part. Let the Google search I described show you how to the find the professional reviews. Newegg.com is one of my favorite places to read personal reviews.

Read the Fine Print

Learn everything you can about the part. Take some time to read the technical specifications. Check the return and warranty policy of the manufacturer and the retailer. Make sure you have some recourse if the part breaks or doesn't function as advertised.

Compare

Before you buy a part, see what folks say about the competitors' parts. Are there other parts that cost less, have better reviews, or use less power?

Put It in Your Hand

If you're lucky enough to live near a big retailer like Fry's Electronics or Micro Center, get in your car and go check out the part. Look for a display model. Look at the back of the box. See what extra parts are included. Talk to the salespeople about their experiences and the returns they've seen; ask about alternatives they like better.

Thick Client

CompTIA wants to call a general-purpose SOHO computer a **thick client**. Fine—let's have a laugh at the guy wearing the belt and suspenders, and then come up with some guidelines for building a thick client.

Thick clients are general-purpose machines. That means they don't have the fastest drives or the best video cards, but, by the same token, they don't

use low-end parts, either. You need to create a platform that will support 90 percent of the folks wanting to use a computer in the home or office.

To begin researching parts for a thick client, look at the recommended hardware requirements for the operating system you intend to use. In this case, I want to install Windows 7 Ultimate 64-bit. I like Ultimate because it gives me the most flexibility, and the extra cost means nothing down the road if I later decide to join a Windows domain.

Here are the recommended system requirements for Windows 7 Ultimate 64-bit edition:

- 1 gigahertz (GHz) or faster 64-bit (x64) processor
- 2 GB RAM
- 20 GB available hard disk space
- DirectX 9 graphics device with WDDM 1.0 or higher driver

• **Figure 21.2** Mike laughing uncontrollably

See Figure 21.2 for my opinion of the requirements. You can do a lot better. Here's my opinion of reasonable and modest hardware for a 64-bit thick client. These values aren't on the exam, but they should be.

- 2 GHz or faster 64-bit (x64) processor with at least two cores
- 4 GB RAM
- Blank 500-GB hard disk
- DirectX 11 video card

> You should always go for a 64-bit edition of Windows when building a new PC—why limit yourself?

Size Matters

You can get into all kinds of mental confusion trying to decide how large of a case you want to use, but do yourself a favor and just get a mid-tower. Mid-towers have plenty of drive bays for future expansion without being so massive that they get in the way. A mid-tower will also support almost any motherboard you might choose to install. Take your time finding that perfect case. Unlike manufacturers of most other components, case manufacturers tend to keep making the same case model for many years (see Figure 21.3).

CPU and Motherboard

You begin the system build by deciding on the CPU/motherboard combination for your new system. I'm not going to tell you to buy an Intel or an AMD CPU. Do your own research and draw your own conclusions. I use plenty of both brands. Because this is a thick client and we don't need the most powerful CPU available, consider the following:

- Get a modern socket. You can get great deals on CPUs that use older sockets, but try to stick to whatever socket is current. This makes it possible to upgrade the CPU in the future.

- Avoid the low end *and* the high end. Both Intel and AMD make three levels of CPUs. Try to stick to the middle. Avoid the slowest and the fastest. Don't buy the CPU with the most cores or the fewest cores.

- When it comes to price, the sweet spot should be around $150 to $300. It's amazing, but CPU price points haven't changed much in over a decade. You can spend a lot more or a lot less, but either way is a waste of money or cheating yourself on power.

Now that you've got a CPU, it's time to find that magic motherboard. Your first big choice is the chipset. Take some time to learn about current chipsets that support the CPU of your choice and compare features. Consider the following:

- Total RAM support

- RAID support

- USB, including versions and number of ports

- Onboard video

- Onboard wireless

• **Figure 21.3** My Antec 900 mid-tower (because everything's bigger in Texas)

Once you narrow down your choice to a particular chipset, see which motherboards fit your plans:

- Just because a chipset supports certain features, don't assume the motherboard will as well. Double-check RAM limits, RAID support, USB ports and types, and so on.

- Check the manufacturer's reputation. Good names like ASUS and Intel are going to be better quality motherboards, but there are plenty of other good manufacturers, too.

- Read reviews of the motherboards you like. What are people saying about them?

- Think about how many expansion slots you need. Your motherboard should have at least one PCIe ×16 slot and a few smaller PCIe slots.

- Do you want to use integrated video? Many folks will think the onboard video is acceptable, and certainly well above Windows 7's Aero requirements. If not, you've always got that PCIe ×16 slot waiting for a new, dedicated video card.

Video

Regardless of whether you choose onboard or a dedicated video card, a thick client isn't going to push a graphics card very hard. Even lower-end cards include at least 1 GB of GDDR3 (or better) video RAM, solid processors, and plenty of extras like HDMI ports. You probably don't need to spend any more than about $150. If you spend more money than that, you're stretching into gaming PC territory.

Be sure to check the reviews on a prospective video card and always be sure to do a Google search for a card's model number followed by "noise." Some videos cards are too loud—they'll drive you bonkers.

Monitors

Monitors are a personal choice, but remember that a good monitor will outlast several system builds, so don't be afraid to get a better monitor. A good-quality, wide-screen, LED-backlit LCD monitor no smaller than 20 inches diagonally across will serve you well for a long time.

Storage

A thick client will do just fine with a single hard drive. Today's multiple-terabyte drives will store anything you might imagine and then some, and if you actually manage to fill a drive, your mid-tower will easily accept a second or even third drive.

Setting up a RAID array is probably not necessary. Of course, the system needs backup capability, but RAID might be overkill. At the same time, the low cost of drives and the ease of RAID installation makes at least RAID 1 a compelling option for your thick client.

Applications

The typical thick client is going to need a Web browser (or two) and some Microsoft Office–type applications. The recommended 4 GB of RAM won't have any difficulty supporting these types of applications or much more.

 Try This!

Finding the Right Graphics Card

If you hadn't noticed already, there are a lot of PC components to choose from, covering all levels of price and performance. In the case of the average thick client, you need to keep costs down. If you want or need the power of a dedicated graphics card, however, you should be ready to research prices for your clients, so Try This!

1. Go to www.tomshardware.com. Following the *Articles* link at the top or using the available search box, find their latest "Best Graphics Cards for the Money" article.

2. Read through the list of recommended cards. Using a budget of about $150, which graphics cards do they recommend? What if you spend a little bit more money? What if you spend less?

■ Workstation PCs

In modern times, people need computers to get work done. The type of computer you need is defined by the work you do and the way that your IT department decides to organize and network. For the most part, the thick client described earlier is the "go to" workstation PC, but CompTIA defines two other workstation types: the thin client and the virtualization work-station.

Thin Client

A **thin client** is a system designed to handle only very basic applications with an absolute minimum amount of hardware required by the oper-ating system. Thin clients often serve as single-purpose systems, like point-of-sale machines (cash registers). Thin clients can be very small

compared to a thick client, which makes them perfect when you want the PC tucked away.

Virtualization Workstations

Virtualization has taken the world of computing by storm over the past few years. As discussed in the previous chapter, virtualization is a powerful technology that enables you to run more than one operating system at the same time on a single computer. With virtualized servers, you can consolidate multiple, power-hungry machines into one box, saving floor space, electricity, and a lot of running around. With workstations, virtualization is most often used to run a second OS on top of the OS installed on the computer's hard drive.

For good performance on a virtualization workstation, install lots and lots of RAM. Each virtualization workstation needs enough memory to run the native operating system, the guest operating system, and any applications running in either OS, so RAM is the most important thing in virtualization. A powerful 64-bit CPU that supports hardware virtualization will also help virtual machines run smoothly. Many desktop computers can run virtual machines, but if you want the best possible performance, you want lots of RAM and a good CPU.

You'll need lots of RAM and a fast CPU to get good performance out of a virtualization workstation.

Media Workstations

When George Lucas made the first *Star Wars* movie, he used camera tricks, miniature models, and stop-motion animation to create the illusion of massive spaceships and robots battling it out in a galaxy far, far away. Twenty years later, he filmed the *Star Wars* prequels in front of massive green screens and used computer-generated imagery (CGI) to transform the bland sets into exotic planets and space stations. I won't get into an argument about which approach produced better movies, but the fact remains that the act of creating films has changed. It's not just films, either—computers have changed the way we create all types of media, including movies, television shows, photography, music, and more.

Computer-aided design (CAD) and computer-aided manufacturing (CAM) software enable engineers to create and build components in an industrial setting.

If you want to get involved in this creative revolution, you're going to need a mighty powerful computer. Workstations for creative professionals are customized for the type of media they create. We'll start by looking at graphics workstations (by which I mean workstations for editing still images and using computer-aided design/computer-aided manufacturing software), then move on to audio workstations and video workstations.

Graphics Workstations

Professional photographers and graphic designers first and foremost need to have the clearest view possible of their images and image editing software. Whether you're editing photos in Adobe Photoshop or drafting mechanical components in SolidWorks, you need to make sure you can see what you're working on! Because of this, the primary need for a graphics workstation is a large, high-quality monitor. A $200 LCD panel

from Best Buy won't help you here—you need to make sure that the colors you see on the screen are as accurate as possible. Expensive monitors will have higher contrast ratios for more vibrant images and they'll also give you more control over the image they output.

You learned in Chapters 13 and 17 that monitors and video cards use different techniques to display colors. For a workstation to display colors accurately on a monitor, you must properly calibrate the monitor. This is a simple process of using a small sensor, like the tool shown in Figure 21.4, on the screen to create a **profile** that enables the monitor to display more accurate colors. You can use a similar device with a printer to create a profile for it, too. That way, your printouts will match what you see on the monitor.

• **Figure 21.4** A monitor calibrator

With a good enough monitor, almost any computer can be used as a graphics workstation, but ideally you'll want a fast, multicore 64-bit CPU and lots of RAM. If the processor is too slow or if the computer doesn't have enough RAM, it can take a long time to make changes to an image you're editing. A large hard drive is also a plus, since CAD files and photographs take up a lot of space. You'll also want to have an external drive to back up your work. If you're working with CAD/CAM software, you'll want a professional-level graphics card, such as an NVIDIA Quadro card (see Figure 21.5), though photo editing software won't see much of an advantage from such a card. Unlike typical graphics cards, these professional cards can cost thousands of dollars.

• **Figure 21.5** An NVIDIA Quadro graphics card (photo courtesy of NVIDIA)

Graphic designers frequently make use of specialized input devices, too, such as digitizer tablets. These tablets enable designers to paint on their computers as if they were painting on a canvas, as shown in Figure 21.6.

Digital Audio Workstations

The requirements for audio workstations are very similar to those for graphics workstations—a fast, multicore CPU, gobs of RAM, a large monitor, and a big, high-speed hard drive. The difference is that you'll also need a high-quality audio interface.

An **audio interface** is a box that you hook up to your PC with inputs that enable you to connect professional microphones and instruments (see Figure 21.7). Functionally, an audio interface is just a really high-end sound card, though they usually connect to your computer via USB or FireWire

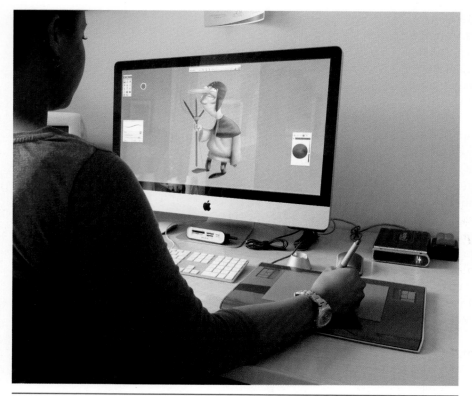

• **Figure 21.6** Painting with a Wacom tablet

• **Figure 21.7** Audio interface device
(photo courtesy of PreSonus)

rather than plugging into the motherboard. Audio interfaces range in size from a device you can fit in your hand, to one that will take up most of your desk. A more expensive interface includes more inputs and produces higher-quality sound, though you'll also need some expensive speakers to hear the difference.

Just like with graphics workstations, audio workstations frequently make use of specialized input devices. These devices, referred to as *control surfaces*, mimic the look and feel of older, analog mixing consoles. They have a large number of programmable inputs that make controlling the software much faster and more accurate than with just a mouse and keyboard. These control surfaces range in size from small desktop units, all the way up to room-filling behemoths that are used in recording studios. Some of these boards also contain an audio interface.

Video Workstations

Video workstations combine the requirements of a graphics workstation and an audio workstation. Video editors often use two or more color-calibrated monitors so they can view the video stream they're working on with one monitor and see their video editor open on the other, making multiple monitors very useful. Video workstations require a very powerful CPU paired with as much RAM as possible, since video editing is a far more intensive process than graphics or audio editing. High-speed, high-capacity hard drives are also life-savers, since video files often take up multiple gigabytes

of space. Many video workstations have multiple hard drives set up in a RAID for added storage capacity and read/write speed.

Video workstations, like CAD/CAM workstations, benefit enormously from a professional-level graphics card. This is almost as important as the fast CPU and piles of RAM, and you'll rarely see a video workstation without one.

Because video workstations are frequently used as audio workstations, too, you will often find video workstations with the same audio interfaces and control surfaces as you'd see on an audio workstation. There are also video interfaces that enable editors to connect to various cameras. Additionally, many video editors use custom keyboards that have special labels and controls for popular video editing software.

■ Specialized Consumer PCs

Once you move away from the office and into the house, your computing needs change. Home is for leisure, and the workplace is for, well, work! The three common types of home systems are home servers that store everything from your music collection to last year's income tax return, home theater PCs to play your music and your movies, and gaming PCs to play powerful, video-intensive games.

Building a Home Server PC

How many computing devices are in your house right now? If you're like me, the answer is "a lot." Between multiple smartphones, iPods, tablets, portables, and desktop computers, you might shock yourself with the count.

As more and more computing devices move into the home environment, there's a need for a centralized storage space, a **home server PC** to dish out files and folders on demand—a place for all your media to stream to multiple devices. This home server PC has very specialized needs that take it beyond the typical thick client.

A home server PC supplies three discrete functions: media streaming, file sharing, and print sharing. Media streaming often uses specialized software. Just like file and print sharing, though, it works fine through the default tools in Windows and Mac OS X. The home server PC has to have a very fast network connection and gobs of storage. Plus, that storage needs to be fault tolerant. Losing your video collection because of a hard drive crash would make for a very bad day.

Software

Any modern operating system enables you to share files and folders through standard sharing features. The same is true of sharing a printer. To turn that PC into a print server, open the Devices and Printers applet in the Control Panel, right-click on an installed printer, choose *Printer properties*, and then check the *Share this printer* checkbox on the Sharing tab (see Figure 21.8).

Microsoft makes a perfectly fine server OS called Windows Home Server that you can use to set up a sweet home server machine. You probably won't find the OS on the CompTIA A+ 220-801 exam, however.

You can easily turn a Windows 7 PC into a media streaming server by selecting that option in the Control Panel. Open the Network and Sharing Center, select the *Change advanced sharing settings* link from the left Task menu, and then click the *Home or Work* option to get to the Advanced sharing settings screen (see Figure 21.9).

Halfway down the screen you'll find a link to *Choose media streaming options*. Click it. Figure 21.10 shows the Media streaming options screen. By default, Windows wants to share everything, though you can customize what's shared in case you have young children and don't want them to have access to inappropriate content.

Finally, both Windows Media Player and iTunes have a feature to share media files on a local network. Figure 21.11 shows iTunes sharing via the Bonjour protocol.

Hardware

Hardware needs on a home server apply primarily to the network speed and hard drive capacity, at least according the CompTIA objectives. If you have a very active server, you should also pay attention to the amount of RAM it has and the speed of the CPU. Beefing both up above the standard thick client can help if you start getting some lag.

• **Figure 21.8** Sharing a printer

• **Figure 21.9** Advanced sharing settings

• **Figure 21.10** Media streaming options

• **Figure 21.11** Streaming with iTunes

Chapter 21: The Right PC for You

669

For the network, a wired Gigabit Ethernet NIC should be standard issue. Although it sounds cool to go wireless, you should limit the use of wireless to the single connection between the WAP and the client. The home server should connect via Ethernet to minimize any lag or dropped frames.

A file server's hard drives do the heavy and sustained lifting for the PC, so you should not stint on them. At a minimum, get two drives of identical size that have as much capacity as you can afford. No one *reduces* the amount of media in his or her collection over time, after all, especially if it's stored electronically. Plus, because you need fault tolerance on the data, you simply must use a RAID 1 configuration at a minimum (and thus the need to get two identical drives). If your budget can afford it and your motherboard supports it, get three identical drives and run in RAID 5.

Alternatives

Instead of building a custom home server box (the fun method), you can also purchase preconfigured devices that contain multiple hard drives and attach them to your network. Referred to as **network attached storage (NAS)**, these devices usually connect via Ethernet. Instead of connecting to the hard drive(s) on a server PC on the network, you connect to the NAS's hard drives. It plays the same role as a home server without all the fuss.

Setting Up a Home Theater PC

A home theater system enables you to play music and watch movies and television. If done well, the experience can rival that of watching a movie at a fine movie house. When coupled with a home theater PC, the home theater system enables the full computing experience as well.

An optimal home theater has five components:

- A monitor, television, or projector
- Surround sound speakers
- A stereo receiver
- A home theater PC
- Network connectivity (such as a cable box or Ethernet)

This section looks at the specific components and issues involved with creating a home theater PC and connecting it to other components.

Output Killer Video

A home theater PC must provide support for large monitors at high resolution, a requirement that usually involves an HDMI connector on the video card (see Figure 21.12). The HDMI cable connects the home theater box to the stereo receiver, which then pushes the signal to the television. Figure 21.13 shows the basic home theater schematic.

• **Figure 21.12** HDMI output on video card

Both DVI and DisplayPort can support 1080p HDTV resolution, as you'll recall from Chapter 13. Many televisions today have a DVI port, so this is a viable solution, especially if you don't have a stereo receiver (see the following section).

Play It Loudly

A great home theater system simply must have surround sound and a thumping subwoofer, so the home theater PC needs a sound card or built-in sound processor that supports 5.1 or 7.1 stereo. For the best output, the sound card connects to the stereo

• **Figure 21.13** Television, receiver, home theater PC

receiver via S/PDIF, through either the optical connector or coaxial connector. The speakers then connect to the receiver. Figure 21.14 shows the schematic with speakers added.

HDMI carries both the video signal and the surround sound audio signal, so if you plug it into the television directly from the PC, the rig will use the television's speakers by default. If you have the surround sound speakers plugged into the computer rather than a receiver, you need to go into the Sound applet in the Control Panel to select the playback device you prefer (see Figure 21.15).

• **Figure 21.14** PC, receiver, speakers

● **Figure 21.15** Sound applet for choosing playback device

Look Cool in the Process

Home theater components look like traditional stacking stereo components, such as a receiver, equalizer, DVD player, and so on. It simply won't do to put a beige office computer case alongside your sleek, black-clad components (see Figure 21.16).

You can get a case for a PC that stacks nicely with other home theater components (see Figure 21.17). CompTIA calls this style of case an **HTPC**, although that's not an industry-standard form factor. I assume the letters stand for *home theater PC*.

Access the Media—Streaming and TV

The home theater PC needs access to content, usually through Gigabit Ethernet to get streaming media through the home server PC you created in the previous section of the chapter. The home theater could use Wi-Fi (802.11n or better), though wired is best, especially for HD content.

The home theater PC wouldn't normally have anything to do with a signal from the cable company or from a dedicated optical disc player, like a Blu-ray Disc box. Those signals go from the applicable box to the stereo receiver directly.

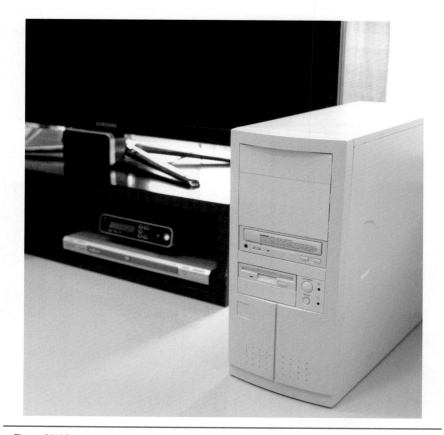

● **Figure 21.16** This is not right!

• **Figure 21.17** HTPC case

The only time the home theater PC should receive a television signal directly is through broadcast over the air. For this signal, the PC needs a television tuner, like you learned about in Chapter 17. You would use this to catch local news or sports programs.

Figure 21.18 shows the home theater schematic with all the media access methods included.

DLNA

Before we leave the hardware to look at software, I want to mention one topic that's outside the scope of the CompTIA A+ exams, but that you might run into in the field.

• **Figure 21.18** Final home theater

Digital Living Network Alliance (DLNA) certified devices connect to your home network, discover each other, and share media. In theory, DLNA devices should work with minimal setup or fuss, even if sourced from different manufacturers. If you share media files on a Windows PC, for example, a DLNA-equipped television, PlayStation 3, or other home theater device should be able to view those files. Look for the DLNA logo on devices as diverse as digital cameras, Blu-ray Disc players, network storage boxes, printers, and more.

Software Tools for Playback

Once you have the media center hardware set up properly, you need software to access streaming media. Microsoft includes Windows Media Center in some editions of Windows. If you don't have one of those editions (see Table 21.1), then you need to use a third-party tool, such as the excellent XBMC or Plex.

Table 21.1	Versions of Windows That Include Media Center	
Windows XP	**Windows Vista**	**Windows 7**
Media Center	Home Premium	Home Premium
	Ultimate	Professional
		Ultimate

Windows Media Center enables you to stream content from a home server and watch content stored locally. You can even access some television shows broadcast over the Internet (see Figure 21.19). Most of the setup happens via wizards that run when you select an option. If you want to add content from networked computers, you'll need to add it to the appropriate library (in Windows 7) or connect to the shared folder(s) in Windows XP or Windows Vista.

As cool as Windows Media Center is, you can find absolutely beautiful and functional third-party software for free, such as XBMC and Plex. XBMC in particular enables you to customize the look and feel of the interface, and many people have made awesome skins available too. Figure 21.20 shows the default skin for XBMC; Figure 21.21 shows the same content but displayed with a completely different skin. Plex is not flashy, but it's totally functional. There are versions of XBMC and Plex available for Windows, Mac OS X, and Linux. You can download XBMC from xbmc.org. Get Plex at www.plexapp.com.

• **Figure 21.19** Windows Media Center

• Figure 21.20 Default XBMC

• Figure 21.21 XBMC sporting the Aeon skin

Gaming PC

And now for the grand finale, the PC you've been waiting for, the system you've always wanted to build. As an aspiring PC tech, you probably took your first apprehensive steps into the dark underbelly of PCs with a game: *Doom, Quake, Myst, The Sims, World of Warcraft* . . . you've played at least one of them. While casual gamers can get by with a standard desktop PC (like the thick client you read about earlier), those who take their gaming seriously want a powerful PC ready to pump out the latest graphics. A gamer goes through a game's graphics settings and sets everything to the max. And since games aren't all about how good they look, you'll also want a good sound card and headphones. (Okay—you also need a good game, but one thing at a time.)

First, I'm going to tell you about the optimal gaming PC—the best bang-for-your-buck gaming PC that will play every game out there without breaking your wallet. (It's cheaper than you think! You can get a lot for about $1000.) Then I'll show you how you can take PC gaming from a hobby to a lifestyle—your only lifestyle—with beyond-bleeding-edge components that you don't need but should buy anyway.

A Gaming PC That Won't Break Your Wallet

A gaming PC isn't that different from your run-of-the-mill thick client: all of the components are the same, but taken to the next level. The Windows recommended system requirements no longer cut it. Instead, you might turn your attention to the system requirements in a favorite PC game. Find a game that came out in the last year or two and see what it needs from your PC. You'll find that most games actually have pretty low system requirements.

A lot of modern PC games are *ports* or copies of console games (originally created for the Xbox 360 or PlayStation 3, for example). Because the consoles were launched so long ago—before Windows Vista!—their old hardware makes it easy for modern PCs to run ported games. Games designed specifically for PCs, however, can take advantage of every core and gigabyte you give them. Take a PC game's system requirements and bump them up a notch or two to keep your gaming PC future-proof. **Future-proofing** means building a PC in a way that keeps it relevant for a few years. You don't want your PC to be out of date a week after you build it. Going beyond the current requirements for a game will make it ready for new games that come out a year or two from now.

The Internals Most of the big improvements over a standard thick client will happen inside the case. Every game is coded differently—just like any other application—so each game will take advantage of your hardware to varying degrees. Some games, for example, are designed to use quad-core CPUs and others are not. If a game can only use one core, those three other cores in a quad-core CPU can't play along. But you want a quad-core CPU anyway. Why? Future-proofing and price. Why limit yourself now when more and more games can take advantage of multiple cores? And these days, the price is right. Find a quad-core Intel processor with a speed of 3 GHz or more. If you have a tighter budget, get the AMD equivalent.

For a budget-minded gaming PC, the processor is the first place you want to splurge a little bit. You don't need a special case or motherboard.

Make sure you get a motherboard and CPU that are compatible with one another. I'll talk more about gaming motherboards later in this section.

You don't need more than 4 GB of RAM, and you only need enough hard drive space to store all your games. You don't need an extra monitor. Powering games revolves around two elements, so you'll spend the most money on these parts. I already told you about CPUs, so now let's talk about the biggest-ticket item, the graphics card.

A powerful graphics card (combined with a quality CPU) enables you to do two things: turn up the graphics quality and increase the performance (see Figure 21.22). The graphics quality of the game depends as much on the graphics card as it does on the designers of the game. A good graphics card can't make an ugly game look pretty, but it can make a pretty game look gorgeous. At higher settings, all sorts of smoothing and filtering happens that would make weaker systems choke. At the same time, you also want to maximize performance. In games, we measure performance by the number of frames per second (FPS) displayed. Most games are designed to run at about 30 FPS, though the sky's the limit on the top end. If you're getting fewer than 20 FPS, everything will look very choppy and it will be difficult to play the game. In this case, you'd need to turn down the game's graphics settings, and no one wants to do that!

So what should you look for in a graphics card? This can be a very "you get what you pay for" proposition, but NVIDIA and AMD—the two dominant graphics processing unit (GPU) manufacturers—have helpfully divided their products by number to show you at a glance how powerful they are. Yes, there are buses, cores, shaders, bandwidths, and so on, but it's all encapsulated into a (slightly random) number. The NVIDIA and AMD numbering systems, however, are entirely different, a little confusing, and sometimes loop back around to the beginning. I owned an NVIDIA GeForce4 MX 460 back in 2002. This is, of course, not the same as the NVIDIA GeForce GTX 460 released in 2010. And the NVIDIA GeForce GTX 460 is more powerful than an AMD Radeon 4850, even though AMD's number is bigger. Use each GPU manufacturer's Web site to learn about the latest available graphics processors. When it comes time to buy, look for the third- or fourth-best card available in the latest generation's lineup. If the best card available is the "690," look for the "650" or "670" model. You can usually save hundreds of dollars and still get the best graphics and performance with modern games.

While the CPU and GPU will satisfy your eyes, don't forget about your ears. More and more games can take advantage of high-end sound cards that produce true surround sound rivaling blockbuster movies. Hear the squeal of your tires, the noise of your jet engine, and the fiery power of a wizard's spell in 5.1 surround sound! You'll need to spend a bit of money (almost as much as that graphics card you just found) to hear the difference, but if you're an audio geek, it's worth it. Look for sound cards that support extra channels (7.1), more bits (24-bit), and higher sample rates (192 KHz).

All of this power inside your case means it needs to handle a lot of extra heat. A more powerful CPU and GPU will put out more heat, and you'll need a cooling system that can handle it (see Figure 21.23). For a budget setup, you don't need to jump straight to liquid cooling (though it's always an option). Most cases have a few extra spots for fans that you can buy

• **Figure 21.22** An NVIDIA 680 graphics card (photo courtesy of NVIDIA)

Graphics card model numbers are organized by generations. As of 2012, NVIDIA cards were divided between the 500 and 600 generations, while AMD cards used the 6000 and 7000 series. Within each generation, a lower number means less power (and lower price), while a higher number means more power (and a higher price). The top NVIDIA card, for example, might be the 690 model, while the low-end model would use the 620 name. For the latest model information, check out the NVIDIA and AMD Web sites.

The key components of a great gaming PC include: a high-end processor, a powerful video card, a good sound card, and enough cooling (fans, heat sinks, liquid cooling) to keep all those parts from melting your machine.

• **Figure 21.23** Powerful CPU fan and heat sink

Like keyboards and mice, cases are a very personal choice. Some people like wild colors. Other people want lights and windows showing off their internal devices. Personally, I prefer a plain black case. No lights. No windows. No distractions.

separately. Get some 120-mm fans and go to town. Your case cannot be too cool (and neither can you).

The Externals For a budget gaming PC, there's not much to improve outside of your case. One monitor will work fine, but make sure it has a resolution of at least 1920 × 1080 and is 24 inches diagonally. That will enable you to easily watch 1080p HD video content and play console ports at or above their intended resolution. Likewise, a basic 2.1 or 5.1 speaker setup will work just fine with your nice sound card. Don't use cheap headphones, though. Invest in something nice (with a microphone, if you like to voice chat while gaming) that is comfortable and produces sounds that aren't tinny or hollow (see Figure 21.24).

Many gamers like to buy fancy keyboards and mice, covered in extra buttons that can be customized to launch your wizard's fireball with a single click. Some keyboards even add little LCD screens that show you exactly how your keys have been customized and enable you to adjust your custom keyboard layout on the fly (see Figure 21.25). Keyboards and

• **Figure 21.24** Sennheiser HD 598

mice are very personal—get whatever best helps you game.

A Gaming PC That Will Set Your Wallet on Fire

If money is no object, go buy a yacht, and on that yacht, set up your dream gaming PC. Here, no price is too high, no technology too frivolous, and no monitor too big. If it exists, you should have it, even if you'll never use it. Some of this will sound extreme, and that's the point. I'll point out the best places to spend too much money and transform your budget box into the ultimate gaming PC.

• **Figure 21.25** A nice keyboard with built-in LCD screen

The Internals With the budget box, I told you why buying a quad-core processor was a good investment for future games that will take advantage of the technology. Now, quad-core isn't nearly enough. As of 2012, six-core processors like the Intel Core i7 Extreme Edition sit at the top of the CPU heap and will future-proof your PC for years to come. No game needs it, but at $1000, you can't afford not to get it.

If that wasn't extreme enough, get ready for your graphics card purchase, or should I say graphics *cards*? That's right: you'll need more than one high-end graphics card if you want the best of the best PC gaming experience. (And forget about not getting the very best card available—just look for the highest model number available and hand over your credit card.)

NVIDIA and AMD have both developed their own technology for linking multiple graphics cards. NVIDIA calls their technology **Scalable Link Interface (SLI)**, while AMD calls theirs **CrossFire**. Using a special cable (it looks sort of like a ribbon cable), the graphics cards can combine their power to increase graphical quality and performance (see Figure 21.26). With either technology, you can link up to four video cards together for more power than any current PC game could use. (But that's not the point.) Gamers will argue how effective these multicard setups really are—in fact, some games are so poorly optimized that they will run worse with more than one graphics card. Read up on how each game you play works with multiple graphics cards and proceed accordingly.

While you're at it, you might as well get a bunch of extra RAM (16 GB sounds comfy). A solid-state drive (or two) will help load game levels into RAM that much faster. When you need a break from gaming, a Blu-ray Disc optical drive enables you to watch HD movies. Add to that a 7.1 sound card and Gigabit networking card for high-speed connections to other gamers, and you have the start of an unmatched gaming-performance machine.

The Externals If you have multiple video cards, why not buy multiple monitors? You learned about multiple monitor setups when you read about audio/video workstations earlier in this chapter, and many games can take

Installing multiple graphics cards requires a motherboard that can handle two or more PCIe cards, a power supply that produces enough wattage, a case it will all fit in, and a cooling system powerful enough to keep your PC from overheating (a liquid-cooling setup sounds nice right about now). Keep these things in mind when upgrading or building your PC.

• **Figure 21.26** An SLI cable

advantage of this feature. Picture, if you will, three monitors, side by side: the nose of your race car speeds down the track on the center monitor while the crowd whips by on the left and right monitors. With multiple monitors, your field of view doubles, triples, or more!

Instead of expanding your view left and right, you can also improve your display forward and backward with 3-D technology. More and more PC games are including support for 3-D displays. You'll need the slightly silly glasses to make it work, but for gaming, the effect is amazing. Lots of action games require a good sense of (virtual) depth perception to play. You can't hit the enemy warlock with your fireball if you can't aim it properly. With 3-D displays, distant enemies will *look and feel* distant. Everything becomes much more natural with 3-D technology. To use it, you'll need a display and video card that supports the technology.

For sound, why stop at puny PC speakers? Jump to big home theater surround sound speakers (see Figure 21.27). Get a gamepad, too (for the PC games that support it). While you're at it, buy a nice chair with good back support and padding. When you game for hours on end in a good chair, your neck, back, and bottom will thank you.

That's it! Who knew it was so easy to spend $10,000 on a gaming PC? While most gamers will stick with something closer to the budget box, keep in mind that there is so much more power available—more than most games can handle. Whether you spend $100, $1000, or $10,000, don't forget to look for what *you* want out of your gaming PC. What games do you play? What do they require? What do you want? When you answer those questions, finding the parts you need becomes easy. Finding the right game, however, is an entirely different challenge.

• **Figure 21.27** 5.1 surround sound speakers (photo courtesy of Klipsch Group, Inc.)

Chapter 21 Review

■ Chapter Summary

After reading this chapter and completing the exercises, you should understand the following about building your own PC.

Research and build a standard thick client

- Before you build your first PC, you need to do some research on the parts you are going to use. Read reviews online, written by both industry experts and users. Learn everything you can about the part. Check with the manufacturer and retailer for warranties and return policies. Compare the device you like with others that are available—which is better? Visit a local brick-and-mortar store so you can play with the parts and see them in person.

- Thick clients are general-purpose devices. They don't use the best components or the worst components. Thick clients should be able to handle the majority of home and office tasks.

- Start your search for thick client components by reading the Windows recommended system requirements. Then forget about those and make sure your thick client has at least a 2-GHz, dual-core CPU, 4 GB of RAM, a hard drive with 500-GB capacity, and a DirectX 11 video card. Use a mid-tower case to ensure you have room for expansion later.

- Pick the CPU and motherboard first. Make sure you use a current socket that you can use with newer CPUs a few years down the road. Find a middle-of-the-road processor from either AMD or Intel. Make sure the motherboard you pick supports the same features as the CPU. The motherboard should have plenty of expansion slots so you can add more components to your thick client later.

- Depending on your needs, you can either use the onboard video device built into your motherboard or add a dedicated PCIe video card. Avoid noisy video cards. You should find a 20-inch widescreen monitor with an LED backlight.

- Get a hard drive with a capacity of 1 TB. You probably don't need a RAID array, but make sure you can make backups.

- Download a Web browser or two and some office-suite applications like Microsoft Office.

Customize a professional PC

- A thin client is similar to a thick client, except it is designed with the most limited of hardware in mind. These devices usually have a single purpose, such as operating as a point-of-sale device.

- Virtualization workstations enable a user to install a second virtual machine onto their local system. You can run an entirely separate OS inside your original OS. For good performance, you'll need lots of RAM and a powerful 64-bit CPU.

- Photographers and graphic designers need high-performance monitors so they can properly and accurately see their work. Monitors should be calibrated to display the correct colors. You'll want a 64-bit CPU and lots of RAM. If you work with CAD/CAM applications, you may want to add a professional-level graphics card, such as one of the NVIDIA Quadro cards. Graphic designers also often use digitizer tablets to draw directly into the computer.

- Audio workstations have similar requirements to graphics workstations: lots of RAM and a fast, multicore CPU. You'll want a large monitor for more workspace and big hard drives to store all of your files. Audio professionals also need an audio interface box that enables them to connect microphones and other instruments. Audio workstations can include control surfaces, which mimic the look and feel of analog mixing consoles.

- A video workstation combines the requirements of an audio and graphics workstation. Video professionals need multiple color-calibrated monitors to view their work. The workstation needs a powerful CPU paired with as much RAM as possible. High-speed, high-capacity hard drives will enable you to store more video files. A professional-level graphics card will also help the video software run more smoothly. Like audio and graphics workstations, special control surfaces are available for video editing. You can also purchase custom keyboards with special labeling that matches the controls for popular video editing software.

Build a specialized consumer PC

- With so many computing devices floating around your home, having a central storage space can make accessing your files and media a lot easier. Home server PCs supply media streaming, file sharing, and print sharing. Media streaming can use special software, though Windows has built-in sharing capabilities.

- The home server PC should have a fast network connection and gobs of storage. The storage should also be fault tolerant in a RAID array. If you have a more active server, pay attention to the amount of RAM and speed of your CPU.

- Instead of building a custom home server PC, you can also use a network attached storage (NAS) device that replicates many of the duties of a home server PC in a prebuilt box. The NAS attaches to your network via Ethernet and serves files stored on its hard drives.

- A home theater should include a display, surround sound speakers, stereo receiver, home theater PC, and network connectivity.

- Most home theater setups use HDMI to send audio and video between devices. If you are connecting directly from your home theater PC to your TV or other display, you can also use DVI or DisplayPort.

- Your sound setup should include 5.1 or 7.1 surround sound speakers, connected to a receiver. The receiver controls the speakers, unless you plug the speakers directly into the PC.

- To match the rest of your home theater components, make sure your home theater PC uses an HTPC form factor.

- Home theater PCs receive content over Gigabit Ethernet, perhaps streamed from a home server PC. Wired connections are best for streaming HD content.

- DLNA enables you to easily share media on your computer with devices that support the standard. Using a DLNA device, you can browse the shared drives and folders on your PC and play back various media formats.

- To access your media on your home theater PC, you can either use the Windows Media Center or download third-party applications such as XMBC and Plex.

- A gaming PC isn't that different from a standard thick client. The components are the same, but taken to the next level. Upgrade to a quad-core processor with a speed of at least 3 GHz. You should find the latest generation of video cards and find a model one or two steps below the most powerful version. Use NVIDIA's and AMD's model numbers to help you sort out which cards are high-end and which cards are low-end. The video card and CPU will be where you spend the most money on your gaming PC.

- The power of the graphics card determines how high you can push the game's graphic details and how well it will perform. The performance of a PC game is measured in frames per second (FPS).

- Make sure you have at least 4 GB of RAM. You need enough hard drive space to hold your PC games.

- To improve the sound quality, purchase a dedicated sound card. If you are an audiophile, you'll definitely hear the difference.

- Because of all these advanced components, you'll need to upgrade your cooling setup. You'll need a large CPU fan and heat sink. You can also consider water-cooling your system.

- Get a nice 24-inch monitor with a resolution of at least 1920 × 1080. A basic 2.1 or 5.1 speaker setup should also suffice for most games. Optionally, you can get a nice set of headphones with an attached microphone for voice chatting with your friends while you game.

- Gaming keyboards and mice are available that include extra buttons and fancy LCD screens. These components are entirely a personal choice.

- Advanced (and expensive) gaming machines can use advanced technology to increase the performance and visual fidelity. These include connecting multiple graphics cards via SLI and CrossFire, connecting multiple monitors, and purchasing 3-D monitors.

- Other components can be upgraded, too: you can upgrade your CPU to more than four cores, quadruple your RAM, and add solid-state drives. You can also get better speakers and gamepads and joysticks.

■ Key Terms

<div style="display: flex; justify-content: space-between;">

audio interface *(666)*
CrossFire *(679)*
Digital Living Network Alliance (DLNA) *(674)*
future-proofing *(676)*
home server PC *(667)*
HTPC *(672)*

network attached storage (NAS) *(670)*
profile *(665)*
Scalable Link Interface (SLI) *(679)*
thick client *(660)*
thin client *(663)*

</div>

■ Key Term Quiz

Use the Key Terms list to complete the sentences that follow. Not all terms will be used.

1. You can store files remotely without a home server by using a(n) _____ device.

2. A(n) _____ is a system designed to handle only very basic applications with an absolute minimum amount of hardware required by the operating system.

3. A(n) _____ is a box that you hook up to your PC with inputs that enable you to connect professional microphones and instruments.

4. CompTIA calls a general-purpose SOHO computer a(n) _____.

5. _____ cases are used to make your computer blend in with the rest of your home theater equipment.

6. Overbuilding your gaming PC to handle games that aren't out yet is called _____.

7. Connecting multiple graphics cards in your PC uses _____ technology if you're using NVIDIA cards and CrossFire technology if you're using AMD cards.

8. _____ certified devices connect to your home network, discover each other, and communicate over the Internet.

9. To ensure that the color output matches between your monitor and your printer, you can use a calibration device to create a(n) _____ both for your monitor and for your printer.

10. If you want to share files and printers over your home network, you can set up a(n) _____.

■ Multiple-Choice Quiz

1. What is a thin client?

 A. A computer with a 32-bit-wide address bus

 B. A portable computer

 C. A system designed to handle only very basic applications with the minimum hardware required by the operating system

 D. A computer in a narrow, small form-factor case

2. What three functions does a home server PC provide? (Select three.)

 A. Media streaming

 B. File sharing

 C. Web hosting

 D. Print sharing

3. What's a good guide to use when deciding on hardware for a basic thick client?

 A. Buy whatever is on sale.

 B. Always start with the most expensive hardware.

 C. Check the recommended requirements for the OS you want to use.

 D. Check the MSDS for the OS you want to use.

4. How can you make sure that your printouts match the colors displayed on your monitor?

 A. Calibrate your GPU with a GPU calibrator.

 B. Calibrate your monitor and printer to use the same profile.

C. Just buy an expensive monitor and printer; no setup is needed.

D. Use RGB ink in your LaserJet printer.

5. How do you share a printer in Windows 7?

 A. Open Device Manager, right-click on the printer, select Properties, and select Share this printer.

 B. You have to install special drivers for your printer.

 C. Open the Devices and Printers applet in the Control Panel, right-click on the printer, select Printer properties, and then check the Share this printer checkbox on the Sharing tab.

 D. You have to have Windows Home Server in order to share printers.

6. What program that comes with some versions of Windows turns your PC into a home theater PC?

 A. XBMC

 B. Windows Media Center

 C. Plex

 D. Windows Home Theater

7. What term defines building your PC to run games that aren't out yet?

 A. Future-proofing

 B. Next-gen proofing

 C. Overbuilding

 D. Prebuilding

8. What does CompTIA call a PC case built for a home theater?

 A. Media center case

 B. XBMC

 C. HTPC

 D. Stereo case

9. Bob wants to build a new gaming computer, but he doesn't want to spend a ton of money. What parts should he spend the most money on? (Select two.)

 A. CPU

 B. Case

 C. Power supply

 D. Graphics card

10. What is the most important component for building a virtualization workstation?

 A. CPU

 B. Power supply

 C. RAM

 D. Large monitor

11. What are the high-end sound output devices on audio workstations called?

 A. Sound cards

 B. Audio interfaces

 C. Consoles

 D. Calibrators

12. What three things does a video workstation benefit from? (Select three.)

 A. High-end motherboard

 B. Fast, multicore CPU

 C. Lots of RAM

 D. Professional-level GPU

13. What device can store your files remotely if you don't want to build a home server PC?

 A. NAS

 B. WAP

 C. PCI

 D. NIC

14. Your friend Susan just won the lottery! After spending a few weeks buying mansions and European sports cars, she decides that what she wants most out of her limitless fortune is to be able to play computer games all day. Not knowing anything about building PCs, she comes to you for help building the Ultimate Gaming Rig. What features would help Susan get the absolute most performance out of her games? (Select three.)

 A. A quad-SLI or quad-CrossFire graphics card setup

 B. A top-of-the-line CPU

 C. One or more SSDs

 D. A case with a window on the side

15. Which of the following editions of Windows comes with Windows Media Center?

 A. Windows 7 Home Premium

 B. Windows XP Professional

 C. Windows Vista Home Basic

 D. Windows Vista Business

■ Essay Quiz

1. Write an essay describing your ideal PC. If you're into music, write about an audio workstation; if you're into games, write about a gaming PC; and so on. What components are important to the type of PC you want to build? Is there anything you want on your PC that's not covered in this chapter? Do you need your PC to do more than one thing?

2. Write about your personal process for researching and purchasing PC components. Which Web sites do you visit? Do you read PC magazines? How do you comparison shop? Are there any local stores that you visit?

Lab Projects

• Lab Project 21.1

Pretend you've been saving money to build yourself a gaming PC. You've managed to scrape together $1000, and it's burning a hole in your pocket. Go on the Internet and shop for components to put together the best home theater PC you can within your budget. Remember to research any components before deciding on which to purchase, and definitely don't forget to include shipping costs in your budget. Write down in a spreadsheet each component, its price, and your reasons for purchasing it.

• Lab Project 21.2

Using your classroom PCs, download and install XBMC from www.xbmc.org. Using the resources available on the XBMC Web site, configure your copy of XBMC with custom skins and background images. Set up XBMC to play a DVD or CD when you put one in your optical drive. If you have a smartphone and you're allowed to use it in class, download and install a free XBMC remote app and set it up to control XBMC on your PC. Look through the available add-ons and try installing any that sound interesting to you. When you're finished customizing, write a short summary of what you did and how you did it.

• Lab Project 21.3

Turn one of your classroom PCs into a home server PC by setting up file and printer sharing. If you've got a printer available, plug it into the server PC and share it with the other PCs in the classroom. Download a video file of some sort (you can download a free, open source, 3-D short film at www.sintel.org/download) and stream it from the server PC to other classroom PCs. When you're finished, write a short guide to sharing media and printers in Windows.

appendix A

Mapping to the CompTIA A+ Objectives

220-801 Exam Objectives

Competency	Chapter	Page(s)
1.0 PC Hardware		
1.1 Configure and apply BIOS settings.		
Install firmware upgrades – flash BIOS	7	160
BIOS component information	7	164
RAM	7	168
Hard drive	7	164
Optical drive	7	164
CPU	7	168
BIOS configurations	7	164, 167-170
Boot sequence	7	167
Enabling and disabling devices	7	168
Date/time	7	164
Clock speeds	7	168
Virtualization support	7	167
BIOS security (passwords, drive encryption: TPM, lo-jack)	7	169, 170
Use built-in diagnostics	7	167
Monitoring	7	169
Temperature monitoring	7	169
Fan speeds	7	170
Intrusion detection/notification	7	168
Voltage	7	169
Clock	7	169
Bus speed	7	168
1.2 Differentiate between motherboard components, their purposes, and properties.		
Sizes	8	181
ATX	8	185
Micro-ATX	8	185
ITX	8	186
Expansion slots	8	191
PCI	8	194
PCI-X	8	195

Competency	Chapter	Page(s)
PCIe	8	195
miniPCI	8	195
CNR	8	191
AGP 2x, 4x, 8x	8	195
RAM slots	6	132
CPU sockets	5	113-115
Chipsets	7	155
North Bridge	7, 8	155, 188
South Bridge	7, 8	155, 188
CMOS battery	7	163
Jumpers	8	210
Power connections and types	9	231
Fan connectors	8	190
Front panel connectors	8	208
USB	8	208
Audio	8	208
Power button	8	208
Power light	8	208
Drive activity lights	8	208
Reset button	8	208
Bus speeds	8	210
1.3 Compare and contrast RAM types and features.		
Types	6	131-138
DDR	6	133-135
DDR2	6	135
DDR3	6	136
SDRAM	6	131-132
SODIMM	6	132
RAMBUS	6	132-133
DIMM	6	131
Parity vs. non-parity	6	138
ECC vs. non-ECC	6	138
RAM configurations	6	132, 136
Single channel vs. dual channel vs. triple channel	6	132, 136
Single sided vs. double sided	6	137
RAM compatibility and speed	6	133-136
1.4 Install and configure expansion cards.		
Sound cards	17	538-542
Video cards	13	385-387
Network cards	14	438
Serial and parallel cards	12, 19	324, 618

Competency	Chapter	Page(s)
2.6 Install, configure, and deploy a SOHO wireless/wired router using appropriate settings.		
MAC filtering	15	463
Channels (1 – 11)	15	884
Port forwarding, port triggering	14	426
SSID broadcast (on/off)	15	463
Wireless encryption	15	463-464
Firewall	14	437
DHCP (on/off)	4, 14, 20	432
DMZ	20	643
NAT	16	491
WPS	15	464
Basic QoS	16	494
2.7 Compare and contrast Internet connection types and features.		
Cable	16	487-488
DSL	16	487
Dial-up	16	481-486
Fiber	16	488-489
Satellite	16	490
ISDN	16	486
Cellular (mobile hotspot)	16	489-490
Line of sight wireless internet service	16	490
WiMAX	16	490
2.8 Identify various types of networks.		
LAN	4	76
WAN	4	76
PAN	15	469
MAN	16	488
Topologies	4	68-69
Mesh	4	68-69
Ring	4	68-69
Bus	4	68-69
Star	4	68-69
Hybrid	4	68
2.9 Compare and contrast network devices and their functions and features.		
Hub	4	72
Switch	4	72
Router	4	76
Access point	15	460
Bridge	14	414
Modem	16	481-482
NAS	14, 21	414, 672

Competency	Chapter	Page(s)
Listen and do not interrupt the customer	2	26
Be culturally sensitive	2	25
Be on time (if late contact the customer)	2	23
Avoid distractions	2	25
Personal calls	2	25
Talking to co-workers while interacting with customers	2	25
Personal interruptions	2	25
Dealing with difficult customer or situation	2	26
Avoid arguing with customers and/or being defensive	2	26
Do not minimize customer's problems	2	27
Avoid being judgmental	2	27
Clarify customer statements (ask open ended questions to narrow the scope of the problem, restate the issue or question to verify understanding)	2	27
Set and meet expectations/timeline and communicate status with the customer	2	28-29
Offer different repair/replacement options if applicable	2	24
Provide proper documentation on the services provided	2	29
Follow up with customer/user at a later date to verify satisfaction	2	29
Deal appropriately with customers confidential materials	20	654
Located on a computer, desktop, printer, etc.	20	654
5.4 Explain the fundamentals of dealing with prohibited content/activity.		
First response		
Identify	20	654
Report through proper channels	20	654
Data/device preservation	20	654
Use of documentation/documentation changes	20	654
Chain of custody	20	
Tracking of evidence/documenting process	20	654

About the CD-ROM

The disc included with this book comes with:

- An introduction to CompTIA A+ video from the author, Mike Meyers

- Digital copy of the CompTIA A+ 220-801 objectives

- Total Tester practice exam software with hundreds of practice exam questions

- A link to hours of Mike Meyers video training

- Links to a collection of Mike's current favorite tools and utilities for PC troubleshooting

- A PDF copy of the book

The software can be installed on any Windows 98/NT/2000/XP/Vista/Windows 7 computer and must be installed to access the Total Tester practice exam software.

Playing the Mike Meyers Introduction Video

If your computer's optical drive is configured to auto-run, the menu will automatically start up upon inserting the disc. If the auto-run feature did not launch the disc, browse to the disc and double-click the Launch.exe icon.

From the opening screen you can launch the video message from Mike by clicking the **Mike Meyers Introduction Video** button. This launches the video file using your system's default video player.

Viewing the CompTIA Exam Objectives

To view the CompTIA A+ exam objectives, select the **CompTIA Exam Objectives** button from the main menu of the disc. On the next page, clicking the **CompTIA A+ (220-801) Objectives** button will open a PDF of the appropriate objectives. The objectives map is the official exam objective list from CompTIA as of the date of publication. Please visit the CompTIA Web site for the most up-to-date exam objectives. A PDF-viewing program must be installed to view the objectives list. Adobe Acrobat Reader is available from www.acrobat.com.

System Requirements

The software requires Windows XP or higher, Internet Explorer 7 or higher or Firefox with Flash Player, and 30 MB of hard disk space for full installation.

Installing and Running Total Tester

From the main screen you may install the Total Tester by clicking the **Software and Videos** button, then selecting the **Total Tester A+ Practice Exams** button. This will begin the installation process and place an icon on your desktop and in your Start menu. To run Total Tester, navigate to **Start | (All) Programs | Total Seminars** or double-click the icon on your desktop.

To uninstall the Total Tester software, go to **Start | Settings | Control Panel | Add/Remove Programs** (XP) or **Programs and Features** (Vista / 7), and then select the **A+ Total Tester** program. Select **Remove** and Windows will completely uninstall the software.

Total Tester

Total Tester provides you with a simulation of the CompTIA A+ 801 exam. You may select practice exams for CompTIA A+ Exam 801. The exams can be taken in either Practice mode or Exam Simulation mode. Practice mode provides an assistance window with hints, references to the book, an explanation of the answer, and the option to check your answer as you take the test. Both Practice mode and Exam Simulation mode provide an overall grade and a grade broken down by certification objective. To take a test, launch the program, select CompTIA A+ from the Installed Question Packs list, then select the 801 exam. You can then select either Practice Exam or Exam Simulation.

Mike's Cool Tools

Mike loves freeware/open source PC tools! Most of the utilities mentioned in the text can be downloaded from the Internet using URLs provided on the disc on the Mike's Cool Tools page. You can access the menu by clicking on the **Software and Videos** button on the main page of the disc and then selecting the **Access Mike's Cool Tools** link.

Please read the Cool Tools page for a description of the utilities.

> ⚠ While all of the tools are "Mike Meyers Approved," there is no guarantee they will work for you. Read any and all documentation that comes with each utility before downloading and using that program.

Mike's Video Training

Your disc comes with a link to hours of free PC video training starring Mike Meyers. On the main page of the disc, click the **Software and Videos** link and then select **Access Mike Meyers Video Training**. You'll have access to several training segments, with an option to purchase even more of Mike's instructional videos.

■ Free PDF Copy of the Book

The contents of this book are provided in PDF format on the CD. This file is viewable on your computer and many portable devices.

To view the file on your computer, Adobe's Acrobat Reader is required and has been included on the CD.

To view the electronic book on a portable device, copy the PDF file to your computer from the CD, and then copy the file to your portable device using a USB or other connection. Adobe offers a mobile version of Adobe Reader, the Adobe Reader mobile app, which currently supports iOS and Android. The Adobe web site also has a list of recommended applications.

For more information on Adobe Reader and to check for the most recent version of the software, visit Adobe's web site at www.adobe.com and search for the free Adobe Reader or look for Adobe Reader on the product page.

■ Technical Support

For questions regarding the Total Tester software or operation of the CD, visit www.totalsem.com or e-mail support@totalsem.com.

For questions regarding the PDF book or video, e-mail techsolutions @mhedu.com or visit http://mhp.softwareassist.com.

For questions regarding book content, please e-mail customer.service @mheducation.com. For customers outside the United States, e-mail international_cs@mheducation.com.

%SystemRoot% The path where the operating system is installed.

10BaseT Ethernet LAN designed to run on twisted pair cabling. 10BaseT runs at 10 megabits per second. The maximum length for the cabling between the NIC and the switch (or hub, repeater, etc.) is 100 meters. It uses baseband signaling. No industry standard spelling exists, so sometimes it's written 10BASE-T or 10Base-T.

100BaseT Ethernet cabling system designed to run at 100 megabits per second on twisted pair cabling. It uses baseband signaling. No industry standard spelling exists, so sometimes it's written 100BASE-T or 100Base-T.

1000BaseT Gigabit Ethernet on UTP.

110 block The most common connection used with structured cabling, connecting horizontal cable runs with patch panels.

16-bit (PC Card) Type of PC Card that can have up to two distinct functions or devices, such as a modem/network card combination.

2.1 speaker system Speaker setup consisting of two stereo speakers combined with a subwoofer.

3.5-inch floppy drive Size of all modern floppy disk drives; the format was introduced in 1986 and is one of the longest surviving pieces of computer hardware.

34-pin ribbon cable Type of cable used by floppy disk drives.

3-D graphics Video technology that attempts to create images with the same depth and texture as objects seen in the real world.

40-pin ribbon cable PATA cable used to attach EIDE devices (such as hard drives) or ATAPI devices (such as optical drives) to a system. (*See* PATA.)

5.1 speaker system Speaker setup consisting of four satellite speakers plus a center speaker and a subwoofer.

64-bit processing A type of processing that can run a compatible 64-bit operating system, such as Windows 7, and 64-bit applications. 64-bit PCs have a 64-bit-wide address bus, enabling them to use more than 4 GB of RAM.

8.3 naming system File-naming convention that specified a maximum of eight characters for a filename, followed by a three-character file extension. Has been replaced by LFN (long filename) support.

80-wire ribbon cable PATA cable used to attach fast EIDE devices (such as ATA/100 hard drives) or ATAPI devices (such as optical drives) to a system. (*See* PATA.)

802.11a Wireless networking standard that operates in the 5-GHz band with a theoretical maximum throughput of 54 Mbps.

802.11b Wireless networking standard that operates in the 2.4-GHz band with a theoretical maximum throughput of 11 Mbps.

802.11g Wireless networking standard that operates in the 2.4-GHz band with a theoretical maximum throughput of 54 Mbps and is backward compatible with 802.11b.

802.11n Wireless networking standard that can operate in both the 2.4-GHz and 5-GHz bands and uses multiple in/multiple out (MIMO) to achieve a theoretical maximum throughput of 100+ Mbps.

A/V sync Process of synchronizing audio and video.

AC (alternating current) Type of electricity in which the flow of electrons alternates direction, back and forth, in a circuit.

AC'97 Sound card standard for lower-end audio devices; created when most folks listened to stereo sound at best.

accelerometer Feature in smartphones and tablets that rotates the screen when the device is physically rotated.

access control Security concept using physical security, authentication, users and groups, and security policies.

ACPI (Advanced Configuration and Power Interface) Power management specification that far surpasses its predecessor, APM, by providing support for hot-swappable devices and better control of power modes.

Action Center A one-page aggregation of event messages, warnings, and maintenance messages in Windows 7.

activation Process of confirming that an installed copy of a Microsoft product (most commonly Windows or a Microsoft Office application) is legitimate. Usually done at the end of software installation.

active matrix Type of liquid crystal display (LCD) that replaced the passive matrix technology used in most portable computer displays. Also called TFT (thin film transistor).

active partition On a hard drive, primary partition that contains an operating system.

active PFC (power factor correction) Circuitry built into PC power supplies to reduce harmonics.

activity light An LED on a NIC, hub, or switch that blinks rapidly to show data transfers over the network.

ad hoc mode Decentralized wireless network mode, otherwise known as peer-to-peer mode, where each wireless node is in meshed contact with every other node.

Add or Remove Programs Applet allowing users to manually add or remove a program to or from the system.

address bus Set of wires leading from the CPU to the memory controller chip (traditionally the Northbridge) that enables the CPU to address RAM. Also used by the CPU for I/O addressing. On current CPUs with built-in memory controllers, the address bus refers to the internal electronic channel from the microprocessor to RAM, along which the addresses of memory storage locations are transmitted. Like a post office box, each memory location has a distinct number or address; the address bus provides the means by which the microprocessor can access every location in memory.

address space Total amount of memory addresses that an address bus can contain.

administrative shares Administrator tool to give local admins access to hard drives and system root folders.

Administrative Tools Group of Control Panel applets, including Computer Management, Event Viewer, and Reliability and Performance Monitor.

administrator account User account, created when the OS is first installed, that is allowed complete, unfettered access to the system without restriction.

Administrators group List of members with complete administrator privileges.

ADSL (asymmetric digital subscriber line) Fully digital, dedicated connection to the telephone system that provides average download speeds of 7 Mbps and upload speeds of 512 Kbps.

Advanced Encryption Standard (AES) A block cipher created in the late 1990s that uses a 128-bit block size and a 128-, 192-, or 256-bit key size. Practically uncrackable.

Advanced Startup Options menu Menu that can be reached during the boot process that offers advanced OS startup options, such as to boot to Safe Mode or boot into Last Known Good Configuration.

adware Type of malicious program that downloads ads to a user's computer, generating undesirable network traffic.

Aero The Windows Vista/7 desktop environment. Aero adds some interesting aesthetic effects such as window transparency and Flip 3D.

AGP (Accelerated Graphics Port) 32/64-bit expansion slot designed by Intel specifically for video that runs at 66 MHz and yields a throughput of at least 254 Mbps. Later versions (2×, 4×, 8×) give substantially higher throughput.

algorithm Set of rules for solving a problem in a given number of steps.

ALU (arithmetic logic unit) CPU logic circuits that perform basic arithmetic (add, subtract, multiply, and divide).

AMD (Advanced Micro Devices) CPU and chipset manufacturer that competes with Intel. Produces the popular Phenom, Athlon, Sempron, Turion, and Duron microprocessors; also produces video card processors under its ATI brand.

AMI (American Megatrends, Inc.) Major producer of BIOS software for motherboards, as well as many other computer-related components and software.

amperes (amps or A) Unit of measure for amperage, or electrical current.

amplitude Loudness of a sound card.

AMR (audio modem riser) Proprietary slot used on some motherboards to provide a sound interference–free connection for modems, sound cards, and NICs.

analog Device that uses a physical quantity, such as length or voltage, to represent the value of a number. By contrast, digital storage relies on a coding system of numeric units.

Android Smartphone and tablet OS created by Google.

anti-aliasing In computer imaging, blending effect that smoothes sharp contrasts between two regions—e.g., jagged lines or different colors. Reduces jagged edges of text or objects. In voice signal processing, process of removing or smoothing out spurious frequencies from waveforms produced by converting digital signals back to analog.

anti-static bag Bag made of anti-static plastic into which electronics are placed for temporary or long-term storage. Used to protect components from electrostatic discharge.

anti-static mat Special surface on which to lay electronics. These mats come with a grounding connection designed to equalize electrical potential between a workbench and one or more electronic devices. Used to prevent electrostatic discharge.

anti-static wrist strap Special device worn around the wrist with a grounding connection designed to equalize electrical potential between a technician and an electronic device. Used to prevent electrostatic discharge.

antivirus program Software designed to combat viruses by either seeking out and destroying them or passively guarding against them.

API (application programming interface) Software definition that describes operating system calls for application software; conventions defining how a service is invoked.

APIPA (Automatic Private IP Addressing) Feature of Windows that automatically assigns an IP address to the system when the client cannot obtain an IP address automatically.

APM (Advanced Power Management) BIOS routines that enable the CPU to turn on and off selected peripherals.

app A program for a tablet or smartphone. Also, a program written for Windows 8 Metro interface.

applet Generic term for a program in the Windows Control Panel.

Applications Name of the tab in Task Manager that lists running applications.

archive To copy programs and data onto a relatively inexpensive storage medium (disk, tape, etc.) for long-term retention.

archive attribute Attribute of a file that shows whether the file has been backed up since the last change. Each time a file is opened, changed, or saved, the archive bit is turned on. Some types of backups turn off this archive bit to indicate that a good backup of the file exists on tape.

ARP (Address Resolution Protocol) Protocol in the TCP/IP suite used with the command-line utility of the same name (arp) to determine the MAC address that corresponds to a particular IP address.

ASCII (American Standard Code for Information Interchange) Industry-standard 8-bit characters used to define text characters, consisting of 96 upper- and lowercase letters, plus 32 nonprinting control characters, each of which is numbered. These numbers were designed to achieve uniformity among computer devices for printing and the exchange of simple text documents.

aspect ratio Ratio of width to height of an object. Standard television has a 4:3 aspect ratio.

ASR (Automated System Recovery) Windows XP tool designed to recover a badly corrupted Windows system; similar to the ERD in Windows 2000.

assertive communication Means of communication that is not pushy or bossy but is also not soft. Useful in dealing with upset customers as it both defuses their anger and gives them confidence that you know what you're doing.

AT (Advanced Technology) Model name of the second-generation, 80286-based IBM computer. Many aspects of the AT, such as the BIOS, CMOS, and expansion bus, have become de facto standards in the PC industry. The physical

organization of the components on the motherboard is called the AT form factor.

ATA (AT Attachment) Type of hard drive and controller designed to replace the earlier ST506 and ESDI drives without requiring replacement of the AT BIOS—hence, AT attachment. These drives are more popularly known as IDE drives. (*See* IDE.) The ATA/33 standard has drive transfer speeds up to 33 MBps; the ATA/66 up to 66 MBps; the ATA/100 up to 100 MBps; and the ATA/133 up to 133 MBps. (*See* Ultra DMA.)

ATA/ATAPI-6 Also known as ATA-6 or "Big Drive." Replaced the INT13 extensions and allowed for hard drives as large as 144 petabytes (144 million GB).

ATAPI (ATA Packet Interface) Series of standards that enables mass storage devices other than hard drives to use the IDE/ATA controllers. Popular with optical drives. (*See* EIDE.)

ATAPI-compliant Devices that utilize the ATAPI standard. (*See* ATAPI.)

Athlon Name used for a popular series of CPUs manufactured by AMD.

attrib.exe Command used to view the specific properties of a file; can also be used to modify or remove file properties, such as read-only, system, or archive.

attributes Values in a file that determine the hidden, read-only, system, and archive status of the file.

ATX (Advanced Technology Extended) Popular motherboard form factor that generally replaced the AT form factor.

audio interface High-end external sound device used by audio engineers and recording artists.

authentication Any method a computer uses to determine who can access it.

authorization Any method a computer uses to determine what an authenticated user can do.

autodetection Process through which new disks are automatically recognized by the BIOS.

Automatic Private IP Addressing (APIPA) A networking feature of operating systems that enables DHCP clients to self-configure an IP address and subnet mask automatically when a DHCP server isn't available.

Automatic Updates Feature allowing updates to Windows to be retrieved automatically over the Internet.

AutoPlay Windows XP/Vista/7 setting, along with autorun.inf, enabling Windows to automatically detect media files and begin using them. (*See* autorun.inf.)

autorun.inf File included on some media that automatically launches a program or installation routine when the media is inserted/attached to a system.

autosensing Used by better-quality sound cards to detect a device plugged into a port and to adapt the features of that port.

auto-switching power supply Type of power supply able to detect the voltage of a particular outlet and adjust accordingly.

Award Software Major brand of BIOS software for motherboards. Owned by Phoenix Technologies.

backlight One of three main components used in LCDs to illuminate an image.

backside bus Set of wires that connects the CPU to Level 2 cache. First appearing in the Pentium Pro, all modern CPUs have a backside bus. Some buses run at the full speed of the CPU, whereas others run at a fraction. Earlier Pentium IIs, for example, had backside buses running at half the speed of the processor. (*See also* frontside bus and external data bus.)

Backup and Restore Center Windows Vista/7's backup utility (Windows 7 drops "Center" from the name). It offers two options: create a backup or restore from a backup.

Backup or Restore Wizard Utility contained within Windows that allows users to create system backups and set system restore points.

Backup Utility (ntbackup) Windows XP's tool for creating and restoring backups.

ball mouse Input device that enables users to manipulate a cursor on the screen by using a ball and sensors that detect the movement and direction of the ball.

bandwidth Piece of the spectrum occupied by some form of signal, such as television, voice, or fax data. Signals require a certain size and location of bandwidth to be transmitted. The higher the bandwidth, the faster the signal transmission, allowing for a more complex signal such as audio or video. Because bandwidth is a limited space, when one user is occupying it, others must wait their turn. Bandwidth is also the capacity of a network to transmit a given amount of data during a given period.

bank Total number of SIMMs or DIMMs that can be accessed simultaneously by the chipset. The "width" of the external data bus divided by the "width" of the SIMM or DIMM sticks. DIMM slots that must be populated to activate dual- or triple-channel memory.

bar code reader Tool to read Universal Product Code (UPC) bar codes.

basic disk Hard drive partitioned in the "classic" way with a master boot record (MBR) and partition table. (*See also* dynamic disks.)

baud One analog cycle on a telephone line. In the early days of telephone data transmission, the baud rate was often analogous to bits per second. Due to advanced modulation of baud cycles as well as data compression, this is no longer true.

bcdedit A command-line tool that enables you to view the BCD store, which lists the Windows boot options.

BD-R (Blu-ray Disc-Recordable) Blu-ray Disc format that enables writing data to blank discs.

BD-RE (Blu-ray Disc-REwritable) Blu-ray Disc equivalent of the rewritable DVD, allows writing and rewriting several times on the same BD. (*See* Blu-ray Disc.)

BD-ROM Blu-ray Disc equivalent of a DVD-ROM or CD-ROM. (*See* Blu-ray Disc.)

beep codes Series of audible tones produced by a motherboard during the POST. These tones identify whether the POST has completed successfully or whether some piece of system hardware is not working properly. Consult the manual for your particular motherboard for a specific list of beep codes.

binary numbers Number system with a base of 2, unlike the number systems most of us use that have bases of 10 (decimal numbers), 12 (measurement in feet and inches), and 60 (time). Binary numbers are preferred for computers for precision and economy. An electronic circuit that can detect the difference between two states (on–off, 0–1) is easier and more inexpensive to build than one that could detect the differences among ten states (0–9).

biometric device Hardware device used to support authentication; works by scanning and remembering a unique aspect of a user's various body parts (e.g., retina, iris, face, or fingerprint) by using some form of sensing device such as a retinal scanner.

BIOS (basic input/output services) Classically, software routines burned onto the system ROM of a PC. More commonly seen as any software that directly controls a particular piece of hardware. A set of programs encoded in read-only memory (ROM) on computers. These programs handle startup operations and low-level control of hardware such as disk drives, the keyboard, and monitor.

bit Single binary digit. Also, any device that can be in an on or off state.

bit depth Number of colors a video card is capable of producing. Common bit depths are 16-bit and 32-bit, representing 65,536 colors and 16.7 million colors (plus an 8-bit alpha channel for transparency levels), respectively.

BitLocker Drive Encryption Drive encryption software offered in Windows Vista/7 Ultimate and Enterprise editions. BitLocker requires a special chip to validate hardware status and to ensure that the computer hasn't been hacked.

Bluetooth Wireless technology designed to create small wireless networks preconfigured to do specific jobs, but not meant to replace full-function networks or Wi-Fi.

Blu-ray Disc (BD) Optical disc format that stores 25 or 50 GB of data, designed to be the replacement media for DVD. Competed with HD DVD.

boot To initiate an automatic routine that clears the memory, loads the operating system, and prepares the computer for use. Term is derived from "pull yourself up by your bootstraps." PCs must do that because RAM doesn't retain program instructions when power is turned off. A cold boot occurs when the PC is physically switched on. A warm boot loads a fresh OS without turning off the computer, lessening the strain on the electronic circuitry. To do a warm boot, press the CTRL-ALT-DELETE keys twice in rapid succession (the three-fingered salute).

Boot Configuration Data (BCD) file File that contains information about the various operating systems installed on the system as well as instructions for how to actually load (bootstrap) them.

boot sector First sector on a PC hard drive or floppy disk, track 0. The boot-up software in ROM tells the computer to load whatever program is found there. If a system disk is read, the program in the boot record directs the computer to the root directory to load the operating system.

boot.ini Text file used during the boot process that provides a list of all OSs currently installed and available for ntldr (NT Loader). Also tells where each OS is located on the system. Used in Windows XP and earlier Microsoft operating systems.

bootable disk Disk that contains a functional operating system; can also be a floppy disk, USB thumb drive, or optical disc.

bootmgr Windows Vista/7's Boot Manager.

bootrec A Windows Recovery Environment troubleshooting and repair tool that repairs the master boot record, boot sector, or BCD store. It replaces the fixboot and fixmbr Recovery Console commands used in Windows XP and earlier operating systems.

bootstrap loader Segment of code in a system's BIOS that scans for an operating system, looks specifically for a valid boot sector, and, when one is found, hands control over to the boot sector; then the bootstrap loader removes itself from memory.

bps (bits per second) Measurement of how fast data is moved from one place to another. A 56K modem can move ~56,000 bits per second.

bridge A device that connects two networks and passes traffic between them based only on the node address, so that traffic between nodes on one network does not appear on the other network. For example, an Ethernet bridge only looks at the MAC address. Bridges filter and forward packets based on MAC addresses and operate at Level 2 (Data Link layer) of the OSI seven-layer model.

broadband Commonly understood as a reference to high-speed, always-on communication links that can move large files much more quickly than a regular phone line.

broadcast A network transmission addressed for every node on the network.

browser Program specifically designed to retrieve, interpret, and display Web pages.

BSoD (Blue Screen of Death) Infamous error screen that appears when Windows encounters an unrecoverable error.

BTX (Balanced Technology eXtended) Motherboard form factor designed as an improvement over ATX.

buffer underrun Inability of a source device to provide a CD burner with a constant stream of data while burning a CD-R or CD-RW.

buffered/registered DRAM Usually seen in motherboards supporting more than four sticks of RAM, required to address interference issues caused by the additional sticks.

bug Programming error that causes a program or a computer system to perform erratically, produce incorrect results, or crash. The term was coined when a real bug was found in one of the circuits of one of the first ENIAC computers.

burn Process of writing data to a writable optical disc, such as a DVD-R.

burn-in failure Critical failure usually associated with manufacturing defects.

bus Series of wires connecting two or more separate electronic devices, enabling those devices to communicate. Also, a network topology where computers all connect to a main line called a bus cable.

bus mastering Circuitry allowing devices to avoid conflicts on the external data bus.

bus topology Network configuration wherein all computers connect to the network via a central bus cable.

byte Unit of 8 bits; fundamental data unit of personal computers. Storing the equivalent of one character, the byte is also the basic unit of measurement for computer storage.

CAB files Short for cabinet files. These files are compressed and most commonly used during OS installation to store many smaller files, such as device drivers.

cache (disk) Special area of RAM that stores the data most frequently accessed from the hard drive. Cache memory can optimize the use of your systems.

cache (L1, L2, L3, etc.) Special section of fast memory, usually built into the CPU, used by the onboard logic to store information most frequently accessed by the CPU.

calibration Process of matching the print output of a printer to the visual output of a monitor.

capacitive touchscreen Type of touchscreen that uses electrical current in your body to determine movement of your fingers across the screen.

card reader Device with which you can read data from one of several types of flash memory.

card services Uppermost level of PCMCIA services. The card services level recognizes the function of a particular PC Card and provides the specialized drivers necessary to make the card work. (*See also* socket services.)

CardBus 32-bit PC cards that can support up to eight devices on each card. Electrically incompatible with earlier PC cards (3.3 V versus 5 V).

CAT 5 Category 5 wire; a TIA/EIA standard for UTP wiring that can operate at up to 100 megabits per second.

CAT 5e Category 5e wire; TIA/EIA standard for UTP wiring that can operate at up to 1 gigabit per second.

CAT 6 Category 6 wire; TIA/EIA standard for UTP wiring that can operate at up to 10 gigabits per second.

CAT 6a Category 6a wire; augmented CAT 6 UTP wiring that supports 10GBaseT networks at the full 100 meter distance between a node and a switch.

catastrophic failure Describes a failure in which a component or whole system will not boot; usually related to a manufacturing defect of a component. Could also be caused by overheating and physical damage to computer components.

CCFL (cold cathode fluorescent lamp) Light technology used in LCDs and flatbed scanners. CCFLs use relatively little power for the amount of light they provide.

cd (chdir) Shorthand for "change directory." Allows you to change the focus of the command prompt from one directory to another.

CD (compact disc) Originally designed as the replacement for vinyl records, has become the primary method of long-term storage of music and data.

CD quality Audio quality that has a sample rate of 44.4 KHz and a bit rate of 128 bits.

CDDA (CD-Digital Audio) Special format used for early CD-ROMs and all audio CDs; divides data into variable-length tracks. A good format to use for audio tracks but terrible for data because of lack of error checking.

CD-R (CD-recordable) CD technology that accepts a single "burn" but cannot be erased after that one burn.

CD-ROM (compact disc/read-only memory) Read-only compact storage disc for audio or video data. CD-ROMs are read by using CD-ROM drives and optical drives with backward compatibility, such as DVD and Blu-ray Disc drives.

CD-RW (CD-rewritable) CD technology that accepts multiple reads/writes like a hard drive.

Celeron Lower-cost brand of Intel CPUs.

cellular wireless networks Networks that enable cell phones, smartphones, and other mobile devices to connect to the Internet.

Centrino Marketing name for an Intel laptop solution including the mobile processor, support chips, and wireless networking.

Centronics connector Connector used with older printers.

certification License that demonstrates competency in some specialized skill.

Certified Cisco Network Associate (CCNA) One of the certifications demonstrating a knowledge of Cisco networking products.

chain of custody A documented history of who has been in possession of a system.

CHAP (Challenge Handshake Authentication Protocol) Common remote access protocol; the serving system challenges the remote client, usually by means of asking for a password.

chassis intrusion detection Feature offered in some chassis that trips a switch when the chassis is opened.

chipset Electronic chips, specially designed to work together, that handle all of the low-level functions of a PC. In the original PC, the chipset consisted of close to 30 different chips; today, chipsets usually consist of one, two, or three separate chips embedded into a motherboard.

chkdsk (CheckDisk) Hard drive error detection and, to a certain extent, correction utility in Windows. Originally a DOS command (chkdsk.exe); also the executable for the graphical Error-checking tool.

clean installation Installing an operating system on a fresh drive, following a reformat of that drive. Often it's the only way to correct a problem with a system when many of the crucial operating system files have become corrupted.

cleaning kit Method for cleaning floppy or optical drives.

client Computer program that uses the services of another computer program. Also, software that extracts information

from a server; your auto-dial phone is a client, and the phone company is its server. Also, a machine that accesses shared resources on a server.

client/server Relationship in which client software obtains services from a server on behalf of a person.

client/server network Network that has dedicated server machines and client machines.

clock cycle Single charge to the clock wire of a CPU.

clock-multiplying CPU CPU that takes the incoming clock signal and multiples it inside the CPU to let the internal circuitry of the CPU run faster.

clock speed Speed at which a CPU executes instructions, measured in MHz or GHz. In modern CPUs, the internal speed is a multiple of the external speed. (*See also* clock-multiplying CPU.)

clock (CLK) wire A special wire that, when charged, tells the CPU that another piece of information is waiting to be processed.

closed source Software that is solely controlled by its creator or distributor.

cluster Basic unit of storage on a floppy or hard disk. Multiple sectors are contained in a cluster. When Windows stores a file on a disk, it writes those files into dozens or even hundreds of contiguous clusters. If there aren't enough contiguous open clusters available, the operating system finds the next open cluster and writes there, continuing this process until the entire file is saved. The FAT or MFT tracks how the files are distributed among the clusters on the disk.

CMOS (complementary metal-oxide semiconductor) Originally, the type of nonvolatile RAM that held information about the most basic parts of your PC, such as hard drives, floppies, and amount of DRAM. Today, actual CMOS chips have been replaced by flash-type nonvolatile RAM. The information is the same, however, and is still called CMOS—even though it is now almost always stored on Flash RAM.

CMOS setup program Program enabling you to access and update CMOS data.

CNR (communications and networking riser) Proprietary slot used on some motherboards to provide a sound interference–free connection for modems, sound cards, and NICs.

coaxial cable Cabling in which an internal conductor is surrounded by another, outer conductor, thus sharing the same axis.

code Set of symbols representing characters (e.g., ASCII code) or instructions in a computer program (a programmer writes source code, which must be translated into executable or machine code for the computer to use).

code names Names that keep track of different variations within CPU models.

codec (compressor/decompressor) Software that compresses or decompresses media streams.

color depth Term to define a scanner's ability to produce color, hue, and shade.

COM port(s) Serial communications ports available on your computer.

command A request, typed from a terminal or embedded in a file, to perform an operation or to execute a particular program.

command-line interface User interface for an OS devoid of all graphical trappings.

command prompt Text prompt for entering commands.

CompactFlash (CF) One of the older but still popular flash media formats. Its interface uses a simplified PC Card bus, so it also supports I/O devices.

compatibility modes Feature of Windows 2000 and beyond to allow software written for previous versions of Windows to operate in newer operating systems.

compliance Concept that members of an organization must abide by the rules of that organization. For a technician, this often revolves around what software can or cannot be installed on an organization's computer.

component failure Occurs when a system device fails due to a manufacturing or some other type of defect.

Component Services Programming tools in Windows for the sharing of data objects between programs.

compression Process of squeezing data to eliminate redundancies, allowing files to use less space when stored or transmitted.

CompTIA A+ 220-801 One half of the CompTIA A+ certification for PC technicians. The 801 exam focuses primarily on hardware and networking.

CompTIA A+ 220-802 The second half of the CompTIA A+ certification for PC technicians. The 802 exam focuses primarily on software, security, and troubleshooting.

CompTIA A+ certification Industry-wide, vendor-neutral computer certification program that demonstrates competency as a computer technician.

CompTIA Network+ certification Industry-wide, vendor-neutral certification for network technicians, covering network hardware, installation, and troubleshooting.

Computer Default interface in Windows Vista and Windows 7 for Windows Explorer; displays hard drives and devices with removeable storage. (*See* My Computer.)

computer administrator One of three types of user accounts in Windows XP, has access to all resources on the computer. A member of the local Administrators group.

Computer Management Applet in Windows' Administrative Tools that contains several useful snap-ins, such as Device Manager and Disk Management.

computing process Four parts of a computer's operation: input, processing, output, and storage.

Computing Technology Industry Association (Comp-TIA) Nonprofit IT trade association that administers the CompTIA A+, CompTIA Network+ exams and many other vendor-neutral IT certification exams.

conditioning charger Battery charger that contains intelligent circuitry that prevents portable computer batteries from being overcharged and damaged.

connectors Small receptacles used to attach cables to a system. Common types of connectors include USB, PS/2, and DB-25.

consumables Materials used up by printers, including paper, ink, ribbons, and toner cartridges.

container file File containing two or more separate, compressed tracks, typically an audio track and a moving-picture track. Also known as a *wrapper*.

context menu Small menu brought up by right-clicking on objects in Windows.

Control Panel Collection of Windows applets, or small programs, that can be used to configure various pieces of hardware and software in a system.

controller card Card adapter that connects devices, such as a disk drive, to the main computer bus/motherboard.

convergence Measure of how sharply a single pixel appears on a CRT; a monitor with poor convergence produces images that are not sharply defined.

copy backup Type of backup similar to a normal or full backup, in that all selected files on a system are backed up. This type of backup does not change the archive bit of the files being backed up.

copy command Command in the command-line interface for making a copy of a file and pasting it in another location.

Core Name used for the family of Intel CPUs that succeeded the Pentium 4.

counter Used to track data about a particular object when using the Performance console in Windows XP.

CPU (central processing unit) "Brain" of the computer. Microprocessor that handles primary calculations for the computer. CPUs are known by names such as Core i5 and Phenom II.

CRC (cyclic redundancy check) Very accurate mathematical method used to check for errors in long streams of transmitted data. Before data is sent, the main computer uses the data to calculate a CRC value from the data's contents. If the receiver calculates from the received data a different CRC value , the data was corrupted during transmission and is re-sent. Ethernet packets use the CRC algorithm in the FCS portion of the frame.

C-RIMM or CRIMM (continuity RIMM) Passive device added to populate unused banks in a system that uses Rambus RIMMs.

crimper A specialized tool for connecting UTP wires to an RJ-45 connector. Also called a *crimping tool*.

CrossFire Technology that combines the power of multiple AMD graphics cards in a system.

crossover cable Special UTP cable used to connect hubs or to connect network cards without a hub. Crossover cables reverse the sending and receiving wire pairs from one end to the other.

CRT (cathode ray tube) Tube of a monitor in which rays of electrons are beamed onto a phosphorescent screen to produce images. Also, a shorthand way to describe a monitor that uses CRT rather than LCD technology.

CSMA/CA (carrier sense multiple access/collision avoidance) Networking scheme used by wireless devices to transmit data while avoiding data collisions, which wireless nodes have difficulty detecting.

CSMA/CD (carrier sense multiple access/collision detection) Networking scheme used by Ethernet devices to transmit data and resend data after detection of data collisions.

cylinder Single track on all the platters in a hard drive. Imagine a hard drive as a series of metal cans, nested one inside another; a single can would represent a cylinder.

daily backup Backup of all files that have been changed on that day without changing the archive bits of those files. Also called *daily copy backup*.

daisy-chaining Method of connecting several devices along a bus and managing the signals for each device.

data classification System of organizing data according to its sensitivity. Common classifications include public, highly confidential, and top secret.

data roaming A feature of cellular data systems that enables the signal to jump from cell tower to cell tower and

from your provider to another provider without obvious notice.

data structure Scheme that directs how an OS stores and retrieves data on and off a drive. Used interchangeably with the term file system. (*See also* file system.)

DB connectors D-shaped connectors used for a variety of connections in the PC and networking world. Can be male (with prongs) or female (with holes) and have a varying number of pins or sockets. Also called D-sub, D-subminiature, or D-shell connectors.

DB-15 connector A two- or three-row D-sub connector (female) used for 10Base5 networks, MIDI/joysticks, and analog video.

DB-25 connector D-sub connector (female), commonly referred to as a parallel port connector.

DC (direct current) Type of electricity in which the flow of electrons is in a complete circle in one direction.

DDR SDRAM (double data rate SDRAM) Type of DRAM that makes two processes for every clock cycle. (*See also* DRAM.)

DDR2 SDRAM Type of SDRAM that sends 4 bits of data in every clock cycle. (*See also* DDR SDRAM.)

DDR3 SDRAM Type of SDRAM that transfers data at twice the rate of DDR2 SDRAM.

debug To detect, trace, and eliminate errors in computer programs.

decibels Unit of measurement typically associated with sound. The higher the number of decibels, the louder the sound.

dedicated server Machine that is not used for any client functions, only server functions.

default gateway In a TCP/IP network, the nearest router to a particular host. This router's IP address is part of the necessary TCP/IP configuration for communicating with multiple networks using IP.

definition file List of virus signatures that an antivirus program can recognize.

defragmentation (defrag) Procedure in which all the files on a hard disk are rewritten on disk so that all parts of each file reside in contiguous clusters. The result is an improvement in disk speed during retrieval operations.

degauss Procedure used to break up the electromagnetic fields that can build up on the cathode ray tube of a monitor; involves running a current through a wire loop. Most monitors feature a manual degaussing tool.

del (erase) command Command in the command-line interface used to delete/erase files.

desktop User's primary interface to the Windows operating system.

desktop extender Portable computer that offers some of the features of a full-fledged desktop computer but with a much smaller footprint and lower weight.

desktop replacement Portable computer that offers the same performance as a full-fledged desktop computer; these systems are normally very heavy to carry and often cost much more than the desktop systems they replace.

device driver Program used by the operating system to control communications between the computer and peripherals.

Device Manager Utility that enables techs to examine and configure all the hardware and drivers in a Windows PC.

DHCP (Dynamic Host Configuration Protocol) Protocol that enables a DHCP server to set TCP/IP settings automatically for a DHCP client.

differential backup Similar to an incremental backup. Backs up the files that have been changed since the last backup. This type of backup does not change the state of the archive bit.

digital camera Camera that simulates film technology electronically.

digital certificate Form in which a public key is sent from a Web server to a Web browser so that the browser can decrypt the data sent by the server.

Digital Living Network Alliance (DLNA) devices Devices that connect to a home network, discover each other, and share media. In theory, DLNA devices should work with minimal setup or fuss, even if sourced from different manufacturers.

digital zoom Software tool to enhance the optical zoom capabilities of a digital camera.

digitally signed driver A driver designed specifically to work with Windows that has been tested and certified by Microsoft to work stably with Windows.

digitizer A tablet that enables users to paint, ink, pencil, or otherwise draw on a computer.

DIMM (dual inline memory module) 32- or 64-bit type of DRAM packaging, similar to SIMMs, with the distinction that each side of each tab inserted into the system performs a separate function. DIMMs come in a variety of sizes, with 184- and 240-pin being the most common on desktop computers.

dipole antennas Standard straight-wire antennas that provide the most omnidirectional function.

dir command Command used in the command-line interface to display the entire contents of the current working directory.

directory Another name for a folder.

directory service Centralized index that each PC accesses to locate resources in the domain.

DirectX Set of APIs enabling programs to control multimedia, such as sound, video, and graphics. Used in Windows Vista and Windows 7 to draw the Aero desktop.

Disk Cleanup Utility built into Windows that can help users clean up their disks by removing temporary Internet files, deleting unused program files, and more.

disk cloning Taking a PC and making a duplicate of the hard drive, including all data, software, and configuration files, and transferring it to another PC. (*See* image installation.)

disk duplexing Type of disk mirroring using two separate controllers rather than one; faster than traditional mirroring.

disk initialization A process that places special information on every hard drive installed in a Windows system.

Disk Management Snap-in available with the Microsoft Management Console that enables techs to configure the various disks installed in a system; available in the Computer Management Administrative Tool.

disk mirroring Process by which data is written simultaneously to two or more disk drives. Read and write speed is decreased but redundancy in case of catastrophe is increased.

disk quota Application allowing network administrators to limit hard drive space usage.

disk striping Process by which data is spread among multiple (at least two) drives. Increases speed for both reads and writes of data. Considered RAID level 0 because it does not provide fault tolerance.

disk striping with parity Method for providing fault tolerance by writing data across multiple drives and then including an additional drive, called a parity drive, that stores information to rebuild the data contained on the other drives. Requires at least three physical disks: two for the data and a third for the parity drive. This provides data redundancy at RAID levels 3–5 with different options.

disk thrashing Hard drive that is constantly being accessed due to lack of available system memory. When system memory runs low, a Windows system will utilize hard disk space as "virtual" memory, thus causing an unusual amount of hard drive access.

diskpart A fully functioning command-line partitioning tool.

display adapter Handles all the communication between the CPU and the monitor. Also known as a video card.

Display applet Tool in Windows XP and Windows 7 used to adjust display settings, including resolution, refresh rate, driver information, and color depth. (For the comparable tool in Windows Vista, *see* Personalization applet.)

DisplayPort Digital video connector used by Apple Mac desktop models and some PCs, notably from Dell. Designed by VESA as a royalty-free connector to replace VGA and DVI.

DMA (direct memory access) modes Technique that some PC hardware devices use to transfer data to and from the memory without using the CPU.

DMA controller Resides between the RAM and the devices and handles DMA requests.

DNS (domain name service) TCP/IP name resolution system that translates a host name into an IP address.

DNS domain Specific branch of the DNS name space. First-level DNS domains include .com, .gov, and .edu.

docking station Device that provides a portable computer extra features such as a DVD drive or PC Card, in addition to legacy and modern ports. Similar to a port replicator.

document findings, actions, and outcomes Recording each troubleshooting job: what the problem was, how it was fixed, and other helpful information. (One of the steps a technician uses to solve a problem.)

Documents folder Windows Vista/7 folder for storing user-created files. Replaces the My Documents folder previously used in Windows 2000/XP. (*See* My Documents.)

Dolby Digital Technology for sound reductions and channeling methods used for digital audio.

domain Groupings of users, computers, or networks. In Microsoft networking, a domain is a group of computers and users that share a common account database and a common security policy. On the Internet, a domain is a group of computers that share a common element in their hierarchical name. Other types of domains exist—e.g., broadcast domain, etc.

domain-based network Network that eliminates the need for logging on to multiple servers by using domain controllers to hold the security database for all systems.

DOS (Disk Operating System) First popular operating system available for PCs. A text-based, single-tasking operating system that was not completely replaced until the introduction of Windows 95.

dot-matrix printer Printer that creates each character from an array of dots. Pins striking a ribbon against the paper, one pin for each dot position, form the dots. May be a serial printer (printing one character at a time) or a line printer.

dot pitch Value relating to CRTs, showing the diagonal distance between phosphors measured in millimeters.

double-sided RAM RAM stick with RAM chips soldered to both sides of the stick. May only be used with motherboards designed to accept double-sided RAM. Very common.

dpi (dots per inch) Measure of printer resolution that counts the dots the device can produce per linear (horizontal) inch.

DPMS (display power-management signaling) Specification that can reduce CRT power consumption by 75 percent by reducing/eliminating video signals during idle periods.

DRAM (dynamic random access memory or dynamic RAM) Memory used to store data in most personal computers. DRAM stores each bit in a "cell" composed of a transistor and a capacitor. Because the capacitor in a DRAM cell can only hold a charge for a few milliseconds, DRAM must be continually refreshed, or rewritten, to retain its data.

DriveLock CMOS program enabling you to control the ATA security mode feature set. Also known as *drive lock*.

driver signing Digital signature for drivers used by Windows to protect against potentially bad drivers.

DS3D (DirectSound3D) Introduced with DirectX 3.0, DS3D is a command set used to create positional audio, or sounds that appear to come from in front, in back, or to the side of a user. Merged with DirectSound into DirectAudio in DirectX 8. (*See also* DirectX.)

DSL (digital subscriber line) High-speed Internet connection technology that uses a regular telephone line for connectivity. DSL comes in several varieties, including asynchronous (ADSL) and synchronous (SDSL), and many speeds. Typical home-user DSL connections are ADSL with a download speed of 7 Mbps and an upload speed of 512 Kbps.

D-subminiature *See* DB connectors.

DTS (Digital Theatre Systems) Technology for sound reductions and channeling methods, similar to Dolby Digital.

dual boot Refers to a computer with two operating systems installed, enabling users to choose which operating system to load on boot. Can also refer to kicking a device a second time just in case the first time didn't work.

dual-channel architecture Using two sticks of RAM (either RDRAM or DDR) to increase throughput.

dual-channel memory Form of DDR, DDR2, and DDR3 memory access used by many motherboards that requires two identical sticks of DDR, DDR2, or DDR3 RAM.

dual-core CPUs that have two execution units on the same physical chip but share caches and RAM.

dual-scan passive matrix Manufacturing technique for increasing display updates by refreshing two lines at a time.

DualView Microsoft feature enabling Windows to use two or more monitors simultaneously.

dumpster diving To go through someone's trash in search of information.

DUN (Dial-up Networking) Software used by Windows to govern the connection between the modem and the ISP.

duplexing Similar to mirroring in that data is written to and read from two physical drives, for fault tolerance. Separate controllers are used for each drive, both for additional fault tolerance and for additional speed. Considered RAID level 1. Also called *disk duplexing* or *drive duplexing*.

Duron Lower-cost version of AMD's Athlon series of CPUs.

DVD (digital versatile disc) Optical disc format that provides for 4–17 GB of video or data storage.

DVD-ROM DVD equivalent of the standard CD-ROM.

DVD-RW/DVD+RW Incompatible rewritable DVD media formats.

DVD-Video DVD format used exclusively to store digital video; capable of storing over 2 hours of high-quality video on a single DVD.

DVI (Digital Visual Interface) Special video connector designed for digital-to-digital connections; most commonly seen on PC video cards and LCD monitors. Some versions also support analog signals with a special adapter.

dxdiag (DirectX Diagnostics Tool) Diagnostic tool for getting information about and testing a computer's DirectX version.

dye-sublimation printer Printer that uses a roll of heat-sensitive plastic film embedded with dyes, which are vaporized and then solidified onto specially coated paper to create a high-quality image.

dynamic disks Special feature of Windows that enables users to span a single volume across two or more drives. Dynamic disks do not have partitions; they have volumes. Dynamic disks can be striped, mirrored, and striped or mirrored with parity.

EAX (Environment Audio eXtensions) 3-D sound technology developed by Creative Labs but now supported by most sound cards.

ECC (error correction code) Special software, embedded on hard drives, that constantly scans the drives for bad sectors.

ECC RAM/DRAM (error correction code DRAM) RAM that uses special chips to detect and fix memory errors. Commonly used in high-end servers where data integrity is crucial.

effective permissions User's combined permissions granted by multiple groups.

EFI (Extensible Firmware Interface) Firmware created by Intel and HP that replaced traditional 16-bit BIOS and added several new enhancements.

EFS (encrypting file system) Encryption tool found in NTFS 5 and later.

EIA/TIA *See* TIA/EIA.

EIDE (Enhanced IDE) Marketing concept of hard drive–maker Western Digital, encompassing four improvements for IDE drives, including drives larger than 528 MB, four devices, increase in drive throughput, and non–hard drive devices. (*See* ATAPI, PIO mode.)

electric potential The voltage differential between any two objects, one of which is frequently ground or earth, resulting in a degree of attraction for the electrons to move from one of the objects to the other. A large difference between a person and a doorknob, for example, can lead to a shocking experience when the two touch. *See* electrostatic discharge (ESD).

electromagnetic interference (EMI) Electrical interference from one device to another, resulting in poor performance of the device being interfered with. Examples: Static on your TV while running a blow dryer, or placing two monitors too close together and getting a "shaky" screen.

electrostatic discharge (ESD) Uncontrolled rush of electrons from one object to another. A real menace to PCs, as it can cause permanent damage to semiconductors.

eliciting answers Communication strategy designed to help techs understand a user's problems better. Works by listening to a user's description of a problem and then asking cogent questions.

e-mail (electronic mail) Messages, usually text, sent from one person to another via computer. Can also be sent automatically to a group of addresses (mailing list).

emergency repair disk (ERD) Saves critical boot files and partition information and is the main tool for fixing boot problems in Windows 2000.

emulator Software or hardware that converts the commands to and from the host machine into an entirely different platform.

encryption Making data unreadable by those who do not possess a key or password.

equipment rack A metal structure used in equipment rooms to secure network hardware devices and patch panels. Most racks are 19 inches wide. Devices designed to fit in such a rack use a height measurement called *units*, or simply *U*.

erase lamp Component inside laser printers that uses light to make the coating of the photosensitive drum conductive.

Error-checking Windows graphical tool that scans and fixes hard drive problems. Often referred to by the name of the executable, chkdsk, or Check Disk.

eSATA Serial ATA-based connector for external hard drives and optical drives.

escalate Process used when person assigned to repair a problem is not able to get the job done, such as sending the problem to someone with more expertise.

Establish a plan of action and implement the solution After establishing and testing a theory about a particular problem, techs solve the problem. (One of the steps a technician uses to solve a problem.)

Establish a theory of probable cause After identifying a problem, techs question the obvious to determine what might be the source of the problem. (One of the steps a technician uses to solve a problem.)

Ethernet Name coined by Xerox for the first standard of network cabling and protocols. Based on a bus topology.

Ethic of Reciprocity Golden Rule: Do unto others as you would have them do unto you.

EULA (End User License Agreement) Agreement that accompanies a piece of software, to which the user must agree before using the software. Outlines the terms of use for the software and also lists any actions on the part of the user that violate the agreement.

event auditing Feature of Event Viewer's Security section that creates an entry in the Security Log when certain events happen, such as a user logging on.

Event Viewer Utility made available as an MMC snap-in that enables users to monitor various system events, including network bandwidth usage and CPU utilization.

expand Command-line utility included with Windows used to access files within CAB files.

expansion bus Set of wires going to the CPU, governed by the expansion bus crystal, directly connected to expansion slots of varying types (PCI, AGP, PCIe, etc.).

expansion bus crystal Controls the speed of the expansion bus.

expansion slots Connectors on a motherboard that enable users to add optional components to a system. (*See also* AGP, PCI, and PCIe.)

ExpressCard The high-performance serial version of the PC Card that replaced PC Card slots on laptop PCs over the past decade. ExpressCard comes in two widths: 34 mm and 54 mm, called *ExpressCard/34* and *ExpressCard/54*.

extended partition Type of nonbootable hard disk partition. May only have one extended partition per disk. Purpose is to divide a large disk into smaller partitions, each with a separate drive letter.

Extensible Authentication Protocol (EAP) Authentication wrapper that EAP-compliant applications can use to accept one of many types of authentication. While EAP is a general-purpose authentication wrapper, its only substantial use is in wireless networks.

extension Two, three, four, five or more letters that follow a filename and identify the type of file. Common file extensions are .zip, .exe, .doc, .java, and .xhtml.

external data bus (EDB) Primary data highway of all computers. Everything in your computer is tied either directly or indirectly to the external data bus. (*See also* frontside bus and backside bus.)

Fast User Switching Account option that is useful when multiple users share a system; allows users to switch without logging off.

FAT (file allocation table) Hidden table that records how files on a hard disk are stored in distinct clusters; the only way DOS knows where to access files. Address of first cluster of a file is stored in the directory file. FAT entry for the first cluster is the address of the second cluster used to store that file. In the entry for the second cluster for that file is the address for the third cluster, and so on until the final cluster, which gets a special end-of-file code. There are two FATs, mirror images of each other, in case one is destroyed or damaged. Also refers to the 16-bit file allocation table when used by Windows 2000 and later NT-based operating systems.

FAT16 File allocation table that uses 16 bits for addressing clusters. Used as the primary hard drive format on DOS and early Windows 95 machines; currently used with smaller (2 GB or less) capacity flash media devices.

FAT32 File allocation table that uses 32 bits for addressing clusters. Commonly used with Windows 98 and Windows Me systems. Some Windows 2000 Professional and Windows XP systems also use FAT32, although most modern Windows systems use the more robust NTFS. Default format for flash media devices larger than 2 GB.

FAT64 (exFAT) A Microsoft-proprietary file system that breaks the 4-GB file-size barrier, supporting files up to 16 exabytes (EB) and a theoretical partition limit of 64 zettabytes (ZB). Envisioned for use with flash media devices with a capacity exceeding 2 TB.

FCS (Frame Check Sequence) Portion of an Ethernet frame used for error checking, most commonly with the CRC algorithm.

FDISK Disk-partitioning utility used in DOS and Windows 9*x* systems.

fiber-optic cable High-speed cable for transmitting data, made of high-purity glass sealed within an opaque tube. Much faster than conventional copper wire such as coaxial cable.

file Collection of any form of data that is stored beyond the time of execution of a single job. A file may contain program instructions or data, which may be numerical, textual, or graphical information.

file allocation unit Another term for cluster. (*See also* cluster.)

file association Windows term for the proper program to open a particular file; for example, the file association for opening .MP3 files might be Winamp.

file format How information is encoded in a file. Two primary types are binary (pictures) and ASCII (text), but within those are many formats, such as BMP and GIF for pictures. Commonly represented by a suffix at the end of the filename; for example, .txt for a text file or .exe for an executable.

file server Computer designated to store software, courseware, administrative tools, and other data on a LAN or WAN. It "serves" this information to other computers via the network when users enter their personal access codes.

file system Scheme that directs how an OS stores and retrieves data on and off a drive; FAT32 and NTFS are both file systems. Used interchangeably with the term "data structure." (*See also* data structure.)

filename Name assigned to a file when the file is first written on a disk. Every file on a disk within the same folder must have a unique name. Filenames can contain any character (including spaces), except the following: \ / : * ? " < > |

Files and Settings Transfer Wizard Windows XP's system for moving files and settings to a new PC.

firewall Device that restricts traffic between a local network and the Internet.

FireWire (IEEE 1394) Interconnection standard to send wide-band signals over a serialized, physically thin connector system. Serial bus developed by Apple and Texas Instruments; enables connection of 63 devices at speeds up to 800 megabits per second.

firmware Embedded programs or code stored on a ROM chip. Generally OS-independent, thus allowing devices to operate in a wide variety of circumstances without direct OS support. The system BIOS is firmware.

Flash ROM ROM technology that can be electrically reprogrammed while still in the PC. Overwhelmingly the most common storage medium of BIOS in PCs today, as it can be upgraded without a need to open the computer on most systems.

flatbed scanner Most popular form of consumer scanner; runs a bright light along the length of the tray to capture an image.

FlexATX Motherboard form factor. Motherboards built in accordance with the FlexATX form factor are very small, much smaller than microATX motherboards.

Flip 3D In the Aero desktop environment, a three-dimensional replacement for ALT-TAB. Accessed by pressing the WINDOWS KEY-TAB key combination.

floating point unit (FPU) Special CPU circuitry that handles complex numbers.

floppy disk Removable storage media that can hold between 720 KB and 1.44 MB of data.

floppy drive System hardware that uses removable 3.5-inch disks as storage media.

flux reversal Point at which a read/write head detects a change in magnetic polarity.

FM synthesis Producing sound by electronic emulation of various instruments to more-or-less produce music and other sound effects.

Folders list A tree menu in Windows Explorer for Windows 2000 and XP that displays the file structure on the left side of the window; toggled on with the Folders button. In Windows Vista and 7, the Folders list is active by default.

form factor Standard for the physical organization of motherboard components and motherboard size. Most common form factors are ATX and BTX.

format command Command in the command-line interface used to format a storage device.

formatting Magnetically mapping a disk to provide a structure for storing data; can be done to any type of disk, including a floppy disk, hard disk, or other type of removable disk.

FPU (floating point unit) Formal term for math coprocessor (also called a numeric processor) circuitry inside a CPU. A math coprocessor calculates by using a floating point math (which allows for decimals). Before the Intel 80486, FPUs were separate chips from the CPU.

fragmentation Occurs when files and directories get jumbled on a fixed disk and are no longer contiguous. Can significantly slow down hard drive access times and can be repaired by using the defrag utility included with each version of Windows. (*See also* defragmentation.)

frame A data unit transferred across a network. Frames consist of several parts, such as the sending and receiving MAC addresses, the data being sent, and the frame check sequence.

freeware Software that is distributed for free, with no license fee.

frequency Measure of a sound's tone, either high or low.

frontside bus Wires that connect the CPU to the main system RAM. Generally running at speeds of 66–133 MHz. Distinct from the expansion bus and the backside bus, though it shares wires with the former.

front-view projector Shoots the image out the front and counts on you to put a screen in front at the proper distance.

FRU (field replaceable unit) Any part of a PC that is considered to be replaceable "in the field," i.e., a customer location. There is no official list of FRUs—it is usually a matter of policy by the repair center.

FTP (File Transfer Protocol) Rules that enable two computers to talk to one another during a file transfer. Protocol used when you transfer a file from one computer to another across the Internet. FTP uses port numbers 20 and 21.

fuel cells Power source that uses chemical reactions to produce electricity. Lightweight, compact, and stable devices expected to replace batteries as the primary power source for portable PCs.

full-duplex Any device that can send and receive data simultaneously.

Full-Speed USB USB standard that runs at 12 Mbps. Also known as USB 1.1.

Function (fn) key Special key on many laptops that enables some keys to perform a third duty.

fuser assembly Mechanism in laser printers that uses two rollers to fuse toner to paper during the print process.

future-proofing Configuring a PC so that it will run programs (especially games) released in the coming years.

gain Ratio of increase of radio frequency output provided by an antenna, measured in decibels (dB).

GDI (graphical device interface) Component of Windows that utilizes the CPU rather than the printer to process a print job as a bitmapped image of each page.

general protection fault (GPF) Error code usually seen when separate active programs conflict on resources or data.

geometry Numbers representing three values: heads, cylinders, and sectors per track; defines where a hard drive stores data.

geotracking Feature in cellular phones that enables the cell phone companies and government agencies to use the ID or MAC address to pinpoint where your phone is at any given time.

giga Prefix for the quantity 1,073,741,824 (2^{30}) or for 1 billion. One gigabyte would be 1,073,741,824 bytes, except with hard drive labeling, where it means 1 billion bytes. One gigahertz is 1 billion hertz.

Global Positioning System (GPS) Technology that enables a mobile device to determine where you are on a map.

globally unique identifier (GUID) partition table (GPT) Partitioning scheme that enables you to create more than four primary partitions without needing to use dynamic disks.

GPU (graphics processing unit) Specialized processor that helps the CPU by taking over all of the 3-D rendering duties.

grayscale depth Number that defines how many shades of gray the scanner can save per dot.

grayware Program that intrudes into a user's computer experience without damaging any systems or data.

group Collection of user accounts that share the same access capabilities.

Group Policy Means of easily controlling the settings of multiple network clients with policies such as setting minimum password length or preventing Registry edits.

guest account Very limited built-in account type for Windows; a member of the Guest group.

GUI (graphical user interface) Interface that enables user to interact with computer graphically, by using a mouse or other pointing device to manipulate icons that represent programs or documents, instead of using only text as in early interfaces. Pronounced "gooey."

gyroscope Device that can detect the position of the tablet or phone in 3-D space.

HAL (hardware abstraction layer) Part of the Windows OS that separates system-specific device drivers from the rest of the NT system.

handshaking Procedure performed by modems, terminals, and computers to verify that communication has been correctly established.

hang When a computer freezes and does not respond to keyboard commands, it is said to "hang" or to have "hung."

hang time Number of seconds a too-often-hung computer is airborne after you have thrown it out a second-story window.

hard drive Data-recording system using solid disks of magnetic material turning at high speeds to store and retrieve programs and data in a computer. Abbreviated HDD for *hard disk drive*.

hardware Physical computer equipment such as electrical, electronic, magnetic, and mechanical devices. Anything in the computer world that you can hold in your hand. A floppy drive is hardware; Microsoft Word is not.

hardware profile Feature in Windows XP that enables the user to switch several hardware configurations at once during the Windows boot process.

hardware protocol Defines many aspects of a network, from the packet type to the cabling and connectors used.

HBA (host bus adapter) Connects SATA devices to the expansion bus. Also known as the SATA controller.

HD (Hi-Definition) Multimedia transmission standard that defines high-resolution images and 5.1, 6.1, and 7.1 sound.

HDA (High Definition Audio) Intel-designed standard to support features such as true surround sound with many discrete speakers. Often referred to by its code name, Azalia.

HDD (hard disk drive) Data-recording system using solid disks of magnetic material turning at high speeds to store and retrieve programs and data in a computer.

HDMI (High Definition Multimedia Interface) Single multimedia connection that includes both high-definition video and audio. One of the best connections for outputting to television. Also contains copy protection features.

head actuator Mechanism for moving the arms inside a hard drive on which the read/write heads are mounted.

heads Short for read/write heads used by hard drives to store data.

heat dope *See* thermal compound.

hex (hexadecimal) Base-16 numbering system using ten digits (0 through 9) and six letters (A through F). In the computer world, shorthand way to write binary numbers by substituting one hex digit for a four-digit binary number (e.g., hex 9 = binary 1001).

hibernation Power management setting in which all data from RAM is written to the hard drive before going to sleep. Upon waking up, all information is retrieved from the hard drive and returned to RAM.

hidden attribute File attribute that, when used, does not allow the dir command to show a file.

hierarchical directory tree Method by which Windows organizes files into a series of folders, called directories, under the root directory. (*See also* root directory.)

high gloss Laptop screen finish that offers sharper contrast, richer colors, and wider viewing angles than a matte finish, but is also much more reflective.

high-level formatting Format that sets up a file system on a drive.

high-voltage anode Component in a CRT monitor that has very high voltages of electricity flowing through it.

Hi-Speed USB USB standard that runs at 480 Mbps. Also referred to as USB 2.0.

home screen The default "desktop" of a mobile device.

home server PC A computer built to store files on a small office/home office (SOHO) network.

HomeGroup A Windows 7 feature that connects a group of computers using a common password—no special user names required. Each computer can be a member of only one homegroup at a time. Homegroups enable simple sharing of documents and printers between computers.

honesty Telling the truth—a very important thing for a tech to do.

horizontal cabling Cabling that connects the equipment room to the work areas.

host On a TCP/IP network, single device that has an IP address—any device (usually a computer) that can be the source or destination of a data packet. In the mainframe world, computer that is made available for use by multiple people simultaneously. Also, in virtualization, a computer running one or more virtual operating systems.

hot-swappable Any hardware that may be attached to or removed from a PC without interrupting the PC's normal processing.

HRR (horizontal refresh rate) Amount of time it takes for a CRT to draw one horizontal line of pixels on a display.

HTML (Hypertext Markup Language) ASCII-based, script-like language for creating hypertext documents such as those on the World Wide Web.

HTPC A home theater PC designed to attach to a TV or projector for movie and TV viewing.

HTTP (Hypertext Transfer Protocol) Extremely fast protocol used for network file transfers in the WWW environment. Uses port 80.

HTTPS (HTTP over Secure Sockets Layer) Secure form of HTTP used commonly for Internet business transactions or any time when a secure connection is required. Uses port 443. (*See also* HTTP.)

hub Electronic device that sits at the center of a star topology network, providing a common point for the connection of network devices. Hubs repeat all information out to all ports and have been replaced by switches, although the term is still commonly used.

hybrid A network topology that combines features from multiple other topologies, such as the star-bus topology.

hyperthreading CPU feature that enables a single pipeline to run more than one thread at once.

hypervisor Software that enables a single computer to run multiple operating systems simultaneously.

I/O (input/output) General term for reading and writing data to a computer. "Input" includes data entered from a keyboard, identified by a pointing device (such as a mouse), or loaded from a disk. "Output" includes writing information to a disk, viewing it on a CRT, or printing it to a printer.

I/O addressing Using the address bus to talk to system devices.

I/O advanced programmable interrupt controller (IOAPIC) Typically located in the Southbridge, acts as the traffic cop for interrupt requests to the CPU.

I/O base address First value in an I/O address range.

ICH (I/O Controller Hub) Official name for Southbridge chip found in Intel's chipsets.

icon Small image or graphic, most commonly found on a system's desktop, that launches a program when selected.

ICS (Internet Connection Sharing) Windows feature that enables a single network connection to be shared among several machines. ICS was first introduced with Windows 98.

IDE (integrated drive electronics) PC specification for small- to medium-sized hard drives in which the controlling electronics for the drive are part of the drive itself, speeding up transfer rates and leaving only a simple adapter (or "paddle"). IDE only supported two drives per system of no more than 504 MB each, and has been completely supplanted by Enhanced IDE. EIDE supports four drives of over 8 GB each and more than doubles the transfer rate. The more common name for PATA drives. Also known as *intelligent drive electronics*. (*See* PATA.)

identify the problem To question the user and find out what has been changed recently or is no longer working properly. (One of the steps a technician uses to solve a problem.)

IEC-320 Connects the cable supplying AC power from a wall outlet into the power supply.

IEEE (Institute of Electronic and Electrical Engineers) Leading standards-setting group in the United States.

IEEE 1284 IEEE standard governing parallel communication.

IEEE 1394 IEEE standard governing FireWire communication. (*See also* FireWire.)

IEEE 1394a FireWire standard that runs at 400 Mbps.

IEEE 1394b FireWire standard that runs at 800 Mbps.

IEEE 802.11 Wireless Ethernet standard more commonly known as Wi-Fi.

image deployment Operating system installation that uses a complete image of a hard drive as an installation media. Helpful when installing an operating system on a large number of identical PCs.

image file Bit-by-bit image of data to be burned on CD or DVD—from one file to an entire disc—stored as a single file on a hard drive. Particularly handy when copying from CD to CD or DVD to DVD.

IMAP4 (Internet Message Access Protocol version 4) An alternative to POP3 that retrieves e-mail from an e-mail server, like POP3; IMAP uses TCP port 143.

impact printer Uses pins and inked ribbons to print text or images on a piece of paper.

impedance Amount of resistance to an electrical signal on a wire. Relative measure of the amount of data a cable can handle.

incident report Record of the details of an accident, including what happened and where it happened.

incremental backup Backs up all files that have their archive bits turned on, meaning that they have been changed since the last backup. Turns the archive bits off after the files have been backed up.

Information Technology (IT) Field of computers, their operation, and their maintenance.

infrastructure mode Wireless networking mode that uses one or more WAPs to connect the wireless network nodes to a wired network segment.

inheritance NTFS feature that passes on the same permissions in any subfolders/files resident in the original folder.

ink cartridge Small container of ink for inkjet printers.

inkjet printer Uses liquid ink, sprayed through a series of tiny jets, to print text or images on a piece of paper.

installation disc Typically a CD-ROM or DVD that holds all the necessary device drivers.

instruction set All of the machine-language commands that a particular CPU is designed to understand.

integrated memory controller (IMC) Memory controller circuitry built into the CPU. An IMC enables faster control over things like the large L3 cache shared among multiple cores.

integrity Always doing the right thing.

interface Means by which a user interacts with a piece of software.

Interrupt 13 (INT13) extensions Improved type of BIOS that accepts EIDE drives up to 137 GB.

interrupt/interruption Suspension of a process, such as the execution of a computer program, caused by an event external to the computer and performed in such a way that the process can be resumed. Events of this kind include sensors monitoring laboratory equipment or a user pressing an interrupt key.

inverter Device used to convert DC current into AC. Commonly used with CCFLs in laptops and flatbed scanners.

iOS The operating system of Apple mobile devices.

IP address Numeric address of a computer connected to the Internet. An IPv4 address is made up of four octets of 8-bit binary numbers translated into their shorthand numeric values. An IPv6 address is 128 bits long. The IP address can be broken down into a network ID and a host ID. Also called *Internet address*.

ipconfig Command-line utility for Windows servers and workstations that displays the current TCP/IP configuration of the machine. Similar to winipcfg and ifconfig.

IPsec (Internet Protocol security) Microsoft's encryption method of choice for networks consisting of multiple networks linked by a private connection, providing transparent encryption between the server and the client.

IPv4 (Internet Protocol version 4) Internet standard protocol that provides a common layer over dissimilar networks; used to move packets among host computers and through gateways if necessary. Part of the TCP/IP protocol suite. Uses the dotted-decimal format—xxx.xxx.xxx.xxx.

IPv6 (Internet Protocol version 6) Protocol in which addresses consist of eight sets of four hexadecimal numbers, each number being a value between 0000 and FFFF, using a colon to separate the numbers. Here's an example: FEDC:BA98:7654:3210:0800:200C:00CF:1234.

IrDA (Infrared Data Association) protocol Protocol that enables communication through infrared devices, with speeds of up to 4 Mbps.

IRQ (interrupt request) Signal from a hardware device, such as a modem or a mouse, indicating that it needs the CPU's attention. In PCs, IRQs are sent along specific IRQ channels associated with a particular device. IRQ conflicts were a common problem in the past when adding expansion boards, but the plug-and-play specification has removed this headache in most cases.

ISA (Industry Standard Architecture) Industry Standard Architecture design was found in the original IBM PC for the slots that allowed additional hardware to be connected to the computer's motherboard. An 8-bit, 8.33-MHz expansion bus was designed by IBM for its AT computer and released to the public domain. An improved 16-bit bus was also released to the public domain. Replaced by PCI in the mid-1990s.

ISDN (integrated services digital network) CCITT (Comité Consultatif Internationale de Télégraphie et Téléphonie) standard that defines a digital method for communications to replace the current analog telephone system. ISDN is superior to POTS telephone lines because it supports a transfer rate of up to 128 Kbps for sending information from computer to computer. It also allows data and voice to share a common phone line. DSL reduced demand for ISDN substantially. (*See also* POTS.)

ISO-9660 CD format to support PC file systems on CD media. Supplanted by the Joliet format.

ISO file Complete copy (or image) of a storage media device, typically used for optical discs.

ISP (Internet service provider) Company that provides access to the Internet, usually for money.

jack (physical connection) Part of a connector into which a plug is inserted. Also referred to as ports.

Joliet Extension of the ISO 9660 format. Most popular CD format to support PC file systems on CD media.

joule Unit of energy describing (in this book) how much energy a surge suppressor can handle before it fails.

joystick Peripheral often used while playing computer games; originally intended as a multipurpose input device.

Jump List A Windows 7 menu that shows context-sensitive information about whatever is on the taskbar.

jumper Pair of small pins that can be shorted with a shunt to configure many aspects of PCs. Often used in configurations that are rarely changed, such as master/slave settings on IDE drives.

Kerberos Authentication encryption developed by MIT to enable multiple brands of servers to authenticate multiple brands of clients.

kernel Core portion of program that resides in memory and performs the most essential operating system tasks.

keyboard Input device. Three common types of keyboards exist: those that use a mini-DIN (PS/2) connection, those that use a USB connection, and those that use wireless technology.

Knowledge Base Large collection of documents and FAQs that is maintained by Microsoft. Found on Microsoft's Web site, the Knowledge Base is an excellent place to search for assistance on most operating system problems.

KVM (keyboard, video, mouse) switch Hardware device that enables multiple computers to be viewed and controlled by a single mouse, keyboard, and screen.

LAN (local area network) Group of PCs connected via cabling, radio, or infrared that use this connectivity to share resources such as printers and mass storage.

laptop Traditional clamshell portable computing device with built-in LCD monitor, keyboard, and trackpad.

laser Single-wavelength, in-phase light source that is sometimes strapped to the head of sharks by bad guys. Note to henchmen: Lasers should never be used with sea bass, no matter how ill-tempered they might be.

laser printer Electro-photographic printer in which a laser is used as the light source.

Last Known Good Configuration Option on the Advanced Startup Options menu that enables your system to revert to a previous configuration to troubleshoot and repair any major system problems.

latency Amount of delay before a device may respond to a request; most commonly used in reference to RAM.

LBA (logical block addressing) Translation (algorithm) of IDE drives promoted by Western Digital as a standardized method for breaking the 504-MB limit in IDE drives. Subsequently universally adopted by the PC industry and now standard on all EIDE drives.

LCD (liquid crystal display) Type of display commonly used on portable PCs. Also have mostly replaced CRTs as the display of choice for most desktop computer users, due in large part to rapidly falling prices and increasing quality. LCDs use liquid crystals and electricity to produce images on the screen.

LED (light-emitting diode) Solid-state device that vibrates at luminous frequencies when current is applied.

LED monitor LCD monitor that uses LEDs instead of CCFL tubes for backlighting, creating much higher contrast ratios and image quality.

Level 1 (L1) cache First RAM cache accessed by the CPU, which stores only the absolute most-accessed programming and data used by currently running threads. Always the smallest and fastest cache on the CPU.

Level 2 (L2) cache Second RAM cache accessed by the CPU. Much larger and often slower than the L1 cache, and accessed only if the requested program/data is not in the L1 cache.

Level 3 (L3) cache Third RAM cache accessed by the CPU. Much larger and slower than the L1 and L2 caches, and accessed only if the requested program/data is not in the L2 cache. Seen only on high-end CPUs.

Li-Ion (Lithium-Ion) Battery commonly used in portable PCs. Li-Ion batteries don't suffer from the memory effects of Nickel-Cadmium (Ni-Cd) batteries and provide much more power for a greater length of time.

Library Feature in Windows 7 that aggregates folders from multiple locations and places them in a single, easy-to-find spot in Windows Explorer.

Lightweight Directory Access Protocol (LDAP) Protocol used by many operating systems and applications to access directories.

limited user account User account in Windows XP that has limited access to a system. Accounts of this type cannot alter system files, cannot install new programs, and cannot edit settings by using the Control Panel.

link light An LED on NICs, hubs, and switches that lights up to show good connection between the devices.

Linux Open-source UNIX-clone operating system.

liquid cooling A method of cooling a PC that works by running some liquid—usually water—through a metal block that sits on top of the CPU, absorbing heat. The liquid gets heated by the block, runs out of the block and into something that cools the liquid, and is then pumped through the block again.

Live DVD The Windows installation media, which loads the Windows Preinstallation Environment (WinPE) directly from disc into memory and doesn't access or modify the hard drive.

Local Security Policy Windows tool used to set local security policies on an individual system.

local user account List of user names and their associated passwords with access to a system, contained in an encrypted database.

Local Users and Groups Tool enabling creation and changing of group memberships and accounts for users.

log files Files created in Windows to track the progress of certain processes.

logical drives Sections of an extended partition on a hard drive that are formatted and (usually) assigned a drive letter, each of which is presented to the user as if it were a separate drive.

logon screen First screen of the Windows interface, used to log on to the computer system.

loopback plug Device used during loopback tests to check the female connector on a NIC.

Low-Speed USB USB standard that runs at 1.5 Mbps. Also called USB 1.1.

LPT port Commonly referred to as a printer port; usually associated with a local parallel port.

LPX First slimline form factor; replaced by NLX form factor.

lumens Unit of measure for amount of brightness on a projector or other light source.

Mac (Also **Macintosh**.) Apple Computers' flagship operating system, currently up to OS Xv10.8 "Mountain Lion" and running on Intel-based hardware.

MAC (media access control) address Unique 48-bit address assigned to each network card. IEEE assigns blocks of possible addresses to various NIC manufacturers to help ensure that the address is always unique. The Data Link layer of the OSI model uses MAC addresses for locating machines.

MAC address filtering Method of limiting wireless network access based on the physical, hard-wired address of the units' wireless NIC.

machine language Binary instruction code that is understood by the CPU.

maintenance kits Set of commonly replaced printer components provided by many manufacturers.

mass storage Hard drives, CD-ROMs, removable media drives, etc.

matte Laptop screen finish that offers a good balance between richness of colors and reflections, but washes out in bright light.

MBR (master boot record) Tiny bit of code that takes control of the boot process from the system BIOS.

MCC (memory controller chip) Chip that handles memory requests from the CPU. Although once a special chip, it has been integrated into the chipset or CPU on modern PCs.

MCH (Memory Controller Hub) Intel-coined name for what is now commonly called the Northbridge.

md (mkdir) command Command in the command-line interface used to create directories.

mega- Prefix that stands for the binary quantity 1,048,576 (2^{20}) or the decimal quantity of 1,000,000. One megabyte is 1,048,576 bytes. One megahertz, however, is a million hertz. Sometimes shortened to *Meg*, as in "a 286 has an address space of 16 Megs."

megapixel Term used typically in reference to digital cameras and their ability to capture data.

memory Device or medium for temporary storage of programs and data during program execution. Synonymous with storage, although it most frequently refers to the internal storage of a computer that can be directly addressed by operating instructions. A computer's temporary storage capacity is measured in kilobytes (KB), megabytes (MB), or gigabytes (GB) of RAM (random-access memory). Long-term data storage on disks is also measured in kilobytes, megabytes, gigabytes, and terabytes.

memory addressing Taking memory address from system RAM and using it to address nonsystem RAM or ROM so the CPU can access it.

Memory Stick Sony's flash memory card format; rarely seen outside of Sony devices.

mesh topology Network topology where each computer has a dedicated line to every other computer, most often used in wireless networks.

MFT (master file table) Enhanced file allocation table used by NTFS. (*See also* FAT.)

microATX (µATX) Variation of the ATX form factor, which uses the ATX power supply. MicroATX motherboards are generally smaller than their ATX counterparts but retain all the same functionality.

microBTX Variation of the BTX form factor. MicroBTX motherboards are generally smaller than their BTX counterparts but retain all the same functionality.

microdrive Tiny hard drives using the CompactFlash form factor. (*See also* CompactFlash (CF).)

microprocessor "Brain" of a computer. Primary computer chip that determines relative speed and capabilities of the computer. Also called CPU.

Microsoft Certified IT Professional (MCITP) An advanced IT certification specifically covering Microsoft products.

MIDI (musical instrument digital interface) Interface between a computer and a device for simulating musical instruments. Rather than sending large sound samples, a computer can simply send "instructions" to the instrument describing pitch, tone, and duration of a sound. MIDI files are therefore very efficient. Because a MIDI file is made up of a set of instructions rather than a copy of the sound, modifying each component of the file is easy. Additionally, it is possible to program many channels, or "voices," of music to be played simultaneously, creating symphonic sound.

MIDI-enabled device External device that enables you to input digital sound information in the MIDI format; for example, a MIDI keyboard (the piano kind).

migration Moving users from one operating system or hard drive to another.

MIMO (multiple in/multiple out) Feature of 802.11n devices that enables the simultaneous connection of up to four antennas, greatly increasing throughput.

mini-audio connector Very popular, 1/8-inch diameter connector used to transmit two audio signals; perfect for stereo sound.

mini connector One type of power connector from a PC power supply unit. Supplies 5 and 12 volts to peripherals. Also known as a floppy connector.

mini-DIN Small connection most commonly used for keyboards and mice. Many modern systems implement USB in place of mini-DIN connections. Also called *PS/2*.

Mini-ITX The largest and the most popular of the three ITX form factors. At a miniscule 6.7 by 6.7 inches, Mini-ITX competes with microATX and proprietary small form factor (SFF) motherboards.

Mini-PCI Specialized form of PCI designed for use in laptops.

Mini-PCIe Specialized form of PCIe designed for use in laptops.

mini power connector Connector used to provide power to floppy disk drives.

mirror set A type of mirrored volume created by Windows 7 Professional, Enterprise, and Ultimate editions. (*See also* mirroring.)

mirrored volume Volume that is mirrored on another volume. (*See also* mirroring.)

mirroring Reading and writing data at the same time to two drives for fault tolerance purposes. Considered RAID level 1. Also called *drive mirroring*.

MMC (Microsoft Management Console) Means of managing a system, introduced by Microsoft with Windows 2000. The MMC allows an administrator to customize management tools by picking and choosing from a list of snap-ins. Available snap-ins include Device Manager, Users and Groups, and Computer Management.

MMX (multimedia extensions) Specific CPU instructions that enable a CPU to handle many multimedia functions, such as digital signal processing. Introduced with the Pentium CPU, these instructions are used on all ×86 CPUs.

mode Any single combination of resolution and color depth set for a system.

modem (modulator/demodulator) Device that converts a digital bit stream into an analog signal (modulation) and converts incoming analog signals back into digital signals

(demodulation). Analog communications channel is typically a telephone line, and analog signals are typically sounds.

module Small circuit board that DRAM chips are attached to. Also known as a "stick."

Molex connector Computer power connector used by optical drives, hard drives, and case fans. Keyed to prevent it from being inserted into a power port improperly.

monaural Describes recording tracks from one source (microphone) as opposed to stereo, which uses two sources.

monitor Screen that displays data from a PC. Can use either a cathode ray tube (CRT) or a liquid crystal display (LCD) to display images.

motherboard Flat piece of circuit board that resides inside your computer case and has a number of connectors on it. Every device in a PC connects directly or indirectly to the motherboard, including CPU, RAM, hard drives, optical drives, keyboard, mouse, and video cards.

motherboard book Valuable resource when installing a new motherboard. Normally lists all the specifications about a motherboard, including the type of memory and type of CPU usable with the motherboard.

mount point Drive that functions like a folder mounted into another drive.

mouse Input device that enables users to manipulate a cursor on the screen to select items.

move command Command in the command-line interface used to move a file from one location to another.

MP3 Short for MPEG Audio Layer 3. A type of compression used specifically for turning high-quality digital audio files into much smaller, yet similar sounding, files.

MPA (Microsoft Product Activation) Introduced by Microsoft with the release of Windows XP, prevents unauthorized use of Microsoft's software by requiring users to activate the software.

MPEG-2 (Moving Pictures Experts Group) Standard of video and audio compression offering resolutions up to 1280 × 720 at 60 frames per second.

MPEG-4 (Moving Pictures Experts Group) Standard of video and audio compression offering improved compression over MPEG-2.

MS-CHAP Microsoft's variation of the CHAP protocol, which uses a slightly more advanced encryption protocol. Windows Vista uses MS-CHAP v2 (version 2), and does not support MS-CHAP v1 (version 1).

msconfig (System Configuration Utility) Executable file that runs the Windows System Configuration utility, which enables users to configure a system's boot files and critical system files. Often used for the name of the utility, as in "just run msconfig."

MSDS (material safety data sheet) Standardized form that provides detailed information about potential environmental hazards and proper disposal methods associated with various PC components.

msinfo32 Provides information about hardware resources, components, and the software environment. Also known as System Information.

multiboot installation OS installation in which multiple operating systems are installed on a single machine. Can also refer to kicking a device several times in frustration.

multicore processing Using two or more execution cores on one CPU die to divide up work independently of the OS.

multimedia extensions (MMX) Originally an Intel CPU enhancement designed for graphics-intensive applications (such as games). It was never embraced but eventually led to improvements in how CPUs handle graphics.

multimeter Device used to measure voltage, amperage, and resistance.

multisession drive Recordable CD drive capable of burning multiple sessions onto a single recordable disc. A multisession drive also can close a CD-R so that no further tracks can be written to it.

multitasking Process of running multiple programs or tasks on the same computer at the same time.

multitouch Input method on many smartphones and tablets that enables you to use multiple fingers to do all sorts of fun things, such as using two fingers to scroll or swipe to another screen or desktop.

music CD-R CD using a special format for home recorders. Music CD-R makers pay a small royalty to avoid illegal music duplication.

My Computer Default interface in Windows XP for Windows Explorer; displays hard drives and devices with removeable storage. (*See* Computer.).

My Documents Introduced with Windows 98 and used in Windows 2000 and Windows XP; folder that provides a convenient place for users to store their documents, log files, and any other type of files.

My Network Places Folder in Windows XP that enables users to view other computers on their network or workgroup.

Nano-ITX A 4.7 inch by 4.7 inch variation of the ITX form factor.

NAT (Network Address Translation) A means of translating a system's IP address into another IP address before sending it out to a larger network. NAT manifests itself by a NAT program that runs on a system or a router. A network using NAT provides the systems on the network with private IP addresses. The system running the NAT software has two interfaces: one connected to the network and the other connected to the larger network.

The NAT program takes packets from the client systems bound for the larger network and translates their internal private IP addresses to its own public IP address, enabling many systems to share a single IP address.

native resolution Resolution on an LCD monitor that matches the physical pixels on the screen. CRTs do not have fixed pixels and therefore do not have a native resolution.

navigation pane Windows 7's name for the Folders list in Windows Explorer.

net command Command in Windows that enables users to view a network without knowing the names of the other computers on that network.

NetBIOS (Network Basic Input/Output System) Protocol that operates at the Session layer of the OSI seven-layer model. This protocol creates and manages connections based on the names of the computers involved.

NetBIOS Extended User Interface (NetBEUI) The default networking protocol for early versions of Windows.

netbook Small, low-power laptop used primarily for Web browsing.

network Collection of two or more computers interconnected by telephone lines, coaxial cables, satellite links, radio, and/or some other communication technique. Group of computers that are connected and that communicate with one another for a common purpose.

Network Interface in Windows Vista and Windows 7 for Windows Explorer; displays networked computers and other devices, such as network printers.

network attached storage (NAS) A device that attaches to a network for the sole purpose of storing and sharing files.

network ID Number that identifies the network on which a device or machine exists. This number exists in both IP and IPX protocol suites.

network printer Printer that connects directly to a network.

network protocol Software that takes the incoming data received by the network card, keeps it organized, sends it to the application that needs it, and then takes outgoing data from the application and hands it to the NIC to be sent out over the network.

network technology A practical application of a topology and other critical standards to provide a method to get data from one computer to another on a network. It defines many aspects of a network, from the topology, to the frame type, to the cabling and connectors used.

NIC (network interface card or controller) Expansion card or motherboard interface that enables a PC to connect to a network via a network cable. A *wireless NIC* enables connection via radio waves rather than a physical cable.

Ni-Cd (Nickel-Cadmium) Battery used in the first portable PCs. Heavy and inefficient, these batteries also suffered from a memory effect that could drastically shorten the overall life of the battery. (*See also* Ni-MH, Li-Ion.)

Ni-MH (Nickel-Metal Hydride) Battery used in early portable PCs. Ni-MH batteries had fewer issues with the memory effect than Ni-Cd batteries. Ni-MH batteries have been replaced by Lithium-Ion batteries. (*See also* Ni-Cd, Li-Ion.)

nit Value used to measure the brightness of an LCD display. A typical LCD display has a brightness of between 100 and 400 nits.

NLQ (near-letter quality) Designation for dot-matrix printers that use 24-pin printheads.

NLX Second form factor for slimline systems. Replaced the earlier LPX form factor. (NLX apparently stands for nothing; it's just a cool grouping of letters.)

NMI (non-maskable interrupt) Interrupt code sent to the processor that cannot be ignored. Typically manifested as a BSoD.

NNTP (Network News Transfer Protocol) Protocol run by news servers that enable newsgroups.

non-system disk or disk error Error that occurs during the boot process. Common causes for this error are leaving a nonbootable floppy disk, CD, or other media in the drive while the computer is booting.

nonvolatile memory Storage device that retains data even if power is removed; typically refers to a ROM or flash ROM chip, but also could be applied to hard drives, optical media, and other storage devices.

normal backup Full backup of every selected file on a system. Turns off the archive bit after the backup.

Northbridge Chip that connects a CPU to memory, the PCI bus, Level 2 cache, and AGP activities. Communicates with the CPU through the frontside bus. Newer CPUs feature an integrated Northbridge.

notebook *See* laptop.

notification area Contains icons representing background processes, the system clock, and volume control. Located by

default at the right edge of the Windows taskbar. Most users call this area the system tray.

nslookup Command-line program in Windows used to determine exactly what information the DNS server is providing about a specific host name.

ntdetect.com One of the critical Windows NT/2000/XP startup files.

NTFS (NT file system) Robust and secure file system introduced by Microsoft with Windows NT. NTFS provides an amazing array of configuration options for user access and security. Users can be granted access to data on a file-by-file basis. NTFS enables object-level security, long filename support, compression, and encryption.

NTFS permissions Restrictions that determine the amount of access given to a particular user on a system using NTFS.

ntldr (NT Loader) Windows NT/2000/XP boot file. Launched by the MBR or MFT, ntldr looks at the boot.ini configuration file for any installed operating systems.

NVIDIA Corporation One of the foremost manufacturers of graphics cards and chipsets.

object System component that is given a set of characteristics and can be managed by the operating system as a single entity.

object access auditing Feature of Event Viewer's Security section that creates an entry in the Security Log when certain objects are accessed, such as a file or folder.

ODBC Data Source Administrator Programming tool for configuring the Open Database Connectivity (ODBC) coding standard. Data Source Administrator enables you to create and manage entries called Data Source Names (DSNs) that point OBDC to a database. DSNs are used by ODBC-aware applications to query ODBC to find their databases.

offline files Windows 7 feature that enables storing a local, duplicate copy of files and folders on a hard drive. When the laptop connects to a network, Windows automatically syncs those offline files with the files and folders on a file server or other PC.

ohm(s) Electronic measurement of a cable's impedance.

open source Software environment that is not controlled by a central creator or distributer.

OLED (organic light-emitting diode) Display technology where an organic compound provides the light for the screen, thus eliminating the need for a backlight or inverter.

OpenGL One of two popular APIs used today for video cards. Originally written for UNIX systems but now ported to Windows and Apple systems. (*See also* DirectX.)

optical disc/media Types of data discs (such as DVDs, CDs, BDs, etc.) that are read by a laser.

optical drive Drive used to read/write to optical discs, such as CDs or DVDs.

optical mouse Pointing device that uses light rather than electronic sensors to determine movement and direction the mouse is being moved.

optical resolution Resolution a scanner can achieve mechanically. Most scanners use software to enhance this ability.

optical zoom Mechanical ability of most cameras to "zoom" in as opposed to the digital ability.

option ROM Alternative way of telling the system how to talk to a piece of hardware. Option ROM stores BIOS for the card in a chip on the card itself.

OS (operating system) Series of programs and code that creates an interface so users can interact with a system's hardware; for example, DOS, Windows, and Linux.

OS X Current operating system on Apple Macintosh computers. Based on a UNIX core, early versions of OS X ran on Motorola-based hardware; current versions run on Intel-based hardware. Pronounced "ten" rather than "ex."

OSI seven-layer model Architecture model based on the OSI protocol suite that defines and standardizes the flow of data between computers. The seven layers are:

> **Layer 1 The Physical layer** Defines hardware connections and turns binary into physical pulses (electrical or light). Repeaters and hubs operate at the Physical layer.
>
> **Layer 2 The Data Link layer** Identifies devices on the Physical layer. MAC addresses are part of the Data Link layer. Bridges operate at the Data Link layer.
>
> **Layer 3 The Network layer** Moves packets between computers on different networks. Routers operate at the Network layer. IP and IPX operate at the Network layer.
>
> **Layer 4 The Transport layer** Breaks data down into manageable chunks. TCP, UDP, SPX, and NetBEUI operate at the Transport layer.
>
> **Layer 5 The Session layer** Manages connections between machines. NetBIOS and Sockets operate at the Session layer.
>
> **Layer 6 The Presentation layer** Can also manage data encryption; hides the differences between various types of computer systems.
>
> **Layer 7 The Application layer** Provides tools for programs to use to access the network (and the lower layers). HTTP, FTP, SMTP, and POP3 are all examples of protocols that operate at the Application layer.

overclocking To run a CPU or video processor faster than its rated speed.

P1 power connector Provides power to ATX motherboards; 20-pin with original ATX motherboards, 24-pin on current units.

P4 12V connector Provides additional 12-volt power to motherboards that support Pentium 4 and later processors.

P8 and P9 connectors Provide power to AT-style motherboards.

packet Basic component of communication over a network. Group of bits of fixed maximum size and well-defined format that is switched and transmitted as a single entity through a network. Contains source and destination address, data, and control information.

page fault Minor memory-addressing error.

page file Portion of the hard drive set aside by Windows to act like RAM. Also known as *virtual memory* or *swap file*.

PAN (personal area network) Small wireless network created with Bluetooth technology and intended to link PCs and other peripheral devices.

parallel execution When a multicore CPU processes more than one thread.

parallel port Connection for the synchronous, high-speed flow of data along parallel lines to a device, usually a printer.

Parental Controls Tool to allow monitoring and limiting of user activities; designed for parents to control the content their children can access.

parity Method of error detection where a small group of bits being transferred is compared to a single parity bit set to make the total bits odd or even. Receiving device reads the parity bit and determines if the data is valid, based on the oddness or evenness of the parity bit.

parity RAM Earliest form of error-detecting RAM; stored an extra bit (called the parity bit) to verify the data.

partition Section of the storage area of a hard disk. Created during initial preparation of the hard disk, before the disk is formatted.

partition boot table Sector of a partition that stores information important to its partition, such as the location of the OS boot files. Responsible for loading the OS on a partition.

partition table Table located in the boot sector of a hard drive that lists every partition on the disk that contains a valid operating system.

partitioning Electronically subdividing a physical hard drive into groups called partitions (or volumes).

passcode lock Mobile device security feature that requires you to type in a series of letters, numbers, or motion patterns to unlock the mobile device each time you press the power button.

passive matrix Technology for producing colors in LCD monitors by varying voltages across wire matrices to produce red, green, or blue dots.

password Key used to verify a user's identity on a secure computer or network.

Password Authentication Protocol (PAP) Oldest and most basic form of authentication. Also the least safe, because it sends all passwords in clear text.

password reset disk Special type of floppy disk with which users can recover a lost password without losing access to any encrypted, or password-protected, data.

PATA (parallel ATA) Implementation that integrates the controller on the disk drive itself. (*See also* ATA, IDE, SATA.)

patch Small piece of software released by a software manufacturer to correct a flaw or problem with a particular piece of software.

patch cables Short (2 to 5 feet) UTP cables that connect patch panels to the hubs.

patch panel A panel containing a row of female connectors (ports) that terminate the horizontal cabling in the equipment room. Patch panels facilitate cabling organization and provide protection to horizontal cabling.

path Route the operating system must follow to find an executable program stored in a subfolder.

PC bus Original 8-bit expansion bus developed by IBM for PCs; ran at a top speed of 4.77 MHz. Also known as the XT bus.

PC Card Credit card–sized adapter card that adds functionality in many notebook computers, PDAs, and other computer devices. PC Cards come in 16-bit and CardBus parallel format and ExpressCard serial format. (*See also* PCMCIA.)

PC tech Someone with computer skills who works on computers.

PCI (Peripheral Component Interconnect) Design architecture for the expansion bus on the computer motherboard that enables system components to be added to the computer. Local bus standard, meaning that devices added to a computer through this port will use the processor at the motherboard's full speed (up to 33 MHz) rather than at the slower 8-MHz speed of the regular bus. Moves data 32 or 64 bits at a time rather than the 8 or 16 bits the older ISA buses supported.

PCIe (PCI Express) Serialized successor to PCI and AGP that uses the concept of individual data paths called lanes.

May use any number of lanes, although a single lane (×1) and 16 lanes (×16) are the most common on motherboards.

PCI-X (PCI Extended) Enhanced version of PCI, 64 bits wide. Typically seen in servers and high-end systems.

PCL (printer control language) Printer control language created by Hewlett-Packard and used on a broad cross-section of printers.

PCM (pulse code modulation) Sound format developed in the 1960s to carry telephone calls over the first digital lines.

PCMCIA (Personal Computer Memory Card International Association) Consortium of computer manufacturers who devised the PC Card standard for credit card–sized adapter cards that add functionality in many notebook computers, PDAs, and other computer devices. (*See also* PC Card.)

PDA (personal digital assistant) Handheld computer that blurred the line between calculators and computers. Early PDAs were calculators that enabled users to program in such information as addresses and appointments. Later PDAs, such as the Palm and PocketPC, were fully programmable computers. Most PDAs used a pen/stylus for input rather than a keyboard. A few of the larger PDAs had a tiny keyboard in addition to the stylus. Smartphones and tablets have supplanted PDAs for almost all uses.

Pearson VUE The company that administers the CompTIA A+ exams.

peer-to-peer network Network in which each machine can act as both a client and a server.

pen-based computing Input method used by many PDAs that combines handwriting recognition with modified mouse functions, usually in the form of a pen-like stylus.

Pentium Name given to the fifth and later generations of Intel microprocessors; has a 32-bit address bus, 64-bit external data bus, and dual pipelining. Also used for subsequent generations of Intel processors—the Pentium Pro, Pentium II, Pentium III, and Pentium 4. Pentium name was retired after the introduction of the Intel Core CPUs.

Performance Tab in Task Manager that tracks PC performance.

Performance console Windows XP tool used to log resource usage over time.

Performance Information and Tools Applet that provides a relative feel for how your computer stacks up against other systems using the Windows Experience Index.

Performance Logs and Alerts Snap-in enabling the creation of a written record of most everything that happens on the system.

Performance Monitor Windows 7's tool for observing a computer's performance.

Performance Options Tool enabling users to configure CPU, RAM, and virtual memory settings.

peripheral Any device that connects to the system unit.

permission propagation Term to describe what happens to permissions on an object when you move or copy it.

persistence Phosphors used in CRT screens continuing to glow after being struck by electrons, long enough for the human eye to register the glowing effect. Glowing too long makes the images smeary, and too little makes them flicker.

Personalization applet Windows Vista applet with which users can change display settings such as resolution, refresh rate, color depth, and desktop features. The Windows 7 version focuses on managing themes, desktop icons, mouse pointers, and account pictures. For other options, *see* Display.

PGA (pin grid array) Arrangement of a large number of pins extending from the bottom of the CPU package. There are many variations on PGA.

Phillips-head screwdriver Most important part of a PC tech's toolkit.

phishing The act of trying to get people to give their usernames, passwords, or other security information by pretending to be someone else electronically.

Phoenix Technologies Major producer of BIOS software for motherboards.

phosphor Electro-fluorescent material that coats the inside face of a cathode ray tube (CRT). After being hit with an electron, it glows for a fraction of a second.

photosensitive drum Aluminum cylinder coated with particles of photosensitive compounds. Used in a laser printer and often contained within the toner cartridge.

picoBTX Variation of the BTX form factor. picoBTX motherboards are generally smaller than their BTX or microBTX counterparts but retain the same functionality.

Pico-ITX A 3.8 by 2.8 inch version of the ITX form factor.

pin 1 Designator used to ensure proper alignment of floppy drive and hard drive connectors.

pinch Multitouch gesture that enables you to make an image bigger or smaller.

pinned application Windows 7's method of attaching programs to the taskbar. A pinned application gets a permanent icon displayed on the taskbar.

ping (packet Internet groper) Slang term for a small network message (ICMP ECHO) sent by a computer to check for the presence and aliveness of another. Used to verify the presence of another system. Also, the command used at a prompt to ping a computer.

PIO (programmed I/O) mode Series of speed standards created by the Small Form Factor Committee for the use of PIO by hard drives. Modes range from PIO mode 0 to PIO mode 4.

pipeline Processing methodology where multiple calculations take place simultaneously by being broken into a series of steps. Often used in CPUs and video processors.

pixel (picture element) In computer graphics, smallest element of a display space that can be independently assigned color or intensity.

plug Hardware connection with some sort of projection that connects to a port.

plug and play (PnP) Combination of smart PCs, smart devices, and smart operating systems that automatically configure all necessary system resources and ports when you install a new peripheral device.

polygons Multisided shapes used in 3-D rendering of objects. In computers, video cards draw large numbers of triangles and connect them to form polygons.

polymorph virus Virus that attempts to change its signature to prevent detection by antivirus programs, usually by continually scrambling a bit of useless code.

polyphony Number of instruments a sound card can play simultaneously.

POP3 (Post Office Protocol) Refers to the way e-mail software such as Eudora gets mail from a mail server. When you obtain a SLIP, PPP, or shell account, you almost always get a POP account with it. It is this POP account that you tell your e-mail software to use to get your mail. Uses port 110.

pop-up Irritating browser window that appears automatically when you visit a Web site.

port (networking) In networking, the number used to identify the requested service (such as SMTP or FTP) when connecting to a TCP/IP host. Examples: 80 (HTTP), 20 (FTP), 69 (TFTP), 25 (SMTP), and 110 (POP3).

port (physical connection) Part of a connector into which a plug is inserted. Physical ports are also referred to as jacks.

port forwarding Preventing the passage of any IP packets through any ports other than the ones prescribed by the system administrator.

port replicator Device that plugs into a USB port or other specialized port and offers common PC ports, such as serial, parallel, USB, network, and PS/2. By plugging your notebook computer into the port replicator, you can instantly connect the computer to non-portable components such as a printer, scanner, monitor, or full-sized keyboard. Port replicators are typically used at home or in the office with the non-portable equipment already connected.

port triggering Router function that enables you to automatically open an incoming connection to one computer based on a specific outgoing connection.

positional audio Range of commands for a sound card to place a sound anywhere in 3-D space.

POST (power-on self test) Basic diagnostic routine completed by a system at the beginning of the boot process to make sure a display adapter and the system's memory are installed; it then searches for an operating system. If it finds one, it hands over control of the machine to the OS.

PostScript Language defined by Adobe Systems, Inc. for describing how to create an image on a page. The description is independent of the resolution of the device that will actually create the image. It includes a technology for defining the shape of a font and creating a raster image at many different resolutions and sizes.

power conditioning Ensuring and adjusting incoming AC wall power to as close to standard as possible. Most UPS devices provide power conditioning.

power good wire Used to wake up the CPU after the power supply has tested for proper voltage.

Power over Ethernet Technology that provides power and data transmission through a single network cable.

power plans Windows Vista/7 feature that enables better control over power use by customizing a balanced, power saver, or high performance power plan.

PowerShell *See* Windows PowerShell.

power supply fan Small fan located in a system power supply that draws warm air from inside the power supply and exhausts it to the outside.

power supply unit Provides the electrical power for a PC. Converts standard AC power into various voltages of DC electricity in a PC.

Power Users group Second most powerful account and group type in Windows after Administrators.

ppm (pages per minute) Speed of a printer.

PPP (Point-to-Point Protocol) Enables a computer to connect to the Internet through a dial-in connection and enjoy most of the benefits of a direct connection.

preboot execution environment (PXE) Technology that enables a PC to boot without any local storage by retrieving an OS from a server over a network.

primary corona Wire that is located near the photosensitive drum in a laser printer and is charged with extremely high voltage to form an electric field, enabling voltage to pass to the photosensitive drum, thus charging the photosensitive

particles on the surface of the drum. Also called the *primary charge roller*.

primary partition Partition on a Windows hard drive that can store a bootable operating system.

print resolution Quality of a print image.

print spooler Area of memory that queues up print jobs that the printer will handle sequentially.

printed circuit board (PCB) Copper etched onto a nonconductive material and then coated with some sort of epoxy for strength.

printer Output device that can print text or illustrations on paper. Microsoft uses the term to refer to the software that controls the physical print device.

printhead Case that holds the printwires in a dot-matrix printer.

printwires Grid of tiny pins in a dot-matrix printer that strike an inked printer ribbon to produce images on paper.

PRML (Partial Response Maximum Likelihood) Advanced method of RLL that uses powerful, intelligent circuitry to analyze each flux reversal on a hard drive and to make a best guess as to what type of flux reversal it just read. This allows a dramatic increase in the amount of data a hard drive can store.

Problem Reports and Solutions Control Panel applet in Windows Vista that lists all Windows Error Reporting issues (plus a few easy-to-check items like firewall and antimalware status).

Processes Tab in Task Manager that lists all running processes on a system. Frequently a handy tool for ending buggy or unresponsive processes.

product key Code used during installation to verify legitimacy of the software.

profile A list of settings that a calibration device creates when calibrating monitors and printers.

program/programming Series of binary electronic commands sent to a CPU to get work done.

Programs and Features Windows Vista/7 replacement for the Add or Remove Programs applet; enables uninstalling programs and altering Windows features.

projector Device for projecting video images from PCs or other video sources, usually for audience presentations. Available in front- and rearview displays.

prompt A character or message provided by an operating system or program to indicate that it is ready to accept input.

proprietary Technology unique to a particular vendor.

protocol Agreement that governs the procedures used to exchange information between cooperating entities. Usually includes how much information is to be sent, how often it is sent, how to recover from transmission errors, and who is to receive the information.

proxy server Device that fetches Internet resources for a client without exposing that client directly to the Internet. Usually accepts requests for HTTP, FTP, POP3, and SMTP resources. Often caches, or stores, a copy of the requested resource for later use. Common security feature in the corporate world.

Public folder Folder that all users can access and share with all other users on the system or network.

punchdown tool A specialized tool for connecting UTP wires to an punchdown block.

Quality of Service (QoS) Policies that control how much bandwidth a protocol, PC, user, VLAN, or IP address may use.

queue Area where objects wait their turn to be processed. Example: the printer queue, where print jobs wait until it is their turn to be printed.

Quick Launch toolbar Enables you to launch commonly used programs with a single click.

QVGA Video display mode of 320 × 240.

RAID (redundant array of independent disks) Seven-level (0–6) way of creating a fault-tolerant storage system:

Level 0 Uses byte-level striping and provides no fault tolerance.

Level 1 Uses mirroring or duplexing.

Level 2 Uses bit-level striping.

Level 3 Stores error-correcting information (such as parity) on a separate disk, and uses data striping on the remaining drives.

Level 4 Level 3 with block-level striping.

Level 5 Uses block-level and parity data striping.

Level 6 Same as RAID 5 but with double distributed parity.

Also known as *redundant array of inexpensive disks*.

RAID 5 volume Striped set with parity. (*See also* RAID).

rails Separate DC voltage paths within an ATX power supply.

RAM (random access memory) Memory that can be accessed at random; that is, memory which you can write to or read from without touching the preceding address. This term is often used to mean a computer's main memory.

RAMDAC (random access memory digital-to-analog converter) Circuitry used on video cards that support analog monitors to convert the digital video data to analog.

raster image Pattern of dots representing what the final product should look like.

raster line Horizontal pattern of lines that forms an image on the monitor screen.

RDRAM (Rambus DRAM) Patented RAM technology that uses accelerated clocks to provide very high-speed memory.

read-only attribute File attribute that does not allow a file to be altered or modified. Helpful when protecting system files that should not be edited.

rd (rmdir) command Command in the command-line interface used to remove directories.

rearview projector Projector that shoots an image onto a screen from the rear. Rearview projectors are usually self-enclosed and very popular for TVs, but are virtually unheard of in the PC world.

Recovery Console Command-line interface boot mode for Windows that is used to repair a Windows XP system suffering from massive OS corruption or other problems.

Recycle Bin Location to which files are moved when they are deleted from a modern Windows system. To permanently remove files from a system, they must be emptied from the Recycle Bin.

regedit.exe Program used to edit the Windows Registry.

region code Encoding that restricts you from playing DVD or Blu-ray Disc movies on a player that doesn't share the same region code.

register Storage area inside the CPU used by the onboard logic to perform calculations. CPUs have many registers to perform different functions.

registration Usually optional process that identifies the legal owner/user of the product to the supplier.

Registry Complex binary file used to store configuration data about a particular system. To edit the Registry, users can use the applets found in the Control Panel or regedit.exe or regedt32.exe.

Reliability and Performance Monitor Windows Vista's extended Performance applet.

remediation Repairing damage caused by a virus.

remnant Potentially recoverable data on a hard drive that remains despite formatting or deleting.

Remote Assistance Feature of Windows that enables users to give anyone control of his or her desktop over the Internet.

Remote Desktop Windows tool used to enable a local system to graphically access the desktop of a remote system.

Remote Desktop Protocol Protocol used for Microsoft's Remote Desktop tool. Uses port 3389.

remote network installation A common method of OS installation where the source files are placed in a shared directory on a network server. Then, whenever a tech needs to install a new OS, he can boot the computer, connect to the source location on the network, and start the installation from there.

removable media Any storage on a computer that can be easily removed. For example, CD-ROM discs, flash drives, or memory cards.

ren (rename) command Command in the command-line interface used to rename files and folders.

resistance Difficulty in making electricity flow through a material, measured in ohms.

resistive touchscreen Type of touchscreen that responds to the pressure applied to the screen.

resistor Any material or device that impedes the flow of electrons. Electronic resistors measure their resistance (impedance) in ohms. (*See* ohm(s).)

resolution Measurement for CRTs and printers expressed in horizontal and vertical dots or pixels. Higher resolutions provide sharper details and thus display better-looking images.

resources Data and services of a PC.

respect How all techs should treat their customers.

response rate Time it takes for all of the sub-pixels on the panel to go from pure black to pure white and back again.

restore point System snapshot created by the System Restore utility that is used to restore a malfunctioning system. (*See also* System Restore.)

RET (resolution enhancement technology) Technology that uses small dots to smooth out jagged edges that are typical of printers without RET, producing a higher-quality print job.

RFI (radio frequency interference) Another form of electrical interference caused by radio-wave emitting devices, such as cell phones, wireless network cards, and microwave ovens.

RG-58 Coaxial cabling used for 10Base2 networks.

RIMM Individual stick of Rambus RAM. The letters don't actually stand for anything; they just rhyme with SIMM and DIMM.

ring Network topology where the computers form a circle and all data flows in one direction only.

RIP (raster image processor) Component in a printer that translates the raster image into commands for the printer.

riser card Special adapter card, usually inserted into a special slot on a motherboard, that changes the orientation of expansion cards relative to the motherboard. Riser cards are used extensively in slimline computers to keep total depth and height of the system to a minimum. Sometimes called a daughterboard.

RJ (registered jack) connector UTP cable connector, used for both telephone and network connections. RJ-11 is a connector for four-wire UTP; usually found in telephone connections. RJ-45 is a connector for eight-wire UTP; usually found in network connections.

RJ-11 *See* RJ (registered jack) connector.

RJ-45 *See* RJ (registered jack) connector.

robocopy command Powerful command-line utility for copying files and directories, even over a network.

ROM (read-only memory) Generic term for nonvolatile memory that can be read from but not written to. This means that code and data stored in ROM cannot be corrupted by accidental erasure. Additionally, ROM retains its data when power is removed, which makes it the perfect medium for storing BIOS data or information such as scientific constants.

root directory Directory that contains all other directories.

root keys Five main categories in the Windows Registry:
HKEY_CLASSES_ROOT
HKEY_CURRENT_USER
HKEY_USERS
HKEY_LOCAL_MACHINE
HKEY_CURRENT_CONFIG

router Device connecting separate networks; forwards a packet from one network to another based on the network address for the protocol being used. For example, an IP router looks only at the IP network number. Routers operate at Layer 3 (Network) of the OSI seven-layer model.

RS-232 Standard port recommended by the Electronics Industry Association for serial devices.

run A single piece of installed horizontal cabling.

Run dialog box Command box in which users can enter the name of a particular program to run; an alternative to locating the icon in Windows.

S.M.A.R.T. (Self-Monitoring, Analysis, and Reporting Technology) Monitoring system built into hard drives.

S/PDIF (Sony/Philips Digital Interface Format) Digital audio connector found on many sound cards. Users can connect their computers directly to a 5.1 speaker system or receiver. S/PDIF comes in both a coaxial and an optical version.

Safe Mode Important diagnostic boot mode for Windows that only runs very basic drivers and turns off virtual memory.

sampling Capturing sound waves in electronic format.

SATA (serial ATA) Serialized version of the ATA standard that offers many advantages over PATA (parallel ATA) technology, including thinner cabling, keyed connectors, and lower power requirements.

SATA bridge Adapter that allows PATA devices to be connected to a SATA controller.

SATA power connector 15-pin, L-shaped connector used by SATA devices that support the hot-swappable feature.

satellites Two or more standard stereo speakers to be combined with a subwoofer for a speaker system (i.e., 2.1, 5.1, etc.).

Scalable Link Interface (SLI) Technology for connecting two or more NVIDIA GPUs together in a system.

scan code Unique code corresponding to each key on the keyboard, sent from the keyboard controller to the CPU.

Scheduled Tasks Windows XP's utility enabling users to set tasks to run automatically at certain times.

SCSI (small computer system interface) Powerful and flexible peripheral interface popularized on the Macintosh and used to connect hard drives, CD-ROM drives, tape drives, scanners, and other devices to PCs of all kinds. Normal SCSI enables up to seven devices to be connected through a single bus connection, whereas Wide SCSI can handle 15 devices attached to a single controller.

SCSI chain Series of SCSI devices working together through a host adapter.

SCSI ID Unique identifier used by SCSI devices. No two SCSI devices may have the same SCSI ID.

SD (Secure Digital) Very popular format for flash media cards; also supports I/O devices.

SDRAM (synchronous DRAM) DRAM that is synchronous, or tied to the system clock and thus runs much faster than traditional FPM and EDO RAM. This type of RAM is used in all modern systems.

SEC (single-edge cartridge) CPU package where the CPU was contained in a cartridge that snapped into a special slot on the motherboard called Slot 1.

sector Segment of one of the concentric tracks encoded on the disk during a low-level format. A sector holds 512 bytes of data.

sector translation Translation of logical geometry into physical geometry by the onboard circuitry of a hard drive.

sectors per track (sectors/track) Combined with the number of cylinders and heads, defines the disk geometry.

segment The connection between a computer and a switch.

serial port Common connector on a PC. Connects input devices (such as a mouse) or communications devices (such as a modem).

server Computer that shares its resources, such as printers and files, with other computers on a network. Example: network file system server that shares its disk space with a workstation that does not have a disk drive of its own.

service A program that runs in the background of a PC but displays no icons anywhere. You can view a list of services in the Task Manager Windows Vista and Windows 7. Also, a program stored in a ROM chip.

service pack Collection of software patches released at one time by a software manufacturer.

Services Tab in Windows Vista/7's Task Manager that lists all running services on a system.

setupapi.log Log file that tracks the installation of all hardware on a system.

setuplog.txt Log file that tracks the complete installation process, logging the success or failure of file copying, Registry updates, and reboots.

sfc (System File Checker) Command-prompt program (sfc.exe) that scans, detects, and restores Windows system files, folders, and paths.

shadow mask CRT screen that allows only the proper electron gun to light the proper phosphors.

share-level security Security system in which each resource has a password assigned to it; access to the resource is based on knowing the password.

Shared Documents Windows pre-made folder that is accessible by all user accounts on the computer.

shared memory Means of reducing the amount of memory needed on a video card by borrowing from the regular system RAM, which reduces costs but also decreases performance.

shareware Program protected by copyright; holder allows (encourages!) you to make and distribute copies under the condition that those who adopt the software after preview pay a fee to the holder of the copyright. Derivative works are not allowed, although you may make an archival copy.

shunt Tiny connector of metal enclosed in plastic that creates an electrical connection between two posts of a jumper.

SID (security identifier) Unique identifier for every PC that most techs change when cloning.

sidebanding Second data bus for AGP video cards; enables the video card to send more commands to the Northbridge while receiving other commands at the same time.

signal-to-noise ratio Measure that describes the relative quality of an input port.

signature Code pattern of a known virus; used by antivirus software to detect viruses.

SIMM (single in-line memory module) DRAM packaging distinguished by having a number of small tabs that install into a special connector. Each side of each tab is the same signal. SIMMs come in two common sizes: 30-pin and 72-pin.

simple file sharing Allows users to share locally or across the network but gives no control over what others do with shared files.

simple volume Volume created when setting up dynamic disks. Acts like a primary partition on a dynamic disk.

single-sided RAM Has chips on only one side as opposed to double-sided RAM.

single source *See* closed source.

sleep timers A feature that enables you to put the computer into Standby after a set period of time, or to turn off the monitor or hard drive after a time, thus creating your own custom power scheme.

slimline Motherboard form factor used to create PCs that were very thin. NLX and LPX were two examples of this form factor.

slot covers Metal plates that cover up unused expansion slots on the back of a PC. Useful in maintaining proper airflow through a computer case.

smart battery Portable PC battery that tells the computer when it needs to be charged, conditioned, or replaced.

smart card Hardware authentication involving a credit card–sized card with circuitry that can be used to identify the bearer of that card.

SmartMedia Format for flash media cards; no longer used with new devices.

smartphone A cell phone enhanced to do things formerly reserved for fully grown PCs, such as Web browsing, document viewing, and media consumption.

SMM (System Management Mode) Special CPU mode that enables the CPU to reduce power consumption by selectively shutting down peripherals.

SMTP (Simple Mail Transport Protocol) Main protocol used to send electronic mail on the Internet. Uses port 25.

snap-ins Small utilities that can be used with the Microsoft Management Console.

snapshot Virtualization feature that enables you to save an extra copy of the virtual machine as it is exactly at the moment the snapshot is taken.

SNMP (Simple Network Management Protocol) A set of standards for communication with devices connected to a TCP/IP network. Examples of these devices include routers, hubs, and switches. Uses port 161.

social engineering Using or manipulating people inside the networking environment to gain access to that network from the outside.

socket services Device drivers that support the PC Card socket, enabling the system to detect when a PC Card has been inserted or removed, and providing the necessary I/O to the device.

SO-DIMM (small-outline DIMM) Memory used in portable PCs because of its small size.

soft power Characteristic of ATX motherboards, which can use software to turn the PC on and off. The physical manifestation of soft power is the power switch. Instead of the thick power cord used in AT systems, an ATX power switch is little more than a pair of small wires leading to the motherboard.

software Single group of programs designed to do a particular job; always stored on mass storage devices.

solid core A cable that uses a single solid wire to transmit signals.

solid ink printers Printer that uses solid sticks of nontoxic "ink" that produce vibrant color documents with much less waste than color laser printers.

sound card Expansion card that can produce audible tones when connected to a set of speakers.

Southbridge Part of a motherboard chipset; handles all the inputs and outputs to the many devices in the PC.

spam Unsolicited e-mails from both legitimate businesses and scammers that account for a huge percentage of traffic on the Internet.

spanned volume Volume that uses space on multiple dynamic disks.

SPD (serial presence detect) Information stored on a RAM chip that describes the speed, capacity, and other aspects of the RAM chip.

speaker Device that outputs sound by using magnetically driven diaphragm.

sprite Bitmapped graphic such as a BMP file used by early 3-D games to create the 3-D world.

spyware Software that runs in the background of a user's PC, sending information about browsing habits back to the company that installed it onto the system.

SRAM (static RAM) RAM that uses a flip-flop circuit rather than the typical transistor/capacitor of DRAM to hold a bit of information. SRAM does not need to be refreshed and is faster than regular DRAM. Used primarily for cache.

SSD (solid-state drive) Data storage device that uses flash memory to store data.

SSH (Secure Shell) Terminal emulation program similar to Telnet, except that the entire connection is encrypted. Uses port 22.

SSID (service set identifier) Parameter used to define a wireless network; otherwise known as the network name.

SSL (Secure Sockets Layer) Security protocol used by a browser to connect to secure Web sites.

standard user account User account in Windows Vista that has limited access to a system. Accounts of this type cannot alter system files, cannot install new programs, and cannot edit some settings by using the Control Panel without supplying an administrator password. Replaces the Limited accounts in Windows XP.

standouts Small connectors that screw into a computer case. A motherboard is then placed on top of the standouts, and small screws are used to secure it to the standouts.

star bus A hybrid network topology where the computers all connect to a central bus—a switch—but otherwise take the form of a star topology.

star topology Network topology where the computers on the network connect to a central wiring point, usually called a hub.

Start button Button on the Windows taskbar that enables access to the Start menu.

Start menu Menu that can be accessed by clicking the Start button on the Windows taskbar. Enables you to see all programs loaded on the system and to start them.

Startup Repair A one-stop, do-it-all troubleshooting option that performs a number of boot repairs automatically.

static charge eliminator Device used to remove a static charge.

static IP address Manually set IP address that will not change.

stealth virus Virus that uses various methods to hide from antivirus software.

stepper motor One of two methods used to move actuator arms in a hard drive. (*See also* voice coil motor.)

stereo Describes recording tracks from two sources (microphones) as opposed to monaural, which uses one source.

stick Generic name for a single physical SIMM, RIMM, or DIMM.

STP (shielded twisted pair) Cabling for networks, composed of pairs of wires twisted around each other at specific intervals. Twists serve to reduce interference (also called crosstalk)—the more twists, the less interference. Cable has metallic shielding to protect the wires from external interference.

stranded core A cable that uses a bundle of tiny wire strands to transmit signals. Stranded core is not quite as good a conductor as solid core, but it will stand up to substantial handling without breaking.

stream loading Process a program uses to constantly download updated information.

streaming media Broadcast of data that is played on your computer and immediately discarded.

stripe set Two or more drives in a group that are used for a striped volume.

striped volume RAID 0 volumes. Data is spread across two drives for increased speed.

strong password Password containing at least eight characters, including letters, numbers, and punctuation symbols.

structured cabling Standards defined by TIA/EIA that define methods of organizing the cables in a network for ease of repair and replacement.

stylus Pen-like input device used for pen-based computing.

subnet mask Value used in TCP/IP settings to divide the IP address of a host into its component parts: network ID and host ID.

sub-pixels Tiny liquid crystal molecules arranged in rows and columns between polarizing filters used in LCDs.

subwoofer Powerful speaker capable of producing extremely low-frequency sounds.

Super I/O chip Chip specially designed to control low-speed, legacy devices such as the keyboard, mouse, and serial and parallel ports.

SuperSpeed USB A fast form of USB, with speeds up to 5 Gbps. Also called USB 3.0.

surge suppressor Inexpensive device that protects your computer from voltage spikes.

SVGA (super video graphics array) Video display mode of 800 × 600.

swap file *See* page file.

swipe Gesture for mobile devices where you hold your finger on the screen and slide it across the screen, either right to left or top to bottom, depending on the type of application.

switch Device that filters and forwards traffic based on some criteria. A bridge and a router are both examples of switches.

SXGA Video display mode of 1280 × 1024.

SXGA+ Video display mode of 1400 × 1050.

sync The process of keeping files on mobile devices up to date with the versions on desktop PCs or over the Internet.

synchronize *See* sync.

syntax The proper way to write a command-line command so that it functions and does what it's supposed to do.

Sysprep (System Preparation Tool) Windows tool that makes cloning of systems easier by making it possible to undo portions of the installation.

system BIOS Primary set of BIOS stored on an EPROM or flash ROM chip on the motherboard. Defines the BIOS for all the assumed hardware on the motherboard, such as keyboard controller, floppy drive, basic video, and RAM.

system bus speed Speed at which the CPU and the rest of the PC operates; set by the system crystal.

system crystal Crystal that provides the speed signals for the CPU and the rest of the system.

system disk Any device with a functional operating system.

system fan Any fan controlled by the motherboard but not directly attached to the CPU.

System File Checker *See* sfc.

System Monitor Utility that can evaluate and monitor system resources, such as CPU usage and memory usage.

System Protection Feature in Windows Vista/7 that enables you to restore any previous version of a file or folder.

system resources In classic terms, the I/O addresses, IRQs, DMA channels, and memory addresses. Also refers to other computer essentials such as hard drive space, system RAM, and processor speed.

System Restore Utility in Windows that enables you to return your PC to a recent working configuration when something goes wrong. System Restore enables you to select a restore point and then returns the computer's system settings to the way they were at that restore point—all without affecting your personal files or e-mail.

system ROM ROM chip that stores the system BIOS.

system setup utility *See* CMOS setup program.

System Tools Menu containing tools such as System Information and Disk Defragmenter, accessed by selecting Start | Programs or All Programs | Accessories | System Tools.

system tray Contains icons representing background processes and the system clock. Located by default at the right edge of the Windows taskbar. Accurately called the notification area.

system unit Main component of the PC, in which the CPU, RAM, CD-ROM, and hard drive reside. All other devices—the keyboard, mouse, and monitor—connect to the system unit.

T568A Wiring standard for Ethernet cable.

T568B Wiring standard for Ethernet cable.

tablet A mobile device consisting of a large touchscreen, enabling the user to browse the Web, view media, or even play games.

Tablet PC Small portable computer distinguished by the use of a touchscreen with stylus and handwriting recognition as the primary modes of input. Also the name of the Windows XP–based operating system designed to run on such systems.

tailgating Form of infiltration and social engineering that involves following someone else through a door as if you belong in the building.

Take Ownership Special permission allowing users to seize control of a file or folder and potentially prevent others from accessing the file/folder.

tap Touchscreen gesture where you press a spot on the screen to start an app or interact with a running app.

Task Manager Shows all running programs, including hidden ones, and is accessed by pressing CTRL-SHFT-ESC. Able to shut down an unresponsive application that refuses to close normally.

Task Scheduler Windows Vista/7's utility enabling users to set tasks to run automatically at certain times.

taskbar Contains the Start button, the system tray, the Quick Launch toolbar, and buttons for running applications. Located by default at the bottom of the desktop.

tasklist A command-line version of the Task Manager.

TCP/IP (Transmission Control Protocol/Internet Protocol) Communication protocols developed by the U.S. Department of Defense to enable dissimilar computers to share information over a network.

tech toolkit Tools a PC tech should never be without, including a Phillips-head screwdriver, a pair of tweezers, a flat-head screwdriver, a hemostat, a Torx wrench, a parts retriever, and a nut driver or two.

telecommunications room Area where all the cabling from individual PCs in a network runs to.

telephone scams Social engineering attack in which the attacker makes a phone call to someone in an organization to gain information.

Telnet Terminal emulation program for TCP/IP networks that allows one machine to control another as if the user were sitting in front of it. Uses port 23.

Temporal Key Integrity Protocol (TKIP) Deprecated encryption standard that provided a new encryption key for every sent packet.

tera- Prefix that usually stands for the binary number 1,099,511,627,776 (2^{40}). When used for mass storage, it's often shorthand for 1 trillion bytes.

terminal Dumb device connected to a mainframe or computer network that acts as a point for entry or retrieval of information.

terminal emulation Software that enables a PC to communicate with another computer or network as if the PC were a specific type of hardware terminal.

termination Using terminating resistors to prevent packet reflection on a network cable.

terminator Resistor that is plugged into the end of a bus cable to absorb the excess electrical signal, preventing it from bouncing back when it reaches the end of the wire. Terminators are used with coaxial cable and on the ends of SCSI chains. RG-58 coaxial cable requires resistors with a 50-ohm impedance. Also, a humanoid robot from the future designed by Skynet to destroy all human life. He'll be back.

test the theory Attempt to resolve the issue by either confirming the theory and learning what needs to be done to fix the problem, or by not confirming the theory and forming a new one or escalating. (One of the steps a technician uses to solve a problem.)

texture Small picture that is tiled over and over again on walls, floors, and other surfaces to create the 3-D world.

TFT (thin film transistor) Type of LCD screen. (*See also* active matrix.)

theory of probable cause One possible reason why something is not working; a guess.

thermal compound Paste-like material with very high heat-transfer properties. Applied between the CPU and the cooling device, it ensures the best possible dispersal of heat from the CPU. Also called heat dope.

thermal printer Printers that use heated printheads to create high-quality images on special or plain paper.

thermal unit Combination heat sink and fan designed for BTX motherboards; blows hot air out the back of the case instead of just into the case.

thick client CompTIA's name for a standard desktop computer.

thin client A system designed to handle only very basic applications with an absolute minimum amount of hardware required by the operating system.

thread Smallest logical division of a single program.

throttling Power reduction/thermal control capability allowing CPUs to slow down during low activity or high heat build-up situations. Intel's version is known as Speed-Step, AMD's as PowerNow!.

throw Size of the image a projector displays at a certain distance from the screen.

TIA/EIA (Telecommunications Industry Association/ Electronic Industries Alliance) Trade organization that provides standards for network cabling and other electronics.

tiers Levels of Internet providers, ranging from the Tier 1 backbones to Tier 3 regional networks.

timbre Qualities that differentiate the same note played on different instruments.

tone generator *See* toner.

tone probe *See* toner.

toner A fine powder made up of plastic particles bonded to iron particles, used to create the text and images on a laser printer. Also, generic term for two devices used together—a tone generator and a tone locator (probe)—to trace cables by sending an electrical signal along a wire at a particular frequency. The tone locator then emits a sound when it distinguishes that frequency.

toner cartridge Object used to store the toner in a laser printer. (*See also* laser printer, toner.)

topology The way computers connect to each other in a network.

touch interface The primary user interface on modern mobile devices where keys are replaced with tactile interaction.

touchpad Flat, touch-sensitive pad that serves as a pointing device for most laptops.

touchscreen Monitor with a type of sensing device across its face that detects the location and duration of contact, usually by a finger or stylus.

tracert Command-line utility used to follow the path a packet takes between two hosts. Also called traceroute.

traces Small electrical connections embedded in a circuit board.

track Area on a hard drive platter where data is stored. A group of tracks with the same diameter is called a cylinder.

trackball Pointing device distinguished by a ball that is rolled with the fingers.

TrackPoint IBM's pencil eraser–sized joystick used in place of a mouse on laptops.

transfer corona Thin wire, usually protected by other thin wires, that applies a positive charge to the paper during the laser printing process, drawing the negatively charged toner particles off of the drum and onto the paper. Newer printers accomplish the same feat using a *transfer roller* that draws the toner onto the paper.

transparency Effect in the Aero desktop environment (Windows Vista/7) that makes the edges of windows transparent.

triad Group of three phosphors—red, green, blue—in a CRT.

Trojan horse Program that does something other than what the user who runs the program thinks it will do. Used to disguise malicious code.

troubleshooting theory Steps a technician uses to solve a problem: identify the problem, establish a theory of probable cause, test the theory, establish and implement a plan of action, verify functionality, and document findings.

Trusted Platform Module A hardware platform for the acceleration of cryptographic functions and the secure storage of associated information.

tunneling Creating an encrypted link between two programs on two separate computers.

TV tuner Typically an add-on device that allows users to watch television on a computer.

TWAIN (technology without an interesting name) Programming interface that enables a graphics application, such as a desktop publishing program, to activate a scanner, frame grabber, or other image-capturing device.

U (Units) The unique height measurement used with equipment racks; 1 U equals 1.75 inches.

UAC (User Account Control) Windows Vista and Windows 7 feature that enables standard accounts to do common tasks and provides a permissions dialog box when standard and administrator accounts do certain things that could potentially harm the computer (such as attempt to install a program).

UART (universal asynchronous receiver/transmitter) Device that turns serial data into parallel data. The cornerstone of serial ports and modems.

UDF (universal data format) Replaced the ISO-9660 formats, enabling any operating system and optical drive to read UDF formatted disks.

UEFI (Unified Extensible Firmware Interface) Consortium of companies that established the UEFI standard that replaced the original EFI standard.

Ultra DMA Hard drive technology that enables drives to use direct memory addressing. Ultra DMA mode 3 drives—called ATA/33—have data transfer speeds up to 33 MBps. Mode 4 and 5 drives—called ATA/66 and ATA/100, respectively—transfer data at up to 66 MBps for mode 4 and 100 MBps for mode 5. Mode 6 pushed the transfer rate to 133 MBps. Modes 4, 5, and 6 require an 80-wire cable and a compatible controller to achieve these data transfer rates.

Ultrabook Thin, powerful laptop powered by Intel processors and built according to the Intel design specification. Competes directly with the Apple Mac Air.

unattended installation A type of OS installation where special scripts perform all the OS setup duties without human intervention.

unauthorized access Anytime a person accesses resources in an unauthorized way. This access may or may not be malicious.

UNC (Universal Naming Convention) Describes any shared resource in a network using the convention \\<server name>\<name of shared resource>.

Unicode 16-bit code that covers every character of the most common languages, plus several thousand symbols.

unsigned driver Driver that has not gone through the Windows Certification Program to ensure compatibility. The Windows Certification Program was formerly know as the Windows Hardware Quality Labs and the Microsoft Windows Logo Program.

UPC (Universal Product Code) Bar code used to track inventory.

update Individual fixes for Windows that come out fairly often, on the order of once a week or so.

Upgrade Advisor The first process that runs on the Windows XP installation CD. It examines your hardware and installed software (in the case of an upgrade) and provides a list of devices and software that are known to have issues with XP. It can also be run separately from the Windows XP installation, from the Windows XP CD. The Upgrade Advisor is also available for Windows Vista and Windows 7.

upgrade installation Installation of Windows on top of an earlier installed version, thus inheriting all previous hardware and software settings.

UPS (uninterruptible power supply) Device that supplies continuous clean power to a computer system the whole time the computer is on. Protects against power outages and sags.

URL (uniform resource locator) An address that defines the location of a resource on the Internet. URLs are used most often in conjunction with HTML and the World Wide Web.

USB (universal serial bus) General-purpose serial interconnect for keyboards, printers, joysticks, and many other devices. Enables hot-swapping of devices.

USB host controller Integrated circuit that is usually built into the chipset and controls every USB device that connects to it.

USB hub Device that extends a single USB connection to two or more USB ports, almost always directly from one of the USB ports connected to the root hub.

USB root hub Part of the host controller that makes the physical connection to the USB ports.

USB thumb drive Flash memory device that uses the standard USB connection.

user account Container that identifies a user to an application, operating system, or network, including name, password, user name, groups to which the user belongs, and other information based on the user and the OS being used. Usually defines the rights and roles a user plays on a system.

User Accounts applet Windows XP (and later versions) applet for creating and modifying user accounts.

user interface Visual representation of the computer on the monitor that makes sense to the people using the computer, through which the user can interact with the computer. This can be a graphical user interface (GUI) like Windows 7 or a command-line interface like the Windows PowerShell or the Recovery Console.

user profiles Settings that correspond to a specific user account and may follow users regardless of the computers where they log on. These settings enable the user to have customized environment and security settings.

User's Files Windows Vista and Windows 7 default location for content specific to each user account on a computer. It is divided into several folders such as Documents, Pictures, Music, and Video. Similar to My Documents folder structure in Windows XP.

Users and Passwords applet Windows 2000 application that allowed management of user accounts and passwords.

Users group List of local users not allowed, among other things, to edit the Registry or access critical system files. They can create groups, but can only manage the groups they create.

USMT (User State Migration Tool) Advanced application for file and settings transfer of multiple users.

UTP (unshielded twisted pair) Popular type of cabling for telephone and networks, composed of pairs of wires twisted around each other at specific intervals. The twists serve to reduce interference (also called crosstalk). The more twists, the less interference. Unlike its cousin, STP, UTP cable has no metallic shielding to protect the wires from external interference. 1000BaseT uses UTP, as do many other networking technologies. UTP is available in a variety of grades, called categories, as follows:
CAT 1 UTP Regular analog phone lines—not used for data communications.
CAT 2 UTP Supports speeds up to 4 megabits per second.
CAT 3 UTP Supports speeds up to 16 megabits per second.
CAT 4 UTP Supports speeds up to 20 megabits per second.
CAT 5 UTP Supports speeds up to 100 megabits per second.
CAT 5e UTP Supports speeds up to 1000 megabits per second.
CAT 6 UTP Supports speeds up to 10 gigabits per second.
CAT 6a UTP Supports speeds up to 10 gigabits per second.

V standards Standards established by CCITT for modem manufacturers to follow (voluntarily) to ensure compatible speeds, compression, and error correction.

vendor specific Stores that only sell products from one manufacturer, like the Apple store.

verify full system functionality Making sure that a problem has been resolved and will not return. (One of the steps a technician uses to solve a problem.)

vertices Used in the second generation of 3-D rendering; have a defined X, Y, and Z position in a 3-D world.

VESA (Video Electronics Standards Association) Consortium of computer manufacturers that standardize improvements to common IBM PC components. VESA is responsible for the Super VGA video standard and the VLB bus architecture.

VGA (video graphics array) Standard for the video graphics adapter that was built into IBM's PS/2 computer. It supports 16 colors in a 640 × 480 pixel video display.

video capture Computer jargon for the recording of video information, such as TV shows or movies.

video card Expansion card that works with the CPU to produce the images displayed on your computer's display.

video display *See* monitor.

virtual machine (VM) A complete environment for a guest operating system to function as though that operating system were installed on its own computer.

virtual machine manager (VMM) *See* hypervisor.

virus Program that can make a copy of itself without your necessarily being aware of it. Some viruses can destroy or damage files. The best protection is to back up files regularly.

virus definition or data file Files that enable the virus protection software to recognize the viruses on your system and clean them. These files should be updated often. They are also called signature files, depending on the virus protection software in use.

virus shield Passive monitoring of a computer's activity, checking for viruses only when certain events occur.

VIS (viewable image size) Measurement of the viewable image that is displayed by a CRT rather than a measurement of the CRT itself.

voice coil motor One of two methods used to move actuator arms in a hard drive. (*See also* stepper motor.)

VoIP (Voice over Internet Protocol) Collection of protocols that make voice calls over a data network possible.

volatile Memory that must have constant electricity to retain data. Alternatively, any programmer six hours before deadline after a nonstop, 48-hour coding session, running on nothing but caffeine and sugar.

volts (V) Measurement of the pressure of the electrons passing through a wire, or voltage.

volume Physical unit of a storage medium, such as tape reel or disk pack, that is capable of having data recorded on it and subsequently read. Also, a contiguous collection of cylinders or blocks on a disk that are treated as a separate unit.

volume boot sector First sector of the first cylinder of each partition; stores information important to its partition, such as the location of the operating system boot files.

voucher Means of getting a discount on the CompTIA A+ exams.

VPN (Virtual Private Network) Encrypted connection over the Internet between a computer or remote network and a private network.

VRM (voltage regulator module) Small card supplied with some CPUs to ensure that the CPU gets correct voltage. This type of card, which must be used with a motherboard specially designed to accept it, is not commonly seen today.

VRR (vertical refresh rate) The amount of time it takes for a CRT to draw a complete screen. This value is measured

in hertz, or cycles per second. Most modern CRTs have a VRR of 60 Hz or better.

wait state Occurs when the CPU has to wait for RAM to provide code. Also known as pipeline stall.

WAP (wireless access point) Device that centrally connects wireless network nodes.

wattage (watts or W) Measurement of the amps and volts needed for a particular device to function.

wave table synthesis Technique that supplanted FM synthesis, wherein recordings of actual instruments or other sounds are embedded in the sound card as WAV files. When a particular note from a particular instrument or voice is requested, the sound processor grabs the appropriate prerecorded WAV file from its memory and adjusts it to match the specific sound and timing requested.

Web browser Program designed to retrieve, interpret, and display Web pages.

Web server A computer that stores and shares the files that make up Web sites.

webcam PC camera most commonly used for Internet video.

Welcome screen Logon screen for Windows XP. Enables users to select their particular user account by clicking on their user picture.

WEP (Wired Equivalent Privacy) Wireless security protocol that uses a standard 40-bit encryption to scramble data packets. Does not provide complete end-to-end encryption and is vulnerable to attack.

Wi-Fi Common name for the IEEE 802.11 wireless Ethernet standard.

Wi-Fi Protected Setup (WPS) A standard included on many WAPs and clients to make secure connections easier to configure.

wide area network (WAN) A widespread group of computers connected using long-distance technologies.

wildcard Character used during a search to represent search criteria. For instance, searching for ***.doc** will return a list of all files with a .doc extension, regardless of the filename. The * is the wildcard in that search.

WiMAX (Worldwide Interoperability for Microwave Access) An updated wireless standard (also known as 802.16) with a range of up to 30 miles.

Windows 2000 Windows version that succeeded Windows NT; it came in both Professional and Server versions.

Windows 7 Version of Windows; comes in many different editions for home and office use, but does not have a Server edition.

Windows 7 Compatibility Center Microsoft's current Web site that lists the hardware and software that work with Windows 7.

Windows 8 Version of Windows noted for the Metro interface. Used for desktop and portable PCs and for mobile devices.

Windows 9*x* Term used collectively for Windows 95, Windows 98, Windows 98 SE, and Windows Me.

Windows Certification Program A rigorous testing program for hardware manufacturers. Hardware and drivers that survive the testing get to wear the *Designed for Windows* logo. The drivers get a digital signature that says Microsoft tested them and found all was well.

Windows Easy Transfer Windows Vista/7's method of transferring files and settings to a new PC.

Windows Explorer Windows utility that enables you to manipulate files and folders stored on the drives in your computer.

Windows Logo'd Products List List of products that have passed the Microsoft Windows Logo Program and are compatible with Windows operating system. Formerly called the Hardware Compatibility List (or HCL).

Windows NT Precursor to Windows 2000, XP, Vista, and 7, which introduced many important features (such as HAL and NTFS) used in all later versions of Windows.

Windows PowerShell Command-line tool included with Windows 7 and available for earlier versions from Microsoft. Offers a number of powerful scripting tools for automating changes both on local machines and over networks.

Windows Preinstallation Environment (WinPE) The installation program for Windows Vista and 7.

Windows Recovery Environment (WinRE) An special set of tools in the Windows Vista/7 setup that enables you to access troubleshooting and repair features.

Windows Sidebar User interface feature in Windows Vista that enables users to place various gadgets, such as clocks, calendars, and other utilities, on the right side of their desktop.

Windows Update Microsoft application used to keep Windows operating systems up to date with the latest patches or enhancements. (*See* Automatic Updates.)

Windows Vista Version of Windows; comes in many different editions for home and office use, but does not have a Server edition.

Windows XP Version of Windows that replaced both the entire Windows 9x line and Windows 2000; does not have a Server version.

Windows XP Mode A Windows XP virtual machine that ships with Professional, Enterprise, and Ultimate editions of Windows 7 to enable users to run programs that don't work on Windows 7.

work area In a basic structured cabling network, often simply an office or cubicle that potentially contains a PC attached to the network.

workgroup A simple, decentralized network that Windows PCs are configured to use by default.

worm Very special form of virus. Unlike other viruses, a worm does not infect other files on the computer. Instead, it replicates by making copies of itself on other systems on a network by taking advantage of security weaknesses in networking protocols.

WPA (Wi-Fi Protected Access) Wireless security protocol that uses encryption key integrity-checking and EAP and is designed to improve on WEP's weaknesses.

WPA 2 (Wi-Fi Protected Access 2) Wireless security protocol, also known as IEEE 802.11i. Uses the Advanced Encryption Standard (AES) and replaces WPA.

WQUXGA Video display mode of 2560 × 1600.

wrapper *See* container file.

WSXGA Video display mode of 1440 × 900.

WSXGA+ Video display mode of 1680 × 1050.

WUXGA Video display mode of 1920 × 1200.

WVGA Video display mode of 800 × 480.

WWW (World Wide Web) System of Internet servers that supports documents formatted in HTML and related protocols. Can be accessed by applications that use HTTP and HTTPS, such as Web browsers.

www.comptia.org CompTIA's Web site.

WXGA Video display mode of 1280 × 800.

x64 Describes 64-bit operating systems and software.

x86 Describes 32-bit operating systems and software.

xcopy command Command in the command-line interface used to copy multiple directories at once, which the copy command could not do.

xD (Extreme Digital) picture card Very small flash media card format.

Xeon Line of Intel CPUs designed for servers.

XGA (extended graphics array) Video display mode of 1024 × 768.

XPS (XML Paper Specification) print path Improved printing subsystem included in Windows Vista. Has enhanced color management and better print layout fidelity.

XT bus *See* PC bus.

ZIF (zero insertion force) socket Socket for CPUs that enables insertion of a chip without the need to apply pressure. Intel promoted this socket with its overdrive upgrades. The chip drops effortlessly into the socket's holes, and a small lever locks it in.

Advanced Communication Riser
(ACR) slots, 480
Advanced Configuration and Power
Interface (ACPI) standard, 575–578
Advanced Encryption Standard
(AES), 462
Advanced Host Controller Interface
(AHCI)
 CMOS setup, 281
 overview, 263
Advanced Micro Devices (AMD)
 chipsets, 189
 CPUs, 55, 100–101
 GPUs, 381–382
 graphics cards, 677, 679
 processing units, 111–112
 sockets, 113–114
 virtualization support, 167
Advanced Power Management
(APM) specification, 575–578
Advanced Research Projects Agency
Network (ARPANET), 77
Advanced tab in Internet
Explorer, 498
advanced technology attachment.
 See ATA (advanced technology
 attachment) interface
advanced technology attachment
 packet interface (ATAPI), 257, 302
adversity, dealing with, 26
AES (Advanced Encryption
Standard), 462
Age of the Blow-off, 23
AGP (Accelerated Graphics Port)
 display adapters, 378–380
 slots, 195
AHCI (Advanced Host Controller
Interface)
 CMOS setup, 281
 overview, 263
AIFF (Audio Interchange File
Format), 525
air quality, 639–640
airflow
 hard drives, 251
 power supplies, 235–236
airport security and portable
 computers, 583
Allow other network users to
 connect through this computer's
 Internet connection option, 493

Allow this device to wake the
 computer option, 438
alpha channels, 376
alternating current (AC) power
 adapters, 223
 description, 220
 spikes and sags, 224–226
 supplying, 221–223
 testing, 222–223
ALUs (arithmetic logic units), 99, 106
Always available offline option, 580
AMD. See Advanced Micro Devices
 (AMD)
AMD Virtualization Technology, 167
American Megatrends (AMI) BIOS,
 162–163
American National Standards
 Institute (ANSI) committees, 253
American Power Conversion Web
 site, 225
American Standard Code for
 Information Interchange (ASCII)
 language, 613–614
AMI (American Megatrends) BIOS,
 162–163
amperage, 219
amperes (A), 219
amplitude, sound, 523
AMR (Audio/Modem Riser) slots,
 191, 480
Analog/digital out connection, 531
analog LCD monitors, 371
analog meters, 222
analog video cards, 372
analog video signals, 371
anonymous FTP logon, 502
ANSI (American National Standards
 Institute) committees, 253
answers, eliciting, 27–28
anti-aliasing for LCD monitors, 366
anti-glare screens, 560
anti-static bags, 30
anti-static mats, 30
anti-static tools, 30–31
anti-static wrist straps, 30
Apache HTTP Server, 65
APIPA (Automatic Private IP
 Addressing) function, 424, 431
APIs (application programming
 interfaces)
 3-D graphics, 398, 400

games, 523, 532
APM (Advanced Power
 Management) specification,
 575–578
APM Enabled level, 576
APM Standby level, 576
APM Suspend level, 576
appearance, 21
Appearance tab for video, 388
Apple Final Cut program, 543
application programming interfaces
 (APIs)
 3-D graphics, 398, 400
 games, 523, 532
applications, 41
 Internet protocols, 493–495
 optical drives, 310
 thick clients, 663
APUs (accelerated processing units),
 111–112, 382
arithmetic logic units (ALUs), 99, 106
ARPANET (Advanced Research
 Projects Agency Network), 77
ASCII (American Standard Code
 for Information Interchange)
 language, 613–614
ASF containers, 545
ASM (Assembly Language Source)
 format, 525
aspect ratio
 CRT monitors, 360
 portable computing
 displays, 559
Assembly Language Source (ASM)
 format, 525
assertive communication, 25–26
ASX sound format, 525–526
asynchronous DSL (ADSL), 485
AT form factor, 182–183
ATA (advanced technology
 attachment) interface, 253
 ATA-1, 253–255
 ATA-2, 255–258
 ATA-3, 259
 ATA-4, 259
 ATA-5, 260
 ATA-6, 260–261
 ATA-7, 261
 ATA/66 controller
 connections, 260
 ATA/133, 261

manufacturers, 100–103
memory, 94–99
model names, 101
modern, 99
multicore processing, 110–111
multithreading, 109–110
overclocking, 92, 118–120
parallel execution, 105–110
pipelining, 105–106
portable computers, 592–593
power connectors, 231
quizzes, 122–124
registers, 88–90
selecting, 112–113
socket types, 112–114
summary, 121–122
thick clients, 661–662
virtualization support, 104
workstations, 664–667
Centronics connectors, 616
certification, 1
basic exam structure, 5–8
exam cost, 9
exam strategies, 9–11
exam taking, 8–9
importance, 2–4
lifetime, 4–5
paths, 3–4
Certiport IC³ certification, 3
CEUs (continuing education units), 5
CF (CompactFlash) cards, 294–295
CGI (computer-generated imagery), 664
chain of custody, 652
chains, SCSI, 264–265
chamfers, 227
Change adapter settings link, 427, 430, 438–439, 493
Change advanced power settings link, 579
Change advanced sharing settings link, 668
Change desktop icons option, 388
Change display settings link, 392, 395, 567
Change power settings option, 390, 577
channels
alpha, 376
controllers, 279
charge rollers, 610

charging step in laser printing, 619
chassis intrusion detection, 168
chat, 511–513
chipsets, 155, 181, 187–190
Choose media streaming option, 668
CHS values for hard drives, 250
circuit breakers, 220
circuit testers, 224
Cisco Certified Network Associate (CCNA), 4
CITE (color infrastructure and translation engine), 626
civil conversation, 26
CL (clock cycle delays), 138
Clarke, Arthur C., 246
class licenses for IP addresses, 423–424
classification of data, 649–650
cleaning
expansion card slots, 198–199
keyboards, 334–335
portable computers, 582
cleaning step in laser printing, 620
Clearwire, Inc., 488
client-side DNS, 80
clients, 65, 67
network, 438–439
thick and thin, 659–664
CLK wire
CPU speed, 91–93
expansion bus, 193
clock cycles, 91–92
delays, 138
display adapters, 379
clock multipliers, 103–104
clock wire
CPU speed, 91–93
expansion bus, 193
clothing safety, 33
CMOS clear jumper setting, 120
CMOS settings
accessing, 164
Advanced BIOS Features, 167–168
Advanced Chipset Features, 168
APM/ACPI, 577
CPU overclocking, 118–119
exiting and saving settings, 170
fans, 237
floppy drives, 292–293

hard drives, 277–281
Integrated Peripherals, 168
MB Intelligent Tweaker, 166–167
on/off switches, 229
overclocking, 168
overview, 162–163
PnP/PCI configurations, 169
Power Management Setup, 168
for security, 643
settings, 164–166
Trusted Platform Module, 170
CMYK color for printers, 606, 608, 626
CNR (communications and networking riser) slots, 191, 480
coaxial cable, 410–411
code division multiple access (CDMA), 487
code names for CPUs, 101–102
codecs
sound, 524
video, 544, 546
cold cathode fluorescent lamp (CCFL) technology, 365
collisions, 458–459
color
cable, 74
connectors, 48
correction, 394
CRT monitors, 361
LCD monitors, 361–364
printers, 606–608, 613, 620
profiles, 626, 665
sound connections, 50
color books for optical drives, 313–314
color depth
display adapters, 375–376
scanners, 339
color infrastructure and translation engine (CITE), 626
color inkjet printers, 606–607
color laser printers, 609
column array strobe (CAS), 138
.com domain, 79
COM ports, 323
Comcast ISP, 477
command prompt access, 649
communication, 25
assertive, 25–26

publishing multimedia, 550
pulse code modulation (PCM), 524
punchdown tools, 417
PVC cabling, 74

■Q

quad-channel memory, 136
quad-pumped frontside buses, 108
quad words, 95
Quake games, 511
quality
 digital cameras, 346–347
 monitors, 549
 sound, 529, 541
 video, 546
quartz oscillators, 92–93
questions for eliciting answers, 27–28
queues for CD burning, 312
QuickTime files, 304
quizzes
 BIOS, 177–179
 CPUs, 122–124
 custom PC builds, 683–685
 hard drives, 285–287
 input devices, 352–354
 Internet, 518–519
 LANs, 453–455
 motherboards, 213–215
 multimedia, 553–555
 networks, 83–84
 operational procedures, 36–38
 PC overview, 60–62
 PC tech overview, 16–18
 portable computing, 600–602
 power supplies, 242–244
 printers, 630–632
 RAM, 151–153
 removable media, 317–319
 security, 654–656
 video, 405–407
 wireless networking, 471–472

■R

racks, equipment, 416
radio frequency identification
 (RFID), 641, 644
radio frequency interference (RFI),
 31–32

radio frequency (RF) technologies,
 463–464
radio power for access points,
 462–463
RAID. *See* redundant array of
 independent disks (RAID)
RAID 0+1, 270
RAID 1+0, 270
rails, 230–231
RAM (random access memory),
 126–127
 address bus, 96–99
 CPUs, 94–99
 current capacity, 142, 146–147
 DDR SDRAM, 133–135
 DDR2, 135
 DDR3, 136
 display adapters, 375
 DRAM, 127–130
 exam objectives, 687
 gaming PCs, 679
 home server PCs, 668
 installing, 145–147
 key terms, 150–151
 lab projects, 153
 laser printers, 612, 618
 overview, 55
 portable computers, 587–588
 quizzes, 151–153
 RDRAM, 132–133
 requirements, 139–143
 SDRAM, 131–132
 selecting, 143–145
 summary, 149–150
 variations, 136–138
 video, 381–382
 workstations, 664–667
RAM cache, 139–141
Rambus DRAM (RDRAM), 132–133
random access memory digital-to-
 analog converter (RAMDAC), 371
range issues in wireless
 networking, 463
RAs (router advertisements), 434
raster image processors (RIPs), 618
raster images with laser printing, 618
raster lines in CRT monitors, 358
RDRAM (Rambus DRAM), 132–133
read-only memory (ROM), 160–161
read speed of Blu-ray Disc, 307
read/write heads, 247–248
Readme files, 625

ReadyBoost feature, 142–144
RealMedia (RM) files, 526
Rear out connector, 530
rearview projectors, 368
rechargeable batteries, 574
recognition of biometric devices, 340
recordable (CD-R) devices, 58
recordable DVD standard, 305
recorded sound formats, 524
recording quality of sound, 529
recycling
 batteries, 574–575
 electronic components, 641
Red book for optical drives, 313–314
redundant array of independent
 disks (RAID), 191, 267–270
 future, 273
 hardware vs. software, 271–273
 implementing, 271–272
 personal, 273
 types, 270–271
refresh rate
 CRT monitors, 358–359
 LCD monitors, 367
region codes for DVDs, 313
registered jack (RJ) connectors, 48,
 73–74
registers
 CPU, 88–90
 keyboard controller, 157–158
Registry
 device drivers, 172
 edit policies, 649
REL (Rights Expression
 Language), 304
Remote Assistance, 506
Remote Desktop, 506
Remote Desktop Connection dialog
 box, 506
remote desktops, 505–507
removable media, 288–289
 digital cameras, 346
 flash memory, 293–296
 floppy drives, 289–293
 key terms, 317–318
 lab projects, 320
 optical drives. *See* optical
 drives
 quizzes, 317–319
 summary, 315–317
removing drivers, 200–201
rendered 3-D graphics, 397

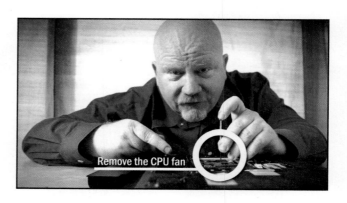